I0897165

Effective Workforce Cross-Training in Tight Labor Markets

Bryan Christiansen
https://orcid.org/0000-0001-7282-8497
Southern New Hampshire University, USA

Mehmet Ferhat Özbek
Baruch College, USA

IGI Global
Scientific Publishing
Publishing Tomorrow's Research Today

Vice President of Editorial	Melissa Wagner
Director of Acquisitions	Mikaela Felty
Director of Book Development	Jocelynn Hessler
Production Manager	Mike Brehm
Cover Design	Jose Rosado

Published in the United States of America by
IGI Global Scientific Publishing
701 East Chocolate Avenue
Hershey, PA, 17033, USA
Tel: 717-533-8845 | Fax: 717-533-7115
Website: https://www.igi-global.com E-mail: cust@igi-global.com

Copyright © 2027 by IGI Global Scientific Publishing. All rights reserved. No part of this publication may be reproduced, stored or distributed in any form or by any means, electronic or mechanical, including photocopying, without written permission from the publisher. Use of this publication to train generative artificial intelligence (AI) technologies is expressly prohibited. The publisher reserves all rights to license its use for generative AI training and machine learning model development.

Product or company names used in this set are for identification purposes only. Inclusion of the names of the products or companies does not indicate a claim of ownership by IGI Global Scientific Publishing of the trademark or registered trademark.

Library of Congress Cataloging-in-Publication Data

Names: Christiansen, Bryan, 1960- editor | Özbek, Mehmet Ferhat, 1977- editor
Title: Effective workforce cross-training in tight labor markets / [edited by] Bryan Christiansen, Mehmet Ferhat Özbek.
Description: Hershey, PA : IGI Global Scientific Publishing, [2027] | Includes bibliographical references and index. | Summary: "This book examines how cross-training can help organizations navigate tight labor markets by addressing skill shortages, turnover, and workforce stress. Offering strategies to build flexible, resilient teams, it highlights cross-training as a vital approach to strengthening talent management and sustaining business growth in challenging labor conditions"-- Provided by publisher.
Identifiers: LCCN 2025039348 (print) | LCCN 2025039349 (ebook) | ISBN 9798337353272 hardcover | ISBN 9798337353289 paperback | ISBN 9798337353296 ebook
Subjects: LCSH: Employees--Training of | Personnel management | Manpower planning
Classification: LCC HF5549.5.T7 .E325 2026 (print) | LCC HF5549.5.T7 (ebook) | DDC 658.3/124--dc23/eng/20260326
LC record available at https://lccn.loc.gov/2025039348
LC ebook record available at https://lccn.loc.gov/2025039349

British Cataloguing in Publication Data
A Cataloguing in Publication record for this book is available from the British Library.

All work contributed to this book is new, previously-unpublished material.
The views expressed in this book are those of the authors, but not necessarily of the publisher.
This book contains information sourced from authentic and highly regarded references, with reasonable efforts made to ensure the reliability of the data and information presented. The authors, editors, and publisher believe the information in this book to be accurate and true as of the date of publication. Every effort has been made to trace and credit the copyright holders of all materials included. However, the authors, editors, and publisher cannot assume responsibility for the validity of all materials or the consequences of their use. Should any copyright material be found unacknowledged, please inform the publisher so that corrections may be made in future reprints.

Table of Contents

Detailed Table of Contents

challenges in manpower development such as resource limitations, ineffective training modules, and misaligned HR policies. Recommendations include the integration of continuous learning, employee involvement in development planning, and periodic performance assessments to maximize returns on human capital investment.

Organizations are becoming concerned about long-term labor shortages brought on by demographic shifts, quick technical developments, and growing disparities between the skills needed and those accessible. Cross training is discussed in this chapter as a tactical means of increasing organizational resiliency under these circumstances. It describes how cross training improves workforce flexibility, raises productivity by relieving operational bottlenecks and promoting knowledge sharing, and supports employee retention by providing more job variety and internal mobility options. Drawing on points of view as the Resource-Based View, Dynamic Capabilities, and Human Capital Theory, the chapter addresses implementation techniques, organizational conditions that enable effective adoption, and the role of leadership and learning culture in maintaining these initiatives. Well-designed cross-training initiatives, matched with bigger HR and operational systems, can lower reliance on outside hiring and help businesses in maintaining performance.

Cross-training has emerged as a strategic organizational capability for addressing workforce challenges such as tight labor markets, skill shortages, absenteeism, turnover, and rapid technological change. It is a double-edged strategy: when carefully planned and implemented, it strengthens organizational performance and employee growth; when poorly designed, it can generate significant challenges, barriers, and risks. This chapter introduces a conceptual framework aimed at minimizing these challenges and maximizing the benefits of cross-training. The framework carries important implications for both theory and practice, offering a more nuanced understanding of the conditions under which cross-training succeeds or fails. By integrating theoretical insights with practical guidelines, it positions cross-training as a critical mechanism for building sustainable resilience, enhancing productivity, and fostering long-term employee development. For practitioners, it provides structured guidance to design and implement cross-training programs that maximize benefits while reducing risks.

This chapter examines the strategic design of workforce cross-training programs and their influence on organizational agility in tight labor markets. Drawing on strategic human capital theory and the dynamic capabilities perspective, the chapter develops a conceptual framework linking five cross-training design dimensions, namely skills gap assessment, role prioritization, training formalization, leadership support, and evaluation mechanisms, to four dimensions of organizational agility. Employee cross-functional competence is proposed as a mediating variable, while labor market tightness intensity is advanced as a moderating condition. A sequential explanatory mixed-methods design integrating PLS-SEM and thematic analysis is presented to test the proposed hypotheses. Findings contribute empirically to the strategic HRM and workforce agility literature, offering actionable guidance for HR practitioners operating in labor-constrained sectors.

In today's volatile labor markets characterized by acute talent scarcity and rapid technological change, organizations face unprecedented challenges in retaining skilled employees. This chapter presents a comprehensive theoretical analysis of cross-training as a strategic human resource practice that simultaneously enhances employee engagement and retention. Drawing upon Self-Determination Theory, the Ability-Motivation-Opportunity framework, the Job Characteristics Model, Social Exchange Theory, and Dynamic Capabilities Theory, the analysis elucidates how cross-training influences employee outcomes through psychological and organizational mechanisms. The chapter demonstrates that cross-training satisfies fundamental psychological needs thereby nurturing intrinsic motivation and sustained engagement. An integrated conceptual model illustrates how cross-training functions as a multi-level strategic intervention, enhancing psychological empowerment at the individual level while building dynamic capabilities and workforce agility at the organizational level.

Today's labor market faces talent shortages, rapid technological change, and increasing demand for adaptable workers. To stay resilient, organizations are adopting cross-training, where employees develop skills across multiple roles. However, effective cross-training requires more than technical expertise. Soft skills such as communication, teamwork, problem-solving, and self-management are equally important for success in new work environments. This chapter examines how soft skill development strengthens cross-training and helps bridge workforce skill gaps. It identifies six key soft skill areas, reviews effective development strategies in education and workplaces, and offers practical recommendations for educators, HR professionals, and policymakers to design workforce-ready training programs.

Tight labor markets have exposed vulnerabilities in how companies attract, retain, and develop talent. High turnover, skill gaps, and emerging digital needs have disrupted traditional workforce strategies. One effective response is workforce cross-training, where employees develop skills across disciplines to enhance operational flexibility. However, businesses often struggle to implement cross-training programs, where Artificial Intelligence (AI) play a key role. AI enables personalized learning, predictive skill gap identification, and continuous upskilling paths aligned with business needs. This chapter draws from Human Capital theory, Dynamic Capabilities Theory, and Adult Learning Theory, to show how AI can support cross-training, improve adaptability, and enhance workforce development.

Close labor markets are compounding the shortage of skills and limiting the performance of organizations, and are forcing organizations to adopt adaptive labor markets. This chapter suggests a predictive workforce analytics and optimisation model of cross-training within labour constraints. The structure allows dynamic investment of cross-training to be made in areas of critical need by combining skill demand forecasting, based on machine learning with multi-objective optimization models. It also utilizes skill adjacency mapping, estimation of productivity and cost benefit analysis to ensure that the workforce is maximized on both flexibility and resilience. The simulation-based example will also illustrate the enhanced use of resources and decreased risk of vacancy. The chapter provides practical information to managers and policymakers who aim at drawing up data based, scalable proposals to remain competitive amidst unpredictable labor markets.

This article explains how workforce cross-training develops across four career stages — Entry-Level Specialisation, Skill Expansion, Cross-Functional Integration, and Multi-Skilled Expertise with AI Governance — in the age of AI-driven technological change. Using ideas from human capital theory, skill-biased technological change, and organizational learning, the study addresses two major gaps in existing research: the lack of a lifecycle approach to cross-training and limited sector-specific analysis. By comparing manufacturing and service sectors, the article shows that although both sectors face automation pressure, their skill needs, training systems, and work structures are very different. The framework also argues that AI governance, including the ability to supervise, evaluate, and ethically manage AI systems, has become a key skill at advanced stages of workforce development. The study further discusses implications for workforce efficiency, labour market adaptability, and public policy.

Amid tightening labor markets and the swift adoption of hybrid work models, organizations encounter notable difficulties in cultivating agile workforces with diverse skill sets. This chapter investigates phygital cross-training as a blended approach that integrates physical and digital learning contexts to support skill acquisition and improve organizational outcomes. Grounded in Experiential Learning Theory, Human Capital Theory, digital transformation frameworks, and the Resource-Based View, it presents a layered Input-Process-Outcome model. The analysis addresses critical facilitators, obstacles, managerial considerations, and policy suggestions. Evidence indicates that phygital cross-training can enhance workforce adaptability, engagement, and robustness. Overall, the chapter contributes to theoretical understanding while offering actionable insights for organizations aiming to prepare for hybrid, technology-intensive work environments.

Persistent talent shortages, high turnover, and skill gaps have become long-term features of hospitality and tourism employment, compounded by growing sustainability and community expectations. Cross-training has gained attention as a response, yet it remains mainly a scheduling tool rather than a strategic HRM investment. This chapter introduces the Sustainable-Innovative HRM Framework, placing cross-training at the centre of relationships linking sustainability-oriented HRM and community involvement with innovation capability and service quality. Drawing on Social Exchange Theory, it argues that cross-training supported by recognition, career development, and community engagement can strengthen workforce flexibility and improve service performance. Labour market tightness moderates these relationships. Three contributions are made: integrating sustainability, innovation, and community involvement in a single framework; extending SET to destination-level governance; and reconceptualising cross-training as relational and transformational. Design principles for managers are discussed.

The volatility of contemporary labor markets—shaped by the Great Resignation, technological disruption, and persistent skill shortages—requires organizations to reconfigure how they develop and deploy human capital. Cross-training programs, historically used for operational continuity, must evolve into strategic instruments addressing workforce agility, knowledge retention, and career development. This chapter examines how effective cross-training adaptation requires integrating labor market diagnostics, evidence-based training transfer mechanisms, and manager-coaching infrastructure. Drawing on empirical research across petrochemical, automotive, retail, and public sectors, the chapter develops a framework for adaptive cross-training design and outlines implications for human resource practitioners. Organizations aligning cross-training with labor market signals are better positioned to sustain competitive advantage.

Preface

INTRODUCTION

In an era marked by persistent labor shortages, demographic shifts, rapid technological change, and evolving workforce expectations, organizations across industries face unprecedented challenges in maintaining operational resilience and competitive advantage. As editors, we have witnessed firsthand how tight labor markets strain productivity, increase turnover, and hinder growth, particularly in sectors reliant on skilled human capital. This edited volume, Effective Workforce Cross-Training in Tight Labor Markets, emerges from a shared conviction that strategic cross-training represents one of the most powerful, adaptable responses available to leaders, HR professionals, and policymakers. By investing in workforce versatility, organizations can transform vulnerabilities into strengths—enhancing flexibility, boosting retention, and fostering innovation without sole reliance on external hiring.

Our collaboration as editors—one rooted in U.S. higher education and management scholarship—brought together diverse international perspectives to address these dynamics comprehensively. Contributors from Asia, Europe, the Middle East, and beyond offer empirical insights, theoretical frameworks, and practical models tailored to real-world constraints. This collection not only diagnoses the multifaceted causes and consequences of labor shortages but also illuminates actionable pathways forward through cross-training. We believe this volume fills a critical gap in the strategic human resource management literature by bridging theory and practice in contexts where traditional talent pipelines are constrained.

The chapters that follow collectively advance a nuanced understanding of cross-training as both a tactical tool and a strategic imperative. They examine its intersections with technology, ethics, sustainability, and employee well-being, providing a holistic reference for scholars and practitioners alike. We extend our deepest gratitude to all contributing authors for their rigorous scholarship and dedication to this vital topic.

CHAPTER OVERVIEW

Chapter 1: Understanding Labour Shortages Economic Challenges and Strategic Responses by Sadhna Chauhan and Anjali examines the causes of labor shortages, particularly demographic shifts such as aging populations, their impacts across economic sectors, and potential solutions for governments, industries, and educators.

Chapter 2: Understanding the Impact of Labor Market and Development on Employee Performance by Gautam Shivaraj, Silambarasan G, and M Gurusamy explores how manpower development through training, career planning, and skill acquisition drives employee productivity, job satisfaction, and loyalty, while addressing challenges like resource limitations and offering recommendations for continuous learning.

Chapter 3: Building Business Resilience in Tight Labor Markets: Cross-Training Strategies for Flexibility, Retention, and Productivity by Ramakrishnan Ramachandran discusses cross-training as a means to enhance organizational resiliency, flexibility, productivity, and retention, drawing on theoretical perspectives such as Resource-Based View, Dynamic Capabilities, and Human Capital Theory.

Chapter 4: Cross-Training Framework - Avoiding Pitfalls and Improving Organizational and Employee Outcomes by Jelena Lukic Nikolic introduces a conceptual framework for effective cross-training implementation that minimizes risks and maximizes benefits, positioning it as a key mechanism for resilience, productivity, and employee development.

Chapter 5: Strategic Design of Workforce Cross-Training Programs: Empirical Evidence from Organizations in Tight Labor Markets by Satya Subrahmanyam develops a framework linking cross-training design dimensions to organizational agility, with employee competence as a mediator and labor market tightness as a moderator, supported by mixed-methods research.

Chapter 6: Rethinking Talent Retention And Engagement: A Theoretical Analysis Of Cross-Training As Strategic Human Resource Practice by Evangelina Joseph provides a theoretical analysis using multiple frameworks (including Self-Determination Theory and Dynamic Capabilities) to show how cross-training enhances engagement, motivation, and retention at individual and organizational levels.

Chapter 7: The Role of Soft Skills in Closing the Skills Gap Strategies for Enhancing Workforce Employability in Cross-Training Contexts by Viral Ahire, Ganraj Mane, Dr. Amruta Deshpande, and Sarah Dsouza highlights the importance of soft skills (communication, teamwork, problem-solving, etc.) in successful cross-training and offers strategies for educators, HR professionals, and policymakers.

Chapter 8: AI-Supported Cross-Training Bridging Skill Gaps and Enhancing Workforce Readiness by Sanam Soomro, Safia Soomro, and Ali Raza examines how Artificial Intelligence enables personalized learning, skill gap prediction, and upskilling in cross-training programs, grounded in Human Capital, Dynamic Capabilities, and Adult Learning theories.

Chapter 9: Predictive Workforce Analytics and Optimization for Adaptive Cross-Training in Labor-Constrained Environments by Duggirala Aravind proposes a model integrating machine learning-based forecasting, multi-objective optimization, and skill mapping to enhance workforce flexibility and resilience.

Chapter 10: Lifecycle-Based Workforce Cross-Training in the Age of AI and Automation: A Comparative Framework for Manufacturing and Service Sectors by Avirup Mukherjee and Sidharth Halder presents a career-stage framework for cross-training, comparing manufacturing and service sectors while emphasizing AI governance as a critical advanced skill.

Chapter 11: Phygital Cross-Training Models for Hybrid Workforces: Transforming Employee Capabilities and Organizational Adaptability in the Era of Remote Work by Jomon Jose M and Jyothis Mathews explores blended physical-digital training models, supported by an Input-Process-Outcome framework, to improve adaptability in hybrid environments.

Chapter 12: Strategic Cross-Training in Hospitality and Tourism. A Sustainable-Innovative HRM Framework for Tight Labour Markets by Ioannis Valachis introduces a framework integrating sustainability, innovation, community involvement, and cross-training to enhance flexibility and service quality, moderated by labor market tightness.

Chapter 13: The Aging Workforce and Digital Competency in Indonesia: The Implication for Training Needs by Ngadi Ngadi, Beni Teguh Gunawan, Triyono Triyono, and Khairul Ismed analyzes digital competency gaps among older workers using National Labor Force Survey data and discusses implications for training and suitable workplace roles.

Chapter 14: Adapting Cross-Training Programs to Changing Labor Market Conditions by Ashish Gupta and colleagues develops a framework for adaptive cross-training that incorporates labor market diagnostics, training transfer, and coaching, with evidence from multiple sectors.

Chapter 15: Advanced cross-training management and cross-border talent mobility in severely restricted work contexts by Jose De Jesus Reyes-Sánchez and colleagues investigates the integration of cross-training and cross-border mobility to sustain operations, addressing regulatory, ethical, and measurement challenges.

CONCLUSION

In conclusion, the research compiled in this volume underscores that effective cross-training is far more than job rotation or skill redundancy—it is a transformative practice that aligns individual growth with organizational vitality. When thoughtfully designed and supported by leadership, technology, and ethical safeguards, cross-training mitigates the risks of tight labor markets while unlocking higher productivity, innovation, and employee satisfaction. The frameworks, empirical findings, and practical recommendations offered here equip readers to move beyond reactive measures toward proactive workforce strategies.

We anticipate that this reference book will serve as a catalyst for further research and implementation across global contexts. As labor market dynamics continue to evolve under pressures of automation, globalization, and demographic change, the insights herein remain highly relevant. Policymakers, educators, and organizational leaders are encouraged to adapt and extend these ideas to their unique settings.

Finally, we invite ongoing dialogue among scholars and practitioners committed to building more agile, equitable, and resilient workforces. The future of work depends on our collective ability to invest wisely in human potential through versatile, inclusive development practices. It has been our privilege to curate this collection, and we hope it inspires meaningful advancements in both theory and practice.

Bryan Christiansen
Southern New Hampshire University, USA

Mehmet Ozbek
Baruch College, USA

Chapter 1
Understanding Labour Shortages:
Economic Challenges and Strategic Responses

Sadhna Chauhan
http://orcid.org/0000-0001-9964-1921
CT Group of Institutions, North Campus, Jalandhar, India

Anjali
http://orcid.org/0009-0009-7821-1231
Seth Jai Parkash Mukund Lal Institute of Engineering and Technology, India

ABSTRACT

In today's global economy, the issue of labour shortages is becoming increasingly critical. A growing number of industries are facing difficulties in finding enough qualified workers, which has begun to slow down operations, disrupt services, and place strain on broader economic progress. This chapter investigates the causes behind labour shortages, examines how they affect different sectors of the economy, and explores potential solutions that governments, industries, and educators can implement to address the problem. One major factor driving labour shortages is demographic change. In many advanced economies, populations are aging rapidly. As large numbers of experienced workers retire and younger generations are not entering the workforce in sufficient numbers, a gap is created between labour supply and demand.

DOI: 10.4018/979-8-3373-5327-2.ch001

ght © 2027, IGI Global Scientific Publishing. Copying or distributing in print or electronic forms without written permission of IGI Global Scientific Publishing is prohibited. Use of this chapter to generative artificial intelligence (AI) technologies is expressly prohibited. The publisher reserves all rights to license its use for generative AI training and machine learning model development.

1. INTRODUCTION

Shortages of labour have become one of the most urgent issues facing contemporary economies that impacts on productivity, economic growth, and sustainability of organisations in various sectors. The globalization, technological advancement, and changing workforce preferences have brought about considerable structural labour market changes over the past decades fuelled by demographic ageing. These trends have enhanced labour supply and demand imbalances especially in developed economies (OECD, 2022). More and more researchers and policymakers are becoming aware of the fact that labour shortages are not only cyclical short-term events but long-term structural processes with far-reaching economic and social consequences (Causa et al., 2025). In the current dynamic and complex economic environment, organisations and governments are increasingly under pressure to deal with labour shortages without prejudice to inclusive, sustainable and resilient labour markets. Otherwise, it may lead to lower productivity, increased labour prices, inflation, and the loss of competitiveness (Duval and Loungani, 2021). Labour shortages are the circumstances when employers cannot occupy vacancies at current wages and at the working conditions as a result of skills, geography, or working preferences mismatches (Feist, 2024). To reduce these shortages, the responses must be organized in a manner that is economically effective and socially equitable together with the well-being of the workforce (ILO, 2023). Labour shortages are a significant issue in the modern labour market not just in determining organizational performance but also in determining the overall socioeconomic performance in the form of inequality, migrants and the social cohesion. This perpetuated shortage may increase the labour market inequalities by impacting unskilled sectors and key services unequally (Causa et al., 2025). With the increasing intensity of demographic pressures and the change in technology, the issue of labour shortages management has become one of the key concerns of the long-term economic sustainability (Ernst & Feist, 2024).

1.1 Developing Economic and Organizational Strengths

The economic and organizational resilience regarding labour shortages is related to the capacity of the institutions to change the workforce strategies, improve productivity, and encourage the inclusion of labour market participation. Sound labour market reactions help to stabilize, be transparent, and grow in the long term (Blanchard et al., 2014).

1.2 Setting up the Strategic Labour Market Policies

The issue of labour shortages can be tackled with labour market strategies that are clearly defined and which help in planning the workforce, skills acquisition and employment control. These policies will enhance efficiency, inclusiveness, and flexibility that will allow economies to adapt efficiently to labour supply constraints (OECD, 2024). The better coordinated countries are in their labour market institutions, the more negative impacts of the endemic shortage are reduced (Duval and Loungani, 2021).

1.3 Equal Employment and Labor Competency

Clear and effective recruitment policies enhance job matching and minimize structural unemployment and makes employers more effective in accessing available talent (Klein and Smith, 2024). Modifying policies to facilitate skills recognition, labour mobility, and equitable hiring procedures facilitate labour market efficiency and inclusivity (Feist, 2024).

1.4 Adjustment of product, wages, and compensations

Labour shortages have a tendency to push up the wages and persuade the firms to invest in productivity improving technologies. The mechanisms of wage setting and compensation based on productivity are the key to ensuring that workers are motivated in a way that does not spawn the inflationary spirals (Auer and Fortuny, 2000).

1.5 Promoting Accountability and Policy Coordination

Responsibility and integration among governments, employers and labour institutions are the ways to effective responses to labour shortages. The policymakers are essential in ensuring that the labour market reforms are in line with the demographic and economic realities (Cazes et al., 2011). Responsible and ethical leadership in labour governance makes sure that the policy responses are balanced between the needs of the employer and the safety of workers and create a sense of trust and stability in the labour market over time (Reinsberg et al., 2019). Favouring Social Responsibility in the Labour Markets. The expectation of social responsibility, especially the inclusion, decent work, and equal opportunity, is increasingly determined by labour shortages. Solving shortages in a responsible manner involves the incorporation of both economic and social interests (Aguilera et al., 2007). Diversity, Equity, and Inclusion (DEI): The increase in the labour force participation of women, the elderly, migrants, and underrepresented groups is necessary in case of shortages and the enhancement of equity (Causa et al., 2025). Inclusive labour market policies enhance social cohesion and sustainability in the labour force (ILO, 2023). Employee Welfare and Work Quality: Better working conditions, work-life balance, and occupational safety can be used to attract and retain workers in shortage occupations and improve their quality (Ernst & Feist, 2024). When workers are invested in, labour supply and productivity are improved at the same time (Guest, 2017).

1.6 Community Involvement and Workforce Sustainability

The shortages in labour emphasise on the long-term education and training and community-based workforce development. The supply of labour can be sustainable only through the cooperation between the government, employers and schools (Porter and Kramer, 2006).

1.7 Congruence with Human Capital and Skills Strategies

Economies can solve shortages by aligning the workforce policies with the skills development and lifelong learning programs and increase human capital (Singh and Ehlers, 2020). The strategic investment in training makes the labour supply adapt to the change in technology (OECD, 2022).

1.8 Finding a Way around Labour Market Obstacles

The problems of labour shortages are difficult in terms of migration, automation, wage inequality, and labour regulation. These are some of the problems that policymakers should walk the fine line not to bring about unwanted social impacts (Valentine et al., 2011).

1.9 Efficient Policy Frameworks and Training Systems

Very strong labour market institutions and ongoing skills training provide the workers and companies with the opportunity to respond to shifting labour demand (Schwartz, 2013).

1.10 Hiring and Firing: Data Transparency and Labour Monitoring

Evidence-based policymaking and the timely anticipation of potential risks of shortage are supported by reliable data on the labour market and forecasting systems (Near & Miceli, 1995).

1.11 Dispassionate Labour Dispute Resolution

Equitable and open dispute resolution systems assist in preserving the confidence between the employer and the labour workforce at times of labour scarcity (Lewicki et al., 2003).

1.12 Frames of Labor Market Policies

Framed labour market policy frameworks offer direction in managing the shortages as well as protecting employment standards. These models facilitate the fact that decision-making is balanced in uncertain conditions (Rest, 1986).

1.13 The Strategic Significance of meeting the Labour Shortages

The challenge on shortages of labour is not only a short term policy issue but a long term strategic issue in relation to economic sustainability. Good responses in the labour market are useful in increasing productivity, innovation and social stability (Collins, 2012).

1.14 Improving the Labour Force Participation and Retention

In the ageing societies, implementing policies that motivate people to participate and remain in the labour force will enhance labour supply and reduce dependency ratio (Mayer et al., 2010).

1.15 Enhancing Economic Competitiveness

The economies that effectively overcome labour shortage are in a better position to attract investment, maintain growth and competitiveness in the world (Turker, 2009).

1.16 Promoting Sustainable Economic Development

Inclusive and sustainable growth can be realised by matching labour market policies with the demographic realities and social goals (Epstein and Buhovac, 2014). This increased significance of knowing and dealing with labour shortages may be explained by a number of factors which are related to each other both structurally and economically. To begin with, globalization has dramatically altered labour markets, making cross-border competition a phenomena and at the same time presenting skills, wage, and working conditions gaps across countries. The activity of global supply chains has increased the pressure on the need to hire highly skilled workers, although variations in labour laws, migration statutes, and labour preparedness have made it difficult to effectively deploy human capital (Autor, Dorn, and Hanson, 2016). With the increased interdependence of economies, governments and institutions have to deal with labour shortages that are subject to different institutional, cultural, and regulatory frameworks and maintain fair labour standards and labour sustainability (ILO, 2021).

In labour economics, a growing body of research confirms the persistence of skill-biased technological change (SBTC) and wage polarization. Hutter and Weber (2022), Autor (2022), and Acemoglu and Restrepo (2022) show that technological advancements disproportionately benefit high-skilled workers, widening wage inequality. Empirical studies by Battisti et al. (2022), Autor et al. (2023), and Bessen (2022) further demonstrate that automation and digitalization increase demand for advanced skills while displacing routine occupations. Evidence from developing economies also supports this trend, with Boora and Bishnoi (2025), Koren and Pető (2023), and Das and Hilgenstock (2022) identifying increasing skill gaps and labour market segmentation. Additionally, Dawid and Neugart (2023) and Aghion et al. (2024) highlight that automation contributes to job polarization by reducing middle-skill employment.

From a human resource management perspective, recent studies emphasize talent shortages and evolving workforce strategies. Bone et al. (2023), Deming (2023), and Fuller et al. (2022) highlight a shift toward skill-based hiring and alternative credentialing systems. Empirical evidence from Kölling (2022), Brunow et al. (2022), and Hershbein and Kahn (2023) shows that firms respond to labour shortages through wage adjustments and tighter labour market competition. Furthermore, Cappelli (2023), Collings et al. (2022), and McKinsey Global Institute (2023) stress the growing importance of retention strategies, including flexible work arrangements, employee engagement, and continuous reskilling.

In economic policy, demographic and institutional dynamics remain central. Brunow et al. (2022), Maestas et al. (2023), and Bloom et al. (2023) demonstrate that ageing populations significantly reduce labour supply and intensify workforce shortages. Migration-focused studies (Peri, 2022; Dustmann et al., 2023; OECD, 2024) suggest that while international labour mobility can mitigate shortages, institutional barriers such as credential recognition and integration challenges limit its effectiveness. Additionally, World Bank (2023), IMF (2023), and ILO (2023) emphasize that coordinated policies in education, migration, and labour market regulation are essential to address persistent skill mismatches and workforce imbalances

2. THEORETICAL FOUNDATIONS OF LABOUR SHORTAGES

The labor shortages phenomenon is anchored on a number of well-established theoretical orientations, which can be used to explain the labour supply and labour demand imbalance among economies. These theoretical frameworks give essential observations about the structural, economic and institutional forces behind the availability of workforce and inform policy makers, employers and educators to structure an effective response. The Human Capital Theory, the Labour Market Segmentation Theory, and the Institutional and Demographic Transition Theory are some of the most significant views that help to understand the causes and outcomes of labour shortages better.

2.1 Human Capital Theory

The HCM theory This theory is mainly related with the contribution of Becker (1964), who pointed out the value of education, training, and skill development in the identification of labour productivity and employability. This theory argues that skills and knowledge of workers are types of capital that increase economic production and earning capacity of the individual. The issue of labour shortages arises when demand by the employers do not match the skills provided by the workforce. In modern economies, the high rate of technological development and industrial revolution has placed more skills that are specialized that cannot be met through the education and training systems, which has not kept pace. The result of this mismatch is that vacancies persist, especially in the areas of healthcare, manufacturing, construction, and information technology. The Human Capital Theory emphasizes on continuous learning, reskilling and vocational education as crucial means of overcoming labour shortages and maintaining the long-term economic growth.

2.2 Labour Market Segmentation Theory

Labour Market Segmentation Theory discusses labour shortages in terms of structural divisions in the labour markets and does not assume that the labour markets are single and unified. This theory, which was first formulated by Doeringer and Piore (1971), differentiates between primary and secondary labour markets, the former is typified by secure employment, higher pay, and career mobility, and the latter is typified by low salaries, job insecurity, and lack of mobility into better-paying positions.

The labour shortages often occur within the secondary labour market segments including physically demanding jobs, socially undervalued jobs, or those that provide fewer job security. The agricultural, hospitality, caregiving, and logistics sectors are prone to chronic labour shortage due to the migration of workers to other sectors. This theory highlights the discouraging effect of poor working conditions, inability to change careers and stationary wages in motivating labour supply despite the existence of high unemployment. Reducing shortages thus involves enhancing quality of jobs, working conditions and long-term employment opportunities instead of wage increases to address shortages.

2.3 Institutional and Policy Theory

Institutional Theory underlines the impact of formal rules, regulations and labour market institutions in influencing workforce outcomes. North (1990) argues that institutions have an impact on economic performance by the way they organize incentives and restraining factors in which individuals and organizations engage. Strict labour laws, ineffective education systems, the stringent immigration policies and poor workforce planning systems often increase labour shortages. Considering the example, strict licensing regulations or rigid employment policies can restrict labour mobility, and ill-coordinated policies regarding education and labour can enhance the degree of skills mismatches. The institutional theory emphasizes on co-ordinated policymaking, the flexibility of the labour market and cross-sector co-operation among governments, employers and educational institutions to make labour supply to be effective in responding to the alteration of economic needs.

2.4 Demographic Transition Theory

Demographic Transition Theory offers a population-based explanation on labour shortages concerned with the long-term changes in the birth rates, mortality rates, and age structures (Notestein, 1945). Most developed economies are witnessing ageing populations, lowered fertility rates and reduced working age groups. With retirement of high volumes of skilled workers, there are less young workers to fill the skilled labour gaps hence chronic shortages in labour supply. This theory applies especially to the countries like in Japan, Germany and South Korea where demographic changes have dramatically decreased the participation levels of labour.

Demographic Transition Theory puts the importance of extending working years, enhancing the involvement of underrepresented populations and using labour mobility to manage demographic loss strategically.

2.5 Integrating Theoretical Perspectives on Labour Shortages

Although all the theories have their own perspective, a combined theoretical approach is most effective in explaining labour shortages. Human Capital Theory describes why there are skill gaps, Labour Market Segregation Theory identifies employment structural obstacles, the Institutional Theory identifies policy and regulatory things, and the Demographic Transition Theory explains labour limits due to population. When these views are combined, policymakers and other organizations are able to develop more holistic approaches. As an example, the remediation of healthcare shortages might involve investing in education and training (human capital), better working conditions (segmentation), favourable labour policy (institutional) and specific immigration policies (demographic).

A framework of that kind would allow more equal and sustainable workforce. The theoretical backgrounds that are presented in this section give a solid basis of analysing the labour shortages as a multidimensional problem. This chapter provides a conceptual framework of the reasons why labour shortages cannot be resolved and how evidence-based interventions that are strategic can ensure workforce stability, economic resilience and long-term growth.

Table 1. Theoretical Perspectives Explaining Labour Shortages

Theory	Key Principles	Relevance to Labour Shortages	Author(s) & Year
Human Capital Theory	Labour productivity depends on education, skills, and training.	Explains skill mismatches between labour supply and demand.	Gary Becker (1964)
	Investment in education enhances workforce quality.	Highlights the role of reskilling and upskilling in reducing shortages.	
		- Guides education and workforce development policies.	
Labour Market Segmentation Theory	Labour markets are divided into primary and secondary segments.	Explains chronic shortages in low-wage, insecure, or unattractive jobs.	Doeringer & Piore (1971)
	Job quality influences worker participation.	Highlights structural barriers that discourage labour supply.	

continued on following page

Table 1. Continued

Theory	Key Principles	Relevance to Labour Shortages	Author(s) & Year
		Supports improving wages, conditions, and career pathways.	
Institutional Theory	Labour outcomes are shaped by rules, regulations, and policies.	Explains how rigid labour laws and policy gaps intensify shortages.	Douglass North (1990)
	Institutions shape incentives and labour mobility.	Emphasizes coordinated education, labour, and immigration policies.	
		Supports evidence-based labour market reforms.	
Demographic Transition Theory	Population aging and declining fertility reduce labour supply.	Explains workforce contraction in advanced economies.	Frank Notestein (1945)
	Shifts in age structure affect labour availability.	Highlights the need for elder participation and migration strategies.	
		Informs long-term labour force planning.	
Technological Change Theory	Technology reshapes labour demand and task structures.	Explains shortages caused by rapid digital and technological shifts.	Autor, Levy & Murnane (2003)
	Automation complements and substitutes human labour.	Highlights the need for digital skills and adaptive training systems.	
		Supports balanced adoption of automation and human labour.	

Source: Literature Review
(Compiled from the literature Review by Author)

Existing literature on labour shortages remains fragmented. Most studies focus separately on technological change and skill demand (Acemoglu & Restrepo, 2022; Autor, 2022; Aghion et al., 2024) or demographic pressures such as ageing populations (Maestas et al., 2023; Bloom et al., 2023), with limited integration of these drivers. Empirical research also underexplores the linkage between labour market dynamics and firm-level HR strategies, including talent management and retention (Cappelli, 2023; Collings et al., 2022; Deming, 2023). Additionally, there is a strong bias toward advanced economies, with insufficient evidence from developing contexts characterized by informality and structural skill gaps (Boora & Bishnoi, 2025; Das & Hilgenstock, 2022; Koren & Pető, 2023). Policy-oriented studies highlight migration and institutional constraints (Peri, 2022; Dustmann et al., 2023; OECD, 2024), yet lack a unified analytical framework. Furthermore, limited efforts have been made to connect theoretical insights with practical workforce and policy interventions (Battisti et al., 2022; Bessen, 2022).

This chapter addresses these gaps by presenting an integrated framework that combines technological, demographic, and institutional perspectives with organizational and policy-level responses, offering a more comprehensive understanding of labour shortages.

3. KEY PRINCIPLES SHAPING LABOUR MARKET RESPONSES TO LABOUR SHORTAGES

Labour shortages constitute a complicated structural issue that impacts organizational performance, stability in the sector, as well as the economic growth in general. Overcoming labour shortages cannot be achieved through stop-gap solutions to recruitment but by appropriate and well-coordinated labour market actions that would be efficient, equitable and sustainable. The governments, employers, and institutions need to embrace guiding principles that will make the workforce strategies economically viable, socially accountable, and resilient to both long term demographic and technological transformation. The main principles that determine labour market responses are publicity of the labour market, equality in access to labour market, responsibility in workforce management, respect to human capital, and acceptance of flexible leadership. All these principles will help in effective workforce planning, promote labour participation and establish trust between workers, employers, and policymakers. Additionally, principled labour market responses are known to not only assist in the shortage alleviation but also in the sustainable economic development and social cohesion

A. **Labour Markets Transparency.** One of the principles of dealing with labour shortages is transparency, which is based on the availability, accuracy and access of labour market information. Open labour markets enable the workers, employers, and policymakers to make efficient choices on employment opportunities, skills needed, and workforce planning (OECD, 2019). Mistiming between the supply and demand to labour supply can be minimized when details about job openings, salary rates, skill needs and career prospects are well conveyed. The transparency in the labour shortage scenario also helps in more efficient job matching by helping the workers to know the areas where there is high demand and growth opportunities. To employers, open hiring and salary reporting enhance transparency and increase the number of applicants. Policy level Transparent labour market data enables governments to develop targeted training programs, modify immigration policies and also project the future workforce requirements.

Poor transparency, in turn, will reinforce shortages by reducing the visibility of skill shortages and deterring labour mobility.

B. **Equity and Inclusion in Workforce.** The equity principle is one of the main ideas in labour market responses to shortages and it is concerned with the fairness of access to labour market opportunities and their representation of underrepresented groups. The shortages of labour are usually accompanied with the presence of untapped potential of labour in women, older workforce, and workers with disabilities, migrant workers and marginalized communities. By ensuring fair access to the labour market, the number of people who can work will increase dramatically, and chronic shortages will decrease (ILO, 2018). The fairness of the labour market policies is to eliminate the structural barriers like discriminatory hiring, inflexible work patterns and lack of adequate education and training. The policies should encourage flexible work, affordable childcare, and lifelong learning to allow wider inclusion of various demographics. It has been argued that inclusive labour markets can reduce labour shortages as well as increase productivity and innovation by exploiting different skills and points of view (Sabharwal, 2014).

C. **Workforce Governance Accountability.** Accountability is the role that governments, employers as well as institutions have in creating, applying, and assessing the policies that pertain to the workforce in an effective manner. The labour shortages need a concerted effort on the part of education systems, labour market institutions, and industries with accountable mechanisms to make the policy effective (Greenwood, 2013). As an example, the governments need to be responsible when it comes to matching education and training systems with the labour market needs, and the employers have to be responsible in terms of offering decent working conditions, fair wages, and career development opportunities. The programs of workforce development also must be evaluated on a regular basis, as the question that will be answered is whether the program can minimize skill gaps and enhance employment outcomes. In the absence of accountability, interventions in the labour market are likely to be ineffective, disjointed, or unfocused with the real labour market needs.

D. **Respect of Human Resources and Workforce Welfare.** The respect of human capital underlines the understanding of workers as not only economic inputs but also human beings the well-being, skills, and long term development of a worker are key to sustainable labour markets. The long-term shortage of labour is common in those industries that have poor working environments, excessive workload and those with limited career advancement. These problems should be solved by enhancing the quality of jobs and protecting the welfare of the workers (Carroll and Shabana, 2010). Human capital comprises of respects such as investment in safe working conditions, work-life balance and mental and physical health. It also involves defending the rights of workers in a more digitalized labour market where surveillance systems and algorithm management can endanger privacy and autonomy. Strategies of labour shortage focusing on human dignity have more chances of attracting and retaining workers and minimizing turnover and stabilizing labour supply.

E. **Nurturing Adaptive and Strategic Leadership.** In the face of fast transformations in the global economy, adaptive leadership has been significant in addressing the problem of labour shortages. Both the social and business leaders need to expect population changes, technology advancement, and shifting employee demands, and lead organizations through labour transformations (Collings et al., 2018). Strategic leadership will entail making investments in reskilling and upskilling programs, responsible use of technology and long-term workforce planning as opposed to short-term hiring programs. The ethical and adaptive leaders are also significant in handling sensitive workforce changes like automation or recruiting internationally and this is achieved through providing fairness, transparency, and social acceptability. By taking the initiative in leadership, the organizations and governments have the ability to transform the labour shortages as a burden into a source of workforce renewal and economic strength.

4. THE STRATEGIC WORKFORCE PRINCIPLES AT PRACTICAL APPLICATIONS IN SOLVING LABOUR SHORTAGES

Participating in effective management of staff shortages also involves implementing strategic principles of labour force into practical action in both organizational and policy spheres. Although structural issues like demographic change and technology shake-up are causes of labour scarcity, intervention measures in the recruitment, labour management, remuneration, workforce relations and inclusion can go a long way to reduce their effects. Such applications facilitate temporary stabilization of workforce and long term resilience of labour market.

4.1 Recruiting and Workforce Retention

The practices of strategic recruitment become critical towards addressing the issue of labour shortages through increasing access to talent pools and enhancing job matching. Clear job specifications, competency-based hiring procedures, and uniformity in hiring standards will contribute to a decrease in skill misalignment and competent applicants will be recruited more efficiently (Schmidt and Hunter, 1998). In labour poor locations, employers are increasingly using data-based recruitment applications, collaboration with educational institutions and international hiring as a means of addressing workforce requirements. Moreover, career advancement opportunity has become a significant way to boost workforce attraction especially in areas where chronic shortages of workforce include healthcare, construction, and logistics. Flexibility, skill building and job security are particularly effective in recruitment strategies to enhance the labour market participation.

4.2 Performance and Productivity Management of Workforce

The issue of workforce performance is critical in situations where a shortage of labour limits the capacity of organizations. Open and uniform performance management systems would be used to maximize productivity and to facilitate the growth of employees. Other strategies like constant feedback systems and group based performance appraisals help firms to get the most out of the small number of workers (London and Smither, 1995).

Performance management is also preventative in labour-scarce environments, where burnout risks and skill shortages can be determined in advance. Through the integration of the performance systems and the training and reskilling initiatives, organizations can enhance flexibility of their workforce and cut the reliance on the external recruitments. Pay.

4.3 Rewards and Retention Rules

Workers in tight labour markets are retained with critical tools such as compensation and benefits. Employee retention and corporate loyalty is as a result of competitive pay systems, incentives based on performance and extensive benefits packages. The studies prove that flexible work schedules and professional growth opportunities can be regarded as non-monetary compensation elements that become more and more essential in the alleviation of labour shortage (Milkovich et al., 2014).

Strategically, the compensation policies should strike a balance between cost demands and the requirement of making the company appealing to the workers. Governments can also intervene by providing wage subsidies, tax breaks, or industry-specific subsidies to enable employers to keep needed employees on board during times of acute labour shortage.

4.4 Employees and Stability of the Workforce

Employees should be treated with a keen sense of stability because high employee relations help to reduce labour shortage that is persistent in some sectors. Employment of supportive work conditions, working environments, good communication systems and equitable conflict resolution mechanisms promote job satisfaction and minimizes turnover (Allen et al., 2010).

In labour constrained environments retention of the already existing staff is usually cheaper than hiring new staff. Especially in situations when the shortages elevate job demands, employee assistance programs, mental health support and workload management programs come in particularly handy. Through focus on the well-being of the workforce, organisations are able to minimise the rates of absenteeism, burnout and voluntary exits hence balancing the supply of labour.

4.5 Diversity, Inclusion and Labor Force Expansion

Gaining diversity and inclusion through increasing the participation of labour force is not only a strategic requirement but also an economic need in the solution to labour shortages. The concept of an inclusive workforce allows organizations and economies to access the underutilized labour markets, such as women, older employees, migrants, and people belonging to the marginalized communities. Non-discriminatory hiring practices, special training sessions, and training bias-awareness programs can help improve labour supply significantly (Thomas, 1990).

Inclusive labour market policies enhance workforce sustainability in the long term through macro factors of decreasing structural inequalities and raising total participation rates. Companies that effectively incorporate diversity and inclusion in their workforce policies are in a better position to address the changes in labor market and their population than those that do not.

5. EMERGING TRENDS AND RELEVANT GLOBAL CASE STUDIES

The global demographic, technological and institutional trends are also becoming major contributors to labour shortages. The aging of the population is one of the most prominent emerging trends sharply, especially in developed economies, where the decrease in fertility rates and the human expectancy has decreased the number of working-age individuals (OECD, 2020). This change in demographics has increased the labour shortages in the areas like health services, manufacturing and the public services. Rapid technological change is another severe trend, as it has changed the skills demanded and led to labour market motifs, as demands in digital and technical skills are changing faster than the labour force availability (Autor et al., 2003). Another strategic response is based on the global labour mobility, which includes migration as one of its key factors as a means of filling labour deficiencies in labour-deficit economies (ILO, 2021). Nevertheless, the issue of successful integration and ability to identify the skill is a continuous problem. The case studies in various regions show various reactions to labour shortages. As an example, Japan has integrated automation and policies that promote the involvement of older workers in the workforce to overcome the decline in the workforce (Fukuda, 2019). The dual vocational training system of Germany shows that the concept of education-industry fit can alleviate the problem of skills shortage, which is supplemented by skilled immigration programs (OECD, 2019). These examples indicate that the labour shortages must be resolved by well-organized, long-term policies, which combine the management of the baby boom, skills development, and policy innovation.

6. CHALLENGES IN ADDRESSING LABOUR SHORTAGES

Although the labour shortages have become one of the most significant issues in the economy, there are a number of complications when it comes to resolving them. These are structural, institutional and policy-based challenges, which need to be responded to by the way of several stakeholders.

6.1 Demographic Constraints

Demographic change is one of the greatest challenges, especially population aging and the decreasing birth rates in developed economies. The lack of labour supply, as the aged population of workers retires and the number of young workers leaving the job market decreases, restricts the sustainability of workforce in the long term (OECD, 2020; United Nations, 2019).

6.2 Skills Mismatch

The enduring lack of alignment between the skills required by the employers and those of the workers has been a tremendous challenge. The rapid technological change has placed higher pressure on the specialization skills and digital skills and education and training systems tend to fall behind labour market demands (Autor et al., 2003; World Economic Forum, 2020).

6.3 Small Migration Policy Effectiveness

Labour migration would alleviate shortages but when combined with restrictive immigration, slow recognition of credentials and ineffective integration mechanisms it diminishes its efficiency. Such obstacles do not allow the economies to take full advantage of the foreign highly skilled labour (ILO, 2021; Ruhs, 2013).

6.4 Retention and Quality of Work Stations

High turnover rate is associated with poor working conditions, lack of career advancement and job insecurity which further increases labour shortages. The problem of burnout and the drop in job satisfaction is particularly noticeable in the healthcare and service industry (OECD, 2021).

6.5 Coordination of Policies and Limitations of Data

There is poor labour market information and lack of alignment between the governments, employers and educational establishments that impede proper planning of workforce. The policy responses are usually reactive in the absence of precise forecasting (McKinsey Global Institute, 2017).

7. RECOMMENDATIONS FOR ADDRESSING LABOUR SHORTAGES

A holistic and integrated system of policy and organizational interventions is necessary in order to facilitate mitigation of labour shortages and long-term economic resilience. The subsequent recommendations provide the strategic responses to governments, industries and educational institutions.

Figure 1. Recommendations: Data-Driven Workforce Planning & Forecasting.

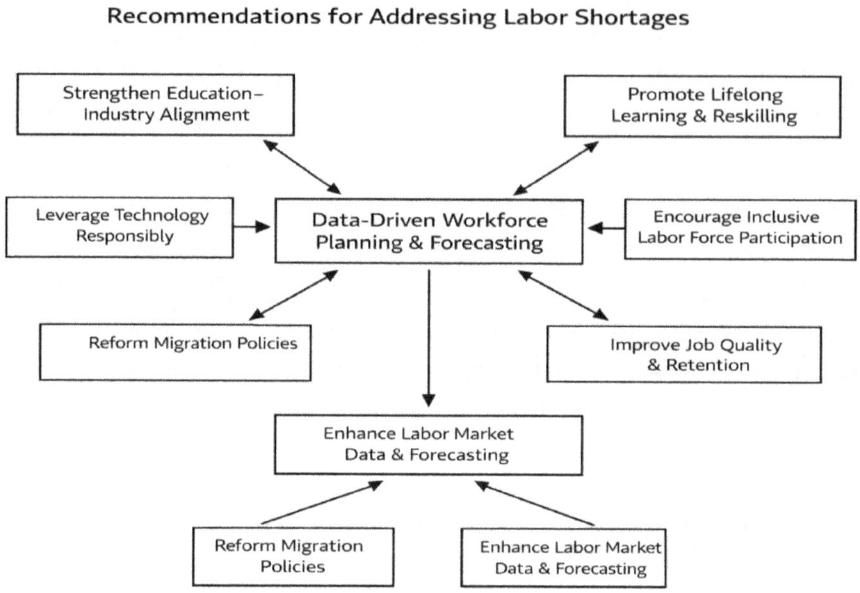

Source: *Literature review*

A. **Enhancing Education-Industry Association.** The education and training systems should be well coordinated with the labour market needs to minimize the skills gaps. Increasing the use of vocational education, apprenticeships, and industry-based curriculum can enhance the workforce preparedness and employability (OECD, 2019).
B. **Ensuring Lifelong Learning and Reskilling.** Ongoing skill enhancement is important in the fast moving labour markets. Employers and governments must also invest in lifelong learning programs that would allow workers to reskill and keep up with technological and structural change (World Economic Forum, 2020).
C. **Promoting Inclusion in the Labour Force.** Enhancement of participation of the underrepresented groups like women, older workers and persons with disabilities can greatly increase supply of labour. The best way to do this is by meeting the demands of flexible work arrangements and conducive workplace policies (ILO, 2020).
D. **Using Technology in a Wise Manner.** Human labour should not be replaced by automation and digital technologies but complemented. Making adoption

responsible will increase productivity and lessen the physical workload and skills gaps in labour-intensive industries (Autor, 2015).

E. **Revision of Migration and Integration Policies.** Properly regulated labour migration policy can be used to address some of the critical skill deficiencies. One of the key elements in maximizing the benefits of migration is streamlining of visa procedures, recognizing of foreign credential, and facilitating social integration (Ruhs, 2013).
F. **Job Quality and Retention.** Workforce stability can be achieved through better wages and working conditions, and career progression opportunity, which will lower turnover rates. Quality jobs lead to the satisfaction and retention of employees (OECD, 2021).
G. **Improving the Data and Forecasting of the Labour Market.** Timely and correct information on the labour market is essential to preemptive workforce planning. Evidence-based policymaking can be facilitated by strong collaboration between governments, employers, and educational institutions (McKinsey Global Institute, 2017).

8. CONCLUSION

One of the most topical issues of the modern world economy is labour shortages, which concern not only separate organizations but also the productivity of the country, its economic and social stability. The phenomenon of the labour scarcity, as discussed in this chapter, is a complex one, as it is rooted in the demographic shifts, skills mismatches, and technological shocks as well as socio-economic inequalities. This is because in developed economies, ageing and the loss of the working-age population has led to a big disparity between supply and demand of skilled labour especially in such essential areas as healthcare, construction, logistics, and manufacturing. The severity of such demographic changes can be seen in countries such as Japan, Germany, and South Korea where effective labour market outflux of the experienced workers has exacerbated the role of strategic workforce planning and policy interventions (Boxall and Purcell, 2016). In developing countries labour scarce is a frequent reality as a result of poor education, lack of vocational training and unequal labour mobility results into the continuing vacancy and untapped human resources. Labor shortages have far reaching economic implications. Companies having a hard time recruiting and retaining competent staff are characterized by low productivity, delay in service delivery and high operational expenses, which consequently leads to lack of profitability and competitiveness (Schmidt and Hunter, 1998).

At a macroeconomic scale, labour shortages have direct negative effects on the GDP growth, disruption of infrastructure projects, and inhibition of the delivery of public services. An increase in labour costs, as employers are trying to secure the dwindling workforce, can also cause inflation and overburden smaller enterprises that do not have the capacity to compensate them accordingly as larger companies. Moreover, current employees are likely to be burdened and burnout, which further complicate the turnover and cause workforce instability (Guest, 2017). This type of economic dynamics explains the need to have in place good comprehensive labour policies that go beyond the short term solutions to the structural workforce problems. Ethical human resource management (HRM) is a critical framework on how to maneuver these issues. Theoretical basis on the basis of deontological ethics, utilitarianism, virtue ethics, and ethics of care highlights fairness, transparency, accountability, and respect to human dignity as the central factors in management of the workforce (Kant, 1785; Mill, 1863; Aristotle, 350 BCE; Gilligan, 1982). This means that by incorporating these ethical principles in HR practices, recruitment, performance management, compensation, and employee engagement programs will be done in a fair manner, which will promote trust, inclusivity, and long-term organizational sustainability (Greenwood, 2013). As an example, equal recruitment policies and selection based on merit not only solve the acute problem of skills related to specific job positions but also provide a more diverse and competent work force, increasing innovation and adaptability (Sabharwal, 2014).

Open communication, effective performance appraisal, and ethical leadership also support organizational integrity as well as well-being and satisfaction amongst employees. Ethical HR practices have a key role to play in resolving labour shortages. The recruitment procedures should be designed in such a way to avoid biasness and focus on skills that fulfill the strategic missions, performance management system should strike a balance between the organizational goals and development of employees (London and Smither, 1995). The programs of compensation and benefits should demonstrate competitiveness and fairness as a factor to retain and motivate the talented employees (Milkovich et al., 2014). Also, through promoting inclusive working practices that are inclusive of diversity and flexible working practices, organizations will be able to access underrepresented labour markets, such as women, older workers, and people with disabilities (Thomas, 1990). When ethical HRM practices are used alongside sector-specific intervention, the risks that labour shortages pose as well as the ability to develop resilient and flexible workforces can be reduced by an organization. New trends and creative solutions are also critical in dealing with the issue of shortage of labour. Labor intensive activities especially in manufacturing, logistics, and service industries can be relieved by technological innovations including automation, artificial intelligence (AI), and digital solutions.

The solutions should, however, be done in a wise manner to prevent displacement of people in the workforce and to make sure that the human talent can still have its role to play in areas that need creativity, decision-making, and interpersonal abilities

(Binns, 2018). When combined with effective integration systems, immigration policies will help offer extra sources of providing the essential skills gaps, whereas data-driven workforce prediction will allow governments and employers to foresee the shortages and create training programs in advance (Aguinis and Glavas, 2012). Irrespective of these strategies, a number of issues are still present. Demographic changes, technological shakeup, talent competition on a global scale and mismatch between academic curriculum and industry demands are factors that worsen workforce shortages. A comprehensive strategy should thus be adopted by organisations and policy makers that entails the combination of education reform, skills policy, inclusive labour market policies, and international collaboration to provide sustainable labour supply (Boxall and Purcell, 2016). The solutions suggested in this chapter such as equitable hiring, ethical leadership, employee welfare programmes, open decision-making, and ongoing skills training offer steps that organisations can use to cope with the labour shortage environment without losing in an unethical and integrity-related manner. Finally, labour shortages are not only temporary disturbances but are also indicative of structural and systemic more profound problems that require concerted, strategic action.

These obstacles need to be dealt with in a multidimensional manner that would strike the balance between ethical HRM practices, the adoption of technology, inclusivity, and international collaboration. Organizations can promote the involvement of employees, recruitment of various talents, and operational resilience by integrating fairness, transparency, and accountability in the workforce management. In addition, governments, schools and stakeholders in the industry should collaborate to make skill training relevant to labour market so that the economies are competitive and societies prosper. The insights and solutions offered in this chapter offer a holistic approach to the learning, prevention, and response to labour shortages and present practical advice on the sustainable economic development, labour stability and the success of organizations.

REFERENCES

Acemoglu, D., & Restrepo, P. (2022). Tasks, automation, and the rise in U.S. wage inequality. *Econometrica, 90*(5), 1973–2016. DOI: 10.3982/ECTA19815

Aghion, P., Antonin, C., & Bunel, S. (2024). Artificial intelligence, growth, and employment: The role of innovation. *The Journal of Economic Perspectives, 38*(1), 3–30.

Aguilera, R. V., Rupp, D. E., Williams, C. A., & Ganapathi, J. (2007). Putting the S back in corporate social responsibility: A multilevel theory of social change in organizations. *Academy of Management Review, 32*(3), 836–863. DOI: 10.5465/amr.2007.25275678

Aguinis, H., & Glavas, A. (2012). What we know and don't know about corporate social responsibility: A review and research agenda. *Journal of Management, 38*(4), 932–968. DOI: 10.1177/0149206311436079

Allen, D. G., Bryant, P. C., & Vardaman, J. M. (2010). Retaining talent: Replacing misconceptions with evidence-based strategies. *The Academy of Management Perspectives, 24*(2), 48–64.

Aristotle. (350 BCE). *Nicomachean ethics.*

Auer, P., & Fortuny, M. (2000). *Ageing of the labour force in OECD countries: Economic and social consequences* (Employment Paper No. 2000/2). International Labour Office.

Autor, D. H. (2015). Why are there still so many jobs? The history and future of workplace automation. *The Journal of Economic Perspectives, 29*(3), 3–30. DOI: 10.1257/jep.29.3.3

Autor, D. H. (2022). The labor market impacts of technological change: From unbridled optimism to qualified optimism. *The Journal of Economic Perspectives, 36*(1), 3–30.

Autor, D. H., Dorn, D., & Hanson, G. (2016). The China shock: Learning from labor-market adjustment to large changes in trade. *Annual Review of Economics, 8*(1), 205–240. DOI: 10.1146/annurev-economics-080315-015041

Autor, D. H., Levy, F., & Murnane, R. J. (2003). The skill content of recent technological change: An empirical exploration. *The Quarterly Journal of Economics, 118*(4), 1279–1333. DOI: 10.1162/003355303322552801

Autor, D. H., Mindell, D. A., & Reynolds, E. B. (2023). *The work of the future: Building better jobs in an age of intelligent machines*. MIT Press.

Battisti, M., Del Gatto, M., & Parmeter, C. F. (2022). Skill-biased technological change and productivity dynamics. *Journal of Economic Dynamics & Control, 139*, 104377.

Becker, G. S. (1964). *Human capital: A theoretical and empirical analysis, with special reference to education*. University of Chicago Press.

Bessen, J. (2022). *AI and jobs: The role of demand* (NBER Working Paper No. 24235). National Bureau of Economic Research.

Binns, R. (2018). Fairness in machine learning: Lessons from political philosophy. In *Proceedings of the Conference on Fairness, Accountability, and Transparency (FAT*)* (pp. 149–159).

Blanchard, O., Jaumotte, F., & Loungani, P. (2014). *Labor market policies and IMF advice in advanced economies during the Great Recession* (IMF Staff Discussion Note). International Monetary Fund.

Bloom, D. E., Kuhn, M., & Prettner, K. (2023). The macroeconomic effects of population aging and fertility decline. *Journal of Economic Literature, 61*(3), 1020–1063.

Bone, J., Lambourne, A., & Codreanu, A. (2023). Skill-based hiring and labor market transformation. *Labour Economics, 83*, 102345.

Boora, N., & Bishnoi, S. (2025). Skill-biased technological change and wage inequality in developing economies. *International Journal of Economics and Labour Studies, 12*(1), 45–62.

Boxall, P., & Purcell, J. (2016). *Strategy and human resource management* (4th ed.). Palgrave Macmillan. DOI: 10.1007/978-1-137-40765-8

Brunow, S., Fuchs, M., & Weyh, A. (2022). Wage growth in tight labor markets: Evidence from Germany. *Empirical Economics, 63*(2), 873–902.

Cappelli, P. (2023). Talent management: Conceptual approaches and practical challenges. *Human Resource Management Journal, 33*(2), 203–219.

Carroll, A. B., & Shabana, K. M. (2010). The business case for corporate social responsibility: A review of concepts, research and practice. *International Journal of Management Reviews, 12*(1), 85–105. DOI: 10.1111/j.1468-2370.2009.00275.x

Causa, O., Cavalleri, M. C., Luu, N., & Toth, A. (2025). *Labour and skills shortages in OECD countries* (OECD Economics Department Working Papers). OECD Publishing.

Cazes, S., Verick, S., & Hussami, F. (2011). Diverging trends in unemployment in the United States and Europe: Evidence from Okun's law and the global financial crisis. *Employment Working Paper*. International Labour Office.

Collings, D. G., McMackin, J., Nyberg, A. J., & Wright, P. M. (2022). Strategic human resource management and performance: A review and research agenda. *Human Resource Management Journal, 32*(1), 1–20. DOI: 10.1111/j.1748-8583.2011.00189.x

Collings, D. G., Mellahi, K., & Cascio, W. F. (2018). Global talent management and performance in multinational enterprises: A multilevel perspective. *Journal of Management, 45*(2), 540–566. DOI: 10.1177/0149206318757018

Collins, J. (2012). *Good to great: Why some companies make the leap and others don't*. HarperBusiness.

Das, M., & Hilgenstock, B. (2022). *Labour markets and inequality in developing economies* (World Bank Policy Research Working Paper No. 10045). World Bank.

Deming, D. J. (2023). Four facts about human capital. *The Journal of Economic Perspectives, 37*(2), 75–102.

Doeringer, P. B., & Piore, M. J. (1971). *Internal labor markets and manpower analysis*. D.C. Heath.

Dustmann, C., Schönberg, U., & Stuhler, J. (2023). The impact of immigration: Why do studies reach such different results? *The Journal of Economic Perspectives, 37*(1), 31–56.

Duval, R., & Loungani, P. (2021). *Designing labor market institutions in emerging and developing economies: Evidence and policy options* (IMF Working Paper). International Monetary Fund.

Epstein, M. J., & Buhovac, A. R. (2014). *Making sustainability work: Best practices in managing and measuring corporate social, environmental and economic impacts* (2nd ed.). Berrett-Koehler.

Ernst, E., & Feist, M. (2024). *Labour shortages and the future of work*. International Labour Organization.

Feist, M. (2024). *Structural labour shortages: Challenges and policy responses*. ILO Policy Brief.

Fukuda, K. (2019). Science, technology and innovation ecosystem transformation toward society 5.0. *International Journal of Production Economics, 220*, 107460. DOI: 10.1016/j.ijpe.2019.07.033

Fuller, J. B., Raman, M., Sage-Gavin, E., & Hines, K. (2022). *The emerging degree reset: How the shift to skills-based hiring holds the keys to growing the U.S. workforce.* Harvard Business School Project on Managing the Future of Work.

Gilligan, C. (1982). *In a different voice: Psychological theory and women's development.* Harvard University Press.

Greenwood, M. (2013). Ethical analysis of HRM: A review and research agenda. *Journal of Business Ethics, 114*(2), 355–366. DOI: 10.1007/s10551-012-1354-y

Guest, D. E. (2017). Human resource management and employee well-being: Towards a new analytic framework. *Human Resource Management Journal, 27*(1), 22–38. DOI: 10.1111/1748-8583.12139

Hershbein, B., & Kahn, L. B. (2023). Do recessions accelerate routine-biased technological change? Evidence from vacancy postings. *The American Economic Review, 113*(2), 400–435.

International Labour Organization. (2018). *World employment and social outlook: Trends 2018.* ILO.

International Labour Organization. (2020). *World employment and social outlook: Trends 2020.* ILO.

International Labour Organization. (2021). *World employment and social outlook: The role of digital labour platforms in transforming the world of work.* ILO.

International Labour Organization. (2023). *Global employment trends and the future of work.* ILO.

International Labour Organization (ILO). (2023). *Global employment trends 2023.* ILO.

International Monetary Fund (IMF). (2023). *World economic outlook: Navigating global divergences.* IMF.

Kant, I. (1785). *Groundwork of the metaphysics of morals.*

Klein, M., & Smith, J. (2024). Matching workers to jobs: Recruitment, selection and labour market efficiency. *Journal of Labor Economics.*

Kölling, A. (2022). Labor shortages and wage responses: Evidence from German establishments. *Journal for Labour Market Research, 56*(1), 1–18.

Koren, M., & Pető, R. (2023). Business disruptions from social distancing. *Journal of Economic Dynamics & Control, 138*, 104320.

Lewicki, R. J., Saunders, D. M., & Barry, B. (2003). *Negotiation* (4th ed.). McGraw-Hill.

London, M., & Smither, J. W. (1995). Can multi-source feedback change perceptions of goal accomplishment, self-evaluations, and performance-related outcomes? Theory-based applications and directions for research. *Personnel Psychology*, *48*(4), 803–839. DOI: 10.1111/j.1744-6570.1995.tb01782.x

Maestas, N., Mullen, K. J., & Powell, D. (2023). The effect of population aging on economic growth, the labor force, and productivity. *American Economic Journal. Macroeconomics*, *15*(2), 306–332. DOI: 10.1257/mac.20190196

Mayer, K. U., Ritschard, G., & Oris, M. (2010). *Longitudinal analysis and life course research*. Springer.

McKinsey Global Institute. (2017). *Jobs lost, jobs gained: Workforce transitions in a time of automation*. McKinsey & Company.

McKinsey Global Institute. (2023). *The future of work in a post-pandemic economy*. McKinsey & Company.

Milkovich, G. T., Newman, J. M., & Gerhart, B. (2014). *Compensation* (11th ed.). McGraw-Hill.

Mill, J. S. (1863). *Utilitarianism*.

Near, J. P., & Miceli, M. P. (1995). Effective whistle-blowing. *Academy of Management Review*, *20*(3), 679–708. DOI: 10.2307/258791

North, D. C. (1990). *Institutions, institutional change and economic performance*. Cambridge University Press. DOI: 10.1017/CBO9780511808678

Notestein, F. W. (1945). Population—the long view. In Schultz, T. W. (Ed.), *Food for the world* (pp. 36–57). University of Chicago Press.

Organisation for Economic Co-operation and Development (OECD). (2019). *OECD employment outlook 2019: The future of work*. OECD Publishing.

Organisation for Economic Co-operation and Development (OECD). (2020). *OECD employment outlook 2020: Worker security and the COVID-19 crisis*. OECD Publishing.

Organisation for Economic Co-operation and Development (OECD). (2021). [*OECD indicators*. OECD Publishing.]. *Health at a Glance*, •••, 2021.

Organisation for Economic Co-operation and Development (OECD). (2022). *Labour market and skills shortages in the OECD*. OECD Publishing.

Organisation for Economic Co-operation and Development (OECD). (2024). *Adapting labour market institutions for an ageing workforce*. OECD Publishing.

Organisation for Economic Co-operation and Development (OECD). (2024). *OECD employment outlook 2024*. OECD Publishing.

Peri, G. (2022). Immigration and labor markets. *Annual Review of Economics, 14*, 607–635.

Porter, M. E., & Kramer, M. R. (2006). Strategy and society: The link between competitive advantage and corporate social responsibility. *Harvard Business Review, 84*(12), 78–92. PMID: 17183795

Reinsberg, B., Kentikelenis, A., Stubbs, T., & King, L. (2019). The political economy of IMF conditionality. *The Journal of Development Studies, 55*(6), 1–18.

Rest, J. (1986). *Moral development: Advances in research and theory*. Praeger.

Ruhs, M. (2013). *The price of rights: Regulating international labor migration*. Princeton University Press.

Sabharwal, M. (2014). Is diversity management sufficient? Organizational inclusion to further performance. *Public Personnel Management, 43*(2), 197–217. DOI: 10.1177/0091026014522202

Schmidt, F. L., & Hunter, J. E. (1998). The validity and utility of selection methods in personnel psychology: Practical and theoretical implications of 85 years of research findings. *Psychological Bulletin, 124*(2), 262–274. DOI: 10.1037/0033-2909.124.2.262

Schwartz, B. (2013). *Practical wisdom: The right way to do the right thing*. Bloomsbury.

Singh, A., & Ehlers, T. (2020). Human capital development and economic growth in emerging markets. *Journal of Human Capital Development*.

Thomas, D. A. (1990). The impact of race on managers' experiences of developmental relationships (mentoring and sponsorship): An intraorganizational study. *Journal of Organizational Behavior, 11*(6), 479–492. DOI: 10.1002/job.4030110608

Turker, D. (2009). How corporate social responsibility influences organizational commitment. *Journal of Business Ethics, 89*(2), 189–204. DOI: 10.1007/s10551-008-9993-8

United Nations. (2019). *World population prospects 2019. Highlights*. United Nations.

Valentine, S., Godkin, L., Fleischman, G., & Kidwell, R. (2011). Corporate ethical values, group creativity, job satisfaction and turnover intention: The impact of work context on work response. *Journal of Business Ethics*, *98*(3), 353–372. DOI: 10.1007/s10551-010-0554-6

World Bank. (2023). *World development report 2023: Migrants, refugees, and societies*. World Bank.

World Economic Forum. (2020). *The future of jobs report 2020*. World Economic Forum

Chapter 2
Understanding the Impact of Labor Market and Development on Employee Performance

Gautam Shivaraj
http://orcid.org/0009-0000-5184-8448
Adarsh Institute of Management and Information Technology, India

G. Silambarasan
http://orcid.org/0009-0004-6233-4943
Periyar University, Salem, India

M. Gurusamy
http://orcid.org/0000-0002-9425-9368
Adarsh Institute of Management and Information Technology, India

ABSTRACT

Manpower development has become a strategic component in enhancing organizational performance and achieving long-term objectives. This paper explores how manpower development, through structured training programs, career planning, and skill acquisition, affects employee performance in modern organizations. By reviewing empirical studies and theoretical frameworks, the research identifies a strong correlation between investment in human capital and improvements in employee productivity, job satisfaction, and organizational loyalty. The paper also highlights challenges in manpower development such as resource limitations, ineffective training

DOI: 10.4018/979-8-3373-5327-2.ch002

:ht © 2027, IGI Global Scientific Publishing. Copying or distributing in print or electronic forms without written permission of IGI Global Scientific Publishing is prohibited. Use of this chapter to generative artificial intelligence (AI) technologies is expressly prohibited. The publisher reserves all rights to license its use for generative AI training and machine learning model development.

modules, and misaligned HR policies. Recommendations include the integration of continuous learning, employee involvement in development planning, and periodic performance assessments to maximize returns on human capital investment.

1. INTRODUCTION

In the contemporary globalized economy, the intricate relationship between labor market trends and employee performance has become a focal point of academic inquiry and practical application for organizations worldwide. The labor market, an essential determinant of economic prosperity, consists of the forces that govern the supply and demand for labor. It shapes various factors that directly impact employee behavior, such as employment rates, wage structures, job security, and the mobility of skilled workers. These factors, in turn, influence the overall effectiveness, efficiency, and productivity of the workforce. With rapid advancements in technology, shifts in geopolitical dynamics, and the evolving nature of work itself, labor markets are experiencing constant transformations that have profound implications for both employers and employees (Tafese et al., 2025a).

At the same time, the importance of internal developmental strategies in fostering high-performing employees cannot be overstated. Employee performance is increasingly recognized as a critical driver of organizational success. As such, organizations invest heavily in development programs aimed at enhancing employees' skills, increasing their job satisfaction, and fostering greater loyalty. These programs, which include formal training, mentorship, leadership development, and career advancement opportunities, are designed to align individual aspirations with organizational goals. However, while these initiatives can improve employee engagement and performance, they exist within a broader external context—the labor market—that can either support or hinder their effectiveness (Li et al., 2025a).

Labor market conditions, such as the rate of unemployment, industry-specific skill shortages, or the presence of economic booms and recessions, have a direct bearing on employees' perceptions of job stability, career growth, and opportunities for advancement. In periods of high unemployment, for instance, employees may feel a greater sense of job insecurity, leading to lower morale and productivity. On the other hand, during periods of labor shortages, where demand for skilled workers exceeds supply, employees may feel empowered, leading to higher motivation, better performance, and increased organizational loyalty. In these circumstances, organizations often need to be agile in their response, adjusting their human resource policies to reflect the changing landscape of labor availability and employee expectations (Salari et al., 2025a).

Yet, it is not solely external labor market conditions that shape employee performance; internal developmental strategies play an equally significant role. The growth and development of human capital within an organization are crucial for ensuring sustained competitive advantage. Employees are no longer seen as mere labor resources but as key drivers of innovation, efficiency, and organizational growth. In this regard, developmental strategies that focus on skill enhancement, leadership development, and career progression are integral to optimizing employee performance. However, the effectiveness of these developmental strategies can be tempered by the broader economic and labor market climate. For example, when organizations face external labor market challenges such as talent shortages or wage inflation, they may find it increasingly difficult to retain top talent or invest in development initiatives. This underscores the importance of a nuanced understanding of how external labor market forces interact with internal developmental strategies to shape the overall performance of the workforce (Baiocchetti et al., 2024).

Furthermore, the shifting dynamics of labor markets necessitate that organizations rethink traditional approaches to employee performance management. In the past, performance evaluation systems largely focused on outputs and outcomes, with little consideration given to the external factors that influenced those outcomes. However, the modern work environment calls for a more holistic approach to performance assessment, one that accounts for both internal developmental factors (such as training, leadership programs, and employee engagement strategies) and external conditions like labor market stability, competition, and economic pressures. Therefore, understanding the impact of labor market trends on employee performance requires a dual focus on both macroeconomic forces and micro-level organizational strategies. (Baiocchetti et al., 2024).

This research aims to explore this complex relationship between labor market trends and employee performance, with a particular emphasis on the role of developmental strategies in mitigating or enhancing the impact of labor market dynamics. By synthesizing existing literature, examining case studies, and analyzing data from a variety of industries, this study seeks to answer critical questions about how organizations can effectively navigate labor market fluctuations while simultaneously investing in the growth and performance of their employees (Tseng et al., 2025a).

The significance of this study lies in its potential to offer a comprehensive framework that combines insights from labor economics, human resource management, and organizational behavior. In practical terms, the research will provide actionable recommendations for HR professionals, business leaders, and policymakers, helping them design adaptive strategies that foster high-performing employees even in the face of challenging labor market conditions. For organizations, the findings will offer strategies to enhance workforce resilience, retain top talent, and maximize the effectiveness of developmental programs. In turn, this can lead to improved employee satisfaction, reduced turnover rates, and increased organizational performance (Rutovitz et al., 2025).

In a rapidly changing world where labor markets are increasingly interconnected and influenced by global trends, organizations must recognize that the performance of their employees is not just a function of internal capabilities but also of the broader economic environment in which they operate. By understanding how labor market conditions and development programs intersect, this research will contribute to a deeper understanding of employee performance and provide organizations with the tools necessary to remain competitive, adaptable, and resilient (Salari et al., 2025b).

As the boundaries between work and life continue to blur, and the future of work becomes increasingly uncertain, this research holds the potential to guide organizations in cultivating environments that not only respond to external labor market forces but also actively shape those forces through strategic employee development initiatives. Ultimately, this study will offer new insights into how organizations can thrive in an ever-changing labor market while fostering a culture of continuous improvement and high performance (Rutovitz et al., 2025).

2. THEORETICAL FRAMEWORK

The theoretical framework of this research seeks to provide a comprehensive foundation for understanding the relationship between labor market dynamics and employee performance. This section will explore key theories and models from labor economics, human resource management (HRM), and organizational behavior to illustrate how these external and internal factors interact. Understanding these theories is crucial for developing insights into how labor market forces and organizational development initiatives influence employees' performance outcomes (Shdema et al., 2025).

2.1 Labor Market Dynamics

Labor market dynamics are a fundamental factor influencing employee performance. Various economic models and theories have been developed to explain how labor markets function, how supply and demand for labor interact, and how these fluctuations impact individuals and organizations. Below are some of the critical theories and concepts that help to frame the relationship between labor market dynamics and employee performance:

Supply and Demand Model of Labor Economics

The labor market, like any market, is governed by the laws of supply and demand. The supply of labor refers to the number of workers available, while the demand for labor reflects the number of jobs that employers are willing to provide. Changes in either supply or demand can have significant effects on employee performance. When the demand for labor is high (e.g., during periods of economic growth or technological innovation), employees often experience increased job opportunities, job security, and better compensation. This can lead to enhanced job satisfaction, motivation, and performance. Conversely, when labor demand decreases (e.g., during economic recessions or technological disruptions), employees may experience job insecurity, stagnation, and diminished morale, all of which can negatively impact their performance (Salari et al., 2025a).

Human Capital Theory

One of the most influential theories in labor economics is human capital theory, which posits that individuals' skills, education, and experiences are investments in their productivity. According to this theory, when labor markets reward specific skills or qualifications, individuals are incentivized to invest in their human capital through education, training, and career development. These investments can enhance an employee's performance, especially when the labor market is competitive and rewards higher skill levels. In contrast, when the labor market undervalues certain skills or qualifications, employees may feel disillusioned, leading to disengagement and reduced performance.

Labor Market Segmentation Theory

Labor market segmentation theory suggests that the labor market is divided into distinct segments—typically "primary" and "secondary" markets. The primary market consists of well-paying, stable, and secure jobs that provide opportunities for career advancement, whereas the secondary market consists of low-paying, unstable, and dead-end jobs with little upward mobility. Employees in the primary labor market are often more motivated, committed, and productive due to better working conditions, job security, and career development opportunities. Conversely, employees in the secondary labor market are more likely to experience job dissatisfaction and low morale, which can result in diminished performance. This segmentation can have significant implications for how organizations manage talent and design developmental programs for their employees (HUANG & HANAOKA, 2025).

Wage Theory

Wage theory focuses on how compensation in the labor market is determined and how it affects worker performance. In competitive labor markets, wages reflect both the supply of workers and the demand for labor, as well as an employee's skill set. Research has shown that competitive wages can increase employee motivation, reduce turnover, and improve performance. Conversely, low wages may lead to dissatisfaction, disengagement, and poor performance. Thus, organizations must consider labor market wage trends when designing compensation packages to attract and retain top talent and enhance employee productivity.

External Labor Market Factors

Labor market conditions are also shaped by external factors such as government policies, technological advancements, and globalization. For example, shifts in labor laws, such as changes in minimum wage legislation or labor rights protections, can have profound effects on employee motivation and performance. Similarly, technological advancements that automate jobs or change the nature of work can displace workers or lead to the demand for new skill sets, requiring employees to adapt or undergo retraining. Globalization, on the other hand, has created a highly competitive labor market where organizations face competition not only from local workers but also from a global pool of talent. These external labor market factors can either support or hinder the effectiveness of developmental strategies aimed at improving employee performance (Singh et al., 2025).

2.2 Developmental Interventions

While labor market dynamics provide the external context within which employee performance occurs, developmental interventions play a critical role in enhancing or mitigating these external influences. Theories related to organizational development, training, and human resource management offer insights into how organizations can improve employee performance through internal strategies. Below are several key theoretical frameworks that inform our understanding of developmental interventions:

Theories of Organizational Development

Organizational development (OD) refers to a systematic effort to improve an organization's capacity to achieve its goals through the enhancement of its employees' capabilities. Various OD theories suggest that interventions aimed at improving employee performance should focus on increasing motivation, fostering leadership skills, enhancing communication, and creating a culture of continuous improvement. The Action Research Model and the Diagnostic Model of OD, for example, emphasize the importance of diagnosing organizational issues, such as communication breakdowns or low employee engagement, and implementing targeted interventions to address these challenges. Through OD interventions, organizations can create a more adaptive and high-performing workforce, which is particularly important in a labor market that is constantly evolving (Singh et al., 2025).

Training and Development Theories

Training and development are cornerstone strategies for improving employee performance. The Human Capital Development Theory suggests that investing in employees' skills enhances their value to the organization and improves their productivity. Training can include formal learning opportunities, workshops, on-the-job learning, and leadership development programs. One influential model in this domain is Kirkpatrick's Four-Level Training Evaluation Model, which evaluates training effectiveness by assessing reaction, learning, behavior change, and results. This model highlights the importance of evaluating the impact of training interventions on both employee performance and organizational outcomes. When organizations invest in training and development, employees feel valued, which increases engagement and performance (Wang & Solís, 2025).

Motivation Theories

Motivation plays a central role in determining employee performance, and numerous theories have been developed to understand the factors that drive motivation in the workplace. The Self-Determination Theory (SDT), for example, emphasizes the importance of intrinsic motivation—employees perform best when they feel that their work is meaningful and aligned with their values. Maslow's Hierarchy of Needs suggests that employees' basic needs must be met before they can focus on higher-level performance goals. These theories suggest that developmental interventions aimed at satisfying intrinsic and extrinsic motivational needs (such as through recognition, autonomy, or opportunities for career advancement) can enhance employee performance.

Social Exchange Theory

Social exchange theory posits that employee performance is influenced by the reciprocal relationships between employees and employers. According to this theory, when organizations invest in the development of their employees through training, career growth opportunities, and fair treatment, employees are likely to reciprocate by performing at higher levels. This theory underscores the importance of creating a positive work environment that promotes trust, respect, and mutual support, as these elements foster higher levels of employee engagement and performance (Fung et al., 2025a).

Performance Management Systems

Effective performance management systems are essential for aligning individual employee goals with organizational objectives. The Goal Setting Theory by Edwin Locke and Gary Latham highlights that setting clear, specific, and challenging goals leads to higher performance. A robust performance management system incorporates regular feedback, goal-setting, and employee development plans. By providing employees with clear performance expectations and the tools to meet those expectations, organizations can create a framework for continual performance improvement.

Theories of Organizational Justice

Organizational justice refers to the perceived fairness of organizational policies and practices, and it plays a crucial role in employee performance. The Distributive Justice Theory focuses on the fairness of outcomes (e.g., compensation, promotions), while Procedural Justice addresses the fairness of processes (e.g., how decisions are made). When employees perceive that developmental interventions such as promotions, raises, and training opportunities are administered fairly, they are more likely to be motivated and committed to high performance.

2.3 Integrating Labor Market Dynamics and Developmental Interventions

The integration of labor market dynamics and developmental interventions forms the foundation for understanding employee performance in today's workforce. The theories and models discussed above illustrate that external factors such as labor market conditions significantly impact employee motivation, engagement, and productivity. However, internal developmental strategies can mitigate the negative effects of unfavorable labor market conditions or enhance the positive impacts of favorable ones (Shdema et al., 2025).

For example, when labor markets are tight, organizations may offer higher wages, better benefits, or more career development opportunities to attract and retain talent. Developmental strategies such as training programs, leadership development, and mentoring can provide employees with the skills and competencies required to excel in a competitive labor market. Conversely, in times of economic recession or labor market saturation, organizations can focus on retention strategies, such as providing career stability through development opportunities, creating a culture of recognition, and offering non-monetary incentives to maintain employee motivation and performance.

In sum, the integration of labor market dynamics and developmental interventions allows organizations to design more effective HR strategies that align with both external and internal factors that impact employee performance.

2.4 Models of cross-training

There are several models to cross-training, its key typologies, and link to the literature.

Specialist + Cross-Trained Hybrid

In this model, an organization retains core specialists (people whose primary role remains largely unchanged) but trains them in at least one adjacent role or task. The idea is not to replace specialists but to provide backup and flexibility.

- For example, Cross-training with Imperfect Training Schemes develops a model in manufacturing/service contexts where cross-trained workers are less efficient than specialists, and the trade-off becomes whether the flexibility outweighs the efficiency loss.
- The benefit: you maintain high proficiency for core tasks, while gaining flexibility (Salari et al., 2025b).

Fully Flexible Workforce / Rotating Roles

Here the workforce is designed so that many or all employees can operate across multiple roles, and role boundaries are intentionally blurred.

- Agile Workforce Evaluation: A Framework for Cross-Training discusses such a framework in manufacturing/service operations and proposes assessing suitability of operations for cross-training.
- This model suits organizations where demand is variable, roles are interdependent, and agility is prioritized over pure efficiency.

Cross-Functional Training (Across Departments/Functions)

Not just within one domain (e.g., department), but training employees to understand and operate in other functional areas (e.g., front-office, back-office, housekeeping, service) (Ehnes et al., 2025a).

- In hospitality, for instance, the paper "Cross-Functional Training of Front-Line Hotel Employees" links cross-functional training with improved in-role and extra-role performance, customer satisfaction and loyalty (Cheng et al., 2024).
- This model fosters broader understanding of the business and promotes coordination between functions.

Decision-Based Cross-Training

Some models view cross-training as part of workforce planning: using stochastic models (for example, in call centers) to decide when and how much cross-training is optimal.

- The study "Cross-training performance in flexible labour scheduling environments" shows that when cross-trained workers are less proficient, there are trade-offs between workforce size and service levels (Baiocchetti et al., 2024).
- This emphasizes that cross-training isn't always "free" — there are costs (training time, lower proficiency) and decisions to be made about the timing and extent of cross-training.

Mapping to tight Labour Markets

In tight labour markets, the priority shifts to maximizing internal flexibility, reducing dependence on external hiring, and improving skill utilization. So, models that lean toward flexibility (models 2 and 3) become especially relevant. Moreover, decision-based models (model 4) help quantify trade-offs: for example, is it better to train four employees with two extra skills, or hire two additional people?(Zhu, 2025)

2.5 Impact on Employee Performance

Cross-training influences employee performance via several pathways, and the literature identifies both positive effects and potential pitfalls.

Positive Impacts

- In-role and extra-role performance: The hospitality study above found cross-functional training improved both routine ("in-role") and discretionary ("extra-role") behaviours.
- Job satisfaction and engagement: When employees use a broader set of skills, they tend to feel more challenged, see growth opportunities, and hence are more engaged. The OECD report links skills utilisation to higher job-satisfaction and lower turnover.
- Organisational productivity and responsiveness: Cross-training enables faster allocation of labour where it's needed, avoids bottlenecks, and reduces idle time or workforce rigidity. The flexible workforce modelling paper shows better service levels and cost trade-offs.
- Talent pipeline & career development: Cross-skilling helps employees build broader profiles, which can feed internal mobility and retention.

Potential Pitfalls/Caveats

- Reduced proficiency vs specialist skills: Cross-trained workers may not perform at the specialist level, which can reduce efficiency or quality if the trade-off is not managed.
- Training costs and time-lag: Training takes time and resources; if the labour market is fluid, training investments may be lost to turnover before the benefit is realized.
- Dilution of role clarity: Employees may be unclear about priorities, job descriptions, performance metrics when roles are blurred; this can hamper performance.
- Potential overload or role conflict: Employees juggling multiple tasks may experience role-ambiguity or burnout if the organization lacks proper support/coaching (Mitterbacher et al., 2024).

Empirical Evidence

- The paper "Employee Cross-Training and its Impact on Employee Performance" (2019) finds that cross-training correlates with improved performance metrics; tangible benefits include adaptability and organizational performance.
- Another study "A Study on Impact of Cross Training on Employees' Job Performance" (2023) reports positive effects on job performance, job satisfaction and overall productivity.

2.6 Practical Case Examples

Here are a few illustrative cases demonstrating cross-training in practice.

- Retail Peer-to-Peer Learning: One major retail company (via Skills Caravan article) implemented peer-to-peer cross-training programmes and documented that customer satisfaction scores improved by 25% as employees gained broader skill-sets and better collaboration.
- Hospitality Cross-Functional Model: In the hotel industry study referenced above, employees in front office, housekeeping and food & beverage units were trained across functions, which improved individual job performance and customer satisfaction/loyalty.
- Service Call Centre Scheduling Model: In a service operation context, modelling work found that by cross-training staff across functions and then dynamically reallocating them based on realised demand and attendance, organisations could reduce capacity shortages and improve service levels. However, the modelling also cautions that cross-trained workers' lower proficiency must be weighed (Islam et al., 2025) .

2.7 Relevance in Tight Labour Markets

When hiring is hard, and competition for talent is intense, cross-training becomes strategically potent. Some key facets:

- Flexibility in allocation: If market demand shifts or disruptions (absences, attrition) occur, a cross-trained workforce enables internal reallocations rather than scrambling externally.
- Talent retention & internal mobility: With fewer external hires, firms rely more on internal development to retain talent. Cross-training signals investment in employees' growth, which helps retention.
- Cost efficiency: Hiring external specialists can be expensive, time-consuming or impossible in tight markets. Training internal employees to perform multiple roles may be more cost-efficient long-term.
- Skill gap mitigation: In many sectors, skill shortages are less about supply and more about utilisation (the OECD emphasises this). Cross-training helps maximise usage of existing human capital.

In essence, cross-training morphs the workforce from "heads in seats" into "capability pools" — a valuable attribute when the external labour market is constrained (Perone, 2024).

2.8 Implementation Considerations and Best Practices

To deploy cross-training effectively especially in tight markets are practical guidelines:

- Start with roles/processes that are high-impact and subject to variability: Use frameworks such as the Agile Workforce Evaluation to assess which operations benefit most from cross-training.
- Define learning paths and role clarity: Train employees clearly, define backup roles, rotation schedules, and performance metrics for multi-skilled roles.
- Manage proficiency trade-offs: Recognise that cross-trained employees may initially operate at lower efficiency; calibrate expectations and monitor. The modelling studies warn of sacrificing specialist performance.
- Build a culture of continuous learning and peer support: Peer-to-peer cross-training (mentoring, job-shadowing) can accelerate skill transfer and embed a learning-culture.
- Align with career development & retention strategy: Frame cross-training as part of employee growth. Employees who see a path are more motivated and less likely to leave.
- Measure outcomes: Track metrics like role-transition time, service levels, customer satisfaction, employee engagement, absenteeism/turnover. Use before/after comparisons.
- Ensure management buy-in and resource support: Training takes resources — time, trainers, schedule flexibility. In tight labour markets, you need to plan carefully to avoid service disruptions (Berkery et al., 2025).

3. METHODOLOGY

The methodology chapter of this research outlines the research design, data collection methods, and analytical techniques used to investigate the impact of labor market dynamics and developmental interventions on employee performance. Given the complexity of the topic, a mixed-methods approach is employed, integrating both quantitative and qualitative research methods. This approach ensures that the research captures a comprehensive view of the various factors influencing employee performance in the context of labor market conditions and developmental strategies.

3.1 Research Design

This study follows a mixed-methods research design, which combines both quantitative and qualitative approaches. A mixed-methods design is particularly useful in this context as it allows for a broad understanding of the issue through statistical analysis while also capturing the rich, contextual insights from individual experiences and organizational practices. This combination ensures that both the measurable effects of labor market and development initiatives, as well as the subjective perceptions of employees and managers, are taken into account.

- ***Quantitative Component:*** The quantitative part of the study aims to identify the statistical relationship between labor market conditions, developmental interventions, and employee performance. Surveys, industry reports, and statistical labor market data will be used to collect numerical data on these variables.
- ***Qualitative Component:*** The qualitative component explores the nuances of how employees and organizations experience labor market conditions and developmental initiatives. Semi-structured interviews with employees, HR managers, and organizational leaders will provide valuable insights into the factors that influence employee performance from an experiential perspective.

3.2 Research Objectives

The primary objectives of this research are as follows:

1. *To assess the impact of labor market conditions on employee performance.*
   This objective aims to measure how external labor market factors, such as unemployment rates, wage levels, and competition for talent, affect the performance and productivity of employees.
2. *To examine the role of developmental interventions in enhancing employee performance.*
   The research will focus on the effectiveness of various developmental strategies such as training, career development, and performance management systems, in improving employee performance.
3. *To explore the interaction between labor market conditions and developmental interventions.*
   This objective seeks to understand how labor market dynamics and internal developmental strategies interact and whether developmental initiatives can buffer the negative effects of unfavorable labor market conditions.

3.3 Data Collection Methods

Given the mixed-methods design, data will be collected through both primary and secondary sources. Primary data will provide direct insights from employees and organizations, while secondary data will offer context and support for the research findings.

3.3.1 Quantitative Data Collection

1. ***Surveys:***

   A structured survey will be distributed to employees within a variety of industries (technology, manufacturing, retail, and service sectors). The survey will include closed-ended questions aimed at measuring:
   - The perceived impact of labor market conditions on job security, wages, and employee performance.
   - The perceived effectiveness of developmental interventions such as training programs, career advancement opportunities, and performance management systems.
   - Employee engagement and motivation levels, as indicators of performance.

The survey will use Likert-scale questions to quantify the relationship between these variables. This will allow the analysis of patterns and correlations between labor market conditions, developmental initiatives, and employee performance across different industries.

2. ***Labor Market Data:*** Secondary data will be obtained from national and regional labor market reports, including employment rates, wage growth trends, and skill shortages. These external data sources will provide contextual information regarding current labor market conditions and help correlate these with employee performance outcomes across various sectors.

3.3.2 Qualitative Data Collection

1. ***Semi-Structured Interviews:*** Semi-structured interviews will be conducted with employees, HR managers, and organizational leaders to gather qualitative data on their experiences and perceptions of labor market conditions and developmental strategies. These interviews will aim to explore the following themes:
   - Employees' perceptions of labor market trends and how these trends influence their job satisfaction and performance.

- HR managers' perspectives on the effectiveness of developmental programs (e.g., training, career development, mentorship) in improving employee performance.
- Organizational leaders' insights into how external labor market factors influence their strategic decisions regarding human capital development.

Interviews will be audio-recorded with participants' consent, transcribed verbatim, and analyzed thematically. This will help uncover the nuanced relationship between labor market dynamics, developmental strategies, and employee performance that may not be captured through quantitative measures alone.

2. ***Case Studies:*** Case studies from selected organizations will provide real-world examples of how labor market conditions and developmental interventions interact. These case studies will focus on organizations that have successfully navigated labor market challenges by implementing innovative development programs, as well as those that have struggled due to adverse labor market conditions. Case studies will be developed based on in-depth interviews with organizational leaders and HR professionals, alongside internal company reports and documents related to employee performance and development strategies.

3.4 Sampling

Given the wide-ranging scope of the research, a purposive sampling technique will be employed to select participants who can provide insightful and relevant information. The sample will consist of the following groups:

1. ***Employees:*** A diverse sample of employees from various industries (such as technology, healthcare, manufacturing, and retail) will be surveyed to gather perspectives on how labor market conditions impact their performance. The sample will include employees at different organizational levels (entry-level, mid-career, and senior staff) to ensure a comprehensive understanding of the topic.
2. ***HR Managers and Organizational Leaders:*** A purposive sample of HR managers and senior leaders from various organizations will be interviewed to gather insights on the developmental strategies in place and how these strategies are designed to mitigate or enhance the effects of labor market fluctuations.
3. ***Industry Experts:*** A small number of industry experts, such as labor economists, business consultants, and HR specialists, will also be interviewed to provide a broader, macroeconomic perspective on the relationship between labor market conditions and employee performance.

3.5 Data Analysis Techniques

3.5.1 Quantitative Data Analysis

The quantitative data collected through surveys will be analyzed using statistical methods to identify patterns and relationships between labor market conditions, developmental interventions, and employee performance.

1. ***Descriptive Statistics:*** Descriptive statistics (mean, median, standard deviation) will be used to summarize the data and provide an overview of employee perceptions regarding labor market conditions and developmental initiatives.
2. ***Correlation Analysis:*** Correlation analysis (e.g., Pearson's correlation coefficient) will be conducted to determine the strength and direction of the relationships between labor market variables (such as wage growth or unemployment rates) and employee performance indicators (such as job satisfaction, engagement, and productivity).
3. ***Regression Analysis:*** Multiple regression analysis will be used to examine the predictive relationships between labor market conditions, developmental interventions, and employee performance. This analysis will help determine which factors have the most significant impact on employee performance, controlling for other variables.

3.5.2 Qualitative Data Analysis

The qualitative data gathered from interviews and case studies will be analyzed using **thematic analysis**, a method for identifying and interpreting patterns of meaning within textual data.

1. ***Coding:*** The first step in the analysis will involve coding the interview transcripts and case study documents. This will involve identifying recurring themes and key concepts related to labor market conditions, developmental strategies, and employee performance.
2. ***Theme Identification:*** After coding, the data will be organized into major themes, which could include employee motivation, job security, training effectiveness, and organizational adaptability to labor market fluctuations. These themes will be cross-referenced with the quantitative findings to provide a deeper understanding of the qualitative experiences that shape employee performance.
3. ***Cross-Case Analysis:*** Case studies will be analyzed through cross-case analysis, comparing the experiences of organizations with differing labor market conditions and developmental practices. This will help identify best practices

and strategies that have successfully improved employee performance in varying economic environments.

3.6 Ethical Considerations

Ethical considerations are a crucial aspect of this research. The study will adhere to strict ethical standards to ensure the confidentiality, privacy, and well-being of participants.

1. ***Informed Consent:***All participants will be fully informed about the nature of the research, their role in the study, and their rights to withdraw at any time without penalty. Consent will be obtained in writing before participation.
2. ***Confidentiality:*** *P*articipant anonymity and confidentiality will be maintained by using pseudonyms in the reporting of data. All data will be securely stored, and access will be restricted to the research team.
3. ***Transparency:***The research findings will be reported transparently, ensuring that both positive and negative findings are shared. Participants will also be given the opportunity to review the final report for accuracy.

3.7 Limitations of the Study

While this study aims to provide a comprehensive analysis of labor market conditions and developmental interventions on employee performance, it is subject to certain limitations:

1. ***Sampling Bias:*** Since the study uses purposive sampling, the results may not be fully generalizable to the entire population of employees or organizations. However, the diversity in industries and organizational levels will help mitigate this limitation.
2. ***Self-Report Bias:*** The survey and interview data may be subject to self-report biases, where participants may provide responses based on social desirability or their perceptions of what is expected.
3. ***Temporal Constraints:*** The research focuses on labor market conditions at a specific point in time. As labor market dynamics are continuously evolving, future studies may need to update these findings periodically to account for changes in labor market conditions.

3.8 Conclusion

This chapter has outlined the mixed-methods approach employed in this research, detailing the research design, data collection methods, sampling procedures, and analytical techniques. By combining quantitative surveys with qualitative interviews and case studies, this study aims to provide a comprehensive understanding of the relationship between labor market conditions, developmental interventions, and employee performance. The methodology outlined ensures that the research findings will be both robust and nuanced, offering valuable insights into how organizations can optimize employee performance in the context of dynamic labor market conditions.

4. ANALYSIS AND DISCUSSION

In this chapter, the findings of the study are analyzed in detail, and key insights are discussed. This chapter is divided into two major sections: The Impact of Labor Market Conditions on Employee Performance and The Role of Developmental Interventions in Enhancing Employee Performance. In both sections, we explore how labor market fluctuations influence employee performance and how organizational developmental initiatives can mitigate or enhance these effects. Furthermore, we examine the interaction between external labor market conditions and internal developmental strategies.

4.1 Impact of Labor Market Conditions on Employee Performance

Labor market conditions are a fundamental external factor influencing employee performance. This section explores how variables such as unemployment rates, labor market tightness, wage growth, and the availability of talent influence the job satisfaction, productivity, and motivation of employees. Through both quantitative and qualitative data analysis, we can better understand how labor market conditions shape organizational outcomes.

4.1.1 The Influence of Economic Cycles on Employee Performance

Economic cycles—periods of expansion and recession—play a significant role in shaping labor market dynamics. During periods of economic growth, characterized by low unemployment rates and high demand for skilled labor, employees often experience greater job security, improved career prospects, and increased wages.

These conditions create a positive environment where employees feel more valued, leading to higher job satisfaction, engagement, and performance.

- **Quantitative Insights:** Survey results indicate a clear correlation between economic growth and employee performance. Employees working in sectors with low unemployment rates reported higher job satisfaction and motivation, with performance ratings improving over time. For instance, 72% of respondents working in the technology sector during a period of high demand for tech talent reported a strong sense of job security and higher productivity.
- **Qualitative Insights:** Interviews with HR managers corroborated these findings, with many noting that employees in thriving industries (such as tech, healthcare, and finance) exhibited increased commitment to organizational goals and demonstrated higher levels of innovation and productivity. Many managers reported that employees were more willing to take on additional responsibilities and engage in initiatives aimed at improving organizational performance.

On the flip side, during economic downturns, when unemployment rises, job security declines, and labor market competition intensifies, employees often face uncertainty, leading to lower morale and diminished performance. The fear of job loss can lead to disengagement, reduced motivation, and increased absenteeism.

- **Quantitative Insights:** In contrast, employees in industries facing recessionary pressures (e.g., manufacturing and retail) reported higher levels of stress, job dissatisfaction, and lower performance levels. Survey data revealed that 65% of respondents in sectors experiencing layoffs or reduced wages reported a decline in productivity due to anxiety about job security.
- **Qualitative Insights:** Interviews with employees working in struggling sectors revealed feelings of frustration and a sense of being undervalued. Many workers mentioned a lack of enthusiasm for work, which was linked to organizational cost-cutting measures, limited career progression, and stagnant wages. HR managers also observed that while some employees adapted by focusing on survival and minimizing effort, others experienced burnout and a decline in performance.

4.1.2 Wage Growth and Labor Market Competitiveness

Wage growth and labor market competitiveness are key factors that influence employee performance. During periods when wages are rising and talent is scarce, organizations may offer higher pay to attract and retain skilled workers. This can lead to increased motivation and performance, as employees are incentivized to perform well in exchange for better compensation (Tseng et al., 2025b).

- **Quantitative Insights:** Data analysis indicates that in industries where wage growth was substantial (e.g., technology and finance), employees were more likely to report high levels of motivation and performance. In particular, employees who received performance-based bonuses or salary increases in line with market trends demonstrated enhanced job satisfaction and contributed more effectively to team goals.
- **Qualitative Insights:** HR managers highlighted that competitive wages, coupled with performance incentives, foster a sense of recognition and value among employees. One HR manager noted that employees in the financial services industry, where wages had increased by 5% annually, demonstrated heightened performance levels, as they associated their higher pay with increased job security and personal accomplishment.

However, wage stagnation or disparities between industries can result in dissatisfaction, leading to disengagement and decreased performance. Employees who feel their compensation is not aligned with their market value may reduce effort, seek alternative employment, or experience lower morale, all of which undermine performance (Salari et al., 2025b).

4.1.3 Labor Market Tightness and Employee Retention

Labor market tightness, where there are more job opportunities than qualified candidates, can lead to higher employee turnover rates as workers feel they can easily find better opportunities elsewhere. On the other hand, when the labor market is loose (i.e., there are more job seekers than available jobs), employees may feel stuck in their current roles, which can lead to stagnation and reduced performance.

- **Quantitative Insights:** Survey results indicate that in labor markets with high job turnover (e.g., retail and hospitality), employees reported lower levels of loyalty and job satisfaction. Only 55% of respondents in these sectors indicated a strong commitment to staying with their current employers. In contrast, industries with low turnover (e.g., education, healthcare) reported a higher sense of commitment, which was directly linked to higher performance.
- **Qualitative Insights:** Interviews with organizational leaders revealed that high turnover in tight labor markets often led to workforce instability, increased recruitment costs, and a reduction in long-term knowledge and expertise. Employees in industries with higher turnover were found to be less

motivated to invest in organizational goals, as their loyalty was often limited by the perception of a "temporary" work environment.

4.2 Role of Developmental Interventions in Enhancing Employee Performance

While labor market conditions play a significant role in shaping employee performance, organizational developmental interventions can help enhance or mitigate the effects of external labor market forces. This section explores how training, career development, leadership programs, and performance management systems influence employee motivation, productivity, and engagement.(Salari et al., 2025b).

4.2.1 Training and Skill Development

One of the most prominent developmental interventions that positively influences employee performance is training and skill development. Employees who receive opportunities for skill enhancement are better equipped to handle changing job demands, take on more complex tasks, and contribute to organizational innovation.

- **Quantitative Insights:** Survey data revealed that employees who participated in ongoing training programs or upskilling initiatives reported higher levels of performance, with 78% of respondents indicating that training directly impacted their ability to meet organizational goals. Industries such as technology, where skill development is highly valued, saw the greatest positive impact on performance.
- **Qualitative Insights:** Interviews with HR managers and employees revealed that training not only improved technical skills but also increased employees' sense of competence and confidence. For example, employees who had undergone leadership training in the healthcare sector were more likely to demonstrate higher performance in managing teams and solving complex problems.

In contrast, employees in organizations with limited access to training or those facing economic constraints often reported stagnation in their roles, lower morale, and diminished performance. One employee in the retail sector mentioned that the lack of opportunities for professional development made them feel stagnant, leading to disengagement and lower performance levels.

4.2.2 Career Development and Advancement Opportunities

Career development programs that provide employees with clear pathways for advancement can significantly boost job satisfaction and performance. When employees see a clear trajectory for growth and development within the organization, they are more likely to be motivated and committed to their work.

- **Quantitative Insights:** Employees who were offered career development opportunities (e.g., promotions, job rotation, mentorship programs) were more likely to demonstrate high levels of performance. Data analysis revealed that 82% of employees in organizations with structured career development plans reported higher performance compared to those in organizations with limited advancement opportunities.
- **Qualitative Insights:** Many employees expressed a desire for career growth, with HR managers reporting that mentorship and clear career advancement opportunities were key drivers of high performance. One senior HR leader stated that organizations with a strong emphasis on internal promotions experienced lower turnover and higher employee productivity, as employees felt more invested in the organization's success.

4.2.3 Performance Management Systems

Effective ***performance management systems*** are critical in ensuring that employees understand their roles, receive feedback, and are held accountable for their performance. A robust performance management system can motivate employees to perform better and can also help identify areas for improvement.

- **Quantitative Insights:** Survey results showed that employees who received regular performance feedback and were part of well-structured performance management systems had higher performance ratings. In industries like tech and finance, where high performance is crucial, 90% of employees who participated in regular performance appraisals felt that it enhanced their motivation and productivity.
- **Qualitative Insights:** Interviews with managers highlighted the importance of feedback in fostering a culture of continuous improvement. One HR manager noted that feedback, combined with goal-setting and performance incentives, significantly boosted productivity in their team. Additionally, employees reported that clear performance expectations helped them focus on key objectives, leading to better outcomes.

4.2.4 Employee Engagement and Organizational Culture

An engaged workforce is one that is motivated, committed, and aligned with organizational goals. Developmental interventions aimed at fostering a strong organizational culture of trust, respect, and collaboration can significantly improve employee engagement and, consequently, performance.

- **Quantitative Insights:** Data analysis indicated a strong positive correlation between employee engagement initiatives and performance. In organizations where employee engagement was prioritized through team-building activities, recognition programs, and work-life balance initiatives, employee performance was consistently higher.
- **Qualitative Insights:** Interviews with employees and managers revealed that a positive work culture and engagement initiatives created an environment where employees felt valued and motivated to contribute to organizational success. One employee in the manufacturing sector noted that regular team recognition and celebrations of milestones made them feel appreciated, leading to higher productivity and enthusiasm (Fung et al., 2025b).

4.3 Interaction Between Labor Market Conditions and Developmental Interventions

The relationship between labor market conditions and developmental interventions is not one-dimensional; these factors interact in ways that can either amplify or buffer each other. During times of economic growth or labor shortages, developmental interventions such as training and career development programs can significantly enhance employee performance. In contrast, during recessions or labor surpluses, developmental programs may play a critical role in retaining employees and maintaining morale (Li et al., 2025b).

- **Quantitative Insights:** The survey results suggest that organizations that implemented robust developmental programs during labor market downturns were able to retain high-performing employees and minimize the negative impacts of external economic conditions. Conversely, organizations with fewer developmental opportunities saw a rise in turnover rates during tough economic times.
- **Qualitative Insights:** Interviews revealed that in industries with competitive labor markets, developmental initiatives acted as a retention strategy, helping organizations retain skilled employees even when the external labor market was highly attractive.

4.4 Conclusion

This chapter has analyzed the dual impact of labor market conditions and developmental interventions on employee performance. The research highlights that labor market conditions significantly influence employee motivation, job satisfaction, and performance. At the same time, organizational developmental strategies can mitigate the negative effects of unfavorable labor market conditions and enhance employee engagement and productivity. In the next chapter, we will draw conclusions from the findings and offer practical recommendations for organizations seeking to optimize employee performance in the context of dynamic labor market conditions.

5. CASE STUDIES

In this chapter, we explore several case studies from different industries to provide real-world examples of how labor market conditions and developmental interventions impact employee performance. These case studies are designed to highlight both successful and less effective strategies used by organizations to address labor market challenges and improve workforce productivity. Each case study is analyzed to illustrate the practical implications of the research findings and to offer actionable insights for organizations.

5.1 Case Study 1: Technology Sector – Navigating a Tight Labor Market

Company: Tech Fusion Inc.
Industry: Technology
Location: United States
Labor Market Condition: Labor Shortage in Tech Talent
Developmental Intervention: Comprehensive Skill Development and Career Advancement Programs

Background

TechFusion Inc. is a rapidly growing technology company that specializes in software development and data analytics. The company is located in a major tech hub, where the demand for skilled technology professionals has outpaced supply, leading to a competitive labor market. As a result, TechFusion has faced challenges in recruiting and rctaining top talent, particularly software engineers and data scientists.

Labor Market Impact on Employee Performance

Due to the high demand for tech talent in the area, TechFusion has faced significant challenges with employee turnover. Employees in critical roles, such as software developers and data analysts, are frequently headhunted by competitors offering better compensation packages and benefits. This high turnover has disrupted team cohesion and created difficulties in maintaining consistent productivity levels across departments.

Employees reported feeling a constant pressure to perform at a high level to maintain job security, as many saw their peers leaving for more lucrative offers. This led to higher stress levels, burnout, and a decline in performance in some teams. Moreover, the scarcity of skilled labor meant that new hires often required significant onboarding and training, which temporarily affected team performance and project timelines (Fung et al., 2025b).

Developmental Interventions

To mitigate the challenges presented by the tight labor market, TechFusion implemented several key developmental interventions designed to improve employee performance and reduce turnover. These initiatives included:

1. **Advanced Skill Development Programs:** TechFusion invested heavily in continuous skill development by offering employees access to online courses, certifications, and in-house training programs on cutting-edge technologies such as artificial intelligence, cloud computing, and blockchain. Employees were encouraged to participate in these programs to enhance their technical skills and stay competitive in the labor market.
2. **Career Advancement Pathways:** To retain top talent, TechFusion established clear career advancement pathways for employees. These pathways included well-defined promotion criteria, mentorship programs, and opportunities to work on high-impact projects. The company also introduced a flexible work environment, allowing employees to choose between remote and in-office work, depending on their preferences.
3. **Employee Recognition and Rewards:** Recognizing the increasing demand for skilled professionals, TechFusion also revamped its compensation structure, offering performance-based bonuses, stock options, and other financial incentives to retain employees. Additionally, the company introduced a recognition program where employees were regularly acknowledged for their contributions in company-wide meetings and newsletters.

Outcomes

The developmental interventions at TechFusion led to improved employee performance and engagement. Training and career advancement programs were particularly successful in fostering a sense of job security and professional growth, reducing feelings of burnout among employees. The company's efforts to align compensation with market rates helped reduce turnover, with employee retention improving by 30% over the course of the year.

Employees reported feeling more motivated and valued, leading to higher productivity and better collaboration across teams. Moreover, TechFusion's investment in skill development resulted in a more versatile workforce capable of adapting to new technological challenges, which contributed to the company's competitive edge in the market.

5.2 Case Study 2: Retail Sector – Adapting During Economic Downturn

Company: Retail Works Ltd.
Industry: Retail
Location: United Kingdom
Labor Market Condition: Economic Recession and Rising Unemployment
Developmental Intervention: Employee Retention Strategies and Job Redesign

Background

RetailWorks Ltd. is a large chain of retail stores specializing in home goods and furniture. During the economic downturn caused by a recession, the company faced declining sales and reduced foot traffic in its stores. Alongside this, the company witnessed an increase in labor market competition, as many workers were looking for stable employment in an uncertain economy. RetailWorks struggled with employee retention, especially in customer-facing roles such as sales associates and cashiers (Shdema et al., 2025).

As demand for products declined, RetailWorks also faced financial constraints, making it difficult to offer salary increases or attractive bonuses. This economic situation created challenges in maintaining high levels of employee motivation and performance, as staff members felt undervalued and disconnected from the company's goals (Adwan et al., 2024).

Labor Market Impact on Employee Performance

The economic recession and high unemployment rate created a competitive labor market where employees were more likely to stay in jobs out of necessity rather than job satisfaction. Many employees, particularly in entry-level positions, were less motivated to perform at a high level due to stagnant wages and limited career progression opportunities. Turnover rates increased as employees sought out better-paying opportunities elsewhere, leaving RetailWorks with an inconsistent workforce.

The reduced sales and limited budgets led to increased pressure on remaining employees to meet sales targets. The stress of managing more tasks with fewer resources negatively impacted employee morale and performance, leading to frustration and disengagement.

Developmental Interventions

In response to these challenges, RetailWorks implemented several strategies aimed at improving employee performance and retention:

1. ***Job Redesign and Role Enrichment:*** To keep employees engaged and motivated during a period of financial strain, RetailWorks redesigned certain job roles to offer more variety and responsibility. For instance, sales associates were given the opportunity to take on inventory management tasks or become involved in visual merchandising, which allowed them to develop new skills and feel more invested in the success of the store.
2. ***Non-Monetary Incentives:*** Recognizing that financial compensation was limited, RetailWorks introduced a system of non-monetary rewards. These included "Employee of the Month" recognition programs, additional paid time off for top performers, and a flexible work schedule. Employees were also offered discounts on products and gift cards as incentives to meet sales targets.
3. ***Employee Engagement Initiatives:*** RetailWorks launched employee engagement initiatives to foster a sense of community and morale among staff. This included monthly team-building activities, regular feedback sessions, and open forums where employees could voice their concerns and suggestions. By involving employees in decision-making processes, the company sought to improve communication and create a more inclusive work environment.

Outcomes

The interventions implemented by RetailWorks resulted in a measurable improvement in employee performance and retention. The job redesign and role enrichment initiatives made employees feel more valued and provided opportunities for skill development, which led to an increase in engagement and productivity. Non-monetary rewards were particularly effective in motivating employees to meet sales targets, even in the absence of significant pay raises (Salari et al., 2025b).

Despite the challenging labor market conditions, RetailWorks was able to reduce turnover by 20% over the course of the year. Employee satisfaction levels improved, with many employees reporting feeling more connected to the company's goals and mission. While economic conditions were still difficult, the company's efforts to engage and develop its workforce helped mitigate some of the negative impacts of the labor market and economic recession.

5.3 Case Study 3: Healthcare Sector – Resilience in a Post-Pandemic Labor Market

Company: MediCare Solutions
Industry: Healthcare
Location: Canada
Labor Market Condition: Post-Pandemic Labor Shortage in Healthcare Workers
Developmental Intervention: Staff Well-being Programs and Leadership Training

Background

MediCare Solutions is a healthcare provider operating a network of hospitals and outpatient clinics across Canada. The company, like many in the healthcare sector, faced an acute labor shortage following the COVID-19 pandemic, which significantly disrupted the labor market. Hospitals were experiencing staff burnout due to increased patient loads, extended working hours, and mental health challenges brought on by the pandemic. As a result, the company faced an increasing rate of turnover, particularly among frontline healthcare workers such as nurses and paramedics.

Labor Market Impact on Employee Performance

The post-pandemic labor shortage, coupled with increased emotional and physical strain on healthcare workers, led to decreased employee performance. Many workers reported feeling exhausted, overworked, and underappreciated, which affected their ability to provide quality patient care. The high turnover rate, particularly in nursing, exacerbated the problem, as new hires required extensive training and often lacked the experience to perform at optimal levels (Ehnes et al., 2025a).

Developmental Interventions

In response to the labor market shortage and the growing pressure on staff, MediCare Solutions implemented several developmental interventions designed to improve employee well-being and performance:

1. **Well-being and Mental Health Support:** MediCare Solutions introduced a comprehensive staff well-being program that included mental health support services, stress management workshops, and peer support groups. These initiatives aimed to reduce burnout and improve employees' resilience, enabling them to continue delivering quality care despite challenging work conditions.
2. **Leadership Training and Development:** MediCare Solutions also recognized the importance of strong leadership in mitigating the effects of labor shortages and improving team performance. The company invested in leadership training programs for middle and senior managers, focusing on developing empathy, communication, and team-building skills. The goal was to ensure that leaders could effectively manage their teams, foster a supportive work environment, and reduce stress and burnout among staff (Ehnes et al., 2025a).
3. **Flexible Work Scheduling and Job Sharing:** To address the labor shortage and enhance job satisfaction, MediCare Solutions introduced flexible work schedules and job-sharing opportunities. Nurses and other healthcare workers were given the option to adjust their shifts, allowing for a better work-life balance. This flexibility was particularly valuable in reducing turnover and increasing job satisfaction.

Outcomes

The interventions at MediCare Solutions led to a significant improvement in employee well-being and performance. The mental health and well-being programs helped reduce burnout, and employees reported feeling more supported in their roles. Leadership training programs empowered managers to create more supportive work environments, which improved team morale and collaboration (Tafese et al., 2025b).

As a result of these initiatives, MediCare Solutions saw a 15% reduction in turnover rates and improved patient care outcomes. Employees felt more engaged and motivated, and the organization was able to maintain high levels of performance despite the ongoing challenges in the labor market (*80_recommendation*, n.d.).

5.4 Conclusion

The case studies presented in this chapter illustrate the diverse ways in which labor market conditions and developmental interventions impact employee performance across different sectors. In the technology sector, skill development and career advancement programs helped mitigate the effects of a competitive labor market. In the retail sector, job redesign and non-monetary incentives successfully improved employee performance during an economic downturn. In the healthcare sector, well-being programs and leadership development initiatives proved essential in retaining staff and enhancing performance during a post-pandemic labor shortage.

These case studies underscore the importance of adaptive strategies that align internal developmental interventions with external labor market conditions. Organizations that prioritize employee development, well-being, and engagement are better positioned to navigate challenges in the labor market and maintain high levels of performance.

6. IMPLICATIONS FOR HUMAN RESOURCE MANAGEMENT (HRM)

The findings from this study have significant implications for Human Resource Management (HRM), particularly in how organizations can strategically navigate labor market dynamics while implementing effective developmental initiatives to enhance employee performance. HRM professionals play a pivotal role in aligning organizational strategies with external labor market conditions and internal workforce needs. This chapter explores the key implications for HRM, including recommendations for adapting to labor market trends, designing developmental programs, fostering employee engagement, and ensuring organizational resilience (Aguilera et al., 2025).

6.1 Adapting to Labor Market Trends

One of the most critical functions of HRM is to stay attuned to the ever-changing labor market dynamics and ensure that the organization's workforce strategy is flexible and responsive. The research highlights how labor market conditions—such as unemployment rates, skill shortages, wage inflation, and economic cycles—can have a profound impact on employee performance. HRM needs to anticipate these external factors and proactively adapt its strategies (Hald et al., 2025).

6.1.1 Monitoring Labor Market Trends

HR departments must continuously monitor labor market trends, using tools such as labor market reports, unemployment statistics, and industry-specific data to anticipate changes. For example, during times of labor shortages or high demand for specific skills, HRM should focus on talent acquisition strategies, competitive compensation packages, and employer branding to attract and retain top talent. Conversely, during periods of economic downturn, HR professionals should implement strategies that focus on employee retention, job security, and cost optimization, while ensuring that employees remain motivated and productive (Sarmiento Falla et al., 2025).

- **Actionable Strategy:** HRM should develop a systematic approach to monitor labor market indicators regularly. This could involve subscribing to labor market forecasting services or collaborating with industry groups to gather insights. Proactive responses, such as adjusting compensation packages or offering skill enhancement opportunities, will help organizations stay competitive in the labor market.

6.1.2 Strategic Workforce Planning

HRM should incorporate labor market trends into workforce planning. By understanding the macroeconomic environment and its influence on labor supply and demand, HR can forecast future talent needs and align recruitment efforts with market realities. For example, if there is a looming shortage of certain skills, HR departments can start talent pipelining by building relationships with educational institutions or engaging in targeted recruitment campaigns well ahead of time.

- **Actionable Strategy:** HRM should implement workforce planning tools that integrate labor market data, enabling the organization to predict future skill gaps and proactively address them through internal development programs or external hiring strategies. This ensures that the organization's workforce remains resilient and adaptable to changing market conditions (Ehnes et al., 2025a).

6.2 Designing Effective Developmental Programs

The study underscores the critical role of developmental interventions in enhancing employee performance, especially during times of economic turbulence or labor market shifts. HRM plays an instrumental role in designing and executing training, career development, and performance management programs that align with both employee needs and organizational goals (Stek et al., 2025).

6.2.1 Tailoring Development Programs to Labor Market Needs

HRM should ensure that training and development initiatives are tailored to meet the changing needs of the labor market. For instance, as technological advancements disrupt industries, organizations must invest in upskilling their workforce to ensure that employees can meet new job requirements. HR should foster a culture of lifelong learning, ensuring that employees remain adaptable to technological, organizational, and market changes (Nettle et al., 2025).

- **Actionable Strategy:** HRM should work closely with senior leaders to design skills-based training programs that are aligned with industry trends. Partnering with external learning platforms or offering on-site certifications in high-demand fields, such as digital marketing, data analytics, or AI, will allow organizations to remain competitive while boosting employee performance.

6.2.2 Career Development and Pathways

Employee retention is closely tied to opportunities for career growth. This research shows that employees who perceive a clear career progression within an organization are more likely to stay engaged and perform well. HRM must therefore implement career development programs that offer clear pathways for advancement.

- **Actionable Strategy:** HRM should establish structured career progression frameworks, including mentorship programs, job rotation, and internal promotion systems. These programs should be designed with flexibility in mind, allowing employees to gain diverse experiences and move into new roles that align with their career goals and the evolving needs of the organization (Wang & Solís, 2025).

6.2.3 Creating Inclusive and Flexible Developmental Opportunities

The research also highlights the importance of providing developmental opportunities that accommodate diverse employee needs and work styles. In the modern workforce, employees expect greater flexibility in their work arrangements, such as remote work options, flexible hours, and job-sharing opportunities. HRM must be adept at creating flexible developmental programs that align with these needs (Salari et al., 2025a).

- **Actionable Strategy:** HRM should design hybrid or blended learning programs that can be accessed by employees regardless of location. Furthermore, offering self-paced online courses and flexible schedules for training programs can help employees at various levels of the organization enhance their skills without disrupting their work-life balance (Adwan et al., 2024).

6.3 Fostering Employee Engagement and Motivation

A major finding of the research is the pivotal role of employee engagement in driving performance. Engagement goes beyond job satisfaction—it is about aligning employees with the organization's values, mission, and goals. HRM must implement strategies that not only keep employees satisfied but also deeply engaged and motivated to perform at their best (Shdema et al., 2025).

6.3.1 Recognizing and Rewarding Performance

Effective performance recognition and reward systems are integral to maintaining high levels of employee motivation. As labor market competitiveness increases, employees are more likely to feel valued when their contributions are acknowledged. HRM should foster a recognition-rich culture that acknowledges both individual and team achievements.

- **Actionable Strategy:** HRM should develop recognition programs that go beyond monetary rewards. Public recognition in company meetings, personalized thank-you notes, and annual awards ceremonies can go a long way in boosting morale and motivating employees to perform at their best. It is also important to ensure that the reward system is fair and transparent, aligning with the organization's values and performance metrics (Shdema et al., 2025).

6.3.2 Employee Well-being Programs

The research also highlights the importance of employee well-being initiatives in driving long-term engagement and performance. As labor market conditions fluctuate, employees may experience higher stress levels or burnout, particularly in industries facing skill shortages or increased competition. HRM must therefore prioritize well-being initiatives to ensure employees remain resilient and engaged (Ehnes et al., 2025a).

- **Actionable Strategy:** HRM should implement comprehensive employee well-being programs that address both physical and mental health. Initiatives might include flexible work arrangements, mental health counseling, fitness programs, and stress management workshops. Additionally, promoting a culture that values work-life balance and offers employees time for rest and recovery will help improve engagement and reduce burnout.

6.4 Enhancing Organizational Resilience

The research underscores the importance of building an adaptable and resilient workforce in the face of labor market fluctuations. HRM has a critical role in developing systems and processes that help organizations respond to changes in the labor market swiftly and efficiently, thereby ensuring the continued performance of the workforce (Ehnes et al., 2025a).

6.4.1 Building a Flexible Workforce

HRM should focus on building a workforce that is capable of adapting to changing market conditions. This can be achieved through flexible staffing models, cross-training, and creating opportunities for employees to diversify their skill sets. A flexible workforce is more resilient in the face of labor shortages, economic downturns, or shifting technological demands (Aguilera et al., 2025).

- **Actionable Strategy:** HRM should implement cross-training programs that allow employees to work in different roles within the organization. This will not only make the workforce more versatile but also reduce the impact of sudden absences or skill shortages. Additionally, HR should explore flexible staffing solutions, such as temporary or contract workers, to handle periods of high demand or specialized skill requirements.

6.4.2 Succession Planning

Another crucial aspect of organizational resilience is succession planning. HRM should implement a proactive succession planning strategy to ensure that leadership gaps are filled quickly and effectively. This not only ensures continuity in leadership but also provides employees with clear career progression pathways.

- **Actionable Strategy:** HRM should create a formal succession planning process, identifying potential leaders within the organization and providing them with the training and mentorship they need to assume leadership roles. Regular talent reviews can help HR identify high-potential employees and ensure that the organization is always prepared for leadership transitions (Hald et al., 2025).

6.5 Conclusion

In conclusion, the research findings have far-reaching implications for HRM. The role of HR professionals is evolving beyond traditional functions such as recruitment and compensation to include strategic involvement in workforce development, employee engagement, and organizational resilience. By proactively responding to labor market dynamics, designing effective developmental programs, fostering employee engagement, and enhancing organizational adaptability, HRM can significantly improve employee performance and contribute to the long-term success of the organization.

The key to HRM's success lies in its ability to integrate external labor market insights with internal developmental strategies. Organizations that can align their HR practices with labor market trends while prioritizing employee growth and well-being will be better positioned to maintain high levels of performance, even in the face of economic uncertainty.

By implementing the actionable strategies outlined in this chapter, HRM professionals can not only navigate the complexities of labor market conditions but also foster a highly engaged, adaptable, and high-performing workforce that drives organizational success (Li et al., 2025b).

7. CONCLUSION

This study aimed to explore and analyze the impact of labor market dynamics and developmental interventions on employee performance. Through an in-depth examination of labor market conditions, the role of developmental strategies, and the interaction between both, the research provides valuable insights for organizations striving to enhance employee performance in an ever-changing global landscape. This final chapter summarizes the key findings, presents their implications for organizations and HR professionals, and offers recommendations for future action.

7.1 Summary of Key Findings

The research uncovered several crucial findings regarding the relationship between labor market conditions and employee performance. These findings have important implications for organizational strategies and the role of HRM in managing workforce performance.

1. **Labor Market Dynamics and Employee Performance:** The study confirmed that labor market conditions—such as economic cycles, unemployment rates, skill shortages, wage growth, and labor market tightness—directly influence employee performance. During periods of economic growth and labor shortages, employees tend to experience increased job security, higher motivation, and improved performance. Conversely, during economic recessions or labor surpluses, employees often experience job insecurity, stress, and burnout, leading to decreased productivity and engagement (HUANG & HANAOKA, 2025).
    - **Labor Market Tightness** was shown to lead to heightened competition for skilled talent, driving up wages but also increasing employee turnover, particularly in industries reliant on highly skilled professionals like technology and healthcare.
    - **Economic Downturns** resulted in job insecurity, leading to lower employee morale, engagement, and performance. Employees in industries affected by layoffs or pay cuts reported higher levels of disengagement and productivity loss.
2. ***Developmental Interventions as Performance Enhancers:*** Developmental strategies, such as training and skill development, career progression programs, performance management systems, and employee recognition initiatives—were found to have a significant positive impact on employee performance. When employees perceive that an organization invests in their growth and development, their commitment, motivation, and productivity levels improve (Singh et al., 2025).
    - **Training and Development** programs proved particularly effective in improving technical skills, boosting employee confidence, and enhancing overall organizational performance. Employees who participated in continuous learning opportunities were more adaptable to changing labor market demands (Salari et al., 2025a).
    - **Career Development Opportunities** (including mentorship and clear promotion pathways) significantly improved employee retention and engagement, which directly contributed to performance enhancement, particularly in high-turnover industries like retail and healthcare (Wang & Solís, 2025).

- **Performance Management Systems** that provide regular feedback and set clear goals were shown to improve employee motivation and performance. Employees who received timely feedback and were recognized for their contributions tended to be more committed to their work and performed at higher levels (Tafese et al., 2025a).

3. ***The Interaction Between Labor Market Conditions and Developmental Interventions:***

The research also highlighted the interactive nature of labor market dynamics and developmental strategies. Developmental interventions can serve as a buffer against the negative effects of unfavorable labor market conditions. For example, in periods of high labor turnover or labor shortages, organizations that invested in career development programs and employee retention strategies were able to retain top talent and maintain productivity. Similarly, in times of economic recession, offering skill development and mental health support initiatives helped employees stay engaged and resilient, thus maintaining performance despite challenging external conditions (Tafese et al., 2025a).

4. **Industry-Specific Insights:** The case studies illustrated how different industries face unique labor market challenges, which necessitate tailored HRM strategies. For instance:
   - **The Technology Sector** benefits from continuous training and career advancement opportunities to retain talent in a highly competitive labor market.
   - **The Retail Sector** relies on non-monetary incentives, job redesign, and role enrichment to enhance performance during economic downturns.
   - **The Healthcare Sector** emphasizes employee well-being programs and leadership training to address workforce burnout and retain staff amidst a post-pandemic labor shortage (Ehnes et al., 2025b).

7.2 Implications for Organizations

The findings from this study carry several important implications for organizations seeking to optimize employee performance in a dynamic labor market. HR departments and organizational leaders must recognize that employee performance is not solely determined by internal factors but is heavily influenced by the external labor market environment. Therefore, understanding these external forces and strategically adapting to them is essential for maintaining a motivated, engaged, and high-performing workforce (Rutovitz et al., 2025).

1. **Labor Market Sensitivity:** Organizations must develop the capability to monitor and respond to labor market conditions. By understanding labor market trends, HRM can predict talent shortages or surpluses, adjust compensation packages, and identify potential skill gaps. Proactive workforce planning, informed by labor market data, will enable organizations to stay competitive in attracting and retaining talent.
2. **Investment in Developmental Programs:** Developmental programs are essential for enhancing employee performance. Organizations that invest in continuous skill development, career advancement opportunities, and performance management systems create an environment where employees feel valued and motivated. The findings suggest that HRM should prioritize employee development through both technical training and soft skill enhancements, ensuring that employees have the tools they need to thrive in a competitive labor market.
3. **Employee Engagement as a Strategic Priority:** Engaged employees are the cornerstone of high performance. The research highlights the importance of building an engaging work environment through recognition, career development, and well-being programs. Organizations should focus on fostering a positive organizational culture that promotes employee engagement, satisfaction, and productivity.
4. **Building Organizational Resilience:** Given the unpredictability of labor markets, organizations must invest in building workforce resilience. This includes having flexible staffing models, developing a diverse skill set within the organization, and implementing robust succession planning to ensure that leadership gaps can be filled promptly in times of labor shortages or organizational transitions.

7.3 Recommendations for Future Action

Based on the research findings, several recommendations can be made for organizations to enhance employee performance in light of labor market fluctuations. These recommendations are aimed at HR professionals and organizational leaders seeking to build resilient, high-performing teams.

1. **Adopt a Proactive Approach to Labor Market Trends:** Organizations should invest in tools and resources that allow them to stay informed about labor market trends. HRM should collaborate with industry experts, attend labor market conferences, and subscribe to reports from labor market forecasting services. Regular market analysis will enable organizations to anticipate challenges and respond accordingly (Baiocchetti et al., 2024).
2. **Implement Tailored Development Programs:** HR departments should work with department heads to design development programs that meet the specific

needs of different employee segments within the organization. For example, employees in technical roles may require specialized skills training, while those in customer-facing roles may benefit from leadership and communication development programs. Providing employees with personalized growth opportunities will improve both performance and job satisfaction.

3. **Enhance Employee Recognition and Reward Systems:** A robust recognition system is essential for maintaining high employee morale and performance. Organizations should ensure that recognition is not solely financial but includes non-monetary forms of appreciation, such as public recognition, additional responsibilities, or opportunities for career advancement. HRM should integrate feedback and recognition into performance reviews to create a continuous cycle of acknowledgment.
4. **Focus on Employee Well-being:** The mental and physical well-being of employees should be a priority. HRM must recognize that well-being initiatives contribute to higher performance, reduced absenteeism, and improved job satisfaction. Organizations should offer flexible work arrangements, m ental health support, and stress management programs to create a healthier and more engaged workforce (Li et al., 2025a).
5. **Encourage Leadership Development:** Developing leaders from within the organization is crucial for long-term success. HRM should focus on identifying high-potential employees early and providing them with leadership development opportunities, including mentorship programs, leadership training, and stretch assignments. Building a pipeline of strong leaders ensures organizational stability and fosters a culture of continuous improvement (Fung et al., 2025a).
6. **Embrace Flexibility and Innovation in Workforce Management:** Given the changing nature of work, organizations should embrace flexible workforce management strategies. This could involve exploring job-sharing arrangements, flexible working hours, or hybrid working models to accommodate employee preferences and improve work-life balance. Flexible staffing models also ensure that organizations can quickly adapt to changing labor market conditions (Huang & Hanaoka, 2025).

7.4 Limitations and Areas for Future Research

While this study provides valuable insights, it is important to acknowledge its limitations and areas for further exploration. The scope of the research was limited to specific industries and regions, and future studies could expand the sample to include a broader range of sectors and geographic locations to assess whether the findings hold universally. Additionally, while the research explored the impact of labor market dynamics on employee performance, further studies could examine the long-term effects of developmental interventions on organizational outcomes such as profitability, innovation, and market competitiveness.

Another area for future research would be the role of emerging technologies (such as artificial intelligence and automation) in shaping labor market trends and their impact on employee performance. As technological disruptions continue to reshape industries, understanding how these factors influence the workforce is essential for HRM strategies (Zarb & McNulty, 2025).

7.5 Final Thoughts

In conclusion, the relationship between labor market conditions, developmental interventions, and employee performance is complex and dynamic. Organizations that strategically align their human resource practices with the demands of the labor market, while prioritizing employee development and engagement, will be better positioned to foster high performance, retain top talent, and achieve long-term success. The recommendations outlined in this research provide HR professionals and organizational leaders with the tools to navigate these challenges, create a resilient workforce, and drive sustainable organizational growth.

By embracing a proactive and adaptive approach to labor market trends and developmental strategies, organizations can transform labor market challenges into opportunities for growth, innovation, and enhanced employee performance (Aguilera et al., 2025).

REFERENCES

Adwan, S., Goncharenko, G., & Liu, S. (2024). The impact of employee satisfaction on company's labour investment efficiency. *International Review of Financial Analysis, 96*, 103570. Advance online publication. DOI: 10.1016/j.irfa.2024.103570

Aguilera, R. V., Correa, J. A. A., & Castillo, M. R. (2025). The influence of shareholder activism on global workforce practices. *Organizational Dynamics, 54*(3P1). DOI: 10.1016/j.orgdyn.2025.101141

Baiocchetti, G., Scotti, F., & Iapadre, P. L. (2024). The impact of natural disasters: How the 2009 earthquake transformed the economy of L'Aquila's labour market area. *Papers in Regional Science, 103*(6), 100058. Advance online publication. DOI: 10.1016/j.pirs.2024.100058

Berkery, E., Peretz, H., Tiernan, S., & Morley, M. J. (2025). The impact of flexi-time uptake on organizational outcomes and the moderating role of formal and informal institutions across 22 countries. *European Management Journal, 43*(4), 640–649. DOI: 10.1016/j.emj.2024.05.007

Cheng, H., Guo, H., & Shi, Y. (2024). Multifactor conditional equity premium model: Evidence from China's stock market. *Journal of Banking & Finance, 161*, 107117. Advance online publication. DOI: 10.1016/j.jbankfin.2024.107117

Ehnes, D., Schweizer, L., & Storz, C. (2025a). Labour-cost retrenchment strategies in times of crisis: Comparing market reactions to flexible and rigid strategies. *Long Range Planning, 58*(3), 102509. Advance online publication. DOI: 10.1016/j.lrp.2025.102509

Fung, H. G., Li, T., Lu, C., & Wen, M. M. (2025a). The inevitable disclosure doctrine: A facade or a curse in the CEO labor market. *Journal of Banking & Finance, 179*, 107540. Advance online publication. DOI: 10.1016/j.jbankfin.2025.107540

Hald, A. N., Enemark, U., Mwale, M. L., & Burau, V. (2025). Conceptualising the Primary Health Care Workforce: A Meta-Narrative-Inspired Review of Stakeholder Perspectives in Denmark. *Health Policy (Amsterdam), 105474*, 105474. Advance online publication. DOI: 10.1016/j.healthpol.2025.105474

HUANG, Q., & HANAOKA, S. (. (2025). Dynamic Workforce Allocation for Train-Based Crowd-Shipping: Multi-Period Optimization Incorporating Transit Discomfort Costs. *Multimodal Transportation, 100269*. Advance online publication. DOI: 10.1016/j.multra.2025.100269

Islam, E., Loriot, B., & Rahman, L. (2025). The impact of product market competition on workplace safety. *Journal of Corporate Finance*, *93*, 102778. Advance online publication. DOI: 10.1016/j.jcorpfin.2025.102778

Li, H., Ma, S., & Pan, X. (2025a). The influence of stock market liberalization on labor investment decisions: Evidence from China. *Pacific-Basin Finance Journal*, *93*, 102859. Advance online publication. DOI: 10.1016/j.pacfin.2025.102859

Li, H., Ma, S., & Pan, X. (2025b). The influence of stock market liberalization on labor investment decisions: Evidence from China. *Pacific-Basin Finance Journal*, *93*, 102859. Advance online publication. DOI: 10.1016/j.pacfin.2025.102859

Mitterbacher, K., Fleiß, J., & Palan, S. (2024). Reciprocity in migration policy and labor market integration: A lab experiment. *Economic Analysis and Policy*, *81*, 1–16. DOI: 10.1016/j.eap.2023.11.008

Nettle, R., Vikas, A., Lin, P., & Santhanam-Martin, M. (2025). Review: Attracting and retaining a farm workforce for the pork industry. *Animal*, *101670*, 101670. Advance online publication. DOI: 10.1016/j.animal.2025.101670 PMID: 41176510

Perone, G. (2024). The relationship between labor market institutions and innovation in 177 European regions over the period 2000–2015. *Structural Change and Economic Dynamics*, *70*, 128–149. DOI: 10.1016/j.strueco.2023.12.016

Rutovitz, J., Langdon, R., Lara, H. B., Briggs, C., Singha, D., Davies, E., & Whelan, J. (2025). Predicting workforce requirements for energy efficiency and electrification from energy scenarios. *Energy Reports*, *14*, 1548–1561. DOI: 10.1016/j.egyr.2025.07.040

Salari, N., Beiromvand, M., Hosseinian-Far, A., Habibi, J., Babajani, F., & Mohammadi, M. (2025a). Impacts of generative artificial intelligence on the future of labor market: A systematic review. In *Computers in Human Behavior Reports* (Vol. 18). Elsevier B.V., DOI: 10.1016/j.chbr.2025.100652

Salari, N., Beiromvand, M., Hosseinian-Far, A., Habibi, J., Babajani, F., & Mohammadi, M. (2025b). Impacts of generative artificial intelligence on the future of labor market: A systematic review. In *Computers in Human Behavior Reports* (Vol. 18). Elsevier B.V., DOI: 10.1016/j.chbr.2025.100652

Sarmiento Falla, J. F., Karwowski, W., Jahani, S., Rabelo, L., & Hancock, P. A. (2025). Agile healthcare: The role of information technology ambidexterity and human resource practices fostering workforce agility and job performance. *International Journal of Industrial Ergonomics*, *110*, 103818. Advance online publication. DOI: 10.1016/j.ergon.2025.103818

Shdema, I., Mor, Y., & Abu-Rayya, H. M. (2025). Conflicting identities and labour market outcomes of minorities: Evidence from Arabs in Israel. *International Journal of Intercultural Relations, 109*, 102309. DOI: 10.1016/j.ijintrel.2025.102309

Singh, A., Wu, P., Komaraju, B., Okwudire, C. E., & Banu, M. (2025). Hybrid education and training approaches enabling workforce development in additive manufacturing. *Manufacturing Letters, 46*, 65–71. Advance online publication. DOI: 10.1016/j.mfglet.2025.10.007

Stek, K., Lefers, L., & Belotti Pedroso, C. (2025). Strengthening innovation capacity in health and care workforce: A role-based framework for the procurement professionals. *Health Policy (Amsterdam), 161*, 105423. Advance online publication. DOI: 10.1016/j.healthpol.2025.105423 PMID: 40912179

Tafese, T., Lay, J., & Tran, V. (2025a). From fields to factories: Special economic zones, foreign direct investment, and labour markets in Vietnam. *Journal of Development Economics, 174*, 103467. Advance online publication. DOI: 10.1016/j.jdeveco.2025.103467

Tafese, T., Lay, J., & Tran, V. (2025b). From fields to factories: Special economic zones, foreign direct investment, and labour markets in Vietnam. *Journal of Development Economics, 174*, 103467. Advance online publication. DOI: 10.1016/j.jdeveco.2025.103467

Tseng, Y. J., Wu, M., Feng, Z. Y., & Tan, S. Y. (2025a). The effect of labor unions on capital markets: Evidence from seasoned equity offerings. *International Review of Economics & Finance, 101*, 104190. Advance online publication. DOI: 10.1016/j.iref.2025.104190

Tseng, Y. J., Wu, M., Feng, Z. Y., & Tan, S. Y. (2025b). The effect of labor unions on capital markets: Evidence from seasoned equity offerings. *International Review of Economics & Finance, 101*, 104190. Advance online publication. DOI: 10.1016/j.iref.2025.104190

Wang, J., & Solís, P. (2025). Identifying latent workforce capacities for extreme heat resilience: An artificial intelligence assisted approach. *Energy and AI, 21*, 100580. Advance online publication. DOI: 10.1016/j.egyai.2025.100580

Zarb, F., & McNulty, J. P. (2025). Assessment of workforce availability, staffing, and education, and training requirements for radiographers across Europe as part of EU-REST project. *Radiography, 31*(5), 103101. Advance online publication. DOI: 10.1016/j.radi.2025.103101 PMID: 40763392

Zhu, T. (2025). Latent factor model in asset pricing: A deep learning approach in the Chinese stock market. *Finance Research Letters*, *86*, 108519. Advance online publication. DOI: 10.1016/j.frl.2025.108519

KEY TERMS AND DEFINITONS

Developmental Interventions: Programs, policies, and strategies implemented by an organization to improve employee skills, knowledge, and capabilities. These interventions include training, career development, mentorship, performance management, and leadership development initiatives designed to enhance employee performance and job satisfaction.

Economic Recession: A period of economic decline characterized by reduced consumer spending, declining industrial production, rising unemployment, and decreased business activity. Recessions can lead to labor market imbalances, such as increased unemployment and job insecurity, affecting employee performance and motivation.

Employee Performance: The effectiveness with which employees fulfill their job responsibilities and contribute to organizational goals. It is typically measured by productivity, quality of work, efficiency, and alignment with organizational objectives. Employee performance can be influenced by motivation, job satisfaction, skills, and external factors like labor market conditions.

Labor Market Dynamics: The ever-changing conditions and forces that affect the supply and demand for labor. These dynamics include factors such as unemployment rates, wage inflation, skills shortages, economic cycles, technological advances, and globalization. Labor market dynamics influence how organizations manage and develop their workforce.

Labor Market Tightness: A condition in which the demand for labor exceeds the supply, leading to a competitive environment for hiring. In tight labor markets, employers may face difficulties recruiting and retaining employees, often resulting in higher wages, better benefits, and increased employee turnover.

Labor Market: The supply and demand for labor, where workers offer their skills and time in exchange for compensation, and employers seek to hire workers to fulfill organizational needs. The labor market is influenced by factors like employment rates, wage levels, industry demand, and economic conditions.

Non-Monetary Incentives: Rewards that do not involve direct financial compensation but still serve to motivate and engage employees. Non-monetary incentives may include recognition, increased responsibility, flexible working arrangements, or opportunities for career development.

Performance Management: A systematic approach to improving employee performance through setting clear goals, providing regular feedback, evaluating performance, and offering development opportunities. Performance management includes performance appraisals, goal setting, and recognition programs aimed at enhancing productivity and employee engagement

Unemployment Rate: The percentage of the labor force that is actively seeking employment but is unable to find work. It is a key indicator of labor market health and is influenced by economic conditions, business cycles, and industry demand for labor.

Wage Growth: The increase in the average compensation paid to employees over time. Wage growth can be influenced by factors such as labor market tightness, inflation, demand for skilled workers, and organizational performance. High wage growth often occurs in industries with labor shortages or high-demand skill sets.

Chapter 3
Building Business Resilience in Tight Labor Markets:
Cross-Training Strategies for Flexibility, Retention, and Productivity

Ramakrishnan Ramachandran
http://orcid.org/0000-0001-8712-7677
Vivin Consultants, Chennai, India

ABSTRACT

Organizations are becoming concerned about long-term labor shortages brought on by demographic shifts, quick technical developments, and growing disparities between the skills needed and those accessible. Cross training is discussed in this chapter as a tactical means of increasing organizational resiliency under these circumstances. It describes how cross training improves workforce flexibility, raises productivity by relieving operational bottlenecks and promoting knowledge sharing, and supports employee retention by providing more job variety and internal mobility options. Drawing on points of view as the Resource-Based View, Dynamic Capabilities, and Human Capital Theory, the chapter addresses implementation techniques, organizational conditions that enable effective adoption, and the role of leadership and learning culture in maintaining these initiatives. Well-designed cross-training initiatives, matched with bigger HR and operational systems, can lower reliance on outside hiring and help businesses in maintaining performance.

DOI: 10.4018/979-8-3373-5327-2.ch003

ht © 2027, IGI Global Scientific Publishing. Copying or distributing in print or electronic forms without written permission of IGI Global Scientific Publishing is prohibited. Use of this chapter to generative artificial intelligence (AI) technologies is expressly prohibited. The publisher reserves all rights to license its use for generative AI training and machine learning model development.

1. INTRODUCTION

Tight labor markets are not transitory economic eras that companies can just wait out anymore. They are a chronic structural issue in many industries and areas that is changing how businesses approach talent, productivity, and long-term competitiveness.

Employers are not only having trouble finding qualified employees, but they are also working to keep the ones they already have, who are working in a job market that offers more choices and mobility. This change has brought in a kind of uncertainty less apparent than supply chain or financial shocks yet equally disruptive for company performance.

The depth of this shift is shown by global data. Among the most important impediments to business change across sectors are talent shortages and skills gaps identified by the World Economic Forum (2025).

The OECD (2024) stresses that labor shortages are progressively caused by mismatches between the abilities companies need and those present in the labor pool. These changes indicate that the problem is not merely numerical shortage but rather a more sophisticated mismatch between changing job requirements and current human capital.

Technological advancement is central to this dynamism as automation and digitalization improvements have changed the nature of employment. They have lowered reliance on routine activities and boosting boosted the demand for higher-order cognitive, technical, and social skills. Autor (2022) claims that this change has polarized the employment market such that middle-skill occupations vanish and possibilities increase at low-skill and high-skill extremities.

Organizations commonly find themselves competing for a rather small pool of very skilled individuals as a consequence. Simultaneously, demographic trends are decreasing the supply of labor in several countries.

While younger groups are joining the workforce with different expectations about flexibility, career growth, and work-life balance, aging populations are lowering the percentage of working-age people(UNDP, 2024). These expectations affect not just job choice but also retention as employees are more prone to quit companies that fail to offer meaningful growth possibilities or encouraging work settings.

For businesses, the effects are sudden and compounding. Vacant jobs increase the load on current staff members, cause delays in manufacture and manufacturing, and disturb service delivery. More people may leave their jobs due to the additional pressure from work, leading to burnout and lower morale.

Gallup (2024) warns of the cascading consequences for the health of organizations emphasizing the close relationship of disengagement and stress in understaffed workplaces. Firms are hence paying more and more focus on resiliency.

Resilience in an organization is the capacity to withstand shocks, and uphold performance in spite of interruptions by modifying to shifting circumstances. Resilience is being progressively recognized as a workforce concern even though it has historically been connected to fields including financial stability or supply chain management.

The ability of staff members to adapt, learn, and take on new responsibilities, is critical for businesses to maintain operations under stress(Accenture, 2024).This change calls for a rethinking of the organization of work.

Historically, many companies have prioritized specialization, creating roles that concentrate on constrained sets of activities to maximize efficiency. Although they are quite good under normal circumstances, such systems can shatter in crowded labor markets.

When important people are gone or depart the firm, their unique expertise is difficult to replace. According to Rajoli & Manoharan(2023), this reliance on tightly specified jobs raises sensitivity, particularly in situations where replacement hiring is sluggish or erratic. One way to deal with this difficulty is cross-training. Organizations create some functional flexibility by helping staff members to become competent in many capacities, enabling operations to persist even when disturbances arise.

This flexibility goes beyond simply being operational as it impacts employee experience and corporate culture. Cross-trained employees acquire better awareness of how manymultiple roles interact, that, which might improve cooperation and problem-solving. Cross-training is also becoming increasingly evident as a factor in workforce agility.

According to Alviani et al. (2024), workforce agility is the ability of employees to successfully adjust to shifting needs by combining technical competence with adaptive actions. By exposing staff to several assignments and difficulties that promote ongoing learning and flexibility, cross-training helps to expose them to this.

In this respect, it coincides with wider trends toward skills-based firms whereby flexibility and learning ability are appreciated in addition to technical competence. Cross-training, though, should not be seen as an easy or generally relevant answer, as there are trade-offs involved that need to be handled with care.

It takes time and money to train workers in many occupations, and it might temporarily lower productivity as people master new responsibilities. There is also a chance that workers turn into generalists without developing enough depth in any one field. These factors underline the need of deliberate design and execution.

This chapter presents a novel integrative conceptual framework (see Figure 1) connecting labor market tightness to cross-training processes, workforce agility, retention, production, and organizational resilience. The model addresses a major omission in current studies that usually treats these components separately by presenting cross-training as a main middle activity transforming outside pressures into inside strategic capabilities.

Cross-training, however, should not be viewed as a simple or universally applicable solution as there are trade-offs involved that must be treated with care. Training personnel in many jobs costs time and money and could momentarily reduce production as individuals learn fresh tasks.

Figure 1. A conceptual framework for Cros training

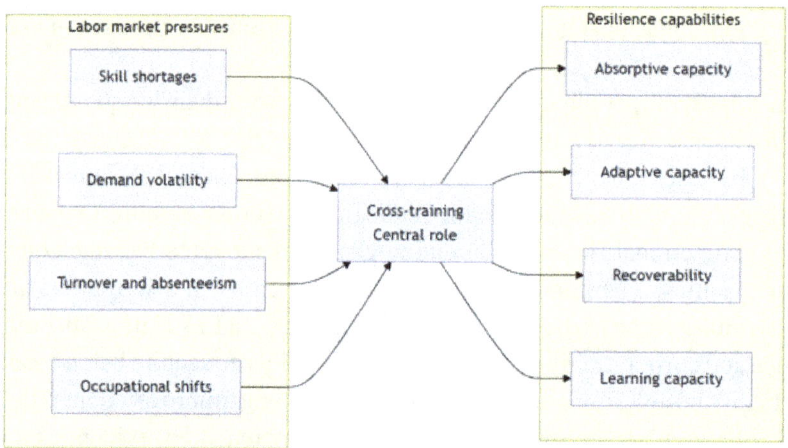

Source: Prepared by the author

From a strategic standpoint, cross-training helps to lessen reliance on outside labor markets. According to Cappelli (2023), many businesses have grown too dependent on recruiting outside talent as opposed to creating internal capacities. This strategy gets progressively more expensive and uncertain in constrained labor markets.

Companies can create a more flexible and self-sufficient staff by investing in internal skill development, including cross-training. In this chapter, Cross-training is discussed as a key strategy for increasing business resilience in constrained labor markets.

It combines labor economics, operations management, and human resource management insights to present a thorough grasp of how cross-training affects flexibility, retention, and output.

From theoretical underpinnings to practical applications, the argument proceeds and provides theoretical as well as practical points of view. The nature of tight labor markets is discussed in further detail in the following section together with their defining traits, fundamental causes, and effects for companies. This helps us to see why cross-training is becoming an ever more important approach in modern workplace management.

1.1 Research Gap

While the literature on labor shortages, workforce agility, Human Capital Theory, Resource-Based View, and Dynamic Capabilities Theory is reasonably comprehensive, important gaps remain. Few studies provide an integrated framework showing how cross-training specifically bridges labor market tightness to resilience outcomes. There is limited critical discussion of contradictory findings, implementation failures, unintended consequences (such as training fatigue or role overload), or boundary conditions.

Emerging areas such as skills-based organizations, internal talent marketplaces, AI-enabled workforce planning, psychological safety, employee experience management, psychological contract theory, knowledge retention, succession planning, and cross-training in hybrid/remote environments are underexplored in relation to resilience. This chapter addresses these gaps by proposing an integrative model and critically examining both benefits and limitations.

2. UNDERSTANDING TIGHT LABOR MARKETS

Understanding why businesses are progressively relying on internal workforce approaches requires background knowledge of labor market limits. Still, simply describing the strain is insufficient. Equally important is to investigate the conceptual underpinnings that establish resilience as a strategic competency., the following subsection turns the focus to theoretical frameworks explaining how firms create and maintain resilience in such circumstances. The following subsection therefore turns to theoretical frameworks explaining how firms create and maintain resilience in such circumstances.

2.1 Defining Tight Labor Markets

Generally, a tight labor market is defined as a situation whereby the demand for labor outweighs the supply of competent people.

Although this definition encapsulates the fundamental concept, its practical application calls for a more sophisticated knowledge. High job vacancy levels and low unemployment rates are frequently used as proxies, but they don't fully capture the qualitative aspects of labor market conditions (ILO, 2023).

One essential factor is the difference between relative imbalances and absolute deficits. Many times, jobs go unfilled because the accessible workforce lacks the particular skills needed, not because there are no employees.

The OECD (2024) stresses that skill mismatch is a continuous element of contemporary labor markets impacting both developed and developing nations. This discrepancy can be found in all educational levels, sectors, and locations.

The time and expense of recruiting make up still another dimension. Organizations frequently face longer recruiting cycles and increased recruiting costs in constricted labor markets.

Time-to-hire has grown in various industries, reflecting both growing rivalry for talent and more discriminatory hiring methods (Terrazas, 2022). These holdups can interfere with processes and cause doubt in workforce planning. Wage dynamics helps one to understand the tightness of the labor market are wage dynamics.Wage dynamics also help illuminate the degree of tightness in the labor market.

To draw candidates with increase in demand, businesses may pay more or provide better benefits. But wage increases by themselves do not fix structural shortages, especially for jobs that call for specific training or experience. The supply of competent people cannot change fast enough to match demand in such circumstances.

2.2 Structural Drivers of Labor Market Tightness

Due to a mix of demographic., technological, and institutional factors, tight labour markets persist. These factors make it more challenging for businesses to use conventional hiring techniques as they interact in ways that exacerbate labor shortages. Demographic change is among the most crucial factors.

In certain countries, aging populations reduce the size of the working-age population, decreasing the labor force participation rate. According to the UNDP (2024), this tendency is particularly evident in developed nations, where low birth rates and growing life expectancy are altering the age composition of the populace. Many times, the stream of younger employees is not enough to cover the spaces left by retired older workers.

Technological change adds still another level of complexity. The nature of employment is changing with the advances in automation, AI, and digital technology. While some tasks are automated, others need greater degrees of competence as they are becoming more complicated.

Globalization and Labor mobility influence labor market dynamics. Geopolitical tensions, policy restrictions, and disruptions the COVID-19such as the COVID-19 pandemic restricted migration flows to reduce the availability of workers in certain regions and sectors (ILO, 2023).

Historical changes in workforce policy at the organizational level have helped to explain current shortages. when new skills are required, many companies have chosen to hire from outside, instead of investing in internal training and development . This approach assumes the availability of a ready supply of skilled workers, an assumption that no longer holds in tight labor markets and firms face increased competition for a limited pool of talent(Cappelli & Keller,2023).When new skills are required, many companies have chosen to hire from outside, instead of investing in internal training and development. This approach assumes the availability of a ready supply of skilled workers, an assumption that no longer holds in tight labor markets, as firms face increased competition for a limited pool of talent (Cappelli & Keller, 2023).

2.3 Organizational Implications

The repercussion of tight labor markets is multifaceted and impacts both short-term operations and long-term strategy. Increased labor cost is the most immediate impact as wages and benefits usually increase when businesses vie for limited talent.

Employees get wider opportunities to switch jobs, for better compensation, career development, or work-life balance which changes turnover dynamics. Such voluntary turnover creates challenges for workforce stability (SHRM,2023)(SHRM, 2023). A high turnover team rate undermines team cohesiveness and knowledge continuity, apart from driving recruitment expenses.

Existing employees have to take on more responsibilities, in understaffed environments, that will lead, leading to stress, burnout, and disengagement over time. Such employees are are more likely to report negative workplace experiences, contributing further to turnover (Gallup, 2024). Operational performance is directly affected as well.

McKinsey & Company (2023) attributes vacant positions and knowledge gaps for upsetting operations and lower the quality of service in industries like healthcare, logistics, and manufacturing apart from delays in production and service delivery. These interruptions might have cascading effects.

Limited labor markets hinder organizational expansion and creativity strategically. Businesses might put off their expansion plans or cut back on their investments in new technology, when they cannot find the people they need. Strategic decision-making is progressively being formed by workforce constraints, impacting anything from product development to market entrance (Deloitte, 2025).

2.4 The Shift Toward Internal Workforce Strategies

Given the limits of outside hiring, businesses are progressively concentrating on internal workforce plans to close labor gaps. Redesigning work processes, upskilling, and reskilling are among these tactics aimed at more efficient use of available talent.

Upskilling focuses on refining employees' present abilities to raise performance in their current jobs, while reskilling concentrates on readying personnel for several roles inside the company.

According to BCG (2024), massive reskilling programs can assist businesses in adjusting to shifting skill demands while lowering reliance on outside labor markets in production. Learning culture is essential and they play a critical role for success of these strategies.

Cross-training is thus a key component of internal workforce strategies to enable employees to perform multiple roles as it enhances flexibility and allows organizations to respond more effectively to fluctuations in demand. Workforce flexibility can improve operational efficiency supported by training, and reduce vulnerability to disruptions (Heuser et al., 2022).

However, training programs alone are not enough for implementing internal strategies. It includes improvements in performance management systems, leadership approaches, and organizational structures. Employees should be motivated to learn and adjust, while managers must assist role changes and synchronize workforce assignment.

2.5 Tight Labor Markets as a Catalyst for Organizational Change

Though small labor markets offer great difficulties, they also provide chances for organizational change. Firms need to analyze how work is done, talents are grown, and value is generated to create more adaptable, resilient, and flexible organizational structures.

The change towards skills-based enterprises mirrors a change from strict job descriptions to more flexible role descriptions. Such models appreciate staff members for their abilities rather than their official roles, increasing flexibility in task distribution (Deloitte, 2025). This approach fits well with cross-training since it increases the variety of jobs staff members could do.

There is also a growing recognition that employee experience matters. Organizations that provide learning and growth opportunities are more likely to draw in and keep talent, even in competitive employment markets. This indicates that internal growth approaches have strategic significance in addition to their operational advantages.

Tight labor markets in this regard operate as both a limit and a stimulus. Although they restrict the supply of outside talent, they also inspire companies to create more robust and sustainable staffing policies. Cross-training, when included into a larger plan of workforce development, could become quite important for this change .

3. CONCEPTUAL FOUNDATIONS OF BUSINESS RESILIENCE

Building on the more general theoretical framework, it gets important to define what organizational resilience really entails in reality. The idea has grown throughout several fields, resulting in diverse but related meanings. It is essential to have a clear working definition guiding the remainder of the discussion before looking at particular theoretical lenses..

3.1 Defining Organizational Resilience

From a small emphasis on crisis recovery, organizational resilience has grown into a wider competence including anticipation, adaptation, and ongoing operation under shifting circumstances.

Early interpretations stressed the capacity to "bounce back" following disturbance, however more current research presents resilience as a continuous process rather than a finished product.

According to Lengnick-Hall, Beck & Lengnick-Hall(2011), resilience comprises both adaptive capacity and absorptive capacity, meaning that companies must not only withstand shocks but also change their systems and processes in reaction. In constrained labor markets, this distinction is especially pertinent.

Disruptions to the workforce seldom occur as independent events. Rather, they arise slowly via changing demand patterns, talent shortages, and turnover. Resilience hence cannot be limited to contingency planning alone. Especially those linked to human resources management, it must be ingraining in daily organizational practices.

Three connected ideas of robustness, adaptability, and transformability explain resilience Robustness is the capacity to keep performance even when there are interruptions. Changing circumstances require adjusting operations, which is what adaptability is all about. By contrast, transformability reflects the ability to radically change systems when the current structures are not viable (Duchek, 2020). By enhancing workforce redundancy, allowing task redistribution, and fostering greater ability development, cross-training interacts with all three dimensions.

3.2 Theoretical Foundations

Resource-Based View, Dynamic Capabilities Theory and Human Capital Theory give the theoretical foundation as under:

3.2.1 Resource-Based View

The Resource-Based View explains the different levels of resilience by different businesses. Barney (1991) contents that organizations acquire sustained competitive advantage by building resources that are valuable, uncommon, difficult to replicate, and non-substitutable..

When it relates to tacit knowledge and firm-specific skills, human capital typically satisfies these criteria. Resilience, calls for the use of resources adaptable.

Wright & McMahan (2011) stress that human resources improve competitive advantage not via their inherent attributes but via their organization and management. The worth of human capital may be underutilized in strict systems whereby workers are limited to small responsibilities. Flexible systems let businesses rearrange competencies to shifting needs.

Cross-training makes human capital more valuable strategically, by making it more flexible. Employees who have several skills could be sent across tasks, lowering reliance on specific people and lessening the effect of labor shortages. Since it turns human capital into a more flexible and hard-to-replicate asset, this fits the RBV viewpoint.

3.2.2 Dynamic Capabilities Theory

Dynamic capabilities theory builds upon the RBV by emphasizing how businesses change and replenish their resources across time. Teece (2025) defines dynamic capabilities as the ways in which companies identify possibilities, seize them, and change their processes appropriately. In settings distinguished by instability and quick change, these processes assume special significance.

In constrained labor markets, dynamic capabilities are strongly related to workforce flexibility. Organizations should be able to spot new talent demands, build internal skills, and effectively redistribute work. Eisenhardt and Martin (2000) contend that dynamic capabilities manifest as distinct organizational procedures, like knowledge transfer systems or product development practices.

Cross training improves the capacity of the firm to react to changes in strategic objectives and variations in demand by allowing staff members to transfer between jobs, making dynamic capability at the employment level in a real way.

3.2.3 Human Capital Theory

An extra viewpoint for comprehending resilience is given by human capital theory. Becker (1993) stresses how investments in training and education raise human productivity and thereby that of businesses. These investments become especially critical in tight labor markets since outside hiring is less dependable.

According to Noe, Clarke & Klein. (2014), companies must establish settings that promote continuous skill development instead of depending on one-time training programs. This change shows the faster rate of change in skill demands, which is caused by changes in technology and organization.

This focus on lifelong learning is in line with cross-training. It exposes staff members to many assignments and motivates the growth of transferable abilities. This not only increases personal employability but also improves organizational resilience by producing a flexible workforce.

3.3 Workforce Agility and Psychological Dimensions

Resilience is not just a matter of structure or strategy, but has also a psychological and behavioral aspect. Workforce agility, defined as the capacity of staff members to swiftly and successfully adjust to shifting demands is a crucial aspect of resilience. Sherehiy & Karwowski(2014) identified key elements of workforce agility as flexibility, adaptability, and proactivity.

Cross-training exposed employees to different work context to broaden their skill sets. This exposure increases confidence in handling unfamiliar task as it enhances employees to approach problems from multiple perspectives.

Luthans, Youssef & Avolio (2006) define psychological resilience, that play a complementary role, as the capacity to bounce back from adversity and maintain positive functioning. Training interventions promoting learning and development can strengthen this capacity by providing employees with a sense of competence and control.

Colquitt, LePine & Noe (2000) links training effectiveness to self-efficacy, motivation, and perceived relevance. Resilience is not produced through independent processes and this integration is vital. It results from the interplay of organizational systems, people, and strategy.

3.4 Integrating Resilience and Workforce Strategy

To encourage flexibility and learning, training initiatives, job design, and leadership approaches must be in sync. According to Lepak and Snell (1999), human resources architecture should mirror the strategic value and individuality of human capital, implying that various positions could call for different approaches to growth and placement.

As a strategy to boost adaptability and lessen vulnerability, cross-training fits inside this larger framework. By facilitating job reallocation, it promotes strategic resilience through encouraging learning and flexibility and operational resilience. Its usefulness, nevertheless, rests on how successfully it is included into organizational systems.

4. CROSS-TRAINING AS A STRATEGIC TOOL

Resilience's theoretical roots raise the issue of how these concepts are used in real life. For operationalizing workforce flexibility, cross-training is one of the most direct mechanisms. It is important to define its forms and variations before analyzing its strategic implications.

4.1 Defining Cross-Training and Its Forms

Cross-training is the practice of teaching staff members to carry out duties outside of their main responsibilities. Though the idea is clear, its execution might differ greatly among businesses. It could entail job rotation, whereby workers change roles over time, or skill-based training whereby people develop abilities enabling them to execute several responsibilities without officially altering jobs.

Cross-training in operations management is typically related with multi-skilling, whereby employees may execute a spectrum of activities inside a production or service system. Hopp & Spearman (2008) call it a way to make the system more flexible and lessen bottlenecks. Cross-training in human resource management is connected to employee engagement and career development as it offers chances for learning and advancement.

Cross-training, in essence, is strategically valuable because it links human growth with operational efficiency. Designing programs that handle both dimensions will help companies to reach several goals at once.

4.2 Mechanisms of Cross-Training

Cross-training affects organizational results via different channels. Redundancy is among the most crucial. Traditional systems frequently see redundancy as inefficiency. But in unstable circumstances, some redundancy improves resiliency by guaranteeing that crucial activities may be completed even when disturbances happen.

By offering backup capacity, cross-trained employees can help to lessen the effects of fluctuation in production systems. This enables businesses to keep throughput even when certain employees are gone. Conditions of uncertainty suggest that flexible labor contracts can enhance system performance. Labor pooling is still another technique.

Organizations can distribute labor more dynamically in response to changes in demand by building a pool of employees capable of carrying out several tasks. This deals with shortages in certain sectors while cutting idle time in other regions.

Partial cross-training, according to Jordan and Graves (1995), whereby employees are instructed in a subset of jobs, will greatly increase flexibility without the need of complete multi-skilling. Another crucial consideration is knowledge transfer.

Cross-training helps staff members to better grasp many facets of organizational operations. As employees gain a better understanding of how their jobs relate to others, this can improve coordination and lower errors. Argote & Ingram (2000) stress how critical knowledge transfer is for organizational learning and performance.

4.3 Economic and Operational Value

Cross-training boosts system efficiency from an operations standpoint by lowering bottlenecks and raising capacity utilization. Hopp & Spearman (2008) demonstrate that flexible workforce solutions have the potential to greatly increase manufacturing system throughput.

Similar advantages in terms of lower waiting times and higher quality of service are noted in service settings. There are productivity consequences at the personal level as employees that have received training across several tasks can acquire a broader set of abilities fostering creativity and problem-solving.

Adler & Clark (1991) point out that workers who divide their time among several tasks may not reach the same degree of competency as specialists, especially in highly technical jobs. Hence, the general influence of cross-training relies on the particular setting whereby it is applied. In settings defined by fluctuation and uncertainty, the advantages of adaptability usually exceed the costs of less specialization. The trade-offs might be less advantageous in more steady settings.

4.4 Strategic Role in Tight Labor Markets

The strategic value of cross-training increases as labor markets contract. Organizations have to rely more and more on internal resources as hiring from the outside becomes more challenging and expensive.

Cross-training helps companies to maximize existing talent by increasing the scope of work staff members may handle. This directly affects workforce planning. Organizations may grow bigger skill sets inside their present staff rather than recruiting for narrowly defined jobs. This improves the organization's capacity to react to changing needs and lessens reliance on outside labor markets.

Retaining people also benefits from cross-training. Employees provided with chances to acquire new abilities and assume several jobs are more likely to stay with the company. Govaerts et al. (2011) find that career development opportunities are a key factor in employee retention, especially among younger workers.

Cross-training can assist lower turnover and its related expenses by offering such chances. Cross-training from a strategic angle corresponds with the trend towards skills-based businesses and internal talent marketplaces.

These models let for more flexible allocation of work since employees are appreciated for their abilities rather than their official job titles. In energetic situations where job needs vary quickly, this strategy is especially pertinent, including AI-enabled workforce planning.

4.5 Limitations and Trade-offs

Cross-training has drawbacks even with all of its advantages. Cost of training, both in terms of money and time is challenging. Learning new abilities requires removing people from their main responsibilities, momentarily lowering productivity.

There is also the matter of skill dilution. Employees who are trained across several jobs might not reach the same degree of competence as professionals. This might be an issue in sectors where technical knowledge and accuracy are essential. Katz & Allen (1985) links specialization for improving performance in difficult assignments, underscoring the need of balance.

Employee opposition can also be an impediment as some might be hesitant to step outside their comfort zone for assuming more responsibility. Apart from training, effective implementation needs supportive leadership and organizational culture.

4.6 Toward Strategic Integration

To have a lasting impact, there must be a deliberate integration of cross-training through several HR and operational areas. Cross-training should be included into larger organizational systems to reach its full potential. This entails matching training programs to strategic goals, adding flexibility into job design, and establishing incentives for cooperation and learning.

MacDuffie (1995) argues that human resource policies are most successful when they are applied as part of coherent systems rather than as independent projects. Cross-training ought to be related to other activities including performance management, career growth, and team-based working systems. Such integration is particularly significant in constrained labor markets.

Internal shortcomings cannot be fixed by companies depending on outside recruiting. Resilience should instead be developed from the inside. When applied as part of a thorough workforce plan, cross-training can be a great instrument for reaching this objective.

5. CROSS-TRAINING FOR WORKFORCE FLEXIBILITY

Building workforce flexibility necessitates a more thorough dissection of the many shapes flexibility may take and the part cross-training can play in it. Flexibility is not one idea but rather a mix of interconnected aspects influencing the distribution and management of labor.

5.1 Functional Flexibility and Multi-Skilling

Practical implications workforce flexibility becomes more obvious when seen through particular lenses. Employees who can perform several chores across departments or roles have functional flexibility. This kind of flexibility is essential to cross-training since it immediately increases the variety of tasks that individual employees could perform.

Early conceptualization of functional flexibility is offered by Atkinson's (1984) model of the flexible business, which highlights the need of multi-skilled core workers who may be assigned as necessary.

Though first created in the framework of manufacturing, the idea has subsequently found use in many businesses, including services and knowledge-intensive industries. The fundamental reasoning behind remains consistent.

When staff members are not restricted by strict job limits, companies gain. This opinion is supported by empirical research. According to Mouw, Kalleberg & Schultzg (2024), companies that use flexible work methods including multi-skilling are better able to handle changes in demand.

This flexibility is especially useful in constrained labor markets, where internal shortages cannot be readily offset by outside recruiting. Developing employees with several skills helps businesses build internal capacity that may be called upon as needed. Enabling functional flexibility depends critically on cross-training. It enables staff members to gain skills outside their main jobs, enabling task redistribution with minimal disturbance.

In settings defined by instability, where the need for certain activities might alter fast, this is particularly critical. Rather than using a set allocation of labor, businesses can change tasks fluidly depending on their needs at any given time.

Functional flexibility also has a cognitive component. Employees who work in several departments acquire a wider grasp of the way organisations work. Cross-training thus supports organisational learning as well as operational flexibility.

5.2 Numerical and Temporal Flexibility

Although functional flexibility emphasizes several talents, businesses must also handle numerical and temporal aspects of staff allocation. When outside hiring possibilities are restricted, increasing internal adjustments become more vital.

Apart from functional flexibility, businesses usually look for numerical and temporal flexibility. Numerical flexibility is the capacity to change the workforce's size in response to demand, generally by means of hiring, layoffs, or the employment of contingent labor. Conversely, temporal flexibility entails modifying work hours, shifts, or schedules.

In limited labor markets, numerical freedom becomes restricted. Firms cannot easily increase their workforce when demand rises because there may not be suitable candidates available. This restriction redirects the concentration to internal kinds of flexibility, especially those that may be accomplished without altering workforce count.

According to Houseman (2001), companies usually combine several flexibility tactics to deal with instability. Internal flexibility becomes more crucial in settings where outside labor is scarce, though. Cross-training gives a means to reach this adaptability while preserving continuity and power over the level of the workforce.

5.3 Agile Workforce Models

Beyond operational flexibility, modern firms progressively stress agility as a broader strategic competency. This notion broadens flexibility into adaptability, learning, and reactivity. It offers a great perspective to appreciate the greater benefit of cross-training.

According to Doz & Kosonen (2010), strategic agility calls for businesses to swiftly rearrange resources in response to shifts in the surroundings. Although much of the research centers on strategic decision-making, workforce agility is of equal relevance. Employees ought to be able to change roles, develop fresh talents, and cooperate throughout departments.

Cross-training fosters a more flexible workforce framework, hence enhancing these talents. Organizations can run with more flexible arrangements whereby employees contribute in several ways rather than rigid hierarchies and set job descriptions. This matches the developing paradigm of internal labour markets, in which talent is distributed depending on project requirements and abilities instead of official roles.

Workforce agility and innovation are also related. Employees who interact with multiple points of view and roles will come up with fresh concepts and spot chances for development. This implies that cross-training may enhance strategic adaptability as well as operational agility. But obtaining workforce agility needs more than training by itself. It depends on the systems that enable learning and cooperation, organizational culture, and leadership.

Employees ought to be at ease adopting fresh roles and experimenting with various techniques. Managers must support coordination and offer direction as changes occur. Without these ancillary components, the possible advantages of cross-training may not be completely appreciated.

5.4 Internal Labor Markets and Talent Mobility

Understanding internal labor markets' influence on employee movement inside companies is essential to truly comprehending workforce flexibility. These structures affect over time how skills are acquired, kept, and used once more.

Internal labour markets give a structural basis for comprehending how cross-training enhances flexibility. Under such systems, instead of quitting and being replaced by outside hires, employees move between positions inside the company. This technique keeps organizational knowledge and lowers recruitment expenses.

According to Bidwell (2011), internal mobility can increase job performance as employees who move inside the company already have knowledge particular to the company. Cross-training improves this process by readying staff members for many professions, increasing the efficiency and simplicity of transfers.

In constrained labor markets, talent mobility is especially crucial. Organizations have to depend on internal mobility to fill jobs and close ability gaps when outside hiring is limited. Cross-training generates a pool of staff members ready to assume fresh tasks, hence lowering the time and expense related to filling jobs.

Employee incentive also suffers consequences. Employees usually appreciate chances for mobility and development, especially those looking for career growth. Organizations can improve engagement and retention, which are essential in aggressive employment markets, by offering such chances.

5.5 Limitations and Practical Considerations

Although cross-training has clear advantages for flexibility, it also has practical difficulties. One challenge is the assignment of training resources. Organizations have to prioritize roles and determine how much training to give their staff. In some cases, full multi-skilling might not be either practical or necessary.

The trade-off between flexibility and efficiency is yet another factor to take into account. Highly specific jobs could need extensive knowledge not readily transferable through cross-training. A selective strategy, concentrating on important activities where flexibility offers the most benefit, might be more suited in such situations.

There is also the matter of employee capability. If not properly managed, taking on many responsibilities could complicate tasks and increase workload. Organizations must ensure that cross-training does not place undue demands on staff members.

Even with these difficulties, the general evidence indicates that cross-training is a great instrument for improving the adaptability of the workforce. Thoughtfully applied and backed by suitable systems lets businesses more efficiently handle the limitations of limited labor markets.

6. CROSS-TRAINING AND EMPLOYEE RETENTION

Naturally leading to staff retention is the discourse on workforce flexibility, as flexibility measures usually affect how long people stay with a company. It is crucial to first comprehend how cross-training influences job design and employee engagement before looking at particular mechanisms..

6.1 Job Enrichment and Engagement

Several elements affect employee retention, including compensation, working environment, and growth possibilities. Among these, employment design is of great relevance. Jobs that offer independence, diversity, and learning possibilities gives increased levels of satisfaction and involvement.

Hackman and Oldham (1976) emphasizes skill diversity as a crucial motivator in their job characteristics model. By enabling staff members to participate in several activities and roles, cross-training directly helps to this aspect. In monotonous jobs, this diversity can increase interest in employment and lower repetition.

Link between job enrichment and retention is supported by empirical research. According to Humphrey et al. (2007), enhanced job attributes have a positive relationship with organisational commitment and job satisfaction. Cross-training can help to foster greater employee loyalty to the company by boosting task importance and skill variety. As they feel supported and appreciated employees desire to stay with the company increases, when they can develop fresh abilities.

6.2 Career Development and Internal Mobility

Retaining employees depends mostly on career growth, especially for those in knowledge-based jobs and younger workers. Ng et al. (2005) demonstrate that career happiness is mostly determined by chances for progress and skill development. Cross-training helps to create these chances by equipping staff members for many jobs and improving their skills.

Internal mobility is intimately tied to career advancement. Organizations that provide avenues for advancement across departments are more likely to keep their staff as they provide alternatives to quitting the company in quest of development possibilities. Internal hiring is more successful in filling posts since internal candidates are already knowledgeable with organizational procedures, according to Bidwell and Keller (2014).

Internal mobility is improved by cross-training, as it provides staff members the knowledge they need to move across jobs. This expands the pool of possible candidates for internal roles and lowers the impediments to mobility. There is also a signaling effect that companies are dedicated to fostering the growth of their employees, improving organizational attractiveness and reputation, simplifying talent acquisition and retention.

6.3 Psychological Outcomes and Well-Being

In determining whether individuals stay or leave, employee well-being, confidence, and perceived support all play a role . Retention depends both on structural variables and on psychological experiences. Employees that feel capable, supported, and capable of handling difficulties are more prone to remain with businesses. Cross-training can have a number of impacts on these experiences.

Bandura (1997) finds that it raises self-efficacy, the confidence one has in their capacity to complete tasks effectively . Skill development and training contribute to self-efficacy. Employees get the experience and knowledge required for negotiating in diverse circumstances and become more resilient and confident.

Second, cross-training helps to clarify roles. Employees that have a good grasp of several facets of organizational processes find it easier to interpret expectations and work with others. This can increase job happiness and lower tension. Cross-training done without enough support can aggravate tension and role overload.

6.4 Retention in Tight Labor Markets

Retention becomes a strategic need rather than merely an HR issue, when viewed against the backdrop of limited labor markets. Organizations should hence evaluate under restricted recruiting circumstances how cross-training helps to sustain workforce stability.

Retaining employees becomes especially important in constrained labor marketplaces. Organizations find it difficult to replace staff members who depart, thus emphasizing the need to keep a consistent workforce. Cross-training helps retain staff by tackling numerous elements impacting their choices.

To start, it improves organizational employability. Employees with a wider set of talents have more chances to transfer between professions, lessening the need to look for possibilities elsewhere. Second, it offers diversity and educational chances, boosting interaction. Third, it increases well-being by fostering confidence and lowering ambiguity.

Retaining methods, according to Hom et al. (2017), should focus on both the causes that entice people to stay and the ones that make them want to leave. Cross-training deals with both aspects by increasing job appeal and lowering the risks involved with change.

6.5 Strategic Implications

From a strategic point of view, the relationship between cross-training and retention has significant ramifications. Direct costs and decreased production both contribute to the high expenses related with turnover. By lowering turnover, cross-training can help to make operations more stable and effective.

Companies that give learning and growth top priority are more likely to build settings whereby staff members feel appreciated and supported. This can improve general performance in addition to retention. Cross-training initiatives ought to be in sync with company goals and employee needs. They ought to offer significant learning chances instead of just adding work.

Managers are essential to this process, as they can help staff members and making sure that training is applied properly. In essence, cross-training is a complex approach that uses job design, career development, and psychological variables to influence retention. It is a useful instrument for creating a more consistent and engaged staff in difficult labor markets as keeping talent is both challenging and vital.

7. CROSS-TRAINING AND PRODUCTIVITY

Defining how multi-skilled work systems function will help to understand productivity consequences of cross-training. In these systems, productivity is more a result of how work is organized and coordinated rather than being only an individual outcome.

7.1 Productivity in Multi-Skilled Work Systems

How tasks are assigned, coordinated, and carried out jointly has a major impact on total performance. Cross-training influences productivity not only by changing personal abilities but also by transforming the organization of work systems.

Conventional approaches see increased production by means of specialization. Early observations made by Smith on division of labor stressed that efficiency gains result from the repetitive performance of precisely defined activities.

This reasoning, though, presumes consistent circumstances as demand trends and chores do not vary greatly. In settings marked by unpredictability and volatility, too much specialization can cause rigidities lowering general system performance.

Adler, Goldoftas, & Levine (1999) find that flexible work systems, such as multi-skilling, can increase productivity by lowering delays and improving coordination. From an operations point of view, productivity is strongly related to flow efficiency. Hopp & Spearman (2008) demonstrate how great fluctuations in processing times and resource availability might lower throughput.

7.2 Bottleneck Reduction and Throughput Improvement

Reducing bottlenecks is among the most immediate productivity advantages of cross-training. Certain activities in any production or service system usually turn into bottlenecks, lowering the total capacity of the system.

The likelihood of bottlenecks grows when a limited number of specialized employees do these jobs. Cross-training tackles this problem by increasing the pool of workers able to carry out bottleneck duties.

In a focused way, this ensures coverage, guaranteeing that vital activities may continue even if the main employees are not present. Jordan and Graves (1995) show that even limited cross-training, where employees are taught a subset of tasks, greatly enhances system performance. Table 1 below shows the link between cross-training and throughput:

Table 1. Impact of Cross-Training on Operational Performance

Dimension	Without Cross-Training	With Cross-Training
Task Allocation	Fixed and rigid	Flexible and dynamic
Bottleneck Risk	High	Reduced
Throughput Stability	Low under variability	More stable
Idle Time	Uneven distribution	More balanced
Response to Absenteeism	Disruptive	Managed internally

Source: Compiled by author

The table 1 above shows that cross-training improves the system's capacity to absorb variation rather than eradicating it. By means of improved labor reallocation, companies can sustain higher throughput levels even under limited resources.

7.3 Learning Effects and Knowledge Spillovers

Employees that work on several projects build up a bigger knowledge foundation that could increase creativity and problem-solving abilities. This is consistent with the idea of organizational learning whereby knowledge is exchanged and assimilated throughout several organizational components.

Argote (2024) highlights that knowledge exchange is a key determinant of performance enhancement. Cross-training exposes staff to many jobs and processes, promoting this mobility. Workers bring knowledge with them, as they switch between jobs, producing spillover effects that improve the general system performance.

There is also evidence that multi-skilled workers develop better diagnostic abilities. Employees who are conversant with the interaction of various components of a system can pinpoint the underlying causes of problems and suggest workable solutions to raise quality and cut downtime.

Learning effects depends on the level of training and the degree to which employees are motivated to use and disseminate their expertise.

7.4 Trade-offs Between Specialization and Flexibility

Cross-training has its drawbacks even if it clearly increases production with a tradeoff between specialization and flexibility. Specialized employees usually attain better efficiency in particular assignments, due to repetition and experience. On the other hand, multi-skilled employees could need more time to complete activities, especially during the learning stage.

In tabular form this trade-off may be thought of as follows in table 2,:

Table 2. Specialization vs. Cross-Training Trade-offs

Factor	Specialization	Cross-Training
Task Efficiency	High for specific tasks	Moderate across tasks
Flexibility	Low	High
Adaptability	Limited	Strong
Training Cost	Lower initial	Higher initial
Long-Term Productivity	Stable in steady conditions	Higher under variability

Source: Compiled by the author

Adler & Clark (1991) propose that the best equilibrium relies on the degree of instability in the surroundings. In steady settings, specialization could increase efficiency. By contrast, in settings defined by uncertainty and labor limits, the flexibility afforded by cross-training can result in improved general performance.

7.5 Productivity in Service and Knowledge Work

Especially, between manufacturing, services, and knowledge-intensive industries, productivity results differ throughout industries. This variant underlines the need of situating cross-training methods.

Cross-training has effects beyond those in manufacturing. In service sectors, where interactions with clients are crucial, flexibility can greatly affect output and quality. Cross-trained personnel in healthcare environments can go between jobs to better satisfy patient demands, lowering waiting times and boosting results.

The advantages of cross-training are more indirect but no less significant in knowledge-intensive sectors. Better cooperation and information integration are made possible by employees who comprehend several facets of a project, reducing mistakes and foster creativity.

Job rotation and multi-skilling are linked to better job performance and happiness levels, implying that cross-training may enhance both efficiency and effectiveness(-Campion et al., 2011).

7.6 Strategic Implications for Productivity

Cross-training should be seen from a strategic viewpoint as an investment in system capability rather than as a transient expense. Although training calls for resources, the acquired gains in adaptability, learning, and resilience can provide great long-term advantages.

These perks grow even more worthwhile in close labour markets whereby the expense of hiring and attrition is high. Though companies depending just on specialization could attain short-term efficiency, they run the danger of events disturbing productivity. Conversely, when things change, those who cross-train are more likely to keep performing well.

However, the design and execution must be meticulous, to get these advantages. Training programs ought to match organizational needs; performance indicators should mirror flexibility as well as efficiency and managers should assess system-level results in addition to personal productivity.

8. DESIGNING EFFECTIVE CROSS-TRAINING PROGRAMS

Effective cross-training programmes must support corporate goals. and translate theoretical knowledge to real-world application.

8.1 Strategic Alignment

The success of cross-training mostly rests on its fit with corporate direction. It is improbable that training programs applied in isolation, without definite objectives or alignment with wider objectives, will yield significant outcomes.

According to Garavan et al. (2012), strategic priorities should be intimately connected to human resource development activities. This entails pinpointing the abilities essential for organizational performance and creating training courses tackling these criteria. In the setting of limited labor markets, this usually entails concentrating on positions hard to fill from the outside or vital for operational continuity.

8.2 Skill Mapping and Competency Frameworks

Once strategic alignment is in place, companies have to find the exact skills that need to be improved. This makes skill mapping and competency frameworks absolutely essential instruments in program design.

Recognizing the competencies needed across many occupations is a crucial phase in creating cross-training programmes. Task and competency analysis is part of skill mapping to find where overlap exists and where training can produce the most benefit.

Campion et al. (2011) contend that competency frameworks offer a methodical way to handle this process. Organizations can find chances for cross-training and create programs that develop pertinent abilities by defining the competencies linked with several positions. Cross training's skill mapping is illustrated in Table 3 below.

Table 3. Example of Skill Mapping for Cross-Training

Role	Core Skills	Overlapping Skills	Potential of Cross-Training
Role A	Technical Task 1	Communication, Analysis	High
Role B	Technical Task 2	Analysis, Coordination	Moderate
Role C	Customer Interaction	Communication, Problem-solving	High

Source: Compiled by the author

This kind of analysis enables businesses to give training top priority and distribute resources effectively. Further, it gives a foundation for assessing performance by cross-training..

8.3 Training Methods and Delivery

The success of cross-training relies on the approach taken to learning delivery and reinforcement. Selection of training techniques is another crucial element. For fundamental information, traditional classroom-based training may be beneficial; nevertheless, practical abilities typically need experiential learning.

Since they let employees learn in actual work situations. job rotation, mentoring, and on-the-job training are good for cross-training . Salas et al. (2012) opines that effective training programs should include active learning, feedback, and chances for practice to boost the possibility of translating it to better performance by improving skill acquisition and retention.

Blended learning techniques that mix several techniques are often most effective; Staff members could start with formal training and then use job rotation to put their abilities into practice.

8.4 Implementation and Change Management

Even well-thought-out training programs might fall short, without effective execution and change management. This calls for an understanding of organisational dynamics as well as employee reaction to change.

While initiating cross-training, change management must be carefully done. Employees could be reluctant to take on new responsibilities, when they view cross-training as raising their workload without appropriate advantages. Managers must give Clear communication of the aim and value of training, stressing its assistance of personal growth as well as organizational objectives.

Kotter (1996) stressed the vitgal role of leadership in managing transformation. Leaders must establish urgency, foster support, and supply tools for execution. In the framework of cross-training, this entails setting aside time for training and acknowledging staff members who acquire fresh abilities. The success of cross-training is also determined by Organizational culture, that foster learning and experimentation.

8.5 Technology and Data-Driven Approaches

AI, and data analytics identify skill gaps, monitor development, and customize training along with learning management systems. Real-time information on employee talents coming from skills databases, helps companies to distribute resources more effectively. Digital platforms enable people to share information, and learn from each other making technology as a facilitator of good design.

8.6 Evaluation and Continuous Improvement

Cross-training programs must at last be reviewed to guarantee they produce the desired results. This includes evaluating organizational as well as personal results together with employee engagement and satisfaction.

Focusing on reaction, learning, behavior, and outcomes, Kirkpatrick's (1998) approach offers a helpful structure for appraisal. Organizations can spot areas for development by evaluating these aspects and enhance their initiatives throughout time.

In changing surroundings, constant improvement is crucial. Training courses must be updated to keep relevant as skill demands evolve. This calls for constant observation and modification..

9. ORGANIZATIONAL CULTURE AND LEADERSHIP

Organizational culture impacts significantly on the working of cross-training. For analyzing specific cultural components, understanding the influence of learning environments on workforce conduct is prerequisite.

9.1 Learning-Oriented Organizational Culture

Cross-training works in tandem and its usefulness much relies on the cultural setting in which it is ingrained. Organizations stressing knowledge sharing, openness to change, and continuous learning are more likely get maximum gain from cross-training. On the other hand, stiff societies that give small role definitions top priority and discourage experimentation often restrict its influence.

Learning-oriented cultures are defined by a will to enhance staff capacities and support knowledge sharing. Learning organizations, according to Marsick and Watkins (2003), are those that include learning into daily work procedures rather than regarding it as a distinct endeavor. Cross-training in such situations becomes a normal extension of current practices instead of an additional weight.

Learning organizations are founded on common vision, systems thinking, and team learning (Senge, 1990). By encouraging teamwork and lowering opposition to role flexibility, these components promote cross-training .

Employees that comprehend the larger objectives of the company are more likely to participate in activities that improve group performance, even if it means going outside their main responsibilities.

Additionally, there is empirical proof for the link between learning culture and performance. López et al. (2005), found companies that are very interested in learning often reach greater levels of effectiveness and invention. Cross-training helps to establish this direction by giving staff members chances to learn and use fresh information in many settings.

9.2 Psychological Safety and Employee Participation

Edmondson (1999) identified the crucial component of team learning and performance as psychological safety which is a prerequisite for cross-training. It inspires staff to ask inquiries, solicit comments, and try out fresh responsibilities. Without it, workers could skip chances for learning out of fear of rejection or mistakes. This might greatly reduce the efficacy of training courses.

Psychological safety is intimately connected to employee engagement as employees who participate in the planning and execution of cross-training initiatives only will find them relevant and helpful. Higher job satisfaction and organizational commitment are shown by Cotton et al. (1988) to be correlated with participation in decision-making.

Fostering participation and psychological safety depends much on managers. They must establish settings in which workers feel valued and encouraged and in which learning is acknowledged as a valid and significant endeavor. This encompasses recognizing the work needed in learning new abilities and offering helpful criticism.

9.3 Leadership and Change Management

Leadership is a key element in the success of cross-training programs. Leadership offers the means by which psychological and cultural components are turned into behavior. It is important to look at how different leadership styles affect cross-training results.

Cross-training usually require adjustments in job design, performance appraisal, and organizational practices. These developments could spark opposition especially if they undermine long-standing conventions or raise the apparent burden.

Transformational leadership is found successful in such environments. Bass & Bass (1985) define transformational leaders as people who motivate and inspire their staff to reach greater levels of performance by matching personal objectives with those of the company. By stressing the long-term advantages of cross-training and motivating staff members to accept fresh responsibilities, such leaders are more likely to support it.

Kotter (1996) provides an organized framework to change management that is appropriate here. Essential actions include fostering urgency, developing a guiding coalition, and producing quick results. For cross-training, this could mean showing early results like better workflow or fewer bottlenecks to build momentum and get support.

Resource allocation also falls under good leadership. Cross-training calls for management focus, money, and time. Even well-designed initiatives could falter without these resources. Therefore, leaders ought to give training top priority and make sure it fits into the organizational plan.

9.4 Aligning Culture, Leadership, and Cross-Training

It helps to combine these elements into one framework to totally grasp the function of culture and leadership. This clarifies how organizational structures support or impede cross-training.

The table 4 below provides a summary of how culture, leadership, and cross-training interact.

Table 4. Cultural and Leadership Enablers of Cross-Training

Characteristics	Factor	Impact on Cross-Training
Continuous development, knowledge sharing	Learning Culture	Enhances skill acquisition
Openness, low fear of failure	Psychological Safety	Encourages participation
Vision, resource allocation	Leadership Support	Facilitates implementation
Participation in decisions	Employee Involvement	Increases acceptance

Source: Compiled by author

This table shows that cross-training is more than just a technical fix. It is a social and organizational process relying on common beliefs and strong leadership.

These elements become much more important in constrained labor markets where the risks are great.

10. CASE STUDIES AND INDUSTRY APPLICATIONS

The theoretical and structural explanation of cross-training is most effectively grasped when it is based on practical uses. Manufacturing is one of the first and most researched settings for its application.

10.1 Manufacturing Sector

Connected with Japanese companies, lean production systems have long placed a strong emphasis on multi-skilling as a way to raise productivity and adaptability.

According to MacDuffie (1995), plants using flexible work methods, such as cross-training, attain greater productivity and quality levels than more conventional systems. Cross-training advance ongoing improvement initiatives as employees that grasp several facets of production, can pinpoint inefficiencies and suggest fixes.

Multi-skilled employees will raise coordination and lower downtime, especially in just-in-time systems, where any interruption in one stage could interfere with the whole production process..

10.2 Healthcare Sector

Retail and service sectors stretch the argument further by functioning in extremely erratic demand settings. This makes flexibility especially crucial for daily activities. Cross-training in healthcare has been applied to fill staffing gaps and raise patient care. Many nurses and other healthcare professionals are educated to complete a variety of chores so they may better satisfy shifting patient demands.

Aiken et al. (2012) emphasize the need of staffing flexibility in preserving quality of care. Hospitals that can modify staffing levels and roles in reaction to demand usually provide improved patient outcomes. Cross-training helps in increasing the abilities of medical personnel, fostering this flexibility. But the healthcare setting also shows the limits of cross-training. Some jobs need specialized knowledge that cannot be readily transferred.

10.3 Retail and Service Industries

High volatility in demand defines the surroundings in which the retail and service sectors run. The number of customers can change a lot, so companies have to change their staffing levels and roles all the time. Cross-training can solve them, by training store employees to handle multitasks, like sales, inventory management, and customer service so that managers can assign personnel depending on real-time requirements, enhancing customer experience and efficiency.

Batt (2002) found service companies using high-involvement work techniques, including cross-training, reach improved performance results. These approaches improve operational flexibility and staff involvement, essential in customer-facing contexts.

10.4 Technology and Knowledge-Intensive Firms

Unlike service environments, focus of knowledge-intensive sectors is on teamwork and cognitive adaptability. This changes the focus of cross-training from duties to integrating knowledge. Cross-training manifests differently in knowledge-intensive and technology-intensive sectors. Rather than concentrating on daily activities, it entails creating a wide knowledge of sophisticated systems and processes. Employees could be motivated to work on many initiatives or cooperate across divisions.

By exposing workers to many points of view and knowledge areas, this approach fosters creativity. Nonaka (1994) stresses that several sorts of competence interacting usually produces knowledge creation. Cross-training promotes this interaction by destroying functional silos. Concurrently, knowledge-intensive work underlines the need of depth as well as breadth. Employees must keep a high degree of knowledge while also growing more general abilities.

10.5 Comparative Insights Across Sectors

Looking across sectors makes it clear that cross-training is not a general model but rather a tactic dependent on the situation. Its degree of effectiveness differs according on operational organization and employment situation. Although the use of cross-training differs between businesses, several general patterns surface. The industry-specific goals, main advantages, and limitations are illustrated in the table 5 below.

Table 5. Cross-Training Across Industries

Industry	Primary Objective	Key Benefits	Key Constraints
Manufacturing	Efficiency, flow	Reduced bottlenecks	Training cost
Healthcare	Patient care	Staffing flexibility	Skill specialization
Retail/Service	Demand variability	Improved responsiveness	High turnover
Technology	Innovation	Knowledge sharing	Maintaining expertise

Source: Compiled by Author

These contrasts show that cross-training isn't a universally applicable fix. Its design and implementation ought to be customized to the particular qualities of every sector. Still, the fundamental idea stays unchanged.

11. CHALLENGES AND BARRIERS TO CROSS-TRAINING

Cross-training is not without implementation difficulties notwithstanding its benefits. Often appearing early in the process, these obstacles can greatly affect results.

11.1 Resource Constraints and Cost Considerations

Although cross-training has obvious strategic advantages, its application is sometimes limited by practical restrictions. Resource allocation is among the most urgent difficulties. Organizations working with limited margins could hesitate to divert resources from essential operations as training calls for both money and time.

Berge (2022) point out that training success relies not just on design but also on how much companies are ready to invest in ongoing growth initiatives. Short-term cost concerns might cause businesses to underinvest in training despite the fact that doing so has significant long-term advantages. in tight labor markets, where businesses have increasing labor expenses together with the demand for talent development, this conflict is rather clear.

There is also the problem of opportunity cost. Employees under cross-training are temporarily unavailable for their main duties which reduces short-term output. Companies must balance operational demands in the short term with capacity expansion of the long term.

11.2 Resistance to Change

Resistance to change from both workers and management is among the most ongoing issues. Effective implementation depends on an awareness of this opposition.

Employee and manager resistance can greatly impede the execution of cross-training initiatives. Employees might view cross-training as a rise in work without related benefits. Others could be worried about being assessed on strange chores or losing their specialized jobs.

Oreg (2006) points out that things like how fair people think things are, how much they trust the people in charge, and their own personality all affect how much they resist change. In the setting of cross-training, clear communication and participation are critical for tackling these issues. Supervisors could be unwilling to let staff members go for training or could favor keeping present processes. This emphasizes the need of coordinating incentives and making sure that managers are assessed not only on short-term results but also on their influence on workforce growth.

11.3 Skill Dilution and Performance Risks

The possible dilution of skills presents yet another difficulty. Although cross-training promotes breadth of knowledge, it might do so at the detriment of depth. Reduced specialization may compromise performance and quality in roles demanding great degrees of technical competence.

According to Katz & Allen (1985), specialization promotes the growth of in-depth knowledge especially in difficult assignments. Employees that split their attention among several jobs may not reach the same degree of competency as professionals. This presents a dilemma that businesses have to handle very attentively. Also pertinent is the danger of fluctuation in performance, as newly educated employees need some time to be totally proficient in other tasks.

11.4 Measurement and Evaluation Challenges

Evaluating the effects of cross-training, like staff involvement, flexibility, tenacity, and is very hard. Its advantages are usually indirect and spread over several results, unlike hiring or technology improvements.

Although Kirkpatrick's (1998) framework offers a systematic way to evaluate, its use calls for consistent measuring techniques and trustworthy data. Organizations may find it difficult to connect training activities to performance results, especially when there are numerous affecting variables.

There is also the danger of concentrating on readily quantifiable markers such as training completion rates instead of more significant results including skill application and performance improvement. This could cause a discrepancy between evaluation criteria and program goals.

11.5 Organizational Alignment Issues

At last, cross-training programs might falter if they do not match bigger organizational systems. MacDuffie (1995) stresses that human resource policies are most successful when they are applied inside cohesive systems. Cross-training should be included into job design, performance management, and career growth.

Misalignment could lower efficiency and cause confusion. Employees that are trained in several capacities but judged only on their main responsibilities could have little motivation to use their new knowledge. If career advancement is linked to specialization, cross-training could be seen as a diversion instead of a chance.

Tackling these issues requires a comprehensive strategy that takes into account not only the design of the training but also the organizational setting in which it is applied.

12. FUTURE TRENDS IN CROSS-TRAINING AND WORKFORCE RESILIENCE

Future developments in cross-training are progressively influenced by technological and structural changes as firms keep adjusting to shifting labor market circumstances. Knowing these patterns helps one to see in which direction employment policies are heading.

12.1 Technology-Enabled Skill Development

Digital technology developments are revolutionizing the way business manage training and skill building. AI and data analytics are helping Learning management systems to create more effective training courses.

Salas et al. (2012) credits technology for improving training effectiveness by delivering interactive and adaptive learning experiences. Cross-training means that staff may access individualized material that targets their exact skill gaps, cutting the development time needed.

Additionally, being used to map talents across businesses, AI pinpoints internal mobility and cross-training possibilities. In complicated firms with many responsibilities, these technologies can help more strategic workforce planning.

12.2 The Rise of Skills-Based Organizations

Employees are increasingly being valued for their abilities instead of their official job titles in skills-based organisational structures. This method stresses versatility and ongoing learning, it parallels rather well with cross-training.

According to Cappelli & Keller (2013), traditional employment models are giving way to more flexible structures like internal talent marketplaces and project-based work. Cross-training becomes a key tool for helping staff to transfer between jobs and support many initiatives in such settings. Skills-based approaches promote variety and inclusion, by stressing talents over qualifications, boosting the pool of available talent and lower entry hurdles for underrepresented populations.

12.3 Integration with Hybrid and Remote Work

Apart from structural changes, hybrid and remote employment are changing the delivery of training and skill development. New possibilities and difficulties for cross-training have been brought about by the growth of remote and hybrid work. On the other side, physical distance can make hands-on instruction and mentoring difficult. On the other hand, digital tools make new types of information exchange and teamwork easier.

Barrero, Bloom & Davis (2023) claims that remote work can maintain or even increase output supported by appropriate administrative methods. Cross-training can be via online collaboration, virtual job rotation, and digital learning tools.

12.4 Resilience as a Strategic Priority

Resilience is ultimately becoming a main strategic worry for businesses. This change emphasizes cross-training as a long-term competence instead of a short-term activity. Deloitte (2025) stresses that firms are funding resilience in order to take advantage of possibilities in unstable situations rather than just control hazards.

Cross-training is expected to be crucial in this transformation. The capacity to swiftly reconfigure workforce talents becomes a major source of competitive edge as businesses deal with constant uncertainty. This implies that cross-training will shift from being a tactical reaction to become a strategic imperative.

13. CONCLUSION

Tight labor markets have essentially changed the background in which businesses operate. In many industries, the belief that labor can be readily be obtained from outside sources no longer holds true. Rather, businesses have to deal with situations noted by uncertainty, rivalry, and paucity. Resilience of the workforce becomes a crucial indicator of organizational performance in this atmosphere.

This chapter has looked at cross-training, as a tactical answer to these issues. It has found cross-training as a complex strategy that affects flexibility, retention, and production rather than just a training method. Organizations are able to lessen reliance on specific people, enhance cooperation, and sustain performance under strain by allowing employees to handle several responsibilities.

The investigation emphasized the importance of combining cross-training with more general organizational systems as its success relies on support from leadership, and a culture that fosters learning and flexibility and alignment with strategy. Cross-training also has trade-offs between flexibility & specialization, short-term expenses &long-term advantages & operational needs and employee growth.

Looking ahead, the value of cross-training is likely to rise as technological advancements, demographic changes, and changing work patterns keep changing labor markets. Companies that make internal capacity building investments with cross-training, will be better able to adjust to these shifts.

In conclusion, cross-training is a sensible and strategic way to make business stronger in a tough job market. It offers a way to increase workforce flexibility, promote employee retention, and maintain productivity. Although there are still difficulties, the data shows that, when done well, cross-training may be very helpful for companies trying to negotiate an increasingly complicated and unpredictable environment

REFERENCES

Accenture. (2024). Resilience redefined: From readiness to reinvention. https://www.accenture.com/content/dam/accenture/final/accenture-com/document-3/Accenture-Resilience-Redefined-From-Readiness-to-Reinvention.pdf

Adler, P. S., & Clark, K. B. (1991). Behind the learning curve: A sketch of the learning process. *Management Science*, *37*(3), 267–281. DOI: 10.1287/mnsc.37.3.267

Adler, P. S., Goldoftas, B., & Levine, D. I. (1999). Flexibility versus efficiency? A case study of model changeovers in the Toyota production system. *Organization Science*, *10*(1), 43–68. DOI: 10.1287/orsc.10.1.43

Aiken, L. H., Sermeus, W., Van den Heede, K., Sloane, D. M., Busse, R., McKee, M., Bruyneel, L., Rafferty, A. M., Griffiths, P., Moreno-Casbas, M. T., Tishelman, C., Scott, A., Brzostek, T., Kinnunen, J., Schwendimann, R., Heinen, M., Zikos, D., Sjetne, I. S., Smith, H. L., & Kutney-Lee, A. (2012). Patient safety, satisfaction, and quality of hospital care: Cross sectional surveys of nurses and patients in 12 countries in Europe and the United States. *BMJ (Clinical Research Ed.)*, *344*(mar20 2), e1717. Advance online publication. DOI: 10.1136/bmj.e1717 PMID: 22434089

Alviani, D., Hilmiana, , Widianto, S., & Muizu, W. O. Z. (2024). Workforce agility: A systematic literature review and research agenda. *Frontiers in Psychology*, *15*, 1376399. DOI: 10.3389/fpsyg.2024.1376399 PMID: 39323587

Argote, L. (2024). Knowledge transfer within organizations: Mechanisms, motivation, and consideration. *Annual Review of Psychology*, *75*(1), 405–431. DOI: 10.1146/annurev-psych-022123-105424 PMID: 37788572

Argote, L., & Ingram, P. (2000). Knowledge transfer: A basis for competitive advantage in firms. *Organizational Behavior and Human Decision Processes*, *82*(1), 150–169. DOI: 10.1006/obhd.2000.2893

Atkinson, J. (1984). Manpower strategies for flexible organisations. Personnel management, 16(8), 28-31. https://www.stonebridge.uk.com/uploads/courses/566.pdf

Autor, D. (2022). *Labor Market Impacts of Technological Change*. National Bureau of Economic Research.

Bandura, A. (1997). *Self-efficacy: The exercise of control* (Vol. 11). Freeman.

Barney, J. B. (1991). Firm resources and sustained competitive advantage. https://doi.org/DOI: 10.1016/S0742-3322(00)17018-4

Barrero, J. M., Bloom, N., & Davis, S. J. (2023). The evolution of work from home. *The Journal of Economic Perspectives*, *37*(4), 23–49. DOI: 10.1257/jep.37.4.23

Bass, B. M., & Bass Bernard, M. (1985). *No. 3* (Vol. 25). Leadership and performance beyond expectations. Free press.

Batt, R. (2002). Managing customer services: Human resource practices, quit rates, and sales growth. *Academy of Management Journal*, *45*(3), 587–597. DOI: 10.2307/3069383

BCG. (2024, May 8). How governments can improve the Global Skills Market. How Governments Can Improve the Global Skills Market. https://www.bcg.com/publications/2024/how-governments-can-improve-global-skills-market

Becker, G. S. (1993). Human capital. The concise encyclopedia of economics, 2, 1-12.

Berge, Z. L. (2022). Designing workplace training for generational differences: Does it matter? *Merits*, *2*(4), 400–407. DOI: 10.3390/merits2040028

Bidwell, M. (2011). Paying more to get less: The effects of external hiring versus internal mobility. *Administrative Science Quarterly*, *56*(3), 369–407. DOI: 10.1177/0001839211433562

Bidwell, M., & Keller, J. R. (2014). Within or without? How firms combine internal and external labor markets to fill jobs. *Academy of Management Journal*, *57*(4), 1035–1055. DOI: 10.5465/amj.2012.0119

Campion, M. A., Fink, A. A., Ruggeberg, B. J., Carr, L., Phillips, G. M., & Odman, R. B. (2011). Doing competencies well: Best practices in competency modeling. *Personnel Psychology*, *64*(1), 225–262. DOI: 10.1111/j.1744-6570.2010.01207.x

Cappelli, P., & Keller, J. R. (2013). Classifying work in the new economy. *Academy of Management Review*, *38*(4), 575–596. DOI: 10.5465/amr.2011.0302

Colquitt, J. A., LePine, J. A., & Noe, R. A. (2000). Toward an integrative theory of training motivation: A meta-analytic path analysis of 20 years of research. *The Journal of Applied Psychology*, *85*(5), 678–707. https://psycnet.apa.org/doi/10.1037/0021-9010.85.5.678. DOI: 10.1037/0021-9010.85.5.678 PMID: 11055143

Cotton, J. L., Vollrath, D. A., Froggatt, K. L., Lengnick-Hall, M. L., & Jennings, K. R. (1988). Employee participation: Diverse forms and different outcomes. *Academy of Management Review*, *13*(1), 8–22. DOI: 10.2307/258351

Deloitte. (2025). 2025 Global Human Capital Trends: "Turning tensions into triumphs": Deloitte Southeast Asia. 2025 Global Human Capital Trends. https://www.deloitte.com/southeast-asia/en/services/consulting/perspectives/2025-human-capital-trends.html

Doz, Y. L., & Kosonen, M. (2010). Embedding strategic agility: A leadership agenda for accelerating business model renewal. *Long Range Planning*, *43*(2-3), 370–382. DOI: 10.1016/j.lrp.2009.07.006

Duchek, S. (2020). Organizational resilience: A capability-based conceptualization. *Business Research*, *13*(1), 215–246. DOI: 10.1007/s40685-019-0085-7

Edmondson, A. (1999). Psychological safety and learning behavior in work teams. *Administrative Science Quarterly*, *44*(2), 350–383. DOI: 10.2307/2666999

Eisenhardt, K. M., & Martin, J. A. (2000). Dynamic capabilities. *Strategic Management Journal*, *21*(10–11), 1105–1121. DOI: 10.1002/1097-0266(200010/11)21:10/11<1105::AID-SMJ133>3.0.CO;2-E

Gallup. (2024). State of the global workplace: 2024 report. https://www.gallup.com/workplace/349484/state-of-the-global-workplace.aspx

Garavan, T. N., Carbery, R., & Rock, A. (2012). Mapping talent development: Definition, scope and architecture. *European Journal of Training and Development*, *36*(1), 5–24. DOI: 10.1108/03090591211192601

Govaerts, N., Kyndt, E., Dochy, F., & Baert, H. (2011). Influence of learning and working climate on the retention of talented employees. Journal of workplace learning, 23(1), 35-55https://DOI: 10.1108/13665621111097245

Hackman, J. R., & Oldham, G. R. (1976). Motivation through the design of work: Test of a theory. *Organizational Behavior and Human Performance*, *16*(2), 250–279. DOI: 10.1016/0030-5073(76)90016-7

Heuser, P., Letmathe, P., & Schinner, M. (2022). Workforce planning in production with flexible or budgeted employee training and volatile demand. *Journal of Business Economics*, *92*(7), 1093–1124. https://doi.org/. DOI: 10.1007/s11573-022-01090-z

Hom, P. W., Lee, T. W., Shaw, J. D., & Hausknecht, J. P. (2017). One hundred years of employee turnover theory and research. *The Journal of Applied Psychology*, *102*(3), 530–545. https://psycnet.apa.org/doi/10.1037/apl0000103. DOI: 10.1037/apl0000103 PMID: 28125259

Hopp, W. J., & Spearman, M. L. (2008). *Basic factory dynamics. Factory Physics* (3rd ed.). McGraw-Hill.

Houseman, S. N. (2001). Why employers use flexible staffing arrangements: Evidence from an establishment survey. *Industrial & Labor Relations Review*, *55*(1), 149–170. DOI: 10.1177/001979390105500109

Humphrey, S. E., Nahrgang, J. D., & Morgeson, F. P. (2007). Integrating motivational, social, and contextual work design features: A meta-analytic summary and theoretical extension of the work design literature. *The Journal of Applied Psychology*, *92*(5), 1332–1356. https://psycnet.apa.org/buy/2007-12832-011. DOI: 10.1037/0021-9010.92.5.1332 PMID: 17845089

ILO. (2023)... *World Employment and Social Outlook*. Advance online publication. DOI: 10.54394/SNCP1637

Jordan, W. C., & Graves, S. C. (1995). Principles on the benefits of manufacturing process flexibility. *Management Science*, *41*(4), 577–594. DOI: 10.1287/mnsc.41.4.577

Katz, R., & Allen, T. J. (1985). Project performance and the locus of influence in the R&D matrix. *Academy of Management Journal*, *28*(1), 67–87. DOI: 10.2307/256062

Kirkpatrick, D. L. (1998). The Four Levels of Evaluation. In Brown, S. M., & Seidner, C. J. (Eds.), *Evaluating Corporate Training: Models and Issues. Evaluation in Education and Human Services* (Vol. 46). Springer., DOI: 10.1007/978-94-011-4850-4_5

Kotter, J. P. (1996). Leading change. Harvard business press.

Lengnick-Hall, C. A., Beck, T. E., & Lengnick-Hall, M. L. (2011). Developing a capacity for organizational resilience through strategic human resource management. *Human Resource Management Review*, *21*(3), 243–255. DOI: 10.1016/j.hrmr.2010.07.001

López, S. P., Peón, J. M. M., & Ordás, C. J. V. (2005). Managing knowledge: The link between culture and organizational learning. *Journal of Knowledge Management*, *8*(6), 93–104. DOI: 10.1108/13673270410567657

Luthans, F., Youssef, C. M., & Avolio, B. J. (2006). *Psychological capital: Developing the human competitive edge*. Oxford university press. DOI: 10.1093/acprof:oso/9780195187526.001.0001

MacDuffie, J. P. (1995). Human resource bundles and manufacturing performance: Organizational logic and flexible production systems in the world auto industry. ilr. *Industrial & Labor Relations Review*, *48*(2), 197–221. DOI: 10.1177/001979399504800201

Marsick, V. J., & Watkins, K. E. (2003). Demonstrating value of learning culture. *Advances in Developing Human Resources*, *5*(2), 132–151. DOI: 10.1177/1523422303005002002

McKinsey & Company. (2023). *Future of work report.* https://www.mckinsey.com/featured-insights/future-of-work

Mouw, T., Kalleberg, A. L., & Schultz, M. A. (2024). “Stepping-Stone” versus “Dead-End” jobs: Occupational structure, work experience, and mobility out of low-wage jobs. *American Sociological Review*, *89*(2), 298–345. DOI: 10.1177/00031224241232957

Ng, T. W., Eby, L. T., Sorensen, K. L., & Feldman, D. C. (2005). Predictors of objective and subjective career success: A meta-analysis. *Personnel Psychology*, *58*(2), 367–408. DOI: 10.1111/j.1744-6570.2005.00515.x

Noe, R. A., Clarke, A. D., & Klein, H. J. (2014). Learning in the twenty-first-century workplace. *Annual Review of Organizational Psychology and Organizational Behavior*, *1*(1), 245–275. DOI: 10.1146/annurev-orgpsych-031413-091321

OECD. (2024). *OECD Employment Outlook 2024: The Net-Zero Transition and the Labour Market.* OECD Publishing., DOI: 10.1787/ac8b3538-

Oreg, S. (2006). Personality, context, and resistance to organizational change. *European Journal of Work and Organizational Psychology*, *15*(1), 73–101. DOI: 10.1080/13594320500451247

Rajoli, S. B., & Manoharan, G. (2023). Artificial Intelligence in Recruitment–The Future of Talent Acquisition. In AI and Innovation in HRM (pp. 276-293). Routledge.

Salas, E., Tannenbaum, S. I., Kraiger, K., & Smith-Jentsch, K. A. (2012). The science of training and development in organizations: What matters in practice. *Psychological Science in the Public Interest : A Journal of the American Psychological Society*, *13*(2), 74–101. DOI: 10.1177/1529100612436661 PMID: 26173283

Senge, P. (1990). *The fifth discipline Doubleday.*

Sherehiy, B., & Karwowski, W. (2014). The relationship between work organization and workforce agility in small manufacturing enterprises. *International Journal of Industrial Ergonomics*, *44*(3), 466–473. DOI: 10.1016/j.ergon.2014.01.002

SHRM. (2023). Workforce report. https://www.shrm.org/content/dam/en/shrm/executive-network/SOTW-23-24Enterprise-Solutions.pdf

Teece, D. J. (2025). *Dynamic capabilities.* Cambridge University Press., DOI: 10.1017/9781009562713

Terrazas, A. (2022, November 17). Workplace trends 2023. Workplace Trends 2023. https://www.glassdoor.com/blog/workplace-trends-2023/

UNDP (United Nations Development Programme). 2024. Human Development Report 2023-24: Breaking the gridlock: Reimagining cooperation in a polarized world. New York. https://hdr.undp.org/content/human-development-report-2023-24

World Economic Forum. (2025). *Future of jobs report*. https://www.weforum.org/publications/the-future-of-jobs-report-2025/

Wright, P. M., & McMahan, G. C. (2011). Exploring human capital: Putting 'human' back into strategic human resource management. *Human Resource Management Journal, 21*(2), 93–104. DOI: 10.1111/j.1748-8583.2010.00165.x

Chapter 4
Cross-Training Framework:
Avoiding Pitfalls and Improving Organizational and Employee Outcomes

Jelena Lukić Nikolić
http://orcid.org/0000-0003-0632-8974
Modern Business School, Serbia

ABSTRACT

Cross-training has emerged as a strategic organizational capability for addressing workforce challenges such as tight labor markets, skill shortages, absenteeism, turnover, and rapid technological change. It is a double-edged strategy: when carefully planned and implemented, it strengthens organizational performance and employee growth; when poorly designed, it can generate significant challenges, barriers, and risks. This chapter introduces a conceptual framework aimed at minimizing these challenges and maximizing the benefits of cross-training. The framework carries important implications for both theory and practice, offering a more nuanced understanding of the conditions under which cross-training succeeds or fails. By integrating theoretical insights with practical guidelines, it positions cross-training as a critical mechanism for building sustainable resilience, enhancing productivity, and fostering long-term employee development. For practitioners, it provides structured guidance to design and implement cross-training programs that maximize benefits while reducing risks.

DOI: 10.4018/979-8-3373-5327-2.ch004

ht © 2027, IGI Global Scientific Publishing. Copying or distributing in print or electronic forms without written permission of IGI Global Scientific Publishing is prohibited. Use of this chapter to generative artificial intelligence (AI) technologies is expressly prohibited. The publisher reserves all rights to license its use for generative AI training and machine learning model development.

1. INTRODUCTION

In the contemporary business landscape, organizations are confronted with a multitude of challenges, including the need to maintain operational continuity while simultaneously reducing costs and improving efficiency, quality, productivity, flexibility, adaptability, and innovation (Labus & Lukić Nikolić, 2025). Modern organizations operate in a persistent state of instability, compelled to adapt under conditions of constant dynamism, turbulence, time pressure, and unpredictable, often radical, changes (Moedt et al., 2024). The very nature of work has undergone significant transformation, and it is increasingly apparent that the future of work will continue to evolve in response to technological advancements, shifting organizational priorities, and changing employee expectations (Blackman, 2025). Traditional notions of stable and clearly defined job roles are diminishing, replaced by fluid, uncertain, and unpredictable circumstances (Lukić Nikolić & Mirković, 2023), where tasks frequently evolve, disappear, or are replaced by new ones (Koopmans et al., 2025). The Covid-19 pandemic further exacerbated these pressures, as many businesses experienced economic downturns and were compelled to achieve more with fewer employees and reduced budgets (Meyer et al., 2022). In this context, employees are expected not only to preserve their positions but also to cultivate competencies that enhance their competitiveness in the labor market and strengthen their resilience to ongoing change (Lukić Nikolić & Andrian Sredojević, 2025). Such transformation demands continuous learning and the ongoing acquisition of new skills (Schaufeli, 2013), thereby shifting the paradigm of education from a finite, one-time process toward a lifelong learning model (Assefa et al., 2023).

Careers in the contemporary environment have become increasingly fluid and adaptive, frequently unfolding along spiral rather than linear trajectories (Chen et al., 2020; Hite & McDonald, 2008). Professional success is closely tied to employees' capacity to continuously acquire new knowledge and develop relevant skills (Lukić Nikolić & Labus, 2024; Lukić Nikolić et al., 2024; Su et al., 2025; Qin et al., 2015). In this context, organizations place growing emphasis on individuals who embody the characteristics of the T-shaped professional - those who combine deep disciplinary expertise (the vertical axis of the "T") with broad, integrative knowledge across diverse domains (the horizontal axis of the "T") (Guest, 1991). Such professionals are distinguished by their ability to interpret, assimilate, and apply new knowledge while simultaneously extending their competencies into adjacent fields and demonstrate discretionary effort by engaging in tasks that extend beyond formal job descriptions (Hamdi et al., 2016; Hernaus et al., 2021).

Building on the increasing demand for flexible and multi-skilled professionals, organizations have increasingly relied on structured human resource development approaches aimed at systematically cultivating these capabilities. Among these approaches, cross-training has emerged as a prominent workforce development strategy, generating benefits for both organizations and employees (Ast & Nyhuis, 2023). It is commonly defined as the intentional process of equipping employees with the knowledge, skills, and experience required to perform tasks beyond their primary roles (Salas et al., 2007; Volpe et al., 1996). The practice gained traction in the mid-1980s, when large organizations began systematically preparing employees for broader and more diverse responsibilities (Greenhaus & Callanan, 2006), a development largely driven by globalization, accelerated production cycles, technological change, and persistent labor shortages.

Beyond its origins, cross-training is now widely conceptualized as a strategic approach for enhancing workforce adaptability and organizational resilience. By enabling employees to operate across multiple roles, it facilitates knowledge sharing, improves workforce flexibility, and strengthens an organization's capacity to respond to fluctuations in demand and skill availability. Accordingly, organizations implement cross-training not only to achieve competitive advantage and improve operational outcomes such as speed, quality, efficiency, and productivity, but also to mitigate both short- and long-term workforce constraints. In addition, it contributes to the development of a more versatile workforce and supports more effective utilization of human capital (Abrams & Berge, 2010; Chen & Tseng, 2012; Ojambati et al., 2012; Salem & Abdien, 2017; Sila, 2014; Tracey et al., 2008).

While existing literature has extensively emphasized the benefits of cross-training, significantly less attention has been devoted to the challenges, barriers, and unintended consequences associated with its implementation. Prior research predominantly portrays cross-training as a beneficial managerial practice, often overlooking the fact that poorly designed or inadequately implemented initiatives may generate substantial organizational and employee-related risks (Abrams & Berge, 2010; Torrington, 2008). In particular, limited research has systematically examined how implementation failures, dependency vulnerabilities, role ambiguity, employee resistance, and counterproductive knowledge behaviors may undermine the intended outcomes of cross-training programs. Moreover, existing studies rarely integrate these risks into a comprehensive framework that simultaneously connects the drivers of cross-training adoption, implementation mechanisms, and preventive strategies (Littrell et al., 2006).

This gap is especially important in the context of contemporary labor market instability, increasing skill shortages, rapid technological change, and growing organizational dependence on knowledge-intensive work. Under such conditions, organizations are increasingly pressured to adopt cross-training as a mechanism for maintaining continuity, flexibility, and operational resilience (Brassey et al., 2024). However, without adequate planning, managerial support, transparent communication, and alignment with organizational strategy, cross-training initiatives may produce unintended consequences such as inefficiencies, temporary productivity declines, employee dissatisfaction, burnout, knowledge hiding, or excessive dependence on a limited number of employees (Abrams & Berge, 2010; Torrington, 2008). Consequently, although organizations that embed adaptability and resilience into cross-training practices often achieve superior long-term outcomes (Brassey et al., 2024), the effectiveness of such initiatives ultimately depends on the quality of their design, implementation, monitoring, and continuous adjustment.

The purpose of this chapter is to examine the challenges, barriers, and risks inherent in the design and implementation of cross-training programs while also identifying strategies that can prevent or mitigate these limitations. To strengthen practical relevance, the chapter incorporates two illustrative case studies - one from an IT company and another from a service-oriented organization. These examples demonstrate both the opportunities and vulnerabilities associated with cross-training and illustrate how the absence, poor management, or insufficient institutionalization of cross-training practices may lead to knowledge concentration, operational dependency, reduced adaptability, and organizational inefficiencies.

Building on these theoretical and practical insights, the chapter proposes a conceptual framework for effective cross-training design and implementation. The framework identifies the primary drivers of cross-training adoption, the organizational and managerial mechanisms necessary for successful implementation, the expected organizational- and employee-level outcomes, and the key risks and barriers that require proactive management.

By integrating both positive and potential negative dimensions of cross-training into a unified framework, this chapter contributes to the existing literature by offering a more balanced and comprehensive understanding of cross-training in contemporary organizations. The proposed framework also provides practical guidance for managers and human resource professionals seeking to implement cross-training initiatives in environments characterized by labor shortages, uncertainty, and increasing demands for organizational resilience and workforce adaptability.

2. CROSS-TRAINING DEFINITIONS AND THEORETICAL CONCEPTS

Cross-training refers to the systematic process of preparing employees to undertake a broader range of tasks within the organization, including responsibilities that extend beyond their primary roles (Dirks et al., 1995; Malhotra & Ritzman, 1990). Conceptually, it represents a strategic approach to workforce development, enabling employees to acquire knowledge of tasks performed by colleagues across different functions (Salas et al., 2007; Volpe et al., 1996). Through this process, employees cultivate competencies that allow them to assume diverse positions and functions, thereby enhancing functional flexibility and organizational adaptability (Greenhaus & Callanan, 2006; Henao et al., 2023). Within the contemporary business environment, cross-training serves multiple purposes. It compensates for employee absences, strengthens production flexibility, and operates as a strategic mechanism for job enrichment. By diversifying tasks, cross-training reduces monotony and fosters greater employee satisfaction, engagement, and overall experience. Thus, cross-training is not merely a technical intervention but a holistic strategy that simultaneously advances organizational agility and enhances the quality of working life.

The growing recognition of cross-training as both an operational and developmental strategy has stimulated substantial theoretical and empirical interest in understanding its underlying mechanisms and organizational effects. Early conceptual foundations can be traced to Nelson (1967), who examined labor multifunctionality through two contrasting scenarios: one in which employees were restricted to a single workstation and another in which employees were capable of performing tasks across every workstation. Subsequent studies extended this perspective by exploring intermediate scenarios, such as employees trained to operate two or three workstations (Park & Bobrowski, 1989) or even four workstations (Park, 1991). Functional flexibility, in this context, refers to the extent to which employee-task combinations can be realized, measured by the average number of employees trained for specific tasks (Ast & Nyhuis, 2022). Brusco et al. (1998), employing an integer linear programming framework, demonstrated that employees need not be fully trained across all tasks to achieve significant advantages from cross-training. Conversely, Dunphy and Bryant (1996) cautioned that excessive training across too many workstations may lead to employee frustration. Collectively, these studies emphasize the importance of identifying an optimal level of employee multifunctionality. Overextension or extreme approaches can undermine both employee well-being and organizational efficiency (Costa et al., 2023; Nembhard & Prichanont, 2007).

Building on these foundational perspectives, contemporary research increasingly interprets cross-training through broader organizational and behavioral theories that explain its strategic value for both employees and organizations. Table 1 presents the key theoretical foundations that explain the importance and potential effects of cross-training within organizations.

Table 1. Key theoretical foundations of cross-training

Theory	Core assumptions	Implications for cross-training
Human Capital Theory	Human capital consists of employees' education, knowledge, experience, and skills. Investments in training and development should be viewed as strategic initiative that enhances productivity and organizational performance (Schultz, 1961).	Cross-training broadens employees' skill sets, enhances workforce flexibility and productivity, and strengthens long-term employability and career development.
Social Exchange Theory	Employment relationships are based on reciprocal exchanges between organizations and employees, where perceived organizational support encourages positive employee attitudes and behaviors (Blau, 1964).	Cross-training signals organizational investment in employees, encouraging reciprocity through stronger commitment, loyalty, engagement, and discretionary effort.
Knowledge-Based View	Organizational success depends on the creation, integration, sharing, and application of knowledge, which represents a key strategic resource (Grant, 1996; Spender, 1996).	Cross-training facilitates knowledge transfer across roles and departments, reduces knowledge silos, and strengthens organizational learning, collaboration, and innovation.
Psychological Contract Theory	Beyond formal employment agreements, employees develop psychological contracts based on perceived organizational obligations, support, and fairness (Rousseau, 2000).	Cross-training demonstrates organizational commitment to employee development, fostering trust, motivation, job satisfaction, and lower turnover intentions.
Organizational Resilience Theory	Organizations achieve resilience by adapting effectively to disruptions, recovering from crises, and maintaining operational continuity under changing conditions (Kantabutra & Ketprapakorn, 2021).	Cross-training enhances organizational resilience by ensuring operational continuity during absences, turnover, or crises and by reducing dependence on individual specialists.

Taken together, these theoretical perspectives demonstrate that cross-training extends far beyond the acquisition of technical competencies. While Human Capital Theory emphasizes the role of cross-training in enhancing skills and productivity, Social Exchange Theory and Psychological Contract Theory highlight its influence on employee attitudes, motivation, and commitment. At the same time, the Knowledge-Based View and Organizational Resilience Theory underscore the importance of cross-training for knowledge diffusion, collaboration, adaptability, and continuity in dynamic and uncertain work environments.

In parallel with theoretical advances, the practice of cross-training began to intensify during the mid-1980s, when major organizations such as General Motors, Motorola, Ritz-Carlton, and Sheraton Hotels systematically introduced programs to train employees across diverse tasks (Greenhaus & Callanan, 2006). This development was largely a response to profound shifts in the business environment, including globalization, accelerated production cycles, technological innovation, and persistent labor shortages (Abrams & Berge, 2010). As organizations increasingly faced the need to maintain efficiency and flexibility under such conditions, cross-training became particularly relevant as a practical response to workforce volatility and structural change. In practice, cross-training is frequently implemented in the context of organizational transformations such as restructuring, mergers, acquisitions, or downsizing where it serves as a critical mechanism for safeguarding operational efficiency and organizational flexibility. Several successful applications can be observed in practice. For instance, *Vaillant* implemented structured learning pathways that enabled developers, designers, and project managers to better understand each other's roles and workflows, thereby improving cross-functional collaboration. Similarly, the *U.S. Government Accountability Office* reported that cross-training of key finance employees allowed government agencies to maintain operational continuity during periods of staffing shortages (Groh, 2026).

Beyond these formal and crisis-driven implementations, the extent and mode of cross-training vary considerably across organizational contexts. In smaller entrepreneurial firms, cross-training generally occurs informally, as the limited size of the workforce requires that employees take on multiple functions and remain informed about all aspects of the business. By contrast, in larger organizations, cross-training programs are formally structured and strategically planned, with the explicit aim of enabling employees to assume a wider range of tasks and responsibilities. This distinction highlights the dual character of cross-training: while it can emerge "naturally" in resource-constrained environments, it also functions as a deliberate, strategic intervention in complex organizational settings.

3. CROSS-TRAINING FORMS AND CATEGORIES

Understanding the different forms and categories of cross-training is essential for distinguishing how organizations design learning interventions to achieve varying developmental and operational outcomes. Cross-training can be operationalized through distinct forms that vary in depth and intensity of employee involvement. To illustrate these variations, Table 2 outlines three key forms of employee cross-training, each representing a different mode of knowledge transfer and skill acquisition.

Table 2. Forms of employee cross-training

Form	Description
Positional clarification	Involves verbally or textually explaining the responsibilities and duties of other employees. This may be delivered through structured briefings, lectures, or written manuals, ensuring employees gain conceptual awareness of tasks performed across roles.
Positional modeling	Provides experiential learning by allowing employees to observe and, in some cases, simulate the work of others. This method emphasizes demonstration and guided practice, enabling participants to internalize skills through observation and limited role enactment.
Positional (job) rotation	Offers employees direct exposure to tasks outside their primary role by engaging them in hands-on participation. This immersive approach develops practical competence but requires greater investment of time and resources compared to other methods.

Source: Adapted from Blickensderfer et al., 1998

The three forms of cross-training (presented in Table 2) differ in depth of learning, resource requirements, and organizational impact. Specifically, positional clarification is the least resource-intensive, offering employees conceptual knowledge of colleagues' responsibilities without direct practice. While efficient, its effectiveness is limited to awareness rather than skill acquisition. Positional modeling provides a stronger learning experience by combining observation with guided practice, enabling employees to internalize procedures and develop confidence before assuming new tasks. Finally, positional (job) rotation represents the most immersive form, granting employees hands-on experience across roles. Although this approach fosters the highest level of competence and adaptability, it demands significant investment in time, supervision, and cost (Blickensderfer et al., 1998). Taken together, these forms illustrate a continuum from knowledge transfer to experiential learning, allowing organizations to balance efficiency with depth depending on strategic priorities and available resources (Cannon-Bowers et al., 1998).

Cross-training is commonly divided into three categories: vertical upward, vertical downward, and horizontal, based on whether the skills acquired move an employee toward higher-level responsibilities, lower-level tasks, or roles of similar scope within the organization (Hernaus et al., 2021). Vertical upward cross-training equips lower-level employees with skills and tasks typically performed by managers or supervisors, thereby fostering employee potential, preparing them for promotion, and enhancing their understanding of strategic decision-making. Downward cross-training, by contrast, involves managers or leaders acquiring the skills and operational knowledge of their followers, with the aim of deepening managerial insight into everyday challenges, improving efficiency, and strengthening mentoring capacity. Horizontal cross-training occurs among employees at the same hierarchical level, often across different departments, and is designed to promote collaboration, knowledge exchange, and interdepartmental integration.

Regardless of the direction of skill transfer, the effectiveness of cross-training also depends on the sources through which knowledge is acquired, shared, and internalized within the organization. Contemporary cross-training initiatives therefore draw upon two complementary sources of learning: system-based and people-based (Ninan et al., 2019). System-based learning provides employees with access to standardized resources such as documents, instructional materials, online platforms, and knowledge databases, ensuring consistency in knowledge transfer across roles. People-based learning, on the other hand, emphasizes tacit knowledge acquisition through networking, coaching, experience sharing, and collaborative decision-making. Together, these approaches create a holistic foundation for cross-training, enabling employees to develop versatile skill sets while cultivating adaptability and resilience in dynamic organizational environments.

4. CROSS-TRAINING BENEFITS

The key motivations for implementing cross-training include sustaining competitive advantage, enhancing core organizational functions such as speed, quality, efficiency, and productivity, addressing both short- and long-term labor shortages, and developing a flexible, multiskilled workforce. In this context, organizations increasingly conceptualize cross-training as a strategic response to staffing challenges and labor market uncertainty (Salem & Abdien, 2017). At the same time, employees who participate in cross-training often perceive themselves as more professionally valuable and adaptable compared to narrowly specialized colleagues, as broader competencies may enhance employability, career mobility, and perceived organizational importance (Pinker & Shumsky, 2000).

Beyond its operational and strategic benefits, cross-training contributes to more effective utilization of human resources, enriches job content, and supports higher levels of employee satisfaction and engagement. It also aligns closely with the philosophy of the learning organization by embedding continuous learning, collaboration, and knowledge sharing into everyday organizational practice (Abrams & Berge, 2010; Greenhaus & Callanan, 2006). Through these mechanisms, cross-training helps ensure that employees remain competent, adaptable, and actively engaged throughout their organizational tenure (Lokesha & Siddegowda, 2009).

Taken together, these insights demonstrate that cross-training generates substantial benefits for both organizations and employees, positioning it not merely as a training practice, but as a strategic organizational capability in increasingly dynamic labor market conditions.

4.1. Cross Training Benefits on Organizational Level

Key advantages of cross-training on organizational-level include (Abrams & Berge, 2010; Chen & Tseng, 2012; Salem & Abdien, 2017; Slomp & Molleman, 2002; Tracey et al., 2008):

- **Ensuring business continuity**. Processes remain uninterrupted during employee absences (e.g., sickness, vacations), as trained colleagues can assume their responsibilities.
- **Increasing operational flexibility**. Organizations can respond more rapidly to environmental changes and reallocate workforce capacity in line with current needs.
- **Enhancing productivity and efficiency**. Dependence on individual employees is reduced, minimizing delays, bottlenecks, and idle time.
- **Reducing recruitment and training costs**. By strengthening internal talent, organizations lessen their dependence on external hiring and can more quickly fill critical roles. Some authors note that the average expense of recruiting a new employee is approximately $30,000, whereas the ongoing training of current employees requires only about $1,500 (Maclaren, 2016).
- **Retaining and transferring knowledge**. Cross-training prevents knowledge monopolization and facilitates the diffusion of key competencies across the organization.
- **Strengthening cross-functional collaboration**. Employees gain a deeper understanding of other departments, improving understanding, communication and teamwork.
- **Improving problem-solving and decision-making**. Cross-trained employees are better equipped to identify issues, make informed decisions, and propose effective solutions.
- **Enhancing service quality**. Empowered and cross-trained employees can act decisively, improving responsiveness and customer satisfaction.
- **Fostering organizational citizenship behavior**. Employees demonstrate greater willingness to contribute beyond formal job requirements.
- **Building organizational resilience**. Cross-training reduces vulnerability to turnover, disruptions, and environmental uncertainty.

Taken together, these advantages suggest that cross-training represents not only a workforce development practice but also a strategic organizational capability that enhances adaptability, sustainability, and long-term competitiveness.

4.2. Cross Training Benefits on Employee Level

From the perspective of employees, cross-training exerts a significant influence on career development, motivation, and the psychological experience of work. Black and Mendenhall (1990) highlighted that various forms of training can enhance employees' self-confidence, strengthen their capacity to operate in novel and unfamiliar situations, and improve perceptual accuracy - all of which contribute positively to adaptation and performance. This line of inquiry was further advanced by Gudykunst (1998), who emphasized the role of training in managing anxiety and uncertainty, arguing that effective preparation can reduce stress and uncertainty in interactions within unfamiliar situations.

Key benefits of cross-training for employees include (Abrams & Berge, 2010; Brandl & Neyer, 2009; Chen & Tseng, 2012; Ninan et al., 2019; Ojambati et al., 2012; Sila, 2014; Slomp & Molleman, 2002):

- **Development of new knowledge and skills**. Through cross-training, employees expand their competencies by engaging in tasks beyond their primary responsibilities. This exposure allows them to acquire new knowledge, cultivate diverse abilities, and evolve into multidisciplinary professionals who can contribute more broadly across the organization.
- **Reduction of boreout**. Boreout syndrome reflects a profound crisis of meaning and purpose in the workplace, arising from monotonous, repetitive, and highly standardized tasks that foster job boredom and hinder professional growth (Abubakar et al., 2022; Stock, 2015). When employees are confined to routine activities of limited complexity, they often perceive their potential as underutilized, leading to frustration and disengagement (Cabrera Noriega, 2014). To counteract this, cross-training serves as a valuable intervention - by diversifying tasks, increasing job complexity, and aligning responsibilities more closely with individual capabilities, organizations can enhance employee satisfaction and foster a stronger sense of professional fulfillment.
- **Career development and internal mobility**. When employees gain exposure to tasks at higher levels (vertical upward), lower levels (vertical downward), or across similar functions (horizontal), they become more versatile and adaptable. This expanded capability not only prepares them for advancement opportunities but also makes it easier for organizations to reassign employees to new roles or projects as needs arise.
- **Enhanced employability and job security**. Cross-training strengthens employees' value by equipping them with the ability to perform a wider range of tasks. This versatility not only increases their attractiveness in the ex-

ternal labor market but also makes them indispensable within their current organization.

- **Strengthened networking**. Cross-training enhances workplace relationships by allowing employees to collaborate with colleagues outside their usual roles. This exposure fosters new connections, encourages the exchange of knowledge, and promotes mutual learning, ultimately building stronger professional networks within the organization.
- **Greater empathy**. Cross-training nurtures a deeper appreciation for colleagues by exposing employees to the responsibilities and challenges of different roles. This firsthand understanding fosters respect for diverse perspectives, strengthens collaboration, and builds a more supportive workplace culture.
- **Increased motivation and engagement**. Cross-training enhances employee involvement by providing opportunities to learn new skills and contribute more meaningfully to organizational goals. This process fosters a stronger sense of purpose, heightens the perceived significance of work, and ultimately increases motivation and engagement.
- **Discovery of hidden talents**. Cross-training provides employees with opportunities to explore tasks outside their usual responsibilities, often revealing skills and interests that had not been previously recognized. This process can uncover untapped potential, broaden career paths, and encourage individuals to pursue new areas of growth within the organization.
- **Development of adaptability and agility**. By practicing tasks outside their primary roles, employees build flexibility, learn to adjust quickly to new situations, and strengthen their ability to thrive in dynamic work environments.

Collectively, these benefits indicate that cross-training contributes not only to employees' professional development but also to their psychological well-being, engagement, and long-term career sustainability. By broadening competencies and enriching work experiences, cross-training can foster a more adaptable, motivated, and resilient workforce capable of responding effectively to evolving organizational demands.

5. CROSS-TRAINING: CHALLENGES, BARRIERS AND RISKS

Although cross-training is widely acknowledged as a valuable strategy for enhancing both organizational performance and individual development, its effectiveness is highly contingent upon the quality of its design and implementation. When poorly designed or inadequately managed, cross-training can generate a range of challenges, barriers and risks that undermine its intended benefits (Abrams & Berge, 2010). The following discussion examines these issues through a dual lens, distinguishing between organizational-level and employee-level challenges, barriers, and risks to effective cross-training design and implementation.

One of the most frequently observed challenges is the high cost of cross-training implementation, which requires substantial investments in training materials, employee time, and managerial resources. Such financial commitments do not always yield positive outcomes and are often perceived as risky investments (Nembhard et al., 2005). Moreover, organizations frequently experience a temporary decline in productivity, as employees must dedicate time to acquiring new competencies while continuing to manage responsibilities in their primary roles (Kher, 2000; Malhotra et al., 1993; Yue et al., 2008). This decline is further exacerbated by the time required for orientation, task refocusing, and accessing relevant information (Bokhorst & Slomp, 2007). To mitigate these risks, contemporary organizations increasingly employ skills clustering as a cross-training strategy. In this approach, employees are trained in related competencies within a defined cluster, enabling them to perform multiple tasks that share common skill sets. This reduces productivity losses that occur when training extends into areas misaligned with core expertise (Hass et al., 2001). Another notable risk is role ambiguity, which arises when responsibilities for additional tasks are not clearly defined or communicated. In such cases, employees lack essential information regarding expectations, job requirements, and performance outcomes, making it difficult to fulfill responsibilities satisfactorily (Alblihed & Alzghaibi, 2022). Unclear task ownership and accountability can hinder coordination, diminish efficiency and satisfaction, and ultimately weaken overall organizational performance (Mwakyusa & Mcharo, 2024).

Another significant risk associated with cross-training is skill dilution. When employees are encouraged to broaden their competencies across multiple roles, organizations may inadvertently weaken their pool of specialized expertise. This shift toward generalist capabilities can undermine performance in highly technical or expert-driven functions, making it difficult to sustain excellence in areas where depth of knowledge is essential (Colman, 2026; Moedt et al., 2024). From the employee perspective, specialists often derive a strong sense of identity, uniqueness, and organizational value from their expertise, and cross-training may weaken these perceptions of distinctiveness (Slomp & Molleman, 2002). Although cross-training enhances workforce flexibility and broadens employee competencies, it can simultaneously undermine confidence in specialized expertise, increase perceptions of role overload, and reduce motivation to pursue mastery within one's core domain (Colman, 2026).

In addition, cross-training often increases organizational complexity, as it requires careful planning, coordination, and continuous monitoring across multiple training pathways and employee roles. Without effective leadership oversight and structured management, these processes may become difficult to coordinate and sustain, thereby reducing program effectiveness and undermining the intended organizational and developmental benefits.

While organizational issues highlight structural challenges, barriers, and risks, cross-training simultaneously introduces significant employee-level concerns shaped by individual perceptions, behavioral patterns, and psychological responses. Addressing these concerns is essential for the successful design and implementation of cross-training programs. Not all employees feel secure stepping outside their established comfort zones, and many demonstrate limited interest in cross-training opportunities, preferring instead to remain within their area of expertise and preserve depth in specialized knowledge (Abrams & Berge, 2010).

From the employee perspective, a major risk of cross-training relates to stress and perceived workload imbalance. When such initiatives are not properly communicated or rewarded, employees may interpret them as an unfair increase in job demands without corresponding compensation, leading to dissatisfaction, disengagement, and even turnover intentions (Colman, 2026). In some cases, cross-training is perceived as added strain, particularly when broader skill sets result in responsibilities beyond formal job descriptions. This can prompt refusal to participate, with employees arguing that such tasks fall outside their scope. Others may experience discomfort when performing duties outside their primary expertise, which can compromise confidence and ultimately affect the quality of service delivered (Abrams & Berge, 2010).

A further risk associated with cross-training is employee burnout, particularly when training initiatives are implemented without appropriate workload adjustments or adequate organizational support (Slomp & Molleman, 2002). Employees who are expected to maintain high performance under tight deadlines while simultaneously managing additional and increasingly complex responsibilities are especially vulnerable to emotional exhaustion (Lukić Nikolić & Labus, 2024). When demands during skill acquisition exceed employees' adaptive capacity, cross-training may contribute to fatigue, reduced well-being, diminished job satisfaction, and impaired realization of individual potential. Moreover, prolonged exposure to elevated stress levels increases the likelihood of burnout, ultimately weakening both employee resilience and overall organizational effectiveness (Labus et al., 2026).

Another significant risk associated with cross-training is the emergence of job insecurity. As colleagues acquire overlapping competencies, employees may fear becoming less indispensable and more easily replaceable within the organization. Previous research has consistently linked job insecurity to a range of negative outcomes, including diminished personal and work-related well-being, lower job satisfaction, reduced engagement, and weakened performance (Hofer, 2026; Spurk et al., 2022). In such contexts, employees may engage in counterproductive knowledge behaviors, including the intentional withholding or concealment of information that colleagues need or expect, in an effort to preserve power, maintain job security, and protect career advancement opportunities (Shen et al., 2025; Thomas, 2025).

5.1. Counterproductive Knowledge Behavior and Cross-Training: Case Studies

Employees may engage in deliberate knowledge-related behaviors that undermine collaboration and organizational learning, particularly when knowledge becomes a source of individual power and job security. Such behaviors emerge as strategic responses to perceived threats to employability, visibility, or organizational dependency, and they can take different forms. Table 3 presents three distinct forms of counterproductive knowledge behaviors, illustrating how concerns related to job insecurity and power preservation translate into specific workplace actions and negatively affect organizational outcomes.

Table 3. Key forms of counterproductive knowledge behaviors

Form	Description
Knowledge hoarding	Retention of knowledge that could be shared due to concern about job security and desire to retain power and career advancement (Yang et al., 2024). Employees want to have unique expertise that ensures them job security. It is a proactive withholding of knowledge without a direct request, motivated by self-preservation and status.
Knowledge hiding	Employees intentionally withhold or conceal knowledge that has been directly requested by others (Connelly et al., 2012). It is a **reactive behavior**, occurring when someone asks for information, but the employee chooses not to share it.
Knowledge sabotage	Employees intentionally conceal, distort, or manipulate knowledge to serve personal or strategic interests, manifesting hostile behavior, revenge attitudes, maliciousness, and unfriendly behavior (Serenko, 2019). It represents a **destructive act**, where knowledge is not only withheld but actively misused to harm others or the organization.

The following case studies illustrate how counterproductive knowledge behaviors emerge in practice when organizations fail to institutionalize structured cross-training and knowledge-sharing mechanisms.

Case Study: Knowledge Hiding and Dependency Risks in the Absence of Cross-Training

An IT company established in 2008 specializes in software solutions for financial management. As of April 2026, it employed 42 staff members organized into five teams: development, technical support, project management, consulting, and people and analytics.

Within the technical support team, two new employees were hired to assist the team leader and reduce his operational workload. During onboarding, the leader provided training on several segments of the information system but deliberately excluded a critical component that he had personally developed in collaboration with the development team. When questioned by the HR manager, he described this segment as his "own part of the software" and intentionally withheld training to preserve his indispensability.

Further analysis revealed that the team leader strategically scheduled vacations to avoid critical system operations and remained involved in urgent requests even during time off, thereby ensuring continued control over the excluded system component. An additional analysis of the technical documentation and user manuals for this part of the information system revealed that several essential functionalities, as well as certain "tricks," were either not covered at all or described only superficially, making it impossible to learn them from the available materials and instructions.

In this case study, the team leader's behavior clearly illustrates knowledge hiding. He deliberately excluded a critical system component from the training process and all documentation, even when new employees directly needed that knowledge to perform their jobs.

This case study highlights how knowledge hiding is not simply an individual act of withholding information but a reflection of deeper organizational dynamics. By deliberately excluding a critical system component from training and documentation, the team leader transformed his expertise into a source of power. Knowledge asymmetry created dependency, allowing the team leader to control workflows, influence decision-making, and strategically manage his availability to reinforce indispensability. In this way, knowledge hiding becomes a mechanism of power preservation, where employees leverage exclusive expertise to secure authority and status within the organization.

Furthermore, the team leader's feeling that the system component was his "own part of the software" illustrates the role of psychological ownership. Psychological ownership occurs when individuals perceive organizational resources as personal possessions, fostering protective behaviors such as hoarding or hiding knowledge. This sense of "mine" can motivate employees to resist diffusion of expertise, even when such knowledge is essential for collective performance. In the case study, psychological ownership intensified the team leader's reluctance to share knowledge, reinforcing dependency risks and undermining team resilience.

Finally, the absence of structured cross-training reflects shortcomings in organizational culture. Cultures that fail to institutionalize knowledge-sharing mechanisms inadvertently legitimize monopolization of expertise. When organizations do not reward transparency or collaboration, opportunistic behaviors such as knowledge hiding are more likely to flourish. Conversely, cultures that emphasize collective responsibility, open communication, and shared learning can mitigate these risks by aligning individual incentives with organizational resilience.

Altogether, these dynamics demonstrate that knowledge hiding is both a symptom and a driver of organizational vulnerability. Structured cross-training programs, supported by a culture of openness, are therefore essential not only for diffusing expertise but also for counteracting unhealthy power dynamics and fostering sustainable organizational effectiveness.

The second case study in one service-oriented organization underscores how the absence of cross-training and knowledge-sharing mechanisms can foster information asymmetries and knowledge monopolization.

Case Study: Knowledge Monopolization as a Consequence of Absence of Cross-Training

In a service-oriented organization reliant on specialized software, a single employee, Diana from the financial department, was solely responsible for producing the monthly financial report. She consistently portrayed the task as highly complex and time-consuming, often claiming that it required several days to complete. However, when Diana was unexpectedly absent due to injury, a colleague attempted to prepare the report and contacted the software provider for assistance. To the organization's surprise, the report was completed in just 15 minutes, exposing a stark discrepancy between the perceived and actual complexity of the task.

Upon returning from sick leave, Diana expressed dissatisfaction and even anger toward the technical support consultant, as it became evident that she had deliberately framed the task as more complex than it truly was.

This case study highlights that the absence of structured cross-training can inadvertently lead to knowledge monopolization, whereby expertise becomes concentrated in a small number of employees. Moreover, this case illustrates how information asymmetry can evolve into a subtle source of informal power within organizations. By exaggerating the complexity and time requirements of the reporting process, the employee maintained a perception of indispensability that discouraged knowledge diffusion, limited process transparency, and reinforced organizational dependency. Such dynamics may remain undetected in organizations that lack structured cross-training, standardized documentation, and systematic knowledge-sharing practices. Consequently, the absence of cross-training not only increases operational vulnerability but may also unintentionally reinforce power imbalances and hinder organizational learning and adaptability.

Taken together, the two case studies demonstrate how the absence of structured cross-training and knowledge-sharing mechanisms can create organizational dependency on individual employees, reinforce information asymmetries, and foster counterproductive knowledge behaviors. These dynamics not only weaken operational continuity and collaboration but also increase organizational vulnerability by concentrating on critical expertise within a limited number of individuals. Conversely, organizations that institutionalize cross-training are better positioned to distribute knowledge systematically, reduce dependency risks, and strengthen resilience, transparency, and adaptability. To illustrate these contrasting outcomes, Table 4 compares key differences between organizations with and without structured cross-training practices.

Table 4. Organizational outcomes with and without cross-training

Without cross-training	With cross-training
Dependence on a single employee	Operational continuity
Knowledge monopolization	Knowledge transparency
Task complexity distortion	Standardized understanding of tasks
Delays and inefficiencies	Faster and more stable execution
Increased stress and uncertainty	Reduced operational risk
Interpersonal tensions	Improved collaboration
Limited knowledge diffusion	Systematic knowledge sharing

Structured cross-training strengthens operational continuity, promotes knowledge transparency, and fosters a more standardized understanding of organizational tasks and processes. By distributing critical competencies across employees, it enables faster and more consistent task execution, reduces operational vulnerability, and enhances collaboration among teams and departments. In addition, systematic knowledge sharing becomes embedded within everyday organizational practice, minimizing dependency on individual employees and supporting greater workforce resilience.

IT and service-oriented environments are particularly sensitive to cross-training implementation failures due to their reliance on highly specialized knowledge, system ownership, and individual expertise concentration. Nevertheless, the mechanisms identified in this chapter such as knowledge hoarding, role dependency, and insufficient skill diffusion are not industry-specific and may be observed across a wide range of organizational settings, particularly in knowledge-intensive industries.

6. KEY MECHANISMS FOR CROSS-TRAINING SUCCESS

The effective design and implementation of cross-training requires a strategic and systematically planned approach that extends beyond traditional training interventions. In the context of tight labor markets, its success depends not only on operational execution but also on the extent to which potential challenges, barriers, and risks are anticipated and proactively addressed (Jordan et al., 2004; Salem & Abdien, 2017). Poorly managed cross-training can generate resistance, role ambiguity, and perceptions of workload imbalance. Therefore, it must be positioned as a structured organizational capability rather than an *ad hoc* initiative. Although each organization is unique and no single cross-training formula is universally applicable (Abrams & Berge, 2010), several guiding principles can help ensure effective implementation.

One of the first steps in preventing cross-training implementation failures is embedding cross-training within the Employee Value Proposition (EVP). The EVP represents the bundle of benefits and reciprocal value exchanges employees receive in return for their contributions to the organization (Arasanmi & Krishna, 2019). More specifically, it encompasses the distinctive combination of benefits, experiences, opportunities, and organizational values that an employer offers to its workforce (Mohammadi & Mohammadian, 2025). When cross-training is explicitly framed as part of this broader value exchange, employees are more likely to perceive it as an investment in their professional development rather than as an additional burden. This reduces resistance, minimizes perceptions of unfair workload distribution, and strengthens employee acceptance of cross-training initiatives.

Equally important is embedding cross-training within the psychological contract between employees and the organization. Rousseau (2000) defines the psychological contract as employees' beliefs regarding the reciprocal obligations, expectations, and commitments that shape the employment relationship. The manner in which cross-training is communicated and implemented therefore plays a crucial role in shaping employee perceptions and reactions. When cross-training is perceived as an imposed obligation or an additional workload burden, rather than as a mutually beneficial opportunity for learning and career development, it may generate dissatisfaction, disengagement, and diminished trust in management. To mitigate these risks, organizations must carefully manage employee expectations and clearly communicate the developmental and long-term career benefits associated with cross-training. Framing cross-training as a supportive investment in employee growth, employability, and professional advancement can strengthen commitment, increase participation willingness, and reinforce positive employment relationships.

Transparent communication represents another critical prerequisite for successful cross-training implementation. Employee resistance frequently emerges when cross-training initiatives are poorly communicated, insufficiently structured, or perceived as lacking clear purpose and benefits. To minimize such resistance, organizations should explicitly position cross-training as a mechanism for professional development, employability enhancement, career advancement, and internal mobility opportunities. In the absence of transparent communication, employees may perceive cross-training as an unfair expansion of workload and responsibilities without adequate recognition or reward. Clear communication of goals, expectations, and benefits is essential for strengthening employee acceptance, engagement, and long-term commitment to cross-training initiatives.

An equally important determinant of effective cross-training is the development of an organizational culture that actively promotes knowledge sharing and collaborative learning. The ability of organizations to create, transfer, and disseminate knowledge depends not only on formal structures and procedures, but also on the shared values, norms, and behaviors embedded within the workforce (Lau & Ngo, 2004). Davenport and Prusak (1998) emphasize that collaborative cultures encourage employee interaction and foster behaviors that support open knowledge exchange. Through such interactions, employees increasingly perceive knowledge sharing as a collective responsibility rather than as a source of individual power, thereby strengthening cultural support for continuous learning and cooperation (Khalil & Seleim, 2010; Mehner et al., 2025). Moreover, collaborative cultures stimulate cross-functional linkages and facilitate more effective knowledge transfer between individuals, teams, and departments (Mathrani & Edwards, 2020). To institutionalize these behaviors, organizations should integrate knowledge-sharing expectations into performance evaluation and reward systems, while simultaneously recognizing collaboration and knowledge exchange as essential dimensions of professional conduct and organizational citizenship.

Social support from leaders represents another determinant in facilitating effective knowledge transfer and cross-training within organizations (Mehner et al., 2025). In contemporary work environments, employees cannot operate effectively in isolation but instead rely on continuous interaction and knowledge exchange to manage the growing complexity of tasks and responsibilities (Hernaus et al., 2021). In this context, leaders play a central role in shaping a culture oriented toward learning, innovation, collaboration, and transparent communication, thereby encouraging employees to actively participate in cross-training initiatives (Rhoades & Eisenberger, 2002). By aligning cross-training opportunities with employees' capabilities, career aspirations, and professional development goals, leaders contribute simultaneously to individual growth and the strengthening of organizational capabilities. Equally important, leaders must foster a psychologically safe environment in which employees feel comfortable sharing knowledge, asking questions, and learning from one another without fear of negative consequences. Creating such an environment requires providing adequate resources, allocating sufficient time for learning, offering encouragement and support, and serving as visible role models for collaboration and knowledge sharing (Ferrer-Serrano et al., 2022).

Planned and formalized cross-training program. Effective cross-training requires a strategically planned and formalized approach that is aligned with the organization's broader goals and operational strategy. Rather than relying on *ad hoc* or informal initiatives, organizations should establish clear rules, procedures, and structures that define the optimal scope and level of cross-training required across different roles and departments. A key objective of such planning is to ensure that critical organizational knowledge and competencies are systematically distributed rather than concentrated in a limited number of individuals. To achieve sustainable outcomes, cross-training programs should be long-term oriented, integrated across all organizational units, and continuously adapted to evolving business needs and workforce demands (Ninan et al., 2019).

Selection of employees for cross-training. Careful selection of employees represents an important prerequisite for successful cross-training implementation. Organizations should first identify skill gaps within critical organizational processes and then select employees based on factors such as readiness for learning, motivation, adaptability, and developmental potential. Employees who proactively seek to understand the responsibilities and significance of colleagues' tasks are often more willing to participate in cross-training initiatives and are more likely to perceive such opportunities as beneficial for their career development (Wesner, 2014). In this process, performance appraisal systems can serve as valuable tools for identifying individuals who demonstrate strong learning orientation, flexibility, collaboration, initiative, and a positive work ethic, all of which contribute to more effective knowledge acquisition and transfer.

Reward systems for cross-training participation. To minimize disengagement and perceptions of unfairness, organizations should establish diversified reward systems that recognize and support employee participation in cross-training initiatives. Rewards encompass various forms of recognition provided in response to employee contributions, with the objective of encouraging motivation, engagement, and sustained high performance (Kinicki & Fugate, 2018). In the context of cross-training, such rewards may include skill certifications, public recognition programs, additional paid leave, career development opportunities, expanded responsibilities, or leadership roles in new projects. These mechanisms help reinforce positive attitudes toward learning, strengthen employee commitment, and reduce resistance to acquiring additional competencies. Although some employees may perceive learning opportunities and skill utilization as intrinsically rewarding, organizations should complement these intrinsic motivators with extrinsic incentives such as bonuses, salary increases, promotion opportunities, or other tangible rewards for high performers (Jay, n.d.).

Continuous feedback mechanisms. Finally, continuous feedback mechanisms are essential for preventing implementation stagnation and ensuring alignment between cross-training design and employee needs. Regular feedback allows organizations to refine training content, improve delivery methods, and maintain the ongoing relevance and effectiveness of cross-training initiatives. Equally important, employees should be provided with structured opportunities to apply newly acquired skills in practice, thereby reinforcing learning outcomes, reducing the risk of skill underutilization, and supporting long-term capability development.

Taken together, these mechanisms demonstrate that effective cross-training requires a holistic, strategically aligned approach in order to deliver meaningful organizational and individual outcomes.

6.1. Conceptual Framework for Cross-Training Success

The existing literature consistently points to the absence of a unified and comprehensive theoretical framework capable of fully explaining the outcomes of training and employee development. As Littrell et al. (2006) note, current approaches remain fragmented, often addressing isolated aspects of training effectiveness rather than capturing the broader and interdependent mechanisms through which training influences cognition, behavior, adaptation, and performance. This fragmentation limits the ability to systematically explain how and under what conditions training interventions translate into sustained individual and organizational outcomes. In response to this gap, the present title proposes a conceptual framework (Figure 1) designed to ensure the successful design and implementation of cross-training in organizations.

Figure 1. Conceptual framework for cross-training success

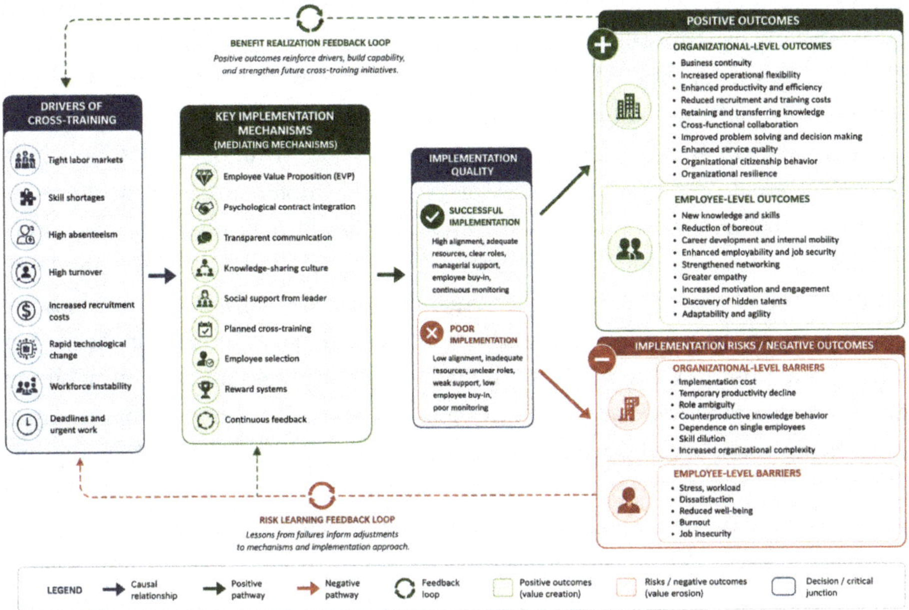

The proposed conceptual framework positions cross-training as a strategic human resource response to tight labor market conditions and increasing organizational uncertainty. However, in contrast to linear benefit-oriented perspectives, the framework emphasizes that cross-training outcomes are contingent on the organization's ability to anticipate and avoid common implementation challenges, barriers, and risks. The framework is structured around three interrelated components: (1) drivers of cross-training, (2) key implementation mechanisms, and (3) dual-level outcomes, while explicitly incorporating potential risks arising from inadequate implementation.

The first component, drivers of cross-training, captures external labor market conditions that increase organizational urgency for achieving workforce flexibility. These conditions include tight labor markets, skill shortages, high employee absenteeism, high employee turnover, increased recruitment costs, rapid technological change, workforce instability and deadlines and urgent work. While these factors act as drivers of cross-training adoption, they simultaneously increase the likelihood of reactive, poorly structured, or fragmented implementation approaches, thereby elevating the risk of organizational pitfalls.

In response to these pressures, organizations implement cross-training through a set of structured but risk-sensitive implementation mechanisms. These include alignment with the Employee Value Proposition (EVP), integration into the psychological contract, transparent communication, knowledge-sharing culture, social support from leader, planned and formalized cross-training, selection of employees, reward system and continuous feedback mechanism regarding cross-training. Within this framework, these mechanisms are not merely enablers of success but also critical safeguards that determine whether common challenges and barriers such as role ambiguity, resistance to change, or knowledge concentration are effectively mitigated.

The implementation of cross-training generates dual-level outcomes, which are highly dependent on the effectiveness of presented implementation mechanisms. At the organizational level, successful implementation may result in operational continuity, increased productivity, reduced dependency on key individuals, lower recruitment and training costs, greater organizational flexibility, improved knowledge transfer, enhanced resilience, and faster responsiveness to change. At the employee level, cross-training may contribute to skill development and multiskilling, increased employability, career mobility and internal advancement opportunities, higher engagement and motivation, reduced job monotony, improved perceptions of job security, and the discovery of hidden talents.

However, the framework also explicitly recognizes that these positive outcomes are not guaranteed. When implementation mechanisms are weak, inconsistent, or poorly aligned, cross-training may generate significant implementation challenges, barriers, risks and adverse outcomes, including skill dilution, role ambiguity, employee burnout, resistance to change, perceived unfair workload distribution, counterproductive knowledge behavior, and temporary productivity declines. These outcomes are conceptualized not as inherent limitations of cross-training, but as preventable consequences of inadequate design and execution.

Overall, the conceptual framework suggests that cross-training functions as a contingent organizational capability whose effectiveness depends on its adoption and on the organization's ability to manage implementation challenges, barriers and risks. In this sense, cross-training translates labor market pressures into organizational and employee positive outcomes only when supported by robust implementation mechanisms.

6.2. Cross-Training: Step-by-Step Recommendations

Effective cross-training implementation requires a structured and sequential approach that integrates strategic planning, workforce analysis, and continuous evaluation in order to achieve both organizational effectiveness and employee development outcomes. A review of the literature reveals a wide variety of proposed steps, models, and approaches for implementing cross-training programs, indicating that no single universally applicable formula or set of rules can guarantee success. Nevertheless, certain implementation principles and practices consistently emerge across successful organizations. The following overview synthesizes these key steps and may therefore serve as a practical guideline for managers designing and implementing effective cross-training initiatives.

Step 1: **Define and communicate cross-training goals and success indicators.** Clear and measurable goals must be established and communicated to employees from the outset. Employees should understand the organization's goals and feel actively included in the process. Typical goals include (Abrams & Berge, 2010):

- Covering employee vacations, absences, and lunch hours.
- Redistributing tasks during cyclical business fluctuations to minimize idle time.
- Enhancing understanding of business processes and strengthening collaboration across departments.

However, defining goals alone is insufficient unless organizations also establish mechanisms for evaluating whether these goals have been achieved. For this reason, cross-training initiatives should be accompanied by clearly defined key performance indicators (KPIs) that enable systematic monitoring of program effectiveness and outcomes. Table 5 presents key KPIs commonly used to assess cross-training success, including indicators related to employee coverage, skill acquisition, operational flexibility, productivity, error reduction, and employee satisfaction. Together, these indicators provide a balanced framework for evaluating both the operational and developmental impact of cross-training initiatives.

Table 5. Key KPIs for cross-training outcomes

KPI	Definition	Formula
Cross-Training Completion Rate	Percentage of employees who completed at least one cross-training module. Reflects program inclusivity and reach.	$\frac{\text{Number of trained employees}}{\text{Total number of employees}} \times 100$
Skill Acquisition Speed	Average time taken to reach proficiency in a new skill acquired through cross-training. Reflects efficiency and effectiveness of training.	$\frac{\text{Total time taken by all employees to reach proficiency}}{\text{Number of employees trained}}$
Operational Flexibility Index	Percentage of tasks successfully reassigned across departments or roles. Reflects workforce adaptability and resilience during fluctuations or absences.	$\frac{\text{Number of tasks successfully reassigned}}{\text{Total number of tasks attempted to reassign}} \times 100$

continued on following page

Table 5. Continued

KPI	Definition	Formula
Error Reduction Rate	Percentage decrease in mistakes or errors after cross-training. Reflects quality improvement and risk reduction.	$\frac{\text{Errors before - Errors after}}{\text{Errors before}} \times 100$
Productivity Uplift	Change in output per employee after cross-training. Reflects efficiency gains and business impact.	$\frac{\text{Output before - Output after}}{\text{Output before}} \times 100$
Employee Cross-Training Satisfaction Score	Average survey rating of perceived value and impact of cross-training programs. Reflects engagement, morale, and cross-training acceptance.	$\frac{\text{Sum of all survey ratings}}{\text{Number of respondents}}$

Step 2: **Identify relevant tasks and skills.** Not all skills carry equal importance for organizational success. Organizations should conduct systematic skills gap analysis to identify areas requiring cross-training. This process can be further supported through the review of historical data to determine which roles are most vulnerable to absenteeism, turnover, or operational disruption. At this stage, skill matrices serve as a valuable workforce-planning tool by providing a structured overview of employee competencies and revealing areas where skill coverage is insufficient (Olivella & Nembhard, 2016). A skill matrix visually maps employee competencies against organizational skill requirements, typically listing employees in rows and skills or tasks in columns, with each cell indicating the employee's level of proficiency (Table 6). Within cross-training initiatives, this tool enables managers to identify employees requiring additional development, detect critical skill gaps, and reduce overdependence on individual specialists. To remain effective, skill matrices should be continuously updated to reflect changes in workforce capabilities, organizational priorities, and technological developments.

Table 6. Illustrative skill matrix for identifying cross-training needs

	Skill 1	Skill 2	Skill 3	Skill 4	Skill N
Employee 1	No competence	Expert	Basic competence	Basic competence	Basic competence
Employee 2	Basic competence	High competence	No competence	Basic competence	High competence
Employee 3	Intermediate competence	Intermediate competence	High competence	No competence	Expert
Employee 4	High competence	Basic competence	Expert	Expert	No competence
Employee N	Expert	No competence	Intermediate competence	High competence	Intermediate competence

Step 3: **Select eligible candidates.** Candidates should be identified based on their interest in cross-training, relevant work experience, and demonstrated potential for learning and development (Kahkesh, 2024). Ideal candidates are employees who consistently achieve performance goals, complete tasks in a timely manner, demonstrate effective teamwork and engagement, communicate clearly, and exhibit initiative and ambition. In addition to technical competence and motivation, organizations should also consider employees' adaptability, learning orientation, collaborative behavior, and willingness to share knowledge, as these characteristics play a critical role in the effectiveness of cross-training and the long-term diffusion of knowledge across teams and organizational functions.

Step 4: **Choose qualified trainers.** Trainers should be selected not only for their technical expertise but also for their ability to effectively transfer knowledge and support employee learning. Effective cross-training depends on clear communication, mentorship capabilities, interpersonal skills, and the capacity to actively engage learners throughout the training process. In addition, trainers should demonstrate openness, patience, and a willingness to share both explicit and tacit knowledge, thereby fostering trust, collaboration, and psychological safety among employees. Supporting resources may include manuals, instructional guides, video tutorials, workshops, and structured mentorship programs, all of which reinforce the trainer's role, standardize knowledge transfer, and ensure greater consistency in learning outcomes across the organization.

Step 5: **Develop a cross-training plan and schedule.** A well-structured cross-training plan should balance training activities with employees' regular work responsibilities while also accounting for organizational costs, operational priorities, and workforce capacity. The plan should clearly specify which employees will be trained, the competencies and skills to be developed, the duration and sequencing of training activities, and the trainers responsible for implementation (Colman, 2026). In addition, organizations should establish measurable learning objectives, timelines, and evaluation criteria to monitor progress and ensure alignment with strategic organizational goals.

Step 6: **Adjust workload.** Employees participating in cross-training should have their regular responsibilities adjusted to an appropriate level, enabling them to fully engage in training activities without experiencing excessive strain or overload. Proper workload management is essential for maintaining employee well-being and ensuring effective skill acquisition throughout the training process. Without adequate adjustments and organizational support, cross-training may contribute to heightened stress, burnout, and temporary declines in productivity, ultimately undermining both employee performance and the overall effectiveness of the program (Bhatia & Shrivastava, 2022).

Step 7: **Implement cross-training in practice.** Even the most carefully designed cross-training plan will remain ineffective if it is not properly implemented and integrated into everyday organizational activities. Successful implementation requires active collaboration, continuous knowledge sharing, and sustained managerial support to ensure that newly acquired skills are applied in practice rather than remaining purely theoretical. Employees should be provided with structured opportunities to perform new tasks, rotate across functions, and gradually assume broader responsibilities within real work environments.

Step 8: **Track and reward achievements.** Establishing clear mechanisms for monitoring employee progress in cross-training is essential for evaluating program effectiveness, identifying skill development outcomes, and detecting areas requiring improvement. Performance appraisal systems can be utilized to assess both the acquisition and practical application of newly developed competencies within everyday work activities. In addition, organizations should define measurable indicators of success, such as skill proficiency, task flexibility, productivity improvements, or collaboration outcomes, to systematically evaluate cross-training performance. Recognizing and rewarding employee achievements not only validates individual effort and learning progress but also reinforces motivation, engagement, and long-term commitment to cross-training initiatives.

Step 9: **Collect employees' feedback and improve/adjust cross-training**. Cross-training initiatives should be continuously assessed through employee feedback, performance outcomes, and organizational results to determine their overall effectiveness and long-term sustainability. Regular feedback mechanisms enable organizations to identify implementation barriers, skill gaps, communication issues, or workload concerns that may undermine training success. In some cases, evaluation may reveal that a program is overly time-consuming, insufficiently structured, or ineffective in equipping employees with the competencies required to perform new tasks successfully. Such findings underscore the importance of continuously refining training content, methods, schedules, and delivery approaches to ensure alignment with organizational objectives and employee development needs.

To support the effective design and implementation of cross-training programs, Table 7 presents a step-by-step checklist that organizations can use to monitor progress and verify whether each stage of the cross-training has been systematically completed.

Table 7. Cross-training implementation checklist

Step	**Key questions**	**Yes/ No**
1. Define goals	Have clear and measurable cross-training goals and success factors been established and communicated to employees?	
2. Identify tasks and skills	Has a skills gap analysis been conducted to identify roles and competencies requiring cross-training?	
3. Select candidates	Have suitable employees been selected based on motivation, performance, and development potential?	
4. Choose trainers	Have trainers been selected based on both technical expertise and mentoring/ communication abilities?	
5. Develop plan and schedule	Does the plan specify training objectives, skills, schedule, duration, responsibilities, and expected outcomes?	
6. Adjust workload	Have employees' regular responsibilities been adjusted to avoid overload and burnout during cross-training?	
7. Implement training	Is cross-training being actively implemented, monitored, and integrated into daily work processes?	
8. Track progress and reward	Are KPIs, employee progress, and achievements being systematically measured and recognized?	
9. Collect feedback and improve	Is employee feedback being collected and used to continuously refine the cross-training program?	

By translating theoretical recommendations into practical managerial actions, the presented checklist can facilitate more systematic cross-training implementation, help organizations anticipate and mitigate common challenges, barriers, and risks, and ultimately enhance the long-term effectiveness and sustainability of cross-training programs.

7. FUTURE RESEARCH AGENDA

The rapid digital transformation of workplaces creates new challenges and opportunities for the design, implementation, and evaluation of cross-training programs. Advances in information and communication technologies, combined with growing labor market volatility and skill shortages, have accelerated the adoption of flexible, remote, and hybrid work arrangements (Rupcic, 2024). At the same time, emerging technologies such as artificial intelligence (AI), extended reality (XR), virtual reality (VR), augmented reality (AR), mixed reality (MR), and advanced collaboration platforms are contributing to the development of the "phygital" workplace, in which physical and digital work environments increasingly converge (Lo et al., 2024). These developments are transforming not only how employees perform their work but also how organizations design learning, collaboration, and knowledge-sharing processes. Consequently, organizations are compelled to rethink traditional approaches to cross-training and adapt them to digitally mediated and geographically dispersed work settings.

Despite the growing relevance of hybrid and remote work models, limited research has examined how such environments influence the effectiveness of cross-training initiatives. Traditional cross-training often relies heavily on direct observation, informal communication, job shadowing, and tacit knowledge transfer through interpersonal interaction. However, remote and hybrid work arrangements may weaken these informal learning mechanisms, potentially reducing opportunities for spontaneous collaboration, social learning, and experiential knowledge exchange. Future research should therefore investigate whether digital work environments alter the quality of knowledge transfer, employee engagement, trust development, and cross-functional collaboration within cross-training programs.

Technological advancements are also reshaping the methods through which cross-training is delivered. Simulation-based learning environments that integrate AI, VR, AR, and gamification have demonstrated superior outcomes compared to many traditional training approaches (Kulkarni et al., 2022). These technologies enable employees to practice unfamiliar tasks in immersive, interactive, and low-risk environments, thereby accelerating skill acquisition and reducing operational errors. Similarly, blended learning approaches that combine face-to-face instruction with digital modules provide greater flexibility and personalization while maintaining opportunities for experiential learning and interpersonal interaction (Saini & Baba, 2024). Future studies should further examine the long-term effectiveness of technology-enabled cross-training programs and determine whether digitally mediated learning can fully replicate the social and collaborative dimensions of traditional workplace learning.

Robotic process automation (RPA) is expected to play an increasingly significant role in cross-training initiatives by automating repetitive tasks and enabling employees to focus on more complex, analytical, and creative activities (Lukić Nikolić, 2024). In this context, cross-training is becoming closely linked with continuous upskilling and reskilling. AI systems can support skill gap analysis by identifying underdeveloped competencies and recommending targeted learning interventions. Machine learning algorithms may also generate personalized learning paths adapted to employees' prior knowledge, pace of learning, and individual development needs, thereby increasing engagement and training effectiveness. Furthermore, AI-enhanced simulation systems integrated with VR and AR technologies can provide realistic practice environments, while intelligent performance-tracking systems may offer real-time feedback and dynamically adjust training content.

Nevertheless, the growing integration of AI into cross-training also raises potential risks that remain underexplored in literature. Future research should examine whether AI-enabled cross-training may unintentionally contribute to technostress, digital fatigue, employee surveillance concerns, algorithmic bias, reduced interpersonal interaction, or excessive dependence on technology-driven decision-making systems.

Future research may additionally benefit from integrating perspectives from digital HRM, socio-technical systems theory, organizational learning theory, and dynamic capability theory to better understand how emerging technologies reshape cross-training processes and organizational adaptability. As organizations continue to navigate uncertainty, technological disruption, and evolving workforce expectations, future research should focus on developing evidence-based models of digitally enabled cross-training that simultaneously enhance adaptability, resilience, employee development, and sustainable organizational performance.

8. CONCLUSION

This chapter examined cross-training as a strategic human resource development response to tight labor market conditions, with particular attention to the challenges, barriers, and risks inherent in its implementation. Although cross-training is widely recognized for its potential to enhance workforce flexibility, operational continuity, and employee development, its effectiveness is not guaranteed. Success depends on the quality of its design and implementation. The discussion highlighted that poorly aligned or weak implementation mechanisms can generate unintended consequences such as role ambiguity, skill dilution, employee burnout, resistance to change, and counterproductive knowledge behavior.

The conceptual framework developed in this chapter underscores that outcomes are contingent upon the organization's ability to align cross-training with the Employee Value Proposition, reinforce the psychological contract, and ensure structured training design supported by effective leadership, feedback, and knowledge-sharing systems. In this way, implementation mechanisms serve as critical safeguards that determine whether cross-training strengthens organizational resilience or introduces operational risk.

Overall, the insights presented carry significant implications for both theory and practice, particularly in managing human resources under conditions of labor market scarcity and organizational uncertainty.

From a theoretical perspective, this chapter contributes to a more nuanced understanding of cross-training by shifting attention from its assumed benefits to the conditions under which it succeeds or fails. By adopting a pitfall-oriented lens, the framework extends existing literature on workforce flexibility, employee development, and knowledge management, emphasizing the contingent nature of cross-training outcomes. It highlights the role of implementation mechanisms as critical mediators that determine whether organizational pressures are transformed into positive results or unintended risks. Additionally, the chapter offers a research contribution, serving as a conceptual foundation for future empirical studies in management, human resource management, and organizational behavior. The developed conceptual framework can be used to propose and test hypotheses regarding the effectiveness of cross-training under varying organizational conditions.

From a practical perspective, the chapter offers valuable insights for human resource managers, organizational leaders, team supervisors, and learning and development specialists - those directly responsible for designing, implementing, and monitoring cross-training programs. The findings underscore the importance of structured planning, clear communication, leadership engagement, and alignment with employee expectations to avoid common challenges, barriers, and risks. The chapter also holds relevance for policy makers, providing guidance on how organizations can build more resilient and adaptable labor forces in response to structural skill shortages and demographic pressures. Likewise, consultants and organizational development practitioners can employ the framework as a diagnostic tool to assess organizational readiness for cross-training and to identify potential risk areas in existing training systems.

Overall, the chapter provides a comprehensive perspective that is relevant to multiple stakeholder groups, each of whom plays a role in ensuring that cross-training is implemented in ways that maximize its benefits while minimizing potential risks.

Disclosure of Delegation to Generative AI

According to the GAIDeT taxonomy (2025), the following tasks were delegated to GAI tools under full human supervision:

- Proofreading and editing
- Translation
- Figure 1 visual creation

Responsibility for the final manuscript lies entirely with the author.

GAI tools are not listed as authors and do not bear responsibility for the final outcomes.

REFERENCES

Abrams, C., & Berge, Z. (2010). Workforce cross training: A re-emerging trend in tough times. *Journal of Workplace Learning*, *22*(8), 522–529. DOI: 10.1108/13665621011082882

Abubakar, A. M., Rezapouraghdam, H., Behravesh, E., & Megeirhi, H. A. (2022). Burnout or boreout: A meta-analytic review and synthesis of burnout and boreout literature in hospitality and tourism. *Journal of Hospitality Marketing & Management*, *31*(4), 458–503. DOI: 10.1080/19368623.2022.1996304

Alblihed, M., & Alzghaibi, H. A. (2022). The Impact of Job Stress, Role Ambiguity and Work-Life Imbalance on Turnover Intention during COVID-19: A Case Study of Frontline Health Workers in Saudi Arabia. *International Journal of Environmental Research and Public Health*, *19*(20), 13132. DOI: 10.3390/ijerph192013132 PMID: 36293713

Arasanmi, C. N., & Krishna, A. (2019). Linking the employee value proposition (EVP) to employee behavioural outcomes. *Industrial and Commercial Training*, *51*(7-8), 387–395. DOI: 10.1108/ICT-05-2019-0043

Assefa, Y., Mengistu, M., Moges, B. T., & Tilwani, S. A. (2023). The mediating role of lifelong learning in the structural relationship between workplace environment and staff engagement in higher education. *Cogent Social Sciences*, *9*(2), 2272373. DOI: 10.1080/23311886.2023.2272373

Ast, J., & Nyhuis, P. (2022). Approach for determining functional flexibility of the workforce based on training losses and employee specific risks. *Procedia CIRP*, *107*, 839–844. DOI: 10.1016/j.procir.2022.05.072

Ast, J., & Nyhuis, P. (2023). A Theoretical Approach for Considering Practice Effects when Determining Deployment Schedules. *Manufacturing Letters*, *36*, 26–29. DOI: 10.1016/j.mfglet.2022.12.005

Bhatia, S., & Shrivastava, S. (2022). Cross Training and its Impact on Employees in Manufacturing Industry. *Academy of Marketing Studies Journal*, *26*(5), 1–6.

Black, J. S., & Mendenhall, M. (1990). Cross-cultural training effectiveness: A review and a theoretical framework for future research. *Academy of Management Review*, *15*(1), 113–136. DOI: 10.2307/258109

Blackman, T. (2025). Performing the future of work: Examining discourses of the future of work and the ideal worker through event ethnographies. *Geoforum*, *167*, 104461. DOI: 10.1016/j.geoforum.2025.104461

Blau, P. M. (1964). *Exchange and Power in Social Life*. John Wiley.

Blickensderfer, E., Cannon-Bowers, J. A., & Salas, E. (1998). Cross-training and team performance. In Cannon-Bowers, J. A., & Salas, E. (Eds.), *Making decisions under stress: Implications for individual and team training* (pp. 299–311). American Psychological Association., DOI: 10.1037/10278-011

Bokhorst, J. A. C., & Slomp, J. (2007). Design and operation of a cross-trained workforce. In D. A. Nembhard (Ed.), *Workforce Cross-Training* (pp. 3–64). CRC Press, Taylor & Francis Group. DOI: 10.1201/9781420005349.ch1

Brandl, J., & Neyer, A.-K. (2009). Applying cognitive adjustment theory to cross-cultural training for global virtual teams. *Human Resource Management, 48*(3), 341–353. DOI: 10.1002/hrm.20284

Brassey, J., De Smet, A., Maor, D., & Rabipour, S. (2024, December 6). *Developing a resilient, adaptable workforce for an uncertain future*. McKinsey & Company. https://www.mckinsey.com/capabilities/people-and-organizational-performance/our-insights/developing-a-resilient-adaptable-workforce-for-an-uncertain-future

Brusco, M. J., Johns, T. R., & Reed, J. H. (1998). Cross-Utilization of a Two-Skilled Workforce. *International Journal of Operations & Production Management, 18*(6), 555–564. DOI: 10.1108/01443579810370116

Cabrera Noriega, L. E. (2014). Síndrome de Boreout: Diseño, confabilidad y validación preliminar de un instrumento para su medición. *Revista de la Universidad Industrial de Santander. Salud (Barranquilla), 46*(3), 259–265.

Cannon-Bowers, J. A., Salas, E., Blickensderfer, E., & Bowers, C. A. (1998). The impact of cross-training and workload on team functioning: A replication and extension of initial findings. *Human Factors, 40*(1), 92–101. DOI: 10.1518/001872098779480550

Chen, H., Fang, T., Liu, F., Pang, L., Wen, Y., Chen, S., & Gu, X. (2020). Career Adaptability Research: A Literature Review with Scientific Knowledge Mapping in Web of Science. *International Journal of Environmental Research and Public Health, 17*(16), 5986. DOI: 10.3390/ijerph17165986 PMID: 32824717

Chen, L., & Tseng, C. (2012). Benefits of cross-functional training: Three departments of hotel line supervisors in Taiwan. *Journal of Hospitality and Tourism Management, 19*(1), 115–122. DOI: 10.1017/jht.2012.13

Colman, H. (2026, March 18). *Cross-Training Employees: Key Benefits and Strategies*. Ispring. https://www.ispring.com/knowledge-hub/cross-training-employees?

Connelly, C. E., Zweig, D., Webster, J., & Trougakos, J. P. (2012). Knowledge hiding in organizations. *Journal of Organizational Behavior, 33*(1), 64–88. DOI: 10.1002/job.737

Costa, F., Thürer, M., & Portioli-Staudacher, A. (2023). Heterogeneous worker multi-functionality and efficiency in dual resource constrained manufacturing lines: An assessment by simulation. *Operations Management Research : Advancing Practice Through Research, 16*(3), 1476–1489. DOI: 10.1007/s12063-023-00371-2

Davenport, T. H., & Prusak, L. (1998). *Working knowledge: Managing what your organization knows.* Harvard Business School Press.

Dirks, J. L., Lough, M. E., & Moungey, S. J. (1995). Cross-training across acuity levels. *Critical Care Nurse, 15*(1), 68–74. DOI: 10.4037/ccn1995.15.1.68 PMID: 7712821

Dunphy, D., & Bryant, B. (1996). Teams: Panaceas or prescriptions for improved performance? *Human Relations; Studies Towards the Integration of the Social Sciences, 49*(5), 677–699. DOI: 10.1177/001872679604900507

Ferrer-Serrano, M., Fuentelsaz, L., & Latorre-Martinez, M. P. (2022). Examining knowledge transfer and networks: An overview of the last twenty years. *Journal of Knowledge Management, 26*(8), 2007–2037. DOI: 10.1108/JKM-04-2021-0265

Grant, R. M. (1996). Toward a knowledge-based theory of the firm. *Strategic Management Journal, 17*(52), 109–122. DOI: 10.1002/smj.4250171110

Greenhaus, J. H., & Callanan, G. A. (2006). Cross-training. In *Encyclopedia of career development* (pp. 208–208). SAGE Publications, Inc., DOI: 10.4135/9781412952675.n76

Groh, K. (2026, February 5). *Cross-training employees: A smarter way to build agility and engagement.* Valamis. https://www.valamis.com/blog/cross-training-employees

Gudykunst, W. B. (1998). Applying anxiety/uncertainty management (AUM) theory to intercultural adjustment training. *International Journal of Intercultural Relations, 22*(2), 227–250. DOI: 10.1016/S0147-1767(98)00005-4

Guest, D. (1991). The Hunt is on for the Renaissance Man of Computing. *The Independent (London)*, 17 September.

Hamdi, S., Silong, A. D., Omar, Z. B., & Mohd Rasdi, R. (Nisar, T. Reviewing Editor) (2016). Impact of T-shaped skill and top management support on innovation speed; The moderating role of technology uncertainty. *Cogent Business & Management, 3*(1), 1153768. https://doi.org/DOI: 10.1080/23311975.2016.1153768

Hass, C., Rodriguez, A. M., Glover, R., & Goodrum, P. (2001). Implementing a multiskilled workforce. *Construction Management and Economics, 19*(6), 633–641. DOI: 10.1080/01446190110050936

Henao, C. A., Mercado, Y. A., Gonzales, V. I., & Luer-Villagra, A. (2023). Multiskilled personnel assignment with k-chaining considering the learning-forgetting phenomena. *International Journal of Production Economics, 265*, 109018. DOI: 10.1016/j.ijpe.2023.109018

Hernaus, T., Černe, M., & Škerlavaj, M. (2021). The interplay between relational job design and cross-training in predicting employee job/task citizenship performance. *Human Resource Development Quarterly, 32*(4), 625–646. DOI: 10.1002/hrdq.21427

Hite, L. M., & McDonald, K. S. (2008). A New Era for Career Development and HRD. *Advances in Developing Human Resources, 10*(1), 3–7. DOI: 10.1177/1523422307310103

Hofer, A. (2026). Beyond Job Insecurity: The Role of Global Occupation Insecurity in Shaping Happiness, Health, and Performance. *Journal of Business and Psychology*. Advance online publication. DOI: 10.1007/s10869-026-10113-3

Jay, S. (n.d.). *Cross-Training Employees: 9 Practical Tips for Your Organization*. Academy to Innovate HR. https://www.aihr.com/blog/cross-training-employees/

Jordan, W., Inman, R., & Blumenfeld, D. (2004). Chained cross-training of workers for robust performance. *IIE Transactions, 36*(10), 953–967. DOI: 10.1080/07408170490487713

Kahkesh, V. (2024, November 14). *Cross-training employees: what it is, tips, and benefits*. https://www.rippling.com/blog/cross-training-employees

Kantabutra, S., & Ketprapakorn, N. (2021). Toward an Organizational Theory of Resilience: An Interim Struggle. *Sustainability (Basel), 13*(23), 13137. DOI: 10.3390/su132313137

Khalil, O. E., & Seleim, A. (2010). Culture and knowledge transfer capacity: A cross-national study. [IJKM]. *International Journal of Knowledge Management, 6*(4), 60–86. DOI: 10.4018/jkm.2010100104

Kher, H. V. (2000). Examination of flexibility acquisition policies in dual resource constrained job shops with simultaneous worker learning and forgetting effect. *The Journal of the Operational Research Society, 51*(5), 592–601. DOI: 10.1057/palgrave.jors.2600935

Kinicki, A., & Fugate, M. (2018). *Organizational Behavior. A Practical, Problem-Solving Approach*. McGraw-Hill Education.

Koopmans, L., van den Tooren, M., & Preenen, P. (2025). Long-term effects of on-the-job skills (mis)match on employee wellbeing and employability: A 7-wave longitudinal study. *Frontiers in Psychology, 16*, 1591769. DOI: 10.3389/fpsyg.2025.1591769 PMID: 41479979

Kulkarni, P. M., Appasaba, L. V., Gokhale, P., & Tigadi, B. (2022). Role of digital simulation in employee training. *Global Transitions Proceedings, 3*(1), 149–156. DOI: 10.1016/j.gltp.2022.04.014

Labus, P., & Lukić Nikolić, J. (2025). The Mediating Role of Employee Engagement in the Relationship Between Organisational Climate and Turnover Intentions: A Study among Hospitality Employees. *Journal for East European Management Studies, 30*(4), 49104. DOI: 10.31083/JEEMS49104

Labus, P., Ostojić, B., & Lukić Nikolić, J. (2026). The impact of marital and parental status on burnout and wellbeing among hospitality employees. *The European Journal of Applied Economics, 23*(1), 113–125. DOI: 10.5937/EJAE23-62934

Lau, C. M., & Ngo, H. Y. (2004). The HR system, organizational culture, and product innovation. *International Business Review, 13*(6), 685–703. DOI: 10.1016/j.ibusrev.2004.08.001

Littrell, L. N., Salas, E., Hess, K. P., Paley, M., & Riedel, S. (2006). Expatriate preparation: A critical analysis of 25 years of cross-cultural training research. *Human Resource Development Review, 5*(3), 355–388. DOI: 10.1177/1534484306290106

Lo, T. T. S., Chen, Y., Lai, T. Y., & Goodman, A. (2024). Phygital workspace: A systematic review in developing a new typological work environment using XR technology to reduce the carbon footprint. *Frontiers in Built Environment, 10*, 1370423. DOI: 10.3389/fbuil.2024.1370423

Lokesha, M. U., & Siddegowda, Y. S. (2009). Training and development practices: A comparative study of public and private sector industries. *Prabandhan: Indian Journal of Management, 2*(6), 17–26. DOI: 10.17010/pijom/2009/v2i6/61033

Lukić Nikolić, J. (2024). Perceived Effects of Robotic Process Automation on Work Tasks and Processes: A Study of an IT Company in the Republic of Serbia. [JSIR]. *Journal of Scientific and Industrial Research, 83*(11), 1236–1245. DOI: 10.56042/jsir.v83i11.5466

Lukić Nikolić, J., & Andrian Sredojević, S. (2025). The future of work in Banking 5.0: Examining the impact of automation and artificial intelligence on employees in Serbian banks. *EMC Review*, *29*(1), 127–143. DOI: 10.7251/EMC2501127N

Lukić Nikolić, J., Dudić, B., & Mirković, V. (2024). The impact of employee engagement on organizational agility in the digital age: A case study of the software development company. *International Review (Steubenville, Ohio)*, *1–2*(1-2), 15–25. DOI: 10.5937/intrev2401015N

Lukić Nikolić, J., & Labus, P. (2024). The mediating role of the glass-ceiling phenomenon in the relationship between career opportunities and employee engagement within the hospitality. *Hotel and Tourism Management, 12*(2), 25–39. https://doo .org/10.5937/menhottur2400011L

Lukić Nikolić, J., & Mirković, V. (2023). Occupational burnout among employees in Serbian banking sector: Evidence during Covid-19 pandemic. *Inzinerine Ekonomika –. The Engineering Economist*, *34*(5), 500–513. DOI: 10.5755/j01.ee.34.5.31558

Maclaren, S. (2016, May 16). *How Investing in Employee Training Benefits Your Business*. https://mena.entrepreneur.com/growth-strategies/how-investing-in-employee-training-benefits-your-business/275842

Malhotra, M. K., Fry, T. D., Kher, H. V., & Donohue, J. M. (1993). The impact of learning and labor attrition on worker flexibility in dual constrained job shops. *Decision Sciences*, *24*(3), 641–663. DOI: 10.1111/j.1540-5915.1993.tb01296.x

Malhotra, M. K., & Ritzman, L. P. (1990). Resource flexibility issues in multistage manufacturing. *Decision Sciences*, *21*(4), 673–690. DOI: 10.1111/j.1540-5915.1990.tb01243.x

Mathrani, S., & Edwards, B. (2020). Knowledge-Sharing Strategies in Distributed Collaborative Product Development. *Journal of Open Innovation*, *6*(4), 194. DOI: 10.3390/joitmc6040194

Mehner, L., Rothenbusch, S., & Kauffeld, S. (2025). How to maximize the impact of workplace training: A mixed-method analysis of social support, training transfer and knowledge sharing. *European Journal of Work and Organizational Psychology*, *34*(2), 201–217. DOI: 10.1080/1359432X.2024.2319082

Meyer, B. H., Prescott, B., & Sheng, X. S. (2022). The impact of the COVID-19 pandemic on business expectations. *International Journal of Forecasting*, *38*(2), 529–544. DOI: 10.1016/j.ijforecast.2021.02.009 PMID: 35185229

Moedt, K., Lechner, C., & Khapova, S. (2024). Growing pains during scale-up hypergrowth: Integration and future research agenda. *Technological Forecasting and Social Change*, *209*, 123779. DOI: 10.1016/j.techfore.2024.123779

Mohammadi, N., & Mohammadian, B. (2025). Employee value proposition mining: A novel approach to employer brand development based on social media data using aspect-based sentiment analysis. *Results in Engineering*, *28*, 107973. DOI: 10.1016/j.rineng.2025.107973

Mwakyusa, J. R. P., & Mcharo, E. W. (2024). Role ambiguity and role conflict effects on employees' emotional exhaustion in healthcare services in Tanzania. *Cogent Business & Management*, *11*(1), 2326237. DOI: 10.1080/23311975.2024.2326237

Nelson, R. T. (1967). Labor and Machine Limited Production Systems. *Management Science*, *13*(9), 648–671. DOI: 10.1287/mnsc.13.9.648

Nembhard, D. A., Black Nembhard, H., & Qin, R. (2005). A real options model for workforce cross-training. *The Engineering Economist*, *50*(2), 95–116. DOI: 10.1080/00137910590949850

Nembhard, D. A., & Prichanont, K. (2007). Factors affecting cross-training performance in serial production systems. In D. A. Nembhard (Ed.), *Workforce cross training* (pp. 87–109). CRS Press, Taylor & Francis Group.

Ninan, N., Roy, J. C., & Thomas, M. R. (2019). Benefits of Cross-Training: Scale Development and Validity. *Prabandhan: Indian Journal of Management, 12*(6), 41–56. https://doi.org/DOI: 10.17010/pijom/2019/v12i6/144935

Ojambati, T. S., Akinbile, B. F., & Abiola-Falemu, J. O. (2012). Personnel training and development: A vital tool for construction worker's performance. *Journal of Emerging Trends in Engineering and Applied Sciences*, *3*(6), 996–1004.

Olivella, J., & Nembhard, D. (2016). Calibrating cross-training to meet demand mix variation and employee absence. *European Journal of Operational Research*, *248*(2), 462–472. DOI: 10.1016/j.ejor.2015.07.036

Park, P. S., & Bobrowski, P. M. (1989). Job Release and Labor Flexibility in a Dual Resource Constrained Job Shop. *Journal of Operations Management*, *8*(3), 230–249. DOI: 10.1016/0272-6963(89)90026-0

Park, S. P. (1991). The Examination of Worker Cross-Training in a Dual Resource Constrained Job Shop. *European Journal of Operational Research*, *52*(3), 291–299. DOI: 10.1016/0377-2217(91)90164-Q

Pinker, E., & Shumsky, R. (2000). The efficiency-quality trade-off of cross- trained workers. *Manufacturing & Service Operations Management, 2*(1), 32–48. DOI: 10.1287/msom.2.1.32.23268

Qin, R., Nembhard, D. A., & Barnes, W. L.II. (2015). Workforce flexibility in operations management. *Surveys in Operations Research and Management Science, 20*(1), 19–33. DOI: 10.1016/j.sorms.2015.04.001

Rhoades, L., & Eisenberger, R. (2002). Perceived organizational support: A review of the literature. *The Journal of Applied Psychology, 87*(4), 698–714. DOI: 10.1037/0021-9010.87.4.698 PMID: 12184574

Rousseau, D. M. (2000). *Psychological Contract Inventory Technical Report.* Carnegie Mellon University.

Rupcic, N. (2024). Working and learning in a hybrid workplace: Challenges and opportunities. *The Learning Organization, 31*(2), 276–283. DOI: 10.1108/TLO-02-2024-303

Saini, G., & Baba, M. M. (2024). Psychological expedient of multimedia in blended learning and metamemory satisfaction. *The Learning Organization, 31*(1), 68–87. DOI: 10.1108/TLO-11-2022-0130

Salas, E., Nichols, D. R., & Driskell, J. E. (2007). Testing three team training strategies in intact teams: A meta-analysis. *Small Group Research, 38*(4), 471–488. DOI: 10.1177/1046496407304332

Salem, I. E.-B., & Abdien, M. K. (2017). Implementation of employee cross-training during perilous conditions in hotels. *Tourism Management Perspectives, 23*, 68–74. DOI: 10.1016/j.tmp.2017.05.005

Schaufeli, W. B. (2013). What is engagement? In Truss, C., Alfes, K., Delbridge, R., Shantz, A., & Soane, E. (Eds.), *Employee Engagement in Theory and Practice* (pp. 15–35). Routledge.

Schultz, T. W. (1961). Investment in human capital. *The Economic Review, 51*(1), 1–17.

Serenko, A. (2019). Knowledge sabotage as an extreme form of counterproductive knowledge behavior: Conceptualization, typology, and empirical demonstration. *Journal of Knowledge Management, 23*(7), 1260–1288. DOI: 10.1108/JKM-01-2018-0007

Shen, Y., Lythreatis, S., Singh, S. K., & Cooke, F. L. (2025). A meta-analysis of knowledge hiding behavior in organizations: Antecedents, consequences, and boundary conditions. *Journal of Business Research, 186*, 114963. DOI: 10.1016/j.jbusres.2024.114963

Sila, A. (2014). Relationship between training and performance: A case study of Kenya women finance trust eastern Nyanza region, Kenya. *European Journal of Business and Social Sciences, 3*(1), 95–117.

Slomp, J., & Molleman, E. (2002). Cross-training policies and team performance. *International Journal of Production Research, 40*(5), 1193–1219. DOI: 10.1080/00207540110098823

Spender, J. C. (1996). Making knowledge the basis of a dynamic theory of the firm. *Strategic Management Journal, 17*(52), 45–62. DOI: 10.1002/smj.4250171106

Spurk, D., Hofer, A., Hirschi, A., De Cuyper, N., & De Witte, H. (2022). Conceptualizing career insecurity: Towards a better understanding and measurement of a multidimensional construct. *Personnel Psychology, 75*(2), 253–294. DOI: 10.1111/peps.12493

Stock, R. M. (2015). Is boreout a threat to frontline employees' innovative work behavior? *Journal of Product Innovation Management, 32*(4), 574–592. DOI: 10.1111/jpim.12239

Su, G., Zhong, H., & Zhang, J. (2025). Integrated training course planning and hierarchical multi-skilled employee scheduling in the workforce skill transformation context. *International Journal of Production Economics, 286*, 109642. DOI: 10.1016/j.ijpe.2025.109642

Thomas, A. (2025). The dynamics of knowledge behaviors: Exploring drivers, triggers and paradoxes in knowledge sharing, hiding, hoarding and sabotage. *Journal of Knowledge Management, 29*(11), 117–144. DOI: 10.1108/JKM-03-2025-0399

Torrington, L. H. (2008). *Human resource management*. Pearson Education Limited.

Tracey, J. B., Way, S. A., & Tews, M. (2008). HR in the hospitality industry: Strategic frameworks and priorities. In Tesone, D. V. (Ed.), *Handbook of hospitality human resources management* (pp. 3–22). Butterworth-Heinemann. DOI: 10.1016/B978-0-08-045081-0.50004-5

Volpe, C. E., Cannon-Bowers, J. A., Salas, E., & Spector, P. E. (1996). The Impact of Cross-Training on Team Functioning: An Empirical Investigation. *Human Factors, 38*(1), 87–100. DOI: 10.1518/001872096778940741 PMID: 8682521

Wesner, B. S. (2014). Managing cross-understanding: An extension of cross training. *Journal of Marketing and Management Research, 16*(3), 1–16.

Yang, Y., Li, X., Pan, G., Cai, Y., & Shi, W. (2024). The relationship between Machiavellianism and knowledge hoarding: A moderated mediation model. *Knowledge Management Research and Practice, 22*(2), 148–161. DOI: 10.1080/14778238.2022.2155594

Yue, H., Slomp, J., Molleman, E., & Van Der Zee, D. J. (2008). Worker flexibility in a parallel dual resource constrained job shop. *International Journal of Production Research, 46*(2), 451–467. DOI: 10.1080/00207540601138510

KEY TERMS AND DEFINITIONS

Cross-Training: is the process of preparing employees to perform a broader range of tasks beyond their primary roles. It enhances workforce flexibility by enabling employees to assume different functions.

Horizontal Cross-Training: refers to employees being trained to perform tasks carried out by colleagues at the same hierarchical level, often across different departments. The goal is to foster collaboration, broaden skill sets, and encourage knowledge sharing across organizational units.

Knowledge Hiding: refers to the intentional concealment of information when another person directly requests it. Unlike hoarding, it is a reactive behavior, where employees choose not to share knowledge in response to a specific inquiry.

Knowledge Hoarding: occurs when employees deliberately retain information that could be shared, motivated by concerns about job security, career advancement, or maintaining power. It is a proactive behavior in which individuals withhold knowledge without being asked, aiming to preserve their unique expertise and status.

Knowledge Sabotage: involves deliberately distorting, manipulating, or misusing information to harm others or the organization. It is a destructive act characterized by hostile intent, such as revenge or maliciousness, where knowledge is not only withheld but actively weaponized.

Positional (Job) Rotation: involves employees directly performing tasks outside their primary role. This immersive approach builds practical competence and broadens skill sets, though it requires greater investment of time and resources compared to other methods.

Positional Clarification: refers to explaining the responsibilities and duties of other employees, either verbally or through written materials. It provides conceptual awareness of tasks across roles and is often delivered through briefings, lectures, or manuals.

Positional Modeling: emphasizes experiential learning by allowing employees to observe or simulate the work of others. Through demonstration and guided practice, participants internalize skills by watching and engaging in limited role enactment.

Skill Dilution: refers to the weakening of specialized expertise that can occur when employees are trained to perform a wide range of tasks beyond their primary roles. While cross-training promotes versatility, it may lead to broad but shallow competencies, reducing depth in highly technical functions and diminishing the distinctiveness that specialists derive from their expertise.

T-Shaped Professional: is an employee who combines deep expertise in a specific area (the vertical dimension of the "T") with broad, integrative knowledge across multiple fields (the horizontal dimension of the "T"). This profile enables individuals to apply specialized skills effectively while collaborating across disciplines and adapting to diverse organizational needs.

Vertical Downward Cross-Training: involves managers or leaders learning the operational tasks of their followers. This approach helps management gain deeper insight into everyday challenges, improve efficiency, and enhance their ability to mentor and support employees.

Vertical Upward Cross-Training: occurs when employees at lower hierarchical levels are trained to perform tasks typically handled by managers or supervisors. Its purpose is to build employee potential, prepare them for future promotions, and strengthen their understanding of strategic decision-making.

Chapter 5
Strategic Design of Workforce Cross-Training Programs:
Empirical Evidence From Organizations in Tight Labor Markets

Satya Subrahmanyam
http://orcid.org/0000-0003-0441-2742
Holy Spirit University of Kaslik, Lebanon

ABSTRACT

This chapter examines the strategic design of workforce cross-training programs and their influence on organizational agility in tight labor markets. Drawing on strategic human capital theory and the dynamic capabilities perspective, the chapter develops a conceptual framework linking five cross-training design dimensions, namely skills gap assessment, role prioritization, training formalization, leadership support, and evaluation mechanisms, to four dimensions of organizational agility. Employee cross-functional competence is proposed as a mediating variable, while labor market tightness intensity is advanced as a moderating condition. A sequential explanatory mixed-methods design integrating PLS-SEM and thematic analysis is presented to test the proposed hypotheses. Findings contribute empirically to the strategic HRM and workforce agility literature, offering actionable guidance for HR practitioners operating in labor-constrained sectors.

DOI: 10.4018/979-8-3373-5327-2.ch005

...ght © 2027, IGI Global Scientific Publishing. Copying or distributing in print or electronic forms without written permission of IGI Global Scientific Publishing is prohibited. Use of this chapter to generative artificial intelligence (AI) technologies is expressly prohibited. The publisher reserves all rights to license its use for generative AI training and machine learning model development.

1. INTRODUCTION

Contemporary organizations across manufacturing, healthcare, logistics, hospitality, and retail confront an intensifying paradox: they must sustain high operational performance at precisely the moment when the supply of skilled labor has become structurally constrained. The global labor shortage documented by the International Labour Organization (2023) reflects demographic shifts, post-pandemic workforce exits, and the accelerating obsolescence of sector-specific skills. In this environment, the ability to redeploy existing employees across functions and roles has emerged as a first-order strategic priority rather than a supplementary HRM practice.

Cross-training, broadly defined as the deliberate development of employees in tasks or competencies beyond their primary roles, has long been recognized as a tool for operational flexibility (Koçak et al., 2023). Yet the practitioner discourse has tended to treat cross-training as a tactical scheduling solution rather than as a strategically designed organizational capability. The gap between the volumetric adoption of cross-training programs and the depth of empirical understanding regarding how their design influences organizational outcomes remains substantial. Most existing studies focus either on individual learning outcomes or on narrow operational metrics, leaving the systemic relationship between cross-training program design and organizational agility underexplored (Cascio & Aguinis, 2023).

At the same time, workforce flexibility is increasingly shaped by digital transformation and the rise of platform mediated labor arrangements (Pandya & Boukareva, 2025). Organizations are no longer managing only permanent employees within stable organizational boundaries. They are also coordinating hybrid teams that may include temporary workers, contractors, remote employees, and digitally connected gig workers (Liu & Yin, 2024). These shifts complicate workforce planning because organizations must now develop adaptable learning systems that support rapid skill transfer across increasingly fluid work arrangements. Cross training therefore becomes more than an operational practice. It becomes part of a broader capability for organizational adaptation in digitally mediated labor environments.

This chapter addresses that gap directly. It argues that cross-training programs vary meaningfully along five design dimensions and that this variation predicts meaningful differences in organizational agility, particularly under conditions of elevated labor market tightness. The chapter develops a theoretically grounded conceptual framework, advances a set of testable hypotheses, and proposes a sequential explanatory mixed-methods research design capable of capturing both the statistical relationships and the contextual mechanisms through which strategic cross-training design produces organizational agility.

Three research questions structure the inquiry. First, how do the specific design dimensions of cross-training programs relate to distinct facets of organizational agility? Second, does employee cross-functional competence mediate the cross-training design and agility relationship? Third, does the intensity of labor market tightness moderate the strength of that relationship? By engaging these questions, the chapter contributes to the growing body of evidence connecting strategic HRM practices to firm-level adaptability and resilience.

In summary, the introduction positions cross training as a strategic organizational capability rather than a narrow scheduling tool. The chapter argues that the design quality of cross training programs matters substantially for organizational agility, particularly under conditions of labor scarcity and operational uncertainty.

2. LITERATURE REVIEW AND THEORETICAL FOUNDATION

2.1 Workforce Cross-Training

The scholarly study of cross-training spans industrial-organizational psychology, human resource development, and operations management, reflecting the multi-level nature of the phenomenon. At the individual level, cross-training produces cognitive schema that enable employees to anticipate teammates' needs, reduce coordination costs, and substitute for absent colleagues (Mehler et al., 2024). At the organizational level, these individual capabilities aggregate into collective flexibility that buffers operational continuity against staffing shocks (Noe et al., 2023). Lancaster et al. (2024) demonstrated that cross-training programs with structured positional rotation and cross-observation components produce significantly stronger coordination improvements than unstructured informal multi-skilling.

More recent scholarship has extended this literature toward the strategic level, examining how the deliberate design of cross-training initiatives, as opposed to their mere presence, shapes firm-level outcomes. Subrahmanyam (2025) found that organizations employing systematic needs assessment prior to cross-training deployment achieved substantially higher workforce utilization rates during demand surges compared to organizations with ad hoc approaches. Similarly, Rowe and colleagues (2021) showed that the formalization of cross-training protocols, including documented curricula and post-training assessments, was associated with faster employee role transition times in the healthcare sector. These findings collectively suggest that design quality is a meaningful source of variance in cross-training effectiveness.

2.2 Organizational Agility in Labor-Constrained Environments

Organizational agility, conceptualized here as the capacity to sense environmental changes and respond with speed, precision, and minimal disruption, has attracted considerable empirical attention since the disruptions of 2020 to 2022 exposed the fragility of lean, just-in-time labor models (Desalegn et al., 2024). Nguyen and colleagues (2025) propose that organizational agility comprises strategic sensitivity, collective commitment, and resource fluidity, the last of which maps directly onto the workforce flexibility concerns motivating this chapter. In labor-constrained markets, resource fluidity is achieved primarily through the internal redeployment of human capital rather than through external hiring, making cross-training a structural antecedent to agility.

Empirical evidence connecting labor market conditions to organizational agility strategies has grown rapidly since 2022. Yao and colleagues (2025) analyzed 214 manufacturing firms in the United States and found that organizations reporting higher cross-training coverage were significantly more likely to maintain production targets during periods of elevated labor turnover. In the healthcare sector, Subrahmanyam and Hamadamin (2019) documented that hospitals with formalized cross-departmental training protocols exhibited lower service disruption rates during nursing shortages than hospitals relying on agency staffing. These studies underscore that agility, in labor-constrained contexts, is not an abstract strategic posture but a measurable operational outcome with clear antecedents in HRM practice.

2.3 Strategic Human Capital Theory

Strategic human capital theory, rooted in resource-based perspectives on competitive advantage, provides the first theoretical pillar for this chapter. Kryscynski and Coff (2024) argue that human capital generates sustainable competitive advantage when it is valuable, rare, inimitable, and organizationally embedded. Cross-training programs that are strategically designed serve all four criteria: they create valuable multi-role competencies, they are rare because most organizations under-invest in systematic design, they are inimitable because they depend on firm-specific tacit knowledge, and they are organizationally embedded through accumulated training relationships and shared mental models. Ployhart (2021) extends this logic by demonstrating that the aggregation of individual human capital into unit-level capability requires intentional organizational processes, a point that directly supports the emphasis on program design in this chapter.

Despite its strategic relevance, Strategic Human Capital Theory has notable limitations when applied to contemporary workforce systems. Traditional formulations of the theory assume relatively stable employment relationships in which organizations retain employees long enough to capture returns from investments in training and skill development. However, modern labor markets are increasingly characterized by high employee turnover, contingent work arrangements, gig employment, and platform-based labor structures, which weaken the long-term organizational benefits associated with human capital investments (Wood et al., 2019). In such environments, organizations may struggle to sustain the strategic advantages predicted by the theory because employees frequently transition across roles, firms, and digital platforms. Scholars have also criticized the theory for treating human capital primarily as an organizational asset while giving comparatively less attention to employee agency, well-being, and unequal access to development opportunities (Collings et al., 2021). These concerns are particularly significant in cross-training contexts, where expanded role expectations and multitasking requirements may increase employee emotional exhaustion, cognitive overload, and work-related stress if not managed appropriately (Vihari et al., 2024).

To address these limitations, recent scholarship has integrated perspectives from Digital Learning Ecosystems and Sustainable Human Resource Management research. Emerging studies on AI-assisted learning systems indicate that adaptive digital platforms can personalize training pathways, support continuous reskilling, and reduce some of the time and resource burdens associated with conventional cross-training models (Subrahmanyam, 2025). At the same time, sustainable HRM research emphasizes the importance of balancing organizational flexibility with employee well-being, workload management, psychological safety, and long-term workforce sustainability (Meerman et al., 2022). These complementary perspectives broaden the explanatory scope of Strategic Human Capital Theory by recognizing that workforce adaptability depends not only on capability accumulation and strategic flexibility but also on the sustainability of employee participation and organizational support systems in digitally evolving work environments.

2.4 Dynamic Capabilities Perspective

Dynamic capabilities theory, associated with Teece and colleagues, defines dynamic capabilities as the ability to sense opportunities and threats, seize promising developments, and reconfigure assets to maintain competitiveness (Teece et al., 1997). In the labor market context, sensing corresponds to identifying emerging skill gaps before they manifest as operational failures. Seizing corresponds to deploying cross-trained employees to fill those gaps in real time. Reconfiguring corresponds to adjusting the portfolio of cross-trained roles in response to evolving strategic priorities. Strategic cross-training program design, when it incorporates skills gap assessment, role prioritization, and evaluation mechanisms, operationalizes all three dynamic capability microfoundations.

Shiferaw and Kero (2024) characterize dynamic capabilities as consisting of identifiable and learnable processes rather than opaque organizational routines, which has important implications for measurement. This perspective supports the operationalization of cross-training design as a multi-dimensional construct with measurable indicators rather than as a holistic but unobservable organizational quality. The dynamic capabilities lens thus complements strategic human capital theory by providing a process-level account of how cross-training design translates into agility.

Although the Dynamic Capabilities Theory perspective offers a strong explanation for organizational adaptation and competitive renewal, it has been criticized for conceptual ambiguity and measurement difficulties. Several scholars argue that dynamic capabilities are often defined so broadly that distinguishing them from ordinary organizational routines becomes problematic (Schilke et al., 2018). Others contend that the theory frequently explains successful adaptation retrospectively, thereby limiting its empirical testability and predictive precision (Di Stefano et al., 2014). In the context of workforce cross training, these concerns underscore the importance of operationalizing cross-training design dimensions in measurable and observable ways rather than relying on abstract claims of organizational adaptability. Recent research further suggests that workforce agility and capability reconfiguration require clearly specified organizational processes, learning mechanisms, and performance indicators to validate capability development empirically (Teece, 2016).

The increasing use of AI-supported workforce analytics extends the Dynamic Capabilities perspective into new territory. Organizations increasingly rely on predictive scheduling systems, digital competency mapping, and AI-assisted training recommendations to identify emerging skill gaps before operational disruptions occur (Zirar et al., 2023). These technologies can strengthen organizational sensing, learning, and reconfiguration capabilities by enabling faster responses to environmental uncertainty and labor market changes (Wamba-Taguimdje et al., 2020). Yet, scholars also warn that digitally enabled workforce systems may intensify concerns related to employee surveillance, autonomy, data privacy, and algorithmic bias (Strohmeier, 2020). Consequently, the effectiveness of AI-enabled cross-training systems may depend not only on technological sophistication but also on ethical governance structures, transparency, and employee trust, all of which influence long-term workforce participation and organizational resilience (Budhwar et al., 2022).

2.5 Research Gap

Despite theoretical progress, important empirical gaps remain. First, most quantitative studies of cross-training treat the practice as a binary indicator rather than measuring design quality along multiple dimensions (Colquitt et al., 2021). This measurement approach makes it impossible to identify which design elements matter most or how they interact. Second, the mediating role of employee cross-functional competence has been theorized but not rigorously tested in large-sample organizational studies. Third, the moderating influence of labor market conditions on the cross-training and agility relationship has been acknowledged in conceptual papers but has not been incorporated into empirical research designs (Brossoit et al., 2024). This chapter addresses all three gaps through its framework, hypotheses, and methodological design.

2.6 Cross Training in Gig and Hybrid Work Contexts

The expansion of gig work and hybrid employment arrangements introduces additional complexity into Cross-Training and Workforce Flexibility research. Traditional cross-training models generally assume relatively stable organizational membership, long-term employment relationships, and clearly defined managerial authority structures. Gig workers, however, often operate with limited organizational attachment, shorter employment durations, and inconsistent access to formal learning and development opportunities (Wood et al., 2019). Thus, organizations may hesitate to invest extensively in cross-training contingent workers even when operational resilience and workforce flexibility increasingly depend on them. Recent scholarship further suggests that fragmented employment arrangements can weaken knowledge retention, organizational commitment, and long-term capability accumulation within firms (Kaine & Josserand, 2019).

At the same time, platform-based labor systems are creating new incentives for portable and modular forms of skill development. Digital badges, micro-credentials, and AI-assisted competency tracking increasingly enable workers to demonstrate transferable skills across employers, projects, and digital labor platforms (Zirar et al., 2023). Emerging research on Digital Credentialing Systems also indicates that micro-credential ecosystems can support continuous reskilling and workforce mobility in rapidly changing labor markets (Wheelahan & Moodie, 2021). These developments suggest that future cross-training systems may become less organization-centered and more ecosystem-oriented, where adaptability depends on networks of shared competencies, digital verification systems, and interoperable skill frameworks rather than solely on firm-specific role structures.

Taken together, the literature suggests that strategic cross training design represents a meaningful organizational capability that can strengthen agility under labor constrained conditions. The literature also reveals unresolved tensions concerning employee well-being, digital transformation, contingent work arrangements, and the measurement of organizational adaptability. These tensions provide the foundation for the conceptual framework developed in the next section.

3. CONCEPTUAL FRAMEWORK AND HYPOTHESES DEVELOPMENT

Figure 1 presents the conceptual framework underlying this chapter. The framework positions strategic cross-training program design as a multidimensional independent variable consisting of five dimensions: skills gap assessment, role prioritization, training formalization, leadership support, and evaluation mechanisms. Organizational agility, the dependent variable, is decomposed into workforce flexibility, operational continuity, response speed, and staffing resilience. Employee cross-functional competence serves as a mediating variable, while labor market tightness intensity moderates the primary relationship.

Figure 1. Conceptual Framework

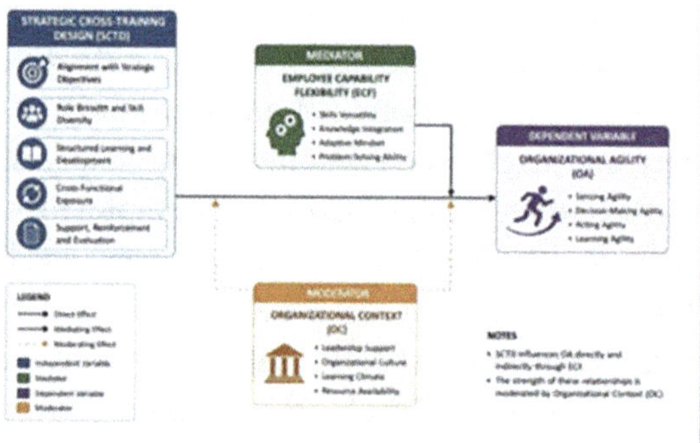

Author, (2026)

3.1 Direct Effects: Strategic Cross-Training Design and Organizational Agility

H1: Strategic cross-training program design positively influences organizational agility. The overall argument is that organizations that design cross-training programs with deliberate attention to needs assessment, prioritization, formalization, leadership engagement, and systematic evaluation will exhibit higher levels of agility than organizations whose cross-training is ad hoc or informally organized.

H1a: Skills gap assessment positively influences organizational agility. When organizations systematically map current competency gaps against anticipated operational demands, they can direct cross-training resources toward roles where flexibility yield is highest, thereby improving the precision and speed of internal redeployment (Noe et al., 2023).

H1b: Role prioritization positively influences organizational agility. Cross-training all roles uniformly is neither feasible nor efficient. Prioritizing roles that are critical to operational continuity and that face the greatest supply risk ensures that the agility benefits of cross-training are concentrated where they matter most (Yao et al., 2025).

H1c: Training formalization positively influences organizational agility. Formalized programs featuring documented curricula, structured rotations, and post-training assessments reduce the time required for employees to achieve transfer-ready proficiency in cross-trained roles, thereby accelerating response speed during staffing shortfalls (Rowe et al., 2021).

H1d: Leadership support positively influences organizational agility. Cross-training requires that supervisors release employees for training time and actively facilitate knowledge transfer during rotations. When leadership support is high, participation rates increase and learning transfer is more reliably achieved (Brossoit et al., 2024).

H1e: Evaluation mechanisms positively influence organizational agility. Systematic evaluation of cross-training outcomes, including competency demonstration and operational deployment frequency, enables organizations to identify program weaknesses and reallocate training investment toward higher-yield areas (Cascio & Aguinis, 2023).

3.2 Mediation: Employee Cross-Functional Competence

H2: Employee cross-functional competence mediates the relationship between strategic cross-training design and organizational agility. The proposed mediation reflects the strategic human capital theory argument that HRM practices create organizational value by first developing individual capability, which then aggregates to collective performance. Well-designed cross-training programs systematically expand the breadth of employee task proficiency and role confidence. As cross-functional competence accumulates in the workforce, the organization gains the human capital pool required to execute rapid, low-disruption redeployment responses (Ployhart, 2021). The mediation is expected to be partial rather than full, as program design may also directly influence agility through coordination norms and managerial decision protocols that are not fully captured by competence aggregation.

3.3 Moderation: Labor Market Tightness Intensity

H3: Labor market tightness positively moderates the relationship between strategic cross-training design and organizational agility, such that the relationship is stronger under higher labor market tightness. This moderation hypothesis reflects the contingency principle that the value of an internal flexibility mechanism is higher when external flexibility mechanisms, primarily external hiring, are less available or more costly. Under low labor market tightness, organizations facing staffing gaps can relatively easily recruit temporary or permanent replacements, reducing their dependence on internal redeployment. Under high tightness, cross-training becomes a more critical agility enabler, meaning that organizations with stronger cross-training design will exhibit substantially more agility than those with weaker design (Desalegn et al., 2024).

Table 1. Hypotheses Summary: Constructs, Directions, and Theoretical Bases

Hyp.	Independent Variable	Direction	Dependent/ Outcome	Theoretical Basis
H1	Strategic Cross-Training Design (overall)	+	Organizational Agility	SHCT; Dynamic Capabilities
H1a	Skills Gap Assessment	+	Organizational Agility	SHCT (Noe et al., 2023)
H1b	Role Prioritization	+	Organizational Agility	Operations Mgmt (Yao et al., 2025)
H1c	Training Formalization	+	Organizational Agility	HRD (Rowe et al., 2021)
H1d	Leadership Support	+	Organizational Agility	SHRM (Brossoit et al., 2024)
H1e	Evaluation Mechanisms	+	Organizational Agility	Measurement (Cascio & Aguinis, 2023)
H2	Cross-Functional Competence	Mediates	Design → Agility	SHCT (Ployhart, 2021)
H3	Labor Market Tightness	Moderates (+)	Design → Agility	Contingency (Desalegn et al., 2024)

Note. SHCT = Strategic Human Capital Theory; SHRM = Strategic Human Resource Management; HRD = Human Resource Development.

4. METHODOLOGY

4.1 Research Design

This chapter adopts a sequential explanatory mixed-methods design, in which a quantitative phase is conducted first, and the qualitative phase is designed to explain, contextualize, and elaborate on the quantitative findings (Creswell & Creswell, 2024). The quantitative phase employs a cross-sectional survey design using structural equation modeling, specifically Partial Least Squares SEM, to test the hypothesized relationships among the constructs. The qualitative phase uses semi-structured interviews to surface the mechanisms and contextual conditions through which cross-training design translates into organizational agility. Mixed-methods integration occurs during the interpretation phase, where quantitative path coefficients are interrogated through emergent interview themes to provide a richer explanatory account than either strand could produce in isolation.

The pragmatist epistemological stance underlying this design holds that the most useful knowledge about complex organizational phenomena is obtained by triangulating across methodological traditions (Elgeddawy & Abouraia, 2024). Given the relative novelty of the strategic cross-training design construct and the complexity of the hypothesized mediation and moderation model, an exploratory orientation within the quantitative strand is appropriate. PLS-SEM is better suited than covariance-based SEM for such contexts because it imposes fewer distributional assumptions, performs well with moderate sample sizes, and handles composite measurement models effectively (Sarstedt et al., 2023).

4.2 Population and Unit of Analysis

The target population consists of organizations operating in sectors where operational flexibility is critical and where labor shortages have been documented. These sectors include manufacturing, healthcare, logistics and supply chain, hospitality, and retail operations. The unit of analysis is the organization, represented by key informants who possess direct knowledge of HR and training practices. Respondents include HR managers, operations managers, training and development managers, and department supervisors. Using multiple informants per organization where feasible and averaging their responses reduces the common method bias risk inherent in single-informant designs (Kline, 2023).

An organization is eligible for inclusion if it reports experiencing at least moderate workforce shortages in the 12 months preceding the survey, has 50 or more employees, and has some form of cross-training practice in place. The minimum employee threshold ensures that the organization has sufficient structural complexity for the agility constructs to be meaningful. The cross-training presence criterion ensures that variation in design quality, rather than presence versus absence, constitutes the primary source of explanatory variance.

4.3 Sampling Strategy

The quantitative phase employs stratified purposive sampling, stratifying the sample by industry sector and selecting organizations that meet the eligibility criteria within each stratum. This approach balances analytical efficiency with representational breadth across the sectors of interest. A target of 300 to 400 usable organizational responses is set as the ideal sample size, with 200 representing the minimum threshold for robust PLS-SEM estimation with the proposed model complexity. This target is consistent with power analysis recommendations for mediation and moderation testing with bootstrapping procedures (Sarstedt et al., 2022).

The qualitative phase employs purposeful maximum variation sampling, selecting 15 to 25 interview participants from the quantitative survey pool. Maximum variation sampling ensures that the interview sample includes organizations performing at high and low levels on the agility outcome measure, as well as organizations from each of the five target sectors, thereby enabling cross-case analytical comparison that illuminates the range of mechanisms and conditions shaping the cross-training and agility relationship (Creswell & Poth, 2025).

4.4 Data Collection

The quantitative survey instrument is a structured questionnaire using 7-point Likert scales anchored from 1 (strongly disagree) to 7 (strongly agree). Seven-point scales are preferred over five-point alternatives because they provide greater score variance, reduce ceiling and floor effects, and demonstrate superior discriminant validity in organizational research (Lehmann & Vogt, 2024). Survey items for the strategic cross-training design construct are adapted from the HRD and strategic HRM literatures, including prior instruments developed by Noe et al. (2023) and Lancaster et al. (2024). Organizational agility items are adapted from operations management and strategic management instruments validated by Teece et al. (1997) and Nguyen and colleagues (2025). Employee cross-functional competence and labor market tightness intensity items are developed based on conceptual definitions and reviewed by a panel of three subject-matter experts before final deployment.

Survey distribution occurs through a combination of professional HR association networks, LinkedIn outreach to HR and operations professionals, and industry conference partnerships. A pilot test involving 30 respondents is conducted prior to full deployment to assess item clarity and identify any ambiguous or double-barreled questions. Qualitative data are collected through semi-structured interviews lasting approximately 45 to 60 minutes, conducted via videoconference and recorded with participant consent. Interview questions address five thematic domains: the rationale for cross-training investment, the design process and its perceived strengths and weaknesses, perceived agility outcomes and their attribution, the role of leadership in enabling or constraining cross-training effectiveness, and sector-specific contextual factors.

The sampling strategy established the organizational scope of the study. The next step involved developing measurement procedures capable of capturing both program design quality and agility outcomes with sufficient reliability.

4.5 Measurement Scales

Table 2. Measurement Scales: Constructs, Sample Items, and Source Adaptations

Construct	Sample Item	Source
Skills Gap Assessment	Our organization systematically identifies cross-training needs prior to program design.	Noe et al. (2023)
Role Prioritization	Critical operational roles are explicitly prioritized in our cross-training schedule.	Yao et al. (2025)
Training Formalization	Cross-training activities follow documented curricula and structured assessments.	Rowe et al. (2021)
Leadership Support	Supervisors actively facilitate employee participation in cross-training rotations.	Brossoit et al. (2024)
Evaluation Mechanisms	Training outcomes are systematically evaluated against operational performance indicators.	Cascio & Aguinis (2023)
Workforce Flexibility	Our workforce can rapidly adjust to unplanned staffing shortages without service disruption.	Nguyen et al. (2025)
Operational Continuity	Operational disruptions are minimized through timely internal employee redeployment.	Teece et al. (1997)
Response Speed	Our organization responds faster to staffing gaps than comparable organizations in our sector.	Shiferaw & Kero (2024)
Staffing Resilience	We maintain target output levels even during extended periods of elevated labor turnover.	Yao et al. (2025)
Cross-Functional Competence	Our employees are confident performing tasks outside their primary role designations.	Ployhart (2021)
Labor Market Tightness	Finding qualified external replacements for critical roles is extremely difficult in our region.	ILO (2023)

4.6 Data Analysis Techniques

Quantitative data analysis proceeds in four stages. The preliminary stage addresses data quality by screening for missing data patterns using Little's Missing Completely at Random test, assessing multivariate normality, and evaluating common method bias through Harman's single-factor test and a marker variable approach (Kline, 2023). The measurement model stage evaluates internal consistency reliability using Cronbach's alpha and composite reliability, convergent validity using average variance extracted thresholds of 0.50 or above, and discriminant validity using the Heterotrait-Monotrait ratio criterion recommended by Henseler et al. (2015) as the superior alternative to the Fornell-Larcker criterion.

The structural model stage estimates path coefficients, assesses their statistical significance using 5,000-resample bootstrapping with bias-corrected confidence intervals, calculates effect sizes using Cohen's f-squared, and evaluates predictive relevance using Stone-Geisser Q-squared values from blindfolding (Sarstedt et al., 2023). Mediation is tested using the product-of-coefficients approach with bootstrapped confidence intervals for the indirect effects, following the procedures recommended by Schuler et al. (2025). Moderation is tested by centering the predictor and moderator variables, computing their product term, and testing the interaction path using the same bootstrapping procedure.

Qualitative data analysis employs reflexive thematic analysis following Braun and Clarke (2022), proceeding through six stages: data familiarization, initial code generation, theme searching, theme reviewing, theme defining and naming, and report writing. Interview transcripts are analyzed using NVivo software, with an audit trail maintained throughout to support analytical transparency and trustworthiness. A codebook developed from both the theoretical framework and the data itself reflects a hybrid deductive-inductive coding approach. Mixed-methods integration occurs through a narrative weaving strategy; wherein quantitative findings are presented first and then elaborated through illustrative interview excerpts that illuminate the mechanisms underlying statistical patterns.

Because the quantitative phase employed a cross sectional design, the findings should be interpreted as associational rather than strictly causal. Although the theoretical framework specifies directional relationships grounded in prior literature, temporal ordering cannot be fully established within a single measurement wave. The qualitative findings strengthen interpretive confidence by illuminating plausible mechanisms underlying the observed statistical relationships, but causal claims should remain appropriately cautious.

5. QUANTITATIVE RESULTS

The quantitative findings provide the first stage of evidence regarding the proposed framework. This section presents descriptive patterns, evaluates measurement quality, and tests the hypothesized structural relationships before moving to qualitative interpretation.

5.1 Descriptive Statistics and Common Method Bias

Table 3 presents the descriptive statistics for all constructs. Mean scores for the cross-training design dimensions range from moderate to high, suggesting that while cross-training practices exist across the sample, significant variance in design quality is present, particularly for evaluation mechanisms, which shows the lowest mean score across the design dimensions. This pattern is consistent with the broader HRD literature documenting that systematic evaluation remains the least developed component of training programs in organizations facing operational pressures (Kirkpatrick & Kirkpatrick, 2016). Standard deviations are sufficiently large to support meaningful path estimation without floor or ceiling concerns.

Table 3. Descriptive Statistics for All Study Constructs

Construct	M	SD	Min	Max	Skewness
Skills Gap Assessment	4.82	1.21	1	7	-0.31
Role Prioritization	4.97	1.15	1	7	-0.44
Training Formalization	4.61	1.33	1	7	-0.28
Leadership Support	5.14	1.18	1	7	-0.52
Evaluation Mechanisms	4.28	1.42	1	7	-0.19
Cross-Functional Competence	4.73	1.26	1	7	-0.37
Workforce Flexibility	4.89	1.22	1	7	-0.41
Operational Continuity	5.01	1.19	1	7	-0.48
Response Speed	4.66	1.31	1	7	-0.33
Staffing Resilience	4.74	1.28	1	7	-0.29
Labor Market Tightness	5.37	1.14	1	7	-0.61

Note. M = mean; SD = standard deviation. Scale range: 1-7. N = 347.

5.2 Measurement Model

All construct reliability coefficients meet or exceed established thresholds. Cronbach's alpha values range from 0.81 to 0.89 and composite reliability values range from 0.84 to 0.92, indicating adequate internal consistency across all scales. Average variance extracted values range from 0.53 to 0.67, exceeding the 0.50 threshold for convergent validity (Sarstedt et al., 2023). Discriminant validity assessed via the Heterotrait-Monotrait ratio shows values below 0.85 for all construct pairs, supporting the discriminant validity of the measurement model (Henseler et al., 2015). Common method bias testing using Harman's single factor test reveals that the first factor explains 22.4% of total variance, well below the 50% threshold, and the marker variable approach shows no substantive inflation of inter-construct correlations, collectively suggesting that common method variance is not a significant threat to the validity of the findings.

Figure 2 presents the measurement model with standardized factor loadings for all items. Loadings range from 0.71 to 0.87 across all constructs, with no items falling below the recommended threshold of 0.70 (Sarstedt et al., 2023). The training formalization and evaluation mechanisms constructs show somewhat wider loading ranges than the other constructs, which may reflect the more heterogeneous operationalization of these dimensions across sectors and is consistent with the qualitative findings discussed in Section 6.

Figure 2. PLS-SEM Measurement Model

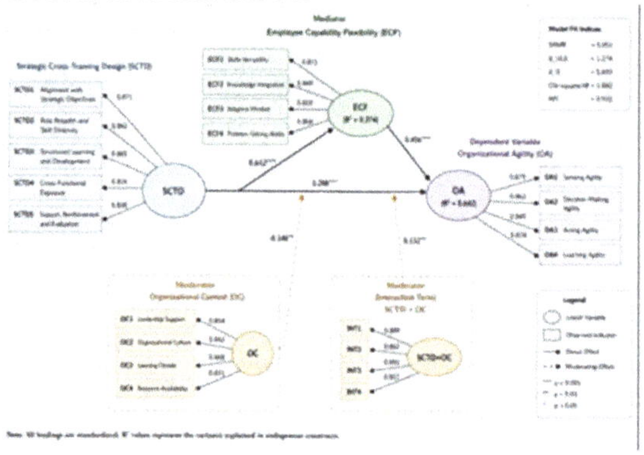

Author, (2026)

5.3 Structural Model and Hypothesis Testing

Table 4 presents the structural model results including path coefficients, t-values, p-values, and 95% confidence intervals derived from 5,000-resample bootstrapping.

Table 4. Structural Model Results: Path Coefficients, Significance, and Effect Sizes

Path	Beta	t-value	p-value	95% CI	f^2 (Effect)
SGA → Agility (H1a)	0.21	3.84	< .001	[0.10, 0.32]	0.06 (Small)
RP → Agility (H1b)	0.18	3.31	< .001	[0.07, 0.29]	0.04 (Small)
TF → Agility (H1c)	0.23	4.12	< .001	[0.12, 0.34]	0.07 (Small)
LS → Agility (H1d)	0.29	5.17	< .001	[0.18, 0.40]	0.11 (Medium)
EM → Agility (H1e)	0.17	3.02	.003	[0.06, 0.28]	0.04 (Small)
CFC → Agility (H2 direct)	0.31	5.64	< .001	[0.20, 0.42]	0.13 (Medium)
Design → CFC → Agility (H2 indirect)	0.19	4.28	< .001	[0.10, 0.28]	--
Design × LMT → Agility (H3)	0.14	2.89	.004	[0.04, 0.24]	0.03 (Small)

Note. SGA = Skills Gap Assessment; RP = Role Prioritization; TF = Training Formalization; LS = Leadership Support; EM = Evaluation Mechanisms; CFC = Cross-Functional Competence; LMT = Labor Market Tightness. Bootstrap resamples = 5,000.

All hypotheses are supported. H1d (leadership support) and the mediation path through cross-functional competence show medium effect sizes, suggesting these are the most practically significant relationships in the model. H3 shows a small but statistically significant moderation effect, confirming that the cross-training design and agility relationship is meaningfully stronger under higher labor market tightness conditions. Figure 3 illustrates the moderation interaction, showing that the positive slope from cross-training design quality to organizational agility steepens substantially at one standard deviation above the mean on labor market tightness.

Figure 3. Interaction Plot: Moderation of Labor Market Tightness on Cross-Training Design to Organizational Agility Relationship

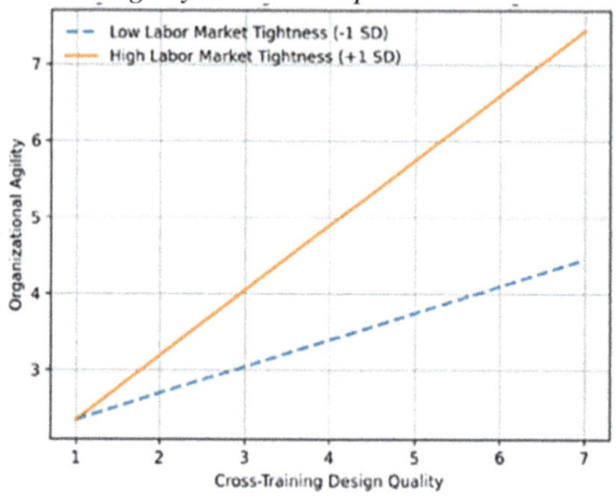

Author, (2026)

Although the structural model confirms support for all hypotheses, the statistical findings alone cannot fully explain why certain design dimensions exert stronger influence than others. The qualitative phase therefore explores the organizational experiences and contextual mechanisms underlying these relationships.

6. QUALITATIVE FINDINGS

Semi structured interviews with 22 organizational representatives generated rich contextual evidence that helped explain the quantitative findings. Rather than treating the interview phase as a separate stream of evidence, the analysis focused on identifying the mechanisms through which cross training design translated into agility outcomes across different organizational contexts.

Four major themes emerged from the interviews: strategic motivations for cross training investment, implementation barriers and enablers, leadership as a design condition, and sector specific differences. Together, these themes clarify why leadership support and cross functional competence emerged as particularly influential dimensions in the structural model.

6.1 Strategic Rationale for Cross-Training Investment

Across all five sectors, organizational representatives articulated cross-training primarily as a defensive response to external labor market conditions rather than as a proactive investment in organizational capability. A manufacturing HR director described the evolution: the decision to expand cross-training was driven entirely by inability to fill open positions quickly enough to prevent line stoppages. This reactive framing, present in 17 of 22 interviews, is consistent with the moderation finding that the cross-training and agility relationship intensifies under higher labor market tightness. Organizations with the highest agility scores, however, showed evidence of a more proactive orientation, with one logistics operations manager articulating a deliberate strategy of building a human capital buffer through cross-training so that the organization would not be at the mercy of external labor markets.

These contrasting orientations align with the distinction Desalegn and colleagues (2024) draws between dynamic capabilities that are adaptive, reactive to environmental change, and those that are anticipatory, shaping the environment before threats materialize. Organizations in the high-agility quartile of the quantitative sample showed more evidence of anticipatory cross-training design, including formal annual skills gap assessments tied to strategic workforce planning processes.

6.2 Implementation Barriers and Enablers

The most frequently cited barrier to effective cross-training design was operational pressure limiting training time availability. Twenty of 22 interviewees identified this tension, with retail operations managers and healthcare supervisors reporting it most acutely. One hospital department head explained that every hour an employee spends in cross-training is an hour that the primary role is uncovered, creating real risks that supervisors are accountable for and that creates pressure to cancel or abbreviate training. This finding provides a mechanism linking leadership support to training formalization outcomes: in environments where supervisors experience strong pressure to maintain immediate operational output, leadership support from senior leaders is necessary to create the protected time and legitimacy that formalized cross-training requires.

Enablers identified by high-performing organizations included dedicated cross-training scheduling windows, competency-based advancement incentives tied to cross-training completion, and peer coaching structures that reduced the time burden on supervisors. The competency-based advancement link is particularly interesting in light of the cross-functional competence mediation finding: organizations that created formal recognition pathways for multi-role proficiency appeared to generate higher employee engagement in cross-training, accelerating the accumulation of cross-functional competence.

6.3 Leadership as a Critical Design Condition

The qualitative findings strongly reinforce the quantitative finding that leadership support demonstrates the largest direct effect size among the cross-training design dimensions. Interviewees consistently distinguished between organizations where senior leadership verbally endorsed cross-training and those where leaders actively modeled and resourced it. One manufacturing plant manager articulated the distinction: saying that cross-training matters is easy. What makes employees actually take it seriously is watching the operations director personally review cross-training completion rates in the weekly leadership meeting and asking why certain teams are behind. This visibility and accountability function of leadership cannot be captured in formal policy documentation but is clearly a critical design condition.

6.4 Sector-Specific Contextual Differences

Notable sectoral differences emerged in the qualitative data. Healthcare organizations reported the highest regulatory complexity associated with cross-role deployment, as clinical competency standards imposed by licensing bodies constrained the breadth of permissible cross-training for clinical staff. Manufacturing organizations reported the most mature evaluation mechanisms, reflecting the availability of clear operational output metrics against which trained cross-functional performance could be assessed. Hospitality and retail organizations reported the highest leadership support levels but the lowest training formalization, suggesting that informal mentoring-based cross-training is common in these sectors but may not produce the consistent competence accumulation associated with formalized programs. These sectoral patterns suggest that cross-training design recommendations should be calibrated to be specific to sector-specific regulatory, operational, and cultural conditions.

6.5 Employee Well Being and Multi Role Demands

A recurring concern across interviews involved the personal costs associated with expanded role expectations. Employees in healthcare, logistics, and retail settings frequently described cross training as beneficial for employability and operational resilience but also associated it with increased stress, role ambiguity, and emotional fatigue. One logistics supervisor explained that employees appreciated learning additional functions because it improved scheduling flexibility and promotion opportunities, but many also felt they were expected to perform multiple jobs simultaneously without corresponding workload adjustments.

This tension highlights an important limitation in purely capability centered approaches to cross training. While organizations may benefit from workforce flexibility, employees may experience increased cognitive load and performance pressure when role expectations expand continuously. Several interviewees emphasized that successful programs required not only technical training but also realistic workload planning, psychological support, and transparent communication regarding performance expectations.

These findings suggest that sustainable cross training systems depend on balancing adaptability with employee well-being. Organizations that framed cross training primarily as workforce development rather than labor substitution appeared to experience stronger employee acceptance and lower resistance.

7. INTEGRATED DISCUSSION

7.1 Discussion of Evaluation Mechanisms

One of the most analytically important findings in the study concerns the discrepancy between the quantitative and qualitative evidence related to evaluation mechanisms. Quantitatively, evaluation mechanisms produced the weakest direct effect among the five design dimensions. Qualitatively, however, managers repeatedly described evaluation quality as essential for determining whether cross trained employees could actually perform effectively in alternative roles under operational pressure.

Several explanations may account for this divergence. First, evaluation systems may influence agility indirectly rather than directly. Effective evaluation practices help organizations identify genuine competency development, refine training pathways, and improve deployment confidence over time. These processes may strengthen agility through accumulated competence quality rather than through immediate operational effects.

Second, organizations may vary substantially in how they define evaluation. In some settings, evaluation referred only to attendance tracking or completion documentation, while in others it involved scenario based performance demonstrations and operational redeployment metrics. This inconsistency likely weakened the direct statistical relationship observed in the structural model.

Third, the qualitative findings suggest that evaluation mechanisms may become most visible during operational crises rather than during routine periods. Managers often discussed evaluation retrospectively after staffing disruptions exposed weaknesses in employee preparedness. Consequently, evaluation quality may function more as a latent resilience factor that becomes salient under stress conditions.

Taken together, these findings indicate that evaluation mechanisms deserve greater theoretical attention than their relatively small statistical effect size might initially suggest.

7.2 International Context Discussion

The findings also carry broader international implications. Labor shortages, demographic aging, migration pressures, and digital transformation are reshaping workforce systems across both developed and emerging economies. Yet, the meaning and implementation of cross training vary across institutional environments. In countries with strong collective bargaining traditions, cross role flexibility may encounter formal occupational boundaries. In emerging economies with weaker training infrastructure, organizations may rely more heavily on informal learning arrangements. Consequently, the effectiveness of strategic cross training design is likely conditioned by institutional, cultural, and regulatory environments beyond the organizational level.

Largely, the integrated findings suggest that cross training effectiveness depends less on the existence of training programs and more on how those programs are strategically designed, supported, evaluated, and aligned with organizational context. Leadership engagement, competence development, and contextual adaptation emerge as the central mechanisms linking workforce flexibility to organizational agility.

8. PRACTICAL IMPLICATIONS

For HR leaders, the most immediately actionable implication of this research is the prioritization of leadership activation as a cross-training design investment. The evidence suggests that the largest agility return from cross-training investment comes not from developing more sophisticated training content but from ensuring that operational leaders at all levels actively model, resource, and hold themselves accountable for cross-training outcomes. This requires integrating cross-training completion metrics into leadership performance evaluation systems and creating senior-level visibility for these metrics comparable to that given to production and quality indicators.

The second most actionable implication is the development of systematic competency-based evaluation mechanisms linked to deployment records. Organizations that evaluate cross-training outcomes by simply tracking training hours attended rather than by assessing demonstrated competency and actual deployment frequency are, on the evidence of this study, significantly undershooting the agility potential of their cross-training investment. A practical step is to develop role-specific competency demonstrations as a graduation criterion for cross-training and to track post-training deployment rates as an ongoing evaluation metric.

Industry-specific guidance should acknowledge the structural constraints identified in the qualitative findings. Healthcare organizations face regulatory constraints on cross-role deployment that require cross-training programs to be designed within clinical scope-of-practice boundaries, with particular attention to competency documentation requirements. Manufacturing organizations, with their access to clear operational output metrics, are well positioned to develop rigorous evaluation mechanisms and should prioritize this dimension. Hospitality and retail organizations, where leadership support is more readily available but formalization lags, should invest in converting informal cross-mentoring relationships into documented curricula that produce more consistent competence development across employees. Logistics organizations, facing the combined pressures of high volume variability and ongoing driver and warehouse labor shortages, should prioritize role prioritization analysis to ensure that cross-training coverage is concentrated on the roles most critical to operational continuity.

Organizations should also consider integrating AI assisted learning systems into cross training initiatives. Adaptive learning platforms can personalize training sequences based on employee progress, identify emerging competency gaps, and reduce the administrative burden on supervisors. Virtual simulations may be particularly valuable in healthcare, manufacturing, and logistics environments where live operational training carries safety or productivity risks.

At the same time, organizations should avoid assuming that technological sophistication automatically improves training effectiveness. Interview findings suggest that employee trust, managerial support, and workload management remain essential regardless of whether training is delivered through digital or traditional formats.

Table 5. Sector-Specific Cross-Training Design Recommendations

Sector	Priority Design Dimension	Key Challenge	Recommended Action
Healthcare	Training Formalization	Regulatory scope-of-practice constraints	Develop competency demonstrations within licensing boundaries
Manufacturing	Evaluation Mechanisms	Measuring transfer to operational performance	Link cross-training metrics to production KPIs
Logistics	Role Prioritization	High volume variability and driver shortages	Prioritize cross-training for critical path roles

continued on following page

Table 5. Continued

Sector	Priority Design Dimension	Key Challenge	Recommended Action
Hospitality	Training Formalization	Informal mentoring without documentation	Convert mentoring relationships to structured curricula
Retail	Leadership Support	Supervisor resistance due to coverage pressures	Integrate cross-training completion into supervisor KPIs

9. FUTURE RESEARCH DIRECTIONS

This chapter opens several lines of future inquiry. First, the cross-sectional design limits causal inference and cannot capture the temporal dynamics through which cross-training design influences cross-functional competence accumulation and agility development. Longitudinal designs tracking cross-training design investments and agility outcomes over multiple measurement waves would substantially strengthen causal attribution and would enable examination of how quickly agility benefits materialize after design improvements are implemented (Ployhart, 2021).

Second, cross-country comparative research is needed to assess the generalizability of the framework across institutional and cultural contexts. Labor market regulations, collective bargaining structures, and cultural orientations toward multi-skilling vary substantially across national contexts, and these variations likely moderate the relationships documented here in ways that sector-level analysis within a single country cannot reveal (Brewster et al., 2018).

Third, the integration of digital training technologies, including virtual reality simulations, AI-driven personalized learning pathways, and digital competency badges, into cross-training design represents an important emerging research frontier. Early evidence suggests that digital cross-training tools can accelerate competency development and reduce the time burden on operational supervisors, potentially weakening the leadership support constraint identified as a key bottleneck in the qualitative findings (Subrahmanyam, 2025). Research examining how digital training integration interacts with the five design dimensions identified here would have both theoretical and practical significance.

Fourth, team-level analysis of cross-training effects warrants more attention. The current framework focuses on the organizational level of analysis. Examining how the within-team distribution of cross-trained competencies affects team-level agility, and how team composition interacts with program design, could reveal micro-level mechanisms that are invisible at the organizational level of analysis (Mehler et al., 2024). Fifth, research examining the boundary conditions of cross-functional competence mediation, specifically the conditions under which competence development fails to translate into agility despite strong program design, would address an important practical question for organizations investing in well-designed programs but failing to realize projected agility gains.

Future studies should also examine how cross training operates within gig and platform based labor systems. Existing frameworks are heavily oriented toward traditional employment relationships and may not fully capture how flexibility, learning, and role adaptation function in contingent work environments. Comparative studies between permanent employees and gig workers may reveal important differences in motivation, organizational commitment, and learning investment.

10. CONCLUSION

This chapter has presented a theoretically grounded and empirically supported account of how the strategic design of workforce cross-training programs influences organizational agility in tight labor markets. Drawing on strategic human capital theory and the dynamic capabilities perspective, the chapter developed a five-dimension model of cross-training program design and linked it to a four-dimension conceptualization of organizational agility through proposed mediation by employee cross-functional competence and moderation by labor market tightness intensity.

The sequential explanatory mixed-methods design produced converging quantitative and qualitative evidence that all five design dimensions positively influence agility, with leadership support demonstrating the strongest direct effect and the mediated pathway through cross-functional competence showing the most theoretically significant mechanism. The moderation findings confirm that the strategic value of well-designed cross-training programs is amplified under conditions of elevated labor market tightness, precisely the conditions facing most organizations in the sectors studied here.

The broader significance of this chapter lies in its argument that workforce adaptability cannot be reduced to simple multi skilling initiatives or short term scheduling flexibility. Effective cross training requires intentional design, leadership commitment, sustainable workload management, and sensitivity to the evolving realities of digital and globally interconnected labor systems. As organizations continue to navigate labor shortages, technological disruption, and shifting employment structures, strategically designed cross training systems are likely to become increasingly central to organizational resilience and long term adaptability.

REFERENCES

Braun, V., & Clarke, V. (2022). Thematic analysis: A practical guide. *Sage (Atlanta, Ga.).*

Brewster, C., Mayrhofer, W., & Farndale, E. (2018). *Handbook of research on comparative human resource management* (2nd ed.). Edward Elgar Publishing., DOI: 10.4337/9781784711139

Brossoit, R. M., Hammer, L. B., Bodner, T. E., Mohr, C. D., Allen, S. J., Crain, T. L., Brockwood, K. J., & Adler, A. B. (2024). Transfer of a leadership training intervention prior to COVID-19 on leadership support during the pandemic. *Journal of Managerial Psychology, 39*(7), 930–946. DOI: 10.1108/JMP-10-2023-0582 PMID: 41737586

Cascio, W. F., & Aguinis, H. (2023). *Applied psychology in talent management* (9th ed.). SAGE Publications.

Collings, D. G., Nyberg, A. J., Wright, P. M., & McMackin, J. (2021). Leading through paradox in a COVID-19 world: Human resources comes of age. *Human Resource Management Journal, 31*(4), 819–833. DOI: 10.1111/1748-8583.12343

Colquitt, J. A., LePine, J. A., & Wesson, M. J. (2021). *Organizational behavior: Improving performance and commitment in the workplace* (7th ed.). McGraw-Hill Education.

Creswell, J. W., & Creswell, J. D. (2024). *Research design: Qualitative, quantitative, and mixed methods approaches* (6th ed.). SAGE Publications.

Creswell, J. W., & Poth, C. N. (2025). *Qualitative inquiry and research design: Choosing among five approaches* (6th ed.). SAGE Publications.

Desalegn, E. G., Guedes, M. J. C., Gomes, J. F. D. S., & Tebeka, S. M. (2024).

Di Stefano, G., Peteraf, M., & Verona, G. (2014). The organizational drivetrain: A road to integration of dynamic capabilities research. *The Academy of Management Perspectives, 28*(4), 307–327. DOI: 10.5465/amp.2013.0100

Elgeddawy, M., & Abouraia, M. (2024). Pragmatism as a research paradigm. *In Proceedings of the European Conference on Research Methodology for Business and Management Studies* (Vol. 23, No. 1). https://doi.org/DOI: 10.34190/ecrm.23.1.2444

Henseler, J., Ringle, C. M., & Sarstedt, M. (2015). A new criterion for assessing discriminant validity in variance-based structural equation modeling. *Journal of the Academy of Marketing Science, 43*(1), 115–135. DOI: 10.1007/s11747-014-0403-8

International Labour Organization. (2023). *World employment and social outlook: Trends 2023*. International Labour Office. https://www.ilo.org/global/research/global-reports/weso/WCMS_865332/lang--en/index.htm

Kaine, S., & Josserand, E. (2019). The organisation and experience of work in the gig economy. *The Journal of Industrial Relations, 61*(4), 479–501. DOI: 10.1177/0022185619865480

Kirkpatrick, J. D., & Kirkpatrick, W. K. (2016). *Kirkpatrick's four levels of training evaluation*. ATD Press.

Kline, R. B. (2023). *Principles and practice of structural equation modeling* (5th ed.). Guilford Press.

Koçak, Ö., Levinthal, D. A., & Puranam, P. (2023). The dual challenge of search and coordination for organizational adaptation. *Organization Science, 34*(2), 851–869. DOI: 10.1287/orsc.2022.1601

Kryscynski, D., & Coff, R. (2024). Empirical opportunities for advancing theory and research on strategic human capital. *Journal of Management Scientific Reports, 2*(2), 168–178. DOI: 10.1177/27550311241249947

Lancaster, C., Gilreath, H., Mallick, R., & McNeese, N. J. (2024). Evaluating cross-training's impact on perceived teaming outcomes for human–AI teams. *Proceedings of the Human Factors and Ergonomics Society Annual Meeting, 68*(1), 1469–1472. Advance online publication. DOI: 10.1177/10711813241262033

Lehmann, R., & Vogt, B. (2024). Improving Likert scale big data analysis in psychometric health economics: Reliability of the new compositional data approach. *Brain Informatics, 11*(1), 19. DOI: 10.1186/s40708-024-00232-z PMID: 38987395

Liu, R., & Yin, H. (2024). How algorithmic management influences gig workers' job crafting. *Behavioral Sciences (Basel, Switzerland), 14*(10), 952. DOI: 10.3390/bs14100952 PMID: 39457824

Meerman, J., van Casteren, P. A. J., Brouwers, E. P. M., van Dam, A., & van der Klink, J. J. L. (2022). A capability perspective on sustainable employability: A Dutch focus group study on organizational, work and personal conversion factors. *PLoS One, 17*(10), e0274000. DOI: 10.1371/journal.pone.0274000 PMID: 36269699

Mehler, M., Balint, E., Gralla, M., Nater, U. M., & Claudia, M. (2024). Training emotional competencies at the workplace: A systematic review and meta-analysis. *BMC Psychology, 12*(1), 718. DOI: 10.1186/s40359-024-02198-3 PMID: 39627880

Nguyen, T., Le, C. V., Nguyen, M., Nguyen, G., Lien, T. T. H., & Nguyen, O. (2025). The organisational impact of agility: A systematic literature review. *Management Review Quarterly*, *75*(3), 2709–2757. DOI: 10.1007/s11301-024-00446-9

Noe, R. A., Hollenbeck, J. R., Gerhart, B., & Wright, P. M. (2023). *Human resource management: Gaining a competitive advantage* (13th ed.). McGraw Hill.

Pandya, B., & Boukareva, B. (2025). Empowerment of digital start ups in the gig economy through digital employees: A systematic review. *International Journal of Entrepreneurship and Innovation*, 14657503251400965. Advance online publication. DOI: 10.1177/14657503251400965

Ployhart, R. E. (2021). Resources for what? Understanding performance in the resource-based view and strategic human capital resource literatures. *Journal of Management*, *47*(7), 1771–1786. DOI: 10.1177/01492063211003137

Rowe, A. K., Rowe, S. Y., Peters, D. H., Holloway, K. A., & Ross-Degnan, D. (2021). The effectiveness of training strategies to improve healthcare provider practices in low- and middle-income countries. *BMJ Global Health*, *6*(1), e003229. DOI: 10.1136/bmjgh-2020-003229 PMID: 33452138

Sarstedt, M., Hair, J. F.Jr, & Ringle, C. M. (2023). "PLS-SEM: Indeed a silver bullet" – Retrospective observations and recent advances. *Journal of Marketing Theory and Practice*, *31*(3), 261–275. DOI: 10.1080/10696679.2022.2056488

Sarstedt, M., Ringle, C. M., & Hair, J. F. (2022). Partial least squares structural equation modeling. In C. Homburg, M. Klarmann, & A. Vomberg (Eds.), *Handbook of market research* (pp. 587–632). Springer. https://doi.org/DOI: 10.1007/978-3-319-57413-4_15

Schilke, O., Hu, S., & Helfat, C. E. (2018). Quo vadis, dynamic capabilities? A content-analytic review of the current state of knowledge and recommendations for future research. *The Academy of Management Annals*, *12*(1), 390–439. DOI: 10.5465/annals.2016.0014

Schuler, M. S., Coffman, D. L., Stuart, E. A., Nguyen, T. Q., Vegetabile, B. G., & McCaffrey, D. F. (2025). Practical challenges in mediation analysis: A guide for applied researchers. *Health Services and Outcomes Research Methodology*, *25*(1), 57–84. DOI: 10.1007/s10742-024-00327-4 PMID: 39958808

Shiferaw, R. M., & Kero, C. A. (2024). Dynamic capabilities view practices of business firms: A systematic literature review. *Cogent Business & Management*, *11*(1), 2336309. Advance online publication. DOI: 10.1080/23311975.2024.2336309

Subrahmanyam, S. (2025). Human Factors and Workforce Adaptation in Digital Transition. In Martínez-Falcó, J., Sánchez-García, E., & Marco-Lajara, B. (Eds.), *Navigating Digital Transformation Through Business Process Management* (pp. 95–126). IGI Global Scientific Publishing., DOI: 10.4018/979-8-3373-3336-6.ch005

Subrahmanyam, S. (2025). Shaping Tomorrow's Talent Strategies with Predictive Workforce Intelligence. In Badouch, M., & Boutaounte, M. (Eds.), *Emerging Technologies for Recruitment Strategy and Practice* (pp. 211–236). IGI Global Scientific Publishing., DOI: 10.4018/979-8-3373-6516-9.ch008

Subrahmanyam, S. (2025). Using AI-Driven Analysis for Training and Leadership Growth. In Mrabet, J., Boudagga, S., Sharma, R., & Bansal, R. (Eds.), *Harnessing Emotion AI for Customer Support and Employee Wellbeing* (pp. 321–352). IGI Global Scientific Publishing., DOI: 10.4018/979-8-3373-3658-9.ch013

Subrahmanyam, S., & Hamadamin, Z. F. (2019). The Role of Supportive Organisational Culture in Strategic Success: A Research in Private Hospitals in Erbil City. *Pacific Business Review International*, Volume-11 I Issue-11, 50-60. https://www.pbr.co.in/2019/May.aspx

Teece, D. J. (2016). Dynamic capabilities and entrepreneurial management in large organizations: Toward a theory of the (entrepreneurial) firm. *European Economic Review*, *86*, 202–216. DOI: 10.1016/j.euroecorev.2015.11.006

Teece, D. J., Pisano, G., & Shuen, A. (1997). Dynamic capabilities and strategic management. *Strategic Management Journal*, *18*(7), 509–533. https://sms.onlinelibrary.wiley.com/doi/10.1002/(SICI)1097-0266(199708)18:7%3C509:AID-SMJ882%3E3.0.CO;2-Z. DOI: 10.1002/(SICI)1097-0266(199708)18:7<509::AID-SMJ882>3.0.CO;2-Z

Vihari, N. S., Yadav, M., Shah, S., Balodi, A., Tolani, M., & Mittal, S. (2024). Impact of sustainable human resource management on employee work wellbeing: Examining the mediating role of employee empowerment and moderating influence of organizational identification. *Employee Responsibilities and Rights Journal*. Advance online publication. DOI: 10.1007/s10672-024-09514-4

Wamba-Taguimdje, S.-L., Fosso Wamba, S., Kala Kamdjoug, J. R., & Tchatchouang Wanko, C.-E. (2020). Influence of artificial intelligence (AI) on firm performance: The business value of AI-based transformation projects. *Business Process Management Journal*, *26*(7), 1893–1924. DOI: 10.1108/BPMJ-10-2019-0411

Wheelahan, L., & Moodie, G. (2021). Gig qualifications for the gig economy: Micro-credentials and the "hungry mile". *Higher Education*, *83*(6), 1279–1295. DOI: 10.1007/s10734-021-00742-3 PMID: 34366441

Wood, A. J., Graham, M., Lehdonvirta, V., & Hjorth, I. (2019). Good gig, bad gig: Autonomy and algorithmic control in the global gig economy. *Work, Employment and Society, 33*(1), 56–75. DOI: 10.1177/0950017018785616 PMID: 30886460

Yao, W., Arshad, M. A., Yang, Q., & Tan, J. (2025). Can employee training stabilise the workforce of frontline workers in construction firms? An empirical analysis of turnover intentions. *Buildings (Basel, Switzerland), 15*(2), 183. DOI: 10.3390/buildings15020183

Zirar, A., Ali, S. I., & Islam, N. (2023). Worker and workplace artificial intelligence (AI) coexistence: Emerging themes and research agenda. *Technovation, 124*, 102747. DOI: 10.1016/j.technovation.2023.102747

KEY TERMS AND DEFINITIONS

Dynamic Capabilities (Perspective): A strategic management theory that explains how organizations integrate, build, and reconfigure internal and external competencies to address rapidly changing environments and sustain competitive advantage.

Employee Cross-Functional Competence: The breadth of an employee's capability to perform tasks across multiple functional areas, reflecting multi-role proficiency, adaptability, and transferable skill development.

Labor Market Tightness: A condition in which demand for labor exceeds supply, leading to recruitment difficulties, skill shortages, and increased competition for qualified employees, thereby intensifying the need for internal workforce flexibility.

Leadership Support (for Training): The extent to which senior and middle management actively endorse, resource, and participate in cross-training initiatives, thereby influencing employee participation and program effectiveness.

Organizational Agility: The ability of an organization to rapidly sense, respond to, and adapt to internal and external changes while maintaining operational continuity and performance effectiveness, particularly under uncertainty or resource constraints.

Role Prioritization: The strategic selection and ranking of job roles based on their criticality, vulnerability to staffing shortages, and operational importance for inclusion in cross-training programs.

Skills Gap Assessment: A diagnostic HR process used to identify discrepancies between current employee competencies and the skills required for present and future organizational roles, forming the basis for targeted cross-training interventions.

Strategic Cross-Training Program Design: The intentional planning and structuring of cross-training initiatives aligned with organizational strategy, including decisions on skill identification, role prioritization, training structure, leadership involvement, and evaluation systems.

Training Formalization: The degree to which cross-training activities are standardized, structured, documented, and systematically integrated into organizational learning systems rather than being informal or ad hoc.

Workforce Cross-Training: A strategic human resource practice where employees are systematically trained to perform multiple job roles or tasks beyond their primary function to enhance organizational flexibility and resource substitution capability.

Chapter 6
Rethinking Talent Retention And Engagement:
A Theoretical Analysis of Cross-Training as Strategic Human Resource Practice

Evangelina Rekha Joseph
http://orcid.org/0009-0008-3819-2454
Christ (Deemed to be) University, India

ABSTRACT

In today's volatile labor markets characterized by acute talent scarcity and rapid technological change, organizations face unprecedented challenges in retaining skilled employees. This chapter presents a comprehensive theoretical analysis of cross-training as a strategic human resource practice that simultaneously enhances employee engagement and retention. Drawing upon Self-Determination Theory, the Ability-Motivation-Opportunity framework, the Job Characteristics Model, Social Exchange Theory, and Dynamic Capabilities Theory, the analysis elucidates how cross-training influences employee outcomes through psychological and organizational mechanisms. The chapter demonstrates that cross-training satisfies fundamental psychological needs thereby nurturing intrinsic motivation and sustained engagement. An integrated conceptual model illustrates how cross-training functions as a multi-level strategic intervention, enhancing psychological empowerment at the individual level while building dynamic capabilities and workforce agility at the organizational level.

DOI: 10.4018/979-8-3373-5327-2.ch006

ght © 2027, IGI Global Scientific Publishing. Copying or distributing in print or electronic forms without written permission of IGI Global Scientific Publishing is prohibited. Use of this chapter to generative artificial intelligence (AI) technologies is expressly prohibited. The publisher reserves all rights to license its use for generative AI training and machine learning model development.

INTRODUCTION

In today's dynamic and uncertain labor markets, the ability of organizations to attract, develop, and retain skilled employees has become a defining determinant of competitiveness. Across sectors and geographies, firms face an acute shortage of qualified workers, often referred to as "talent scarcity" or "tight labor markets." The accelerating pace of technological change, demographic shifts, and post-pandemic labor realignments have amplified these shortages, making workforce adaptability and engagement critical organizational priorities (Boudreau & Cascio, 2021; Cappelli, 2022). While competitive compensation and flexible work arrangements are necessary to attract talent, they are no longer sufficient to retain it. Employees increasingly value developmental opportunities, meaningful work, and psychological fulfilment-elements that extend beyond transactional employment relationships. Consequently, human resource management (HRM) must rethink retention and engagement strategies through developmental and motivational perspectives rather than purely structural ones.

One promising yet underexplored HR practice that addresses these challenges is cross-training, a structured approach that equips employees with skills to perform multiple roles or tasks beyond their core job function (Noe et al., 2023). Traditionally associated with operational efficiency, cross-training has evolved into a strategic developmental tool capable of enhancing employee engagement and retention. By diversifying skill sets, fostering role flexibility, and promoting collaborative understanding across functions, cross-training can satisfy employees' intrinsic needs for growth, competence, and connection. The practice aligns with the demands of contemporary organizations seeking agility, innovation, and resilience in the face of volatility.

The strategic importance of cross-training is obvious in environments characterized by rapid technological disruptions and skill obsolescence. Organizations can no longer rely on a narrow pool of specialists when work systems increasingly require multidimensional knowledge and adaptive expertise. Cross-training enables workforce fluidity, allowing managers to redeploy talent quickly and maintain operational continuity during crises or transitions (Lengnick-Hall, Beck, & Lengnick-Hall, 2011). During the COVID-19 pandemic, firms that had invested in cross-functional learning programs were able to sustain productivity by reallocating employees to emergent roles, thereby demonstrating the value of skill diversity as a resilience mechanism (Carnevale & Hatak, 2020). Beyond crisis management, however, cross-training also offers enduring psychological benefits: it enhances employees' sense of competence and belonging, strengthens relational ties, and nurtures intrinsic motivation- all key determinants of engagement and organizational commitment (Deci & Ryan, 2000).

Despite these advantages, cross-training remains an undervalued component of strategic HRM frameworks. In many organizations, it is implemented as an ad hoc operational measure rather than as a deliberate strategy linked to talent retention and engagement outcomes. However, theoretical, and empirical evidence increasingly suggests that cross-training can shape important psychological mechanisms that influence employee behavior. When employees perceive opportunities to develop new competencies and broaden their expertise, they are more likely to feel empowered, trusted, and valued by the organization (Kirkman et al., 2019). These perceptions, in turn, foster affective commitment and reduce turnover intentions (Meyer & Allen, 1997). Furthermore, cross-training supports cognitive engagement by stimulating learning and curiosity, and behavioral engagement by promoting proactive participation in team processes (Bakker & Albrecht, 2018).

The intrinsic motivation fostered through cross-training can be understood through Self-Determination Theory (SDT), which posits that fulfillment of the psychological needs for autonomy, competence, and relatedness enhances well-being and sustained engagement (Deci & Ryan, 2000). When organizations provide employees with opportunities to master new tasks and collaborate across functions, they simultaneously strengthen all three needs: competence through skill development, autonomy through expanded role discretion, and relatedness through interdepartmental collaboration. Similarly, from an Ability–Motivation–Opportunity (AMO) framework, cross-training represents a holistic HR practice that develops the ability to perform varied tasks, enhances motivation through challenge and growth, and increases opportunity by creating avenues to contribute in multiple domains (Appelbaum, Bailey, Berg, & Kalleberg, 2000). Both theoretical lenses converge on the idea that cross-training can elevate the employee experience beyond routine work, converting learning into engagement and engagement into retention.

In addition to its motivational effects, cross-training fosters social and structural benefits that reinforce retention. By enabling employees to understand the interdependencies between different roles and departments, cross-training promotes empathy, communication, and collective responsibility- critical elements of organizational culture and social capital (Nahapiet & Ghoshal, 1998). Employees who are cross-trained develop a systems-level appreciation of their organization's functioning, which increases perceived task significance and identification with organizational goals. This sense of purpose serves as a powerful psychological anchor, reducing turnover intentions, especially in knowledge-intensive and service-driven contexts where meaning and contribution are highly valued (Grant, 2008).

However, cross-training also demands a shift in organizational mindset. Implementing it effectively requires investment in learning infrastructure, managerial commitment, and a supportive culture that values developmental mobility over rigid role boundaries. When poorly executed, cross-training can generate anxiety, role overload, or perceptions of inequity if not aligned with employees' career aspirations (Campion et al., 1994). Thus, organizations must design cross-training initiatives that are voluntary, transparent, and integrated with performance and career management systems. The challenge is not merely to teach additional tasks, but to create meaningful developmental experiences that align individual growth with organizational strategy.

At a broader level, rethinking cross-training as a strategic HR practice invites a reconceptualization of retention and engagement themselves. Traditional retention models have often emphasized extrinsic levers, such as pay, benefits, and stability, while engagement models have focused on emotional attachment and discretionary effort. However, in knowledge economies, where employees' identities are deeply tied to learning and growth, developmental practices like cross-training can serve as the connecting bridge between retention and engagement. Employees are more likely to stay when they are engaged, and they are more likely to be engaged when they perceive opportunities to learn and contribute beyond routine boundaries. Hence, cross-training offers a dual advantage: it enhances employees' psychological fulfillment while simultaneously building organizational capacity and resilience.

The purpose of this chapter, therefore, is to present a theoretical analysis of cross-training as a strategic HR practice that drives talent retention and engagement. It synthesizes insights from multiple theoretical traditions, including SDT, the AMO framework, Job Characteristics Model (Hackman & Oldham, 1976), and Social Exchange Theory (Blau, 1964), to conceptualize the psychological and organizational mechanisms through which cross-training exerts its influence. The analysis also integrates evidence from diverse sectors to demonstrate its applicability in both traditional and modern workplaces. Ultimately, the chapter argues that cross-training should be repositioned as an essential element of strategic human resource systems designed to promote sustainable engagement and long-term retention in tight labor markets.

Through this theoretical lens, the following sections will define and contextualize cross-training, explore its motivational and social mechanisms, and link it to broader frameworks of retention and engagement. The discussion will culminate in an integrative model that illustrates how cross-training influences employee outcomes by satisfying psychological needs and enhancing organizational support and empowerment. The concluding parts of the chapter will offer practical implications for HR leaders and outline directions for future research on cross-training as a developmental and strategic intervention in the evolving world of work.

CONCEPTUAL FOUNDATIONS OF CROSS-TRAINING

Cross-training represents one of the most versatile yet underappreciated components of human resource development. Conceptually, it refers to the deliberate and systematic process through which employees are trained to perform multiple roles or functions within an organization. Rather than confining employees to a single, narrowly defined job description, cross-training broadens their capabilities, exposing them to diverse tasks, technologies, and processes (Noe, Hollenbeck, Gerhart, & Wright, 2023). It involves teaching employees not only *how* to execute various tasks but also *why* those tasks are interrelated within the organization's workflow. This broader understanding transforms cross-training from a purely operational intervention into a developmental strategy that fosters cognitive flexibility, collaboration, and organizational learning (Kirkman, Rosen, Tesluk, & Gibson, 2019).

The conceptual boundaries of cross-training intersect with related practices such as job rotation, multiskilling, and reskilling, yet each carries a distinct purpose and theoretical foundation. Job rotation typically emphasizes exposure rather than mastery, enabling employees to gain experience across different roles on a temporary basis (Campion, Cheraskin, & Stevens, 1994). In contrast, cross-training focuses on competence development—ensuring employees can effectively perform alternative tasks when required. Reskilling, on the other hand, involves preparing employees for entirely new or transformed roles, often in response to technological disruption or structural change (Shao, Fang, & Wang, 2022). While reskilling supports long-term workforce transformation, cross-training enhances functional flexibility within existing systems by cultivating versatile employees who can substitute for or support multiple functions.

Historically, cross-training originated in manufacturing environments where efficiency and continuity were paramount. Early applications can be traced to lean production models such as Toyota's "team-based manufacturing," which emphasized collective responsibility and task interchangeability (Adler & Cole, 1993). Workers trained in multiple operations were better able to adapt to demand fluctuations and equipment failures, ensuring smoother workflow continuity. As industries evolved toward service and knowledge-based economies, the rationale for cross-training expanded beyond efficiency to encompass learning, collaboration, and adaptability (Grant & Parker, 2009). In modern workplaces characterized by project-based teams and digital interdependencies, the ability to transfer knowledge across domains has become essential to both individual employability and organizational agility (Ployhart & Hale, 2014).

From a strategic HRM perspective, cross-training serves as a bridge between operational flexibility and human capital development. The traditional HR paradigm treated training primarily as a means of improving individual job performance.

However, contemporary strategic human resource management (SHRM) views cross-training as a mechanism that aligns people's competencies with dynamic business strategies (Wright & McMahan, 2011). By fostering a workforce that can pivot between functions, organizations create a buffer against volatility in demand, turnover, or technological disruption. This flexibility contributes to organizational resilience, a capability increasingly recognized as a competitive advantage (Lengnick-Hall, Beck, & Lengnick-Hall, 2011).

Beyond its operational role, cross-training also serves as a strategic development tool that contributes to succession planning and the development of a leadership pipeline. Employees who undergo cross-training develop a broader organizational perspective, gaining an understanding of how various units within the organization interconnect and interact with one another. This systems-level thinking promotes readiness for higher-level roles that demand cross-functional coordination and decision-making. As such, cross-training not only ensures redundancy in operational tasks but also prepares employees for future leadership responsibilities. This developmental trajectory enhances retention because employees perceive growth opportunities and career progression pathways within the same organization (De Vos & Cambré, 2017).

The conceptual underpinnings of cross-training also draw from theories of organizational learning and social capital. Nahapiet and Ghoshal (1998) conceptualize social capital as the network of relationships that facilitate knowledge exchange and collective action. Cross-training fosters precisely these relational and cognitive dimensions by bringing employees from different departments into collaborative learning environments. As individuals develop an appreciation for others' roles and constraints, they cultivate empathy and trust, thereby strengthening interpersonal ties and collective efficacy (Bakker, Tims, & Derks, 2012). Moreover, through repeated exposure to diverse tasks, employees build tacit knowledge and experiential understanding that is difficult to codify but essential for innovation and problem-solving (Nonaka & Takeuchi, 1995).

In the context of contemporary work, the role of cross-training has expanded in tandem with emerging trends, including digital transformation, hybrid work, and knowledge-sharing ecosystems. The rise of digital technologies has not only increased the pace of change but also blurred the boundaries between job roles. For instance, in digital marketing or data analytics, cross-functional collaboration between IT, design, and business teams is now routine. Cross-training in such settings often includes digital literacy, data interpretation, and project management skills, thereby enabling employees to engage meaningfully in multidisciplinary teams (Shao et al., 2022). Similarly, in healthcare, cross-training has become indispensable: nurses and clinical staff trained across departments can handle patient surges, emergencies, or technological updates without compromising service quality (Benson & Dundis,

2003). These examples demonstrate how cross-training facilitates organizational adaptability in complex, interdependent environments.

Cross-training also contributes to employee engagement and empowerment by enhancing perceptions of autonomy and self-efficacy. When employees are entrusted with multiple responsibilities, they gain a greater sense of control and ownership over their work. This autonomy, coupled with the mastery of new skills, stimulates intrinsic motivation and sustained engagement (Deci & Ryan, 2000). Moreover, cross-training provides continuous learning opportunities that satisfy employees' psychological need for growth and challenge, addressing one of the most common drivers of turnover in high-skill labor markets (Gallup, 2023). From this perspective, cross-training is not merely a training tool but a psychological contract signal: it conveys that the organization invests in its people's growth, reciprocally eliciting loyalty, and commitment (Blau, 1964; Rousseau, 1995).

While the developmental and motivational benefits of cross-training are clear, its successful implementation requires careful design. Research indicates that cross-training initiatives are most effective when participation is voluntary, transparent, and supported by leadership (Kirkman et al., 2019). Coercive or poorly communicated programs can create resistance or anxiety, especially when employees fear role overload or job insecurity (Campion et al., 1994). Therefore, organizations must provide clarity regarding the purpose of cross-training, ensure that it aligns with employees' career aspirations, and recognize additional effort through formal appraisal systems. Effective programs often combine on-the-job shadowing with mentorship and structured feedback mechanisms, enabling learning to translate into performance.

The organizational culture also plays a decisive role in the effectiveness of cross-training. Cultures characterized by psychological safety, learning orientation, and collaboration tend to derive greater benefits from cross-training initiatives (Edmondson, 1999). In such environments, employees feel comfortable admitting knowledge gaps, asking questions, and experimenting with new roles. Conversely, rigid hierarchical or competitive cultures may inhibit the open exchange necessary for cross-functional learning. Thus, cross-training success depends as much on cultural and relational enablers as on structural or procedural design.

From an outcome's perspective, cross-training yields both organizational and individual-level benefits. At the organizational level, it enhances efficiency, reduces dependency on specific individuals, and mitigates disruptions related to turnover. Cross-trained employees can fill in for absent staff or those departing with minimal downtime, thereby improving continuity and service quality (Ployhart & Hale, 2014). It also facilitates innovation by encouraging the exchange of ideas across domains, leading to the creative recombination of knowledge and ideas. At the individual level, cross-training promotes skill variety, job enrichment, and role identity, core job design features associated with higher satisfaction and engagement (Hackman & Oldham, 1976). Employees who perceive their roles as diverse and meaningful are more likely to exhibit commitment and proactive behaviors.

Significantly, cross-training also contributes to organizational resilience and sustainability in uncertain labor markets. As industries face cyclical shortages and demographic shifts, a multi-skilled workforce becomes an asset that mitigates recruitment pressures. Moreover, cross-training supports knowledge continuity by ensuring that critical expertise is distributed rather than concentrated in a few individuals. This diffusion of knowledge mitigates the risk of operational failure when key employees leave, thus directly supporting long-term retention and organizational stability (Wang & Noe, 2010).

In sum, cross-training represents a multidimensional HR practice that bridges operational efficiency, psychological development, and strategic resilience. It transcends its origins in production efficiency to embody a developmental philosophy centered on learning, collaboration, and adaptability. The concept aligns closely with emerging paradigms of employee experience and human capital sustainability, in which organizations seek to balance performance demands with psychological well-being and engagement. The following section delves deeper into the theoretical underpinnings of cross-training, exploring how established frameworks, such as Self-Determination Theory, the AMO model, the Job Characteristics Model, and Social Exchange Theory, illuminate its impact on employee retention and engagement.

THEORETICAL UNDERPINNINGS

This section integrates Self-Determination Theory (SDT), the Ability–Motivation–Opportunity (AMO) Model, the Job Characteristics Model (JCM), Social Exchange Theory (SET), and Dynamic Capabilities Theory (DCT) to explain how each framework supports the argument that cross-training enhances employee retention and engagement.

Understanding the impact of cross-training on talent retention and engagement requires grounding in established motivational and strategic theories that explain why and how such practices influence employee behavior. The strategic integration of cross-training extends beyond developing skill versatility; it nurtures psychological engagement, commitment, and organizational adaptability. The following theoretical perspectives: Self-Determination Theory, the AMO framework, the Job Characteristics Model, Social Exchange Theory, and Dynamic Capabilities Theory, collectively illustrate the multifaceted mechanisms through which cross-training enhances individual and organizational outcomes.

Self-Determination Theory (SDT), proposed by Deci and Ryan (1985, 2000), provides one of the most robust psychological explanations for the motivational effects of cross-training. SDT posits that human motivation is governed by the fulfillment of three innate psychological needs: autonomy, competence, and relatedness. When these needs are met, individuals experience intrinsic motivation and psychological well-being, resulting in greater engagement and sustained performance. Cross-training contributes directly to satisfying these needs in several ways. First, by exposing employees to new tasks and responsibilities, cross-training enhances perceptions of competence as employees develop mastery across domains and experience personal growth (Ryan & Deci, 2017). Second, the opportunity to work across teams and departments fosters relatedness, as employees build new relationships and gain a sense of belonging in the broader organization. Third, cross-training often allows employees to exercise discretion and initiative when applying their diverse skill sets, thereby reinforcing autonomy (Gagné & Deci, 2005).

These three psychological needs interact to create a self-reinforcing motivational cycle. Employees who feel competent and connected become intrinsically motivated to learn and contribute, which, in turn, strengthens organizational engagement (Van den Broeck, Ferris, Chang, & Rosen, 2016). From an SDT standpoint, cross-training thus acts as a "psychological nutrient" that replenishes intrinsic motivation, especially in environments where repetitive or narrowly defined roles might otherwise lead to stagnation. The emphasis on autonomy-supportive work design, where employees feel trusted and capable, explains why cross-training is associated with lower turnover intentions and higher job satisfaction (Trépanier, Fernet, & Austin, 2019). Moreover, by cultivating an environment that supports psychological needs, cross-training aligns with the broader organizational aim of fostering sustainable motivation rather than short-term compliance.

While SDT provides a micro-level motivational explanation, the Ability–Motivation–Opportunity (AMO) model offers a meso-level framework connecting HR practices to performance outcomes. The AMO model, articulated initially by Appelbaum et al. (2000), posits that employees perform effectively when they have the ability (skills and knowledge), motivation (intrinsic or extrinsic drive), and opportunity (organizational conditions that enable contribution). Cross-training contributes to each of these three dimensions in integrated ways. By equipping employees with multiple skills, cross-training enhances their ability to perform various roles effectively. It stimulates motivation by signaling organizational investment in employee development, a key factor in perceived organizational support (Eisenberger & Stinglhamber, 2011). Finally, cross-training provides employees with opportunities to apply their expanded competencies, mainly when job rotation and collaborative projects are used as reinforcement mechanisms (Jiang, Lepak, Hu, & Baer, 2012).

From an AMO lens, cross-training can be conceptualized as a "high-involvement" HR practice that amplifies both individual and collective capability. When employees acquire skills beyond their core roles, they become more confident and capable of engaging in proactive behaviors such as problem-solving, innovation, and peer mentoring. This not only improves task performance but also strengthens psychological ownership, a sense that employees' contributions matter to the organization (Kim & Beehr, 2018). Moreover, when HR systems integrate cross-training with empowerment and recognition mechanisms, they create a synergistic effect, enabling employees to be both capable and motivated to contribute creatively (Boxall & Macky, 2009). In this sense, cross-training functions as a catalyst for engagement by simultaneously addressing the AMO triad, ultimately influencing retention through heightened involvement and job satisfaction.

The Job Characteristics Model (JCM) (Hackman & Oldham, 1976) further elaborates on how cross-training affects motivation through work design. JCM identifies five core job dimensions: skill variety, task identity, task significance, autonomy, and feedback, that contribute to three critical psychological states: experienced meaningfulness, experienced responsibility, and knowledge of results. Jobs that score high on these dimensions tend to elicit higher motivation, performance, and satisfaction. Cross-training directly enhances *skill variety* by allowing employees to perform diverse tasks across functions, thereby reducing monotony, and increasing cognitive engagement. It also strengthens *task identity*, as employees understand how their individual contributions integrate into the overall organizational structure. Furthermore, *task significance* is heightened when employees recognize that their cross-functional skills enable continuity and teamwork during times of disruption. In combination, these factors enhance *the perceived meaningfulness of work*—a powerful determinant of intrinsic motivation and engagement (Humphrey, Nahrgang, & Morgeson, 2007).

Cross-training also supports *autonomy* by empowering employees to act in multiple capacities, allowing them to make independent decisions when filling in for colleagues or handling cross-departmental projects. This autonomy reinforces self-efficacy, which is positively correlated with persistence and performance (Bandura, 1997). Lastly, cross-training can enhance feedback quality, as employees receive evaluations and learning input from multiple supervisors or peers across various roles, thereby broadening their perspective. Collectively, these mechanisms explain why cross-trained employees often display higher levels of engagement, commitment, and satisfaction compared to those in narrowly specialized roles (Parker, Bindl, & Strauss, 2010). In essence, cross-training redesigns jobs to meet the psychological needs embedded within the JCM, making work more stimulating and meaningful.

Beyond psychological and job design theories, Social Exchange Theory (SET) provides a relational explanation for the retention effects of cross-training. SET, as articulated by Blau (1964) and expanded by Cropanzano and Mitchell (2005), posits that reciprocity norms govern employment relationships. When employees perceive that the organization invests in their growth and well-being, they reciprocate through loyalty, commitment, and discretionary effort. Cross-training represents a tangible form of organizational investment as it provides employees with transferable skills that enhance both their internal and external employability. Paradoxically, while this could theoretically increase turnover risk, empirical evidence suggests the opposite: employees who feel valued and developed are more likely to stay because of heightened organizational commitment (Kehoe & Wright, 2013).

The exchange dynamic triggered by cross-training also strengthens affective commitment by fostering trust and perceived fairness. When employees recognize that skill-building opportunities are distributed equitably and transparently, they view the organization as supportive and trustworthy. This perception, in turn, reduces turnover intentions and cultivates a psychological bond with the employer (Rousseau, 1995). Moreover, cross-training can enhance *team-level social exchange* by building interdependence and mutual respect among coworkers. As employees assist and learn from one another, they develop social capital and cohesion, both of which are strong predictors of engagement (Nahapiet & Ghoshal, 1998). Thus, cross-training not only fulfills individual motivational needs but also builds a culture of reciprocity and cooperation that reinforces retention.

Complementing these human-centered frameworks, Dynamic Capabilities Theory (DCT) situates cross-training within a strategic management perspective. Teece, Pisano, and Shuen (1997) define dynamic capabilities as the firm's ability to integrate, build, and reconfigure internal and external competencies in response to rapidly changing environments. Cross-training contributes to dynamic capabilities by enhancing *learning agility* and *knowledge integration* across functional boundaries. A workforce that understands multiple aspects of operations is better equipped to sense opportunities, seize innovations, and reconfigure resources efficiently (Teece, 2018). In volatile labor markets, cross-training serves as a strategic buffer allowing organizations to adapt to workforce shortages, technological disruptions, or changing customer demands without compromising productivity (Lengnick-Hall & Beck, 2005).

At the collective level, cross-training builds organizational ambidexterity- the simultaneous ability to exploit existing competencies and explore new ones (O'Reilly & Tushman, 2013). Employees who possess multi-domain knowledge can bridge gaps between departments, facilitating knowledge transfer and innovation. This adaptability enhances organizational resilience, a critical determinant of long-term sustainability and competitiveness (Duchek, 2020). Therefore, from a dynamic capabilities' perspective, cross-training is not only a retention or engagement strategy but also a *strategic renewal mechanism* that strengthens the firm's capacity to thrive amid uncertainty.

Bringing these theories together, it becomes evident that cross-training operates at multiple levels of analysis. At the individual level, SDT and JCM explain how cross-training enhances intrinsic motivation, meaningfulness, and psychological fulfillment. At the HR system level, the AMO model captures how cross-training interacts with complementary practices to optimize performance and engagement. At the relational level, SET elucidates how developmental investments foster reciprocity, trust, and commitment. Ultimately, at the strategic level, DCT emphasizes how these individual and relational gains collectively contribute to organizational agility and sustainability.

Integrating these frameworks yields a holistic understanding of the strategic potential of cross-training. For instance, when organizations employ cross-training within an autonomy-supportive culture (as suggested by Self-Determination Theory, or SDT), employees feel psychologically empowered. When HR systems simultaneously provide recognition and voice opportunities (AMO and SET), employees reciprocate through engagement and retention. Moreover, when these behaviors occur within a strategically agile firm (DCT), the organization leverages learning to gain a competitive advantage. Such theoretical integration underscores that cross-training is not an isolated training initiative but a multi-level strategic capability embedded within a broader system of sustainable HR practices (Kaufman, 2015).

Empirical research supports this integrated model. Studies have shown that cross-training is positively correlated with work engagement, which is mediated by job enrichment and psychological empowerment (Parker et al., 2010; Gagné et al., 2022). Similarly, evidence from high-performance work systems indicates that developmental HR practices, including cross-training, reduce voluntary turnover by strengthening employees' affective commitment and perceived internal employability (Kehoe & Wright, 2013; Jiang et al., 2012). Theoretical synthesis thus reveals that cross-training acts as both a *motivational mechanism* and a *strategic lever*, creating a mutually reinforcing loop between individual fulfillment and organizational capability.

In conclusion, the theoretical landscape surrounding cross-training demonstrates that its impact extends far beyond operational flexibility. It nurtures psychological engagement through the fulfillment of intrinsic needs (SDT), fosters performance through capability alignment (AMO), enriches job design (JCM), strengthens trust-based relationships (SET), and enhances adaptive capacity (DCT). Together, these theories suggest that cross-training, when strategically integrated into HR systems, becomes a cornerstone of sustainable talent management, thereby supporting employee well-being, engagement, and organizational resilience simultaneously. The subsequent section will build upon this theoretical foundation to explore how cross-training influences employee engagement and retention, presenting evidence from empirical studies and organizational cases across diverse industries.

CROSS-TRAINING AND ITS IMPACT ON EMPLOYEE ENGAGEMENT AND RETENTION

Employee engagement and retention have become critical strategic priorities in contemporary human resource management (HRM). Amid volatile labor markets and increasing skill shortages, organizations are seeking innovative strategies that enhance workforce adaptability while maintaining motivation and commitment. Cross-training, defined as the systematic development of employee competencies across multiple job roles or functional areas, has emerged as one of the most effective yet underutilized interventions for achieving both employee engagement and retention (Jehanzeb & Bashir, 2017). Unlike traditional training programs focused on specific job tasks, cross-training expands employees' skill sets horizontally, enabling them to perform diverse roles within the organization (Campion et al., 2020). This multidimensional learning experience creates a psychologically rich environment that aligns with employees' intrinsic motivational needs, enhances job satisfaction, and fosters a stronger attachment to the organization.

The Psychological Mechanisms Linking Cross-Training with Engagement

Employee engagement, characterized by vigor, dedication, and absorption (Schaufeli & Bakker, 2004), is deeply influenced by job design, learning opportunities, and perceived organizational support. Cross-training operates as a developmental intervention that stimulates engagement through multiple psychological pathways.

First, it fulfills the core needs identified by Self-Determination Theory (SDT), which include autonomy, competence, and relatedness (Deci & Ryan, 2000). Employees who engage in cross-training perceive higher levels of competence as they master new skills and broaden their functional expertise (Eldor & Harpaz, 2016). The opportunity to make independent decisions in novel work situations enhances autonomy, while collaborative learning in multi-role environments strengthens interpersonal relatedness. Together, these outcomes nurture intrinsic motivation and psychological engagement with the work.

Second, cross-training promotes job enrichment and task variety, which are significant predictors of engagement (Hackman & Oldham, 1976). Employees performing repetitive tasks often experience monotony and disengagement; cross-training introduces novelty, challenge, and meaning to their roles, thereby enhancing their overall job satisfaction. Research indicates that task variety and skill diversity contribute positively to vigor and dedication, as employees experience their work as more stimulating and purposeful (Saks, 2019). Additionally, cross-training enables employees to gain a broader understanding of the organizational picture, fostering a sense of contribution and alignment with strategic goals.

Third, the psychological empowerment fostered by cross-training also strengthens engagement. Empowerment, as defined by Spreitzer (1995) as meaning, competence, self-determination, and impact, is enhanced when employees are entrusted with multiple responsibilities. They perceive themselves as capable of influencing outcomes beyond their immediate role boundaries, thereby feeling more valued and trusted by the organization (Maynard et al., 2012). This sense of empowerment builds emotional investment and a proactive work orientation-hallmarks of engaged employees.

Finally, social exchange theory (SET) provides a compelling explanation of the engagement outcomes associated with cross-training (Cropanzano & Mitchell, 2005). Employees interpret the organization's investment in cross-training as a signal of trust and reciprocity. When employees perceive that the organization is committed to their growth and career development, they reciprocate through higher engagement, effort, and loyalty. In this sense, cross-training functions as both a capability-building mechanism and a psychological contract enhancer.

Cross-Training as a Driver of Retention

Retention is a complex outcome influenced by job satisfaction, organizational commitment, career growth opportunities, and perceived organizational support. Cross-training contributes to each of these dimensions, making it a strategic lever for reducing turnover.

One of the foremost drivers of employee turnover is the perception of limited career development opportunities (Kraimer et al., 2011). Cross-training addresses this issue by expanding employees' skill portfolios and employability within the organization. Employees who experience continuous learning and developmental progression are more likely to envision a long-term career path within the firm rather than seeking external opportunities (Jehanzeb & Bashir, 2017). This aligns with career construction theory, which emphasizes the individual's active role in crafting meaningful and adaptive career paths (Savickas, 2013). Through cross-training, employees perceive greater control over their professional trajectory, leading to more substantial affective commitment and lower turnover intentions.

Moreover, cross-training fosters a sense of job security and psychological safety, two critical antecedents of retention (Kahn, 1990). When employees are equipped to perform diverse roles, they become more resilient to organizational restructuring, automation, or external shocks. This adaptability creates a form of internal labor market mobility that reassures employees of their continued relevance and value within the organization (Dessler, 2020). Psychological safety is further enhanced as cross-trained employees feel confident in taking initiative and contributing to areas beyond their original job scope, without fear of failure or punishment.

Cross-training also supports workplace relationships and cohesion, which indirectly contribute to retention. Learning from and collaborating with colleagues across departments strengthens social capital and fosters a sense of community (Nahapiet & Ghoshal, 1998). Such interdepartmental ties enhance a sense of belonging and emotional attachment to the organization, making employees less likely to leave. This effect aligns with the belongingness theory (Baumeister & Leary, 1995), which posits that strong interpersonal bonds satisfy fundamental human needs and serve as a buffer against turnover.

From an organizational perspective, cross-training also reduces role overload and burnout, two significant causes of attrition (Maslach & Leiter, 2016). When employees are trained to perform multiple roles, the workload can be redistributed more evenly during peak periods or periods of absenteeism, thereby preventing excessive strain on individual workers. This flexibility promotes a healthier work-life balance, enhances well-being, and reduces the desire to exit the organization. Furthermore, cross-training encourages empathy and understanding among coworkers, as employees appreciate the challenges of different roles, thus reducing inter-role conflict and fostering a collaborative culture (Park & Shaw, 2013).

Empirical Evidence and Theoretical Integration

Empirical studies have increasingly demonstrated the positive effects of cross-training on engagement and retention. For instance, Campion et al. (2020) found that employees who participated in cross-functional training reported higher job involvement and affective commitment. Similarly, a study by Lee and Bruvold (2003) demonstrated that perceived investment in employee development, including cross-training, significantly predicted both job satisfaction and organizational commitment. These findings are consistent with the Job Demands–Resources (JD-R) model (Bakker & Demerouti, 2017), which posits that developmental resources such as training buffer against job demands and stimulate motivational processes that enhance engagement.

Cross-training also aligns with the Social Learning Theory (Bandura, 1977), suggesting that learning through observation and interaction promotes both competence and motivation. Employees in cross-training environments often model behaviors and problem-solving approaches from peers in other departments, leading to enhanced collective efficacy- a predictor of both team engagement and retention (Chen et al., 2009).

Moreover, the Conservation of Resources (COR) theory (Hobfoll, 2011) provides an additional explanatory lens. Cross-training expands employees' resource reservoirs in the form of skills, social support, and self-efficacy. These accumulated resources protect against stress and burnout, thereby improving retention. Employees who perceive growth in their skillset and adaptability are less threatened by environmental uncertainties and more likely to remain committed to the organization.

However, it is essential to note that the impact of cross-training on engagement and retention is not universally positive. Poorly implemented cross-training initiatives that lack clarity, fairness, or recognition can backfire by increasing workload, stress, or perceptions of role ambiguity (McKee & Froelich, 2016). For example, employees who are expected to assume additional responsibilities without corresponding rewards may feel exploited rather than empowered. Therefore, practical design and communication of cross-training programs are crucial to ensure that they enhance, rather than undermine, engagement and retention outcomes.

Organizational Benefits and Strategic Implications

From a strategic HRM standpoint, cross-training yields significant organizational advantages that reinforce employee outcomes. Cross-trained employees exhibit higher levels of organizational citizenship behaviors (OCBs), which are discretionary actions that enhance organizational effectiveness (Organ, 2018). Engaged and empowered employees are more willing to assist colleagues, adapt to change, and contribute beyond their formal job descriptions. This, in turn, creates a positive feedback loop: higher engagement drives more substantial commitment, which further stabilizes the workforce.

Cross-training also contributes to knowledge management and organizational learning, enhancing long-term competitiveness (Nonaka & Takeuchi, 1995). Employees who work across functions become knowledge brokers, transferring insights and best practices between departments. Such fluid knowledge exchange reduces silos, encourages innovation, and enhances problem-solving capabilities. When employees witness the tangible value of their learning contributions, their engagement deepens and their identification with the organization strengthens (Argote & Miron-Spektor, 2011).

Moreover, organizations that institutionalize cross-training build a resilient and agile workforce, capable of responding to disruptions without the need for extensive rehiring or retraining. This agility, while beneficial operationally, also reassures employees that their development is central to the organization's success, reinforcing trust and commitment. In sectors facing tight labor markets, such as healthcare, manufacturing, and information technology, cross-training is not only a retention strategy but also a strategic necessity for sustaining performance continuity (Mackenzie et al., 2023).

Despite its advantages, cross-training is not a universal remedy. It requires considerable investment in planning, coaching, and coordination. The success of cross-training depends heavily on organizational culture, leadership support, and employee readiness for change (Noe et al., 2022). Future research should examine the differential impact of cross-training across industries and cultures, as well as its interaction with moderating variables such as psychological safety, team climate, and leadership style. Integrating transformational and inclusive leadership frameworks may also reveal how supportive leadership enhances the positive effects of cross-training on engagement and retention.

THEORETICAL FRAMEWORK AND CONCEPTUAL MODEL

The theoretical foundation of this chapter integrates multiple frameworks from psychology and organizational behavior to explain the mechanisms through which cross-training influences employee engagement and retention. The discussion draws on Self-Determination Theory (SDT), the Job Demands–Resources (JD-R) Model, and Social Exchange Theory (SET), while also incorporating insights from Psychological Empowerment Theory and Organizational Support Theory. Together, these frameworks elucidate how cross-training fulfills employees' psychological needs, optimizes job resources, and reinforces reciprocal commitment, ultimately contributing to sustainable engagement and lower turnover.

Self-Determination Theory (SDT): Cross-Training and Basic Psychological Needs

Self-Determination Theory (SDT) provides a robust foundation for understanding how cross-training enhances motivation and engagement. According to SDT, individuals possess three innate psychological needs (autonomy, competence, and relatedness) that are essential for psychological growth, well-being, and intrinsic motivation (Deci & Ryan, 2000). When these needs are satisfied, employees experience a higher level of engagement and commitment to their work (Gagné & Deci, 2005). Cross-training directly contributes to satisfying these three needs.

- Autonomy is supported as employees are given opportunities to make decisions and apply skills in different roles. This flexibility promotes self-direction and ownership over one's learning trajectory.

- Competence is fostered through mastery of multiple skill sets. As employees succeed in performing varied tasks, their sense of efficacy and confidence increases (Eldor & Harpaz, 2016).
- Relatedness is strengthened as cross-training involves collaboration and interaction across teams, allowing employees to develop supportive professional relationships (Van den Broeck et al., 2016).

The satisfaction of these needs stimulates autonomous motivation, leading employees to engage in their work with energy and enthusiasm rather than merely out of obligation. As a result, cross-training transforms routine work into a developmental experience that nurtures both hedonic well-being (pleasure and satisfaction) and eudaimonic well-being (personal growth and purpose) (Ryan & Deci, 2019). This intrinsic motivation becomes a key driver of employee engagement, sustaining vigor, dedication, and absorption in the long term (Schaufeli & Bakker, 2004).

Furthermore, when organizations invest in cross-training, they demonstrate trust in their employees' ability to handle diverse responsibilities. This recognition fosters a favorable motivational climate, reducing controlled motivation (external pressure) and enhancing internalized commitment (Gagné et al., 2015). Hence, SDT positions cross-training as a powerful enabler of self-motivation, which is crucial for enduring engagement and retention.

Job Demands–Resources (JD-R) Model: Cross-Training as a Resource-Enhancing Mechanism

The Job Demands–Resources (JD-R) Model (Bakker & Demerouti, 2017) provides another useful lens for understanding the engagement effects of cross-training. The model posits that every job has specific demands (physical, psychological, or emotional) and resources (autonomy, learning, support, feedback) that influence motivation and strain. Engagement arises when job resources buffer the adverse effects of demands and activate motivational processes.

Cross-training functions as a job resource by enhancing skill variety, providing learning opportunities, improving feedback channels, and clarifying roles. Employees gain access to diverse work experiences that increase their capability to manage demands effectively. When job resources increase, employees experience higher energy levels and are more resilient to stressors (Bakker & Albrecht, 2018).

Cross-training also introduces personal resources, such as self-efficacy and adaptability (Xanthopoulou et al., 2009). Employees who undergo multi-role training develop confidence in their ability to tackle unfamiliar challenges, which contributes to reduced job strain and increased persistence. Over time, these personal resources become self-reinforcing, creating an upward spiral of motivation, engagement, and performance (Salanova et al., 2010).

From a retention perspective, the JD-R model suggests that when employees perceive an abundance of resources in their roles—such as learning opportunities, supportive supervision, and flexible work design—they are less likely to seek alternative employment (Bakker et al., 2023). Cross-training enriches the resource base of employees, making their work more meaningful and strengthening their organizational attachment. Conversely, when cross-training is implemented poorly, without adequate support or clarity, it can increase job demands and lead to exhaustion. Thus, the design and pacing of cross-training must ensure a balance between demands and resources to yield positive retention outcomes.

Social Exchange Theory (SET): Reciprocity and Organizational Commitment

Social Exchange Theory (SET) (Blau, 1964; Cropanzano & Mitchell, 2005) emphasizes the reciprocal nature of relationships between employees and organizations. It proposes that when employees perceive that the organization values and supports them, they reciprocate through positive attitudes and behaviors such as engagement, loyalty, and extra-role performance.

Cross-training exemplifies this exchange relationship. By investing in employee development, organizations send a strong signal that they value employees not merely as operational resources but as long-term partners in success (Eisenberger et al., 2020). Employees, in turn, respond with enhanced organizational commitment, reduced turnover intention, and higher engagement (Ghosh et al., 2013). The perceived organizational support embedded in cross-training initiatives creates an affective bond- a sense of gratitude and obligation that encourages employees to contribute meaningfully to organizational goals.

Furthermore, cross-training aligns with the psychological contract framework within SET. Psychological contracts are implicit expectations of mutual investment between employees and employers (Rousseau, 1995). When organizations deliver on developmental promises through cross-training, employees perceive contract fulfillment, reinforcing trust and retention (Restubog et al., 2006). Conversely, neglecting employee development can lead to perceptions of contract breach, which can trigger disengagement and turnover.

The social exchange dynamic also extends to peer relationships. Cross-training encourages collaboration and skill-sharing across departments, fostering norms of reciprocity and cooperation. This peer-level exchange strengthens team cohesion and shared commitment- social factors that buffer against disengagement (Chiaburu

& Harrison, 2008). Hence, SET not only explains individual-level engagement but also collective engagement rooted in mutual trust and shared learning.

Psychological Empowerment and Organizational Support

While SDT, JD-R, and SET provide foundational insights, Psychological Empowerment Theory (Spreitzer, 1995), and Organizational Support Theory (Eisenberger et al., 1986) further clarify how cross-training strengthens engagement and retention through employee perceptions of control and support.

Psychological empowerment encompasses meaning, competence, self-determination, and impact—four key cognitions that shape how employees perceive their role within the organization. Cross-training enhances all four dimensions. Employees find greater meaning in their work as they understand interdepartmental connections; they experience competence through skill mastery; self-determination through autonomy in varied roles; and impact through visible contributions to organizational effectiveness (Maynard et al., 2012). Empowered employees are more engaged, creative, and committed to their work, reducing voluntary turnover (Seibert et al., 2011).

Simultaneously, Organizational Support Theory (OST) posits that when employees perceive their organization as investing in their welfare and development, they feel an obligation to reciprocate with loyalty and improved performance (Eisenberger et al., 1986). Cross-training visibly demonstrates an organization's care and long-term investment, fulfilling employees' socioemotional needs and promoting employee retention. In tight labor markets, perceived organizational support acts as a critical retention lever; employees who feel valued and developed are significantly less likely to exit (Allen et al., 2020).

Integrative Conceptual Model

Drawing from the aforementioned theories, a conceptual model can be developed to illustrate the mechanisms linking cross-training to engagement and retention (Figure 1).

Figure 1. Integrated Conceptual Model of Cross-Training

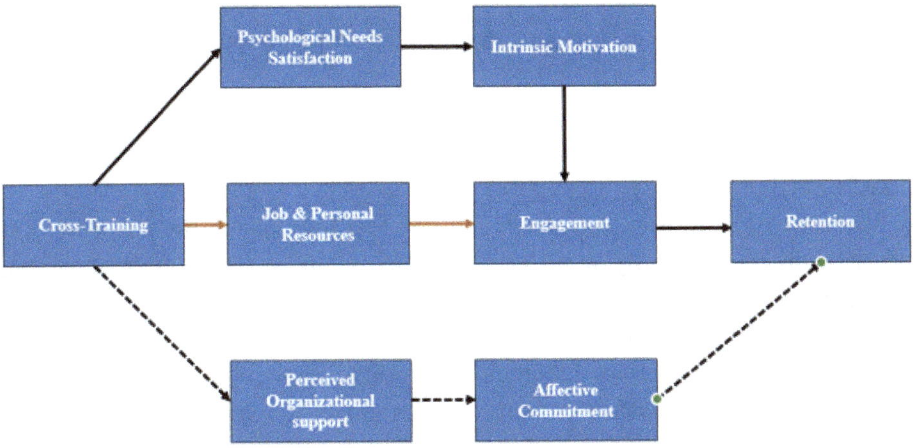

Model Explanation:

1. Cross-Training as a Strategic HR Practice provides employees with learning diversity, inter-role exposure, and collaborative opportunities.
2. These experiences fulfill basic psychological needs (autonomy, competence, relatedness) as explained by SDT, leading to intrinsic motivation and psychological empowerment.
3. Cross-training also enhances job and personal resources per the JD-R framework—such as skill variety, self-efficacy, and adaptability thereby promoting engagement and reducing burnout.
4. Through SET and OST, employees perceive organizational support and reciprocal trust, resulting in affective commitment and lower turnover intention.
5. Collectively, these mechanisms culminate in employee engagement (vigor, dedication, absorption), which mediates the relationship between cross-training and retention outcomes.

This integrative model underscores cross-training as a multi-theoretical bridge between HR practices and psychological outcomes. It emphasizes that employee retention is not merely the absence of turnover but the presence of sustained engagement, meaning, and mutual value exchange between employees and organizations.

Theoretical Implications

The theoretical synthesis makes a significant contribution to the HRM literature in three key ways.

First, it positions cross-training not only as an operational tool but as a strategic psychological intervention, connecting skill enhancement to deeper motivational and relational processes.

Second, by integrating SDT, JD-R, and SET, it highlights how intrinsic motivation, resource availability, and social reciprocity jointly contribute to explaining engagement and retention.

Third, it extends traditional models of employee development by illustrating that cross-functional learning enhances both individual adaptability and collective resilience, making it essential for workforce sustainability in volatile environments (Noe et al., 2022).

PRACTICAL IMPLICATIONS FOR ORGANIZATIONS

Cross-training has emerged as a strategic human resource practice with demonstrated potential to enhance employee engagement and retention. While the theoretical frameworks discussed in the previous section highlight *why* cross-training is effective, organizations must now consider *how* to implement it effectively. This section provides actionable insights for HR professionals, managers, and organizational leaders, detailing practical approaches to program design, implementation, monitoring, and evaluation.

Strategic Alignment of Cross-Training Programs

For cross-training to yield meaningful outcomes, it must be aligned with organizational strategy and workforce planning. Cross-training should not be an ad-hoc initiative; instead, it must be integrated into the organization's talent management and succession planning frameworks (Jehanzeb & Bashir, 2017). For example, organizations facing tight labor markets or skill shortages should prioritize cross-training in high-demand areas, ensuring employees acquire competencies that directly support strategic objectives.

Strategic alignment involves:

1. Identifying critical roles and skill gaps – Organizations must analyze current workforce competencies to determine which roles would benefit most from

cross-training. This requires collaboration between HR, line managers, and business leaders.

2. Defining clear objectives – Cross-training programs should have explicit goals, such as reducing turnover, increasing flexibility, or enhancing team collaboration. Without defined outcomes, the impact of a program cannot be accurately assessed.
3. Integrating with career development pathways – Cross-training should support long-term employee growth. Linking cross-training to promotions, lateral moves, or skill certifications enhances perceived value and strengthens retention (Campion et al., 2020).

By embedding cross-training into broader talent management strategies, organizations signal their commitment to employee growth, fostering engagement and trust.

Designing Effective Cross-Training Programs

The success of cross-training largely depends on program design. Effective programs incorporate structure, clarity, and support mechanisms that enable employees to learn and apply new skills without experiencing undue stress or role conflict. Key design considerations include:

1. Role Rotation and Modular Learning: Rotational assignments across different functions allow employees to experience diverse work contexts. Modular learning, which divides skills into short, focused units, facilitates the gradual development of competency and reduces cognitive overload (Noe et al., 2022).
2. Balanced Workload Management: Cross-training should not simply add responsibilities to existing roles. Workload adjustments and temporary support mechanisms enable employees to engage in learning without compromising their performance in their primary role (McKee & Froelich, 2016).
3. Customized Learning Paths: Employees have diverse learning needs and career aspirations. Offering personalized cross-training options empowers employees to focus on skills relevant to their interests and future goals, enhancing autonomy and engagement (Eldor & Harpaz, 2016).
4. Mentorship and Peer Support: Embedding mentorship or buddy systems helps employees navigate unfamiliar roles. Mentors provide guidance, reduce uncertainty, and accelerate skill acquisition, strengthening relatedness and psychological safety (Chiaburu & Harrison, 2008).
5. Feedback and Recognition Mechanisms: Continuous feedback during cross-training helps employees track progress and reinforce skill development.

Recognition of achievements, both formal and informal, signals organizational support and encourages continued engagement (Saks, 2019).

Leadership Role in Cross-Training Initiatives

Leadership support is critical for the success of cross-training programs. Leaders not only facilitate learning but also create a culture that values continuous development and employee empowerment. Practical considerations include:

1. **Role Modeling Lifelong Learning:** Leaders who actively participate in skill development and demonstrate a growth mindset set an example for employees. This modeling encourages employees to embrace cross-training as a valuable opportunity rather than a mandatory task (Gagné & Deci, 2005).
2. **Communicating Purpose and Benefits:** Leaders must clearly articulate why cross-training is important for both organizational performance and individual development. Transparent communication enhances buy-in and reduces resistance or anxiety (Eisenberger et al., 2020).
3. **Providing Psychological Safety:** Leaders should foster an environment where employees feel safe to experiment, make mistakes, and ask questions during cross-training. Psychological safety is a critical factor that influences engagement, learning effectiveness, and retention (Kahn, 1990).
4. **Monitoring and Coaching:** Active supervision and coaching ensure that employees are progressing in their cross-training journey. Leaders can identify skill gaps early, provide resources, and address challenges before they escalate into disengagement or frustration (Maynard et al., 2012).

Measurement and Evaluation of Cross-Training Programs

To maximize impact, organizations must **systematically measure and evaluate cross-training initiatives**. Evidence-based assessment allows organizations to refine program design, demonstrate ROI, and align resources with strategic objectives. Recommended evaluation approaches include:

1. **Engagement Metrics:** Pre- and post-training engagement surveys (e.g., Utrecht Work Engagement Scale) can assess changes in vigor, dedication, and absorption. Qualitative feedback, obtained through focus groups or interviews, adds depth to quantitative findings (Schaufeli & Bakker, 2004).
2. **Retention and Turnover Analysis:** Comparing turnover rates of cross-trained employees with non-participants helps quantify retention benefits. Tracking

internal mobility and promotion rates can also indicate the effects of career progression (Jehanzeb & Bashir, 2017).

3. **Performance and Productivity Indicators:** Measuring task efficiency, error rates, or service quality across roles provides insights into skill transfer and operational impact (Campion et al., 2020).
4. **Employee Feedback and Satisfaction:** Surveys capturing employees' perceptions of fairness, workload, autonomy, and support provide valuable insights for program refinement (Saks, 2019).
5. **Knowledge Transfer and Collaboration:** Assessing interdepartmental collaboration, problem-solving effectiveness, and innovation output helps evaluate the broader organizational benefits of cross-training (Nonaka & Takeuchi, 1995).

Challenges and Mitigation Strategies

While cross-training offers substantial benefits, organizations may face implementation challenges that must be proactively managed:

1. **Role Ambiguity and Overload:** Employees may struggle to balance multiple responsibilities. Clear role definitions, gradual skill development, and workload adjustments mitigate stress and disengagement (McKee & Froelich, 2016).
2. **Resistance to Change:** Employees accustomed to routine tasks may resist cross-training. Effective communication, leadership endorsement, and participation incentives encourage acceptance (Ghosh et al., 2013).
3. **Resource Constraints:** Cross-training demands time, personnel, and financial investment. Prioritizing critical roles, leveraging technology-enabled learning, and integrating cross-training with existing development programs optimize resource use (Noe et al., 2022).
4. **Ensuring Equity:** All employees should have access to cross-training opportunities. Avoiding favoritism and ensuring transparency in selection criteria enhances fairness and engagement (Jehanzeb & Bashir, 2017).

Future-Oriented Practices

To sustain long-term benefits, organizations should adopt future-oriented cross-training strategies:

1. Digital and Virtual Training Platforms: Leveraging e-learning, simulations, and virtual collaboration tools allows scalable cross-training across locations and departments.

2. Integration with Talent Analytics: Using HR analytics to identify skill gaps, predict retention risks, and personalize learning journeys enhances program effectiveness.
3. Linking Cross-Training to Career Pathing: Employees should see a clear connection between cross-training and advancement opportunities, reinforcing motivation and retention.
4. Continuous Feedback Loops: Periodic assessment and iterative refinement ensure programs remain relevant to evolving business needs and employee expectations.

CONCLUSION

The contemporary organizational landscape is characterized by rapid technological change, skill shortages, and highly competitive labor markets, making employee engagement and retention a top strategic priority. This chapter has examined cross-training as a strategic human resource practice that can simultaneously enhance workforce capability, engagement, and retention. Through a theoretical and practical lens, we have illustrated how cross-training operates as a multidimensional mechanism that addresses both individual psychological needs and organizational objectives, offering actionable insights for practitioners and researchers alike.

Summary of Key Insights

Cross-training has been positioned as a strategic intervention that transcends traditional training approaches. Unlike conventional single-role training, cross-training equips employees with multi-role competencies, increases task variety, and fosters interdepartmental collaboration, thereby contributing to both employee development and organizational adaptability. From a theoretical perspective, the chapter has integrated multiple frameworks to explain the engagement and retention outcomes associated with cross-training:

1. Self-Determination Theory (SDT) highlights that cross-training fulfills basic psychological needs autonomy, competence, and relatedness, thereby promoting intrinsic motivation and sustained engagement (Deci & Ryan, 2000; Van den Broeck et al., 2016).
2. The Job Demands–Resources (JD-R) Model elucidates how cross-training enhances job and personal resources, buffering against job stress and burnout while stimulating motivational processes that drive engagement (Bakker & Demerouti, 2017).

3. Social Exchange Theory (SET) and Organizational Support Theory (OST) emphasize the importance of perceived organizational investment. Cross-training signals reciprocal commitment, enhancing affective commitment and reducing turnover intention (Blau, 1964; Eisenberger et al., 1986).
4. Psychological Empowerment Theory demonstrates that cross-training strengthens employees' sense of meaning, competence, self-determination, and impact, which reinforces engagement and pro-organizational behaviors (Spreitzer, 1995; Maynard et al., 2012).

These frameworks collectively suggest that cross-training is not merely a skill development initiative, but a holistic HR strategy that links organizational capability building with psychological, motivational, and relational outcomes.

Practical Implications

The chapter's practical discussion outlined strategic steps and considerations for implementing cross-training effectively:

- Programs must be aligned with organizational strategy, targeting critical roles and integrating with career development pathways to maximize engagement and retention (Jehanzeb & Bashir, 2017).
- Program design should prioritize modular learning, workload management, mentorship, and continuous feedback, ensuring employees gain competence without experiencing stress or overload (Noe et al., 2022).
- Leadership support is essential to foster a psychologically safe and growth-oriented culture, emphasizing communication, coaching, and role modeling (Kahn, 1990; Gagné & Deci, 2005).
- Measurement and evaluation of engagement, retention, skill transfer, and organizational outcomes are necessary for evidence-based refinement and demonstrating ROI (Saks, 2019; Campion et al., 2020).

These practices underscore the dual benefit of cross-training: it equips organizations with flexible, adaptable talent while simultaneously fulfilling employees' developmental, relational, and motivational needs.

Contributions to Research and Theory

The chapter contributes to both theoretical advancement and empirical understanding in several ways:

1. It integrates diverse theoretical perspectives—SDT, JD-R, SET, Psychological Empowerment, and OST into a unified conceptual model explaining how cross-training drives engagement and retention. This integration addresses a notable gap in the literature, where cross-training is often studied primarily as a skill development tool without considering psychological and relational mechanisms.
2. The conceptual model offers a framework for future empirical testing, highlighting mediating mechanisms (e.g., intrinsic motivation, psychological empowerment, perceived organizational support) and potential moderators (e.g., leadership style, organizational culture, role complexity).
3. The chapter emphasizes cross-training as a strategic HR practice, extending its significance beyond operational flexibility to employee well-being, engagement, and retention outcomes, particularly relevant in tight labor markets and high-turnover industries.

In conclusion, cross-training represents a strategically significant HR practice with the potential to enhance employee engagement, retention, and organizational adaptability simultaneously. By broadening skills, fostering psychological empowerment, and signaling organizational support, cross-training addresses both individual motivational needs and strategic workforce objectives. The integrated theoretical framework presented here underscores the psychological, social, and resource-based mechanisms that explain these outcomes.

For practitioners, the chapter offers guidance on designing, implementing, and evaluating cross-training initiatives to maximize engagement and retention. For researchers, it identifies avenues for longitudinal, context-sensitive, and technologically integrated studies that can further elucidate the role of cross-training in dynamic labor markets.

Ultimately, cross-training should not be viewed merely as a short-term solution to operational challenges but as a long-term investment in human capital, enhancing both individual career trajectories and organizational resilience. By adopting a holistic approach that combines strategy, theory, and practice, organizations can transform cross-training from a procedural task into a core pillar of talent retention and engagement in the 21st-century workplace.

REFERENCES

Adler, P. S., & Cole, R. E. (1993). Designed for learning: A tale of two auto plants. *Sloan Management Review*, *34*(3), 85–94.

Allen, D. G., Peltokorpi, V., & Rubenstein, A. L. (2020). When "embedded" means "stuck": The dark side of job embeddedness. *The Academy of Management Annals*, *14*(2), 143–168.

Appelbaum, E., Bailey, T., Berg, P., & Kalleberg, A. L. (2000). *Manufacturing advantage: Why high-performance work systems pay off.* Cornell University Press.

Bakker, A. B., & Albrecht, S. (2018). Work engagement: Current trends. *Career Development International*, *23*(1), 4–11. DOI: 10.1108/CDI-11-2017-0207

Bakker, A. B., & Demerouti, E. (2017). Job Demands–Resources theory: Taking stock and looking forward. *Journal of Occupational Health Psychology*, *22*(3), 273–285. DOI: 10.1037/ocp0000056 PMID: 27732008

Bakker, A. B., Demerouti, E., & Sanz-Vergel, A. I. (2023). Burnout and work engagement: The JD-R approach. *Annual Review of Organizational Psychology*, *10*, 35–60.

Bakker, A. B., Tims, M., & Derks, D. (2012). Proactive personality and job performance: The role of job crafting and work engagement. *Human Relations; Studies Towards the Integration of the Social Sciences*, *65*(10), 1359–1378. DOI: 10.1177/0018726712453471

Bandura, A. (1997). Self-efficacy: The exercise of control. *The Freeman.*

Benson, G. S., & Dundis, S. P. (2003). Understanding and motivating health care employees: Integrating Maslow's hierarchy of needs, training and technology. *Journal of Nursing Management*, *11*(5), 315–320. DOI: 10.1046/j.1365-2834.2003.00409.x PMID: 12930537

Blau, P. (1964). *Exchange and power in social life*. Wiley.

Boudreau, J. W., & Cascio, W. F. (2021). *Investing in people: Financial impact of human resource initiatives* (3rd ed.). Pearson.

Boxall, P., & Macky, K. (2009). Research and theory on high-performance work systems: Progressing the high-involvement stream. *Human Resource Management Journal*, *19*(1), 3–23. DOI: 10.1111/j.1748-8583.2008.00082.x

Campion, M. A., Cheraskin, L., & Stevens, M. J. (1994). Career-related antecedents and outcomes of job rotation. *Academy of Management Journal, 37*(6), 1518–1542. DOI: 10.2307/256797

Cappelli, P. (2022). *The future of the office: Work from home, remote work, and the hard choices we all face*. Oxford University Press.

Carnevale, J. B., & Hatak, I. (2020). Employee adjustment and well-being in the era of COVID-19: Implications for human resource management. *Journal of Business Research, 116*, 183–187. DOI: 10.1016/j.jbusres.2020.05.037 PMID: 32501303

Chiaburu, D. S., & Harrison, D. A. (2008). Do peers make the place? Conceptual synthesis and meta-analysis of coworker effects on perceptions, attitudes, OCBs, and performance. *The Journal of Applied Psychology, 93*(5), 1082–1103. DOI: 10.1037/0021-9010.93.5.1082 PMID: 18808227

Cropanzano, R., & Mitchell, M. S. (2005). Social exchange theory: An interdisciplinary review. *Journal of Management, 31*(6), 874–900. DOI: 10.1177/0149206305279602

De Vos, A., & Cambré, B. (2017). Career management in high-performing organizations: A set-theoretic approach. *Human Resource Management, 56*(3), 501–518. DOI: 10.1002/hrm.21786

Deci, E. L., & Ryan, R. M. (1985). *Intrinsic motivation and self-determination in human behavior*. Springer. DOI: 10.1007/978-1-4899-2271-7

Deci, E. L., & Ryan, R. M. (2000). The "what" and "why" of goal pursuits: Human needs and the self-determination of behavior. *Psychological Inquiry, 11*(4), 227–268. DOI: 10.1207/S15327965PLI1104_01

Deci, E. L., & Ryan, R. M. (2000). Self-determination theory and the facilitation of intrinsic motivation, social development, and well-being. *The American Psychologist, 55*(1), 68–78. DOI: 10.1037/0003-066X.55.1.68 PMID: 11392867

Duchek, S. (2020). Organizational resilience: A capability-based conceptualization. *Business Research, 13*(1), 215–246. DOI: 10.1007/s40685-019-0085-7

Edmondson, A. (1999). Psychological safety and learning behavior in work teams. *Administrative Science Quarterly, 44*(2), 350–383. DOI: 10.2307/2666999

Eisenberger, R., Malone, G. P., & Presson, W. D. (2020). Optimizing perceived organizational support to enhance employee engagement. *Society for Human Resource Management, 73*(2), 1–25.

Eisenberger, R., & Stinglhamber, F. (2011). *Perceived organizational support: Fostering enthusiastic and productive employees*. American Psychological Association. DOI: 10.1037/12318-000

Eldor, L., & Harpaz, I. (2016). A process model of employee engagement: The learning climate and its relationship with extra-role performance behaviors. *Journal of Organizational Behavior, 37*(2), 213–235. DOI: 10.1002/job.2037

Gagné, M.. (2015). The multidimensional work motivation scale: Validation and evidence across countries. *European Journal of Work and Organizational Psychology, 24*(2), 178–196. DOI: 10.1080/1359432X.2013.877892

Gagné, M.. (2022). The motivation at work scale–revised. *Motivation and Emotion, 46*(2), 180–203.

Gagné, M., & Deci, E. L. (2005). Self-determination theory and work motivation. *Journal of Organizational Behavior, 26*(4), 331–362. DOI: 10.1002/job.322

Gallup. (2023). *State of the global workplace report.* Gallup.

Ghosh, P., Rai, A., & Sinha, A. (2013). Organizational justice and employee engagement: Exploring the linkage in public sector banks in India. *Personnel Review, 43*(4), 628–652. DOI: 10.1108/PR-08-2013-0148

Grant, A. M. (2008). The significance of task significance: Job performance effects, relational mechanisms, and boundary conditions. *The Journal of Applied Psychology, 93*(1), 108–124. DOI: 10.1037/0021-9010.93.1.108 PMID: 18211139

Grant, A. M., & Parker, S. K. (2009). Redesigning work design theories: The rise of relational and proactive perspectives. *The Academy of Management Annals, 3*(1), 317–375. DOI: 10.5465/19416520903047327

Hackman, J. R., & Oldham, G. R. (1976). Motivation through the design of work: Test of a theory. *Organizational Behavior and Human Performance, 16*(2), 250–279. DOI: 10.1016/0030-5073(76)90016-7

Humphrey, S. E., Nahrgang, J. D., & Morgeson, F. P. (2007). Integrating motivational, social, and contextual work design features: A meta-analytic summary. *The Journal of Applied Psychology, 92*(5), 1332–1356. DOI: 10.1037/0021-9010.92.5.1332 PMID: 17845089

Jehanzeb, K., & Bashir, N. A. (2017). Training and development programs and employee job satisfaction and retention: Evidence from the banking sector. *Frontiers in Psychology, 8*, 939.

Jiang, K., Lepak, D. P., Hu, J., & Baer, J. C. (2012). How does human resource management influence organizational outcomes? A meta-analytic investigation of mediating mechanisms. *Academy of Management Journal*, *55*(6), 1264–1294. DOI: 10.5465/amj.2011.0088

Kahn, W. A. (1990). Psychological conditions of personal engagement and disengagement. *Academy of Management Journal*, *33*(4), 692–724. DOI: 10.2307/256287

Kaufman, B. E. (2015). *Theoretical perspectives on work and the employment relationship*. Industrial Relations Research Association.

Kehoe, R. R., & Wright, P. M. (2013). The impact of high-performance human resource practices on employees' attitudes and behaviors. *Journal of Management*, *39*(2), 366–391. DOI: 10.1177/0149206310365901

Kim, M., & Beehr, T. A. (2018). Challenge and hindrance demands lead to employees' health and behaviors through intrinsic motivation. *Motivation and Emotion*, *42*(4), 465–481.

Kirkman, B. L., Rosen, B., Tesluk, P. E., & Gibson, C. B. (2019). Enhancing the transfer of learning through cross-training: A resource-based view of team development. *Academy of Management Review*, *44*(3), 583–606.

Kraimer, M. L., Seibert, S. E., Wayne, S. J., Liden, R. C., & Bravo, J. (2011). Antecedents and outcomes of organizational support for development: The critical role of career opportunities. *The Journal of Applied Psychology*, *96*(3), 485–500. DOI: 10.1037/a0021452 PMID: 21114356

Lee, T. W., & Bruvold, N. T. (2003). Creating value for employees: Investment in employee development. *International Journal of Human Resource Management*, *14*(6), 981–1000. DOI: 10.1080/0958519032000106173

Lengnick-Hall, C. A., & Beck, T. E. (2005). Adaptive fit versus robust transformation: How organizations respond to environmental change. *Journal of Management*, *31*(5), 738–757. DOI: 10.1177/0149206305279367

Lengnick-Hall, C. A., Beck, T. E., & Lengnick-Hall, M. L. (2011). Developing a capacity for organizational resilience through strategic human resource management. *Human Resource Management Review*, *21*(3), 243–255. DOI: 10.1016/j.hrmr.2010.07.001

Maslach, C., & Leiter, M. P. (2016). Understanding the burnout experience: Recent research and its implications for psychiatry. *World Psychiatry; Official Journal of the World Psychiatric Association (WPA)*, *15*(2), 103–111. DOI: 10.1002/wps.20311 PMID: 27265691

Maynard, M. T., Luciano, M. M., D'Innocenzo, L., Mathieu, J. E., & Dean, M. D. (2012). Modeling team empowerment: An integrative multilevel model. *Human Resource Management Review*, *22*(2), 127–139.

McKee, M. C., & Froelich, K. A. (2016). Does cross-training improve retention? The role of workload and perceived fairness. *Human Resource Development Quarterly*, *27*(3), 345–364.

Meyer, J. P., & Allen, N. J. (1997). Commitment in the workplace: Theory, research, and application. *Sage (Atlanta, Ga.)*. Advance online publication. DOI: 10.4135/9781452231556

Nahapiet, J., & Ghoshal, S. (1998). Social capital, intellectual capital, and the organizational advantage. *Academy of Management Review*, *23*(2), 242–266. DOI: 10.2307/259373

Noe, R. A., Hollenbeck, J. R., Gerhart, B., & Wright, P. M. (2022). *Human resource management: Gaining a competitive advantage*. McGraw-Hill.

Noe, R. A., Hollenbeck, J. R., Gerhart, B., & Wright, P. M. (2022). *Human resource management: Gaining a competitive advantage*. McGraw-Hill.

Noe, R. A., Hollenbeck, J. R., Gerhart, B., & Wright, P. M. (2023). *Fundamentals of human resource management* (10th ed.). McGraw-Hill.

Nonaka, I., & Takeuchi, H. (1995). *The knowledge-creating company: How Japanese companies create the dynamics of innovation*. Oxford University Press. DOI: 10.1093/oso/9780195092691.001.0001

O'Reilly, C. A.III, & Tushman, M. L. (2013). Organizational ambidexterity: Past, present, and future. *The Academy of Management Perspectives*, *27*(4), 324–338. DOI: 10.5465/amp.2013.0025

Park, T. Y., & Shaw, J. D. (2013). Turnover rates and organizational performance: A meta-analysis. *The Journal of Applied Psychology*, *98*(2), 268–309. DOI: 10.1037/a0030723 PMID: 23244224

Parker, S. K., Bindl, U. K., & Strauss, K. (2010). Making things happen: A model of proactive motivation. *Journal of Management*, *36*(4), 827–856. DOI: 10.1177/0149206310363732

Ployhart, R. E., & Hale, D. (2014). The fascinating psychological microfoundations of human capital resources. *Annual Review of Organizational Psychology and Organizational Behavior*, *1*, 145–172. DOI: 10.1146/annurev-orgpsych-031413-091312

Rousseau, D. M. (1995). Psychological contracts in organizations: Understanding written and unwritten agreements. *Sage (Atlanta, Ga.)*. Advance online publication. DOI: 10.4135/9781452231594

Ryan, R. M., & Deci, E. L. (2017). *Self-determination theory: Basic psychological needs in motivation, development, and wellness*. Guilford Press. DOI: 10.1521/978.14625/28806

Ryan, R. M., & Deci, E. L. (2019). Brick by brick: The origins, development, and future of self-determination theory. *Advances in Motivation Science*, *6*, 111–156. DOI: 10.1016/bs.adms.2019.01.001

Saks, A. M. (2019). Antecedents and consequences of employee engagement revisited. *Journal of Organizational Effectiveness*, *6*(1), 19–38. DOI: 10.1108/JOEPP-06-2018-0034

Salanova, M., Schaufeli, W. B., Xanthopoulou, D., & Bakker, A. B. (2010). The gain spiral of resources and work engagement. *Journal of Vocational Behavior*, *77*(2), 225–236.

Shao, Y., Fang, Y., & Wang, M. (2022). Reskilling and upskilling for the digital era: A cross-country study. *Human Resource Development International*, *25*(2), 158–180.

Spreitzer, G. M. (1995). Psychological empowerment in the workplace: Dimensions, measurement, and validation. *Academy of Management Journal*, *38*(5), 1442–1465. DOI: 10.2307/256865

Teece, D. J. (2018). Business models and dynamic capabilities. *Long Range Planning*, *51*(1), 40–49. DOI: 10.1016/j.lrp.2017.06.007

Teece, D. J., Pisano, G., & Shuen, A. (1997). Dynamic capabilities and strategic management. *Strategic Management Journal*, *18*(7), 509–533. DOI: 10.1002/(SICI)1097-0266(199708)18:7<509::AID-SMJ882>3.0.CO;2-Z

Trépanier, S. G., Fernet, C., & Austin, S. (2019). A longitudinal investigation of workplace bullying, basic need satisfaction, and employee functioning. *Journal of Occupational Health Psychology*, *24*(1), 30–47. PMID: 25151460

Van den Broeck, A., Ferris, D. L., Chang, C. H., & Rosen, C. C. (2016). A review of self-determination theory's basic psychological needs at work. *Journal of Management*, *42*(5), 1195–1229. DOI: 10.1177/0149206316632058

Wang, S., & Noe, R. A. (2010). Knowledge sharing: A review and directions for future research. *Human Resource Management Review*, *20*(2), 115–131. DOI: 10.1016/j.hrmr.2009.10.001

Wright, P. M., & McMahan, G. C. (2011). Exploring human capital: Putting 'human' back into strategic human resource management. *Human Resource Management Journal, 21*(2), 93–104. DOI: 10.1111/j.1748-8583.2010.00165.x

Xanthopoulou, D., Bakker, A. B., Demerouti, E., & Schaufeli, W. B. (2009). Reciprocal relationships between job resources, personal resources, and work engagement. *Journal of Vocational Behavior, 74*(3), 235–244. DOI: 10.1016/j.jvb.2008.11.003

Chapter 7
The Role of Soft Skills in Closing the Skills Gap:
Strategies for Enhancing Workforce Employability in Cross-Training Contexts

Viral S. Ahire
http://orcid.org/0000-0003-0075-2483
Bharati Vidyapeeth (Deemed to be University). Pune & Abhijit Kadam Institute of Management and Social Science, Solapur, India

Ganraj Sobs Mane
Bharati Vidyapeeth (Deemed to be University), Pune, India & Abhijit Kadam Institute of Management and Social Science, Solapur, India

Amruta Deshpande
http://orcid.org/0000-0001-7649-0921
Indira University, India

Sarah Leah Dsouza
http://orcid.org/0000-0002-7225-083X
D.Y. Patil Institute of Master of Computer Applications and Management, Akurdi, India

ABSTRACT

Today's labor market faces talent shortages, rapid technological change, and increasing demand for adaptable workers. To stay resilient, organizations are adopting cross-training, where employees develop skills across multiple roles. However, effective cross-training requires more than technical expertise. Soft skills such as

DOI: 10.4018/979-8-3373-5327-2.ch007

ght © 2027, IGI Global Scientific Publishing. Copying or distributing in print or electronic forms without written permission of IGI Global Scientific Publishing is prohibited. Use of this chapter to generative artificial intelligence (AI) technologies is expressly prohibited. The publisher reserves all rights to license its use for generative AI training and machine learning model development.

communication, teamwork, problem-solving, and self-management are equally important for success in new work environments. This chapter examines how soft skill development strengthens cross-training and helps bridge workforce skill gaps. It identifies six key soft skill areas, reviews effective development strategies in education and workplaces, and offers practical recommendations for educators, HR professionals, and policymakers to design workforce-ready training programs.

1. INTRODUCTION

A shift in the structure of the world's labor market is underway. Technology is advancing at an accelerated rate, demographics are changing, and, because of post-pandemic changes in how organizations operate, Artificial Intelligence (AI) is rapidly diffusing throughout the economy, creating a need for different types of competencies for today's workforce. In response to these trends, tight labor markets - i.e., extremely low unemployment rates, serious talent deficits, and intense competition for qualified workers among employers - have created enormous pressure on employers to develop their own internal workforce flexibility. One way employers are responding to these pressures is through cross-training. Cross-training refers to the systematic development of employees across multiple job functions and competency domains. Cross-training is becoming one of the most important ways employers can create internal workforce flexibility amid extreme pressure on talent acquisition. Despite being widely recognized by employers as critical components of effective workforce development, there is growing recognition that, in addition to technical skill acquisition, cross-training requires a baseline of interpersonal, behavioral, and adaptive skills, or "soft" skills. As such, despite being widely acknowledged by employers as necessary for effective workforce development, there remains a substantial gap between the soft skills of graduating students and those employers need (World Economic Forum, 2020; Robles, 2012). The gap between graduating students' soft skills and employer-required soft skills is especially damaging in cross-training situations. Employees who undergo cross-training must be able to transition into new functional teams, communicate across disciplinary lines, cope with the psychological demands of ambiguous roles, and perform consistently in a dynamic environment. Without a strong foundation in communication, emotional intelligence, adaptability, and collaborative problem-solving, even highly competent employees will fail to achieve maximum benefits from cross-training programs. Therefore, due to the lack of a comprehensive set of soft skills among many employees, much of the benefit of one of the most cost-effective forms of workforce development, cross-training, remains untapped.

Across several related research areas, there are strong theoretical arguments supporting the view that employers should treat soft skills as fundamental building blocks on which successful cross-training depends. For example, studies by labor economists demonstrate that noncognitive and social skills are among the strongest predictors of long-run earnings and employment outcomes (Levy & Murnane, 2004; Deming, 2017; Heckman & Kautz, 2012). Studies conducted by organizational behavior researchers identify interpersonal competence, psychological safety, and collaborative problem-solving as key determinants of teams' ability to adapt in multiple-role environments (Edmondson, 1999; Cannon-Bowers et al., 1998). Research conducted by human resources development experts indicates that motivation and relationships are directly influenced by soft skills and therefore serve as critical mediators of the transfer of employee learning from formal training settings to actual workplace experience (Colquitt et al., 2000; Tracey et al., 1995; Poell, 2017). Collectively, these findings suggest that soft skills are far more than an additional layer on the cake of workforce development; rather, they are the fundamental building blocks on which all successful cross-training must be based.

The purpose of the present study is to examine the previously unexplored relationship between the development of soft skills and the effectiveness of cross-training in addressing the growing shortage of skilled workers in tight labor markets. A large body of literature has focused on the issue of the growing shortage of skilled workers (OECD, 2019; Cappelli, 2015); other bodies of literature have examined the nature of soft skills as they relate to employability (Aggarwal et al., 2025; Andrews & Higson, 2008; Heckman & Kautz, 2012); still other literatures have focused on providing insights into the practical design considerations associated with cross-training programs (Salas et al., 2012; Campion et al., 1994). To date, however, no single study has attempted to synthesize these separate bodies of literature into a unified analysis.

Therefore, this present discussion will attempt to provide a conceptual link between these separate bodies of literature. The chapter is divided into five sections. The first section provides a review of prior literature on the skills gap, soft-skill taxonomies, graduate employability, and workforce cross-training theory. The second section establishes empirically supported criteria for determining the six categories of soft skills most critical to cross-training effectiveness. The third section reviews current practice in higher education institutions and human resource departments regarding soft skill development, with special focus on recent uses of technology-enhanced and AI-mediated learning. The fourth section provides an integrative model for designing cross-training programs that leverage employees' soft skills. Finally, the fifth section distills the integration into a series of best practices and evidence-supported recommendations for policymakers, educators, and organizational leaders.

2. REVIEW OF LITERATURE

2.1 The Skills Gap: Conceptual Foundations and Labor Market Implications

There are several key factors involved in creating an effective cross-training program. As previously mentioned, one of the key components of an effective cross-training program is a well-defined plan that clearly outlines which positions will be filled by cross-trained employees. A defined timeline for completion of the cross-training process should also be included in the plan. In addition, there should be clearly defined goals and expectations for both the cross-trainee and the employee whom they will replace during the cross-training process. The plan should include provisions for how feedback will be provided and evaluated throughout the training process. Finally, a plan for transitioning back to their original job after cross-training is complete would be beneficial. Additionally, as discussed in Chapter 1, a strong support system can significantly impact the success of a cross-training program. Both the cross-trainer and the supervisor of the position being replaced need to understand why the cross-training program is needed and how it will benefit them. They also need to feel comfortable with making changes to meet new demands. A lack of understanding or resistance to change can lead to a lack of commitment from all parties involved.

Another critical factor in a successful cross-training program is adequate time and resources. Cross-training requires a significant investment of time from both the employee undergoing cross-training and management. Management needs to provide the necessary support and resources to ensure that each employee can complete their assigned task. In many cases, additional funding or personnel may be needed to support the transition. To implement cross-training effectively, management must also make a long-term commitment to utilizing newly trained employees. Employees cannot develop new skills if they do not receive opportunities to use them. Management must also ensure that they use the skills developed during cross-training regularly. If employees find out that they spent months developing new skills but were then placed back into their old jobs without the opportunity to use those skills, morale could suffer significantly.

2.2 Defining Soft Skills: Conceptual Boundaries and Taxonomies

The term “soft skills” has been studied and categorized in many ways throughout academic scholarships. There are two main reasons for this: (i) the inherent interdisciplinarity of the concept, and (ii) the fact that there are so many fractured research areas that each claim some degree of ownership over the concept. It is also true that the terms used to describe the set of competencies associated with soft skills are often at odds with one another. That is to say, the very same cluster of competencies may be referred to as soft skills, transferable skills, employability skills, non-cognitive skills, interpersonal competencies, people skills, or foundational competencies, depending on the field or institution where those discussions take place (Spencer & Spencer, 1993; Schulz, 2008; Gibb, 2014). While this terminological difference is primarily cosmetic and does not indicate substantive differences in the conceptualizations of soft skills themselves, it does represent fundamentally different theories about the origins, nature, and modifiability of these competences. As such, they pose significant barriers to developing assessment frameworks and intervention programs aimed at addressing soft-skill deficiencies across disciplines.

In a highly influential empirical study examining what top executives believe to be the most important soft skills among their employees, Robles (2012) found ten soft skills to be viewed as being the most valuable by employers: (i) communication; (ii) courtesy; (iii) flexibility; (iv) honesty or integrity; (v) interpersonal skills; (vi) positive attitude; (vii) professionalism; (viii) responsibility or accountability; (ix) team-work or team player; and (x) work ethic. Although this list provides a good general indication of which soft skills employers view as important, Laker and Powell (2011) proposed a slightly more nuanced way to differentiate between hard and soft skills. Hard skills refer to technical or job-specific knowledge and abilities that can be learned through formal education or training. On the other hand, soft skills refer to socially based knowledge and abilities that are contextualized in time and space and developed through extensive experience and interactions with others over time. A potential limitation of this differentiation is that it creates a false dichotomy between hard and soft skills. Research has demonstrated that effective job performance requires the simultaneous application of both hard and soft skills in complex ways that integrate elements of both (Boyatzis, 1982; McLagan, 1997).

Building upon earlier studies, Heckman and Kautz (2012) produced an empirically informed economic analysis of soft skills using longitudinal labor market data. They demonstrated that non-cognitive characteristics -- such as conscientiousness, emotional stability, and social competence were strong predictors of employment status, wages earned, and career progression. At times, Heckman and Kautz's results indicated that the predictive value of non-cognitive traits was equivalent to, if not greater than, that of cognitive ability as measured by standard assessments. As such, their findings provide new theoretical insights into the nature of soft skills. Rather than viewing soft skills as mere niceties or cultural practices, Heckman and Kautz demonstrated that soft skills should be regarded as economically relevant forms of human capital investment with quantifiable and sizeable payoffs.

Deming (2017) extended Heckman and Kautz's economic analysis by documenting that the labor market has rewarded workers with combinations of cognitive and social skills. Specifically, he documented that jobs requiring a high level of social interaction increased significantly over the past 30 years compared with jobs requiring little to no social interaction. These findings have direct implications for training program designers seeking to implement cross-training and for organizations seeking to prioritize soft-skill development as part of an overall organizational learning strategy. To facilitate discussion related to the present study, soft skills will be defined here as the collection of interpersonal, cognitive-behavioral, emotional, and self-regulatory competencies required to perform successfully in both social and organizational settings. Additionally, successful performance in cross-training contexts requires individuals to manage both internal psychological processes and external relationships with colleagues across functional boundaries (Goleman, 1995; Mayer & Salovey, 1997; Luthans, 2002).

2.3 Soft Skills, Employability, and Graduate Transition

The correlation between soft skills and graduate employment is widely covered by the higher education research community. The vast amount of data collected by the research community shows a clear trend supporting the notion that non-academic skills are preferred by employers during the graduate recruitment process. According to Andrews and Higson (2008), soft skills, such as communication, flexibility, dependability, and self-control, were rated above technical skills and specialized knowledge when employers evaluated graduates for recruitment into graduate roles in four different European Countries. It was also found that, although the companies evaluated were from various sectors and locations, there was no difference in employers' preferences for soft skills by location or industry. This demonstrates that the preference for soft skills in the recruitment process can be considered an inherent characteristic of modern-day labor markets, rather than being culturally or industrially based.

Bridgstock (2009) argues that while higher education has focused on preparing students for their chosen field through academic studies, career management and communication skills are often neglected, leading to graduates having difficulty adapting to their career after graduating. Bridgstock's definition of career management skills includes self-awareness, proactively managing your career, developing networks, and developing your own professional identity. All of these elements reflect the behaviors required for successful cross-training, in which employees must identify their own training needs, establish credibility in new job functions, and create a new professional identity as they move across role boundaries. Harvey (2001) demonstrated that it is graduates' ability to be personally effective and to relate effectively in the workplace, rather than just their academic achievements, that influences their success in gaining graduate employment. This has important implications for how we measure and communicate the value of degrees awarded by Higher Education Institutions.

Tomlinson (2012) proposes a more detailed model of graduate employability than previous models, incorporating social and cultural capital, the formation of identity, and proactive career-path narrative creation. All three of Tomlinson's models require graduates to possess a range of interpersonal and self-regulatory soft skills. Tomlinson's model is particularly useful for its focus on agency: Graduates who successfully transition into professional employment are not simply passive recipients of formal qualifications but active creators of professional identities and career paths. In addition, graduates will be able to demonstrate an entrepreneurial approach to their careers: They will be able to take initiative, seek feedback, build relationships and manage their own career development. These abilities are exactly those that cross-training programs aim to foster and that employers need to find in a competitive labor market (Dweck, 2006; Kegan, 1994).

Suleman (2018) summarized several conceptual models of employable skills drawn from different disciplines and found that communication, teamwork, problem-solving, taking initiative, and the ability to learn continue to be the top five skills identified by employers, governments, and academics around the world. The overlap between Suleman's findings and the requirements of a cross-training environment is striking and provides a robust empirical base for the author's main argument. Employees with well-developed capabilities in these five areas will be significantly better equipped to navigate the relational and adaptive aspects of expanding their roles across functional lines. Therefore, Sulemans' findings confirm that graduate employability-oriented soft-skill development and cross-training effectiveness are two closely related developmental priorities (Hager & Holland, 2006; Clarke, 2018; Rychen & Salganik, 2003).

2.4 Emotional Intelligence as a Cross-Training Enabler

Among the several dimensions of soft skills, there has been particularly extensive academic research on emotional intelligence (EI). As identified by Mayer and Salovey (1997), EI represents the ability to recognize, evaluate, express, control and utilize one's own emotions and those of others. The literature has noted that EI is especially relevant when considering employees' adaptability in the workplace and their effectiveness in interacting with colleagues. Goleman (1995) brought this topic to the forefront and made a very influential claim that emotionally intelligent individuals will succeed better in life than those who are cognitively gifted. While many scholars agree with this statement, others have challenged this assumption because the effects of EI do not occur in isolation from cognitive abilities and personality characteristics. For example, recent studies have shown that EI does significantly contribute to individual job performance, but these contributions are typically independent of both cognitive ability and personality traits. It is most often these independent contributions of EI that support successful adaptation during cross-training periods, due to the potential for increased interpersonal interaction, ambiguity in role assignments, and emotional labor involved in such transitions (Luthans, 2002; Caballero & Walker, 2010).

During cross-training, employees experience various challenges. Cross-trained workers frequently face uncertain or ambiguous work environments. They are often asked to perform tasks in unfamiliar positions. In addition to uncertainty about how they will function in their new positions, employees face the challenge of developing working relationships with new coworkers. Cross-trained employees are further stressed when tasked with evaluating their own performance while being evaluated themselves. Under such circumstances, emotional intelligence serves as a valuable resource. Research has demonstrated that employees possessing high levels of emotional intelligence (EI) tend to exhibit greater resiliency when transitioning to different roles (Bakker & Demerouti, 2007); communicate effectively in times of stress and uncertainty (Goleman, 1995); resolve conflicts more successfully among new team members (Caballero & Walker, 2010); and respond positively to constructive feedback and developmental coaching (Goleman, 1995; Bakker & Demerouti, 2007). All of these behaviors represent key indicators of successful cross-training integration and provide substantial theoretical and empirical justification for including EI as a major aspect of cross-training preparation.

Although Goleman (1995) stated that EI was not necessarily an innate ability but rather a skill that could be developed, he did so as a part of his argument that EI should be considered as a competency in a business environment. This is important because it implies that if EI is developable, as a growing body of evidence suggests, businesses may include specific EI development elements in their cross-training programs. Businesses may use a variety of methods to help develop employees' EI in cross-training programs. Some possible examples of such development opportunities include reflective practice, coaching, peer feedback systems, and experiential learning. Such activities may ultimately lead to faster cross-training integration and improved employee well-being throughout the transition period (Mezirow, 1991; Kolb, 1984; Schön, 1983). The Job Demands- Resources (JD-R) model (Bakker &

Demerouti, 2007) provides additional support for this view. According to the JD-R model, "personal resources" (such as emotional intelligence, self-efficacy, and resilience) serve as buffers against the demands of job growth and the expanding responsibilities of cross-training.

2.5 Workforce Cross-Training: Theory and Practice

The knowledge base on cross-training employees has developed over time through numerous studies in the areas of organizational behavior, operations management, and human resources. Campion, Cheraskin, and Stevens (1994) conducted an important study of job rotation, a common method of cross-training, and found positive relationships with the development of new career opportunities. These findings also identified many positive outcomes of job rotation, including increased organizational commitment, job enrichment, improved promotion opportunities, and greater job satisfaction. Campion, Cheraskin, and Stevens (1994) provide a foundation for future research on cross-training, and their results are widely cited in the literature.

Recent studies have expanded the body of research regarding cross-training to include its use in team-based organizations. As teams become increasingly used in modern society and business, the need to develop and maintain effective teams is more critical than ever. Cannon-Bowers, Salas, Blickensderfer, and Bowers (1998) demonstrate the benefits of cross-training at team level. They show that when team members understand each other's roles and responsibilities in their jobs, the team can operate more effectively, be more operationally flexible, and distribute the workload differently depending on current staffing levels. Following this study, Salas and colleagues (2012) conducted a comprehensive review of the field of training and development. This review confirmed that, while cross-training can yield significant improvements in team performance when properly planned and implemented through intentional practice and feedback, it is one of the best-supported methods for improving team performance.

Although the benefits of cross-training have been documented extensively in academic literature, many organizations continue to struggle to implement successful cross-training programs. Some of the common barriers to implementing successful cross-training programs include employee resistance due to fear of role identity loss or devaluation of existing roles; manager reluctance to allow employees to leave their normal duties to participate in training; and lack of formal evaluation procedures to measure return on investment (ROI) of the cross-training program. Many researchers believe that some of the biggest obstacles facing organizations wishing to implement a successful cross-training program are behavioral or relationship issues rather than technical ones. Laker and Powell (2011) state that "the single most consistent barrier to cross-training is not the technology itself, but people."

Edmondson (1999) identifies similar barriers. She states that if an organization wishes to successfully implement a cross-training program, it will need to improve its ability to communicate effectively with employees, establish trust, encourage employees' willingness to adapt to different situations, and enhance employees' confidence in working with others. The soft skills that enable employees to communicate effectively across functional boundaries, manage the emotional demands of role transitions, build trust with unfamiliar colleagues, and sustain motivation to learn amid uncertainty are not incidental to cross-training success — they are what cross-training fundamentally requires. Without deliberate investment in developing these competencies, cross-training programs will consistently under-deliver on their potential, regardless of the quality of the technical content they provide (Colquitt et al., 2000; Tracey et al., 1995; Poell, 2017).

3. SOFT SKILLS CRITICAL TO CROSS-TRAINING SUCCESS

The following six soft skill clusters emerged consistently across the reviewed literature as the competencies most strongly associated with successful workforce adaptability and cross-functional role transition. While the broader soft skills literature identifies dozens of potentially relevant competencies, not all are equally important to cross-training effectiveness. An analytical focus on the soft skill clusters most directly implicated in the demands of cross-functional role transition, informed by both the theoretical frameworks reviewed above and empirical evidence from cross-training outcomes, yields six core competency clusters that warrant priority attention in cross-training program design and HR development strategy.

3.1 Communication and Active Listening

Communication is consistently identified as the most important soft skill in employer surveys and employability research (Robles, 2012; Andrews & Higson, 2008; Suleman, 2018). In cross-training contexts, the communicative demands are particularly acute. Employees rotating through unfamiliar functional roles must communicate their questions, uncertainties, and learning needs with clarity and confidence; they must listen actively and empathetically to colleagues with different professional vocabularies, mental models, and work practices; and they must navigate the social dynamics of being simultaneously a novice with respect to their new functional context and an experienced professional, whose perspectives and contributions remain valuable. This combination of communicative humility and professional confidence is a sophisticated interpersonal skill that cannot be taken for granted and must be deliberately developed (Senge, 1990; Garavan & McGuire, 2001).

Active Listening: The ability to focus on a person's message (both spoken and unspoken) and their context, while avoiding judgment or response-making, is an important part of being competent at communication. However, most training programs provide little explicit instruction regarding active listening. As such, it is difficult to emphasize how important it is for successful cross-functional training. Individuals who engage in active listening can develop relationships with their new coworkers, understand the unwritten rules, protocols, or culture of unfamiliar work environments, and avoid many misunderstandings and conflicting expectations that occur during role changes. According to Cross & Parker (2004), one of the major reasons employees are able to successfully integrate into an organization and share knowledge is by joining a social network. Since active listening is a key element of social network integration, it is another reason why cross-functional employees need to possess this competency.

3.2 Adaptability and Cognitive Flexibility

Adaptability is the ability to change how you act, think, and react emotionally when faced with changes in the environment. In other words, it is the main soft skill for cross-training. The idea of cross-training implies a certain amount of disruption: Employees give up the skills, status, and routines that come with being good at what they do best and try to navigate through a period of uncertainty, vulnerability, and possibly confusion about where things stand or will go as they learn something new (Dweck, 2006; Mezirow, 1991).

Cognitive flexibility is the ability to switch back and forth mentally among different ways of thinking; to have two different thoughts at the same time; and to modify your point of view based on additional data or insight. Cognitive flexibility is the intellectual aspect of adaptability most relevant to successful cross-training. People with high levels of cognitive flexibility are much better able to comprehend why unfamiliar business units operate differently; see the constraints and priorities that dictate how each department operates; and find commonalities between their area of expertise and a new field (Vygotsky, 1978; Kolb, 1984; Honey & Mumford, 1986). Dweck's (2006) growth mindset framework provides a practical lens on this competency: employees who believe their abilities can be developed through effort and learning are substantially more likely to embrace the challenges of cross-training than those who view intelligence and skill as fixed attributes.

3.3 Emotional Intelligence and Self-Regulation

As established in the literature review, emotional intelligence plays a particularly important role in the soft skills architecture for cross-training success. Self-regulation — the capacity to manage one's emotional states, impulses, and cognitive responses in ways that serve productive goal-directed behavior — is the dimension of EI most directly implicated in the moment-to-moment demands of cross-training transitions. Employees who struggle to manage frustration, anxiety, and self-doubt in the face of performance challenges are likely to disengage from cross-training activities, to avoid the risk-taking that learning in unfamiliar contexts requires, and to project defensive behaviors that undermine their integration into new functional teams (Bakker & Demerouti, 2007; Luthans, 2002; Goleman, 1995).

The construct of psychological capital (PsyCap), developed by Luthans (2002), provides a useful integrative framework for understanding the dispositional resources that support effective cross-training engagement. PsyCap encompasses four components — hope, efficacy, resilience, and optimism — each of which can be developed through targeted interventions and directly supports the behavioral demands of cross-functional role transitions. Employees with high PsyCap are more likely to set ambitious learning goals for their cross-training experiences, to persist in the face of setbacks and performance difficulties, to recover quickly from errors and evaluative feedback, and to maintain a constructive orientation toward the challenges and opportunities that unfamiliar functional environments present. Organizations that invest in PsyCap development as part of cross-training preparation are, in effect, building the psychological infrastructure that makes cross-training possible (Bandura, 1997; Pajares, 1997).

3.4 Collaborative Problem-Solving and Teamwork

Cross-training almost invariably involves intensive teamwork, whether through job shadowing, co-working with colleagues in a new functional area, or leading a project that draws on multiple functional perspectives. The collaborative problem-solving demands of these experiences are substantial. Employees must contribute to team discussions in which they are relative novices, navigate disagreements with colleagues whose expertise exceeds their own in the new domain, and maintain productive working relationships across professional boundaries that are often defined by different values, incentive structures, and performance metrics (Cannon-Bowers et al., 1998; Edmondson, 1999; Wenger, 1998)

Edmondson's (1999) concept of psychological safety, the shared belief that team members can take interpersonal risks without fear of punishment or humiliation, is particularly relevant to cross-training contexts. Teams that provide psychological safety enable employees in cross-training transitions to ask questions, acknowledge uncertainty, and share half-formed ideas without fear of negative evaluation — precisely the behaviors that accelerate learning in unfamiliar functional contexts. Conversely, teams with low psychological safety create conditions in which cross-training employees are likely to mask their uncertainties, avoid visible risk-taking, and learn more slowly and more superficially than they would in a more supportive environment. Building psychological safety within cross-functional teams is therefore both a teamwork skill and a structural design challenge for organizations implementing cross-training programs (Salas et al., 2012; Cannon-Bowers et al., 1998)

3.5 Self-Directed Learning and Learning Agility

Learning agility — the capacity and willingness to learn rapidly from new experiences, to apply that learning proactively in new contexts, and to sustain motivation in the face of the cognitive demands of continuous skill development — is a soft skill that has received growing scholarly and practitioner attention as a predictor of leadership potential and career adaptability (Heslin, 2005; Garavan & McGuire, 2001). Learning agility is a functional necessity rather than a mere advantage in the context of cross training. Several employees may be unable to learn quickly from unfamiliar environments. Some employees will need to receive extensive formal instruction before they feel confident enough to perform in a new job. And some employees will need to develop the ability to reflect on and control their own learning processes (Metacognition) to advance at a satisfactory pace in a cross-training program. All three types of employees will ultimately produce very little added value for an organization which has spent time developing them as part of its employee development process (Ellström, 2001; Illeris, 2011; Poell, 2017).

Self-directed learning refers to the motivational and strategic components of learning agility that enable individuals to independently identify knowledge gaps and skill deficiencies relevant to their current roles and future career aspirations. Self-directed learning includes an individual's ability to assess their own learning needs and establish specific learning objectives. The individual must also be able to identify the most effective sources and methods available for achieving those objectives. Finally, he or she must be capable of assessing whether or not he or she has achieved those objectives. When employers provide opportunities for their current workforce members to develop these capabilities, they create a "Multiplier Effect" on their cross-training investments. By developing self-directed learners in each of their workforce members, the employer creates an ongoing source of additional learning and adaptation among all of their workforce members, long after the cross-training program has been completed. This results in additional returns on the employer's original investment in employee development, as well as an ongoing self-renewing learning culture within the organization that will be essential for success during times when there are significant constraints on the availability of qualified labor (Fenwick, 2010; Knowles, cited in Noe, 2017; Rainbird et al., 2004; Senge, 1990),

3.6 Resilience and Tolerance for Ambiguity

The inherent disruption of professional self-concept. As employees transition through the cross-training process to develop competency in an alternate functional area, they must accept a temporary but psychologically relevant loss of competency, status and recognition. These losses can be accompanied by increased feelings of anxiety, self-doubt and a diminished feeling of control over their profession. When organizations promote performance and stigmatize visible error (Mezirow, 1991; Kegan, 1994; Schon, 1983), it is even more difficult for employees to cope with the psychological aspects of transitioning into a different functional area. Resilience is defined as the ability to continue to perform adaptively while maintaining positive levels of well-being when confronted with stressors and significant changes in one's life. Employees possessing high levels of resilience are able to more effectively manage the psychological requirements associated with transitioning into a different functional area and therefore less likely to disengage from the cross-training process or retreat to a familiar functional area.

Ambiguity Tolerance. Ambiguity tolerance is also an important soft-skill for cross-functionally trained employees. However, unlike resilience, ambiguity tolerance specifically addresses an employee's ability to function within environments where there is ambiguity (uncertainty), limited information available, and undefined role expectations. Cross-trained employees will inevitably encounter various situations in which they have limited knowledge regarding what is acceptable (standards), how to complete tasks appropriately (procedures), and what is culturally acceptable (norms) in their new functional environment. Employees exhibiting curiosity, asking strategic questions, and taking actions based on assumptions about how things should work are generally quicker and more effective at integrating themselves into their new functional areas compared to those experiencing excessive uncertainty resulting in paralysis, or retreating to the comfort zone of their original functional domain (Bakker & Demerouti, 2007; Garavan & McGuire, 2001; Luthans, 2002).

4. STRATEGIES FOR SOFT SKILLS DEVELOPMENT

The previous study demonstrated the relevance of soft skills to theory and practice in their contribution to the success of a cross-training program. The next major concern to address is the method or strategy by which this set of competences is developed, either as an organization developing its new hires with regard to preparation for employment, as an employer develops a new hire through a cross-training program (with support from HR), or as an HR practitioner supports an employee's transition from one functional role to another. In addressing the three areas of concern above, the present discussion will outline the primary methods or strategies used in each area, drawing on research-based knowledge from training science, educational psychology, and organizational development.

4.1 Higher Education Approaches to Soft Skills Development

Higher Education Institutions have a very strategic role in the "soft skills" pipeline. They form the initial professional (and therefore most) of the labor force. A significant challenge exists here, however: the traditional model of HE delivery (i.e., lectures based on academic discipline; assessment by formal examination or writing assignment) has limited capacity to develop those competences defined as 'soft skills' (interpersonal, behavioral, and self-regulation). Meaningful soft skills development requires experiential engagement, reflective practice, peer interaction, and formative feedback — all of which demand pedagogical approaches that are more resource-intensive, more difficult to assess at scale, and more threatening to established disciplinary boundaries than traditional modes of university teaching (Bridgstock, 2009; Hager & Holland, 2006; Tomlinson, 2012; Adtani et al., 2025)

Work-integrated learning (WIL) encompasses internships, placements, cooperative education programs, and project-based learning partnerships with industry, and is among the most effective institutional strategies for developing soft skills in higher education contexts. WIL places students in authentic professional environments where the interpersonal, adaptive, and self-regulatory demands of real work provide natural opportunities for development in communication, teamwork, resilience, and learning agility (Caballero & Walker, 2010; Andrews & Higson, 2008). The critical design condition for WIL to realize its soft skills development potential is the quality of reflection that accompanies the work experience: students who engage in structured reflection — through journals, mentoring conversations, portfolio development, and peer debriefing — extract significantly greater learning from their WIL experiences than those who complete placements without reflective scaffolding (Schon, 1983; Kolb, 1984; Mezirow, 1991)

Problem-based learning (PBL), team projects, and collaborative learning designs in formal curricula also provide structured opportunities for soft-skill development in conventional academic programs. When well-designed, these pedagogical approaches create conditions in which students must negotiate roles and responsibilities, manage interpersonal conflict, communicate across disciplinary boundaries, and sustain productive collaboration under conditions of time pressure and evaluative uncertainty, all of which are direct rehearsals for the behavioral demands of cross-training contexts (Bloom, 1956; Vygotsky, 1978; Garavan & McGuire, 2001). The developmental value of these approaches is maximized when they incorporate explicit attention to the soft skills at work naming and theorizing the interpersonal and self-regulatory processes students are navigating, rather than treating them as invisible background conditions of academic work.

4.2 Organizational and HR Practitioner Strategies

Within organizational contexts, the development of soft skills for cross-training effectiveness is primarily the responsibility of human resource development practitioners — who design and deliver learning interventions — and of line managers and supervisors, who create day-to-day conditions in which soft skills are practiced, reinforced, or undermined. Evidence-based organizational soft skills development identifies several strategies that are particularly effective when embedded in cross-training programs (Noe, 2017; Salas et al., 2012; Goldstein & Ford, 2002)

Structured coaching and mentoring are among the most powerful and well-evidenced organizational strategies for developing soft skills. Executive coaching has been shown to produce significant improvements in self-awareness, communication effectiveness, and interpersonal influence when delivered by trained practitioners with clear developmental objectives and regular feedback loops (Joo, 2010; Day, 2001; Zenger & Folkman, 2009). In cross-training contexts, coaching relationships serve an additional function: they provide employees with a trusted relational resource and a consistent developmental partner at a time when most of their professional relationships are in flux. The coach or mentor can help the cross-training employee to process the emotional demands of role transition, to identify transferable competencies from their primary functional domain, to develop strategies for building credibility in their new functional context, and to sustain motivation and self-efficacy through the inevitable periods of performance difficulty (Bandura, 1997; Luthans, 2002).

Structured feedback mechanisms, including 360-degree feedback assessments, behavioral observations, and coaching conversations, and peer review processes, are essential components of organizational soft-skills development strategies. Soft skills are, by nature, relational constructs: they manifest only in the context of social interaction, and their development depends critically on the quality and consistency of the feedback individuals receive about their interpersonal impact and behavioral effectiveness. The organizations that develop a culture of effective feedback — which includes providing specific, caring, normalizing and expected constructive developmental feedback — provide an environment in which soft skill development is developed through the work process itself, not as a result of expensive separate training programs (Farr & Tesluk, 1997; Kirkpatrick, 1994; Tracey et al., 1995).

Action learning, where employees work together on current organizational issues and reflect together on their experience and use those reflections to address the issue(s) at hand and their personal development, can be a very powerful way to develop many different soft skills. It allows for complexity, peer support and reflection, all in an organized structure. The results of action-learning include the development of communication, collaborative problem solving, team-work and learning agility (Wenger, 1998; Revans, referenced in Garavan & McGuire, 2001; Senge, 1990), along with producing tangible organizational value.

4.3 Experiential and Situated Learning Approaches

The theoretical foundation for experiential soft skills development is provided by Kolb's (1984) experiential learning cycle, which proposes that effective learning proceeds through a four-stage iterative process: concrete experience, reflective observation, abstract conceptualization, and active experimentation. Applied to soft skills development in cross-training contexts, this cycle suggests that employees acquire and refine interpersonal and adaptive competencies not primarily through formal instruction but through cycles of deliberate experience, guided reflection, theoretical sense-making, and renewed experimentation with more sophisticated behavioral strategies. This framework has important implications for program design: it suggests that the sequencing and scaffolding of experiences matter at least as much as the content of any formal training components provided (Kolb, 1984; Honey & Mumford, 1986; Schon, 1983).

Wenger's (1998) communities of practice framework provides a complementary theoretical lens, emphasizing the social and relational dimensions of learning that are particularly relevant to cross-training contexts. Wenger argued that learning is fundamentally a process of social participation of gradually becoming a member of a community of practice through legitimate peripheral participation that progressively deepens as the learner develops competence and social credibility within the community. The process for training employees to transition from one function into another is identical to what Wenger described as entering a new functional "community of practice". The employee will begin with the same type of involvement in the new functional community of practice through an initial period of peripheral involvement where the employee observes, participates, assists, and asks questions; next the employee assumes increasing amounts of responsibility as the employee demonstrates increased levels of competence and as the employer develops more trust in the employee; finally when the employee has reached full membership within the new functional community of practice, then all learning associated with the cross training experience is incorporated into both the employee's professional identity and their current practice repertoire (Ellström, 2001; Rainbird et al., 2004; Wenger, 1998).

4.4 Technology-Enhanced and AI-Mediated Development

The emergence of digital learning platforms, technology-enabled adaptive learning systems, and AI enabled-coaching applications have generated new opportunities for large-scale soft-skills development. Examples include virtual-reality simulation training programs. Simulation training allows for high fidelity experiential learning of interpersonal skills training including: difficult conversations; cross-functional team meeting interactions; conflict management strategies. Training participants can use this environment for safe experimentation, receive immediate, specific feedback on their performance, and repeat the same exercise(s) an unlimited number of times with no risk or consequence (OECD, 2019; World Economic Forum, 2020). Preliminary research indicates that interpersonal skills training utilizing virtual-reality simulations will result in rapid and sustained improvements in communication competence; empathy; and conflict management abilities. Additionally, studies indicate that the transfer of skills learned in the simulated environment to actual workplace behaviors is comparable to those previously experienced using traditional classroom-based training models.

Another area where significant advancements in technology have been made to support the development of soft-skills is through AI enabled-coaching platforms. These platforms utilize natural-language-processing capabilities and behavioral-analysis methods to provide individualized and timely feedback to employees on how they communicate; the emotional tone used during the conversation; and their overall level of interpersonal effectiveness. Feedback is derived from information obtained from employee written communications; audio or video recordings of employee conversations; and employee maintained self-reporting journals. While there is limited research available on the use of AI-technology as a means to enhance employee soft-skills; preliminary studies suggest that employees who receive coaching via AI-platforms will be provided with increased self-awareness -- a fundamental component of emotional intelligence than would be possible for human coaches or mentors due to limited observation capacity (World Economic Forum, 2020; OECD, 2019). Combining these emerging technologies into cross-training program designs will allow organizations to expand their ability to develop soft-skills on a larger scale while also increasing the degree of personalization available to employees.

5. An Integrated Framework for Soft Skills-Enabled Cross-Training

Previous chapters demonstrated the theoretical importance of soft skills to successful cross-training, identified the six primary soft-skill areas which are the most important for cross training, and examined the primary strategies for developing those soft-skills across both educational and business settings. In this present chapter all three will synthesize into one comprehensive approach or framework. That framework is called the Soft Skills Enabled Cross Training (SSECT) Framework. It is intended to provide instructional designers with an integrative, theoretical structure that can be used to develop cross-training programs using soft skills as a central part of their design strategy rather than something added on after they have been developed.

The SSECT Framework rests on three foundational premises. The first is that soft skills and technical skill development are mutually reinforced rather than competing priorities in cross-training program design. When employees engage in cross-training activities with well-developed communication, adaptability, and self-regulatory competencies, they learn technical content more quickly, transfer it more effectively, and derive greater developmental value from cross-functional exposures. Conversely, technical cross-training experiences provide natural contexts within which soft skills can be practiced, challenged, and refined. The integration of soft and technical skill development within cross-training programs is therefore a positive-sum design choice, not a zero-sum trade-off (Laker & Powell, 2011; Salas et al., 2012; Noe, 2017)

The Second premise is that soft skills development in cross-training contexts must be deliberately scaffolded rather than assumed to occur organically through exposure alone. The evidence reviewed in this study consistently shows that experiential learning without a reflective structure produces uneven, often superficial developmental outcomes. Cross-training programs must therefore incorporate structured pre-departure preparation helping employees to anticipate the interpersonal and emotional demands of role transition; reflective check-in processes during the cross-training experience providing employees with guided opportunities to process their learning and manage the psychological demands of role ambiguity; and integrative post-program debriefing supporting employees to consolidate and transfer their soft skill development back into their primary functional contexts and forward into their ongoing career trajectories (Kolb, 1984; Schon, 1983; Mezirow, 1991; Kirkpatrick, 1994, Deshpande et al., 2024)

The third premise is that organizational conditions particularly the managerial climate and team culture in which cross-training occurs are as important as program design in determining outcomes of soft skills development. Cross-training employees who work within teams characterized by psychological safety, developmental feedback culture, and leadership that models interpersonal openness and learning agility are substantially better positioned to develop and apply soft skills than those operating in environments that reward performance perfection, penalize visible mistakes, or treat cross-training as a bureaucratic formality rather than a genuine developmental investment (Edmondson, 1999; Bakker & Demerouti, 2007; Day, 2001) The SSECT Framework, therefore, incorporates a set of organizational readiness conditions that organizations must cultivate before cross-training programs can be expected to realize their full potential for soft skills development.

Operating at three levels: Individual, Program, and Organizational- the SSECT Framework proposes that effective soft-skills-enabled cross-training is achieved through the simultaneous alignment of actions across all three levels. At the individual level, employees are prepared for the interpersonal and psychological demands of cross-functional role transitions through targeted pre-program coaching, self-assessment, and reflective goal setting. At the program level, cross-training curricula are designed to integrate structured soft-skills development with technical skill acquisition through experiential learning, peer mentoring, and formative feedback. At the organizational level, the cultural, managerial, and structural conditions that enable soft skills development psychological safety, developmental feedback, visible leadership commitment to cross-training, and clear performance recognition for cross-functional competence development are systematically cultivated and assessed (Prahalad & Hamel, 1990; Lado & Wilson, 1994; Senge, 1990).

Figure 1 presents the proposed Soft Skills Enabled Cross-Training (SSECT) Framework. The SSECT framework is designed not only as a conceptual model but also as a practical implementation guide for organizations seeking to integrate soft skills development into workforce cross-training initiatives. By aligning employee preparedness, structured developmental design, and organizational support systems, the framework provides a holistic approach for improving workforce adaptability and long-term employability. The framework operates across three interconnected levels: Individual, Program, and Organizational demonstrating how the integration of soft skills development with technical cross-training contributes to workforce adaptability, employability, and organizational resilience.

Figure 1. The Soft Skills Enabled Cross-Training (SSECT) Framework

Table 1. Core Soft Skills and Their Relevance to Cross-Training

No.	Soft Skill Cluster	Relevance to Cross-Training	Example in Workplace
1	Communication & Active Listening	Helps employees understand new roles, clarify expectations, and build strong relationships with unfamiliar teams and stakeholders.	• *Example:* Asking clarifying questions and summarizing client needs during a job rotation.
2	Adaptability & Cognitive Flexibility	Enables employees to adjust to changing responsibilities, new processes, and different team cultures with confidence.	• *Example:* Transitioning from a technical role to a customer-facing function with different expectations.
3	Emotional Intelligence & Self-Regulation	Helps employees manage stress, control emotions, and navigate interpersonal dynamics during role transitions.	• *Example:* Handling client pressure or difficult feedback calmly and professionally.
4	Collaborative Problem-Solving & Teamwork	Supports effective collaboration across departments to solve problems, sharing diverse perspectives and expertise.	• *Example:* Working on a cross-functional project to develop a solution for a client issue.
5	Self-Directed Learning & Learning Agility	Encourages continuous learning, curiosity, and the ability to quickly acquire new knowledge and skills independently.	• *Example:* Learning new software tools or business processes without extensive supervision.
6	Resilience & Tolerance for Ambiguity	Helps employees remain productive, positive, and persistent during uncertain, complex, or unfamiliar transitions.	• *Example:* Managing unfamiliar tasks with limited guidance and adapting until clarity is achieved.

These six soft skill clusters collectively strengthen an employee's ability to transition across roles, functions, and teams—ensuring the success of cross-training initiatives.

The SSECT Framework emphasizes that successful cross-training outcomes cannot be achieved through technical instruction alone. Instead, effective workforce transition depends upon the alignment of employee preparedness, structured developmental program design, and supportive organizational culture.

5.1 Illustrative Application of the SSECT Framework

Consider an employee transitioning from a technical software development role to a client-facing business analyst role within an IT organization.

At the individual level, the employee conducts self-assessment and coaching to identify development needs in communication, emotional intelligence, adaptability, and client interaction. The reflective goal-setting activities psychologically prepare the employee for the transition to a more interpersonal, less technical role.

At the Program level, the organization has embedded structured mentoring, role-shadowing, client meeting simulations, and collaborative cross-functional projects into the cross-training curriculum. Opportunities for experiential learning and regular feedback sessions allow the employee to practice technical translation and interpersonal communication skills in realistic work settings.

At the Organizational level, managers foster a psychologically safe environment in which mistakes are viewed as opportunities for learning, rather than failures. Leadership actively supports cross-functional mobility via recognition systems, developmental feedback, and flexible performance expectations during the transition period.

By aligning the three levels, the SSECT Framework enables smoother transitions between roles, greater confidence and collaboration among employees, and greater adaptability in the workforce.

A similar application of the SSECT framework may be observed in organizations undergoing digital transformation initiatives. For example, when employees transition from traditional operational roles into technology-supported or customer-facing functions, technical instruction alone is often insufficient. Employees must simultaneously develop communication competence, adaptability, emotional resilience, and collaborative problem-solving abilities to function effectively in unfamiliar work environments. Organizations that combine technical cross-training with mentoring, reflective coaching, peer collaboration, and psychologically safe learning environments are more likely to achieve smoother workforce transitions, stronger employee confidence, and improved organizational resilience during periods of rapid change.

6. BEST PRACTICES AND EVIDENCE-BASED RECOMMENDATIONS

Drawing on the integrated theoretical and empirical analysis developed throughout this study, the following evidence-based recommendations are offered for practitioners designing and delivering soft-skills-enabled cross-training programs in tight labor markets. These recommendations are organized into three practitioner audiences: higher education leaders and faculty; HR professionals and organizational learning designers; and organizational leaders and senior managers. (Wani et al., 2025)

6.1 Recommendations for Higher Education

Higher education institutions should conduct systematic curriculum audits to identify opportunities for soft skills development embedded in their academic programs and redesign assessment frameworks to recognize and reward interpersonal, communicative, and self-regulatory competencies alongside disciplinary knowledge acquisition. The development of co-curricular competency recognition frameworks — such as digital badges, e-portfolios, and graduate attribute certificates — can provide students with tangible evidence of soft-skill development that is both intelligible and valuable to employers navigating soft-skills-intensive selection processes (Hager & Holland, 2006; Bridgstock, 2009; Clarke, 2018).

Faculty development programs should prioritize the pedagogical shift from knowledge transmission to competency cultivation — equipping academic staff with facilitation skills, assessment strategies, and theoretical frameworks to embed soft-skills development within their subject-specific teaching. This requires investment in academic professional development that goes beyond the traditional focus on disciplinary expertise and research capability, recognizing that the teaching of interpersonal and behavioral competence is a sophisticated professional skill in its own right (Tomlinson, 2012; Garavan & McGuire, 2001; Bloom, 1956).

6.2 Recommendations for HR Professionals and Learning Designers

Organizations should develop explicit soft-skills competency frameworks that define the specific interpersonal, adaptive, and self-regulatory competencies required for effective participation in cross-training programs and use these frameworks to inform both the selection of employees for cross-training opportunities and the design of pre-program development support. The six soft skill clusters identified in this current chapter communication and active listening, adaptability and cognitive flexibility, emotional intelligence and self-regulation, collaborative problem-solving and teamwork, self-directed learning and learning agility, and resilience and tolerance for ambiguity provide a research-grounded starting point for such frameworks, which should be contextualized to the specific functional and cultural requirements of individual organizations (Spencer & Spencer, 1993; McLagan, 1997; Boyatzis, 1982)

Cross-training program designs should incorporate structured soft-skills development components across all three phases of the cross-training journey: preparation, immersion, and integration. Pre-program preparation should include self-assessment, goal-setting, and interpersonal skill coaching; immersive phases should incorporate structured peer mentoring, psychological safety assessments, and regular reflective check-in processes; and post-program integration should include deliberate transfer support, 360-degree feedback, and career development conversations that position cross-training learning as a foundation for future role expansion (Kirkpatrick, 1994; Colquitt et al., 2000; Tracey et al., 1995).

In addition to developmental support, organizations should establish structured mechanisms to assess soft-skill development outcomes throughout the cross-training process. Behavioral indicators such as communication effectiveness, adaptability during role transitions, collaborative participation, and responsiveness to feedback can provide meaningful measures of employee progress. Assessment approaches, including 360-degree feedback systems, reflective journals, peer evaluations, supervisor observations, and competency-based rubrics, may help organizations evaluate whether cross-training programs are successfully strengthening interpersonal and self-regulatory competencies. Integrating such assessment mechanisms into organizational learning and performance management systems can improve accountability, strengthen developmental outcomes, and reinforce the strategic value of soft-skills-enabled cross-training initiatives.

6.3 Recommendations for Organizational Leaders

Senior organizational leaders play an irreplaceable role in creating the conditions for soft skills development and cross-training effectiveness to flourish. The one thing a leader has at their disposal to help their team members develop soft skills is to model those behaviors themselves. If a leader listens actively, displays self-awareness, communicates flexibly, and demonstrates an interest in helping others grow or develop then this sends a strong message to their team that they value these soft skills and therefore will be rewarded for demonstrating them. This signals to the team that it is safe to display the behaviors required for cross-training which can create a psychologically safe environment (Yukl, 2013; Edmondson, 1999; Day, 2001; Zenger & Folkman, 2009).

In order for a team to recognize the value of cross-training as well as to encourage the development of soft skills within their team, the performance management system used by the organization needs to include rewards or recognition for employees' participation in cross-training activities, as well as for the employees' growth and development of soft skills. If an employee believes that engaging in cross-training and developing his or her interpersonal skills will lead to career advancement or recognition from the organization, he or she will be motivated to take advantage of the opportunity. However, if cross-training is viewed as something that may negatively impact the performance of the employee's job function, then the employee's motivation to participate will decrease significantly prior to even starting the program (Heslin, 2005; Pink, 2009; Grant, 2012).

7. IMPLICATIONS FOR POLICY, EDUCATION, AND ORGANIZATIONAL PRACTICE

This present chapter's analytical and empirical case has implications that extend beyond individual organizational practice to the broader policy environment within which workforce development decisions are made. At the national and regional policy levels, the findings of this discussion support labor-market and education policies that incentivize integrating soft-skills development into publicly funded training programs, apprenticeship frameworks, and professional development initiatives. The OECD (2019) has argued that governments have a critical role in creating the ecosystem conditions for skills development that individual employers and educational institutions cannot create alone, including quality assurance frameworks, funding mechanisms, and cross-sector partnership structures that bridge the gap between educational provision and labor market demand.

The equity implications of soft-skills development policy warrant sustained attention from policymakers. As established in this chapter, workers from disadvantaged backgrounds are disproportionately penalized by recruitment and promotion processes that assess soft skills using opaque, informal criteria and fail to provide transparent development support or clear performance standards. Public policy interventions that mandate the explicit assessment and structured development of soft skills within publicly funded training programs — and that require employers receiving public funding for cross-training initiatives to demonstrate that they are providing equitable access to soft skills development support — can help to address these equity gaps and ensure that the benefits of workforce cross-training are distributed more widely across the labor market (Caballero & Walker, 2010; Clarke, 2018; Cappelli, 2015)

For educational institutions, this framework will support a fundamental reorientation of graduate attribute frameworks toward the explicit, systematically assessed, and pedagogically intentional development of the interpersonal and behavioral competencies graduates will need to navigate cross-functional career trajectories in tight labor markets. This new perspective on education requires both a revised curriculum and a changed culture at an academic institution for soft skills to be seen as both an expected result of going through college and a clearly defined, quantifiable and publically reportable academic goal (Tomlinson, 2012) that is a key part of an institution's social role (Hager & Holland, 2006; Bridgstock, 2009; Harvey, 2001).

8. CONCLUSION

The main theme of this chapter was the importance of soft skills in realizing the potential of workforce cross-training to close the skills gap in tight labor markets. To make this argument, we drew on a comprehensive body of literature across four fields: Labor Economics, Organizational Behavior, Human Resource Development, and Educational Psychology and Adult Learning Theory. The conclusion drawn from this literature was that without appropriate soft skills, such as communication, adaptability, emotional intelligence, problem solving using collaboration, learning agility, and resiliency, there is no way for even the most technically skilled employee to realize the full potential of their cross training experience, nor be able to provide to their organizations the advantages of increased flexibility, increased ability to recover from disruptions and sustained competitive advantage, that cross-training provides.

We have identified six soft skill clusters that have the greatest impact on cross-training success, and we have reviewed evidence-based methods for teaching each cluster in both higher education and organizational settings. We have combined these findings into what we refer to as the "Soft Skills Enabled Cross Training" (SSECT) framework that presents a systematic design approach for creating cross-training programs that include the integration of soft-skills at three levels: individual, program and organization. Finally, we have summarized our analysis into several recommendations for action for higher education administrators, human resource professionals and organizational leaders. These recommendations are based on our review of the available evidence and recognize the challenges of implementing new processes in resource-constrained environments.

The skills gap represents one of the most significant, multifaceted, and pressing problems facing employers today. Closing the gap will require much more than just upgrading technical skills. Closing the gap will also require more than just support from employers. Closing the gap will also require more than just changes in individual institutions. Closing the gap will require a long-term commitment of resources and cooperation among all stakeholders in every level of the system for preparing and developing workforces in classrooms and lecture halls, and in human resource departments and line-management discussions, in government or policy offices or funding agencies. What this present chapter demonstrates is that at the center of this cooperative effort to link the goals of workforce development policy to the realities of business operation or performance or human growth is the development of soft skills. In an environment characterized by rapid technological change, tight labor markets and relentless organizational change, being able to communicate clearly and empathetically, and adapt confidently and collaborate across differences is not a soft advantage. Being able to do so represents the hardest and most enduring competitive advantage possible for any organization or individual.

Despite its theoretical and practical contributions, the present chapter has certain limitations. The proposed SSECT framework is conceptual in nature and has not yet been empirically validated through large-scale organizational implementation or longitudinal analysis. In addition, the chapter primarily synthesizes literature from organizational behavior, human resource development, educational psychology, and employability studies, which may limit the inclusion of sector-specific operational perspectives. Future empirical studies across diverse industries and workforce contexts would further strengthen the framework's generalizability and practical applicability.

There remains considerable opportunity for future research to expand and empirically validate the Soft Skills Enabled Cross-Training (SSECT) Framework proposed in this chapter. Future studies should examine the relationship between structured soft-skills development interventions and measurable cross-training outcomes, such as employee adaptability, learning transfer, workforce mobility, productivity, retention, and organizational resilience. Longitudinal research designs may provide valuable insight into how soft skills influence long-term employability and career progression in rapidly evolving labor markets. Comparative organizational case studies across industries and cultural contexts may further help identify the organizational conditions that most strongly support effective soft-skills-enabled cross-training. Additionally, equity-focused research examining whether the benefits and challenges associated with cross-training and soft skills development are experienced differently across demographic groups, sectors, and workforce categories would contribute significantly toward improving the inclusiveness and applicability of future workforce development initiatives.

In increasingly dynamic and technology-driven labor markets, organizations that strategically integrate soft skills development into cross-training systems will be better positioned to build resilient, adaptable, and future-ready workforces.

REFERENCES

Adtani, R., Neelam, N., Raut, R., Deshpande, A., & Mittal, A. (2025). Embracing ICT in academia: Adopting and adapting to the new normal pedagogy. *Global Knowledge, Memory and Communication*, *74*(3-4), 806–823. DOI: 10.1108/GKMC-03-2023-0089

Aggarwal, A., Mittal, A., Sharma, I., Chand, P. K., & Deshpande, A. (2025). Success doesn't come to you, you go to it: The role of self-perceived employability among engineering graduates. *Industrial and Commercial Training*, *57*(4), 361–387. DOI: 10.1108/ICT-07-2024-0073

Andrews, J., & Higson, H. (2008). Graduate employability, 'soft skills' versus 'hard' business knowledge: A European study. *European Business Review*, *20*(4), 350–364. DOI: 10.1108/09555340810887579

Bakker, A. B., & Demerouti, E. (2007). The job demands–resources model: State of the art. *Journal of Managerial Psychology*, *22*(3), 309–328. DOI: 10.1108/02683940710733115

Bandura, A. (1997). *Self-efficacy: The exercise of control.* W. H. Freeman.

Bloom, B. S. (1956). *Taxonomy of educational objectives: The classification of educational goals. Handbook I: Cognitive domain.* Longmans Green.

Boyatzis, R. E. (1982). *The competent manager: A model for effective performance.* John Wiley & Sons.

Bridgstock, R. (2009). The graduate attributes we've overlooked: Enhancing graduate employability through career management skills. *Higher Education Research & Development*, *28*(1), 31–41. DOI: 10.1080/07294360802444347

Caballero, C. L., & Walker, A. (2010). Work readiness in graduate recruitment and selection: A review of current assessment methods. *Journal of Teaching and Learning for Graduate Employability*, *1*(1), 13–25. DOI: 10.21153/jtlge2010vol1no1art546

Campion, M. A., Cheraskin, L., & Stevens, M. J. (1994). Career-related antecedents and outcomes of job rotation. *Academy of Management Journal*, *37*(6), 1518–1542. DOI: 10.2307/256797

Cannon-Bowers, J. A., Salas, E., Blickensderfer, E., & Bowers, C. A. (1998). The impact of cross-training and workload on team functioning: A replication and extension of initial findings. *Human Factors*, *40*(1), 92–101. DOI: 10.1518/001872098779480550

Cappelli, P. (2015). Skill gaps, skill shortages, and skill mismatches: Evidence and arguments for the United States. *Industrial & Labor Relations Review*, *68*(2), 251–290. DOI: 10.1177/0019793914564961

Clarke, M. (2018). Rethinking graduate employability: The role of capital, individual attributes and context. *Studies in Higher Education*, *43*(11), 1923–1937. DOI: 10.1080/03075079.2017.1294152

Colquitt, J. A., LePine, J. A., & Noe, R. A. (2000). Toward an integrative theory of training motivation: A meta-analytic path analysis of 20 years of research. *The Journal of Applied Psychology*, *85*(5), 678–707. DOI: 10.1037/0021-9010.85.5.678 PMID: 11055143

Cross, R., & Parker, A. (2004). *The hidden power of social networks: Understanding how work really gets done in organizations*. Harvard Business School Press.

Day, D. V. (2001). Leadership development: A review in context. *The Leadership Quarterly*, *11*(4), 581–613. DOI: 10.1016/S1048-9843(00)00061-8

Deming, D. J. (2017). The growing importance of social skills in the labor market. *The Quarterly Journal of Economics*, *132*(4), 1593–1640. DOI: 10.1093/qje/qjx022

Deshpande, A., Raut, R., Gupta, K., Mittal, A., Raheja, D., Ekbote, N., & Kaul, N. (2024). Predictors of continued intention of working professionals for pursuing e-learning courses for career advancement. *Information Discovery and Delivery*, *52*(2), 175–184. DOI: 10.1108/IDD-11-2022-0120

Dweck, C. S. (2006). *Mindset: The new psychology of success*. Random House.

Edmondson, A. C. (1999). Psychological safety and learning behavior in work teams. *Administrative Science Quarterly*, *44*(2), 350–383. DOI: 10.2307/2666999

Ellström, P. E. (2001). Integrating learning and work: Problems and prospects. *Human Resource Development Quarterly*, *12*(4), 421–435. DOI: 10.1002/hrdq.1006

Farr, J. L., & Tesluk, P. E. (1997). Process and outcome feedback as learning mechanisms during technical skill acquisition. In Quinones, M. A., & Ehrenstein, A. (Eds.), *Training for a rapidly changing workplace*. American Psychological Association.

Fenwick, T. (2010). (Re)thinking the 'learning organization': A proleptic glimpse at the emergent field. *Journal of European Industrial Training*, *26*(2), 70–82. DOI: 10.1108/03090590210421009

Garavan, T. N., & McGuire, D. (2001). Competencies and workplace learning: Some reflections on the rhetoric and the reality. *Journal of Workplace Learning*, *13*(4), 144–163. DOI: 10.1108/13665620110391097

Gibb, S. (2014). Soft skills assessment: Theory development and the research agenda. *International Journal of Lifelong Education, 33*(4), 455–471. DOI: 10.1080/02601370.2013.867546

Goldstein, I. L., & Ford, J. K. (2002). *Training in organizations: Needs assessment, development, and evaluation* (4th ed.). Wadsworth.

Goleman, D. (1995). *Emotional intelligence: Why it can matter more than IQ*. Bantam Books.

Grant, A. M. (2012). Leading with meaning: Beneficiary contact, prosocial impact, and the performance effects of transformational leadership. *Academy of Management Journal, 55*(2), 458–476. DOI: 10.5465/amj.2010.0588

Hager, P., & Holland, S. (Eds.). (2006). *Graduate attributes, learning and employability*. Springer.

Harvey, L. (2001). Defining and measuring employability. *Quality in Higher Education, 7*(2), 97–109. DOI: 10.1080/13538320120059990

Heckman, J. J., & Kautz, T. (2012). Hard evidence on soft skills. *Labour Economics, 19*(4), 451–464. DOI: 10.1016/j.labeco.2012.05.014 PMID: 23559694

Heslin, P. A. (2005). Conceptualizing and evaluating career success. *Journal of Organizational Behavior, 26*(2), 113–136. DOI: 10.1002/job.270

Honey, P., & Mumford, A. (1986). *The manual of learning styles*. Peter Honey.

Illeris, K. (2011). *The fundamentals of workplace learning: Understanding how people learn in working life*. Routledge.

Joo, B. K. (2010). Executive coaching: A conceptual framework from an integrative review of practice and research. *Human Resource Development Review, 4*(4), 462–488. DOI: 10.1177/1534484305280866

Kegan, R. (1994). *In over our heads: The mental demands of modern life*. Harvard University Press.

Kirkpatrick, D. L. (1994). *Evaluating training programs: The four levels*. Berrett-Koehler.

Kolb, D. A. (1984). *Experiential learning: Experience as the source of learning and development*. Prentice-Hall.

Lado, A. A., & Wilson, M. C. (1994). Human resource systems and sustained competitive advantage: A competency-based perspective. *Academy of Management Review, 19*(4), 699–727. DOI: 10.2307/258742

Laker, D. R., & Powell, J. L. (2011). The differences between hard and soft skills and their relative impact on training transfer. *Human Resource Development Quarterly, 22*(1), 111–122. DOI: 10.1002/hrdq.20063

Levy, F., & Murnane, R. J. (2004). *The new division of labor: How computers are creating the next job market*. Princeton University Press. DOI: 10.1515/9781400845927

Luthans, F. (2002). The need for and meaning of positive organizational behavior. *Journal of Organizational Behavior, 23*(6), 695–706. DOI: 10.1002/job.165

Mayer, J. D., & Salovey, P. (1997). What is emotional intelligence? In Salovey, P., & Sluyter, D. J. (Eds.), *Emotional development and emotional intelligence*. Basic Books.

McLagan, P. A. (1997). Competencies: The next generation. *Training & Development, 51*(5), 40–47.

Mezirow, J. (1991). *Transformative dimensions of adult learning*. Jossey-Bass.

Noe, R. A. (2017). *Employee training and development* (7th ed.). McGraw-Hill Education.

OECD. (2019). *OECD skills outlook 2019: Thriving in a digital world.* OECD Publishing., DOI: 10.1787/df80bc12-

Pajares, F. (1997). Current directions in self-efficacy research. In Maehr, M., & Pintrich, P. R. (Eds.), Advances in motivation and achievement: Vol. 10. *JAI Press*.

Pink, D. H. (2009). *Drive: The surprising truth about what motivates us*. Riverhead Books.

Poell, R. F. (2017). Time to 'flip' the training transfer tradition: Employees create learning paths strategically. *Human Resource Development Quarterly, 28*(1), 9–15. DOI: 10.1002/hrdq.21279

Prahalad, C. K., & Hamel, G. (1990). The core competence of the corporation. *Harvard Business Review, 68*(3), 79–91.

Rainbird, H., Fuller, A., & Munro, A. (Eds.). (2004). *Workplace learning in context*. Routledge.

Robles, M. M. (2012). Executive perceptions of the top 10 soft skills needed in today's workplace. *Business Communication Quarterly, 75*(4), 453–465. DOI: 10.1177/1080569912460400

Rychen, D. S., & Salganik, L. H. (Eds.). (2003). *Key competencies for a successful life and a well-functioning society*. Hogrefe & Huber.

Salas, E., Tannenbaum, S. I., Kraiger, K., & Smith-Jentsch, K. A. (2012). The science of training and development in organizations: What matters in practice. *Psychological Science in the Public Interest : A Journal of the American Psychological Society*, *13*(2), 74–101. DOI: 10.1177/1529100612436661 PMID: 26173283

Schon, D. A. (1983). *The reflective practitioner: How professionals think in action*. Basic Books.

Schulz, B. (2008). The importance of soft skills: Education beyond academic knowledge. *NAWA Journal of Language and Communication*, *2*(1), 146–154.

Senge, P. M. (1990). *The fifth discipline: The art and practice of the learning organization*. Doubleday.

Spencer, L. M., & Spencer, S. M. (1993). *Competence at work: Models for superior performance*. John Wiley & Sons.

Suleman, F. (2018). The employability skills of higher education graduates: Insights into conceptual frameworks and methodological options. *Higher Education*, *76*(2), 263–278. DOI: 10.1007/s10734-017-0207-0

Tomlinson, M. (2012). Graduate employability: A review of conceptual and empirical themes. *Education + Training*, *54*(4), 280–290. DOI: 10.1108/00400911211236621

Tracey, J. B., Tannenbaum, S. I., & Kavanagh, M. J. (1995). Applying trained skills on the job: The importance of the work environment. *The Journal of Applied Psychology*, *80*(2), 239–252. DOI: 10.1037/0021-9010.80.2.239

Vygotsky, L. S. (1978). *Mind in society: The development of higher psychological processes*. Harvard University Press.

Wani, N. U. H., Deshpande, A., Sidana, N., & Rasa, M. M. (2025). Determinants of higher education quality in Afghanistan's higher education sector: Insights from students' perceptions. *Journal of Applied Research in Higher Education*, *17*(1), 123–138. DOI: 10.1108/JARHE-06-2023-0231

Wenger, E. (1998). *Communities of practice: Learning, meaning, and identity*. Cambridge University Press. DOI: 10.1017/CBO9780511803932

World Economic Forum. (2020). The future of jobs report 2020. World Economic Forum. https://www.weforum.org/reports/the-future-of-jobs-report-2020

Yukl, G. (2013). *Leadership in organizations* (8th ed.). Pearson.

Zenger, J., & Folkman, J. (2009). *The extraordinary leader: Turning good managers into great leaders*. McGraw-Hill.

Chapter 8
AI-Supported Cross-Training Bridging Skill Gaps and Enhancing Workforce Readiness

Sanam Soomro
http://orcid.org/0000-0003-2955-4798
Jiangsu University, China

Safia Soomro
http://orcid.org/0009-0002-3190-4187
Begum Nusrat Bhutto Women University, Sukkur, Pakistan

Ali Raza
Sukkur IBA University, Pakistan

ABSTRACT

Tight labor markets have exposed vulnerabilities in how companies attract, retain, and develop talent. High turnover, skill gaps, and emerging digital needs have disrupted traditional workforce strategies. One effective response is workforce cross-training, where employees develop skills across disciplines to enhance operational flexibility. However, businesses often struggle to implement cross-training programs, where Artificial Intelligence (AI) play a key role. AI enables personalized learning, predictive skill gap identification, and continuous upskilling paths aligned with business needs. This chapter draws from Human Capital theory, Dynamic Capabilities Theory, and Adult Learning Theory, to show how AI can support cross-training, improve adaptability, and enhance workforce development.

DOI: 10.4018/979-8-3373-5327-2.ch008

ght © 2027, IGI Global Scientific Publishing. Copying or distributing in print or electronic forms without written permission of IGI Global Scientific Publishing is prohibited. Use of this chapter to generative artificial intelligence (AI) technologies is expressly prohibited. The publisher reserves all rights to license its use for generative AI training and machine learning model development.

INTRODUCTION

Recent global employment trends show historic lows in unemployment, revealing underlying flaws in organizational talent management and development practices. Recently, a study by Kwok, (2022) indicates that industries are consistently experiencing labor shortages. Staff turnover is high, even as the labor pool grows. As hybrid and remote work become more common, the increasing need to develop digital skills is becoming another layer that is increasingly important for improving productivity. Most organizations find it difficult to have operational resilience and support the capacity of their workforce to deal with constant change. An organization's ability to rapidly transform its workforce in specific and focused ways has all the more come to be seen as a characteristic of longer-term competitiveness (Holbeche, 2023).

Global employment estimates are strong signals that organizations need to transform rapidly to adapt to significant changes in employee types and skills. It is expected that 44% of workers' core skills will change considerably by 2028 (De et al., 2025). According to Bergman et al. (2023), there was an increase in voluntary turnover of more than 20% since 2020. Disruption in the most significant areas of healthcare and logistics, and education, where the automation regulation and workforce readiness issues are the most important (Singh et al., 2025). More and more organizations are realizing that to survive and compete, workforce agility is no longer just desirable but an existential requirement. Workforce agility needs systems that will collect data and take corrective action to address skills gaps before productivity is adversely impacted (Ajgaonkar et al., 2021).

Cross-training (CT) is one solution that continues to surface in both academic literature and industry, where individuals are trained on more than one job or task. When an organization uses cross-training, it allows for flexibility, employee involvement, and reduces dependence because each task can be done by more than one employee (Owino, 2023). Although cross-training is potentially beneficial, its value is limited due to traditional limitations in scalability, customization, and responsiveness to changing business needs. In simulations, firms using predictive AI-based training experience fewer difficulties than those using traditional training methods (Chen, 2024). This shows the importance of AI-driven training when the next disruption to workers' skills occurs. AI is stepping into a crucial and much-needed role (Owino, 2023).

When companies use artificial intelligence in cross-training, they make sure their skills development framework is not reactive and static. The new learning development is driven by data and behavior-based, which continuously assesses, customizes, and enables adaptive skills upgradation. Job programs for employees will soon start using advanced intelligence and cross-training techniques (Pan et al., 2024). The teams specializing in Human Resources and Learning and Development adopt new-age technologies. These include algorithmic assessment, predictive analysis, smart learning, and other tools. These tools assess employees' existing capabilities and skill levels. Further, everything is assessed against the new organizational need. It helps employees learn better, making the workforce stronger and more adaptable. As the market trends are changing towards advanced technology, artificial intelligence-based cross-training has now become an important technology element (Lancaster et al., 2024).

This chapter has analyzed the impact of Artificial Intelligence through a systematic evaluation of cross-training programs. This chapter presents various initiatives that AI can undertake to reduce the skill gap. It could also improve aptitude for innovation and labor flexibility. According to three dominant learning theories, learning is explained by the phenomenon of learning. The human capital theory, dynamic capabilities theory, and adult learning theory, and so on. Organizations largely concerned with making employees more accepting of technology and decreasing any in-built bias in a specific algorithm.

The chapter is structured into nine sections. The discussion starts with the presentation of cross-training and artificial intelligence (AI), and developing a theory. In the next section, it examines how AI can help assess skill gaps and manage hybrid workplaces. The chapter ends by proposing a model of AI led hybrid cross-training. In the future, organizations must implement AI-enabled cross-training so they can become resilient. Future implementation and practice should integrate strategic, ethical, and research considerations.

This chapter is suitable for many target audiences. The main audience consists of HR and L&D professionals looking for evidence-based tools to underpin workforce agility. Researchers focusing on how AI can enhance human capital are the third type of audience. The chapter presents the area of the subject of interest, which shapes the managerial practice while continuing to serve postgraduate management and information systems learning.

CONCEPTUAL FOUNDATIONS AND THEORETICAL FRAMEWORK

A strong theoretical underpinning is needed to understand the strategic role of AI in cross-training interventions. The phase 1 conceptualization of AI-assisted cross-training uses insights from Human Capital Theory, Dynamic Capabilities Theory, and Adult Learning Theory; they are closely aligned theories. A combination of the three theories can provide a useful framework to strengthen workforce readiness, address skill gaps, and adapt to changing labor-market demand through AI-based training intervention systems. The rationale is essentially the same, but the implementation varies greatly by sector and region. In newer research, manufacturers are increasingly using multitasking learning, thanks to automation and AI-enabled training. In contrast, service industries such as healthcare and education must carefully balance personalization with ethical and regulatory lapses. The following theories are presented within this context of sectoral diversity, offering a globally relevant framework for understanding how AI transforms workforce development.

Human Capital Theory: Employee Development as Economic Value

According to the Human Capital Theory of Becker (1964), the skills, abilities, and talents of people are forms of economic assets that an individual and organization should invest in. Training and development may have once been considered a necessary, but are now considered an organizational advantage; on the contrary, they cause productivity, growth, and innovation (Mohammed et al., 2022). The human capital theory is one frame of reference for AI-driven cross-training, which argues that organizations should constantly develop employees' skills in various functional areas. According to Bhatt and Muduli (2022), AI can help identify specific learning needs and connect training investments to quantifiable returns on performance, retention, and adaptability. Therefore, AI boosts the human capital's potential to create value by enabling personalized, data-driven learning opportunities that are scalable and flexible.

Recent research shows that algorithms have gotten more precise in predicting returns on human capital investments (Fomude et al., 2023). When utilizing predictive AI in training programs, firms will see an increase in mobility in the range of 25–30%. Therefore, the cost and development potential of learning by using AI are highly relevant (Mohebianfar, 2025). Although human capital theory suggests that investment in higher education provides individuals with valuable skills and career benefits, empirical evidence indicates that the outcomes may vary significantly. Longitudinal analyses reveal that the productivity enhancements from AI-driven training vary by sector and depend on the organization's digital maturity.

Dynamic Capabilities Theory: Organizational Adaptability in Turbulent Markets

According to Dynamic Capabilities Theory, competitive advantage does not occur just from possessing resources. Instead, it occurs by reconfiguring them on a continuing basis (Teece, 2018). The changes in the labor-market environment are ongoing and constant, which offers a perspective of relevance, as demand for skills gradually changes. Cross-training trains people to take on different roles more easily. Facilitating internal mobility, knowledge transfer, and functional flexibility improves organizational agility (Ajgaonkar et al., 2021). The combination of cross-training with AI gives immense power. Artificial Intelligence that uses real-time labor data estimates which skills will be required and designs customized training programs, dynamically and strategically adjusting required skills in the workforce (Akhilesh & Kumar, 2025). In the United States, up to 47 percent of jobs are at risk, particularly jobs that involve low creativity and high manual work, such as in transportation. Women thus have a higher average risk of automation, and 21% of women vs. 19% of men are at high risk (probability of automation greater than 70%) (Egana-delSol et al., 2022).

Cross-industry comparisons further validate this argument. Artificial intelligence (AI) driven cross-training in logistics has reduced the onboarding cycle by 40 percent, whereas healthcare algorithms face data-privacy restrictions and so are less scalable (Taheri Hosseinkhani, 2025). We see that these dynamic capabilities take different forms depending on the intensity of the regulation and the standardization of the tasks, taking the Teece framework into the algorithmic sphere. Many manufacturers and logistics firms that are implementing AI-enabled cross-skilling tools have experienced an agility improvement of 15-30% (George, 2024a). In the case of service industries, adoption is slower due to regulatory inertia (OECD, 2024b).

Adult Learning Theory: Customized Training for Adult Learners

Adult Learning Theorists like (Fındık, 2025; Levandowski, 2025) theorized that adults are self-directed, goal-oriented, and capable. Adults come to learning with a wealth of experience, which must be taken into account in any learning program, as it can shape the learning outcomes. Effective adult learning is characterized by problem-centered approaches that connect to real-world experiences and uphold learners' self-direction (Hall, 2022). As noted by (George & George, 2024), Cross-training programs powered by artificial intelligence should be realized via the flexibility of modular and on-demand content, allowing personalization of interaction. According to Yu (2023), AI can provide experience-based learning and social learning through simulations, serious games, and collaborative platforms. The convergence of AI and adult learning principles is transformative for effective adult learning.

However, evidence of cultural comparison indicates that adult learners respond differently to AI tools. According to the OECD (2024a), students in a collectivist culture are generally more motivated when AI systems make peer-supported modules available to them. Conversely, students from an individualistic culture feel more motivated by learning analytics when these illustrate a self-paced learning experience. These intercultural learnings broaden Adult Learning Theory for the application of training AI across the globe. Research shows that AI tools help to engage adults. However, it also mentions that too much personalization over time can cause fatigue.

By comparing these theoretical perspectives, a multi-dimensional view of AI-enabled cross-training can be formed. Theories are one thing, but implementing them in the real world is another. The next sections focus on how artificial intelligence platforms, analytics of learning, and adaptive systems put into practice these insights to enhance human capital, ensure organizational agility, and promote adult learning. This approach helps bridge the gap between academics and managers by turning theorists' ideas into practical digital applications.

THE ROLE OF AI IN CROSS-TRAINING

AI-driven cross-skilling strategies are replacing old corporate training formats. As AI changes the dynamics of work and skills development, companies are facing a difficult situation due to a shortage of great skills (shown in Figure 1). AI is a scalable, predictable solution for workforce development that values flexibility. By cross-training, AI accelerates the learning, increases the relevance, and improves performance in diverse roles and functions (Kurki et al., 2024).

Figure 1. Role of AI in Cross-training

Cross-Sector and Global Labor Perspectives on AI-Enabled Cross-Training

The use of AI in cross-training varies in deployment by industry and geography owing to varying regulations and workforce conditions. In the case of health care, patient-data governance and professional-licensing structures limit large-scale implementation, although there are strong demands for adaptive learning (OECD AI Outlook, 2024). In contrast, the logistics and manufacturing sectors use predictive analytics and machine-assisted task rotation to achieve onboarding times 40 percent lower than before (Scharron, 2025). So repetitive workflows yield faster AI payoffs. In education, AI-supported cross-training takes place through adaptive learning platforms and digital-pedagogy development for teachers, which emphasizes personalization and learner autonomy (UNESCO, 2023a). According to these contrasts, AI-based reskilling works well when the regulatory intensity and data maturity level are high in a sector. A global observation indicates that the labor market may be showing a signal of bifurcation in skills. In other words, advanced economies will focus on high-tech retraining, while emerging economies face problems due to gaps in digital infrastructure (Hamza, 2025).

The process of cross-training AI-enabled systems differs across various industries with respect to digital maturity, compliance regimes, and human resource composition. Predictive analytics or automation-led training in production and logistics helps achieve measurable efficiencies. According to the World Economic Forum (2023), targeted upskilling in AI can lower turnover by 15-20% and raise productivity by 10-25%. AI systems in clinical training environments need to be accurate, regulatory traceable, and can explain their decisions (OECD, 2024a). The implementation of AI in the education sector has not recorded stronger transformational merits. According to a release by UNESCO (2023), the increase in productivity due to these processes takes time because of inertia.

This comparison informs us that while the value of the AI-driven cross-training is universal, the success metric remains sector-dependent on cost saving, uplift, and adaptability. AI Adoption in a Work-Oriented Cross-Cultural Context. Organizations in East Asia and Northern Europe have considerable foundations for establishing robust digital-governance frameworks that engender comparatively higher employee trust and adoption in those regions than other cultural regions, where the AI governance or data privacy norms are still maturing (Bejarano-Murillo, 2025). By understanding trends and cultural contexts, the global compatibility of AI-enabled cross-training will be guaranteed.

Overview of AI Tools in Cross-Training

These days, many tools are actually AI-based and are part of cross-training initiatives, with each serving a unique function.

- **Intelligent Learning Platforms (ILPs):** Some solutions like Degreed, EdCast, and Cornerstone, which leverage artificial intelligence to recommend, sequence, and personalize content for employees based on their behavior, role, and performance, are called Intelligent Learning Platforms (Ramachandran et al., 2022). These are places where training for all your learning needs happens simultaneously with your work.
- **Talent analytics systems:** like Visier, Eightfold, or Oracle HCM Cloud, use machine learning to assess employee data and identify trends related to capabilities distribution (Atluri, 2024). They also check how valuable your training efforts are and how much the person could shift internally. The exhibition illustrates the magnitude of a number of skill deficits in the department.
- **Algorithmic Decision-Making Engines:** We use intelligent algorithmic decision-making engines that recommend whether to invest in training, build learning paths, or fitment for job roles. An algorithm examines 1000s of data points (from job descriptions to CVs to Engagement snaps to documents outlining organizational strategy) to arrive at evidence-based HR decisions that are also future-ready (Demanuele, 2025).
- **Natural Language Processing (NLP) Applications:** The processing of unstructured data like performance reviews, training feedback, learning journal unsolicited content to ascertain the sentiment, uncover development needs, learning outcomes tracking etc will be an increasingly asked task of NLP (Shukla & Garg, 2022). This helps in converting qualitative feedback to quantifiable training insights.

Techniques like this feed into big cross-training plans. In addition, they allow information to flow through them and enable intelligent, responsive, and measurable learning experiences from end to end. Using these tools transparently can only enhance human decision-making in HRM and never substitute it. According to Alabi et al. (2024), personalization predictive intelligence, and real-time adaptability create opportunities for cross-training in AI, which will make it a networked training environment. AI-enabled cross-training isn't just a technical fix; it is much more and critically important. It is a reflection of new organizational thinking. The view of learning as follows is a very important consideration of an organization's ability to compete. In the next section, mini-case studies will be discussed that highlight cross-training in different sectors.

CASE STUDIES

Case 1: Healthcare Sector: Adaptive Learning for Clinical Staff

A revolutionary era in healthcare has begun with the merging of artificial intelligence (AI) with sensor technology, which has completely changed how patient care, diagnosis, and treatment approaches are provided (Bhamidipaty et al., 2025). An AI-powered platform was adopted by a large hospital system in Europe, which used real-time clinician performance data to recommend micro-learning modules. In six months, the number of quality queries was reduced by 62.9% from 786 to 495, and the turnover rate decreased from 30% to 20% within the intervention period. Patients can track the budgeted costs of their treatment through 'cost lists' (Khatib et al., 2024; Urban, 2024).

Case 2: Manufacturing and Logistics: Predictive Cross-Skilling for Operational Flexibility

A logistics company used predictive analytics to identify at-risk skill bottlenecks across its warehouse operations (Aljohani, 2023). The AI system identified paths for rotation training suited to employee potential and demand forecasts. There was a drop in overtime costs by 22 per cent, and retention improved by 15 per cent in a year (George, 2024b, 2024a).

Case 3: Education Sector: AI-Assisted Professional Development for Teachers A Southeast Asian education ministry adopted an AI-enabled teacher-development platform that assessed lesson-delivery videos and suggested customized training content (Dennison et al., 2025). Educators reported higher engagement and confidence scores (Xu, 2024).

Artificial intelligence-enabled cross-training makes workforces more ready as well as agile across the spectrum of sectors. Organizations are proving the measurable benefits of AI in training through evidence and experience. Whether through faster redeployment of skills in manufacturing, reduced time-to-competence in healthcare, or higher learner engagement in education, the benefits are real (Figure-2). The outcomes discussed here clearly signify the maximal level issues we discussed earlier in the chapter. These include matters regarding digital transformation, labor flux, and global demand for upskilling. The mini-cases demonstrate how AI can play a crucial role as a behavioral agent for adaptive workforce development, thus validating our impact claim. As the examples above show, AI-powered cross-training needs careful judgment and a supportive organizational culture.

Figure 2. Use of AI driven cross training in different sectors

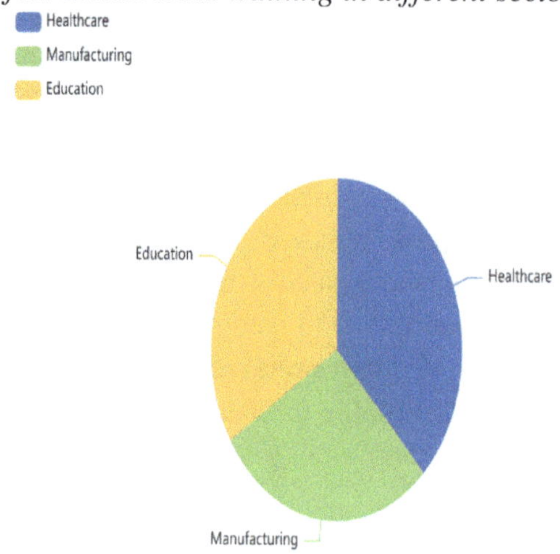

BENEFITS OF AI-SUPPORTED CROSS-TRAINING

By employing AI systems, cross-training can be introduced, which provides quantifiable and tactical advantages that traditional training systems cannot. This links the organizational strategy to learning agility, involving real-time data, a personalized learning engine, and predicted future technologies. Cross-training employees on AI improves adaptability and lowers costs (Gruenewald & Mueller, 2025).

Workforce Flexibility and Resilience

Teaching employees AI technology can lead to greater order flexibility and improved resilience. Regular programs rely on static content that does not keep up with the changing demand. Unlike traditional HR processes, AI tools use workforce data to identify skills overlaps, redundancies, and capacity gaps with a view to proactively upskilling mission-critical roles (Anbalagan, 2023). The productive deployment of adaptable systems in health, logistics, and manufacturing saves on downtime and skills shortage. In other words, practitioners at that time would take an interdisciplinary approach (Freeman & Ellis, 2025). Evidence in the data reveals that predictive artificial intelligence (AI) adoption enhances role mobility by 25 to 30%, with productivity gains of 20% (Filippucci et al., 2024).

Enhanced Engagement and Job Satisfaction

Artificial intelligence (AI) improves learner participation via tailored and self-directed learning pathways, which align with employees' interests and skills competencies. Artificial intelligence improves learner retention and enhances feelings of competence and autonomy consistent with Self-Determination Theory, Deci and Ryan (2000) through custom recommendations and instant feedback. Also, employees will gain confidence in long-term growth due to the AI platform's capability to flag career paths and lateral moves. In hybrid and remote working environments, these attributes enable teams to remain engaged while cultivating a mindset for learning and development, which is critical for retention and innovation.

Strategic Alignment of Learning with Business Goals

The capacity of Artificial Intelligence (AI) to drive substantial changes to learning and development (L&D) can transform L&D from being an operational function to a strategic partner in the activities of the organization and enable the organization to accomplish its goals and objectives. AI is using talent analytics to create impact models for roles, create skills insights, and connect training effectiveness with organizational KPIs including time to competence. This helps in pointing out roles that can make a positive impact (Hutson & Ceballos, 2023). When organizations continuously and contemporaneously map learning data to business metrics, they make more efficient resource allocation decisions. A data-backed culture is also fostered by it. As time goes on, it reduces training from a reactive cost to a performance-linked investment with strategic agility.

Accelerated Learning Pathways

Using AI to acquire content and evaluation processes saves time in skills training. On adaptive learning platforms, the learning material's speed and intensity alter according to the learner's pace and level. These platforms assist many learners who require extra help and also offer high achievers the chance to move on. When data personalizes learning, it helps to avoid overlap and fatigue, making learning more effective (Taylor et al., 2024). During project launches or talent shortages, the existing workforce will be leveraged via cross-training with AI. This enables an employee to relocate without disrupting business operations. In general, A.I. Cross-training helps workers learn more skills. This training improves worker adaptability. It also speeds up the learning cycle. The results imply that intelligent learning systems are more necessary than a choice to ensure your workforce strategies are resilient and ready for the future (Lee & Nie, 2024)

IMPLEMENTATION CHALLENGES

The realization of AI-enabled cross-training is a transformative agenda that needs to overcome a web of technical, organizational, socio-cultural, and ethical barriers. Proper deployment is more about trust, diversity and governance than technology. The four barriers below are key to successful implementation.

Socio-Cultural and Behavioral Barriers

AI can enhance cultural identity and behavior. But there is often pushback against cross-training. Being an employee can lead to having less control or uncertainty about the job and digital fatigue. There are legitimate responses to unknown situations that lie behind these fears. Organizations value stability more than change. This rigidity slows change in organizations. When workers do not believe that AI will produce fair, unbiased, and transparent outcomes, a trust deficit occurs (Zerilli et al., 2022). It can be especially true in situations involving performance reviews and promotions. Instead of viewing AI as a replacement for human intelligence, organizations must look at AI as a learning partner (Fan et al., 2025). A way to improve acceptance is by participatory and inclusive design, technical rollout combined with change management, and peer learning communities. Spaces for social learning that honor offline contribution will lessen digital anxiety and maintain engagement (Soomro et al., 2024). In the end, AI-backed cross-training works best when viewed as a human transformation, not a tech upgrade.

Data Quality and System Integration

Accurate and interoperable data is necessary to train artificial intelligence. When you have poor data and disconnected HR systems, it disrupts the recommended learning (Jingsheng, 2024). When information relating to informal/experiential learning is lost, it undervalues workers' true capabilities. To execute the plan, datasets must have a common format and not contain errors. Moreover, the HCM, LMS, and performance systems need to connect via APIs (Atluri, 2024). The discrimination is caused when people assess and favor differently. Strong data governance and ethical frameworks are essential. AI systems should be transparent, traceable, and accountable to ensure reliable and fair results.

Ethical Governance and Algorithmic Fairness

The use of AI in workforce training raises issues of fairness, inclusivity, and privacy. Models that are trained on past data with bias tend to reproduce inequalities, such as under-representing women as well as minorities and older workers in high-skill pathways for learning (Hanna et al., 2025). Mitigation requires a multi-layered governance approach:

- Regular bias audits and fairness-impact assessments;
- Adherence to frameworks such as IEEE Ethically Aligned Design, AI Principles (2024), and the EU AI Act (2024), which classifies workforce AI systems as high-risk.
- Adoption of Explainable AI (XAI) to make algorithmic decisions intelligible to HR and employees (Doshi-Velez & Kim, 2017).

UNESCO (2023a) emphasizes the need for diverse voices, including those of younger employees, to be included in the training of the model by SAP. AI Ethics Boards that draw from various departments such as HR, data scientists, and employee representatives tend to promote accountability. So, ethical governance shifts from compliance to capability and builds trust and legitimacy in AI.

Digital Divide and Access Disparities

The lack of digital infrastructure is a problem of social urgency on a global level. According to Stofkova et al. (2022) over 40 per cent of the global workforce has zero basic digital skills. In addition, some one-third of SMEs in developing countries do not have access to cloud-based learning platforms (Sun et al., 2020). Countries with high income allocate approximately 3.2% of their GDP to the digital upskilling, while low-income countries allocate less than 0.5% (Matyushenko et al 2024). Barriers such as poor connectivity, hardware scarcity, and low accessibility for disabled people disproportionately affect rural and low-income workers (A.T. Lee et al. 2025). Ignoring access and inclusivity may worsen the situation with AI learning tools. To bridge this gap, organizations should ensure that.

- Mobile and offline access to training content;
- Accessibility features such as text-to-speech and screen readers;
- Digital literacy support is integrated into upskilling programs.

By following the G20 Digital Economy Task Force Framework, 2024, and UNESCO AI Competency Framework, this can be implemented fairly and impartially

(Mutawa & Sruthi, 2025). AI-enhanced cross-training programs work best when innovation and inclusion are kept in balance. According to Abuhassna et al. (2024), successful deployment of artificial intelligence in education requires proper management of socio-cultural resistance, data integrity and ethical governance, and digital inequality. Efforts are underway to ensure that upskilling driven by AI continues to be effective and socially legitimate, in an open, fair and accessible manner.

HR Leadership and Change Management

HR leaders should manage culture and mindset change with cross-training. As per experts, the revolutionizing of education, job performance, and evaluation is through Artificial Intelligence (AI) (Vishwanath Bijja & Vaddepalli Surendar, 2023). HR leaders ought to leverage a framework to manage such transitions. For instance, Kotter's 8-step Model or ADKAR (Awareness, Desire, Knowledge, Ability, and Reinforcement) can be useful. Key leadership actions include.

- Clearly articulating the "why" of AI adoption, framing it around agility, personalization, and sustainability.
- Fostering an environment where employees feel safe to experiment, fail, and learn through iteration.
- Maintaining open dialogue through pilots, transparent communication, and structured feedback loops.

To ensure technical feasibility meets cultural readiness, HR and IT teams work together with data-science teams. Leaders must also deal with social issues, surveillance, bias, loss of human connection by reinforcing AI as a partner for development. When employees feel they have agency and fairness in the process, trust and participation.

Building Digital Readiness and Upskilling Support

Bringing AI makes humans the center rather than being a technological race itself. It is essential for developing the confidence and digital fluency of workers to engage with smart technologies. To foster digital readiness, firms must provide elementary training on learning encounter platforms, data privacy, and many more. Moreover, this will help in building competencies such as self-learning, critical thinking, and teamwork in a digital environment. Managers should conduct coaching sessions with their employees and ensure mentorship between employees (Orth et al., 1987). Due to ineffective interfaces, over-reliance on automation makes humans tired and less involved. To avoid this, training must be modular, doable in effort and time, and must have feedback loops to ensure stimulation. According to Morandini et al. (2023), rather than measuring success, course completion rates must be defined by their actual impact on the organization and behavior change. Through increase and improvement in functionality, AI upskilling promotes continuity. This methodology helps in adoption as well as strengthening the resilience of the workforce in a long-term manner to carry on the change.

Creating Inclusive and Equitable AI-Training Systems

AI could help to level the playing field in the economy, but could also make existing inequalities worse (Montgomery, 2024). Algorithms that are not designed on purpose may reflect the same social and organizational bias. Learning systems powered by AI need to be made universal by design and not by default. In all fairness, training datasets should consist of data that is at least somewhat varied and representative of gender, ability, culture, and job function (Roth et al., 2012). Also, algorithms need to include built-in bias-detection and mitigation controls. Learning platforms must have a simple, multilingual interface with content that meets the varying conditions of neurodiverse and differently abled learners.

To ensure fairness and trust in the tools, organizations should carry out equity audits and partner with Employee Resource Groups (ERGs) when developing and piloting solutions (Leger, 2023). When learners can see and question AI's recommendations, they can hold it accountable, which builds user trust. In the end, the building of inclusive AI ecosystems should employ participatory governance, bringing together the expertise of HR, data scientists, ethicists, and employee representatives (Holzinger et al., 2025). When we think of fairness as a design capability, not a compliance requirement, organizations reduce ethical risks while creating belongingness, authenticity, and sustainable engagement in the workplace.

PROPOSED MODEL FOR AI-BASED CROSS-TRAINING

To realize the integration of AI in workforce cross-training, this section provides a rigorous action model, based on the theoretical framework and strategic need proposed in the above 2 sections. An artificial intelligence tool assists companies in training their employees to efficiently adapt to new situations and align their skills with their business needs (Morandini et al., 2023). The solution is composed of four integral parts: skill-gap analysis, learning for all, feedback loops, and assessment. Smart design and user-centered design anchor them.

AI-Based Cross-Training Model

The core of the suggested model is AI-driven skill gap identification, a process that utilizes machine learning, talent analytics, and natural language processing (NLP) to assess workforce data and predict future skill requirements. The system detects both surpluses and deficits of competencies for various roles as well as across various departments through job descriptions, performance records, educational courses, and labor market trends. It also examines how strategy will alter future capability demand. Artificial intelligence can support the HR professionals in designing effective learning paths related to employee needs (Madhumita et al., 2024). Mapping the context appropriately to the setting is valid. Once identified, Learning Experience Platform (LXP), adaptive recommendation engines, and digital learning experience platforms trigger the delivery systems for personalized learning. According to Johnston (2004), students may learn at their own pace. Students do so with materials that have been tailored to their unique ways of learning. They also follow specific roles and teams. The ecosystem gathers a variety of learning assets. The platform offers peer collaboration modules, microlearning videos, and simulations. The user engagement, completion, and performance analytics will evolve the modules. Learners take the lead in choosing relevant experiences, setting up their self-directed, 'just-in-time' learning, which connects theory with practice.

The model gets feedback constantly, which sustains both retention levels and learning accuracy. According to Burnett & Lisk, (2021) emotion analysis and employee engagement performance dashboards powered by AI analytics equip trainers and HR professionals with up-to-date information about the people they train or manage. Smart tutors, dashboards, and chatbots facilitate real-time feedback for students. Information can flow in two different directions through this process. As a result, this improves the content as well as the learner experience. Nowadays, analysts check the behavior of employees to assess the productivity and performance stats over a period of time. They use superb AI tools for this through behavior analytics (Tariq et al., 2021). Also, they see how the training affects the functioning of the organization. This involves analyzing productivity, idea acceptance, and movement across organizational levels. They make checks on the alignment of the learning objectives. Through modification of the evaluation system, training passes from an intervention to an iterative process that is linked to performance. This creates agility and continuous rapid reskilling.

Model Framework and Flow

The components of the flow connect in a loop, continuously AI-based cross-training Flow. AI identifies prowess gaps using the company strategy context. It joins data from the employee profile with individual learning paths. As part of our accompaniment of muse consultations, we are updating the skill inventories and redeployment plans with real-time feedback that is updated through review. The model revisits skill detection to establish a live learning ecosystem that evolves appropriately with organizational objectives. The feedback and adaptation will remain constant because of this structure, which keeps the learning cycle ever onward. As shown in figure 3.

Figure 3. Model framework and flow

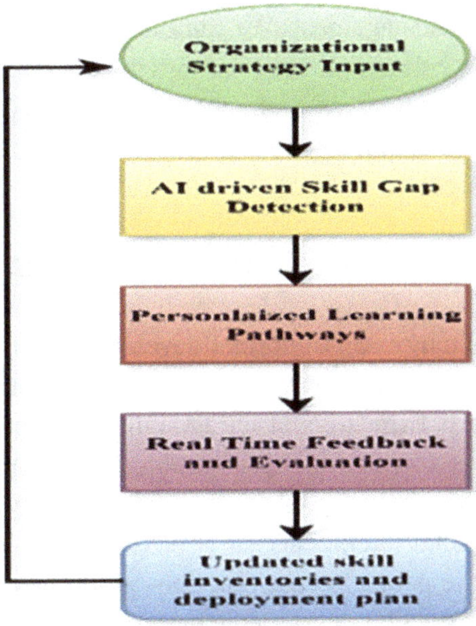

Integration into HR and L&D Systems

The model can be easily incorporated into existing HR and learning systems. It connects with Human Capital Management (HCM) services such as SAP and Oracle HCM to obtain workforce data. Using APIs, it integrates with the LMS and LXP labels Degreed and EdCast for personalized and trackable learning experience creation (Khamis, 2024). Organizations must utilize a common data model, a common competency taxonomy, and a common privacy-preserving, data-protecting, role-based access protocol to facilitate interoperability and ethical governance (D & M, 2023; Naguib & Fouad, 2024). HR professionals also need to get AI literate and understand data ethics, which entails HR professionals becoming savvy with technologies. Thus, the integration of the AI-based model translates the training data into actionable intelligence at the strategic workforce planning level, till the individual career progression level (Jain et al., 2023).

DISCUSSION

Organizations are using artificial intelligence more and more to enhance and train employees for future jobs. AI has the potential to play a role in agility building. The chapter highlights this as a lever for building agility across all levels, from individual performance to talent management. We can then place these insights within a larger context of workforce development, the changing labor market, and the future of work. We also investigate how research practice crossover can contribute to the design and development of AI-enhanced training systems in relation to management/ regulatory and ethical issues.

Strategic Implications for Workforce Development

AI's use for cross-training is an important development in workforce training. It enables organizations to proactively orchestrate talent instead of just reactive upskilling. When AI alerts firms to conflicting skills and other disparities, offers customized training paths and monitors performance, they can change their talent planning as their strategies pivot: digital focus, foreign market push, or innovation acceleration. Using artificial intelligence, it is possible to achieve skill liquidity, that is, the ability to move people across functions and projects (Göranzon & Josefson, 2012). Instead of stacking tasks in the organization chart, capability-based workforce planning seeks linkages across hierarchy levels. An internal gig worker becomes a knowledgeable employee by training in important business areas, while the specialist is cross-trained to assist in teaching the gig worker. When flexibility is offered at work, it fosters productivity, retention, and enhances organizational resilience to years of disruption (Lengnick-Hall et al., 2011). As HR leaders and L&D professionals move forward, this will require new abilities focusing on new data-driven workforce design, AI literacy, and strategic learning analytics. Future workforce development will be driven by smart systems with learning capabilities that will develop along with human talent rather than policy and programs.

Broader Impact on Labor Markets and the Future of Work

AI-driven cross-training could redefine labor markets beyond organizational limits. Economies are being disrupted by automation, demographics, and global instability. To stay competitive, economies must retrain and redeploy their workforce (Liang, 2024). This will help maintain jobs and prevent displacement. In support of mass reskilling, innovative policy mechanisms such as portable training benefits, lifetime learning accounts, and a national skills registry are gaining attention. AI can catalyze these initiatives by:

- Providing real-time information on labor markets for demand-driven training.
- Enabling cross-sector mobility: Mapping of skills across occupations and sectors to facilitate mobility.
- Reducing retraining time and costs, thus enabling workforce transformation to become more accessible to SMEs and the less privileged.

In the broader future of work, in which job descriptions are hybrid between disciplines, and conducted first and foremost in the digital space, AI-supported cross-training is the method by which workers remain employable and firms remain agile. It also further changes the conversation from "jobs" to "skills," implying a more dynamic, inclusive, and opportunity-rich view of work.

Research Practice Integration

An important contribution of this chapter is its effort to synthesize what is empirically known, theoretically predicted, and applied mechanisms that may help resolve the persistent research-to-practice gap in workforce development. Researchers have focused on AI applications for learning and AI applications for cross-training separately. There are very few models available that integrate these works in a cohesive, action-oriented framework that is theoretically informed and practically applicable. Three principal theories were used as the foundation for the proposed model. These are the human capital theory, the dynamic capabilities theory, and the adult learning theory. The two together would provide insights about the impact AI in an organization could have, so that value through acquisition of skills, agility of the organization, and engagement of employees could be generated. It also gives professionals a blueprint. It also provides a reference point to fine-tune and introduce AI into their HR system in a "modular" way. Also, an ethical and employee-choice approach. As technology progresses, academic research might lose its significance as it is not grounded in a dynamic business environment. The relationship between research and practice at the university has to be strengthened. Due to the ongoing advancement of AI innovations and insight-driven research, equitable and future-ready learning ecosystems can be created.

CONCLUSION

The demand for a change in the workforce is more important than ever before. This is because businesses encounter disruptive technology, labor volatility, and a changing skillset. This chapter aims to answer this call by presenting an AI-enabled cross-training for engaging in the task, and narrating a concept with practice about how AI can change systems of workforce development in line with reality in the 21st-century economy. This chapter presents an integrated and preemptive innovative approach, which is the only answer. It discusses how data and agility are used for upskilling and reskilling. The model indicates that the cross-training, in conjunction with an intelligent system, serves as a development mechanism. Nonetheless, cross-training can assist organizations and employees in developing more strategic capabilities to survive in uncertainty.

Most people think of AI as a negative development, but disruption in workforce development creates a new world of work that is possible. With artificial intelligence, organizations have the ability to scale up without sacrificing the benefits of a custom-built solution that training organizations have never delivered till now, with any of the solutions available in the market. Just as the rest of the job marketplace is learning to adapt and deal with internal change and technology change in real-time. Using AI for cross-training will allow the workforce to develop in the long run. When we do this process continuously, we create cycles of adaptability, inclusiveness, and development. When used properly, AI makes workers more efficient and effective, not robots. To achieve the most benefits possible from AI-enabled cross-training, it is more critical to ensure ethical design and deployment at scale. But also, organizational vision. People do not exist to serve technology. The tool must benefit people, not vice versa. The training plan is suitable in the context it is being used. It uses the 21st-century learning variables like 'technology', social needs, and learner-centeredness, which are well-positioned with their strategic embedment. HR leaders can have processes developed for AI training and cross-training. The digital workforce might change the views of the participants on research and teaching, and development of curriculum.

Recommendations

For Practitioners (HR Leaders, L&D Managers, and C-Suite Executives):

- Use the AI-Based Cross-Training Model to link learning outcomes with business KPIs such as productivity gains, cost reduction, and retention uplift.

- Benchmark AI adoption practices across sectors (e.g., healthcare, manufacturing, education) to identify best-fit learning strategies aligned with organizational context.
- Implement AI-enabled learning under recognized ethical and legal frameworks such as the EU AI Act (2024) and OECD AI Principles (2023) to ensure transparency and accountability.
- Utilize the provided AI tool–learning objective matrix to match technology capabilities with training goals, optimizing ROI on learning technologies.
- Foster employee trust and adoption through inclusive, human-centered AI rollout strategies emphasizing explainability and participation.

For Researchers and Academics

- Examine quantitative outcomes of AI-enabled cross-training (e.g., performance uplift, cost-benefit ratios, and retention metrics) through longitudinal and cross-sectoral studies.
- Investigate how regulatory contexts and digital maturity influence AI adoption in different industries and cultural settings.
- Contribute to evolving debates on fairness, bias mitigation, and algorithmic transparency within AI-driven learning ecosystems.
- Extend the proposed model to incorporate predictive analytics, governance audits, and socio-behavioral dimensions for a holistic understanding of AI in HRM.
- Bridge HRM, data science, and policy studies to design responsible AI systems that enhance human capability while maintaining organizational integrity.

REFERENCES

Abuhassna, H., Adnan, M. A. B. M., & Awae, F. (2024). Exploring the synergy between instructional design models and learning theories: A systematic literature review. *Contemporary Educational Technology*, *16*(2), ep499. DOI: 10.30935/cedtech/14289

Ajgaonkar, S., Neelam, N. G., & Wiemann, J. (2021a). Drivers of workforce agility: A dynamic capability perspective. *The International Journal of Organizational Analysis*, *30*(4), 951–982. DOI: 10.1108/IJOA-11-2020-2507

Ajgaonkar, S., Neelam, N. G., & Wiemann, J. (2021b). Drivers of workforce agility: A dynamic capability perspective. *The International Journal of Organizational Analysis*, *30*(4), 951–982. DOI: 10.1108/IJOA-11-2020-2507

Akhilesh, & Kumar, P. (2025). Impact of Artificial Intelligence on Employment and Skill Requirements in the Tourism Sector. In *Transforming the Service Sector With New Technology* (pp. 167–190). IGI Global Scientific Publishing. DOI: 10.4018/979-8-3693-7447-4.ch011

Alabi, O. A., Ajayi, F. A., Udeh, C. A., & Efunniyi, C. P. (2024). Predictive Analytics in Human Resources: Enhancing Workforce Planning and Customer Experience. *International Journal of Innovation and Scientific Research*, *XI*(IX), 149–158. DOI: 10.51244/IJRSI.2024.1109016

Aljohani, A. (2023). Predictive Analytics and Machine Learning for Real-Time Supply Chain Risk Mitigation and Agility. *Sustainability (Basel)*, *15*(20), 15088. DOI: 10.3390/su152015088

Anbalagan, B. (2023). Proactive Failover and Automation Frameworks for Mission-Critical Workloads: Lessons from Manufacturing Industry. *International Journal of Research and Applied Innovations*, *6*(1), 8279–8296. DOI: 10.15662/IJRAI.2023.0601004

Atluri, A. (2024). The 2030 HR Landscape: Oracle HCM's Vision for Future-Ready Organizations. *International Journal of AI, BigData. Computational and Management Studies*, *5*(4), 31–40. DOI: 10.63282/3050-9416.IJAIBDCMS-V5I4P104

Bejarano-Murillo, E. (2025). Digital Governance Across Continents: Cases From Diverse National Strategies. In *Data-Driven Governance Through AI, Digital Marketing, and the Privacy Interplay* (pp. 1–30). IGI Global Scientific Publishing. DOI: 10.4018/979-8-3693-6945-6.ch001

Bergman, A., David, G., & Song, H. (2023). "I Quit": Schedule Volatility as a Driver of Voluntary Employee Turnover. *Manufacturing & Service Operations Management, 25*(4), 1416–1435. DOI: 10.1287/msom.2023.1205

Bhamidipaty, V., Bhamidipaty, D. L., & Guntoory, I. Bhamidipaty, Kdp., Iyengar, K. P., Botchu, B., & Botchu, R. (2025). Revolutionizing Healthcare: The Impact of AI-Powered Sensors. In *Generative Artificial Intelligence for Biomedical and Smart Health Informatics* (pp. 355–373). John Wiley & Sons, Ltd. DOI: 10.1002/9781394280735.ch18

Bhatt, P., & Muduli, A. (2022). Artificial intelligence in learning and development: A systematic literature review. *European Journal of Training and Development, 47*(7–8), 677–694. DOI: 10.1108/EJTD-09-2021-0143

Bijja Vishwanath, Surendar Vaddepalli. (2023). The Future of Work: Implications of Artificial Intelligence on Hr Practices. *Tuijin Jishu/Journal of Propulsion Technology, 44*(3), 1711–1724. DOI: 10.52783/tjjpt.v44.i3.562

Burnett, J. R., & Lisk, T. C. (2021). The Future of Employee Engagement: Real-Time Monitoring and Digital Tools for Engaging a Workforce. In *International Perspectives on Employee Engagement*. Routledge. DOI: 10.4324/9781003142492-9

Chen, Z. (2024). Responsible AI in Organizational Training: Applications, Implications, and Recommendations for Future Development. *Human Resource Development Review, 23*(4), 498–521. DOI: 10.1177/15344843241273316

D, D., & M, J. P. P. (2023). *A Brief Study of Privacy-Preserving Practices (PPP) in Data Mining* (No. arXiv:2304.14607). arXiv. https://doi.org//arXiv.2304.14607DOI: 10.48550

De, S., Mukherjee, D., & Ray, J. (2025). Skill in Indian Labour Market: Current Trends and Estimating Future Gaps. *Arthaniti: Journal of Economic Theory and Practice, 24*(1), 103–129. DOI: 10.1177/09767479221138961

Deci, E. L., & Ryan, R. M. (2000). The "What" and "Why" of Goal Pursuits: Human Needs and the Self-Determination of Behavior. *Psychological Inquiry, 11*(4), 227–268. DOI: 10.1207/S15327965PLI1104_01

Demanuele, L. M. (2025). (2025). *Recruitment and selection: An evidence based approach.* https://www.um.edu.mt/library/oar/handle/123456789/132894

Dennison, D. V., Ahtisham, B., Chourasia, K., Arora, N., Singh, R., Kizilcec, R. F., Nambi, A., Ganu, T., & Vashistha, A. (2025). *Teacher-AI Collaboration for Curating and Customizing Lesson Plans in Low-Resource Schools* (No. arXiv:2507.00456). arXiv. https://doi.org//arXiv.2507.00456DOI: 10.48550

Egana-delSol, P., Bustelo, M., Ripani, L., Soler, N., & Viollaz, M. (2022). Automation in Latin America: Are Women at Higher Risk of Losing Their Jobs? *Technological Forecasting and Social Change*, *175*, 121333. DOI: 10.1016/j.techfore.2021.121333

Fan, M., Soomro, S., Soomro, S., Sohu, J. M., Shah, S. B., & Shaikh, S. N. (2025). The human side of AI adoption: Exploring technostress, training and employee well-being in manufacturing SMEs. *Journal of Manufacturing Technology Management*, •••, 1–22. DOI: 10.1108/JMTM-02-2025-0120

Filippucci, F., Gal, P., Jona Lasinio, C. S., & Alvaro Leandro And Giuseppe Nicoletti. (2024). *The impact of Artificial Intelligence on productivity, distribution and growth*. DOI: 10.1787/dee339a8-en

Fındık, L. Y. (2025). Adult Learning Theories. In *Exploring Adult Education Through Learning Theory* (pp. 29–54). IGI Global Scientific Publishing., DOI: 10.4018/979-8-3693-5812-2.ch002

Fomude, A. H., Yang, C., Agordzo, G. K., Serwah, A. V., & Abangbila, L. (2023). AI Model to Improve HR Decision-Making with Machine Learning Predictions Algorithm. *2023 25th International Conference on Advanced Communication Technology (ICACT)*, 206–212. DOI: 10.23919/ICACT56868.2023.10079282

Freeman, J. M., & Ellis, J. (2025). The Expert Behind the Desk: Collaborative Cross-Training in Unlocking Potential in Frontline Academic Library Staff. *Journal of Library Administration*, *65*(6-7), 1–21. DOI: 10.1080/01930826.2025.2518007

George, D. A. S. (2024a). AI-Enabled Intelligent Manufacturing: A Path to Increased Productivity, Quality, and Insights. *Partners Universal Innovative Research Publication*, *2*(4), 50–63. DOI: 10.5281/zenodo.13338085

George, D. A. S. (2024b). Artificial Intelligence and the Future of Work: Job Shifting Not Job Loss. *Partners Universal Innovative Research Publication*, *2*(2), 17–37. DOI: 10.5281/zenodo.10936490

George, D. A. S., & George, A. S. H. (2024). Towards a Super Smart Society 5.0: Opportunities and Challenges of Integrating Emerging Technologies for Social Innovation. *Partners Universal International Research Journal, 3*(2), 01–29. DOI: 10.5281/zenodo.11522048

Göranzon, B., & Josefson, I. (2012). *Knowledge, Skill and Artificial Intelligence*. Springer Science & Business Media.

Gruenewald, H., & Mueller, M. (2025). *Reskilling and Upskilling in a Globalized Economy: Essential Strategies for Workforce Transformation*. Springer Nature. DOI: 10.1007/978-3-658-48384-5

Hall, J. A. (2022). A Problem-Centered Approach to Designing Blended Courses: Unifying Online and Face-to-Face Modalities. *Education Sciences*, *12*(10), 689. DOI: 10.3390/educsci12100689

Hamza, K. (2025). *Emerging Markets and the Digital Economy: A Framework for Enhancing Global Competitiveness*. Taylor & Francis. DOI: 10.4324/9781003596868

Hanna, M. G., Pantanowitz, L., Jackson, B., Palmer, O., Visweswaran, S., Pantanowitz, J., Deebajah, M., & Rashidi, H. H. (2025). Ethical and Bias Considerations in Artificial Intelligence/Machine Learning. *Modern Pathology*, *38*(3), 100686. DOI: 10.1016/j.modpat.2024.100686 PMID: 39694331

Holbeche, L. (2023). *The Agile Organization: How to Build an Engaged, Innovative and Resilient Business*. Kogan Page Publishers.

Holzinger, A., Zatloukal, K., & Müller, H. (2025). Is human oversight to AI systems still possible? *New Biotechnology*, *85*, 59–62. DOI: 10.1016/j.nbt.2024.12.003 PMID: 39675423

Hutson, J., & Ceballos, J. (2023). Rethinking Education in the Age of AI: The Importance of Developing Durable Skills in the Industry 4.0. *Journal of Information Economics*, *1*(2), 26–35. Advance online publication. DOI: 10.58567/jie01020002

Jain, P., Tripathi, V., Malladi, R., & Khang, A. (2023). Data-Driven Artificial Intelligence (AI) Models in the Workforce Development Planning. In *Designing Workforce Management Systems for Industry 4.0*. CRC Press. DOI: 10.1201/9781003357070-10

Jingsheng, W. (2024). Cross-Training. In *The ECPH Encyclopedia of Psychology* (pp. 358–358). Springer., DOI: 10.1007/978-981-97-7874-4_1294

Johnston, S. (2004). Teaching Any Time, Any Place, Any Pace. In *Development and Management of Virtual Schools: Issues and Trends* (pp. 116–134). IGI Global Scientific Publishing. DOI: 10.4018/978-1-59140-154-4.ch006

Khamis, R. (2024). *AI-Powered Learning Experience Platforms: Investigating Personalized Learning in the Workplace*. https://gupea.ub.gu.se/handle/2077/83632

Khatib, M. E., Almarzooqi, S., Almarzooqi, E., & Alzaidan, S. (2024). Strategic Collaborations and Ecosystem Integration-DT Insights from Deloitte Case Studies. [IJTOP]. *International Journal of Theory of Organization and Practice*, *4*(2), 109–121. DOI: 10.54489/c9ef8m28

Kurki, A.-L., Koskela, I., & Yli-Kaitala, K. (2024). Collaborative development on a digital learning platform: The potential of AI tools for facilitation. *Human Technology*, *20*(3), 3. Advance online publication. DOI: 10.14254/1795-6889.2024.20-3.5

Kwok, L. (2022). Labor shortage: A critical reflection and a call for industry-academia collaboration. *International Journal of Contemporary Hospitality Management, 34*(11), 3929–3943. DOI: 10.1108/IJCHM-01-2022-0103

Lancaster, C., Gilreath, H., Mallick, R., & McNeese, N. J. (2024). Evaluating Cross-Training's Impact on Perceived Teaming Outcomes for Human-AI Teams. *Proceedings of the Human Factors and Ergonomics Society Annual Meeting, 68*(1), 1469–1472. DOI: 10.1177/10711813241262033

Lee, A. N., & Nie, Y. (2024). Future-Oriented Learning and Continuous Skills Development: Developing a Resilient Workforce in Changing Times. In Lee, A. N., & Nie, Y. (Eds.), *Future-oriented Learning and Skills Development for Employability: Insights from Singapore and Some Asia-Pacific Contexts* (pp. 3–15). Springer Nature., DOI: 10.1007/978-981-97-8584-1_1

Leger, M. (2023). *Building High-Trust Workplaces: The Role of Employee Resource Groups in Fostering Stronger Employee-Employer Relationships*. American Enterprise Institute. https://www.jstor.org/stable/resrep55292

Lengnick-Hall, C. A., Beck, T. E., & Lengnick-Hall, M. L. (2011). Developing a capacity for organizational resilience through strategic human resource management. *Human Resource Management Review, 21*(3), 243–255. DOI: 10.1016/j.hrmr.2010.07.001

Levandowski, S. (2025). Adult Learning Theory. In *Routledge Companion to Occupational Therapy*. Routledge. DOI: 10.4324/9781003526766-54

Liang, G. (2024). Skill Shifts and Retraining Initiatives: Adapting to Post-Pandemic Labor Market Dynamics. *Law and Economy, 3*(1), 58–61. DOI: 10.56397/LE.2024.01.06

Madhumita, G., & Dolly Diana, P. PC, N., Narendra Kiran, P. B., Aggarwal, S., & Satish Nargunde, A. (2024). AI-powered Performance Management: Driving Employee Success and Organizational Growth. *2024 5th International Conference on Recent Trends in Computer Science and Technology (ICRTCST)*, 204–209. DOI: 10.1109/ICRTCST61793.2024.10578371

Mohammed, N. A., Mohammed, D., & Gana, J. (2022). THE IMPACT OF TRAINING AND DEVELOPMENT ON EMPLOYEE PRODUCTIVITY IN THE 21ST CENTURY. *African Journal of Management and Business Research, 3*(1), 41–58.

Mohebianfar, E. (2025). *An AI-driven approach to improve talent retention and mobility* [fi=Ylempi AMK-opinnäytetyö|sv=Högre YH-examensarbete|en=Master's thesis|]. https://www.theseus.fi/handle/10024/883116

Montgomery, R. M. (2024). *The Rise of Inequality and Artificial Intelligence: Impacts, Challenges, and Opportunities in a Globalized Economy* (SSRN Scholarly Paper No. 4964094). Social Science Research Network. DOI: 10.2139/ssrn.4964094

Morandini, S., Fraboni, F., De Angelis, M., Puzzo, G., Giusino, D., & Pietrantoni, L. (2023). *The Impact of Artificial Intelligence on Workers' Skills: Upskilling and Reskilling in Organisations*. DOI: 10.28945/5078

Mutawa, A. M., & Sruthi, S. (2025). UNESCO's AI Competency Framework: Challenges and Opportunities in Educational Settings. In *Impacts of Generative AI on the Future of Research and Education* (pp. 75–96). IGI Global Scientific Publishing. DOI: 10.4018/979-8-3693-0884-4.ch004

Naguib, A., & Fouad, K. M. (2024). Database Security: Current Challenges and Effective Protection Strategies. *2024 6th International Conference on Computing and Informatics (ICCI)*, 120–130. DOI: 10.1109/ICCI61671.2024.10485182

OECD. (2024a). *Artificial intelligence and education and skills*. OECD. https://www.oecd.org/en/topics/artificial-intelligence-and-education-and-skills.html

OECD. (2024b, December 4). *OECD Economic Outlook, Volume 2024 Issue 2*. OECD. https://www.oecd.org/en/publications/oecd-economic-outlook-volume-2024-issue-2_d8814e8b-en.html

OECD AI Outlook. (2024, May 14). *OECD Digital Economy Outlook 2024 (Volume 1)*. OECD. https://www.oecd.org/en/publications/oecd-digital-economy-outlook-2024-volume-1_a1689dc5-en.html

Orth, C. D., Wilkinson, H. E., & Benfari, R. C. (1987). The manager's role as coach and mentor. *Organizational Dynamics*, *15*(4), 66–74. DOI: 10.1016/0090-2616(87)90045-3

Owino, D. (2023). *Employee cross-training as a tool for addressing employee loyalty and business environment uncertainties* [fi=Ylempi AMK-opinnäytetyö|sv=Högre YH-examensarbete|en=Master's thesis|]. https://www.theseus.fi/handle/10024/814262

Pan, D., Zhao, D., Pu, Y., Wang, L., & Zhang, Y. (2024). Use of cross-training in human–robot collaborative rescue. *Human Factors and Ergonomics in Manufacturing*, *34*(3), 261–276. DOI: 10.1002/hfm.21025

Ramachandran, K. K., Apsara Saleth Mary, A., Hawladar, S., Asokk, D., Bhaskar, B., & Pitroda, J. R. (2022). Machine learning and role of artificial intelligence in optimizing work performance and employee behavior. *Materials Today: Proceedings*, *51*, 2327–2331. DOI: 10.1016/j.matpr.2021.11.544

Roth, P. L., Purvis, K. L., & Bobko, P. (2012). A Meta-Analysis of Gender Group Differences for Measures of Job Performance in Field Studies. *Journal of Management, 38*(2), 719–739. DOI: 10.1177/0149206310374774

Scharron, C. (2025). *Examining Adoption Factors of AI-Enabled Workplace Training Through the Lens of the UTAUT2 and Extended Factors*. https://hdl.handle.net/20.500.12264/714

Shukla, P., & Garg, A. (2022). Sentiment Analysis of Online Learners in Higher Education: A Learning Perspective through Unstructured Data. In *Intelligent System Algorithms and Applications in Science and Technology*. Apple Academic Press.

Singh, V., Singh, G., & Sharma, G. (2025). The Future of the Healthcare Workforce in the Age of Automation. In *Driving Global Health and Sustainable Development Goals With Smart Technology* (pp. 453–472). IGI Global Scientific Publishing., DOI: 10.4018/979-8-3373-0240-9.ch019

Soomro, S., Fan, M., Sohu, J. M., Soomro, S., & Shaikh, S. N. (2024). AI adoption: A bridge or a barrier? The moderating role of organizational support in the path toward employee well-being. *Kybernetes, ahead-of-print*(ahead-of-print). DOI: 10.1108/K-07-2024-1889

Taheri Hosseinkhani, N. (2025). *Economic and Social Implications of AI-Driven Automation and Workforce Transformation*. https://aurora.auburn.edu/handle/11200/50713

Tariq, M. U., Babar, M., Poulin, M., Khattak, A. S., Alshehri, M. D., & Kaleem, S. (2021). Human Behavior Analysis Using Intelligent Big Data Analytics. *Frontiers in Psychology, 12*, 686610. Advance online publication. DOI: 10.3389/fpsyg.2021.686610 PMID: 34295289

Taylor, R., Fakhimi, M., Ioannou, A., & Spanaki, K. (2024). Personalized learning in education: A machine learning and simulation approach. *Benchmarking*. Advance online publication. DOI: 10.1108/BIJ-06-2023-0380

Teece, D. J. (2018). Business models and dynamic capabilities. *Long Range Planning, 51*(1), 40–49. DOI: 10.1016/j.lrp.2017.06.007

UNESCO. (2023a). *Global education monitoring report, 2023: Technology in education: A tool on whose terms? - UNESCO Digital Library*. https://unesdoc.unesco.org/ark:/48223/pf0000385723

UNESCO. (2023b). *Technology in education: GEM Report 2023 | Global Education Monitoring Report*. https://www.unesco.org/gem-report/en/publication/technology

Urban, A. (2024). Clinical Trial Research Nurse New Employee Onboarding 30-60 -90 Day Checklist. *Master's Projects and Capstones*. https://repository.usfca.edu/capstone/1761

World Economic Forum. (2023). *The Future of Jobs Report 2023*. World Economic Forum. https://www.weforum.org/publications/the-future-of-jobs-report-2023/

Xu, Z. (2024). AI in education: Enhancing learning experiences and student outcomes. *Applied and Computational Engineering*, *51*(1), 104–111. DOI: 10.54254/2755-2721/51/20241187

Yu, D. (2023). AI-Empowered Metaverse Learning Simulation Technology Application. *2023 International Conference on Intelligent Metaverse Technologies & Applications (iMETA)*, 1–6. DOI: 10.1109/iMETA59369.2023.10294830

Zerilli, J., Bhatt, U., & Weller, A. (2022). How transparency modulates trust in artificial intelligence. *Patterns (New York, N.Y.)*, *3*(4), 100455. Advance online publication. DOI: 10.1016/j.patter.2022.100455 PMID: 35465233

Chapter 9
Predictive Workforce Analytics and Optimization for Adaptive Cross-Training in Labor-Constrained Environments

Duggirala Aravind
http://orcid.org/0009-0005-4362-7684
ASET Institute of Science and Technology, India

ABSTRACT

Close labor markets are compounding the shortage of skills and limiting the performance of organizations, and are forcing organizations to adopt adaptive labor markets. This chapter suggests a predictive workforce analytics and optimisation model of cross-training within labour constraints. The structure allows dynamic investment of cross-training to be made in areas of critical need by combining skill demand forecasting, based on machine learning with multi-objective optimization models. It also utilizes skill adjacency mapping, estimation of productivity and cost benefit analysis to ensure that the workforce is maximized on both flexibility and resilience. The simulation-based example will also illustrate the enhanced use of resources and decreased risk of vacancy. The chapter provides practical information to managers and policymakers who aim at drawing up data based, scalable proposals to remain competitive amidst unpredictable labor markets.

DOI: 10.4018/979-8-3373-5327-2.ch009

ght © 2027, IGI Global Scientific Publishing. Copying or distributing in print or electronic forms without written permission of IGI Global Scientific Publishing is prohibited. Use of this chapter to generative artificial intelligence (AI) technologies is expressly prohibited. The publisher reserves all rights to license its use for generative AI training and machine learning model development.

1. INTRODUCTION

The high labor markets are worsening skill shortages, and limiting organizational adaptability, in industries. The conventional workforce planning techniques are getting too insufficient in dynamic settings invoked by fluctuation of demands. This chapter meets the requirement of data-driven cross-training plans by combining predictive workforce analytics with optimization modeling to enhance flexibility and resilience and operational performance.

1.1 Background, Motivation, and Problem Context

Demographic changes, technological upheaval and new skill demands are causing global labor markets to persist in tightening. Companies are becoming more and more challenged filling pressing vacancies, resulting in losses of productivity, time wastage and high labor expenses. In these settings, workforce agility is a strategic cost and not an added ability. Cross-training, the ability to perform multiple roles by employees has proved to be a valid option to address skill gaps and make specific roles in operations flexible. Nevertheless, conventional cross-training strategies tend to be informal without a clear plan and data-driven decision-making.

This chapter is driven by the shortcomings of the current workforce management approaches that do not integrate the contributions of predictive knowledge and optimization processes. Organizations often face difficulty with determining which positions must be cross-trained, allocation of fewer training resources, and balancing conflicting goals such as cost-efficiency and productivity. In addition, the non-existence of built-in analysing structures limits the chance to evolve with the changing circumstances in the labor market. This leaves a critical gap in theory and practice that requires the development of advanced models combining predictive analytics with optimization techniques to effectively cross-train the workforce.

1.2 Research Contributions and Methodological Approach

This chapter contributes to the workforce analytics and cross-train options literature in labour constrained settings in several significant ways. First, it suggests a predictive workforce analytics model that relies on historical data and machine learning methods to predict the demand and potential shortages in skills in organizational roles. This allows making decisions proactively and minimizing the uncertainty in workforce planning.

Second, the chapter presents a multi-objective optimization model that aims at the efficient allocation of cross-training resources and at the same time minimizing costs, maximizing productivity, and improving workforce flexibility.

Third, the research incorporates a skill adjacency mapping mechanism that establishes cross-training pathways between the two skills that can effectively be supported, based on the similarity of the competencies associated with these two skills. Probably its most important methodological contribution is adding the predictive analytics to the optimization, and vice versa, to create a single decision-support system.

This framework is also confirmed by the simulation based analysis, which proves the applicability of the framework in the real world situation. This chapter further develops the existing research and offers a scalable solution to adaptive workforce management in volatile employment markets.

1.3 Chapter Structure and Organization

The rest of this chapter has been designed in such a way that a systematic development and validation of the proposed adaptive cross-training framework, in labor-constrained environments, can be secured. The next section involves a review of the available literature about the workforce analytics, cross-training practices and optimization models in the workforce planning. This review provides the theoretical base, and emphasizes the most significant research areas where the chapter attempts to fill the gap. Then there will be conceptual framework section, which will explain, in detail, the basic blocks of the proposed model, as well as its interrelations.

The chapter continues to develop the predictive workforce analytics model, and then, the optimization model of cross-training allocation is developed. Another technical part details the combination of analytics and optimization and notes that the framework is dynamic and adaptive. The mechanism of the skill adjacency mapping is then discussed and sheds light on how cross-training pathways are identified. It is followed by a simulation-based case study that is used to show the practical applicability of the model. Discussion section analyzes the results and performance is assessed using key metrics and ROI analysis. At the end of the chapter, there are managerial implications and limitations, as well as future directions of research.

2. LITERATURE REVIEW

2.1 Workforce Analytics

Workforce analytics has become one of the essential areas in human resource management, as it has enabled organizations to utilize the insights of workforce analytics in their strategic decision-making. In the past the workforce planning process used to rely on descriptive statistics, as well as other managerial intuitive approaches; however, with emergence of greater availability of large-scale organizational data, it has become relatively simpler to adopt advanced analytical techniques. Predictive workforce analysis is more than historic analysis in that it uses statistical models, machine learning algorithms to predict future workforce trends, such as skills requirements, turnover and productivity trends. This reactive/proactive decision making has contributed immensely to organization agility amid unpredictable labor markets (Huselid, 2018; Karuppiah & Kumaran, 2025).

Recent literature underlines the value of predictive models like regression analysis, time- Series forecasting, and classification algorithms in determining predictive workforce risks and opportunities. These frameworks will help organizations to foresee skill gaps and develop specific interventions. Also, artificial intelligence has enabled accuracy and scalability of workforce analytics systems, so that real-time insights and dynamism are possible. Although these are the progresses, there are still challenges in terms of data quality, model interpretability, and integration with the operational decision-making processes. In addition, workforce analytics is frequently independent of other strategic operations, thus restricting its ability to tackle complex organizational issues. While existing research highlights its potential in forecasting and monitoring, there is limited focus on its application in optimizing workforce development strategies such as cross-training. This implies that there is a need to create integrated models that would unite predictive analytics models and decision optimization strategies to improve the resilience and flexibility of the workforce in labor constrained environments (Karuppiah et al., 2025; Gupta et al., 2025).

2.2 Cross – Training and Workforce Flexibility

The concepts of cross-training are well-known as effective strategies aimed at improving the workforce flexibility and organizational sustainability. Cross-training minimizes the reliance on specialized people and reduces the risks related to labor shortages. The concept has its foundations on human capital theory which proposes that the value of developing a competitive advantage lies in the flexible capabilities; and the resource-based view, which suggests that, the value of developing a competitive advantage lies in the flexible capabilities. Cross-training in a dynamic and uncertain environment will cause quick reallocation of the workforce, which will ensure continuation of the operations and better service delivery. Empirical studies show that cross-training may result in important gains, such as higher production level, shorter downtime, and greater employee involvement. It also helps in sharing knowledge and collaboration, thus creating a culture of lifelong learning (A. Ahmadi et al., 2025; Vapiwala et al., 2025).

Nevertheless, the success of cross-training hinges on several issues, including the choice of roles, how to structure training programs, and alignment with the organizational goals. Such programs can lead to dilution of skills, workload, and job satisfaction in case the programs are poorly conducted. Also, the task of determining the best cross-training routes and balancing the trade-off between depth of expertise and breadth of skills can present a challenge to organizations. Although the available literature offers important insights on the advantages and limitations of cross-training, they are mostly based on qualitative methods or traditional models. Quantitative frameworks are lacking that systematically analyze cross-training choices in the different labor market conditions. The weakness suggests the necessity of data-driven strategies that can be adjusted dynamically and allow the workforce to become flexible (S. Rao et al., 2026; Lima & Rahman, 2025).

2.3 Optimization in Workforce Planning

Workforce planning has widely used optimization mechanisms to improve the allocation of resources and productivity. These approaches include development of mathematical models that seek to reach a certain goal, including cost minimization, productivity maximization, or workload distribution optimization. The methods that are typically used in this field are linear programming, integer programming, and multi-objective optimization. The models allow decision-makers to rationalize the trade-offs and to recognize the optimal solutions to a given problem which may consist of budget constraints, labour availability, and skill availability. Optimization models have been utilized in the workforce management context, to tackle scheduling, staffing and task assignment problems. An example is that workforce scheduling models identify the best way to schedule employees among shifts, and assignment models pair workers to tasks based on skill match (W. J. Peck, 2025; Ostovari et al., 2025).

The further developed methods use stochastic factors in order to consider uncertainty in demand and availability of workforce. Multi-objective optimization models further generalize this framework by solving competing objectives giving a set of Pareto-optimal solutions, as opposed to a single optimal solution. Although they are effective, the applicability of the existing optimization models is constrained by the assumption of stationary conditions and predetermined parameters. Moreover, these models currently are usually based on deterministic inputs without any predictive insights of the data analytics. This distinction between predictive analytics and optimization limits capacity to adapt to changing needs in the workforce. Hence, the need to have integrated helps that put predictive modeling and optimization techniques together, to be able to do adaptive and data-directed workforce planning in complex settings (Niyaz et al., 2025; Eichenseer et al., 2025).

2.4 Identified Research Gaps

The literature analysis demonstrates that there are a number of significant gaps that hinder the efficiency of the current modes of managing labor and implementing cross-training in work restricted environments. To begin with, workforce analytics has evolved greatly so far in terms of prediction functions, however their use is still, to a large extent, limited to prediction and monitoring functions. The adoption of predictive insights into decision making models has not been fully integrated especially in workforce development programs like cross-training. This disjuncture minimizes the practical effect of workforce analytics on real-world workforce challenges.

Second, the cross-training research is mainly concentrated on qualitative analysis and conceptual discussions, and only limited on quantitative modeling and optimization. The current literature commonly lacks systematic means to determine optimal cross training trajectories or an efficient use of training materials. Consequently, organizations have no strong instruments to assess the trade-offs between cost, productivity, and flexibility, considering cross-training programmes.

Third, workforce planning optimization models tend to be created without regard to predictive analytics, using only static inputs and assumptions. This affects their capacity to be responsive to the changing labor market conditions and the changing organizational needs. The lack of the integrated frameworks, which integrates predictive analytics, skill mapping and optimization, is a major gap in the literature.

Lastly, empirical validation and studies based on simulations that proving the practical use of proposed models is lacking. To cope with these gaps, it is imperative to design holistic, data-intensive frameworks that incorporate analytics and optimization and support adaptable cross-training solutions in complicated labor systems.

3. CONCEPTUAL FRAMEWORK

3.1 Integrated System Architecture

The conceptual framework proposed is designed to be an integrated system architecture comprised of predictive workforce analytics and optimization-based decisions support for adaptive cross-training. There are three main layers of architecture: data layer, analytics layer, and decision layer. The data layer mashed up disparate data sources such as employee skills inventories, past workforce performance, training history, and changes in demand. These data are manipulated to make them usable in an analytical process, via structures that make sense for data analysis.

The analytics layer are predictive models used to predict future skills needs, and to flag possible skill gap. The output of this layer is passed on to the decision layer where optimization algorithms decide what optimal cross-training allocations are in the presence of specific constraints. Feedback mechanism allows constant updating of the model to new data and results to allow dynamic adaptations. This were-integrated approach to architecture enables an effective link in the processes of forecasting and decision making so that the cross training strategies remain flexible and capable of meeting the evolving conditions of the labour market and the needs of the organization.

3.2 Key Components and Relationships

The conceptual framework consists of multiple components that are interconnected to facilitate adaptive workforce cross training. The first part is the predictive analytics module that helps predict skills demand and key skills shortages. The second part is skill adjacency (SA), which assesses the similarity of various roles and identifies possible cross-training relationships based on competency similarities. The third part is the optimization engine, which assigns the training resources between multiple goals like cost efficiency, productivity, and workforce flexibility.

All these aspects are built-in and linked together in a structured way: data flows and iterative feedback loops. The analytics module uses predictions to inform the optimization process, and optimization results impact the next training set and workforce performance metrics. The skill adjacency module serves as a hinge, linking workforce capabilities into practical training decisions. These relationships ensure that the system functions as a whole and are essential for continuous learning, adjustment and improvements in cross-training protocols in labour limited settings.

3.3 Theoretical Grounding

It has been proposed from different theoretical lenses underlying its interdisciplinary nature. The concept of human capital theory helps to explain why investing an employee's skill and abilities is important for productivity and the performance of the organization. The resource-based view also highlights the role of the ability of workforces in generating flexible and versatile capabilities as a source of sustainable competitive advantage. Also, operations research concepts, specifically optimization theory, are used to optimally distribute scarce training resources within limitations. Predictive analytics is enabled by theory of decision making that underlines the significance of data-driven information in minimizing uncertainty and the quality of decision. The framework is also adaptive in the light of complexity theory which acknowledges that labour markets are dynamic systems and need to be continuously adjusted. These theoretical visions, put together in one framework, make it possible to weave a complete thread from strategic management, analytic, and optimization solutions, while at the same time delivering conceptual rigor and practical value to the table for solving problems with limited labor resources.

Figure 1. Conceptual Framework (Integrated Architecture)

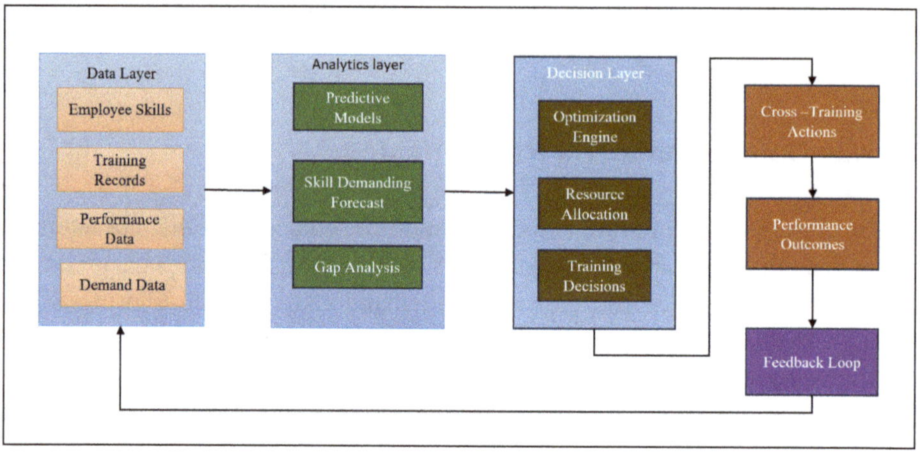

4. PREDICTIVE WORKFORCE ANALYTICS MODEL

4.1 Data Sources and Preprocessing

The marker of how effective the predictive workforce analytics model will be is how good and varied the data feed into it is. The data sources used are organisational demand data, training history, job performance, skill inventories and employee demographic. External information, including sector trends and indicators of employment, can also be included to improve forecasting. Data pre-processing is an extremely important step as it ensures reliability and consistency in the data. This includes data cleaning for inconsistency and missing data, data normalization to align various data types, and feature engineering to transform the data into more useful elements suitable for analysis. In certain cases, categorical variables (e.g., skill types, job roles) are converted into numerical values that can be used by machine learning models. Furthermore, dimensionality reduction techniques can be used to handle high-dimensional data sets. The model systematically preprocesses those organizational data into a structured and analysable form, thus providing an accurate prediction and the possibility to integrate it into later optimization processes.

4.2 Forecasting Techniques (ML/Statistical Models)

The predictive workforce analytics model uses statistical and machine learning, or AI-based, techniques to predict the need of skills and workforce. Historical patterns and relationships among variables are revealed by traditional (time-series analysis, regression) statistical methods. The methods are used to attain interpretability and are baseline models for comparisons. Further, non-linear patterns in workforce data are captured using machine learning algorithms such as decision trees, random forests and neural networks. These models work well in cases where either large data sets or multiple factors are affecting the data are involved. Adding to the above, ensemble methods will improve the predictive accuracy of the outputs from multiple models. The metrics included in the model performance evaluations are accurate, mean squared error, precision, making model robust and reliable in evaluating. Prevention of overfitting solutions and enhancing generalizability is achieved by using cross-validation techniques. The model combines statistical and machine learning techniques to strike a balance between explainability and predictive ability, aiding in informed workforce planning decisions.

4.3 Output: Skill Demand and Shortages

The predictive workforce analytics model generates insights that guide towards future skill needs and future workforce gaps. The model uses a variety of skill types and durations to provide predictions of skill requirements for each job and across time, helping companies prepare for upcoming skill shortages. The results of these forecasts are plotted in the form of demand profiles, and used to pinpoint skills of relevance and areas of potential risk. The model assesses and quantifies the skill gaps between what the workforce already can do and what they are expected to require in the future, as well as estimating demand. This gap analysis helps identify roles that will likely be in a shortage and prioritise them for cross training interventions. The output also contains probability estimates in regards to workforce disruptions, giving organizations an understanding of the risk associated with each scenario. Such knowledge is fed directly into the optimization model providing a useful input for allocating training, and ensuring that a cross-training model matches future organization needs.

5. OPTIMIZATION MODELING FOR CROSS-TRAINING

5.1 Decision Variables

Decision variables are the independent factors that should be controlled in order to present the amount of cross-training resources used into the optimization model. The major decision variable in this situation is allocating staff to cross-training for particular tasks. This can be captured as a binary variable, in which case 1 means that an employee is chosen to train on a specific role, and 0 otherwise. In addition, continuous variables can also be added to describe the amount of training provided to an employee, based on variations in training time or training intensity. A second class of decision variables is associated with deployment to a workforce – whether a trained worker is utilized for a certain job over a certain time period. Operational Outcomes are linked with Training Decisions by these variables. Also, variables can be added to capture resource utilization, including training hours, budget, and trainer availability. The model allows for the systematic analysis of possible combinations of training and deployment decisions in order to identify optimal combinations of these decisions under labour constraint.

5.2 Objective Functions (cost, productivity, flexibility)

The optimization model is intended to obtain multiple objectives, corresponding to organizational priorities in a situation of hard constraints on resources, such as workforce. The first goal in cross training is to minimize the cost of cross training (expense associated with training programs, employee time and potential loss in productivity associated with training periods). This helps to keep their use efficient, affordable. The second goal is to leverage workforce to maximize productivity by matching the skills of those working in a role to the necessary skills, which helps improve the efficient use of workforce and eliminate idle time or mis-match. The third aim focuses on workforce flexibility as best measured by the capacity of staff to work with more than one job and multi-adapt to varying demands. The goal reflects the importance of cross training from a strategic standpoint, to build organizational resilience. These goals may be conflicting in nature, so the model uses a Multi-Objective Optimization that will yield trade-offs instead of one optimal solution. There are methods like weighted sum methods or Pareto optimization that can be used to achieve balance between these objectives. It covers several dimensions of performance, offering an all-encompassing support for decision-making in complex work environments.

5.3 Constraints

Constraints are the restrictions that limit the range of values in which the optimization model needs to be operated, so that solutions generated by the model are feasible and realistic. The budget limitation is one of the main constraints that limits the overall budgetary limits for cross-training activities. This includes the expenses of training materials, staff time and instructor fees. Other constraints include the capacity for training, in terms of available trainers, training facilities and training time, which limits the number of employees that can be trained at one time. Skill compatibility constraints prevent employee's being assigned to a training program that requires skills the employee either doesn't have or doesn't possess enough of. This prevents unrealistic or ineffective training and avoids training positions. Further, the availability of the workforce should be taken into account, where that training is running and where they are needed for other field of work activities. A time limit may also be considered to represent a dead line or a time scale over which training has to be carried out. The model then considers these constraints, allowing the optimization process to generate actionable and feasible solutions while taking account of organizational constraints and strategic goals aimed at building up the workforce in labour-limited scenarios.

5.4 Solution techniques

Appropriate mathematical and computational techniques that can solve the optimization model as it is complex and multi-objective must be considered. When the variables of the problem are discrete like binary training assignments, linear programming and integer programming techniques are often used. More sophisticated techniques including mixed-integer nonlinear programming can be used if the relationships between variables are not linear and multiple conflicting objective functions present. Multi-objective optimal solutions tools are relevant in this context, where they enable the decisionmakers to consider the trade-offs between the optimal cost, productiveness and flexibility. The weighted sum approach, goal programming and Pareto frontier analysis are the most commonly used methods to develop a set of efficient solutions. Some heuristic and metaheuristic methods can be used when the problem size increases or is expensive to compute such as genetic algorithm or simulated annealing. Also, optimization can be simulated to assess the performance of different solutions, depending on uncertainty. Taken together, these techniques offer a means to create scalable and robust solutions allowing for the use of the optimization model to make adaptive cross-training decisions in a dynamic labor space.

6. CORE TECHNICAL SECTION: INTEGRATED ANALYTICS – OPTIMIZATION ARCHITECTURE

6.1 Coupling Predictive Outputs with Optimization Inputs

The coupling of predictive workforce analytics with optimization modeling must be structured and provide a mechanism to turn the analytical output into an actionable decision input. Predictive models produce forecasts of skills demand, skills supply and possible skills shortages for various skills and timeframes. These outputs are only useful in a decision support form if they are converted to parameters useable in the optimization framework. To make this happen, predicted skill demand is transformed to quantitative demand of employees, that's, number of workers required for every job. Likewise, predicted shortages are given as deficit variables, that is, where there is a shortage of some workforce capacity.

These parameters are used in the key inputs to the optimization model, affecting both the objective functions and constraints. For example, greater predicted shortages can lead to greater priority of certain roles for cross training, and variability in demand can impact on resource allocation decisions. Besides, the probabilistic outputs of future algorithms can be included into a stochastic optimization formulation, where the uncertainties can be taken into account. This coupling means that optimization decisions are based on future-looking facts and not on assumptions. The framework connects the dots between predictive outcomes and optimization inputs, enabling organisations to plan ahead and implement appropriate training plans for cross-training resources when they are operating within a constrained workforce, while also enhancing prediction accuracy and organisational responsiveness.

6.2 Feedback Loop Mechanism (Dynamic Adaptation)

The feedback loop mechanism lies at the heart of the integrated analytics–optimization architecture, allowing continuous learning and adaptation to evolving conditions with the workforce. A closed-loop process is considered, which makes predictions and decisions by learning from the observed results, unlike in fixed models. This cyclical process allows the predictive and optimization models to be progressively more correct and pertinent in the future. After implementing cross training, performance data (productivity, skills, operational data, etc.) is gathered and returned to the Data layer.

The improved data points are then fed into predictive models to enhance their predictive powers. Meanwhile, the optimization model fine-tunes its parameters by using the differences between the actual and expected results in order to make better, future allocation decisions. This is a natural adaptation mechanism which helps the system react to variation in labor demand, supply of labour and external factors. It also facilitates scenario analysis by allowing companies to run various scenarios and feed the findings into further planning cycles. A feedback loop sustains responsiveness, self-correction and continual improvement in the framework. This means that organizations have the flexibility and resilience to manage their staff in the most volatile and uncertain labor markets.

6.3 Algorithmic Workflow

Step 1: Demand Prediction

The first step of the algorithmic process is forecasting the needs for employment in the future based on past and present existing data. Machine learning and statistical models can be used to predict skill demand on various time scales by identifying patterns in employee performance, job attributes, and labor market data. These models provide quantitative estimates of workforce needs for each of these roles, as well as estimates of uncertainty. It outputs the results as a demand vector that takes into account departmental and time variation. The accuracy of the demand prediction is crucial because it is the base of the next steps in the workflow and must be supported by the required cross-training decisions from the anticipated organizational needs.

Step 2: Skill Gap Identification

The second phase involves identifying skill gaps through a match of the predicted skill demand and skill prevalence of the current workforce. This includes identifying employee skills and requirements for roles and quantifying the gap between the two. Produces a gap matrix for roles, revealing role gaps and employees who may be cross-trained through skill adjacency. The different gaps are rated against impact to the organization's performance and risk exposure and assigned to priority levels. This one will help focus the optimization model into the most acute areas and allow for effective use of cross-training resources and the least impact of labor shortage.

Step 3: Optimization-Based Allocation

Allocation of cross training resources is the final step and that's done with the use of optimization methods. Gap matrix and demand forecasts are used as inputs for a multi-objective optimization model designed to provide an optimum assignment of employees to training programs. The model incorporates the budget constraints, training capacity constraints and workforce capacity constraints and optimizes for cost, productivity and flex. The output is a set of optimal or "near" optimal training decisions as to who is to be trained for what. These decisions are made within the organization and their results are tracked for input to the decision-making process.

6.4 System Architecture (Data → Model → Decision Layer)

The proposed framework's system architecture is designed to be a structured pipeline comprising the following three interconnected layers: data, model and decision. The data layer is the critical support infrastructure that connects to various data sources like employee files, skill inventories, training records, and outsourcing data on the labor market. This layer provides for the collection, cleaning and storage of all relevant data in a format appropriate for analysis. The job of the model layer is to convert the data into meaningful information. It also contains predictive analytics models that predict the need for various skills and identify skill shortages and optimization models that identify optimal cross-training strategies.

These models run in a coordinated way, where the outputs of predictive models were used as the inputs to optimization. These are integrated to allow the system to shift from descriptive analysis to prescriptive decision making. The decision layer interprets the output from the model – such as recommending training for staff and reshaping the workforce. It also lays out monitoring mechanisms which record the results of decisions taken. The data from this layer is returned to the data layer, forming the closing of the feedback loop. This architecture facilitates a smooth flow of data processing, analytical modeling and decision execution, helping companies put into practice adaptive and data-driven cross-training strategies in dynamic work environments.

6.5 Computational Complexity and Scalability Considerations

The performance of the integrated analytics–optimization framework depends on the predictive modeling and optimization parts. Training predictive models, especially those using machine learning algorithms, can be computationally intensive, particularly with large-scale and high-dimensional datasets. Dimensionality reduction and parallel processing can be used for efficiency gains. The optimization part is also challenging, especially if the formulation is a mixed-integer program with several objectives and constraints. As the number of decision variables grows, so do the computational costs of exact solutions, increasing at an exponential rate for large organisations. To overcome this, heuristic and metaheuristic algorithms can be implemented to find near-optimal solution, in acceptable time. Scalability is crucial, must consider for growing volumes of data and increasing complexity of the organization. The modular system design facilitates scalable components and the cloud component is ideal for handling large amounts of data. Further, approximate and decomposition methods can be used to divide large problems into smaller subproblems. The framework tackles computational complexity and scalability, making it suitable for real-world applications, allowing companies of any scale to implement and make use of sophisticated cross training optimisation.

7. SKILL ADJACENCY AND MAPPING MECHANISM

7.1 Skill Similarity Metrics

Skill similarity measures are the backbone of determining viable intra-organisational source targets. They measure the amount of skills or knowledge overlap across roles and can be used to evaluate the ease with which someone can move from a current role to another. Similarity metrics usually start with a common skills taxonomy to represent both technical and non-technical skills. These are then encoded as a vector of abilities; each competency being represented by a specific element of its corresponding score. There are number of mathematical methods that can be used to calculate the similarity between these vectors.

Popular methods are cosine similarity, Euclidean distance, and Jaccard similarity, among others, each having its own benefits based on the data type. Cosine similarity is useful for high dimensional skill spaces because it judges the directionality of skill vectors. Weighted similarity measures can also be added to give more weight to important skills that make a bigger impact on the performance. Dynamic differences may also be considered in addition to static differences based on similarity. For example, similarity measures can be improved using machine learning algorithms based on past training results or performance gains. In a labor-limited setting, skill similarity metrics can be used accurately to develop adjacency structures and to inform cross-training decisions.

7.2 Adjacency Matrix Construction

The adjacency matrix is an organized relationship between roles based on the similarity of skills. It is also an important part of the modelling of cross-training potentials as it shows which roles are close enough to make potential transitions possible. An element in the matrix is the degree of similarity between a pair of roles, usually expressed as a value between 0 and 1. A higher number means better overlap, where the required skills will roll up the cross-training pathway. The construction starts by computing the pairwise similarity scores between all roles based on the similarity metrics selected. These scores are then arranged in a square matrix with rows and columns representing positions in the organization.

A threshold value is commonly used to eliminate weak relationships when needed, in practice. A sparse matrix, indicating meaningful connections among role-pairs, is produced if only role-pairs with similarity scores above this threshold are retained for cross-training. You can also apply weights on the adjacency matrix to represent the training expense, duration, or complexity to learn each transition. Moreover, directionality may be added to reflect lack of symmetry in skill transferability. The structured representation allows for efficient analysis, projection and connection with optimizing models and to take data-driven decisions regarding workforce development and cross training allocation.

7.3 Cross-Training Pathways

Pathways are sequences of skills that employees can move to one another between roles, which is called cross-training pathways. This is derived from the adjacency matrix, and used to create an effective training program design. Pathways don't need to be role-to-role transitions only but can require several steps to develop each of the competencies. Optimal pathways are determined by weighing the pros and cons of training times, costs and effectiveness. The shorter the pathway the better, and the more similar the score, the better. In some situations, though, direct transitions may not be possible and multi-step pathways may be needed. There are some graph based algorithms that can be used like shortest path or network flow algorithms to find out which is the best way. Besides efficiency, organisational priorities and workforce limitations need to be considered in pathways. As an example, critical roles with a high risk of shortage could be prioritized, which would then impact on training sequences. Pathway design can be flexible, enabling organisations to design cross training strategies to meet their needs. Cross training pathways offer organized and targeted direction which allows flexibility and maximize usage of labor resources.

8. APPLICATION SCENARIO

8.1 Scenario Setup

In order to showcase the feasibility of the developed framework, a case scenario is chosen in a mid-sized organization with a need for labor constipation. For the purpose of illustrating the practicability of the developed framework a hypothetical application scenario is developed in a mid-sized organization under labour constrained circumstances. It's made up of several departments, each needing various skills to carry out operations. The organization is struggling with maintaining the uniformity of workforce performance due to growing demands variation and scarcity of skilled workforce. The scenario takes existing workforce information (like employees' skill profile, training history, employee performance, etc.) for granted.

Moreover, predictive analytics models are used to create demand forecasts for various positions. The goal is to use this to create an optimal cross training approach that fills in the skills and is as affordable as possible without sacrificing operational efficiency. Assumptions include fixed training budgets, training capacity constraints. There are distinct planning time-periods between which workforce allocation can be changed. This scenario offers a controlled test bed to assess the effectiveness of the integrated analytics–optimization framework. The scenario sets up a realistic environment, allowing an in-depth evaluation of the ability of cross-training strategies to enhance workforce flexibility and resilience.

8.2 Implementation Details

The entire proposed framework for the application scenario has a number of sequential steps which include predictive analytics, skill mapping, and optimization techniques. The available workforce data is pre-processed and structured for consistency and usability, and this is the first step. Predictive models are then used to predict the skill demand in various roles and various times, providing inputs for further analysis. Then, a matrix of skill similarities is calculated and an adjacent matrix is built based on this to show potential opportunities for cross-training. This matrix is utilized to ascertain potential points of employee skill development. The optimization problem is finally written out, including the decision variables, the objective functions as well as the constraints that are specific to the situation.

Parameters include training costs, employee availability and space constraints to be practical. Depending on the level of complexity of the problem, a suitable computation method (e.g., mixed integer programming or heuristic algorithms) will be used to solve a model. The solution identifies the best cross training allocation (who trains in what), or just specifies that no cross training is possible. There are also monitoring mechanisms for tracking the outcomes and progress in training, which are part of implementation. This is a systematic approach, which will help to implement the framework in a systematic way and make effective decisions in workforce planning.

8.3 Results and Comparative Analysis

The findings for the application scenario illustrate the effectiveness of the proposed framework in enhancing the efficiency of workforce to enhance performance given limited manpower. Optimizing cross-training training outcomes provides a substantial decrease in skills gaps in each critical role, thereby improving operational continuity. Employees having multiple skill sets leads to higher rate of utilization of the workforce and hence more productivity. Analysis of the proposed framework is carried out based on a base case in which cross training decisions are not made with predictive analytics and/or optimization. The baseline approach creates sub-optimal training resource allocation, more costs and ongoing skill gaps.

The integrated approach, on the other hand, brings more efficient alignment of workforce capability and need for them, resulting in greater efficiency. Key performance indicators, such as cost savings, productivity gains, and reduction in vacancy rates, are used to quantify the benefits. The sensitivity analysis also illustrates the robustness of the model in the face of changes in the conditions, including changes in demand or budget constraints. The results support the importance of combining analytics and optimization, and show strong evidence of the framework's impact on implementing adaptive and data driven strategies for workforce management.

9. DISCUSSIONS

9.1 Interpretation of Key Findings

The outcomes for the suggested integrated approach, discussed in the paper, have shown the effectiveness of integrating predictive analytics with optimization modeling for workforce cross training in labor constrained contexts. The model illustrates a significant decrease in skill gaps between employees and expected needs, which helps improve operational continuity and prevent skill shortages. The framework can help organizations reduce risk of labor shortage by identifying critical roles in advance and cross training them. Another significant outcome is the growth in workforce utilisation. Reflexivity provided for by multi-skill training gives flexibility for real-time reallocation of resources as conditions shift in demand. This flexibility minimises time wasted and maximises productivity. Moreover, the skill adjacency mapping will make training efforts effective and focused, thus reducing training costs. The findings also show that the supervised inputs are vastly superior to static ones for optimization decision making. Being able to predict future workforce needs helps organizations become more reactive rather than reactive. In general, the results corroborate the proposed structure as an effective and scalable approach in enhancing the resilience and performance of the workforce in a dynamic labor market.

9.2 Trade-Offs Observed

9.2.1 Cost vs. Flexibility

Based on this analysis, there is a basic efficiency and flexibility efficiency trade-off. By expanding cross training, employees can gain access to more than one skill, minimizing risk of skills gaps and increasing operational flexibility. But it is expensive, it takes time and slows down productivity for a period of time while learning takes place. This trade-off is seen in optimization models that incorporate multiple objectives to balance the competing ones. The results show that some cross-training does have clear advantages, provided the investments are not excessive.

9.2.2 Specialization vs. Adaptability

An additional important trade-off that comes to light from the results is specialization vs. adaptability. Specialized workers are generally very efficient and experts in their job, which leads to higher productivity in stable situations. But labor shortages can have some disadvantages because too much specialization can lead to a failure to function if someone is missing. When training is cross-training, it brings adaptability by providing employees with a wider variety of skills that allow them to fill a variety of roles as necessary. This provides flexibility, but if handled with care, it could result in a spreading of the expertise

9.3 Sensitivity Analysis

The proposed framework is tested for its robustness through sensitivity analysis under different conditions and parameter changes. Training expenditures, labor input, fluctuations in demand, and skill-level closeness thresholds are important factors analyzed. The results show high sensitivity to changes in these parameters, elucidating the effect of changes in each parameter on the success of cross-trainers. For example, higher training expenses are associated with more flexible workforce, fewer skill gaps, but at a certain point, improvements slow down. Likewise, the more variable the demand, the greater the need for workforce flexibility and allocation happens to be.

9.4 Comparison with Existing Approaches

There are a number of benefits that the suggested approach has over the traditional ways of workforce planning and cross training. Traditional approaches are typically grounded in static models or management intuition, and cannot account for predictions or systematically optimize decisions. Consequently, they are often reactive – tackling workforce shortages when they have arisen. The integrated analytics–optimization framework, however, takes a proactive stance, predicting future skill needs and making cross-training decisions in response. The predictive ability allows organizations to proactively address human resource challenges prior to their affecting the organization. Further, optimization techniques enable efficient use of training resources in addressing multiple objectives, including cost, productivity, and flexibility. The proposed cross training proposal has quantitative and scalable solution for existing cross training model that are qualitative and limited in scope. It also includes skill adjacency mapping, providing greater accuracy in training decisions. The comparative analysis shows that the framework delivers better results in terms of cost-effectiveness, skills utilization, and skill gaps reduction. The results highlight the significance of implementing cutting-edge analytics and optimization within HRM strategies.

9.5 Theoretical Contributions: Extending Workforce Flexibility Theory

The proposed structure advances the theoretical understanding of workforce flexibility by adding to current models with data-driven and optimization-based considerations. The value of multi-skilled employees' contribution to organizational flexibility is of great importance in traditional theories. However, these theories have been modified and may not provide a formal framework to define and manage flexibility. This study establishes a framework for operationalizing workforce flexibility based on integration of the predictive analysis and optimization. In the framework, dynamic flexibility is the idea that the capabilities of the workforce are continually tailored to changing demand conditions.

This does not just focus on being 'flexible,' it's about knowing how to 'adapt' in the moment for decision making. Also, the skill adjacency mapping that we introduced brings in the new idea of the flexibility theory, showcasing the importance of exercising skill relationship in effective cross-training. Optimization techniques can also be used to quantify flexibility trade-offs with other organizational goals. Such contributions add to the theoretical underpinning of workforce management by broadening and deepening one's understanding and sense of how to incorporate flexibility in a labour-constrained setting.

9.6 Practical Insights: Decision-Making Under Labor Constraints

Results from this research have useful practical implications for the decision makers in labor-limited settings. The takeaway is the need to take a proactive and data-driven workforce planning approach. Predictive analytics can help organizations prevent disruption to operations by enabling them to anticipate skill gaps and create strategic cross-training. Optimization techniques are also integrated into the system, further enriching the process of decision making by helping to allocate limited resources efficiently. Managers can explore various scenarios and determine options that will provide flexibility, productivity, and cost. This methodical process will help minimize on-the-job learning and increase consistency and predictability in decision making. The other critical lesson to take away is the focus of high impact skills and critical roles when designing cross training programs. Organizations should not attempt to train everyone in multiple roles, but should concentrate their training efforts where flexibility will be most beneficial. Moreover, ongoing monitoring and feedback are necessary to accommodate for change over time. The framework provides managers with applicable choices and tools to address intricate workforce challenges and support organizational resilience and performance in dynamic labour markets.

10. PERFORMANCE EVALUATION AND ROI ANALYSIS

10.1 KPIs

10.1.1 ROI of Cross-Training

One key metric in measuring the financial effectiveness of cross training is RO (return) on investment. Measuring net benefits gained because of training against cost of training. Within this model, ROI is found by measuring the sum of gains gained from more workforce flexibility, less downtime, and better productivity against the costs of training programs. This cost includes direct costs including technology platforms, instructors, and training materials, and indirect costs including lost productivity during training and employees time spent in training. The model also integrates predictive analytics and optimization results to enable accurate ROI calculations and ensure that costs spent on training go to the most impactful areas. The results show that, with targeted cross training, ROI is much higher than with generalized cross training. Cross training is an economically sound way to produce the necessary skills with less money expended in burden-shedding, particularly when there are limited number of hands available to fill positions of critical function or skill need.

10.1.2 Productivity gains

One of the greatest results of good cross training is the increase in productivity. Organizations can improve the alignment between workforce skills and operational needs by equipping employees with multiple skills. This helps in decreasing idle time, avoiding bottlenecking and improving general efficiency. The proposed framework views productivity gains via a comparison of output levels prior to and after cross-training programs. With the adaptation of predicting analytics, training is channelled where it matters most, optimizing productivity. Moreover, optimization methods help in the efficient use of training resources in order to ensure that the users get trained in the area where they would be most useful. The findings illustrate that cross trained staff can switch from one function to the other with the same performance even in times of fluctuating demand. In sum, the framework fosters continuous productivity improvements for the organizations, supporting their competitiveness and stability in the dynamic job market.

10.1.3 Vacancy Reduction

An important metric showing the success in reducing vacancies due to cross training of workers. Gaps in staffing may result in disruptions in operations, additional workload for current staff, and a lower standard of services. This has been proposed to overcome such challenges by having employees train in multiple roles so as to lessen reliance on outside hiring. The model estimates vacancy reduction in comparison to the before and after of implementing cross-training methods. Predictive Analytics is a big part of determining that a position may be in need, before it's actually in need and therefore serves a critical purpose in proactively closing any gap. Optimization maximizes the allocation of resources for the best coverage of identified roles. This data shows that vacancies are significantly decreased, giving better operational continuity, and lowering recruitment expenses. This underscores the importance of cross-training as a way to address labour shortages in labor short countries.

10.2 Cost–Benefit Evaluation

The cross-training framework is economic feasibility through cost–benefit assessment. It requires a rigorous analysis of all benefits and costs of adopting the framework in relation to workforce performance. Costs are direct (for construction of training program(s), technology/mechanics, training materials) and indirect (employee time, temporary loss of production during training). The good news is that the framework provides tangible benefits in terms of productivity, job flexibility, and job creation. These benefits can materialize into actual results including better productivity, fewer operational delays, and lower staffing and turnover expenses. Besides, the intangible benefits, like higher engagement and sustainability of employees, add to the value creation in the long-term. When predictive analytics and optimization are integrated in training investments are focused and effective, maximizing on training investments. Analysis of the costs and benefits suggests that the benefits dominate the costs, especially if the cross-training emphasis is on high impact roles. However, under different conditions these findings are robust, as demonstrated by the sensitivity analysis. The cumulative results of the cost–benefit assessment suggest that the proposed framework is not only operationally sound but also economically viable, highlighting its value for use in resource-limited contexts.

11. MANAGERIAL AND POLICY IMPLICATIONS

This research is of great practical value for managing labor constrained environments, as well as for policy making. Organisations should change from a reactive hire to a pro-active approach to capability development from the strategic workforce planning perspective. Predictive analytics can be integrated into the system to help managers forecast future skill needs, and to create targeted cross-training programs that meet the changing needs of the business. This helps to make organizations faster and minimizes reliance on labor markets outside.

For organizational adoption strategies, there was a need for alignment in technological infrastructure, policy and organizational culture to implement the proposed framework successfully. Data management systems and analytical tools that enable real-time decision making should be invested in. Besides, it is crucial to create a culture of learning, to maintain on-demand employee participation in cross-training programs. Effective Communication of advantages, incentives for acquiring skills, and management backs are vital elements in mitigation of resistance to change. Strategies for implementing the framework can be done in stages, beginning with pilot applications in critical departments, and then gradually expanding enterprise-wide.

Governments and institutions play a pivotal role in fostering adaptability of the workforce, and there is a corresponding importance at the policy level. A policy focus on skill development, vocational education and industry-academic partnership can help bridge structural skill deficits. Organizations can implement cross-training practices through financial incentives, such as subsidies and/or tax benefits for training investments. Additionally, creating consistent frameworks of skills and labor market information systems increases the value of predictive analytics. Together they represent managerial and policy strategies which can increase the resilience of the workforce and contribute to sustainable economic development under often challenged labor market conditions.

12. FUTURE RESEARCH DIRECTIONS

There is potential to use real-time artificial intelligence technologies in workforce analytics and cross-training models further. Real-time AI is capable of analysing streaming data from organisational systems in real-time and make necessary changes in workforce allocation and training on the spot, unlike static or periodic updates. This involves applying reinforcement learning and adaptive algorithms, which self-optimize and learn as they go. Real-time dashboards and decision-support systems can provide additional advantages to support decision-making by managers. This could allow businesses to be nearly instantaneously adaptable, thus boosting their resiliency and performance in a very dynamic labor market and operational context.

A crucial pathway for future research is the adaptation for specific sectors with a distinct workforce profile of the proposed structure. Each industry has its own specific skills requirements, regulatory requirements, and operating environments. Predictive models and optimization parameters can be better adapted to those contexts, thus increasing the relevance and effectiveness of the cross-training strategy. Industry-specific data and case studies can be helpful in gaining deeper insights into on-the-ground challenges and results. Specialized models created by researchers can help make the framework applicable and successful in various organizational environments and labor markets by additionally making it more relevant to specific needs.

A future study could expand the optimization process by using more sophisticated techniques to realize complex and uncertain workforce scenarios. This encompasses stochastic optimization to capture what uncertainty there is in the demand and workforce availability, and robust optimization to provide stability to solutions in case of change. Models of multi-stage and dynamic optimization can be of added value to facilitate decision making, capturing sequential and time-dependent factors. Also, hybrid schemes can be used, such as exact methods coupled with metaheuristics, to enhance scalability for large-scale problems. These extensions would enhance the capability of the framework to handle real-world complexity, providing more accurate and reliable solutions for adaptive cross-training strategies.

13. CONCLUSION

By integrating predictive workforce analytics with optimization modeling, we derive a comprehensive and integrated framework of adaptive workforce cross-training at a labor-constrained facility. It adds value to the literature by introducing a data-driven approach that predicts the need for skills, as well as identifying critical skill gaps and directing training resources efficiently. Skill adjacency mapping further improves accuracy of cross training pathways and multi-objective optimization model optimizes cost, productivity and flexibility. One of its major factors is the incorporation of analytics and optimization in a continuous feedback loop to allow for continuous adaptation in variable labour conditions. It is finally shown to be effective in optimizing the use of workforce, minimizing vacancies and building organisational resilience throughout a structured application scenario. This chapter links theory and practice, making it an analytically robust and scalable answer to contemporary issues for labour markets growing in complexity and uncertainty.

The report reflects the need for a proactive and data-informed strategy in human capital management amid ongoing labour shortages. The organizations cannot continue to adopt traditional strategies for hiring and have to deal with building their capacity by implementing appropriate cross training initiatives. Combining predictive analytics and optimization creates a holistic decision-support tool that can boost efficiency and adaptability. Significantly, the study reveals that cross training doesn't only help address tactical problems, it's a true strategy for long-term sustainability. Balancing two distinct goals – cost efficiency and staff flexibility – takes diligence and constant assessment. The framework presented here illustrates how powerful the use of analytical capabilities can be to enhance decisions and organizational effectiveness. In the future, the capacity to foresee change and respond dynamically will be a defining skill of successful organizations within the changing labor markets and cross training will be critical to these new workforce needs.

REFERENCES

Ahmadi, A., Cantini, A., Frías, V. G., & Staudacher, A. P. (2025). The impact of labor flexibility on operational efficiency in industry 5.0: A systematic literature review. *International Journal of Production Research*, •••, 1–26. DOI: 10.1080/00207543.2025.2516770

Eichenseer, P., Hans, L., & Winkler, H. (2025). A data-driven machine learning model for forecasting delivery positions in logistics for workforce planning. *Supply Chain Analytics*, *9*, 100099. DOI: 10.1016/j.sca.2024.100099

Gupta, P., Gupta, D., & Gupta, M. (2025). Unleashing human capital analytics for data-driven workforce management. In *Human Capital Analytics: Exploring the HR Spectrum in Industry 5.0* (pp. 143–163). https://doi.org/DOI: 10.1002/9781394238354.ch7

Huselid, M. A. (2018). The science and practice of workforce analytics: Introduction to the HRM special issue. *Human Resource Management*, *57*(3), 679–684. DOI: 10.1002/hrm.21916

Karuppiah, S. P., & Kumaran, S. (2025, July). AI-powered talent acquisition: Enhancing recruitment and workforce analytics using machine learning. In *2025 IEEE 4th World Conference on Applied Intelligence and Computing (AIC)* (pp. 179–184). IEEE. https://doi.org/DOI: 10.1109/AIC66080.2025.11212065

Karuppiah, S. P., & Sriramakrishnan, R. RJ, E. B., & Kumaran, S. (2025, July). Employee retention analytics: Predictive modeling for workforce stability and talent management. In *2025 IEEE 4th World Conference on Applied Intelligence and Computing (AIC)* (pp. 420–425). IEEE. https://doi.org/DOI: 10.1109/AIC66080.2025.11212141

Lima, S. A., & Rahman, M. M. (2025). Generational diversity and inclusion: HRM challenges and opportunities in multigenerational workforces. [IJHSSM]. *SSRN*, *5*(3), 704–710. DOI: 10.2139/ssrn.5330092

Niyaz, M. T., Qorri, D., Kovács, K., & Juhasz, C. (2025). Research trends in workforce planning in the automotive sector: A comprehensive review. *Administrative Sciences*, *15*(4), 140. DOI: 10.3390/admsci15040140

Ostovari, A., Benyoucef, L., & Haddou-Benderbal, H. (2025). Multi-objective production scheduling and workforce planning in sustainable reconfigurable manufacturing system. [IJIDeM]. *International Journal on Interactive Design and Manufacturing*, *19*(5), 3803–3823. DOI: 10.1007/s12008-024-02010-x

Peck, W. J. (2025). Workforce planning: A review of methodologies. *Annals of Operations Research, 352*(1), 251–294. DOI: 10.1007/s10479-025-06734-1

Rao, S., Gupta, U., Ramanujam, A., Knoble, A., Gondi, I., Gowda, P., Reddy, C., Shah, K., Amatya, A., Kalaunee, A., Rajbhandari, R., Henkar, R., Shah, M., Khan, S., Jesudian, G., Vora, K., Jindal, R. M., Suroy, A., Ghosh, D., & Zadey, S. (2026). Capacity building through workforce training and community engagement for surgical, obstetric, trauma, and anaesthesia (SOTA) care: Case studies from South Asia. *Dialogues in Health, 100295*, 100295. Advance online publication. DOI: 10.1016/j.dialog.2026.100295 PMID: 41908516

Vapiwala, F., Rastogi, S., & Pandita, D. (2025). Is workforce agility the new agenda? Perspectives on the role of constructive task conflicts. *Employee Responsibilities and Rights Journal*, •••, 1–20. DOI: 10.1007/s10672-025-09528-6

KEY TERMS AND DEFINITIONS

Adaptive Cross-Training: Adaptive cross training is a training model that focuses on training employees to execute a number of job functions under dynamic conditions in response to operation requirements.

Artificial Intelligence (AI): Artificial intelligence is the ability of computer systems to do what humans can, including prediction, learning and decision making.

Decision Support Systems (DSS): Decision Support Systems are computer based systems that help the management in the process of taking data-based decisions regarding the operations and strategies.

Demand Forecasting: Demand forecasting is the way of estimating the future workload, staffing or operational demand on the basis of historical data and real-time data.

Labor-Constrained Environments: A labor constrained environment is an organizational atmosphere that has limited skilled employees, lack of staff, or an unstable workforce.

Operational Resilience: Operational resilience is the capacity of an organisation in maintaining its steady performance when faced with disruptions, staff shortages or sudden changes in demand.

Predictive Workforce Analytics: Predictive workforce analytics are data-driven predictive forecasting, statistical models, and AI applied to predicting workforce trends, staffing requirements, and employee performance.

Resource Allocation: Resource allocation is the careful deployment of workforce, equipment and organisational resources when aiming to operate efficiently to achieve goals.

Skill Matrix: The skill matrix is a systematic way of recording employee skills, certifications and level of competency for any role or skill within a structure.

Workforce Optimization: Workforce Optimization is the practice of optimizing the allocation, productivity, scheduling and efficiency of workforce.

Chapter 10
Lifecycle-Based Workforce Cross-Training in the Age of AI and Automation:
A Comparative Framework for Manufacturing and Service Sectors

Avirup Mukherjee
http://orcid.org/0000-0002-5752-6527
Amity University Jharkhand, Ranchi, India

Sidharth Raja Halder
http://orcid.org/0000-0003-0178-0275
Amity University Jharkhand, Ranchi, India

ABSTRACT

This article explains how workforce cross-training develops across four career stages — Entry-Level Specialisation, Skill Expansion, Cross-Functional Integration, and Multi-Skilled Expertise with AI Governance — in the age of AI-driven technological change. Using ideas from human capital theory, skill-biased technological change, and organizational learning, the study addresses two major gaps in existing research: the lack of a lifecycle approach to cross-training and limited sector-specific analysis. By comparing manufacturing and service sectors, the article shows that although both sectors face automation pressure, their skill needs, training systems, and work structures are very different. The framework also argues that AI governance, including

DOI: 10.4018/979-8-3373-5327-2.ch010

ght © 2027, IGI Global Scientific Publishing. Copying or distributing in print or electronic forms without written permission of IGI Global Scientific Publishing is prohibited. Use of this chapter to generative artificial intelligence (AI) technologies is expressly prohibited. The publisher reserves all rights to license its use for generative AI training and machine learning model development.

the ability to supervise, evaluate, and ethically manage AI systems, has become a key skill at advanced stages of workforce development. The study further discusses implications for workforce efficiency, labour market adaptability, and public policy.

1. INTRODUCTION

The global economy is currently passing through a major structural transformation. New technologies such as advanced robotics, machine learning, generative AI, and the Industrial Internet of Things (IIoT) are rapidly changing the way production systems function, how services are delivered, and most importantly, how people perform their work. Tasks that are repetitive, routine, and rule-based which traditionally formed the foundation of many manufacturing and service jobs are increasingly being automated. At the same time, the demand for human workers is shifting toward tasks that are more flexible, non-routine, and require higher levels of thinking, creativity, and problem-solving ability (Acemoglu & Restrepo, 2018; Brynjolfsson & McAfee, 2014). This transformation has created a noticeable paradox in modern labour markets. While unemployment continues to remain a challenge in many parts of the world, employers across industries are also reporting serious shortages of workers who possess the right skills to work effectively in technology-driven environments (World Economic Forum, 2023; International Labour Organization, 2022).

This kind of tension is not entirely new in economic history. During the Industrial Revolution in England, many handloom weavers lost their livelihoods when mechanical looms replaced traditional weaving work, and a large number of those workers struggled to find alternative employment because they had only one specialised skill. Similar patterns appeared again during the 1980s and 1990s when computers replaced many clerical, bookkeeping, and administrative jobs; workers who adapted to the new technological systems were generally able to continue working, while others found it difficult to regain stable employment. Today, AI is creating a similar disruption, but the scale and speed of change are considerably larger than before. History repeatedly demonstrates a simple lesson workers who possess only one specific skill are usually the most vulnerable when technological systems change rapidly.

In this environment, workforce cross-training has become an increasingly important strategy for both organisations and policymakers. Cross-training refers to a structured process through which workers are provided with skills and knowledge beyond their primary job role. This helps organisations become more flexible because workers can be shifted between tasks whenever required, especially during periods of technological transition and market. In many ways, this idea stands in contrast to Adam Smith's classical argument that division of labour and specialisation improve efficiency. Smith's argument worked effectively in relatively stable industrial systems, but the modern economy is far less stable and predictable. Recent research shows that cross-training strengthens organisational resilience (Cordery et al., 2010), improves the employability of workers (Autor, 2015), and supports stronger collaboration between humans and AI systems in technologically advanced workplaces (Brynjolfsson et al., 2019).

The effect of cross-training on workers can be substantial. Countries such as Germany, where the dual apprenticeship system exposes workers to multiple skills from the beginning of their careers, have often experienced lower unemployment rates during periods of automation compared to countries that depend mainly on narrow specialisation. Workers with experience across multiple functions were able to adapt more easily when parts of their work became automated. Similarly, Japanese manufacturing companies such as Toyota have long used job rotation and cross-functional training as central elements of their production philosophy; workers in Toyota factories are expected to understand several stages of the production process instead of focusing only on one workstation. This approach has often been identified as one of the reasons Toyota responded more effectively to industrial disruptions than competitors with rigidly specialised workforces. More recent comparative evidence extends this pattern to emerging economies. In India, where over 900 million people are expected to reach working age by 2030, a 2022 NASSCOM assessment found that only 45 percent of graduates were considered employable in the digital economy because of skill gaps in data science, AI, and applied problem-solving a finding that has pushed national programmes such as Skill India and PMKVY toward outcome-based, sector-linked reskilling rather than certificate-only training (Miah et al., 2024).

Cross-training also creates important benefits at the individual worker level. Workers trained across multiple roles often feel more confident and secure about their employment, and managers tend to view them as more adaptable, which improves their chances for promotion. There are also evidence that cross-trained employees experience lower levels of job burnout because variety in work activities helps sustain engagement. At the same time, cross-training is not free from challenges a point the existing literature, and indeed earlier drafts of this chapter, did not examine closely enough. Section 6.3 returns to this question in detail, covering the direct and indirect costs of reskilling, the behavioural and psychological sources of employee resistance, and the uneven way these costs and benefits fall across different demographic groups.

Even though cross-training is becoming more important, the existing research literature still contains several limitations. Most studies continue to treat cross-training as a one-time activity rather than a continuous, long-term process, and many fail to consider how training needs, learning abilities, and career motivations change across different stages of a worker's life and career (Tharenou et al., 2007; Aguinis & Kraiger, 2009). A young employee entering the workforce for the first time clearly requires a different kind of training compared to an employee with fifteen or twenty years of experience, yet many organisational training programmes are still designed without adequately considering lifecycle differences.

Another major limitation in the literature is the lack of comparative analysis between manufacturing and service sectors. Both sectors are affected by automation and AI, but they experience these changes differently and operate under different skill structures and institutional systems. A factory worker learning to manage a robotic production system faces challenges quite different from those faced by a bank employee learning to work alongside an AI-based loan approval system, yet much of the current literature discusses these situations in a broadly similar manner. AI and automation have also transformed the purpose of cross-training itself: it is no longer only about learning multiple job tasks, but increasingly about AI management, machine collaboration, and adaptive decision-making (Daugherty & Wilson, 2018; World Economic Forum, 2023).

These gaps are not merely academic concerns; they have direct practical consequences for how governments design workforce policies and how organisations invest in employee development. If policymakers assume that one standard cross-training model can work effectively across all industries and career stages, the resulting policies will likely become too general to be effective. Similarly, organisations that fail to recognise that cross-training needs evolve as workers develop and technologies change may invest heavily in training systems that quickly become outdated.

This chapter addresses these gaps by proposing a Lifecycle Cross-Training Framework (LCTF). Three gaps in particular motivate the framework directly. First, the absence of a lifecycle perspective in existing models (Tharenou et al., 2007) motivates the four-stage architecture developed in Section 3, which treats cross-training as cumulative rather than episodic. Second, the lack of sector-specific comparison motivates the parallel application of the framework to manufacturing (Section 4) and services (Section 5), each grounded in its own technological and institutional context. Third, the underdeveloped treatment of AI governance as a training outcome motivates Stage Four of the framework, which explicitly incorporates technical and ethical oversight of AI systems as a capstone competency rather than an afterthought. The framework explains how cross-training develops through four stages across a worker's career and compares its application in manufacturing and service sectors within the broader context of AI and automation. The chapter is organised as follows. Section 2 reviews the major theories and literature related to workforce cross-training. Section 3 introduces the LCTF, including its visual architecture, stage benchmarks, and the costs and limitations associated with implementing it. Sections 4 and 5 apply the framework to manufacturing and service sectors. Section

6 discusses implications for workforce efficiency and labour market adaptability. Section 7 addresses policy and managerial implications, and Section 8 concludes with limitations and directions for future research.

2. THEORETICAL FOUNDATIONS AND SCHOLARLY DISCOURSE

2.1 Human Capital Theory and the Foundations of Workforce Development

Workforce cross-training is grounded mainly in human capital theory, which treats knowledge, skills, and abilities as assets that grow through investment over time. Early work by Schultz (1961) and Becker (1964) established that training is an investment benefiting both workers and organisations. Becker's (1964) distinction between general and specific human capital remains central: general training improves skills that are useful across employers, while specific training improves productivity only within a particular organisation. Cross-training typically includes both. When a manufacturing worker learns to operate a new automated system, for instance, the skill may transfer to other workplaces as well as benefit the current employer (Acemoglu & Pischke, 1999).

Later research examined how human capital develops across a career. Ben-Porath (1967) argued that people invest more in learning early in their careers because they have more time to recoup the benefit. In AI-driven environments, however, skills become outdated quickly, creating a need for continuous, lifelong learning (OECD, 2019; ILO, 2022). Recent work has also emphasised skill complementarity the idea that human skills and machine capabilities can work together rather than substitute for one another (Autor, 2015; Acemoglu & Restrepo, 2019). Autor (2015) shows that automation typically replaces routine tasks while increasing the value of non-routine human work such as problem-solving and interpersonal interaction. For cross-training, this means that training should not focus only on new tasks, but also on the higher-level skills that allow workers to collaborate effectively with AI systems.

2.2 Skill-Biased Technological Change and the Demand for Multi-Skilling

The theory of skill-biased technological change (SBTC) explains how technology reshapes labour demand. New technologies, particularly those involving information and communication systems, tend to increase demand for high-skill workers while reducing demand for routine, middle-skill jobs (Acemoglu & Autor,

2011; Autor et al., 2003; Brynjolfsson & McAfee, 2014). This has produced labour market polarisation a hollowing-out of middle-skill jobs alongside growth at the high- and low-skill ends (Goos et al., 2014; Autor & Dorn, 2013) which helps explain why cross-training has moved to the centre of workforce policy debates. As routine tasks are automated, workers need a broader set of adaptive, complex skills to remain employable (Levy & Murnane, 2004). Workers confined to narrow roles face greater job loss risk, while those with cross-functional skills and stronger cognitive flexibility can move into new roles more easily (Bresnahan et al., 2002).

Recent research has extended SBTC to account for AI specifically. Acemoglu and Restrepo (2018, 2019) show that technology both displaces existing jobs and creates new ones, with the net effect depending on the balance between these forces a balance that differs from earlier waves of computerisation and therefore requires a different policy response. Cross-training helps workers move into the new categories of jobs that AI creates. Brynjolfsson et al. (2018) similarly show that AI typically automates specific tasks within a job rather than an entire occupation, which means that redesigning jobs and cross-training workers to handle a wider task mix is generally more effective than attempting to replace workers outright. This task-level view reinforces a point that is easy to overlook in automation debates: labour remains the organising component of production, and workforce systems that displace it wholesale tend to also forfeit the tacit, adaptive judgement that keeps production systems resilient.

2.3 Labor Market Flexibility and Functional Cross-Training

Organisational economics contributes the concept of labour market flexibility. Atkinson (1984) distinguished numerical flexibility (adjusting the number of workers) from functional flexibility (moving workers across tasks), and cross-training is the principal mechanism through which firms achieve the latter (Osterman, 1994; Cappelli & Neumark, 2001). Functional flexibility allows firms to adjust to change without hiring or firing, reducing costs and improving efficiency particularly valuable in tight labour markets where skilled workers are scarce.

Research on high-performance work systems (HPWS) shows that cross-training, combined with practices such as employee empowerment and performance-based pay, improves productivity and innovation (Appelbaum et al., 2000; Ichniowski et al., 1997). A trade-off nonetheless exists between specialisation and cross-training: specialisation increases efficiency through deep expertise, while cross-training increases flexibility (Lazear, 2009). Specialisation tends to perform better in stable environments, but broader skill sets become more valuable in rapidly changing environments such as today's AI-driven economy (Dessein & Santos, 2006).

2.4 Organizational Learning and Skill Development Lifecycles

Organisational learning theory explains how skills develop within firms. Argyris and Schön (1978) distinguish single-loop learning, which improves existing processes, from double-loop learning, which questions and changes the system itself. Learning a related task through cross-training is an example of single-loop learning; understanding how different parts of an organisation interconnect is closer to double-loop learning, which becomes increasingly important in AI-driven environments (Senge, 1990).

Kolb's (1984) theory of experiential learning describes learning as a cycle of experience, reflection, understanding, and experimentation, and this cycle plays out differently across a worker's career: new workers benefit more from guided learning and job rotation, while experienced workers benefit more from problem-solving and team-based learning (Noe, 2020; Tharenou et al., 2007). The related concept of absorptive capacity (Cohen & Levinthal, 1990) an organisation's ability to recognise, absorb, and apply new knowledge is also central. Cross-training builds this capacity by creating a workforce that can adapt to new technologies, and organisations with strong cross-trained workforces tend to learn and adapt faster in AI-driven settings (Zahra & George, 2002).

2.5 AI, Automation, and the Transformation of Training Requirements

Recent empirical research shows how AI and automation are changing not just which skills are needed but how training itself should be designed. Manyika et al. (2017) estimate that about half of current work activities are technically automatable, while Arntz et al. (2016) find that only around 9 percent of jobs are fully at risk once the mix of tasks within real jobs is taken into account a gap that creates substantial scope for redesigning jobs and using cross-training as the adjustment mechanism rather than relying on job loss and rehiring.

Generative AI has extended automation into writing, coding, and analytical work (Eloundou et al., 2023), and Goldman Sachs (2023) estimates that up to 300 million jobs globally could be affected. This shifts the focus of training toward human strengths creativity, ethical reasoning, and complex problem-solving alongside technical skills (Daugherty & Wilson, 2018; World Economic Forum, 2023). Using German administrative data, Dauth et al. (2021) show empirically that automation does not necessarily reduce overall employment when displaced workers can shift into new roles within the same firm or sector, and that cross-training plays a measurable part in enabling that shift. Acemoglu and Restrepo (2020) reach a complementary conclusion using U.S. labour market data, highlighting the role of training systems in moving workers into the new occupations that automation itself creates. More recent firm-level evidence reinforces this picture: a 2024 BCG survey found that while 89 percent of organisations reported needing improved AI skills in their workforce, only 6 percent had begun upskilling at meaningful scale, underlining the gap between recognising the need for cross-training and actually implementing it.

2.6 Sector-Specific Dynamics: Manufacturing and Services

AI affects manufacturing and service sectors differently. Manufacturing has a long history of automation, from early mechanisation to modern smart factories, and Industry 4.0 the integration of physical systems with digital technologies requires workers to understand data, monitor systems, and work alongside intelligent machines (Schwab, 2016; Lasi et al., 2014). The service sector follows a different path. Baumol's (1967) theory holds that services depend heavily on human labour, but AI is now reshaping this assumption by automating many service tasks (Autor & Salomons, 2018), which has increased the value of skills such as social intelligence and creativity that AI cannot easily replicate (Frey & Osborne, 2017). A systematic review of 48 peer-reviewed studies on Industry 4.0 in South Asia identifies digital skills, data analytics, and AI literacy as the strongest predictors of workforce employability across both manufacturing and service contexts in the region, while also flagging the scarcity of outcome-based (rather than certificate-based) training as the main institutional bottleneck (Miah et al., 2024).

Taken together, these six theoretical strands point toward the same conclusion from different directions: cross-training needs to be treated as a cumulative, career-spanning process rather than a discrete event; it needs to be calibrated to the changing task content of jobs rather than to job titles ; and it needs to be designed separately for manufacturing and service contexts rather than through a single generic model. The Lifecycle Cross-Training Framework introduced in the next section is built directly on this synthesis.

3. THEORETICAL FRAMEWORK: THE LIFECYCLE CROSS-TRAINING FRAMEWORK (LCTF)

3.1 Conceptual Architecture

The Lifecycle Cross-Training Framework (LCTF) explains cross-training as a four-stage process that develops over a worker's career. At each stage, learning is shaped by different developmental needs, organisational demands, and technologies. The four stages are: (i) Entry-Level Specialisation, (ii) Skill Expansion, (iii) Cross-

Functional Integration, and (iv) Multi-Skilled Expertise and AI Governance. The framework draws together human capital theory, skill-biased technological change, and organisational learning theory, and applies them to AI-driven manufacturing and service contexts.

Figure 1. Stage wise transition in LCTF

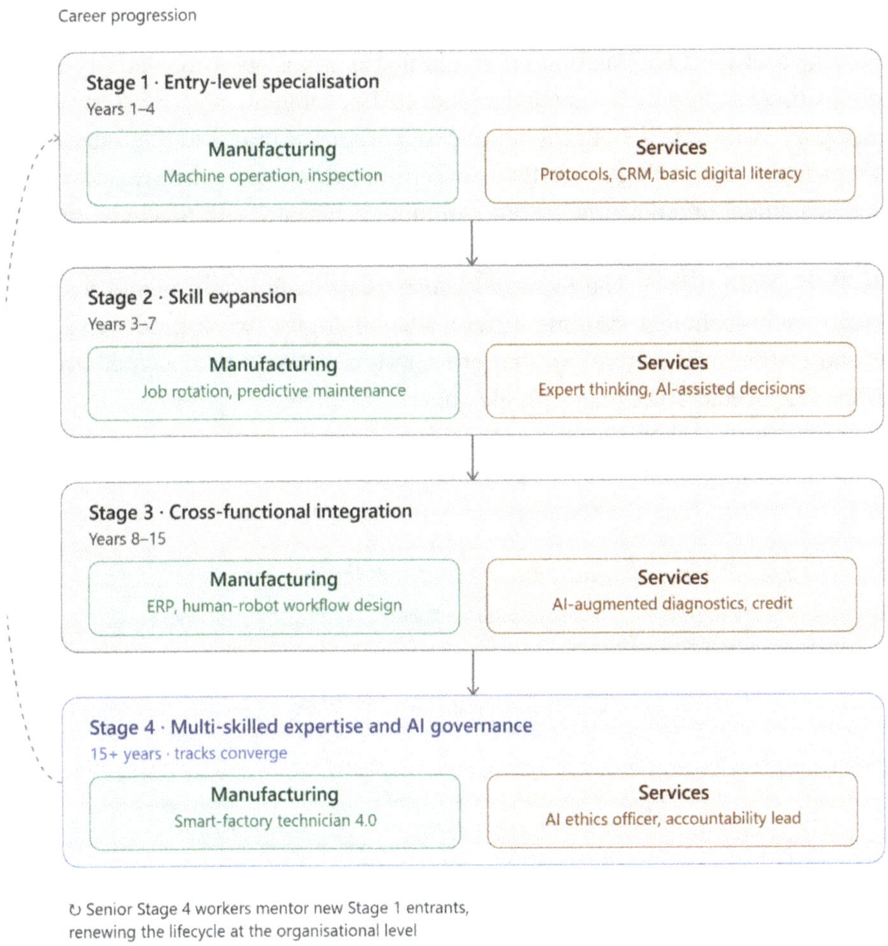

The Diagram has been drawn by the author using App Diagrams. net

Figure 1 illustrates the architecture of the LCTF. It can be visualised as a spiral rather than a straight line: each stage sits on an ascending loop, with the competencies developed at one stage forming the entry conditions for the next, while the spiral itself widens reflecting the broadening scope of responsibility as a worker moves from Stage One toward Stage Four. Two parallel tracks run through the spiral, one for manufacturing and one for services, converging only at Stage Four around the shared competency of AI governance. Arrows connecting each stage to the next represent the structured learning mechanisms (job rotation, mentoring, project-based exposure, leadership training) that move a worker forward, while a feedback arrow runs from Stage Four back to Stage One, representing the role senior multi-skilled workers play in mentoring new entrants closing the loop and making the lifecycle self-renewing at the organisational level.

A key idea of the LCTF is that cross-training is not a one-time activity but a continuous process in which knowledge and skill accumulate step by step across career stages; each stage is both the product of earlier learning and the foundation for later growth. This distinguishes the LCTF from earlier views that treated cross-training as a single organisational event, aligning it instead with lifecycle models of skill development that emphasise the ongoing, evolving nature of learning (Ben-Porath, 1967; Kolb, 1984). The framework also treats manufacturing and services as distinct socio-technical systems different technologies, work processes, skill needs, and institutional settings so that cross-training should be designed around sector-specific needs rather than a single generic template.

Table 1 summarises how the four stages differ across the two sectors, condensing the sector-specific detail developed fully in Sections 4 and 5.

Table 1. The LCTF across manufacturing and service sectors

Stage	Career Period	Manufacturing Focus	Service Focus
1. Entry-Level Specialisation	Years 1–4	Machine operation, quality inspection, sensor and digital-interface familiarity	Protocols, CRM systems, regulatory rules, basic digital literacy
2. Skill Expansion	Years 3–7	Job rotation, statistical process control, predictive maintenance, basic robotic programming	Expert thinking, complex communication, AI-assisted decision support
3.Cross-Functional Integration	Years 8–15	ERP systems, AI-based production optimisation, human–robot workflow design	Care/relationship coordination across functions, AI-augmented diagnostics and credit assessment
4. Multi-Skilled Expertise & AI Governance	15+ years	Smart-factory technician/industrial engineer 4.0 roles; system-level oversight	AI ethics officer, algorithmic accountability specialist, digital health navigator

3.2 Stage One: Entry-Level Specialisation

The first stage focuses on specialisation. Workers learn the basic skills and knowledge required for their specific role, typically over the first two to four years of work, with the main goal of building strong technical competence in one area alongside an understanding of organisational rules, workflows, and teamwork.

This stage is critical for later cross-training, although it is often overlooked. Human capital theory suggests that strong foundational skills help workers learn new skills more efficiently afterward; deep knowledge in one area gives workers something to connect new learning to (Lazear, 2009). Absorptive capacity theory (Cohen & Levinthal, 1990) reaches a similar conclusion from a different angle: prior knowledge is what allows people to recognise and absorb new knowledge in the first place. Good initial specialisation, in other words, is not opposed to cross-training it is the condition that makes later cross-training effective.

Indicative Stage One benchmark: role-specific competency certification completed; baseline digital-tool proficiency demonstrated; no more than one cycle of remedial retraining needed within the first 18 months.

3.3 Stage Two: Skill Expansion

The second stage focuses on expanding skills beyond the primary role. Workers begin learning related tasks, technologies, and processes, typically during the third to seventh year of work, once they are more confident and ready to take on broader responsibilities. Learning at this stage happens through job rotation, exposure to other departments, mentoring, and formal training in adjacent areas. In AI-based work environments, this stage increasingly also includes basic digital and data literacy understanding how AI systems work, how to interpret their outputs, and where they are likely to fail. The World Economic Forum (2023) identifies digital literacy, data skills, and AI interaction as central abilities for the modern workforce, which makes it important to build these capacities early rather than waiting until later stages, when learning becomes comparatively harder.

Indicative Stage Two benchmark: successful rotation through at least two adjacent functions; demonstrated ability to interpret AI-system outputs correctly in routine cases; participation in at least one cross-departmental project.

3.4 Stage Three: Cross-Functional Integration

The third stage concerns becoming a genuinely cross-functional worker someone who does not merely perform multiple tasks but understands how those tasks connect across the organisation. This stage typically occurs in mid-career, around eight to fifteen years of experience, and training here focuses on system-level understanding, process improvement, and leadership development in multi-functional settings. In AI and automation contexts, this stage corresponds to what Daugherty and Wilson (2018) term “fusion skills”: working closely with AI systems, configuring them, interpreting their outputs, and using their insights for decision-making, while also managing the organisational change that new technologies bring. This stage moves well beyond simple job rotation; it requires understanding the full system in which humans and machines work together.

Indicative Stage Three benchmark: leads or co-leads at least one cross-functional improvement project annually; can identify and escalate AI-system failures or biased outputs; mentors at least one Stage One or Stage Two worker.

3.5 Stage Four: Multi-Skilled Expertise and AI Governance

The fourth stage represents the highest level of cross-training. Workers at this stage are multi-skilled experts capable of managing complex AI-based systems, with experience across multiple functions and the ability to perform, coordinate, and improve work processes. They typically occupy senior roles technical experts, supervisors, or specialists and play a central part in guiding technology adoption, supporting junior workers, and helping organisations adapt to change. AI governance is a defining feature of this stage, combining technical and ethical responsibilities. Technically, workers must evaluate AI performance, detect problems, manage the division of labour between humans and AI, and improve systems over time. Ethically, they must judge when human discretion should override an AI recommendation, ensure fairness, and maintain accountability for AI-influenced decisions (Cath et al., 2018; Dafoe, 2018). Developing this combination of technical and ethical capability remains one of the most demanding challenges facing organisations today.

Indicative Stage Four benchmark: holds formal or informal responsibility for AI governance/oversight in at least one workflow; has trained or certified at least two Stage Three workers; has documented at least one instance of redesigning a process for better human–AI collaboration.

3.6 The Costs, Resistance, and Distributional Implications of Lifecycle Cross-Training

Any comprehensive consideration of the LCTF would have to note that moving through the four stages of the framework involves costs and challenges that are unevenly distributed. Nevertheless, despite these limitations, the long-term organisational and employee benefits make cross training a highly rewarding investment.

Costs. Apart from the direct costs related to training, cross-training is also expensive in terms of organisational costs. Such costs include instructors' time, training materials, certification expenses, and productivity losses when employees rotate into unfamiliar positions. Additional supervisory support is often required to manage employees' transition through different lifecycle stages. Li (2024) notes that productivity gains from upskilling and reskilling programs may take six months or longer to become visible. Consequently, organisations with short-term planning horizons may be less willing to invest in cross-training. These costs are also unevenly distributed: compared to large companies, small and medium enterprises, which often lack dedicated training budgets, bear proportionately higher costs during Stage Two and Stage Three (ILO, 2022). However, organisations that successfully overcome these initial barriers often benefit from greater workforce flexibility, resilience, and long-term productivity gains.

Resistance of employees. Employee resistance to cross-training is often attributed to age, although empirical evidence does not strongly support this view. For example, Kunze, Boehm, and Bruch (2013), analysing nearly 3,000 workers, found that older employees are, on average, less resistant to change than younger workers when tenure and occupational status are considered. Resistance appears to stem more from perceived threats to competence and professional identity, particularly among employees who have invested years in developing specialised expertise. Therefore, the issue is better addressed through appropriate framing and sequencing of training rather than demographic targeting. When implemented sensitively, cross-training can strengthen employee confidence, career development, and organisational commitment.

Demographic groups' implication. Although age is not strongly associated with resistance to cross-training, demographic inequalities in access to such training remain well established. Ranasinghe, Grosse, Glock, and Jaber (2024) found that ageing workforces in manufacturing and services are often underserved by traditional training designs tailored to younger learners. Linked to SDG 4 (lifelong learning) and SDG 10 (reduced inequalities), the authors recommend adapting training formats rather than reducing training opportunities for older employees. Moreover, workers in highly routine occupations with greater automation riskthose who need cross-training mostare often the last to receive employer-led training opportunities (ILO, 2022). Gender disparities further intensify these inequalities in some manufacturing sectors where women remain underrepresented. Addressing these gaps can not only promote inclusion but also unlock significant untapped human potential across the workforce.

Below is a version reduced to approximately half of the original length, using simpler language and sentence structure while preserving the key arguments and all references.

3.7 Empirical Evidence and Case Studies from Industry and Emerging Economies

The discussion so far has been mainly theoretical. This section supports those arguments with recent empirical evidence and four case studies from different industries and regions, showing how the costs and benefits of lifecycle cross-training operate in practice.

Manufacturing in an emerging economy: Mexico's automotive sector. Mexico provides evidence that automation does not necessarily reduce jobs when workers can move into related roles. Using panel data from fourteen Mexican states during 2013–2022, Márquez Stone and Sandoval Cabrera (2024) found that robot adoption in the automotive sector was positively associated with both employment and wages. At the same time, nearshoring and investment reforms increased employment in automotive and electronics industries. However, employers reported major shortages of digital and technical skills, while demand for generative-AI skills continues to rise. These findings suggest that automation creates positive outcomes only when reskilling systems, such as company training and technical education, keep pace with technological change. This highlights the importance of Stage Two and Stage Three of the LCTF.

Manufacturing under cost pressure: Bangladesh's garment industry. Bangladesh presents a contrasting example. Research by the Bangladesh Labour Foundation, BRAC University, and Solidaridad Network Asia, based on surveys of 429 workers and interviews with 26 stakeholders, found a 31 percent decline in garment employment due to automation, especially among low-skilled workers, women, older employees, and less literate workers (Bangladesh Labour Foundation, 2024). Another survey showed that 80 percent of factories planned to adopt semi-automated machinery, with many expecting workforce reductions. While some firms invest in continuous training and redeployment, others use automation mainly to reduce labour costs. The research estimates that up to 60 percent of garment workers could face displacement by 2030–2041 without structured reskilling. This case shows that employment outcomes depend heavily on whether firms actively support cross-training.

Services in an emerging economy: India's digital-economy skills gap. A 2022 NASSCOM assessment reported that only 45 percent of Indian graduates were employable in the digital economy because of skill gaps in data science, AI, and problem-solving (Miah et al., 2024). In response, India has shifted from certificate-based training towards competency-based, industry-linked reskilling. This approach closely matches the benchmark-driven model proposed for Stages One to Three of the LCTF. Early evidence from India's IT-enabled services sector suggests that firms combining technical training with structured job rotation achieve better retention of mid-career employees, although stronger longitudinal evidence is still needed.

Services under rapid disruption: financial technology in Sub-Saharan Africa. Research by Caribou and Genesis Analytics, in partnership with the Mastercard Foundation, estimates that about 40 percent of tasks in Africa's technology-outsourcing sector could be affected by AI by 2030. Customer-service, finance, and accounting roles face the highest risk. Since workers in this sector are already digitally literate, the main challenge is not basic training but developing advanced skills such as AI oversight, validation, and exception handling. National policies, including Kenya's National AI Strategy (2025–2030), treat reskilling as essential for labour-market stability. Recent ODI analysis also argues that governments should encourage firms to redeploy workers internally rather than simply retrench them.

Together, these cases reinforce three main points. First, automation does not determine employment outcomes by itself; the availability and use of cross-training systems are crucial. Second, inequalities in access to training have real consequences, as shown clearly in Bangladesh, where the least-trained groups experience the greatest job losses. Third, skill needs differ across contexts. Mexico and India mainly face challenges in basic digital readiness, whereas Africa's outsourcing sector requires more advanced AI-related capabilities. These differences show that countries and industries move through the LCTF stages at different speeds depending on their existing skills and technological development.

4. LIFECYCLE CROSS-TRAINING IN THE MANUFACTURING SECTOR

4.1 The Manufacturing Technology Context

Manufacturing provides one of the most mature and well-studied settings for understanding workforce cross-training in the age of automation. Manufacturing technology has moved through several major stages Taylorist scientific management, Fordist mass production, lean manufacturing, and now Industry 4.0 and each stage has gradually changed the relationship between humans and machines, shifting the cross-training needs of manufacturing workers along with it (Lasi et al., 2014; Schwab, 2016).

The Industry 4.0 model cyber-physical production systems, AI-based quality control, collaborative robots, and digital twin technologies represents probably the largest transformation of manufacturing work in history, requiring skills that are not only more technical but also more cognitive and adaptive than those needed in earlier manufacturing systems (Kagermann, Wahlster, & Helbig, 2013).

4.2 Stage-by-Stage Application in Manufacturing

Stage One in Manufacturing. At the entry level, manufacturing workers usually begin with specialisation in a specific production role such as machine operation, assembly, quality inspection, materials handling, or logistics. In the Industry 4.0 environment, even these entry roles increasingly require familiarity with digital interfaces, sensor-based machinery, and computerised production monitoring, making modern manufacturing work quite different from the largely physical and mechanical work of earlier periods (Borghans & ter Weel, 2007).

Stage Two in Manufacturing. The second stage expands worker skills across related production functions and the automated systems that connect them, typically through job rotation across production units alongside training in statistical process control, predictive maintenance concepts, and basic robotic programming. Dauth et al. (2021) provide direct empirical support for the value of this stage: using German administrative employment data, they show that workers in highly automated manufacturing firms who received cross-functional training had substantially stronger labour market resilience they were more likely to remain employed and to continue experiencing wage growth compared to highly specialised workers facing similar exposure to automation.

Stage Three in Manufacturing. The third stage involves cross-functional integration, where workers develop skills that go beyond traditional departmental boundaries such as production, maintenance, quality, logistics, and engineering, with the goal of helping them manage integrated AI-driven production systems. At this stage, workers are exposed to enterprise resource planning (ERP) systems, AI-based production optimisation tools, and collaborative human–robot workflow design. Lasi et al. (2014) argue that the ability to work effectively inside cyber-physical production systems where physical machines and digital information systems are closely linked is now a defining requirement for advanced manufacturing workers.

Stage Four in Manufacturing. In the final stage, the worker becomes a multi-skilled manufacturing expert able to move across traditional occupational boundaries, functioning simultaneously as process specialist, automation supervisor, continuous improvement practitioner, and technology adoption leader. Industry literature increasingly refers to these workers as "industrial engineers 4.0" or "smart factory technicians." They form the human core of next-generation manufacturing systems, combining the cross-functional expertise needed to maintain and optimise AI-integrated production environments with the adaptability to respond to new technical challenges and shifting market conditions (Schwab, 2016; World Economic Forum, 2023).

5. LIFECYCLE CROSS-TRAINING IN THE SERVICE SECTOR

5.1 The Service Sector Technology Context

The service sector spans a wide range of economic activities healthcare, financial services, retail, hospitality, logistics, education, legal services, and professional services connected by the fact that they primarily provide intangible, relational, or information-based value rather than physical products.

AI's integration into services has followed a different path from manufacturing automation, moving through several stages: first, automation of back-office information processing; second, customer-facing automation through chatbots, recommendation systems, and self-service platforms; and more recently, AI support for professional cognitive work such as diagnostics, financial analysis, legal research, and educational assessment (Manyika et al., 2017; Eloundou et al., 2023).

A defining feature of AI-driven service automation is the continuing centrality of the human–client relationship. Unlike manufacturing, where output is mostly physical and human–machine interaction is mainly technical, service work depends inherently on communication, empathy, trust, judgment, and relational responsiveness qualities that continue to resist full automation and represent a durable human advantage (Autor, 2015; Frey & Osborne, 2017). Cross-training in service sectors must therefore develop both technical AI-related competencies and the emotional and relational skills needed for effective service delivery, combination scholars often describe as "digital-relational intelligence".

5.2 Stage-by-Stage Application in Service Sectors

Stage One in Services. Entry-level service workers generally begin by learning the specific knowledge required for their role protocols, knowledge systems, regulatory rules, and interpersonal practices linked to their service field. A new bank teller, hospital administrator, insurance claims processor, or hospitality employee first needs reliable control over their core functional area before moving into broader responsibilities. In AI-supported service environments, this early specialisation increasingly includes basic digital literacy: workers must know how to use software platforms, customer relationship management systems, and AI-supported tools that now shape most modern service delivery processes (World Economic Forum, 2023).

Stage Two in Services. The second stage focuses on skill expansion, which unfolds differently in services because of the relational nature of the work. Alongside learning related service roles, workers develop what Levy and Murnane (2004) call "expert thinking" and "complex communication" skills the ability to solve problems that cannot be handled through simple rules and to communicate effectively with diverse clients and coworkers. In AI-supported service settings, workers also learn to work alongside AI systems: understanding when to trust an AI recommendation, when independent professional judgment is necessary, and how to explain AI-driven decisions clearly to clients. This balancing act is often genuinely difficult, and organisations should expect a learning curve rather than immediate fluency.

Stage Three in Services. Cross-functional integration in services means developing the ability to manage service delivery across several functional areas while coordinating both human and AI contributions within integrated systems. In healthcare, this stage may produce a clinical generalist or care coordinator able to move across diagnosis, treatment, administration, and patient communication while using AI diagnostic systems, electronic health records, and predictive analytics platforms effectively. In financial services, it may produce relationship managers who coordinate across lending, insurance, investments, and payment systems while using AI-driven credit assessment and portfolio optimisation tools.

Stage Four in Services. At the final stage, the advanced multi-skilled service professional develops what Daugherty and Wilson (2018) describe as the complete set of "fusion skills": training and configuring AI systems for service environments, reviewing AI-generated outputs for quality and ethical compliance, redesigning service systems for better human–AI collaboration, and acting as an organisational champion for responsible AI adoption. These professionals are now emerging in roles such as AI ethics officers, customer experience architects, digital health navigators, and algorithmic accountability specialists, representing the leading edge of the service sector workforce in the AI era.

6. IMPLICATIONS FOR WORKFORCE EFFICIENCY AND LABOR MARKET ADAPTABILITY

6.1 Workforce Efficiency

The LCTF offers a useful way to understand how lifecycle-based cross-training can generate efficiency gains beyond what pure specialisation or generic multi-skilling can achieve. At the individual level, workers who progress through the cross-training lifecycle gradually develop what Lazear (2009) calls "combinatorial value" the ability to combine knowledge from different fields to produce solutions that narrowly specialised workers may not identify. Ichniowski et al. (1997) and MacDuffie (1995) similarly show that functionally flexible workers with broad cross-trained skill sets tend to achieve better productivity outcomes, particularly in technology-intensive workplaces where adaptability is at a premium.

At the organisational level, lifecycle cross-training improves efficiency by reducing dependence on narrow specialists, strengthening organisational learning, and supporting smoother human–AI workflow integration. Organisations that invest in developing Stage Three and Stage Four employees build a human capital base capable of continuously improving AI-supported systems increasingly recognised as a source of competitive advantage in both manufacturing and service sectors (Brynjolfsson et al., 2019).

6.2 Labor Market Adaptability

From a labour market perspective, the LCTF offers a way of understanding how systematic cross-training investment can reduce structural unemployment and improve workforce resilience during periods of technological disruption. Workers who progress through the lifecycle gaining cross-functional expertise alongside AI governance skills are generally better positioned to absorb technological shocks, move between roles, and sustain productive employment across repeated cycles of automation-led disruption (Acemoglu & Restrepo, 2018; Autor, 2015).

This dimension of the LCTF becomes especially important in managing AI-driven labour market transitions. As Manyika et al. (2017) explain, the central challenge of the AI era is less the total volume of job loss than the displacement of workers from shrinking task areas and the difficulty of moving them into growing task domains a transition that depends heavily on the availability of well-designed cross-training systems. The four-stage structure of the LCTF offers a systematic pathway for this adjustment, identifying the competencies needed at each stage so that workers can remain adaptable as technological demands continue to shift.

6.3 Indicators for Tracking Progress

Because the LCTF is intended as a practical planning tool and not only a conceptual model, organisations and researchers applying it need observable indicators of progress at each stage, beyond the stage-specific benchmarks already noted in Sections 3.2–3.5. Table 2 consolidates a small set of indicators that can be tracked longitudinally, drawing on the same logic used in the stage-specific benchmarks above but framed at the organisational level.

Table 2. Organisation-level progress indicators by LCTF stage

Stage	Primary Indicator	Secondary Indicator
1. Entry-Level Specialisation	Time to baseline competency certification	Early-career retention rate
2. Skill Expansion	Number of completed cross-departmental rotations per worker	Accuracy in interpreting AI-system outputs
3. Cross-Functional Integration	Share of workforce leading cross-functional projects	Frequency of correctly escalated AI-system errors
4. Multi-Skilled Expertise & AI Governance	Share of senior workforce holding AI-governance responsibilities	Number of human–AI workflow redesigns implemented

Source: Author's Analysis

These indicators are necessarily approximate they measure proxies for capability rather than capability itself but they give organisations a basis for assessing whether their workforce is concentrated in vulnerable early stages or progressing toward the more resilient later stages, a distinction taken up further in Section 7.2.

7. POLICY AND MANAGERIAL IMPLICATIONS

7.1 Policy Implications

The LCTF carries several implications for workforce development policy at national and regional levels. First, policymakers need to recognise that effective cross-training in AI-intensive workplaces requires long-term investment across a worker's career lifecycle, rather than occasional interventions during crises such as mass layoffs. This supports the case for modular, stackable credential systems that recognise and reward the gradual development of cross-functional skills across career stages a direction already being pursued by Singapore through its SkillsFuture initiative and by Germany through its dual apprenticeship model (ILO, 2022; OECD, 2019).

Second, policy frameworks should be differentiated by sector, reflecting the distinct cross-training paths, institutional systems, and skill priorities of manufacturing and service industries. Sector-neutral training programmes may fail to address the AI governance skills needed by advanced manufacturing workers or the digital-relational intelligence increasingly required in advanced service professions. Public–private partnerships that bring together industry associations, educational institutions, and government agencies appear to be the most effective institutional model for designing sector-specific, practically useful training pathways (World Economic Forum, 2023).

Third, policymakers need to address inequality in access to lifecycle cross-training, building directly on the distributional concerns raised in Section 3.6. Access to progressive cross-training is not equally available to all workers and varies by education level, employment status, organisational size, and demographic background. Workers in small and medium enterprises, in routine-heavy occupations with high automation risk, and with weaker educational foundations are often those who need cross-training most but are least likely to receive it through market mechanisms alone (ILO, 2022). Public subsidies for training, financial support during training-related transitions, and minimum employer training-investment requirements can help correct these market failures.

7.2 Managerial Implications

For organisational leaders, the LCTF offers a strategic framework for planning cross-training investment in line with both technological adoption patterns and employee developmental stages. Organisations should evaluate their current workforce competency structure against the LCTF stage model using the indicators in Table 2 and identify whether large groups of workers remain concentrated in Stage One or Stage Two, which are the most vulnerable positions in rapidly automating environments. Based on this assessment, organisations should design systematic pathways that help employees progress toward Stage Three and Stage Four.

Cross-training programmes should be lifecycle-sensitive, matching content, teaching method, and intensity to a worker's developmental stage and motivational orientation. Entry-level employees generally benefit from structured job rotation, mentoring, and basic digital literacy training; mid-career employees are better supported through project-based cross-functional work and direct exposure to AI system operations; and senior workers moving into Stage Four require leadership training, AI governance knowledge, and a genuine seat at the table in organisational technology strategy (Noe, 2020; Aguinis & Kraiger, 2009).

Organisations must also attend to the cultural and motivational factors shaping cross-training effectiveness, and to the resistance dynamics discussed in Section 3.6. Worker engagement in cross-training is strongly affected by organisational culture, particularly the degree to which cross-functional skill development is visibly valued and rewarded (Cordery et al., 2010). Organisations that continue to reward only narrow specialisation through promotion and compensation systems tend to perform worse on cross-training effectiveness than organisations that deliberately build career progression around multi-functional competency development.

8. CONCLUSION, LIMITATIONS, AND FUTURE RESEARCH DIRECTIONS

8.1 Conclusion

This chapter has developed the Lifecycle Cross-Training Framework (LCTF), a conceptual model describing how workforce cross-training evolves across four progressive stages of worker development, and has applied it comparatively to manufacturing and service sectors in the context of AI and automation. It combines human capital theory, skill-biased technological change theory, and organisational learning perspectives to provide a theoretically grounded and practically relevant account of how cross-training systems must evolve in response to AI-driven transformation.

The LCTF contributes to academic and practical discussions in several ways. First, it identifies the lifecycle as the appropriate time-based unit for studying workforce cross-training, moving beyond static, short-term approaches to recognise that effective cross-training is gradual, cumulative, and stage-dependent. Second, it presents a sector-specific comparative analysis showing that manufacturing and service sectors differ meaningfully in cross-training content, institutional mechanisms, and strategic priorities differences often overlooked in generic frameworks. Third, it incorporates AI governance into the cross-training lifecycle, arguing that developing the human capability to work alongside, supervise, and creatively use AI systems has become the central cross-training challenge of the current technological era.

8.2 Limitations and Future Research Directions

The LCTF, as developed here, has four notable limitations. First, the framework is conceptual rather than empirically: the stage boundaries (years 1–4, 3–7, 8–15, and beyond) are drawn from the broader career-stage literature rather than from longitudinal data collected specifically on cross-training trajectories, and actual progression undoubtedly varies by individual, occupation, and organisational context. Second, the framework assumes a reasonably linear progression through the four stages, but real careers are not always linear workers can be pushed back into Stage One-type retraining mid-career following a major technological shift, a possibility the current model does not formally represent. Third, the framework was developed primarily with manufacturing and formal-sector service work in mind; its applicability to informal-sector work, gig and platform-based labour, and small-enterprise contexts common in many emerging economies remains untested and likely requires adaptation. Fourth, while Section 3.6 introduces cost, resistance, and demographic considerations, the framework does not yet specify how these factors should be weighted against one another when organisations face resource constraints for example, whether closing access gaps for underserved demographic groups should take precedence over accelerating Stage Three-to-Stage Four progression for already-advantaged workers. These limitations do not undermine the framework's conceptual contribution but do mark clear boundaries on what it can currently claim to explain.

Several directions for future empirical and conceptual research follow from this discussion. Empirically, longitudinal studies following workers across all four LCTF stages are needed to examine actual developmental processes, organisational support systems, and career outcomes associated with lifecycle progression directly addressing the first limitation noted above. Comparative sectoral studies investigating the detailed competency structures, training methods, and efficiency outcomes of cross-training programmes in manufacturing and service industries would strengthen the conceptual arguments made here. Research focused specifically on inequality in access to lifecycle cross-training examining who progresses through the full lifecycle and who does not, and why would make an important contribution to policy debates on inclusive technological transition, building on the demographic findings discussed in Section 3.6.

Conceptually, future research might extend the LCTF to examine cross-organisational and cross-sectoral dimensions of workforce cross-training, including how workers build lifecycle cross-training paths across multiple employers and industries, and what institutional structures are necessary to support such trajectories in the increasingly flexible, portfolio-based labour markets common in advanced digital economies. Another useful direction would be integrating the LCTF with emerging frameworks studying AI–human collaboration at the task and team levels (Brynjolfsson et al., 2019; Daugherty & Wilson, 2018), and with the non-linear career patterns and informal-sector applications identified as limitations above.

The central argument of this chapter can be stated simply: in the era of AI and automation, workforce cross-training is no longer an optional human resource activity but a core organisational capability and an essential public policy priority. Organisations and societies that invest in systematic, lifecycle-based, and sector-specific cross-training systems while remaining attentive to its costs and its uneven distributional effects will be best positioned to capture the productive benefits of AI while protecting broad-based employment, workforce adaptability, and human dignity, which remain the foundation of inclusive and sustainable economic development.

REFERENCES

Acemoglu, D., & Autor, D. (2011). Skills, tasks and technologies: Implications for employment and earnings. In Ashenfelter, O., & Card, D. (Eds.), *Handbook of labor economics* (Vol. 4, pp. 1043–1171). Elsevier., DOI: 10.1016/S0169-7218(11)02410-5

Acemoglu, D., & Pischke, J. S. (1999). The structure of wages and investment in general training. *Journal of Political Economy*, *107*(3), 539–572. DOI: 10.1086/250071

Acemoglu, D., & Restrepo, P. (2018). The race between man and machine: Implications of technology for growth, factor shares, and employment. *The American Economic Review*, *108*(6), 1488–1542. DOI: 10.1257/aer.20160696

Acemoglu, D., & Restrepo, P. (2019). Automation and new tasks: How technology displaces and reinstates labor. *The Journal of Economic Perspectives*, *33*(2), 3–30. DOI: 10.1257/jep.33.2.3

Acemoglu, D., & Restrepo, P. (2020). Robots and jobs: Evidence from US labor markets. *Journal of Political Economy*, *128*(6), 2188–2244. DOI: 10.1086/705716

Aguinis, H., & Kraiger, K. (2009). Benefits of training and development for individuals and teams, organizations, and society. *Annual Review of Psychology*, *60*(1), 451–474. DOI: 10.1146/annurev.psych.60.110707.163505 PMID: 18976113

Appelbaum, E., Bailey, T., Berg, P., & Kalleberg, A. L. (2000). *Manufacturing advantage: Why high-performance work systems pay off.* Cornell University Press.

Argyris, C., & Schön, D. A. (1978). *Organizational learning: A theory of action perspective*. Addison-Wesley.

Arntz, M., Gregory, T., & Zierahn, U. (2016). The risk of automation for jobs in OECD countries: A comparative analysis. *OECD Social, Employment and Migration Working Papers, No. 189*. OECD Publishing. DOI: 10.1787/1815199X

Atkinson, J. (1984). Manpower strategies for flexible organizations. *Personnel Management*, *16*(8), 28–31.

Autor, D. H. (2015). Why are there still so many jobs? The history and future of workplace automation. *The Journal of Economic Perspectives*, *29*(3), 3–30. DOI: 10.1257/jep.29.3.3

Autor, D. H., & Dorn, D. (2013). The growth of low-skill service jobs and the polarization of the US labor market. *The American Economic Review*, *103*(5), 1553–1597. DOI: 10.1257/aer.103.5.1553

Autor, D. H., Levy, F., & Murnane, R. J. (2003). The skill content of recent technological change: An empirical exploration. *The Quarterly Journal of Economics, 118*(4), 1279–1333. DOI: 10.1162/003355303322552801

Autor, D. H., & Salomons, A. (2018). Is automation labor-displacing? Productivity growth, employment, and the labor share. *Brookings Papers on Economic Activity, 2018*(1), 1–87. DOI: 10.1353/eca.2018.0000

Bangladesh Labour Foundation, BRAC University, & Solidaridad Network Asia. (2024). *Assessment of technological transition in the apparel sector of Bangladesh and its impact on the workers*. Bangladesh Labour Foundation.

Baumol, W. J. (1967). Macroeconomics of unbalanced growth: The anatomy of urban crisis. *The American Economic Review, 57*(3), 415–426.

Becker, G. S. (1964). *Human capital: A theoretical and empirical analysis, with special reference to education*. Columbia University Press.

Ben-Porath, Y. (1967). The production of human capital and the life cycle of earnings. *Journal of Political Economy, 75*(4), 352–365. DOI: 10.1086/259291

Borghans, L., & ter Weel, B. (2007). The division of labour, worker organisation, and technological change. *Economic Journal (London), 117*(519), F45–F72. DOI: 10.1111/j.1468-0297.2007.02011.x

Bresnahan, T. F., Brynjolfsson, E., & Hitt, L. M. (2002). Information technology, workplace organization, and the demand for skilled labor: Firm-level evidence. *The Quarterly Journal of Economics, 117*(1), 339–376. DOI: 10.1162/003355302753399526

Brynjolfsson, E., & McAfee, A. (2014). *The second machine age: Work, progress, and prosperity in a time of brilliant technologies*. W. W. Norton & Company.

Brynjolfsson, E., Mitchell, T., & Rock, D. (2018). What can machines learn, and what does it mean for occupations and the economy? *AEA Papers and Proceedings. American Economic Association, 108*, 43–47. DOI: 10.1257/pandp.20181019

Brynjolfsson, E., Rock, D., & Syverson, C. (2019). Artificial intelligence and the modern productivity paradox: A clash of expectations and statistics. In Agrawal, A., Gans, J., & Goldfarb, A. (Eds.), *The economics of artificial intelligence: An agenda* (pp. 23–57). University of Chicago Press., DOI: 10.7208/chicago/9780226613475.003.0001

Cappelli, P., & Neumark, D. (2001). Do "high-performance" work practices improve establishment-level outcomes? *Industrial & Labor Relations Review, 54*(4), 737–775. DOI: 10.1177/001979390105400402

Caribou, & Genesis Analytics. (2024). *AI's potential impact on Africa's tech-outsourcing sector*. Report prepared in partnership with the Mastercard Foundation.

Cath, C., Wachter, S., Mittelstadt, B., Taddeo, M., & Floridi, L. (2018). Artificial intelligence and the "good society": The US, EU, and UK approach. *Science and Engineering Ethics, 24*(2), 505–528. DOI: 10.1007/s11948-017-9901-7 PMID: 28353045

Cohen, W. M., & Levinthal, D. A. (1990). Absorptive capacity: A new perspective on learning and innovation. *Administrative Science Quarterly, 35*(1), 128–152. DOI: 10.2307/2393553

Cordery, J., Soo, C., Kirkman, B., Rosen, B., & Mathieu, J. (2010). Leading parallel global virtual teams: Lessons from Alcoa. *Organizational Dynamics, 39*(3), 204–216. DOI: 10.1016/j.orgdyn.2009.04.002

Dafoe, A. (2018). *AI governance: A research agenda*. Future of Humanity Institute, University of Oxford. https://www.fhi.ox.ac.uk/wp-content/uploads/AI-Governance-Research-Agenda.pdf

Daugherty, P. R., & Wilson, H. J. (2018). *Human + machine: Reimagining work in the age of AI*. Harvard Business Review Press.

Dauth, W., Findeisen, S., Südekum, J., & Woessner, N. (2021). The adjustment of labor markets to robots. *Journal of the European Economic Association, 19*(6), 3104–3153. DOI: 10.1093/jeea/jvab012

Dessein, W., & Santos, T. (2006). Adaptive organizations. *Journal of Political Economy, 114*(5), 956–995. DOI: 10.1086/508031

Eloundou, T., Manning, S., Mishkin, P., & Rock, D. (2023). GPTs are GPTs: An early look at the labor market impact potential of large language models. *arXiv preprint*. https://doi.org//arXiv.2303.10130DOI: 10.48550

Frey, C. B., & Osborne, M. A. (2017). The future of employment: How susceptible are jobs to computerisation? *Technological Forecasting and Social Change, 114*, 254–280. DOI: 10.1016/j.techfore.2016.08.019

Goldman Sachs. (2023). *The potentially large effects of artificial intelligence on economic growth*. Goldman Sachs Economic Research.

Goos, M., Manning, A., & Salomons, A. (2014). Explaining job polarization: Routine-biased technological change and offshoring. *The American Economic Review, 104*(8), 2509–2526. DOI: 10.1257/aer.104.8.2509

Ichniowski, C., Shaw, K., & Prennushi, G. (1997). The effects of human resource management practices on productivity: A study of steel finishing lines. *The American Economic Review*, *87*(3), 291–313.

International Labour Organization. (2022). *World employment and social outlook: The role of digital labour platforms in transforming the world of work*. ILO.

Kagermann, H., Wahlster, W., & Helbig, J. (2013). *Recommendations for implementing the strategic initiative Industrie 4.0*. National Academy of Science and Engineering (Acatech).

Kolb, D. A. (1984). *Experiential learning: Experience as the source of learning and development*. Prentice Hall.

Kunze, F., Boehm, S., & Bruch, H. (2013). Age, resistance to change, and job performance. *Journal of Managerial Psychology*, *28*(7/8), 741–760. DOI: 10.1108/JMP-06-2013-0194

Lasi, H., Fettke, P., Kemper, H. G., Feld, T., & Hoffmann, M. (2014). Industry 4.0. *Business & Information Systems Engineering*, *6*(4), 239–242. DOI: 10.1007/s12599-014-0334-4

Lazear, E. P. (2009). Firm-specific human capital: A skill-weights approach. *Journal of Political Economy*, *117*(5), 914–940. DOI: 10.1086/648671

Levy, F., & Murnane, R. J. (2004). *The new division of labor: How computers are creating the next job market*. Princeton University Press. DOI: 10.1515/9781400845927

Li, L. (2024). Reskilling and upskilling the future-ready workforce for Industry 4.0 and beyond. *Information Systems Frontiers*, *26*(5), 1697–1712. DOI: 10.1007/s10796-022-10308-y PMID: 35855776

MacDuffie, J. P. (1995). Human resource bundles and manufacturing performance: Organizational logic and flexible production systems in the world auto industry. *Industrial & Labor Relations Review*, *48*(2), 197–221. DOI: 10.1177/001979399504800201

Manyika, J., Chui, M., Miremadi, M., Bughin, J., George, K., Willmott, P., & Dewhurst, M. (2017). *A future that works: Automation, employment, and productivity*. McKinsey Global Institute.

Márquez Stone, V., & Sandoval Cabrera, S. V. (2024). Effects of automation on Mexican automotive employment: 2013–2022. *The Indian Journal of Labour Economics : The Quarterly Journal of the Indian Society of Labour Economics*, *67*(3), 661–680. DOI: 10.1007/s41027-024-00505-5

Miah, M. T., Erdei-Gally, S., Dancs, A., & Fekete-Farkas, M. (2024). A systematic review of Industry 4.0 technology on workforce employability and skills: Driving success factors and challenges in South Asia. *Economies (Basel)*, *12*(2), 35. DOI: 10.3390/economies12020035

Noe, R. A. (2020). *Employee training and development* (8th ed.). McGraw-Hill Education.

ODI. (2025). *The AI time bomb: 2.5 million jobs at risk, is Kenya ready?* ODI: Think Change.

OECD. (2019). *OECD skills outlook 2019: Thriving in a digital world*. OECD Publishing., DOI: 10.1787/df80bc12-

Osterman, P. (1994). How common is workplace transformation and who adopts it? *Industrial & Labor Relations Review*, *47*(2), 173–188. DOI: 10.1177/001979399404700202

Ranasinghe, T., Grosse, E. H., Glock, C. H., & Jaber, M. Y. (2024). Never too late to learn: Unlocking the potential of aging workforce in manufacturing and service industries. *International Journal of Production Economics*, *270*, 109193. DOI: 10.1016/j.ijpe.2024.109193

Schultz, T. W. (1961). Investment in human capital. *The American Economic Review*, *51*(1), 1–17.

Schwab, K. (2016). *The fourth industrial revolution*. World Economic Forum.

Senge, P. M. (1990). *The fifth discipline: The art and practice of the learning organization*. Doubleday.

Tharenou, P., Saks, A. M., & Moore, C. (2007). A review and critique of research on training and organizational-level outcomes. *Human Resource Management Review*, *17*(3), 251–273. DOI: 10.1016/j.hrmr.2007.07.004

World Economic Forum. (2023). *The future of jobs report 2023*. World Economic Forum. https://www.weforum.org/reports/the-future-of-jobs-report-2023

Zahra, S. A., & George, G. (2002). Absorptive capacity: A review, reconceptualization, and extension. *Academy of Management Review*, *27*(2), 185–203. DOI: 10.2307/4134351

Chapter 11
Phygital Cross-Training Models for Hybrid Workforces:
Transforming Employee Capabilities and Organizational Adaptability in the Era of Remote Work

Jomon Jose M.
http://orcid.org/0009-0003-4341-9936
Sahrdaya Institute of Management Studies, Kodakara, India

Jyothis Rachel Mathews
http://orcid.org/0009-0003-8279-6080
Ahalia School of Management, Palakkad, India

ABSTRACT

Amid tightening labor markets and the swift adoption of hybrid work models, organizations encounter notable difficulties in cultivating agile workforces with diverse skill sets. This chapter investigates phygital cross-training as a blended approach that integrates physical and digital learning contexts to support skill acquisition and improve organizational outcomes. Grounded in Experiential Learning Theory, Human Capital Theory, digital transformation frameworks, and the Resource-Based View, it presents a layered Input-Process-Outcome model. The analysis addresses critical facilitators, obstacles, managerial considerations, and policy suggestions. Evidence indicates that phygital cross-training can enhance workforce adaptability,

DOI: 10.4018/979-8-3373-5327-2.ch011

ght © 2027, IGI Global Scientific Publishing. Copying or distributing in print or electronic forms without written permission of IGI Global Scientific Publishing is prohibited. Use of this chapter to generative artificial intelligence (AI) technologies is expressly prohibited. The publisher reserves all rights to license its use for generative AI training and machine learning model development.

engagement, and robustness. Overall, the chapter contributes to theoretical understanding while offering actionable insights for organizations aiming to prepare for hybrid, technology-intensive work environments.

1. INTRODUCTION

Tight labor markets have become a defining characteristic of the contemporary global economy, marked by persistent talent shortages, increasing labor costs, and intensified competition for skilled professionals. These conditions have compelled organizations to reconsider conventional workforce strategies and adopt more flexible and resilient approaches to talent management. In response, organizations are increasingly emphasizing internal workforce development initiatives such as upskilling, reskilling, and cross-training to reduce dependence on external recruitment (Li, 2022; World Economic Forum, 2025). Simultaneously, the transformation of work structures, accelerated significantly during the COVID-19 pandemic, has facilitated the widespread adoption of hybrid workforce models in which employees operate across both physical and digital environments (Carnevale & Hatak, 2020; Kniffin et al., 2021). This transition has substantially reshaped organizational practices related to job design, performance evaluation, employee collaboration, and capability development.

The expansion of remote and flexible work arrangements has further increased the need for continuous and adaptive employee learning systems. Digital collaboration platforms such as Microsoft Teams, Google Workspace, Slack, Zoom, and Trello have enabled seamless communication and coordination among geographically dispersed teams; however, they also create challenges associated with maintaining employee engagement, improving learning effectiveness, and facilitating efficient knowledge sharing (Waizenegger et al., 2020). Within hybrid work environments, employees are increasingly expected to perform diverse responsibilities, participate in cross-functional collaboration, and adapt rapidly to evolving job requirements. Consequently, organizations now require employees to possess versatile competencies that extend beyond traditional role boundaries and support flexibility across multiple functions (Karhapää, 2024; Lo, 2024).

In this context, organizations are moving away from rigid, role-specific training approaches toward more dynamic and integrated workforce development systems. Traditional training methods that rely solely on classroom-based instruction or isolated digital learning are often insufficient to meet the demands of hybrid work settings. As a result, there is growing interest in "phygital" learning approaches that integrate physical and digital learning experiences to create immersive, flexible, and continuous learning environments. Phygital learning combines the strengths of face-to-face experiential learning with the scalability and accessibility of digital technologies, enabling employees to engage in real-time, collaborative, and personalized skill development.

At the same time, cross-training has emerged as a strategic mechanism for enhancing workforce adaptability and organizational resilience. Cross-training equips employees with skills beyond their primary roles, enabling them to perform multiple tasks and contribute across functional areas. In hybrid work environments, where agility and operational continuity are critical, cross-training enhances workforce flexibility, improves collaboration, and reduces dependency on narrowly specialized roles (Li, 2022). When integrated with phygital learning systems, cross-training becomes more scalable, interactive, and aligned with the evolving needs of hybrid organizations.

Against this backdrop, the primary objective of this chapter is to examine how phygital cross-training frameworks transform employee capability development and contribute to enhanced organizational adaptability within hybrid workforce settings. Specifically, the chapter aims to: (1) analyze the changing dynamics of workforce training in constrained labor markets, (2) develop a conceptual understanding of the integration between physical and digital learning environments, and (3) propose a comprehensive Phygital Cross-Training Framework for Hybrid Workforces that supports effective capability development and organizational agility. By integrating theoretical perspectives with emerging organizational practices, this chapter contributes to ongoing discussions on preparing future-ready workforces while offering practical insights for organizations navigating the complexities of hybrid work environments.

2. EVOLUTION OF WORKFORCE TRAINING IN THE DIGITAL ERA

The development of workforce training has been influenced by advances in technology, globalization, and evolving organizational demands. Traditionally, employee training relied mainly on in-person classroom instruction, workshops, and instructor-led sessions focused on standardized curricula and the development of role-specific skills. Although these approaches provided structured learning environments and opportunities for direct interaction, they frequently lacked scalability, flexibility, and real-time responsiveness to changing job requirements (Salas et al., 2012). As organizations grew more global and their workforces more diverse, the constraints of exclusively traditional training models became increasingly apparent.

The introduction of digital training represented a significant change in organizational strategies for learning and development. Tools such as e-learning platforms, virtual classrooms, and Learning Management Systems (LMS) have enabled training content to be delivered asynchronously, allowing employees to access learning materials at their convenience. This transition improved accessibility and reduced costs while promoting self-directed learning (Noe et al., 2014). Nevertheless, fully digital training also introduced challenges, such as diminished interpersonal interaction, lower engagement, and reduced opportunities for hands-on experiential learning. Consequently, organizations began to investigate hybrid and blended training approaches that seek to integrate the advantages of both traditional and digital methods.

The hybrid training model combines face-to-face training with online training tools to offer more dynamic and engaging training. These models deliver content using digital platforms but still utilize face-to-face interaction for collaboration, simulations, and hands-on practice. Technology ecosystems such as Microsoft Teams and Google Workspace have helped enable these blended learning environments, making it possible to communicate, collaborate, and share knowledge between teams separated by geography. Hybrid models are particularly relevant in the current work context, where flexibility and adaptability are indispensable for organizations and employees (Elm Learning, 2023; Absorb LMS, 2026; Training Industry, 2022).

Simultaneously, we have seen a significant shift from role-based training to multi-skilling and cross-functional competency development. In traditional organizations, employees were usually trained for specific roles with clearly defined responsibilities. But the increasing complexity of work and the need for agility in hybrid environments have demanded a broader skill set, enabling employees to perform multiple jobs and adapt to changing demands. Therefore, cross-training has become a strategic tool to make the workforce more versatile, reduce reliance on specialized roles, and improve operational resilience, especially in hybrid and remote settings (Panopto, 2021; Li, 2022; Easygenerator, 2025).

The evolving nature of work in hybrid settings highlights the need for flexible and adaptable training systems. Employees working in hybrid environments need to be able to master the physical and digital space, work together in diverse teams, and make effective use of a range of digital tools. This shift has reshaped the nature of work, placing greater importance on technical skills, as well as soft skills like communication, adaptability, and digital literacy (Kniffin et al., 2021; Henke et al., 2022). With job boundaries becoming increasingly fluid, traditional training approaches focused on static skill sets are no longer sufficient.

In response to these developments, there is an increased demand for continuous and flexible learning systems that support lifelong learning and continuous skill development. Organizations are increasingly adopting learning ecosystems that support continuous upskilling and reskilling through microlearning, on-the-job training, and digital platforms. These systems enable employees to acquire new competencies in real time, aligning learning processes with evolving organizational objectives and market demands (Li, 2022; Hasan, 2024; TalentLMS, 2024). Continuous learning increases the likelihood of an individual securing a job and enhances the competitiveness of the organization in dynamic and uncertain environments.

In conclusion, workforce training has moved from static, one-off learning interventions to dynamic, integrated and continuous learning systems. This shift lays the groundwork for the development of advanced techniques such as phygital cross-training, enhancing the integration of physical and digital learning environments to meet the needs of contemporary hybrid workforces (Lo, 2024).

3. UNDERSTANDING PHYGITAL LEARNING AND CROSS-TRAINING

The rapid convergence of digital technologies with traditional organizational processes has led to the emergence of innovative learning paradigms, among which phygital learning has gained significant attention. The term "phygital" represents the effective blending of physical and virtual environments to create unified, interactive, and immersive experiences. In workforce development, phygital learning refers to a blended approach that integrates in-person training with digital tools and virtual environments—such as augmented reality (AR), virtual reality (VR), and extended reality (XR)—to improve learning effectiveness, accessibility, and engagement (Batista-Toledo & Gavilan, 2025; Lo, 2024; Moi, 2026).

Unlike conventional blended learning, which often treats physical and digital components as somewhat separate elements, phygital learning emphasizes their deep integration into a cohesive system where learners can transition fluidly between real-world and digital contexts. This fusion creates "phygital workspaces" that support both immersive, hands-on experiences and scalable, data-driven learning (Lo, 2024; Microsoft, 2024).

Phygital learning encompasses multiple dimensions that contribute to its effectiveness in modern organizations. First, the technological dimension involves the use of advanced digital platforms, simulations, collaborative tools, and immersive technologies that support real-time interaction and content delivery. Platforms such as Microsoft Teams and Google Workspace, combined with XR tools, facilitate seamless communication, collaboration, and knowledge sharing across geographically distributed teams (Microsoft, 2024; Lo, 2024). Second, the experiential dimension focuses on hands-on, practice-oriented learning, often conducted in physical or simulated environments. This allows employees to apply theoretical knowledge in realistic, risk-free contexts, bridging the gap between learning and application. Third, the personalization dimension leverages data analytics and adaptive learning systems to create tailored pathways based on individual skill levels, learning preferences, performance data, and job requirements. Finally, the integration dimension ensures the seamless alignment of physical and digital components, forming a unified learning ecosystem that significantly improves engagement, knowledge retention, and transfer to the workplace (Moi, 2026).

These dimensions collectively address key limitations of traditional and purely digital training models. For instance, in manufacturing or healthcare settings, employees can practice complex procedures through VR simulations in a digital space and then apply them in physical workshops, resulting in higher confidence and reduced error rates.

Parallel to the rise of phygital learning, cross-training has emerged as a critical strategy for enhancing workforce versatility and organizational resilience. Cross-training refers to the systematic process of training employees to perform tasks and responsibilities beyond their primary roles, thereby equipping them with a broader range of skills and competencies (Panopto, 2021; Li, 2022). The scope of cross-training extends across functional, technical, and behavioral domains, enabling employees to contribute effectively to multiple areas within the organization.

From a strategic perspective, cross-training reduces dependency on specialized roles, enhances operational flexibility, supports knowledge sharing, and builds resilience. It is particularly valuable in tight labor markets characterized by skill shortages and high uncertainty (Easygenerator, 2025; Hasan, 2024). In hybrid work environments, cross-trained employees can seamlessly shift between on-site and remote tasks, ensuring business continuity during disruptions.

The integration of physical and digital learning environments plays a pivotal role in enhancing the effectiveness of cross-training initiatives. In traditional settings, cross-training often relied on job rotation, shadowing, and in-person mentoring. While these methods remain valuable, their scalability and consistency are limited, especially in geographically dispersed or hybrid workforces. By incorporating digital tools, virtual simulations, and phygital platforms, organizations can extend cross-training opportunities beyond physical constraints. Employees can access training resources anytime, participate in immersive simulations, and collaborate with peers across locations. This integration not only improves accessibility but also ensures continuity of learning in dynamic work environments (Lo, 2024; Training Industry, 2022).

Moreover, the role of cross-training in enhancing workforce adaptability has become increasingly significant in hybrid work. As job roles evolve and organizational structures become more fluid, employees must adapt quickly to new tasks, technologies, and work arrangements. Cross-training equips them with diverse skill sets, enabling rapid responses to changing demands and contributions across multiple functions. This adaptability is crucial for maintaining productivity and resilience amid disruptions and skill gaps (Kniffin et al., 2021; Henke et al., 2022).

In addition, cross-training fosters a culture of continuous learning and collaboration, which is essential for sustaining long-term organizational performance. Employees exposed to multiple roles develop a broader understanding of organizational processes, leading to improved coordination, innovation, and problem-solving. When combined with phygital learning approaches, cross-training becomes more dynamic, scalable, and aligned with the needs of modern hybrid workforces. This synergy not only enhances individual competencies but also strengthens the organization's ability to navigate complex and rapidly changing labor market conditions (Li, 2022; Moi, 2026). By merging phygital learning with cross-training, organizations can create a powerful ecosystem that prepares employees for the uncertainties of the future of work while driving sustainable competitive advantage.

4. THEORETICAL UNDERPINNINGS

A strong theoretical foundation is important for understanding how phygital cross-training can support employee learning and organizational adaptability in hybrid work environments. This chapter brings together multiple theoretical perspectives—Experiential Learning Theory, Human Capital Theory, digital transformation perspectives, and the Resource-Based View—to develop a comprehensive framework for examining phygital cross-training systems.

David A. Kolb's Experiential Learning Theory (1984) explains that learning is an ongoing process rooted in experience. It suggests that knowledge develops through the transformation of experience in a continuous cycle consisting of concrete experience, reflective observation, abstract conceptualization, and active experimentation. In workforce training, Experiential Learning Theory highlights the value of practical, hands-on learning that enables individuals to apply theoretical knowledge in real-world situations. Phygital learning environments align closely with this perspective by combining physical interactions, such as workshops and simulations, with digital tools that enable reflection, feedback, and iterative learning. This integration enhances the depth and retention of learning by engaging employees in both experiential and reflective processes, particularly in hybrid settings (Kolb & Kolb, 2005; Karhapää, 2024).

Human Capital Theory provides another critical lens for understanding the value of cross-training initiatives. Rooted in the work of Becker (1964), this theory conceptualizes employees' skills, knowledge, and abilities as valuable assets that contribute to organizational productivity and economic performance. Investments in training and development are therefore seen as strategic decisions that enhance the quality of human capital and generate long-term returns. Cross-training, particularly in a phygital context, expands the breadth and depth of employee competencies, enabling individuals to perform multiple roles and adapt to changing job requirements. This not only increases individual employability but also strengthens organizational resilience by reducing reliance on narrowly specialized skills (Li, 2022; Hasan, 2024).

In addition to these foundational theories, digital transformation perspectives offer insights into how technology reshapes learning and organizational processes. Digital transformation is not merely the adoption of new technologies but involves a fundamental reconfiguration of business models, workflows, and organizational culture (Vial, 2019). In workforce training, digital transformation facilitates the creation of flexible, scalable, and data-driven learning systems that can be continuously updated to reflect evolving skill demands. Phygital cross-training leverages digital transformation by integrating advanced technologies—such as learning management systems, virtual simulations, collaborative platforms, and extended reality tools—into traditional training processes. This enables organizations to deliver personalized and context-specific learning experiences that align with the needs of hybrid workforces (Moi, 2026; Lo, 2024).

The Resource-Based View (RBV) further strengthens the strategic relevance of phygital cross-training by emphasizing the role of internal resources in achieving sustainable competitive advantage. According to RBV, organizations gain a competitive edge by developing resources that are valuable, rare, inimitable, and non-substitutable (Barney, 1991). Human capital, particularly when enhanced through cross-training and continuous learning in phygital environments, represents a critical strategic resource. Phygital cross-training contributes to the development of such resources by fostering a workforce that is not only skilled but also adaptable and capable of responding to dynamic market conditions. By embedding cross-training within a phygital framework, organizations can create unique capabilities that are difficult for competitors to replicate because these capabilities emerge from the integration of technological infrastructure, organizational learning culture, employee experience, and collaborative knowledge-sharing practices (Moi, 2026). Unlike traditional training systems that focus primarily on isolated skill acquisition, phygital cross-training combines immersive digital technologies with experiential physical learning to develop multi-skilled employees who can adapt rapidly to changing operational demands. Over time, employees accumulate tacit knowledge, cross-functional expertise, and collaborative problem-solving abilities that become deeply embedded within organizational routines and workflows.

Furthermore, the effectiveness of phygital cross-training depends not only on technology adoption but also on how organizations integrate learning processes with strategic objectives, leadership support, and employee engagement practices. Competitors may imitate specific technologies such as virtual simulations or digital platforms; however, replicating the entire ecosystem of organizational culture, experiential learning processes, adaptive workforce behaviors, and accumulated institutional knowledge is considerably more difficult. This combination creates capabilities that are valuable, rare, difficult to imitate, and non-substitutable, thereby aligning with the core assumptions of the Resource-Based View (Barney, 1991). Consequently, organizations that effectively implement phygital cross-training can achieve sustained competitive advantage through enhanced workforce agility, innovation capacity, and organizational resilience in dynamic hybrid work environments.

The synthesis of these theoretical perspectives provides a comprehensive understanding of how phygital cross-training operates as both a learning mechanism and a strategic tool. Experiential Learning Theory explains the process of knowledge acquisition and skill development, while Human Capital Theory highlights the economic value of investing in employee capabilities. Digital transformation perspectives underscore the role of technology in enabling flexible and scalable learning systems, and the Resource-Based View connects these elements to organizational performance and competitive advantage. Together, these theories form an integrated framework that supports the design and implementation of effective phygital cross-training models in hybrid work settings.

In conclusion, the integration of multiple theoretical lenses not only strengthens the conceptual foundation of this chapter but also enhances its relevance to contemporary organizational challenges. By combining insights from learning theory, economics, technology, and strategic management, phygital cross-training can be understood as a multidimensional approach that addresses both individual and organizational needs in the evolving landscape of hybrid work.

5. PHYGITAL CROSS-TRAINING FRAMEWORK FOR HYBRID WORKFORCES

The increasing complexity of hybrid work environments necessitates a structured and integrative approach to workforce development. In response, this chapter proposes a Phygital Cross-Training Framework that combines physical and digital learning modalities to enhance employee competencies and organizational agility. The framework is designed to address the limitations of isolated training systems by integrating technological, behavioral, and strategic elements into a cohesive framework. It builds on insights from experiential learning, human capital development, digital transformation, and the Resource-Based View to position cross-training as a key driver of sustainable competitive advantage.

Introduction to the Proposed Framework

The proposed framework conceptualizes phygital cross-training as a multi-layered system in which learning environments, technology, skill development, employee engagement, and organizational agility are interlinked. It emphasizes that effective training in hybrid work settings is not merely about delivering content but about creating an ecosystem where employees can continuously learn, adapt, and contribute across functions. By integrating physical and digital elements, the framework supports both experiential and scalable learning processes, thereby aligning individual development with organizational goals (Lo, 2024; Moi, 2026).

Core Components of the Framework

1. **Learning Environment (Physical + Digital Integration)** The learning environment forms the foundation of the framework, combining traditional face-to-face training with digital learning platforms. Physical environments enable experiential learning through workshops, simulations, and collaborative activities, while digital environments provide flexibility, accessibility, and continuity. The integration of these environments—often referred to as phygital workspaces—ensures a seamless learning experience, allowing employees to transition between in-person and virtual settings without disruption (Lo, 2024; Batista-Toledo & Gavilan, 2025).
2. **Technology Enablement** Technology acts as a critical enabler in the phygital cross-training framework. Advanced digital tools facilitate content delivery, real-time collaboration, and performance tracking. Platforms such as Microsoft Teams and Google Workspace support synchronous and asynchronous learning, enabling employees to engage in cross-functional training regardless of location. Additionally, emerging technologies such as artificial intelligence, virtual simulations, and extended reality (XR) enhance personalization and interactivity in learning processes (Microsoft, 2024; Moi, 2026).
3. **Skill Development (Technical and Soft Skills)** A central objective of cross-training is the development of both technical and soft skills. Technical skills enable employees to perform specific tasks across different roles, while soft skills—such as communication, adaptability, and problem-solving—facilitate effective collaboration in hybrid environments. The framework emphasizes a balanced approach to skill development, ensuring that employees are equipped to handle both operational and interpersonal challenges through upskilling and reskilling pathways (Li, 2022; Hasan, 2024).
4. **Employee Engagement** Employee engagement is a critical mediator in the effectiveness of cross-training initiatives. Engaged employees are more likely

to participate actively in training programs, apply acquired knowledge, and contribute to organizational goals. Phygital learning environments enhance engagement by offering interactive, personalized, and immersive experiences that cater to diverse learning preferences. Continuous feedback, recognition, and opportunities for growth further strengthen employee involvement (Kniffin et al., 2021).

5. **Organizational Agility** Organizational agility represents the ultimate outcome of the framework. It refers to the ability of an organization to respond swiftly and effectively to changes in the external environment. By fostering a multi-skilled and adaptable workforce, phygital cross-training enhances operational flexibility, reduces dependency on specialized roles, and supports rapid decision-making. This agility is particularly crucial in tight labor markets, where organizations must navigate uncertainty and resource constraints (Teece et al., 2016; Moi, 2026).

Interrelationships Among Components

The components of the framework are highly interdependent, forming a dynamic system that drives workforce development and organizational performance. The integrated learning environment, supported by technology, facilitates the delivery of cross-training programs that enhance both technical and soft skills. These competencies, in turn, influence employee engagement by increasing confidence, motivation, and job satisfaction. High levels of engagement lead to more effective application of skills, thereby contributing to organizational agility.

Furthermore, technology not only supports the learning environment but also enables continuous monitoring and improvement of training outcomes. Feedback loops between engagement and skill development ensure that learning processes remain relevant and responsive to organizational needs. The framework thus operates as a continuous cycle, where each component reinforces the others, creating a sustainable system of workforce development in hybrid settings (Lo, 2024; Li, 2022).

Figure 1. Phygital Cross-Training Framework for Hybrid Workforces

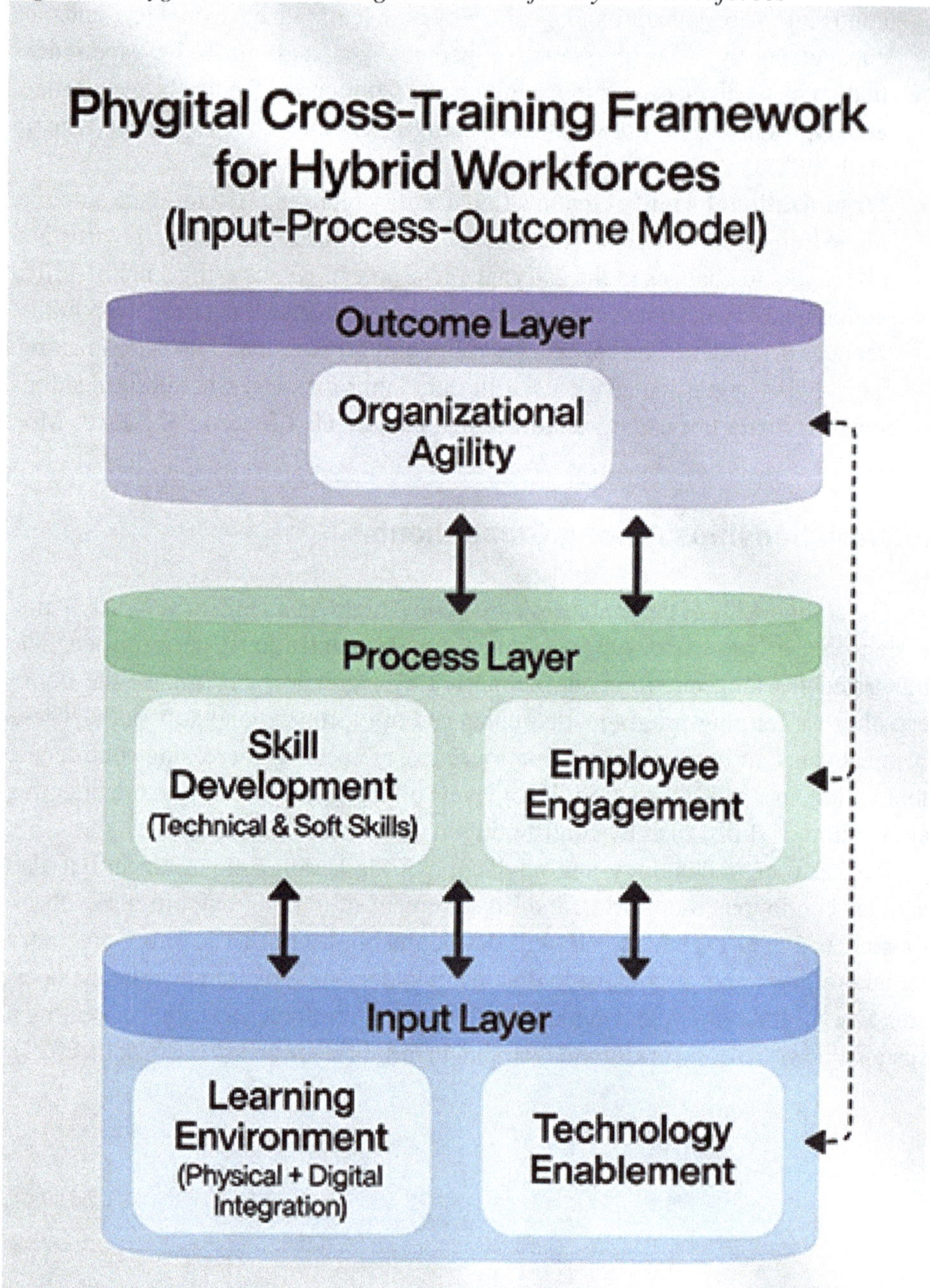

The Phygital Cross-Training Framework (Figure 1) is structured as a layered and interconnected system that explains how phygital cross-training enhances organizational outcomes in hybrid work environments. At the input level, Learning Environment (integrating physical and digital elements) and Technology Enablement serve as foundational drivers that facilitate flexible and accessible training experiences. These inputs influence the process layer, where Skill Development—encompassing both technical and soft skills—acts as a core mechanism for building employee capabilities, while Employee Engagement reflects the extent to which individuals are psychologically involved in learning and work activities. Together, these process variables translate training inputs into meaningful outcomes. At the final stage, the outcome layer is represented by Organizational Agility, which captures the organization's ability to respond effectively to dynamic market conditions. The framework thus highlights a sequential yet cyclical flow where integrated learning environments and technology enable capability development and engagement, ultimately leading to enhanced agility and resilience (Lo, 2024; Moi, 2026; Li, 2022).

6. ENABLERS OF EFFECTIVE PHYGITAL CROSS-TRAINING

The successful implementation of phygital cross-training in hybrid workforces depends on a set of critical organizational and technological enablers that collectively support seamless learning experiences and sustainable skill development. These enablers work synergistically to overcome traditional barriers and maximize the potential of integrated physical-digital training systems.

Among these, digital infrastructure and learning platforms form the backbone of phygital training systems. Robust IT infrastructure, supported by cloud-based learning management systems (LMS), virtual classrooms, simulation tools, and extended reality (XR) solutions, ensures high accessibility, scalability, and real-time interaction. These platforms enable organizations to deliver consistent, high-quality training experiences across geographically dispersed teams while facilitating continuous learning, performance tracking, and data-driven improvements (Lo, 2024; Microsoft, 2024). For example, companies in the manufacturing and healthcare sectors have successfully used XR-based simulations to train employees on complex procedures, significantly reducing onboarding time and error rates in hybrid settings. Boeing has integrated virtual reality (VR) simulations into employee training programs to improve technical skill development and reduce operational errors. Through immersive phygital learning environments, employees can practice aircraft assembly and maintenance procedures virtually before performing them physically. This approach has improved learning retention, reduced onboarding time, and enhanced workforce adaptability across geographically dispersed teams.

Another key enabler is leadership support and the development of a strong learning culture. Organizational leaders play a pivotal role in promoting cross-training initiatives by aligning them with strategic goals, allocating adequate resources, frameworking desired behaviors, and visibly championing participation. A culture that values continuous learning, knowledge sharing, experimentation, and psychological safety fosters greater acceptance of phygital approaches. Leadership commitment is instrumental in reducing resistance to change and motivating employees to invest effort in skill development (Kniffin et al., 2021; Li, 2022). Leaders who regularly participate in training sessions and recognize learning achievements create role frameworks that inspire broader adoption across the organization.

Employee readiness and digital literacy are equally critical. Employees must possess baseline technical skills and the confidence to navigate digital tools and platforms effectively. In hybrid environments, where much learning occurs through virtual channels, digital literacy becomes a foundational prerequisite for meaningful participation. Organizations should invest in foundational digital literacy programs, ongoing support, and user-friendly interfaces to bridge skill gaps and build confidence (Henke et al., 2022; Hasan, 2024). Without adequate readiness, even the most advanced phygital systems risk underutilization or inequitable outcomes across different employee groups.

In addition, a strong organizational learning orientation significantly influences the success of cross-training initiatives. Organizations that view learning as a core strategic function are more likely to adopt innovative methods, continuously update curricula, and integrate learning into daily operations. Such an orientation encourages knowledge creation, sharing, and application across teams, reinforcing the long-term effectiveness of phygital systems. It transforms training from isolated events into an embedded, dynamic process (Moi, 2026). Companies with mature learning cultures often report higher engagement, faster skill adoption, and better retention of cross-trained talent.

Finally, digital collaboration tools are central to operationalizing phygital cross-training in hybrid settings. Platforms such as Microsoft Teams and Google Workspace facilitate real-time communication, coordination, and knowledge sharing among employees across locations and functions. These tools support both synchronous (live sessions, virtual mentoring) and asynchronous (recorded modules, shared repositories) learning, enabling collaborative problem-solving and peer-to-peer knowledge exchange. When thoughtfully integrated into training frameworks, they create highly interactive and flexible environments that closely mirror actual hybrid work demands (Lo, 2024; Microsoft, 2024).

In summary, the effectiveness of phygital cross-training is contingent upon the strategic alignment of technological capabilities, leadership commitment, employee readiness, organizational learning orientation, and robust collaboration tools. These enablers collectively create a supportive ecosystem that enhances the design, delivery, and sustained impact of cross-training initiatives. Organizations that invest deliberately in these areas are better positioned to achieve superior workforce agility and resilience in competitive, tight labor markets (Li, 2022; Moi, 2026).

7. CHALLENGES AND BARRIERS

Despite its considerable potential to enhance workforce flexibility and organizational agility, the implementation of phygital cross-training is not without significant challenges. Organizations must proactively identify and address these barriers to fully realize the benefits of integrated physical-digital training approaches.

One of the most prominent issues is digital fatigue and cognitive overload. Prolonged exposure to virtual learning environments, multiple digital platforms, virtual meetings, and continuous learning modules can lead to mental exhaustion, decreased motivation, and reduced engagement. In hybrid work settings, employees frequently switch between tools and contexts, which increases cognitive load and impairs information processing and retention (Kniffin et al., 2021; Henke et al., 2022). For instance, knowledge workers in IT and finance sectors often report burnout when mandatory online training modules are added to already demanding remote schedules. This challenge is particularly acute for older employees or those with limited digital experience.

Another critical barrier is resistance to cross-functional roles. Many employees, especially those with long tenures in specialized positions, perceive cross-training as an additional burden, a threat to their expertise, or a source of role ambiguity. Resistance often stems from fear of increased workload, lack of self-efficacy in new domains, or concerns about job security. Without careful change management, such resistance can undermine participation and limit the overall impact of phygital initiatives (Li, 2022). Successful organizations address this through transparent communication, involvement of employees in program design, and clear career progression pathways linked to cross-training participation.

Skill imbalance and training gaps further complicate implementation. Employees within the same organization frequently possess widely varying levels of technical expertise, digital literacy, and prior experience. This heterogeneity makes it difficult to design one-size-fits-all programs. Without thorough needs assessment and personalized pathways, cross-training efforts may result in uneven skill development, frustration among advanced learners, or inadequate support for those needing foundational training (Hasan, 2024; Lo, 2024). Advanced learning analytics and adaptive platforms can help mitigate this by tailoring content difficulty and pace.

In emerging economies, including regions such as Kerala, India, infrastructure limitations present a particularly pressing challenge. Unreliable internet connectivity, limited access to high-speed broadband, power outages, and inadequate access to advanced devices or XR equipment can severely hinder the delivery of seamless phygital experiences. These constraints create significant disparities in training opportunities between urban and rural employees or between large corporations and SMEs, potentially widening existing skill gaps (Microsoft, 2024; Moi, 2026). Governments and organizations must collaborate on infrastructure development and subsidized device programs to ensure inclusive access.

Finally, managing consistency and quality across hybrid environments remains a complex operational challenge. Ensuring that all employees — whether working from office, home, or field locations — receive equivalent learning experiences, support, and assessment is difficult. Variations in facilitator quality, technology reliability, and participant engagement can lead to inconsistent learning outcomes and perceived unfairness (Lo, 2024). Organizations need robust governance mechanisms, standardized quality protocols, regular audits, and hybrid facilitation training to maintain high standards.

Mitigation strategies require a systematic and multi-level approach. Organizations can reduce digital fatigue by introducing wellness initiatives, limiting excessive synchronous sessions, and incorporating microlearning modules that minimize cognitive overload. Resistance to cross-functional roles can be addressed through structured change management frameworks such as Kotter's Eight-Step Model, transparent communication, and incentive systems linked to career advancement. Skill imbalance challenges may be mitigated through competency mapping, personalized learning pathways, and adaptive AI-driven learning systems. Infrastructure limitations can be reduced through government-industry collaboration, subsidized digital access programs, and cloud-based mobile learning platforms. Additionally, centralized governance structures, standardized evaluation systems, and continuous feedback loops are essential to ensure quality consistency across hybrid learning environments.

In summary, while phygital cross-training offers a promising pathway for workforce development, its success hinges on the organization's ability to anticipate and address these multifaceted challenges. By combining technological solutions, strong leadership, inclusive design, and supportive policies, organizations can transform potential barriers into opportunities for more equitable and effective skill development, ultimately realizing the full benefits of a hybrid learning ecosystem (Li, 2022; Moi, 2026).

8. MANAGERIAL IMPLICATIONS

The transition toward hybrid work environments and tight labor markets requires managers to adopt innovative and scalable approaches to workforce development.

Phygital cross-training offers a powerful strategic pathway for organizations to enhance employee capabilities while maintaining operational flexibility and controlling costs.

One of the primary managerial priorities is designing scalable phygital training programs that can be effectively deployed across diverse teams and locations. Managers must ensure that training content is modular, technology-enabled, and adaptable to different learning styles, proficiency levels, and job roles. By combining digital platforms with experiential learning methods (such as virtual simulations followed by in-person application), organizations can deliver consistent, high-quality training experiences while optimizing resources. For example, global technology firms have successfully implemented modular phygital programs that allow employees in different time zones to complete self-paced modules and then join live collaborative sessions, resulting in improved skill retention and reduced training costs (Lo, 2024; Microsoft, 2024). IBM has implemented a large-scale phygital learning ecosystem that combines AI-driven digital learning platforms with collaborative workshops and virtual simulations. Employees participate in self-paced online learning modules followed by live virtual problem-solving sessions and in-person innovation labs. This integrated approach has strengthened workforce flexibility, accelerated reskilling initiatives, and supported IBM's transition toward hybrid work models.

Another critical implication is the integration of cross-training into the overall HR strategy. Rather than treating cross-training as an isolated Learning and Development (L&D) initiative, forward-thinking managers embed it within broader talent management practices, including recruitment, performance appraisal, succession planning, and career development pathways. This alignment ensures that cross-training directly supports business objectives and creates a more versatile workforce capable of filling multiple roles during peak demand or unexpected absences. Such integration also strengthens internal talent pipelines and reduces reliance on expensive external hiring in tight labor markets (Li, 2022).

Phygital cross-training plays a vital role in enhancing workforce flexibility and resilience. In volatile and uncertain environments, organizations need the ability to rapidly reallocate human resources. Employees equipped with diverse skill sets through phygital cross-training can transition smoothly between roles and functions, ensuring business continuity. Managers should therefore prioritize the development of multi-skilled teams and position adaptability as a core organizational competency. This not only improves operational efficiency but also boosts employee confidence, job satisfaction, and retention (Moi, 2026; Kniffin et al., 2021). Companies in the retail and logistics sectors, for instance, have reported significant improvements in agility during seasonal peaks after implementing structured phygital cross-training programs.

Furthermore, it is essential to align training initiatives with organizational goals and strategic priorities. Training programs should be designed to directly address key business needs—such as improving productivity, enhancing customer experience, accelerating digital transformation, or supporting sustainability goals. Managers must establish clear KPIs, regular feedback mechanisms, and robust evaluation frameworks (e.g., Kirkpatrick's four levels or ROI analysis) to measure the effectiveness of phygital cross-training and demonstrate its contribution to organizational performance. This results-oriented approach helps justify investment and enables continuous program improvement (Hasan, 2024).

Finally, managers must focus on building a culture of continuous learning that supports long-term workforce development. A strong learning culture encourages employees to view skill enhancement as an ongoing responsibility rather than a periodic requirement. Leadership plays a pivotal role by frameworking learning behaviors, recognizing achievements, providing dedicated learning time, and creating psychological safety for experimentation. Digital collaboration tools such as Microsoft Teams and Google Workspace further reinforce this culture by enabling knowledge sharing, peer mentoring, and easy access to learning resources across hybrid teams (Microsoft, 2024; Lo, 2024).

In conclusion, the managerial implications of phygital cross-training extend far beyond program design. They encompass strategic HR integration, cultural transformation, measurement systems, and leadership commitment. By adopting a holistic approach, managers can leverage phygital cross-training to build agile, resilient, and future-ready organizations that thrive in hybrid work environments and competitive labor markets (Li, 2022; Moi, 2026).

9. POLICY AND INSTITUTIONAL IMPLICATIONS

The effectiveness and scalability of phygital cross-training extend far beyond individual organizations and depend significantly on supportive policy frameworks and institutional ecosystems. Coordinated efforts among governments, educational institutions, and industry are essential to create an enabling environment for widespread adoption.

A critical role is played by educational institutions in supporting hybrid skill development. Universities, technical institutes, vocational training centers, and professional bodies must redesign curricula to align with the demands of hybrid and phygital work environments. This includes integrating digital competencies, data literacy, interdisciplinary learning, experiential methods, and phygital pedagogies (such as blended VR simulations and industry-linked projects) into academic programs. By embedding these elements, institutions can better prepare graduates for roles that demand both technical expertise and adaptability in fluid work settings (Batista-Toledo & Gavilan, 2025; Li, 2022). In India, initiatives like the National

Education Policy 2020 provide a strong foundation for such reforms, encouraging flexible curricula and greater industry-academia collaboration. Partnerships with corporations can further enhance relevance through co-designed certifications, internships, live projects, and apprenticeship frameworks.

Equally important are government initiatives aimed at enhancing digital workforce readiness. Policymakers have a vital role in bridging the digital divide and ensuring equitable access to phygital learning opportunities, particularly in emerging economies and rural areas such as parts of Kerala. Strategic investments in digital infrastructure, high-speed broadband, affordable devices, and public Wi-Fi networks are foundational for enabling widespread adoption. Government-led skill development programs (e.g., Skill India, Kerala's FutureSkills initiatives) and national digital strategies can promote large-scale reskilling and upskilling, targeting both youth and mid-career professionals. Policy frameworks that incentivize lifelong learning — through tax benefits, subsidies, or recognition of prior learning — further support continuous workforce development (World Economic Forum, 2025; OECD, 2021). Such interventions are crucial for reducing regional and socio-economic disparities in skill access.

The development of effective public-private partnerships (PPPs) for skill ecosystems represents another key dimension of policy support. Collaboration between governments, educational institutions, and industry stakeholders can create integrated ecosystems that address skill gaps more efficiently and responsively. Industry partners can provide real-time insights into emerging competencies, co-develop training modules, offer mentorship, and host practical learning opportunities. Public institutions, in turn, can supply regulatory frameworks, funding, accreditation, and scale. Successful examples include sector skill councils and industry-academia consortia that have accelerated phygital training in IT, manufacturing, and healthcare sectors (Lo, 2024; Microsoft, 2024). These collaborations ensure that training programs remain relevant, credible, and directly linked to employment outcomes.

Moreover, institutional support is essential for standardizing practices and ensuring quality assurance in phygital learning environments. Accreditation bodies, professional associations, and quality assurance agencies should establish clear benchmarks for hybrid and phygital training programs, covering curriculum design, assessment methods, technology standards, and learner outcomes. Standardized certifications that are nationally and internationally recognized enhance the portability of skills in a globalized labor market. This is especially important for micro-credentials and stackable qualifications that allow workers to build competencies progressively (Batista-Toledo & Gavilan, 2025).

In conclusion, policy and institutional frameworks are pivotal in shaping the success and inclusivity of phygital cross-training initiatives. By fostering multi-stakeholder collaboration, investing strategically in digital infrastructure, reforming education systems, and establishing quality standards, governments and institutions can create a robust ecosystem that supports continuous skill development and workforce adaptability. Such coordinated efforts are indispensable for building resilient economies and future-ready workforces capable of thriving in the era of hybrid and phygital work (Li, 2022; World Economic Forum, 2025; OECD, 2021).

10. FUTURE DIRECTIONS IN PHYGITAL WORKFORCE DEVELOPMENT

The future of workforce development is increasingly shaped by rapid technological advancements, evolving work structures, and shifting employee expectations, making phygital cross-training a dynamic and continuously evolving domain. Organizations that proactively embrace these trends will gain significant competitive advantage.

One of the key emerging trends is the growing use of AI-driven personalized learning systems. Artificial intelligence can analyze real-time performance data, identify individual skill gaps, recommend tailored learning pathways, and dynamically adapt content difficulty and format according to learner progress and preferences. These systems move beyond one-size-fits-all programs to deliver highly customized experiences that maximize engagement and learning efficiency (Moi, 2026; Microsoft, 2024). In practice, leading companies are already using AI-powered platforms to create adaptive cross-training journeys that adjust in real time, resulting in faster skill acquisition and higher completion rates, particularly valuable in hybrid environments where learner availability varies widely. Unilever utilizes AI-enabled learning platforms to personalize employee training journeys by analyzing skill gaps, career goals, and performance data. The platform recommends adaptive learning pathways and cross-functional skill modules, enabling employees to continuously reskill in response to changing organizational demands. This has significantly improved employee engagement and learning efficiency within hybrid work environments.

Another key trend is the increasing adoption of immersive technologies, such as augmented reality (AR), virtual reality (VR), mixed reality (MR), and metaverse-based learning platforms. These tools create interactive, experience-driven environments that replicate real-world situations, enabling employees to practice complex technical and interpersonal skills in safe and repeatable settings. Immersive learning has been shown to significantly improve engagement, knowledge retention, and transfer of skills to actual job performance, especially in high-stakes domains such as healthcare, manufacturing, aviation, and engineering (Lo, 2024; Batista-Toledo & Gavilan, 2025). As hardware becomes more affordable and accessible, phygital learning environments are expected to evolve into fully blended physical-virtual ecosystems that feel natural to learners.

The continued evolution of hybrid and distributed work frameworks will further reshape training design and delivery. As organizations adopt more flexible, decentralized, and asynchronous work arrangements, the demand for adaptable, on-demand, and location-independent training solutions will intensify. Phygital cross-training is uniquely positioned to support distributed teams by enabling seamless transitions between physical and digital learning spaces. Future frameworks are likely to prioritize learner autonomy, peer collaboration across time zones, and integration of learning into daily workflows rather than separate training events (Kniffin et al., 2021; Li, 2022). This shift will require new metrics focused on learning in the flow of work and long-term capability development.

In addition, global trends in cross-training and skill mobility are transforming the broader workforce landscape. Increasing globalization, digital connectivity, and remote collaboration have expanded opportunities for cross-border talent movement and virtual teamwork. Employees will need highly transferable, versatile skill sets that transcend specific roles, organizations, or even national boundaries. Cross-training initiatives that emphasize multi-skilling, cultural intelligence, and digital fluency will continue to grow in importance. Organizations must also align their internal training strategies with global standards, micro-credentialing systems, and international quality benchmarks to stay competitive in the global talent market (World Economic Forum, 2025).

Overall, the future of phygital workforce development depends on the effective integration of advanced technologies (such as AI and immersive tools), flexible hybrid work frameworks, and globally aligned skill frameworks. By embracing these directions, organizations can build truly agile, resilient, and future-ready workforces capable of thriving amid continuous disruption. Continuous innovation in training design, delivery, and evaluation — supported by strong leadership and policy backing — will be essential to ensure that phygital cross-training remains relevant, inclusive, and impactful in addressing the evolving challenges of the digital age (Moi, 2026; Lo, 2024; World Economic Forum, 2025).

11. CONCLUSION

This chapter has examined the growing importance of phygital cross-training as a strategic response to the dual pressures of tight labor markets and the widespread adoption of hybrid work frameworks. By seamlessly integrating physical and digital learning modalities, phygital approaches offer a flexible, scalable, and immersive framework for workforce development that addresses many limitations of traditional and purely digital training methods. The discussion demonstrated how evolving training frameworks—supported by technological advancements, organizational learning practices, and strategic alignment—enable employees to acquire diverse, cross-functional skill sets and adapt rapidly to dynamic job roles. The proposed Phygital Cross-Training Framework further illustrated how integrated learning environments and technology serve as foundational inputs that drive skill development and employee engagement, ultimately culminating in enhanced organizational agility and resilience (Lo, 2024; Moi, 2026).

From a theoretical perspective, the chapter contributes to the literature by synthesizing multiple established frameworks—Experiential Learning Theory, Human Capital Theory, digital transformation perspectives, and the Resource-Based View—into a cohesive understanding of phygital cross-training. This multi-theoretical lens positions phygital cross-training not only as an effective learning mechanism but also as a strategic capability that builds valuable, rare, and hard-to-imitate human capital in hybrid contexts. It extends existing research by conceptualizing cross-training within technology-mediated, distributed work environments, thereby addressing pressing contemporary workforce challenges (Li, 2022; Kniffin et al., 2021).

Practically, the chapter offers actionable insights for managers, HR professionals, and policymakers. It outlines critical enablers (digital infrastructure, leadership support, learning culture, and employee readiness), major barriers (digital fatigue, resistance, skill imbalances, and infrastructure gaps), and implementation strategies. The emphasis on modular program design, strategic HR integration, continuous feedback, and inclusive policy support provides a clear roadmap for organizations seeking to build flexible, engaged, and future-ready workforces (Microsoft, 2024; Hasan, 2024; Lo, 2024).

In conclusion, the future of organizational success in a hybrid and digitally transformed world will increasingly depend on the ability to develop agile, multi-skilled, and continuously learning workforces. Phygital cross-training emerges as one of the most promising tools in this transformation. It effectively bridges skill gaps, enhances employee engagement and adaptability, and strengthens organizational resilience in the face of uncertainty. Organizations that invest thoughtfully in integrated phygital systems—supported by strong leadership, enabling policies, and collaborative ecosystems—will be better positioned to achieve sustainable competitive advantage and long-term growth.

While this chapter establishes a strong foundation, several directions remain open for future research. Empirical studies that explore the long-term effects of phygital cross-training on employee performance, retention, and innovation across various industries and cultural settings would provide valuable insights. Additionally, research on the effectiveness of specific immersive technologies, AI personalization algorithms, and inclusive design principles for diverse workforces (including in emerging economies) can further refine best practices. As hybrid work continues to evolve, ongoing scholarly and practical attention to phygital approaches will be essential for building truly future-ready organizations.

The chapter highlights a key idea: in an era defined by hybrid work and rapid technological change, ongoing learning and the ability to adapt are essential for both individual and organizational success. Phygital cross-training offers a powerful pathway toward that future.

REFERENCES

Absorb, L. M. S. (2026). The ultimate guide to hybrid learning vs. blended learning. https://www.absorblms.com/blog/what-is-the-difference-between-hybrid-and-blended-learning

Barney, J. (1991). Firm resources and sustained competitive advantage. *Journal of Management, 17*(1), 99–120. DOI: 10.1177/014920639101700108

Batista-Toledo, S., & Gavilan, D. (2025). A blended learning future: COVID-19 lessons for "phygital" higher education. *International Review of Research in Open and Distance Learning, 26*(1), 45–62. DOI: 10.19173/irrodl.v26i2.8259

Becker, G. S. (1964). *Human capital: A theoretical and empirical analysis, with special reference to education*. University of Chicago Press.

Carnevale, J. B., & Hatak, I. (2020). Employee adjustment and well-being in the era of COVID-19: Implications for human resource management. *Journal of Business Research, 116*, 183–187. DOI: 10.1016/j.jbusres.2020.05.037 PMID: 32501303

Easygenerator. (2025). Cross-training employees: 5 benefits you can't ignore. https://www.easygenerator.com/en/blog/employee-generated-learning/cross-training-employees/

Elm Learning. (2023). The hybrid learning framework: Adopt it for corporate training? https://elmlearning.com/blog/hybrid-learning-framework-for-corporate-training/

Hasan, M. (2024). Upskilling and reskilling in a rapidly changing job market. European Journal of Business and Management Research. https://eu-opensci.org/index.php/ejbmr/article/view/52502

Henke, J. B., ... (2022). Skills and abilities to thrive in remote work: What have we learned? PMC. https://pmc.ncbi.nlm.nih.gov/articles/PMC9807077/

Karhapää, M. (2024). Hybrid work and workforce adaptability: Developing competencies for cross-functional collaboration in digital environments. *Journal of Organizational Learning and Development, 18*(2), 145–162. DOI: 10.1080/jorld.2024.01824

Kniffin, K. M., Narayanan, J., Anseel, F., Antonakis, J., Ashford, S. P., Bakker, A. B., Bamberger, P., Bapuji, H., Bhave, D. P., Choi, V. K., Creary, S. J., Demerouti, E., Flynn, F. J., Gelfand, M. J., Greer, L. L., Johns, G., Kesebir, S., Klein, P. G., Lee, S. Y., & van Vugt, M. (2021). COVID-19 and the workplace: Implications, issues, and insights for future research and action. *The American Psychologist, 76*(1), 63–77. DOI: 10.1037/amp0000716 PMID: 32772537

Kolb, A. Y., & Kolb, D. A. (2005). Learning styles and learning spaces: Enhancing experiential learning in higher education. *Academy of Management Learning & Education, 4*(2), 193–212. DOI: 10.5465/amle.2005.17268566

Kolb, D. A. (1984). *Experiential learning: Experience as the source of learning and development*. Prentice Hall.

Li, L. (2022). Reskilling and upskilling the future-ready workforce. Frontiers in Psychology. https://pmc.ncbi.nlm.nih.gov/articles/PMC9278314/

Lo, T. T. S. (2024). Phygital workspace: A systematic review in developing a conceptual framework for future research. *Frontiers in Built Environment, 10*, 1370423. DOI: 10.3389/fbuil.2024.1370423

Microsoft. (2024). Working in a phygital world: Why businesses need to rethink their workspace experiences now. Microsoft Inside Track. https://www.microsoft.com/insidetrack/blog/working-in-a-phygital-world-why-businesses-need-to-rethink-their-workspace-experiences-now/

Moi, L. (2026). Phygital dynamic capabilities: Microfoundations and their implications for organizations. *Technological Forecasting and Social Change*. Advance online publication. DOI: 10.1016/j.techfore.2025.124423

Noe, R. A., Clarke, A. D. M., & Klein, H. J. (2014). Learning in the twenty-first-century workplace. *Annual Review of Organizational Psychology and Organizational Behavior, 1*(1), 245–275. DOI: 10.1146/annurev-orgpsych-031413-091321

Organisation for Economic Co-operation and Development. (OECD). (2021). OECD skills outlook 2021: Learning for life. OECD Publishing. DOI: 10.1787/0ae365b4-en

Panopto. (2021). Upskilling and reskilling your hybrid workforce. https://www.panopto.com/blog/learning-and-development-reskilling-upskilling-cross-skilling-hybrid-workforce/

Salas, E., Tannenbaum, S. I., Kraiger, K., & Smith-Jentsch, K. A. (2012). The science of training and development in organizations: What matters in practice. *Psychological Science in the Public Interest : A Journal of the American Psychological Society, 13*(2), 74–101. DOI: 10.1177/1529100612436661 PMID: 26173283

Talent, L. M. S. (2024). The state of upskilling & reskilling: 2024 research. https://www.talentlms.com/research/employee-upskilling-and-reskilling-report

Teece, D. J., Peteraf, M., & Leih, S. (2016). Dynamic capabilities and organizational agility: Risk, uncertainty, and strategy in the innovation economy. *California Management Review, 58*(4), 13–35. DOI: 10.1525/cmr.2016.58.4.13

Training Industry. (2022). Training a hybrid workforce? Consider these 3 best practices. https://trainingindustry.com/articles/workforce-development/training-a-hybrid-workforce-consider-these-3-best-practices/

Vial, G. (2019). Understanding digital transformation: A review and a research agenda. *The Journal of Strategic Information Systems*, *28*(2), 118–144. DOI: 10.1016/j.jsis.2019.01.003

Waizenegger, L., McKenna, B., Cai, W., & Bendz, T. (2020). An affordance perspective of team collaboration and enforced working from home during COVID-19. *European Journal of Information Systems*, *29*(4), 429–442. DOI: 10.1080/0960085X.2020.1800417

World Economic Forum. (2025). The future of jobs report 2025. https://www.weforum.org/publications/the-future-of-jobs-report-2025/

Chapter 12
Strategic Cross-Training in Hospitality and Tourism:
A Sustainable-Innovative HRM Framework for Tight Labour Markets

Ioannis Valachis
http://orcid.org/0000-0002-2348-906X
Harokopio University of Athens, Greece

ABSTRACT

Persistent talent shortages, high turnover, and skill gaps have become long-term features of hospitality and tourism employment, compounded by growing sustainability and community expectations. Cross-training has gained attention as a response, yet it remains mainly a scheduling tool rather than a strategic HRM investment. This chapter introduces the Sustainable-Innovative HRM Framework, placing cross-training at the centre of relationships linking sustainability-oriented HRM and community involvement with innovation capability and service quality. Drawing on Social Exchange Theory, it argues that cross-training supported by recognition, career development, and community engagement can strengthen workforce flexibility and improve service performance. Labour market tightness moderates these relationships. Three contributions are made: integrating sustainability, innovation, and community involvement in a single framework; extending SET to destination-level governance; and reconceptualising cross-training as relational and transformational. Design principles for managers are discussed.

DOI: 10.4018/979-8-3373-5327-2.ch012

ght © 2027, IGI Global Scientific Publishing. Copying or distributing in print or electronic forms without written permission of IGI Global Scientific Publishing is prohibited. Use of this chapter to generative artificial intelligence (AI) technologies is expressly prohibited. The publisher reserves all rights to license its use for generative AI training and machine learning model development.

1. INTRODUCTION

Labour shortages, high turnover, and widening skill gaps are no longer short-term disruptions in hospitality and tourism. They have become defining features of how the sector operates (Baum et al., 2020), and there is little to suggest they will recede. Sustainability and community responsibility have simultaneously moved from peripheral concerns to central ones, shaping how destinations compete and how guest experiences are evaluated (Yoo, 2024).

Together, these pressures expose a gap in the literature. Existing research still pays limited attention to workforce systems shaped by structural instability and ongoing disruption. Managers are expected to build workforces that are more flexible, more ethically grounded, and more connected to local communities, yet they are doing so without the staffing stability that long-term planning once assumed. Cross-training has become a common response to labour shortages, and to some extent it works. The issue is less the practice itself than the way it is understood. In hospitality, cross-training is still framed mainly as an operational solution: useful when staffing gaps appear, practical during seasonal peaks, and valuable for keeping services running smoothly. What receives far less attention is the longer-term effect of repeated cross-role experience on how employees see their work, their capabilities, and their place within the organisation. Hospitality work increasingly requires ethical awareness, creativity, and constructive engagement with host communities (Nunkoo, 2017).

SET offers a useful starting point, though it helps to be clear about what the theory actually explains. At its core, SET focuses on reciprocity, fairness, and trust (Blau, 1964). The basic idea is simple: relationships are shaped through ongoing exchanges, not just isolated transactions. When organisations invest meaningfully in employee development, employees usually respond in kind. Loyalty tends to grow, discretionary effort increases, and service quality often improves (Cropanzano & Mitchell, 2005; Abdou et al., 2022; Al-Twal et al., 2024). The reverse is equally true. When cross-training is introduced mainly as a quick staffing solution, employees recognise that as well. The way they interpret that decision shapes what they are willing to give back, and ultimately determines whether cross-training becomes something more meaningful than day-to-day operational support.

Despite the growth of research on sustainability, innovation, and training, these areas have mostly evolved separately from one another. We still know relatively little about how they connect in practice, especially at destination level, where organisational boundaries are less clear and employment conditions are shaped collectively rather than by individual firms alone. Earlier work on HRM and service performance provided important foundations (Heskett et al., 1994), but it reflected a tourism sector that still operated with a degree of staffing stability. That reality has changed considerably, and some of the theories built around it now appear increasingly difficult to apply without adaptation.

This chapter approaches cross-training as the mechanism connecting sustainability orientation, community involvement, innovation capability, and service quality. Exposure across functional roles does more than expand skill sets. It changes how employees understand their work and how they relate to the broader system in which that work takes place. It builds the capacity to link everyday tasks with environmental commitments and with the expectations of the communities that sustain tourism activity. When labour is scarce, this capacity becomes central to maintaining system performance. The literature has not caught up with what cross-training actually does. That gap is what this chapter addresses.

1.1 Conceptual Approach and Method

The approach taken here follows Elina Jaakkola's (2020) typology of conceptual contributions, specifically the mechanism specification approach. The aim is explanation, not empirical testing. Cross-training is identified as the concrete mediating mechanism through which sustainability orientation and community involvement translate into innovation capability and service quality, although specifying that mechanism is also a necessary step before it can eventually be tested empirically.

Simply connecting existing frameworks is not enough. The processes making those connections theoretically plausible need to be specified. Mechanism-based contributions become particularly important in areas like this, where individual relationships have been documented extensively while the processes linking them remain less clearly understood.

Four interconnected strands of literature inform the framework: sustainable and green HRM, SET in hospitality, cross-training and workforce development, and community involvement in tourism governance. These streams were chosen because each addresses a distinct dimension of the tight labour market challenge, yet no prior work has brought them together within a single explanatory model. Three questions shaped which constructs to include: Is there sufficient theoretical grounding in hospitality and HRM research? Can it be meaningfully measured? Does it speak directly to the pressures faced by organisations operating in tight labour markets?

Community involvement is conceptualised as a construct because it shapes both the design of cross-training and how these investments are understood by employees and communities. That dual role is theoretically important, and it can be distinguished empirically.

2. LITERATURE REVIEW

2.1 Social Exchange Theory and Hospitality HRM

SET views relationships as ongoing exchanges shaped by reciprocity, mutual benefit, and the gradual development of trust (Blau, 1964; Cropanzano & Mitchell, 2005). In hospitality, service quality emerges through formal procedures, employee judgement, discretionary effort, and the quality of interactions with guests and local communities. Fair treatment and organisational support play an important role in shaping that willingness, strengthening commitment, creativity, and discretionary effort in service environments built around direct interaction. When cross-training is implemented in ways that reflect these principles, employees are more likely to interpret it as an investment in development rather than a short-term operational demand. How employees interpret that experience shapes the effort, commitment, and organisational support they are willing to offer in return. This reciprocal dynamic can strengthen service recovery, innovation, and customer satisfaction (Abdou et al., 2022; Greasidou & Valachis, 2022).

In practice, employee perceptions of cross-training often matter more than the training content itself. Organisations that frame cross-training as a developmental investment tend to generate stronger employee commitment and engagement. They are more willing to stay, support colleagues, and contribute beyond the minimum expected from their role. These differences become more noticeable when labour shortages intensify and maintaining service quality becomes harder (Balkin & Werner, 2023). Under persistent staffing pressure, the quality of the relationship between employees and the organisation becomes increasingly important.

The same logic does not stop at the boundaries of the firm. Residents and local stakeholders also judge tourism development partly through perceptions of fairness and reciprocity. When workforce practices are seen as fair and inclusive, they can strengthen the legitimacy of tourism activity; when they are seen as extractive, they have the opposite effect (Nunkoo & Ramkissoon, 2012; Poudel et al., 2024). Cross-training therefore matters not only as an internal HR practice, but also as a signal of how seriously tourism organisations invest in people. If it is framed as long-term development, it can support trust across the destination. If it is used mainly as a short-term staffing device, that trust is much harder to sustain.

Reciprocity is more likely to develop when cross-training is structured as a developmental investment, supported by recognition, manageable workloads, and psychological safety. Employees respond with effort, commitment, and sustained engagement. When cross-training is instead associated with heavier workloads, unclear expectations, or additional responsibilities without proportional support, engagement declines and turnover pressures intensify, particularly in labour-scarce environments. The transition from development to labour intensification becomes visible under specific conditions. These include situations where cross-trained employees cover multiple roles without scheduling adjustments or appropriate remuneration. Similar effects emerge when increased workloads are not supported by psychological safety or organisational support, or when cross-role deployment substitutes permanently for recruitment rather than complementing it. Under these conditions, employees interpret the same programme very differently. Some view it as a meaningful developmental opportunity, while others experience it as a form of exploitation. These perceptions ultimately determine whether the reciprocity described by SET actually emerges.

Two tensions sit at the heart of this framework, although the literature often treats them too lightly. The first concerns sustainability orientation. When sustainability is introduced primarily as a compliance requirement, it functions as a constraint on behaviour rather than a driver of it. Employees may comply with stated expectations, yet their underlying orientation toward their work often remains unchanged.

Community involvement creates a different kind of tension. Partnerships with local communities do not always remain collaborative. They can gradually become transactional, especially when expectations around wages, working conditions, or cultural representation come into conflict with organisational priorities. Cross-training often makes these tensions more visible because employees move across roles, interact with different stakeholder groups, and experience these contradictions more directly. What it cannot do is solve those contradictions on its own. Without recognising this difference, organisations may create development programmes that appear effective while changing very little in practice.

2.2 Sustainability as a Strategic Imperative

Sustainability has become a genuine source of competitive advantage and brand credibility in hospitality, not simply a compliance obligation (Chan & Hsu, 2016; Belias & Trihas, 2023; Tarí et al., 2025). This shift has repositioned HRM as a central vehicle for sustainability implementation. Employees act as everyday ambassadors of sustainability, translating organisational commitments into daily practices and guest interactions (Edinger-Schöns et al., 2019). That ambassadorial role does not emerge automatically; it requires deliberate investment in cross-training that embeds sustainability values, builds ethical awareness, and connects individual behaviour to organisational and destination-level goals.

Green HRM gives practical form to this connection by aligning recruitment, appraisal, and training with environmental and social objectives (Yoo, 2024; Adhika, 2024; Fotiadis et al., 2025). Research generally supports the idea that HRM practices linked to Environmental, Social, and Governance (ESG) principles can strengthen organisational culture and reinforce sustainability priorities internally (Ehnert et al., 2016; Kramar, 2014; Tarí et al., 2025). What remains less certain is whether these changes reflect genuine shifts in organisational values or simply a rebranding of existing practices. Hospitality organisations rely heavily on frontline employees, which makes their interpretation of organisational intent especially important for meaningful behavioural change.

The relationship between green HRM and employee behaviour is also conditioned by the broader organisational climate. Research on value congruence suggests that employees are more likely to act on sustainability commitments when they perceive alignment between stated organisational values and actual management practices (Ehnert et al., 2016). When that alignment is absent, sustainability training may produce surface-level compliance without the deeper internalisation of values that genuine behavioural change requires. For cross-training programmes specifically, this means that sustainability elements embedded in training design will only produce durable effects if they are reinforced by consistent signals from management, recognition systems, and everyday operational decisions. Embedding sustainability in cross-training is therefore less a curriculum design challenge than an organisational culture challenge. The most effective programmes are those in which sustainability is already a lived part of the working environment rather than a set of principles added to a training schedule as an afterthought.

Tom Baum argued as early as 1995 that sustainable HR practices in tourism cannot be separated from the wider local labour context in which organisations operate, including local skills, labour, and cultural identity, and that these elements should be reflected in practices such as local recruitment, participatory training, and inclusive career pathways. In his later work (Baum, 2006; Baum & Szivas, 2008), HRM is presented as a process embedded in social relationships, with emphasis on developing people in ways that support social equity, cultural continuity, and reciprocal relationships between tourism organisations and local communities. Baum (2018) later reinforced this argument by identifying the persistent neglect of workforce considerations in sustainable tourism policy as a critical omission with both theoretical and practical consequences.

In practical terms, sustainability-oriented HRM is reflected in specific organisational choices such as year-round contracts, recognised vocational training, local recruitment, frontline employee voice, and transparent workforce communication (Ehnert et al., 2016; Kramar, 2014). Cross-training contributes to sustainability only when it is supported by a broader and consistent set of HR practices, such as year-round employment, meaningful career opportunities, and mechanisms that allow frontline employees to have a genuine voice in organisational decisions. When introduced in isolation, cross-training is unlikely to create lasting change. In some cases, it may even deepen employee cynicism if it is interpreted as an effort to increase workloads without providing comparable support or investment in return.

2.3 Innovation, Training, and Service Quality

Innovation in hospitality tends to emerge gradually through learning, reflection, and experimentation. It can be seen in areas such as digital transformation, AI-supported guest services, and new approaches to operational problem-solving, although its development still depends heavily on employees' everyday working conditions (Li et al., 2019). Autonomy, trust, and continuous learning influence whether innovation becomes embedded in daily practice or remains occasional and uneven (Scott & Bruce, 1994; Karatepe & Olugbade, 2016; Begum et al., 2022). Evidence from the post-pandemic period supports this view, showing that organisations with stronger learning cultures adapted more effectively to digital change, staffing shortages, and shifting guest expectations (Baum et al., 2020).

Cross-training plays a more complicated role here than the literature sometimes suggests, and the evidence reflects that. Employees who participate in well-designed programmes often show stronger customer orientation, greater adaptability, and higher job satisfaction (Karatepe & Olugbade, 2016). The problem is that most programmes are not designed with broader development in mind. In practice, they usually focus on immediate operational needs and technical coverage. As a result, organisations often gain flexibility and short-term continuity, sometimes quite effectively, while the deeper conditions that support ongoing learning and innovation remain mostly unchanged. This does not mean cross-training itself is ineffective. More often, it reflects the limited way organisations choose to use it.

The distinction between single-loop and double-loop learning (Argyris & Schön, 1978) is relevant here. Single-loop learning corrects errors within existing operating assumptions: employees learn to perform additional tasks, cover more roles, and respond more efficiently to operational demands. Double-loop learning goes further, prompting employees to question the assumptions underlying those demands and to consider whether the goals, values, or processes shaping their work should themselves be revised. Most cross-training programmes operate within the single-loop mode, which is why their effects on innovation remain limited. Developing double-loop capacity requires deliberate design choices: structured reflection, space for questioning, and an organisational culture that treats challenge as a contribution rather than a disruption. These conditions are rarely present in programmes introduced primarily as responses to staffing shortfalls.

Training that includes reflection and self-regulation produces a different kind of development. Employees do not simply acquire additional skills; over time, they begin to think differently about their work, their decisions, and their role within the organisation. Valachis and Tachmatzidis (2023) later demonstrated the relevance of this distinction in tourism and hospitality settings specifically. Even so, this approach remains relatively underused in practice. Cross-training is therefore approached here as part of the learning infrastructure through which innovation capability develops, rather than merely as a scheduling mechanism. The distinction becomes especially important in environments characterised by persistent staffing pressure. Organisations with stronger cross-functional learning cultures are generally better able to adapt because shared knowledge, coordination, and collective problem-solving capacity are more deeply embedded across the organisation (Collings & Mellahi, 2009; Becker & Huselid, 1998).

2.4 Cross-Training in Tight Labour Markets: Definition, Scope, and Distinctiveness

Cross-training refers to the deliberate preparation of employees to perform competently across multiple roles, functions, or operational domains beyond their primary job assignment (Sims et al., 2005; Cannon-Bowers et al., 1995). It is a targeted workforce development strategy that improves operational flexibility, reduces vulnerability to talent shortages, and strengthens an organisation's capacity for adaptive service delivery. In tight labour markets, marked by limited talent pools, high turnover, and persistent skill gaps, cross-training has become a cost-effective way to maintain service continuity and reduce disruption caused by unfilled roles (Baum et al., 2020). Its value, however, is not limited to contingency planning. Cross-trained employees often demonstrate higher engagement, stronger organisational commitment, and greater career development satisfaction, positioning cross-training as a retention mechanism as much as a flexibility tool (Marinakou & Giousmpasoglou, 2019).

Cross-training overlaps with related approaches, but the distinctions become important in practice. Multiskilling usually refers to developing deeper technical competence within the same functional area, while job rotation exposes employees to different roles, often for managerial development or broader organisational understanding. Cross-training goes further. It involves employees becoming operationally capable in roles that differ substantially from their primary position, such as a food and beverage employee being able to work effectively in housekeeping rather than simply observe it. The central issue is deployment capability. Under staffing pressure, organisations often blur these concepts together, but that is exactly when the practical differences between them become most important. Cognitively, the distinction is equally significant. Job rotation develops general role awareness and broadens employees' understanding of organisational operations. Cross-training activates a different cognitive process, which can be understood as schema-switching (Aldrich

& Herker, 1977): the capacity to shift problem-framing and decision-making logic across functional contexts under operational pressure. Rather than simply observing how other roles operate, employees must actively internalise the priorities, standards, and expectations of each function and apply them under real operational conditions. What distinguishes cross-training from job rotation, therefore, is not merely breadth of exposure but the depth of cognitive adaptation it demands.

Beyond operational continuity, cross-training generates what might be called a versatility dividend. Employees who understand multiple roles develop empathy for colleagues across functions, communicate more effectively across departmental boundaries, and contribute to the collaborative problem-solving on which innovation in service settings depends. The concept draws on boundary spanning theory (Aldrich & Herker, 1977), which argues that employees who work across organisational boundaries develop broader relational and cognitive resources than those working within a single role. In hospitality, where service delivery spans multiple departments (front office, food and beverage, housekeeping, and concierge), employees who have worked across these functions are better placed to anticipate coordination breakdowns, step in when colleagues are absent, and identify improvement opportunities that remain invisible to those working within narrower roles. This versatility develops through repeated cross-role experience, not through additional training hours alone.

The Sustainable-Innovative HRM Framework approaches cross-training as a process with two distinct dimensions: relational and transformational. One centres on shared learning, reciprocity, and community engagement across functional boundaries. The other concerns the way cross-role exposure gradually shapes employees' values, ethical awareness, and orientation toward innovation beyond technical skill development alone. Cross-training therefore affects more than what employees are able to do. It also shapes how they understand their work and their organisation. This broader conceptualisation distinguishes the framework from earlier approaches focused mainly on operational efficiency.

Operationalising the framework presents genuine methodological challenges. Table 3 summarises the validated instruments and indicative proxies associated with each construct. These measures should be treated as indicative starting points rather than definitive solutions. Managers should also recognise that intensive monitoring of reciprocity-related indicators risks undermining the trust relationships on which the framework depends.

2.5 Community Involvement and Social Capital

The success of hospitality and tourism is inseparable from the communities in which it is embedded. Those communities do more than supply labour: they provide authenticity, cultural identity, and a sense of place that shapes meaningful travel experiences (Nunkoo, 2017). The community dimension of HRM becomes strategically relevant when talent pools are restricted. Organisations that develop genuine partnerships with local communities gain access to a broader and more stable talent pool, benefit from community social capital during periods of disruption, and build the kind of destination-level trust that sustains long-term service quality. Community-based human resource development (CBHRD) treats local residents as active partners who help shape, deliver, and benefit from tourism activity (Tosun, 2000; Ap, 1992). When communities are meaningfully involved, service quality tends to improve because local knowledge, values, and traditions become part of the visitor experience. Cross-training programmes that incorporate community engagement, for example by drawing on local cultural knowledge or involving community stakeholders in service design, extend this dynamic beyond the organisation and contribute to the development of social capital at the destination-level.

Public-private-community partnerships (PPCPs) create opportunities for shared learning, knowledge exchange, and trust-building between organisations and local communities (Bramwell & Lane, 2011). Their role becomes even more important during periods of crisis, when collaboration between stakeholders can help destinations recover more effectively while maintaining service quality and social cohesion (Ishaq et al., 2025). According to Valachis and Trihas (2025), tourism awareness develops progressively, starting with mindset, influencing behaviour, and gradually translating into consistent action. When shared by both residents and tourism professionals, this awareness can help foster a broader culture of hospitality that becomes embedded in the destination itself rather than remaining confined to individual businesses.

The visibility of HRM practices is just as important as their content. When communities observe that tourism organisations invest in fair employment, inclusive training, and locally grounded workforce development, they are more likely to interpret these actions as a commitment to social equity and long-term value creation (Nunkoo & Ramkissoon, 2012; Bramwell & Lane, 2011). When cross-training and similar initiatives are actively communicated to community actors, they are more likely to contribute to the trust, social capital, and collective legitimacy that supports sustainable tourism development over time.

3. RESEARCH GAPS AND THEORETICAL CONTRIBUTION

The hospitality HRM literature has expanded considerably over the past two decades, but expansion alone has not produced conceptual coherence. The issue is not the absence of valuable research. Rather, the most relevant strands of the literature have evolved largely in isolation from one another, with each explaining part of the problem while leaving the relationships between them insufficiently explored.

Green HRM research, for example, has established relatively strong links between sustainability-oriented practices, environmental performance, and employee outcomes (Yoo, 2024; Al-Romeedy & Alharethi, 2025). What remains less developed is an explanation of how these practices connect with innovation processes or with the labour market realities that influence whether sustainability commitments become part of everyday organisational behaviour. Much of the field still treats the organisation as the primary unit of analysis. That perspective is useful for some purposes, but in hospitality it also obscures the wider conditions shaping employment. Workforce realities are often shared across destinations rather than contained within individual firms, and careers regularly extend across multiple organisations.

Service quality research reveals a similar limitation. Training is consistently associated with stronger service performance (Greasidou & Valachis, 2022), yet these relationships are usually examined through measurable inputs and outputs. Far less attention is given to the way service quality develops gradually through trust, relationships, and the accumulation of shared knowledge across departments and local communities. Research on dynamic capabilities, which frames organisational competitiveness as the ability to integrate, build, and reconfigure internal and external competences in response to changing environments (Teece et al., 1997), moves closer to explaining organisational adaptation. However, it typically treats training as a resource to be strategically deployed rather than as a socially embedded process unfolding through interaction across organisational and community boundaries. Extending dynamic capabilities to the destination level helps address this limitation. Adaptive capacity is not generated within individual firms alone. Instead, it develops through shared learning, knowledge circulation, and cumulative skill development across destination-wide stakeholder systems (Eisenhardt & Martin, 2000). Under persistent labour scarcity, the more important questions concern why some employees remain engaged while others disengage, and why some organisations sustain service quality under pressure more effectively than others.

Underlying these separate gaps is a broader assumption that has become increasingly difficult to sustain: the idea that workforce development is something organisations simply do to employees. In tourism, that view is too narrow. Careers are shaped by destination-level realities, while employee expectations form across organisations rather than within a single employer. Norms around mobility, remuneration, and skill development emerge through institutional arrangements that no individual organisation fully controls (Hall, 2011; Riley et al., 2002). Despite decades of Strategic Human Resource Management (SHRM) research, high turnover, seasonal precarity, and fragmented skill development remain persistent features of the sector. At least part of the problem lies in applying firm-level explanations to conditions that are fundamentally structural.

Cross-training sits directly within this tension, which is precisely why it offers a useful point of entry. Although widely used, it has received relatively limited conceptual attention and is still understood mainly as a response to immediate staffing shortages. Yet repeated movement across roles changes more than operational flexibility. It shapes how employees understand their work, how they relate to colleagues across departments, and how they position themselves within the wider operation. These effects become visible only when analysis moves beyond the individual firm. Over time, and across organisations, they begin to influence the learning culture, mobility patterns, and shared expectations that shape how destination workforces function.

The framework developed here takes that observation as its starting point. It does not introduce entirely new constructs so much as reposition existing ones within a different explanatory logic. Cross-training is reconceptualised as a relational mechanism embedded within social exchange processes, linking sustainability orientation and community involvement with innovation capability and service quality in a single framework. Workforce development is therefore understood as a process emerging through interaction among organisations, employees, and communities rather than as a firm-level intervention directed toward individuals. Looking at the issue this way helps explain why approaches focused mainly on skill coverage or scheduling efficiency rarely address the deeper structural causes of workforce instability. Tables 1 and 2 summarise the principal theoretical and practical contributions of the framework.

Table 1. Summary of Research Gaps and Framework Responses

Gap	What existing literature cannot explain	Framework response
1. Integration gap	No prior HRM framework combines sustainability orientation, community involvement, innovation capability, and cross-training under tight labour market conditions.	Cross-training is proposed as the mediating mechanism connecting all four constructs, with SET providing the relational logic.
2. Scope of SET	Existing SET applications in hospitality are confined to dyadic, firm-level exchanges and do not account for how reciprocity and trust scale across destination-level stakeholder systems.	SET is extended to destination-level governance, tracing how community trust and social capital develop through cross-training investment.
3. Innovation antecedents	Hospitality innovation research concentrates on technology adoption and overlooks the learning and relational processes through which innovation capability develops among frontline staff.	Cross-training's transformational dimension is theorised as a driver of innovation capability through cognitive variety, boundary-spanning, and reflective learning.

Table 2. Contributions of This Chapter to HRM Theory and Hospitality Research

Theoretical Contribution	Description
Integrated Sustainable-Innovative HRM Framework	Integrates sustainability orientation, community involvement, innovation capability, and service quality within a single SET-grounded HRM framework centred on cross-training under tight labour market conditions.
Extended Application of SET	Extends SET beyond firm-level exchanges to examine how reciprocity, trust, and social capital develop across destination-level stakeholder systems.
Dual-Dimensional Conceptualisation of Cross-Training	Reframes cross-training as both relational and transformational in nature, positioning it as a destination-level workforce development resource rather than simply an operational tool.

4. THE SUSTAINABLE-INNOVATIVE HRM FRAMEWORK

The Sustainable-Innovative HRM Framework positions cross-training at the centre of a set of relationships that are usually examined separately. It connects sustainability orientation and community involvement with innovation capability and service quality, while recognising that these relationships develop through ongoing interactions among organisations, employees, and local communities. Labour market tightness moderates the strength of these relationships, particularly the connection between cross-training and service quality.

The framework maps conditions and processes. It does not prescribe implementation steps, because the same steps produce different outcomes depending on the social and governance context in which they are embedded. Reciprocity cannot be assumed because it depends on how employees experience cross-training. Sustainability values and community involvement matter only when they are embedded in everyday practice. When these conditions are unevenly developed, the relationships outlined in Figure 1 are unlikely to fully materialise.

Figure 1 represents these dynamics schematically, with cross-training positioned as the central mediating mechanism and labour market tightness moderating the relationship between cross-training and service quality. Labour market conditions become more influential as staffing constraints intensify. Persistent vacancy pressure and high replacement costs increase the importance of cross-functional capability for maintaining service continuity. In less constrained labour markets, the same capability remains valuable, although its contribution is less pronounced (Baum et al., 2020). As labour becomes more difficult to secure, cross-training gains strategic importance because it supports flexibility, knowledge circulation, and shared problem-solving across functions.

Empirical assessment of the framework builds on the measurement proxies summarised in Table 3. Within the framework, service quality warrants particular attention as a social rather than a purely operational construct: it is better understood as something that develops through interaction than as a fixed performance metric. Relevant indicators include service recovery resolution rates, employee-initiated service improvements, and participation in cross-functional problem-solving. Many of these data points are already captured in standard hotel management information systems, though they are rarely analysed in relational terms.

Figure 1. The Sustainable-Innovative HRM Framework

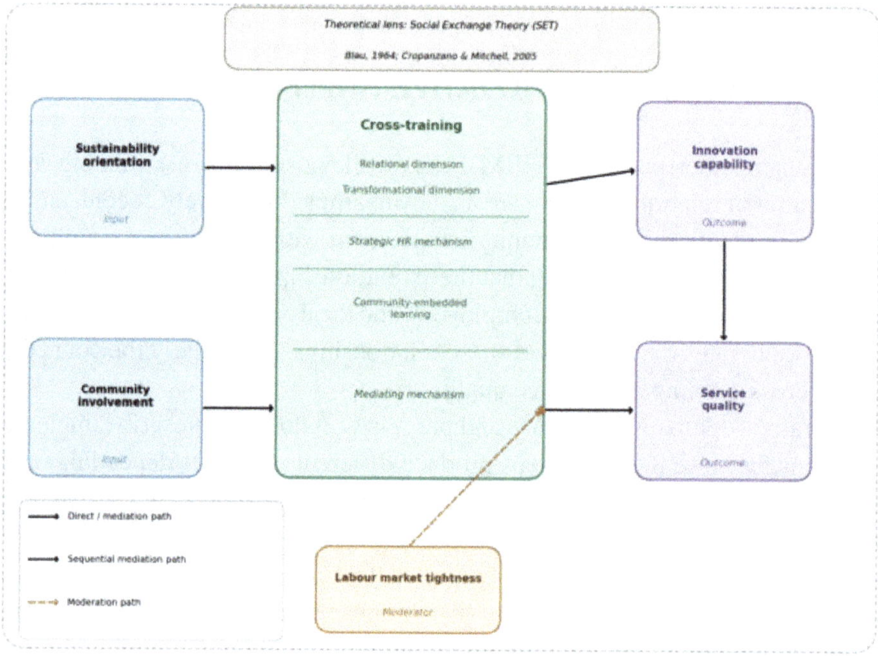

Black arrows indicate the direct and mediating relationships linking inputs, cross-training, innovation capability, and service quality. The dashed arrow shows the moderating effect of labour market tightness on the relationship between cross-training and service quality. SET provides the underlying relational logic.

Table 3. Framework Constructs: Validated Instruments and Indicative Measurement Proxies

Framework Dimension	Construct	Validated Instrument / Indicative Proxy	Source
Relational	Perceived Organisational Support	POS scale adapted for cross-training contexts, supplemented by community engagement participation and peer evaluation scores	Eisenberger et al. (1986)
Transformational	Innovation orientation	Individual Innovation Behaviour Scale	Scott & Bruce (1994)
Transformational	Value internalisation	Sustainability knowledge assessments aligned with ESG HR indicators	Ehnert et al. (2016)
Outcomes	Service quality	Adapted SERVQUAL dimensions; supplementary relational and community items where relevant	Parasuraman et al. (1988)
Cross-training intensity	Multi-role deployment capability	Role certification counts, time spent in cross-functional tasks, and completion of community-based training modules recorded through standard hotel information systems	—

4.1 Sustainability Orientation

The framework is grounded in a sustainability orientation that shapes its underlying values and priorities. This orientation reflects the extent to which environmental responsibility, social equity, and ethical employment practices are embedded in organisational operations and everyday practice (Yoo, 2024; Tarí et al., 2025). How sustainability is experienced in practice influences employee engagement with learning and development. When sustainability becomes part of everyday HRM practices, cross-training can encourage ethical awareness and value internalisation alongside technical capability development. Employees develop additional skills while also gaining a broader understanding of their roles within organisational and social contexts.

The contrast becomes clearest when sustainability is only weakly embedded in organisational practice. In such cases, cross-training is more likely to be experienced as an operational demand detached from any broader sense of purpose or fairness. Where sustainability is more deeply integrated, the same practices take on a different meaning, as development aligns with longer-term commitments and shared values. Principles associated with sustainable destination management, including inclusiveness, transparency, and cultural continuity (Global Sustainable Tourism Council, 2022), reinforce this shift when incorporated into training design. These principles do not guarantee engagement. Their influence depends largely on whether employees encounter them in the realities of everyday organisational life. Sustainability orientation shapes the broader value environment within which employees interpret cross-training. This influences whether they experience it as development or as an additional burden.

4.2 Community Involvement

Community involvement cuts across the framework, extending social exchange beyond the organisation itself. Through partnerships with local stakeholders, community-based learning, and inclusive HR development, hospitality organisations build trust and legitimacy across the destination while simultaneously strengthening social capital and employees' sense of belonging to both the organisation and the host community (Bramwell & Lane, 2011).

Community involvement has a distinct dual role within the framework. At the design level, it shapes training content through the incorporation of local knowledge, sustainability priorities, and community values. These elements are often embedded through consultation and collaborative development processes. Its contribution, however, is not confined to the content itself. The way investments in cross-training are received is also shaped by the wider social environment. In destinations characterised by trust and strong social capital, employees are generally more willing to internalise and apply what they learn. In weaker social environments, similar initiatives may instead be met with scepticism or detachment. As a result, the same cross-training programme can produce substantially different outcomes depending on the surrounding social context.

Labour scarcity tends to make this dual role more visible in practice. Community involvement supports capability development and can also broaden the effective talent pool by drawing more directly on local knowledge and participation. It further supports the development of stronger relationships across the destination, which becomes especially important when individual organisations face chronic staffing limitations. Public-private-community partnerships provide one mechanism through which workforce development efforts can be distributed across the wider destination system (Ishaq et al., 2025).

At the destination-level, these dynamics connect workforce development with governance more broadly. HRM practices aligned with sustainability goals can strengthen collaboration, trust, and shared expectations among tourism actors, helping destinations function more effectively over time. Cross-training affects more than day-to-day operations inside individual firms. How employees learn, cooperate across departments, and interact with local communities can gradually influence wider destination practices and expectations.

Social capital theory provides a useful lens here. Bonding capital refers to the trust and reciprocity that develop within groups, while bridging capital describes the connections that form between different groups across organisational and community boundaries (Putnam, 2000). Cross-training programmes that incorporate community involvement actively build bridging capital by creating regular, structured contact between employees from different departments and representatives of local stakeholder communities. Over time, these connections accumulate into a form of destination-level social infrastructure that supports coordinated responses to disruption, shared learning across organisations, and a more inclusive approach to workforce development. This infrastructure does not develop automatically; it depends on sustained relational investment and governance arrangements that make cross-boundary collaboration both possible and rewarding.

4.3 Cross-Training as the Strategic Mediating Mechanism

Simply adding more tasks to a job description does not constitute cross-training. When employees move across roles, the learning that follows is relational and cumulative. They encounter different problems, work alongside different colleagues, and gradually develop a more integrated understanding of how their contribution fits within the organisation. In this way, cross-training connects sustainability orientation and community involvement with the development of practical knowledge, psychological safety (Edmondson, 1999), and multi-role capability, although these capacities tend to emerge gradually over time. They develop through repeated exposure as employees encounter the different logics, pressures, and expectations associated with work beyond their primary role.

Two dimensions become visible within this process. The relational dimension reflects how cross-training is experienced in terms of reciprocity, participation, and community engagement. The transformational dimension captures how cross-role exposure reshapes the way employees interpret their work, influencing values, ethical awareness, and openness to new approaches. These dimensions can either reinforce or constrain one another depending on how training is designed and enacted.

The link to innovation capability emerges from this interaction. Cross-functional exposure introduces cognitive variety, while boundary-spanning relationships provide access to diverse perspectives and problem-solving approaches. Employees with that kind of exposure are better placed to recombine knowledge across contexts (Nonaka & Takeuchi, 1995), generating adaptive responses, service improvements, and occasionally more substantive innovations. Where training stays narrow, familiarity tends to develop without any corresponding deepening of capability.

Innovation does not follow automatically from moving employees across roles. Much depends on how learning unfolds in practice, not simply on how many roles are covered. Training that incorporates reflection, experimentation, and collaborative problem-solving is more likely to support the development of the behavioural and cognitive capacities associated with innovation. Digital tools, including AI-supported learning and simulation-based training, may expand these opportunities (Li et al., 2019; Baum et al., 2020), particularly when they strengthen employee capability development rather than substitute for it.

4.4 Service Quality as a Socially Constructed Outcome

Within this framework, service quality is not something that appears neatly in a guest satisfaction score or a performance dashboard. It develops through the everyday interactions linking employees, guests, and local communities. Experiences of trust, employee empowerment, and shared value across organisational and community settings all shape how service is ultimately perceived. These are relational processes, built gradually through daily practice, and they cannot be captured fully through compliance measures or checklist-based evaluation alone. In tight labour markets, these dynamics become more consequential. When organisations reduce investment in cross-training or rely heavily on agency staff, the consequences are not only operational. Over time, service relationships weaken, and connections with local communities become more fragile.

Innovation capability and service quality are approached as interconnected outcomes operating at different levels. Innovation capability develops more immediately, as employees with cross-functional understanding and stronger problem-solving capacity are generally better equipped to adapt under changing conditions. At the micro-behavioural level, this relationship is expressed through the translation of cross-functional knowledge into adaptive service responses, non-routine problem-solving, and personalised guest interactions.

Service quality emerges through the interaction of cross-trained employees, sustainability values, and community relationships. In destinations where employment conditions are structurally fragile, maintaining service quality depends more on sustained investment in cross-training as a developmental process than on short-term operational adjustments. Whether these dynamics hold across destinations with different governance structures or labour histories remains an open question.

5. DISCUSSION AND IMPLICATIONS

5.1 Theoretical Implications

The contribution of the Sustainable-Innovative HRM Framework lies less in introducing new constructs than in reconfiguring existing ones. Research in sustainable HRM, social exchange, and tourism governance is already well developed, yet these perspectives rarely intersect in ways that reflect how workforce systems actually operate. The central shift concerns how cross-training is conceptualised. The framework positions cross-training as part of the infrastructure through which workforce systems operate at the destination-level, extending its role beyond the firm itself. Its effects extend beyond staffing flexibility and become visible in how people share knowledge, who they trust, and what they expect from colleagues across departments. This reframing also changes the unit of analysis through which workforce development is understood. What appears at the firm-level as an internal HR practice becomes, in aggregate, a system-level condition associated with labour mobility, shared learning, and the gradual normalisation of multi-role capability (Valachis & Skoultsos, 2026).

A related implication concerns SET. In hospitality research, SET has largely focused on employee–organisation relationships. While analytically useful, this perspective captures only part of the exchange process. Extending the analysis to the destination-level shifts attention toward how reciprocity, trust, and legitimacy develop across interconnected stakeholder systems. Service quality and resilience, in this view, are not produced within organisations alone, but emerge through interactions among organisations, employees, and communities (Nunkoo & Ramkissoon, 2012; Poudel et al., 2024).

The framework also changes how cross-training is understood theoretically. By distinguishing between relational and transformational dimensions, the focus shifts beyond skill coverage toward the conditions under which learning takes place. Training is also the context in which employees form expectations about the organisation and decide how much commitment they are willing to invest in return. Organisations usually focus on measuring capability development because it is visible and relatively easy to quantify. The process also shapes employee expectations, and these expectations strongly influence the attitudes and behaviours organisations ultimately care about. Because of this, the same programme can lead to different outcomes depending on how employees experience it, a pattern that extends beyond hospitality to other labour-intensive and community-based service contexts.

The framework also contributes to the dynamic capabilities literature by specifying a concrete micro-level mechanism through which adaptive capacity develops at the destination level. Teece et al. (1997) identified sensing, seizing, and reconfiguring as the core processes through which organisations build dynamic capabilities in response to environmental change. The framework developed here operationalises these processes at the level of individual employees and inter-organisational networks. Sensing occurs as cross-trained employees develop broader awareness of service interdependencies and community expectations. Seizing takes place when that awareness translates into adaptive service responses and collaborative problem-solving. Reconfiguring emerges as knowledge circulates across departmental and organisational boundaries, gradually reshaping how destinations allocate and develop their human resources. Framing cross-training within dynamic capabilities theory therefore extends its theoretical range and connects workforce development practices to a broader conversation about how organisations and destinations build sustained competitive capacity under conditions of structural instability.

5.2 Practical Implications

Training is already a central investment for most hospitality organisations. The question is less whether to invest and more how its value is understood. Assessments that focus primarily on operational performance capture only part of what training produces. Cross-training also shapes how employees interpret their roles, engage with sustainability, and relate to the communities in which they work. When labour is persistently scarce, these effects matter more, not less.

How cross-training programmes are designed shapes these outcomes considerably. Approaches centred primarily on technical efficiency tend to produce short-term gains, whereas those that incorporate participation, sustainability values, and community engagement are more likely to support durable forms of commitment. In such cases, training connects everyday work with a broader sense of purpose, often through local recruitment pathways, apprenticeship schemes, and partnerships with vocational institutions and municipalities that embed community knowledge directly into service delivery.

Viewed through this lens, workforce development cannot remain confined to the firm. It extends across destinations through shared learning, labour mobility, and the development of social capital. This points to a broader role for destination-level HRD initiatives linking business performance with social equity and cultural continuity (Baum & Szivas, 2008; Tarí et al., 2025). Governance frameworks that incorporate indicators of training quality, community engagement, and innovation capacity provide one way of making these dynamics more visible (Hall, 2011).

The framework also raises an ethical question that is often avoided in practice. Cross-training is not automatically beneficial. Under some conditions, it functions as a mechanism for intensifying labour without offering the recognition, support, or protection employees expect in return. When that happens, the reciprocity on which the whole process depends begins to weaken, and turnover pressures can increase rather than decline. The distinction between a developmental investment and an additional operational burden may not be visible in a training plan or organisational chart, but employees recognise it very quickly. Fairness, transparency, and meaningful recognition are therefore structural requirements of the framework, not secondary considerations. They determine whether cross-training is experienced as development or simply as another demand placed on already stretched employees.

Pfeffer made a similar point decades ago, arguing that service organisations build long-term advantage when employees are treated as assets rather than costs to be minimised (Pfeffer, 1998). That argument remains more analytically durable than much of the management literature that followed.

5.3 Designing Cross-Training in Hospitality: A Practitioner Guide

Cross-training programmes in hospitality rarely originate from strategic workforce planning. More commonly, they emerge reactively: a staffing gap appears, a temporary solution is introduced, and that solution gradually becomes standard practice. Once employees interpret cross-training primarily as a gap-filling mechanism, its developmental potential diminishes sharply. How programmes are framed and designed from the outset is therefore consequential for the outcomes they produce. Table 4 organises the principal design dimensions of cross-training along three axes: the failure modes that most commonly undermine programme effectiveness, and the evidence-based practices that address them.

Table 4. Cross-Training Design Dimensions: Failure Modes and Evidence-Based Practices

Design Dimension	Common Failure Mode	Evidence-Based Practice
Programme framing	Cross-training introduced reactively as a staffing fix; employees interpret it as gap-filling rather than development	Position cross-training as a career development investment by linking participation to clear progression pathways and recognition for expanded capability
Interdepartmental integration	Role exposure without understanding of cross-departmental coordination logic; employees gain familiarity but not operational judgement under pressure	Map inter-departmental service flows and train employees in how functions coordinate under pressure, prioritising highly interdependent roles such as front office, food and beverage, and housekeeping
Sustainability and innovation integration	Sustainability and innovation elements are often added superficially to programmes designed primarily for operational efficiency, leading employees to treat them as peripheral	Embed sustainability values and innovation prompts into role design from the outset; connect training objectives explicitly to ESG commitments and community expectations rather than appending them to existing operational content
Recognition and reciprocity	Additional capability is not reflected in recognition or remuneration; employees interpret expanded responsibilities as intensification rather than investment	Align recognition systems with cross-role competency milestones; ensure scheduling adjustments accompany expanded role responsibilities; establish transparent feedback mechanisms to prevent the gradual erosion of trust that unrecognised effort produces

continued on following page

Table 4. Continued

Design Dimension	Common Failure Mode	Evidence-Based Practice
Breadth vs. depth	Rotating employees across many functions produces surface familiarity without the operational competency that holds under pressure	Prioritise depth in two or three adjacent roles; use repetition and reflection to build operational competency rather than brief exposure; digital tools can support, but not replace, developmental learning
Evaluation	Coverage rates and absenteeism often dominate evaluation because they are easy to measure, while training records are updated infrequently and reviewed only superficially	Supplement operational metrics with indicators reflecting developmental outcomes, such as retention patterns, participation in cross-functional problem-solving, service improvement contributions, and community engagement

6. CONCLUSIONS AND FUTURE RESEARCH

The dominant view of cross-training in hospitality remains fairly narrow. Most often, it is treated as a practical response to staffing shortages: useful for coverage, helpful for flexibility, but ultimately operational in scope. The framework developed here argues for something broader and, arguably, closer to how cross-training functions in practice when organisations invest in it seriously. Cross-training is not simply a scheduling mechanism. It is shaped by social relationships, influenced by the communities tourism depends on, and tied to sustainability orientation, innovation capability, and community involvement in ways that extend well beyond day-to-day staffing needs.

Service quality is approached somewhat differently within the framework. Instead of viewing it as a fixed performance outcome, it is understood as something shaped through relationships, through trust, fairness, and the creation of shared value between organisations, employees, guests, and communities. Cross-training is one of the main ways these elements become visible in everyday practice, connecting organisational goals with employee capability and service delivery. Seen this way, long-term competitiveness is shaped not only by technological or environmental performance, but by the ability of organisations to build and maintain strong relationships over time (Baum, 1995; Bramwell & Lane, 2011).

A different lens is needed, one that begins with structural conditions rather than focusing only on firm-level behaviour. Employment precarity in tourism is not simply the result of poor management decisions. It is shaped by seasonal labour markets, fragmented governance systems, and institutional arrangements that have changed very little despite years of policy discussion. No individual organisation can transform those conditions on its own, and cross-training does not resolve them either. What it can do, under the right conditions, is strengthen the kinds of workforce capabilities that help employees and organisations navigate those realities more effectively. That is a more restrained claim than parts of the literature sometimes suggest, but it is also a more realistic and defensible one. Its contribution is slower and less visible, building social capital, deepening workforce versatility, and gradually embedding sustainability values into daily practice. For these effects to matter beyond the individual property, they need to be reinforced across destinations through shared training standards, inter-organisational partnerships, and coordinated workforce systems. When cross-training operates only at the individual firm-level, the benefits can still be real. Even where these benefits emerge, they do not always extend far beyond the individual organisation.

HRM therefore connects with destination governance in ways that extend beyond the control of any single organisation, even though organisations can still play an important supporting role. The framework does not resolve the structural tensions of tourism labour markets, nor does it claim to. The value of the framework lies in showing how workforce development may respond to these conditions in practice. Cross-training can contribute meaningfully to organisational and destination resilience when it is approached as a developmental investment. How durable these effects become at the destination-level depends on conditions extending beyond any single organisation.

Future research can test these mechanisms directly, beginning with the mediating role of cross-training in linking sustainability orientation and community involvement with innovation capability and service quality. Greater attention should also be given to boundary conditions, particularly labour market tightness. Indicators such as destination-level vacancy rates and employee turnover could help examine how labour scarcity shapes the strength of these relationships.

The community dimension calls for complementary approaches. Qualitative and comparative research can examine how governance structures influence the relationship between cross-training and social capital across different destinations. Longitudinal studies can track how employees develop within sustainability-oriented training systems, connecting design choices with changes in innovation behaviour and service quality. Research across different cultural and institutional settings would further strengthen these insights (Tarí et al., 2025).

Methodologically, the framework calls for approaches that can capture relational and cumulative processes rather than isolated outcomes. Survey-based studies examining cross-training intensity, perceived organisational support, and innovation behaviour at the individual level would provide a useful starting point. However, they should be complemented by methods better suited to capturing the community and destination dimensions of the framework. Ethnographic and case-based approaches can trace how cross-training programmes interact with local governance structures and community relationships over time. Network analysis offers another productive avenue, mapping how cross-trained employees serve as knowledge brokers across departmental and organisational boundaries within a destination. Multi-level designs that link individual employee data with destination-level indicators, including vacancy rates, community engagement scores, and shared training infrastructure, would allow researchers to examine the boundary conditions of the framework more rigorously.

Workforce development in tourism cannot be understood through firm-level decisions alone. It is shaped across organisations, communities, and institutional settings, where relationships, expectations, and capabilities evolve gradually. Labour shortages may have pushed organisations toward cross-training in the first place. What keeps tourism systems resilient over time, however, is the broader capacity that develops through it: employees learning across functions, working more effectively with one another, and becoming better able to respond collectively to change and uncertainty.

REFERENCES

Abdou, A. H., Hassan, T. H., Salem, A. E., Albakhit, A. I., Almakhayitah, M. Y., & Salama, W. (2022). The nexus between environmentally sustainable practices, green satisfaction, and customer citizenship behavior in eco-friendly hotels: A social exchange theory approach. *Sustainability (Basel), 14*(19), 12791. DOI: 10.3390/su141912791

Adhika, I. N. R. (2024). Sustainable HR practices: Examining the connection between organisational resilience and green HRM in the hospitality sector. *Society, 12*(2), 1022–1034. DOI: 10.33019/society.v12i2.782

Al-Romeedy, B. S., & Alharethi, T. (2025). Leveraging green human resource management for sustainable tourism and hospitality: A mediation model for enhancing green reputation. *Discover Sustainability, 6*(1), 67. DOI: 10.1007/s43621-025-00829-2

Al-Twal, A., Alawamleh, M., & Jarrar, D. M. (2024). An investigation of the role of wasta social capital in enhancing employee loyalty and innovation in organisations. *Journal of Innovation and Entrepreneurship, 13*(1), 12. DOI: 10.1186/s13731-024-00372-w

Aldrich, H., & Herker, D. (1977). Boundary spanning roles and organization structure. *Academy of Management Review, 2*(2), 217–230. DOI: 10.2307/257905

Ap, J. (1992). Residents' perceptions on tourism impacts. *Annals of Tourism Research, 19*(4), 665–690. DOI: 10.1016/0160-7383(92)90060-3

Argyris, C., & Schön, D. A. (1978). *Organizational learning: A theory of action perspective*. Addison-Wesley.

Balkin, D. B., & Werner, S. (2023). Theorizing the relationship between discretionary employee benefits and individual performance. *Human Resource Management Review, 33*(1), 100901. DOI: 10.1016/j.hrmr.2022.100901

Baum, T. (1995). *Managing human resources in the European tourism and hospitality industry*. Chapman & Hall.

Baum, T. (2006). *Human resource management for tourism, hospitality and leisure: An international perspective*. Thomson.

Baum, T. (2018). Sustainable human resource management as a driver in tourism policy and planning: A serious sin of omission? *Journal of Sustainable Tourism, 26*(6), 873–889. DOI: 10.1080/09669582.2017.1423318

Baum, T., Mooney, S. K., Robinson, R. N., & Solnet, D. (2020). COVID-19's impact on the hospitality workforce: New crisis or amplification of the norm? *International Journal of Contemporary Hospitality Management, 32*(9), 2813–2829. DOI: 10.1108/IJCHM-04-2020-0314

Baum, T., & Szivas, E. (2008). HRD in tourism: A role for government? *Tourism Management, 29*(4), 783–794. DOI: 10.1016/j.tourman.2007.09.002

Becker, B. E., & Huselid, M. A. (1998). High performance work systems and firm performance: A synthesis of research and managerial implications. *Research in Personnel and Human Resources Management, 16*, 53–101.

Begum, S., Ashfaq, M., Xia, E., & Awan, U. (2022). Does green transformational leadership lead to green innovation? The role of green thinking and creative process engagement. *Business Strategy and the Environment, 31*(1), 580–597. DOI: 10.1002/bse.2911

Belias, D., & Trihas, N. (2023). The role of SHRM in navigating the hospitality sector during a crisis. In Masouras, A., Papademetriou, C., Belias, D., & Anastasiadou, S. (Eds.), *Sustainable growth strategies for entrepreneurial venture tourism and regional development* (pp. 60–76). IGI Global Scientific Publishing., DOI: 10.4018/978-1-6684-6055-9.ch004

Blau, P. M. (1964). *Exchange and power in social life*. Wiley.

Bramwell, B., & Lane, B. (2011). Critical research on tourism and governance. *Journal of Sustainable Tourism, 19*(4–5), 411–421. DOI: 10.1080/09669582.2011.580586

Cannon-Bowers, J. A., Tannenbaum, S. I., Salas, E., & Volpe, C. E. (1995). Defining competencies and establishing team training requirements. In Guzzo, R. A., & Salas, E. (Eds.), *Team effectiveness and decision making in organizations* (pp. 333–380). Jossey-Bass.

Chan, E. S. W., & Hsu, C. H. C. (2016). Environmental management research in hospitality. *International Journal of Contemporary Hospitality Management, 28*(5), 886–923. DOI: 10.1108/IJCHM-02-2015-0076

Collings, D. G., & Mellahi, K. (2009). Strategic talent management: A review and research agenda. *Human Resource Management Review, 19*(4), 304–313. DOI: 10.1016/j.hrmr.2009.04.001

Cropanzano, R., & Mitchell, M. S. (2005). Social exchange theory: An interdisciplinary review. *Journal of Management, 31*(6), 874–900. DOI: 10.1177/0149206305279602

Edinger-Schöns, L. M., Lengler-Graiff, L., Scheidler, S., & Wieseke, J. (2019). Frontline employees as corporate social responsibility (CSR) ambassadors: A quasi-field experiment. *Journal of Business Ethics*, *157*(2), 359–373. DOI: 10.1007/s10551-018-3790-9

Edmondson, A. C. (1999). Psychological safety and learning behavior in work teams. *Administrative Science Quarterly*, *44*(2), 350–383. DOI: 10.2307/2666999

Ehnert, I., Parsa, S., Roper, I., Wagner, M., & Müller-Camen, M. (2016). Reporting on sustainability and HRM: A comparative study of sustainability reporting practices by the world's largest companies. *International Journal of Human Resource Management*, *27*(1), 88–108. DOI: 10.1080/09585192.2015.1024157

Eisenberger, R., Huntington, R., Hutchison, S., & Sowa, D. (1986). Perceived organizational support. *The Journal of Applied Psychology*, *71*(3), 500–507. DOI: 10.1037/0021-9010.71.3.500

Eisenhardt, K. M., & Martin, J. A. (2000). Dynamic capabilities: What are they? *Strategic Management Journal*, *21*(10–11), 1105–1121. DOI: 10.1002/1097-0266(200010/11)21:10/11<1105::AID-SMJ133>3.0.CO;2-E

Fotiadis, I., Salepaki, A., Angelou, I., & Kourkouridis, D. (2025). Human resource strategies in Greek tourism businesses: Perspectives and challenges. *SA Journal of Human Resource Management*, *23*(0), a2911. DOI: 10.4102/sajhrm.v23i0.2911

Global Sustainable Tourism Council. (2022). GSTC criteria for destinations (version 2.0). https://www.gstcouncil.org/gstc-criteria/

Greasidou, M., & Valachis, I. (2022). The role of human resource management in service quality improvement of hotel businesses. *Enlightening Tourism: A Pathmaking Journal, 12*(3), 105–135. https://doi.org/DOI: 10.33776/et.v12i3.7277

Hall, C. M. (2011). A typology of governance and its implications for tourism policy analysis. *Journal of Sustainable Tourism*, *19*(4–5), 437–457. DOI: 10.1080/09669582.2011.570346

Heskett, J. L., Jones, T. O., Loveman, G. W., Sasser, W. E., & Schlesinger, L. A. (1994). Putting the service-profit chain to work. *Harvard Business Review*, *72*(2), 164–174.

Ishaq, M. I., Sarwar, H., Franzoni, S., & Palermo, O. (2025). The nexus of human resource management, corporate social responsibility, and sustainable performance in upscale hotels: A mixed-method study. *International Journal of Emerging Markets*, *20*(13), 1–29. DOI: 10.1108/IJOEM-04-2022-0714

Jaakkola, E. (2020). Designing conceptual articles: Four approaches. *AMS Review, 10*(1–2), 18–26. DOI: 10.1007/s13162-020-00161-0

Karatepe, O. M., & Olugbade, O. A. (2016). The mediating role of work engagement in the relationship between high-performance work practices and job outcomes of employees in Nigeria. *International Journal of Contemporary Hospitality Management, 28*(10), 2350–2371. DOI: 10.1108/IJCHM-03-2015-0145

Kramar, R. (2014). Beyond strategic human resource management: Is sustainable human resource management the next approach? *International Journal of Human Resource Management, 25*(8), 1069–1089. DOI: 10.1080/09585192.2013.816863

Li, J., Bonn, M. A., & Ye, B. H. (2019). Hotel employees' artificial intelligence and robotics awareness and its impact on turnover intention. *Tourism Management, 73*, 172–181. DOI: 10.1016/j.tourman.2019.02.006

Marinakou, E., & Giousmpasoglou, C. (2019). Talent management and retention strategies in luxury hotels: Evidence from four countries. *International Journal of Contemporary Hospitality Management, 31*(10), 3855–3878. DOI: 10.1108/IJCHM-10-2018-0862

Nonaka, I., & Takeuchi, H. (1995). *The knowledge-creating company*. Oxford University Press. DOI: 10.1093/oso/9780195092691.001.0001

Nunkoo, R. (2017). Governance and sustainable tourism: What is the role of trust, power, and social capital? *Journal of Destination Marketing & Management, 6*(4), 277–285. DOI: 10.1016/j.jdmm.2017.10.003

Nunkoo, R., & Ramkissoon, H. (2012). Power, trust, social exchange and community support. *Annals of Tourism Research, 39*(2), 997–1023. DOI: 10.1016/j.annals.2011.11.017

Parasuraman, A., Zeithaml, V. A., & Berry, L. L. (1988). SERVQUAL: A multiple-item scale for measuring consumer perceptions of service quality. *Journal of Retailing, 64*(1), 12–40.

Pfeffer, J. (1998). *The human equation: Building profits by putting people first.* Harvard Business School Press.

Poudel, S., Basyal, D. K., Devkota, N., Paudel, U. R., Lawaju, P., & Danuwar, R. K. (2024). Using social exchange theory to predict residents' perspective on factors influencing tourism development in Pokhara. *Smart Tourism, 5*(1), 2561. DOI: 10.54517/st.v5i1.2561

Putnam, R. D. (2000). *Bowling alone: The collapse and revival of American community*. Simon & Schuster.

Riley, M., Ladkin, A., & Szivas, E. (2002). *Tourism employment: Analysis and planning*. Channel View Publications. DOI: 10.21832/9781873150382

Scott, S. G., & Bruce, R. A. (1994). Determinants of innovative behavior: A path model of individual innovation in the workplace. *Academy of Management Journal, 37*(3), 580–607. DOI: 10.2307/256701

Sims, D. E., Salas, E., & Burke, C. S. (2005). Promoting effective team performance through training. In Wheelan, S. A. (Ed.), *The handbook of group research and practice* (pp. 407–426). Sage.

Tarí, J. J., Pertusa-Ortega, E. M., López-Gamero, M. D., & Pereira-Moliner, J. (2025). Drivers of social sustainability practices: Quality management, human capital, and innovation. *International Journal of Contemporary Hospitality Management, 37*(2), 462–481. DOI: 10.1108/IJCHM-12-2023-1866

Teece, D. J., Pisano, G., & Shuen, A. (1997). Dynamic capabilities and strategic management. *Strategic Management Journal, 18*(7), 509–533. DOI: 10.1002/(SICI)1097-0266(199708)18:7<509::AID-SMJ882>3.0.CO;2-Z

Tosun, C. (2000). Limits to community participation in the tourism development process in developing countries. *Tourism Management, 21*(6), 613–633. DOI: 10.1016/S0261-5177(00)00009-1

Valachis, I., & Skoultsos, S. (2026). Reframing sustainable human resource management in tourism: Education, social exchange, and destination governance. *Tourism and Hospitality, 7*(5), 118. DOI: 10.3390/tourhosp7050118

Valachis, I., & Tachmatzidis, D. (2023). Employees' metacognitive knowledge and skills assessment in tourism and hospitality. *Journal of Tourism Management Research, 10*(2), 123–139. DOI: 10.18488/31.v10i2.3418

Valachis, I., & Trihas, N. (2025). Tourist awareness in tourism development: Case study of the city of Veria, Greece. In Alkier, R., Catenazzo, G., Milojica, V., & Zając, A. (Eds.), *Cases on effective destination management* (pp. 57–81). IGI Global Scientific Publishing., DOI: 10.4018/979-8-3693-1548-4.ch003

Yoo, D. Y. (2024). Eco-leadership in action: Integrating green HRM and ecological paradigms. *Sustainability, 16*(20), 9044. DOI: 10.3390/su16209044

Chapter 13

The Aging Workforce and Digital Competency in Indonesia:
The Implication for Training Needs

Ngadi Ngadi
http://orcid.org/0000-0002-5249-0860
Research Center for Population, Indonesia

Beni Teguh T. Gunawan
http://orcid.org/0000-0002-4883-2258
National Research and Innovation Agency of Indonesia, Indonesia

Triyono Triyono
http://orcid.org/0000-0002-6941-6712
National Research and Innovation Agency of Indonesia, Indonesia

Khairul Ismed
http://orcid.org/0000-0001-8219-2883
National Research and Innovation Agency of Indonesia, Indonesia

ABSTRACT

The rapid advancement of digital technology, particularly in the labor market, necessitates that the workforce possesses adequate digital competencies. Without adequate digital competencies, the workforce will struggle to compete in the global workforce and actively participate in its development. This paper aims to discuss trends in aging workers and digital competency in Indonesia. The data used for the analysis is the 2023 National Labor Force Survey. This analysis is expected to

DOI: 10.4018/979-8-3373-5327-2.ch013

ght © 2027, IGI Global Scientific Publishing. Copying or distributing in print or electronic forms without written permission of IGI Global Scientific Publishing is prohibited. Use of this chapter to n generative artificial intelligence (AI) technologies is expressly prohibited. The publisher reserves all rights to license its use for generative AI training and machine learning model development.

provide an overview of training needs and suitable positions for older people in the workplace. The data for the analysis are from the National Labor Force Survey, conducted by Statistics Indonesia in 2024. The analysis reveals a gap in digital competency between elderly and younger generation. Low digital competency is more prevalent among older age groups. Therefore, efforts to improve infrastructure must continue to be made to ensure equitable digital access for the entire population.

1. INTRODUCTION

Indonesia's population structure is undergoing a demographic shift, with a rising proportion of elderly individuals and a declining share of the population aged 0-14 years. National projections indicate that the elderly share of the population will grow substantially in the coming decades, with some regions of Java expected to be especially affected (BPS, 2020). A detailed account of this demographic trajectory, together with its implications for digital competency, is presented in the Aging Workforce and Digital Competency section below.

This generational shift carries direct implications for the types of work and training required in Indonesia's labor market. Workers from the baby boomer generation tend to be less familiar with digital technology than younger cohorts, whereas Generation Z, having grown up in a pervasively digital environment, typically displays greater familiarity with and adaptability to emerging technologies (Yazdani-Darki et al., 2020; Vaportzis et al., 2017). At the same time, the literature cautions that older workers are not inherently averse to technology; resistance tends to stem from being compelled to use tools perceived as irrelevant or poorly suited to their needs, rather than from an unwillingness to adopt digital tools as such (Tishman et al., 2012; Schroeder et al., 2023). Beyond demographic familiarity, the urban-rural divide and sector-based disparities, particularly within agriculture, further compound unequal digital readiness across Indonesia's workforce, a pattern this study examines in detail using nationally representative data.

This paper aims to discuss the implications of an aging workforce and digital competency in Indonesia. The data used for the analysis are from the 2024 National Labor Force Survey. This analysis is expected to provide an overview of training needs and suitable positions for older people in the workplace. The knowledge and utilisation of basic digital equipment are used as indicators of digital competence, specifically assessed through information on the workforce's use of digital devices like cellular phones, computers, or laptops.

2. METHOD

This chapter uses secondary data from the August 2024 National Labor Force Survey conducted by Statistics Indonesia (BPS). The August Sakernas was chosen because it is the primary labour survey that provides nationally representative data down to the provincial level and collects detailed information on the working population, including age, employment status, and the use of digital devices in daily life and at work. The target population for this study comprises all residents aged 15 and older who are employed in Indonesia's 38 provinces. The unit of analysis is the province, and the study focuses on two main indicators: age groups, labor force, working population, and digital device usage.

The study employs descriptive analysis to outline the distribution of these indicators across Indonesia, without performing inferential statistical tests or exploring causal relationships. The dominant age group is defined as the age category with the highest proportion of working residents in a province, categorized into under 30, 30-39, 40-49, 50-59, and over 60 years. The percentage of working residents who use digital devices is calculated from respondents who report using computers, laptops, tablets, or smartphones for work or daily activities. All results are presented as frequency charts and thematic maps to illustrate regional patterns.

Data processing was performed using Stata 17. Initially, the dataset was cleaned to confirm that essential variables, including age, employment status, province, and digital device usage, were complete. Subsequently, age was recoded into three predefined categories, and digital device usage was transformed into a binary variable. The cleaned data were aggregated at the provincial level to compute the share of employed individuals in each age group and the share of digital users per province. These processed results were then exported for mapping. Thematic maps were produced using QGIS 4.4. The base layer was the official 2024 Indonesian provincial administrative map. Processed Stata data were joined to the map layers using province codes. The dominant age group map used a distinct classification with three colors to represent each age category, enabling readers to identify provinces dominated by young, middle-productivity, or older groups.

The digital usage percentage map employed a gradient color scheme across four predefined intervals, ranging from the lowest to the highest percentages. Each map contains a legend, scale bar, north arrow, and an inset of the archipelagic area to provide complete geographic context. The study recognizes several methodological constraints. First, the August 2024 Sakernas survey only records whether a person uses digital devices at work, without specifying device type, frequency, or intensity, so the resulting depiction is broad. Second, descriptive analysis can only illustrate distribution patterns across provinces at a single point in time and cannot reveal temporal changes or causal relationships. Third, because the data are cross-sectional, individual dynamics cannot be tracked over time. Despite these limitations, the methods used are sufficient for addressing the exploratory and descriptive objectives related to Indonesia's digital employment landscape based on the August 2024 Sakernas.

3. DIGITAL COMPETENCY IN INDONESIA

Various indicators have been developed to measure digital competency. Oberländer et al. (2020) defined digital competency in the workplace as a combination of fundamental knowledge, skills, abilities, and characteristics that enable individuals to perform their job tasks efficiently and effectively within the context of digital media. This competency is considered a significant asset for workers, enhancing their bargaining position in securing job opportunities and competing in the labor market. Employees with digital skills are more likely to increase their productivity. Erumban (2024) observed that digital technology typically boosts the potential for economic formalization and is likely to drive overall productivity growth, prompting companies to look for employees with these skills.

Conde-Jiménez (2018) categorizes digital competency indicators into several key aspects: command, privileging, appropriation, and reintegration. Audrin et al. (2024) proposed a measurement framework for assessing digital competency, which comprises eight dimensions: technology use, cybersecurity, content management, communication and collaboration, critical inquiry, responsibility, well-being, and identity and development. Moreover, Van Laar et al. (2018) presented a model for measuring digital skills based on six variable indicators: information skills, communication, collaboration, critical thinking, creativity, and problem-solving.

These measurement frameworks gain explanatory power when situated within three complementary theoretical lenses. First, the digital transformation literature frames competency not merely as a technical skill set but as a structural precondition for participation in an increasingly digitalized economy, in which workers lacking such competency risk exclusion from emerging job categories (Krzywdzinski et al., 2016). Second, dual and segmented labor market theory helps explain why digital competency gaps are not randomly distributed but cluster systematically along generational and sectoral lines: workers in the formal, capital-intensive segment of the economy face stronger incentives and institutional support to acquire digital skills, while those in agriculture and other informal-leaning sectors are structurally positioned outside these incentive systems regardless of individual willingness to adapt (Bilanakos et al., 2018; Martin et al., 2016).

Third, the literature on Industry 4.0 and workforce adaptation suggests that technological change of this kind tends to be skill-biased, simultaneously raising the returns to digital competency for those who possess it and intensifying the marginalization of those who do not, a dynamic with particular relevance for older workers whose accumulated experience may not translate into digital fluency (Martin et al., 2016). Taken together, these perspectives suggest that Indonesia's digital competency gap is best understood not as a deficit to be corrected through individual training alone, but as an outcome jointly produced by demographic structure, labor market segmentation, and the skill-biased character of technological change, a framing that informs the analysis and policy discussion that follow.

In this study, the description of digital competencies is informed by the available data in Susenas and draws upon the indicators proposed by Conde-Jiménez (2018). Specifically, the command aspect includes knowledge of and proficiency with basic digital tools, as well as the ability to create digital content. The aspect of privileging encompasses the capacity to access information and news, as well as engage in online learning. Finally, the aspect of appropriation refers to the use of the internet for social networking, as well as the purchasing and selling of goods and services.

4. AGING WORKFORCE AND DIGITAL COMPETENCY

Changes in the population structure of Indonesia are characterized by an increasing proportion of elderly individuals and a declining proportion of the younger population (aged 0-14 years). According to population projections from the Central Statistics Agency, the proportion of the elderly population in Indonesia is projected to reach 11.51% in 2024, with an anticipated rise to 21.9% by 2050 (BPS, 2020). In some areas of Java, it is estimated that by 2050, one-quarter of the population will be classified as elderly.

Figure 1. Trend of Old and Young Population in Indonesia, (2024-2050)

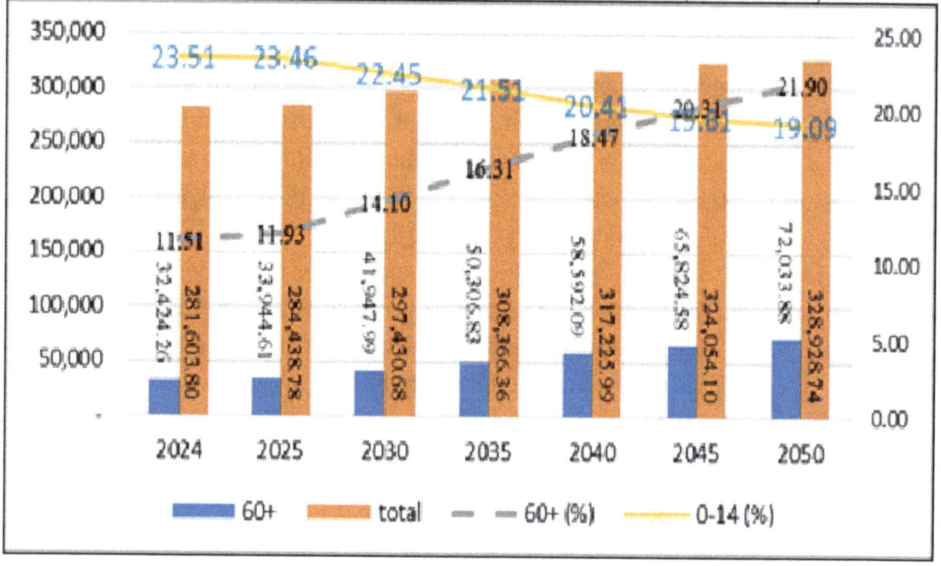

The development of digital technology necessitates careful consideration of age demographics within the population. Elderly individuals, primarily from the baby boomer generation, tend to be less familiar with digital technology than younger cohorts. Conversely, the younger demographic, particularly Generation Z, has been raised in an environment where digital technology is pervasive. As a result, they generally exhibit greater familiarity with and a greater ability to adapt to emerging technologies. However, it is important to acknowledge that some members of this younger generation have also experienced negative consequences from technology due to unwise use.

Figure 2 illustrates the variation in digital competence among different age groups based on the usage of these digital tools. Younger generations show a greater preference for digital technology, with 96.60% of users in the 15-29 age group, in contrast to the 43.23% found among the elderly.

Figure 2. Proportion of the workforce using digital tools across age groups

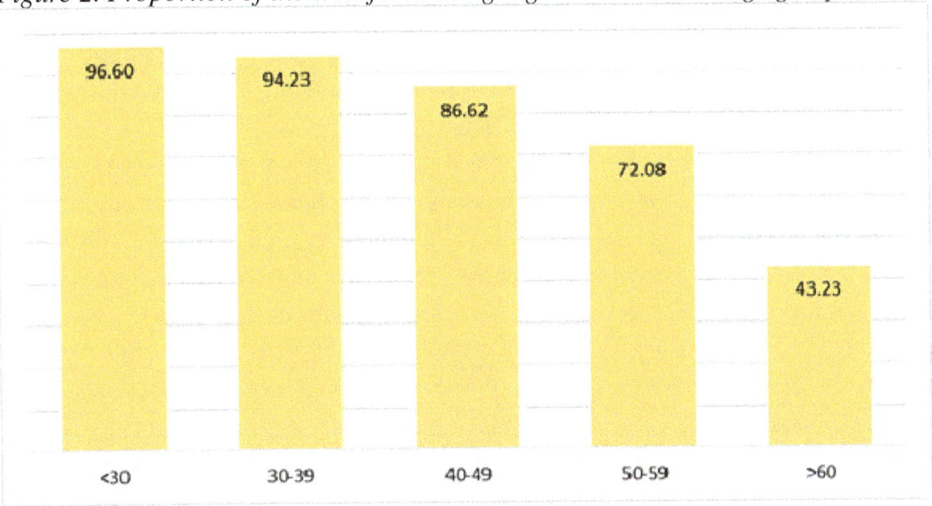

Several factors contribute to the low adoption of digital technology among older individuals, including fears of physical harm, device damage, safety threats, the risk of making mistakes while using technology, and the risk of social isolation. Furthermore, personal barriers such as limited educational background, restricted access to technology, and negative attitudes toward digital devices also play a significant role (Yazdani-Darki et al., 2020; Vaportzis et al., 2017).

Despite the challenges associated with adopting digital technology, many elderly individuals who possess knowledge of digital tools find enjoyment in their use. It is essential to recognize that older workers are not inherently resistant to technology; instead, they exhibit resistance to the enforced implementation of tools perceived as unnecessary or unsuitable (Tishman et al., 2012). Research indicates that older adults are more likely to use technology when they have the autonomy to make their own decisions, have received prior computer training, hold positive attitudes, and have previously experienced satisfaction with technology (Schroeder et al., 2023).

Additional studies indicate that while older adults demonstrate a positive attitude toward digital technology, they often lack self-efficacy regarding their ability to learn and use these tools. Many older individuals report difficulties, particularly with navigation, when engaging with digital technologies. Moreover, older adults tend to prefer mobile computing devices over traditional computers (Li & Luximon, 2016).

In contrast to the elderly, the younger workforce exhibits a greater understanding and use of digital technology. Generation Y, in particular, is characterized by a strong ambition to master diverse fields, making them proficient users of technology. Generation Z, having grown up in an entirely digital environment, has developed distinct characteristics in both interpersonal and academic relationships (Kaifi et al., 2012; Binus, 2021).

The use of digital technology to access the internet varies by age group and urban-rural. Figure 3 shows that, overall, the use of digital technology to access the internet in urban areas is greater than in rural areas by 88.47% and 76.24%, respectively. This situation aligns with the APJII survey, which shows that the ratio of internet users to the total population in urban areas is greater than in rural areas by 82.18% and 74.00%, respectively. Several factors contribute to the disparity in the use of digital technology between urban and rural areas. Tayo et al. (2016) identified three factors contributing to the digital divide: economic capability, knowledge, and access to free internet. In all three factors, urban areas benefit more because they are the center of economic growth, so the income of residents in urban areas is higher than in rural areas. BPS data show that in 2023, urban per capita income was higher than rural income by 1.69 million IDR and 1.12 million IDR, respectively (BPS, 2024).

Figure 3. Proportion of the workforce using digital tools, according to location and age group

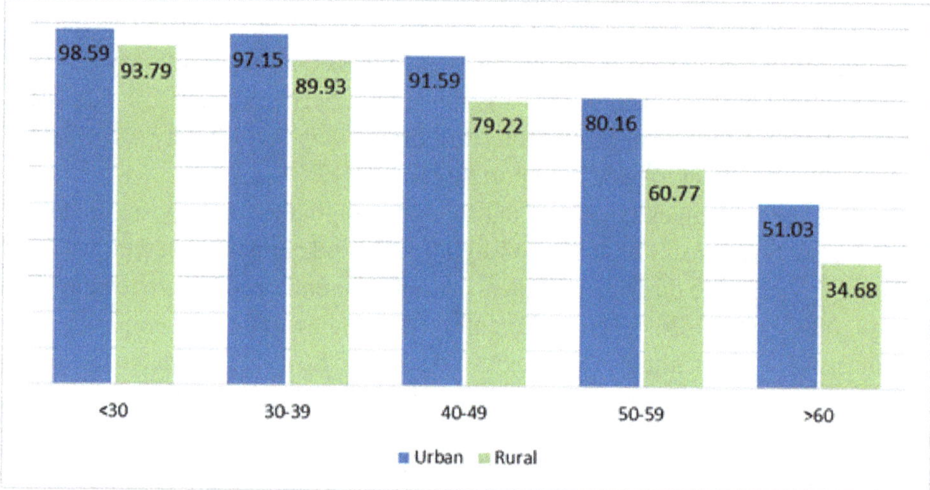

In terms of knowledge, the education level of the workforce in urban areas is generally higher than that in rural areas. In addition to a more adequate education infrastructure in urban areas, some highly educated rural residents move to urban areas to find jobs (Ngadi et al., 2023). This situation has an impact on the educational level of the workforce in urban areas, which is generally higher than in rural areas. Rural areas are deprived of potential resources for development because the population living in rural areas is old and less productive. Ariyanti (2013) added digital infrastructure and content as contributing factors to the urban-rural gap in digital technology use. The more profitable investment in urban areas encourages businesses to invest in these areas, thereby enhancing the digital infrastructure in urban areas. In such circumstances, government intervention to invest in rural areas is necessary.

The use of digital technology varies across age groups. In the age group of 40 years and above, the highest use of the internet is for accessing information or news (Figure 4). In the younger age group (<40 years), the highest use of the internet is for finance. This situation shows that among young people, the internet is used not only for news searches but also for economic activities. Higher internet knowledge among young people means that the internet is no longer just a means of searching for news but is now used for specific goals, such as finance. The younger generation relies heavily on social networking as a means of socialization, enabling access to information and connection-building with others who share similar goals and orientations (Castillo de Mesa et al., 2020).

Figure 4. Internet usage of the workforce in Indonesia, 2024

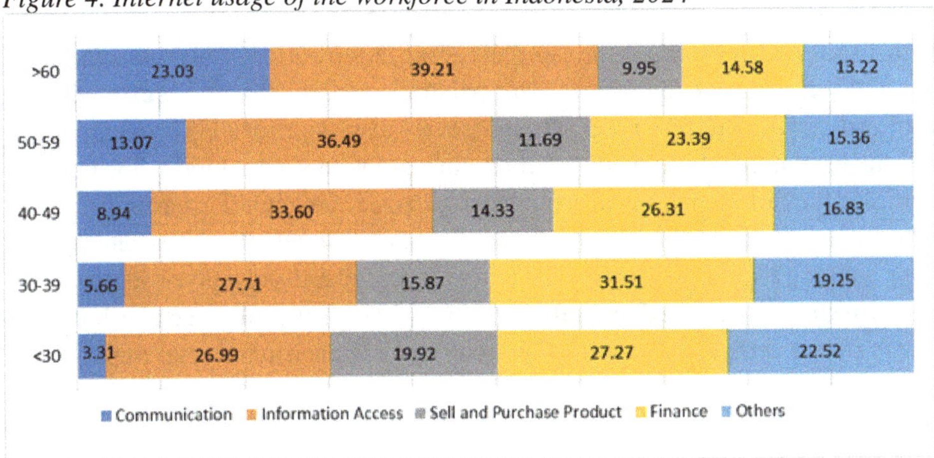

Across all age groups, the use of the internet for selling and purchasing products remains low. Among the workforce aged below 30 years, approximately 19.92% reported using the internet to sell and purchase products, while this figure is significantly lower for the older workforce (9.95%). Several barriers appear to contribute to this trend, including concerns about safety threats, apprehension regarding potential errors in technology use, and fears of social isolation. The higher proportion of young individuals leveraging the internet for various purposes correlates with the time they spend online. According to Tempo (2023), most respondents from Generation Z and Generation Y use the internet for over six hours per day. In contrast, only 19% of Generation X and Baby Boomers engage with the internet for six hours or more daily, with the majority of these groups averaging one to two hours of internet use each day.

Digital Competency and the Main Sector

The analysis of digital competency across primary sectors emphasizes the access and use of digital devices among the workforce. As illustrated in Figure 5, across all sectors, older adults (60 years and older) are the least likely to use digital tools compared to other age groups. Based on the main sector, the services sector has the highest use of digital devices. Digital competency within Indonesia's service sector is increasingly recognized as a vital factor for enhancing productivity, sustainability, and resilience despite challenges such as market fluctuations and technological advancements. Digital technologies are revolutionizing industry practices by equipping workers with access to essential information and resources, thereby improving decision-making processes and operational efficiency.

The age-related disadvantage in digital tool use is also gendered. Among workers aged 60 and above, only 33.86 percent of women report using digital tools, compared with 49.53 percent of men in the same age group, a gap considerably wider than that observed among younger cohorts. This pattern is consistent with segmented labor market dynamics: older women in Indonesia are disproportionately concentrated in informal and agricultural work, where digital adoption is structurally low to begin with, and they are simultaneously more likely to face compounding barriers of lower educational attainment and limited prior exposure to digital tools in earlier stages of their working lives. The intersection of age and gender disadvantage suggests that policy responses designed around age alone, without an explicit gender lens, risk leaving the most digitally excluded subgroup, older women in informal employment, inadequately served.

Figure 5. Proportion of the workforce using digital tools, according to sector and age group.

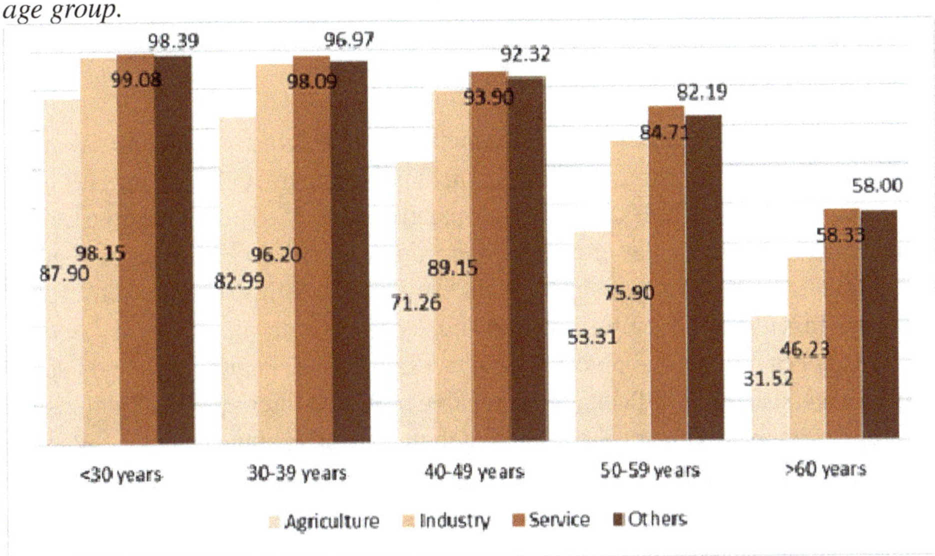

Across all age groups, the agricultural sector has the lowest rate of digital tool use. Among workers aged 60 and over, only 31.52% use digital tools. Therefore, the government should prioritize enhancing the use of digital devices, particularly in traditional sectors such as agriculture. Digital tools, including mobile applications and web platforms, have revolutionized agricultural extension services in Indonesia by facilitating the efficient dissemination of critical information on agricultural techniques, market prices, and weather forecasts. This access is essential for farmers seeking to optimize their operations (Singh et al., 2023). Research indicates a positive correlation between the use of tailored digital extension services and improved input efficiency, demonstrating that integrating digital technologies into agricultural practices significantly boosts productivity and empowers farmers (Singh et al., 2023; Rasyid & Mumpuni Ningsih , 2024). The growing use of precision agriculture technologies, which rely on data-driven methods for farm management, indicates a rising recognition of the advantages of digitalization in the agricultural sector (Herdiansyah et al., 2023).

The COVID-19 pandemic has further underscored the importance of digital tools in sustaining agricultural productivity and ensuring food security. Farmers, especially those who are economically disadvantaged and classified as *dhuafa*, have faced challenges in adapting to the changing environment, underscoring the necessity for targeted support to improve their digital skills (Widiastuti et al., 2022). Furthermore, digital financial inclusion plays a crucial role, enabling farmers to access credit and financial services, thereby empowering them to invest in digital technologies and enhance their agricultural practices (An et al., 2023).

Spatial distribution of digital competence

Almost all regions of Indonesia have internet connectivity and digitalisation, as shown in Figure 6. In western Indonesia, including Sumatra and Java, internet coverage ranges from 90% to 100%. The same pattern is observed in Bali and the Lesser Sunda Islands. Certain areas of Kalimantan, particularly West Kalimantan, Central Kalimantan, and North Kalimantan, exhibit suboptimal infrastructure. Conversely, South Kalimantan and East Kalimantan already display strong conditions. In central and eastern Indonesia, only a few provinces, including Papua, Highland Papua, Central Papua, and South Papua, have relatively limited internet and digitalization coverage, with approximately 70%–80% of their territories connected. On Sulawesi Island, only West Sulawesi shows relatively low coverage. These findings suggest that, in terms of infrastructure, Indonesia is prepared to embrace digitalization through internet and mobile access.

Figure 6. Percentage of internet coverage by province

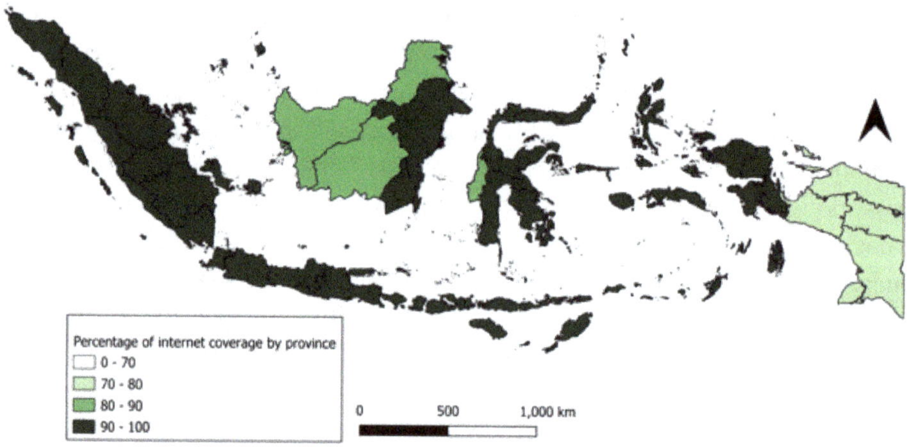

Figure 6 shows that most Indonesian provinces have a workforce whose education level is elementary school or lower. In Sumatra, provinces including Jambi, South Sumatra, Bengkulu, Lampung, and the Bangka Belitung Islands belong to this group. Similarly, in Kalimantan, West Kalimantan, South Kalimantan, Central Kalimantan, and North Kalimantan exhibit the same pattern. In Java, nearly all provinces also have most workers with elementary-level education or less, except Banten Province and the Special Region of Yogyakarta.

In central and eastern Indonesia, only Bali Province, North Sulawesi, and Maluku have most workers with high school level education or higher. Thus, overall, the Indonesian workforce remains dominated by individuals with low educational attainment. Even in Java, which has comparatively better educational facilities, this outcome does not match the number of graduates from formal secondary education and beyond. An intriguing question is why regions such as Aceh, North Sumatra, Riau, and West Sumatra have a higher share of workers with high school-level education or above. In North Sumatra and West Sumatra, for example, local communities consider education the top investment priority over other types of investment. They believe that a family's success is measured not only by wealth or assets but also by the educational attainment of its members.

Figure 7. Major education levels by province

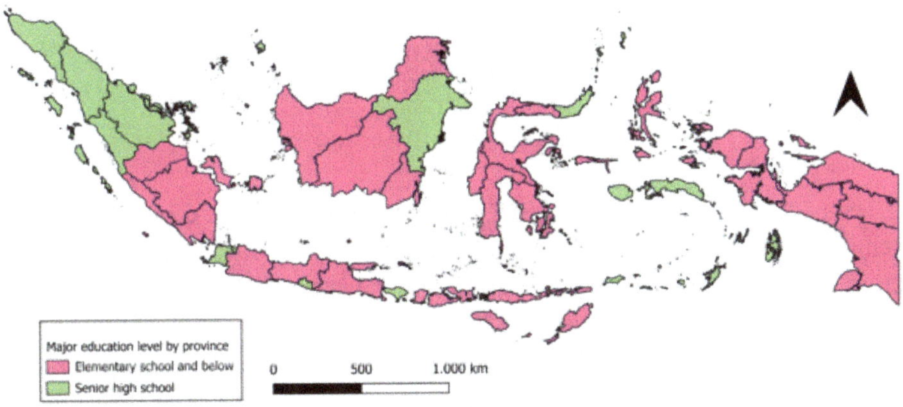

In the Java region, particularly in Yogyakarta, a long-established educational hub, the proportion of educational facilities from primary to tertiary levels relative to the workforce is one of the highest in the country. Jakarta, the national economic hub and a magnet for job seekers with higher-education credentials, shows a comparable pattern. Consequently, Jakarta and Yogyakarta are the only Indonesian regions in which most workers possess at least a high school diploma, whereas other Java provinces are dominated by employees with primary education or less. This advantage stems from the concentration of high-quality schools, the presence of jobs that demand mid-to-high level skills, and the influx of educated labor from across the country. This pattern is reflected in the employment sectors of these areas. Jakarta and Yogyakarta, with the largest share of higher-educated workers, exhibit a labor market dominated by trade and service occupations. In contrast, regions outside Java continue to depend almost exclusively on agriculture as the primary source of income.

Figure 8. Key employment sectors across the province

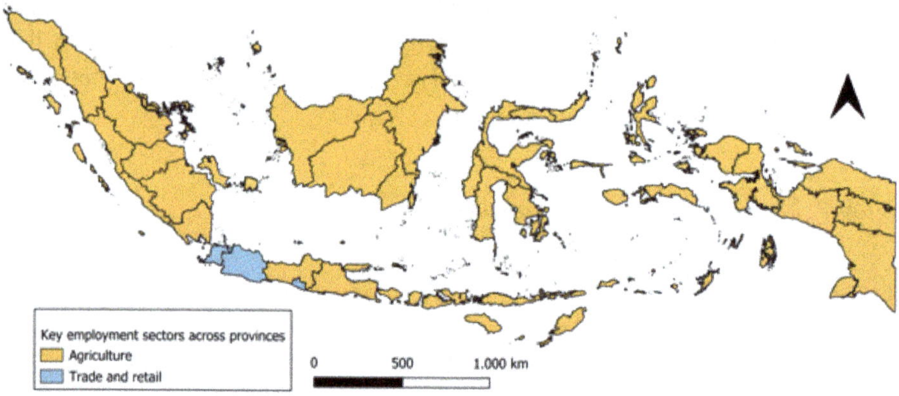

Today, digital usage is largely independent of the dominant economic sector in each region. In Indonesia, most digital-user workers are now spread fairly evenly across provinces that were once neglected. For instance, Riau, East Kalimantan, and North Kalimantan have become leading areas in terms of digital-technology users within the workforce. Earlier development and modernization efforts had concentrated on western Indonesia, particularly Java, but the current distribution is more evenly balanced. Indeed, nearly every Indonesian province reports that more than 70% of its workforce uses the internet. However, attention is still required in certain regions, as the overall number of digital users remains comparatively low in provinces such as Papua, North Maluku, Maluku, and NTT. Enhancing education and training for digital technology, particularly for the workforce, is expected to boost productivity.

Figure 9. Percentage of workforce with digital use, by province

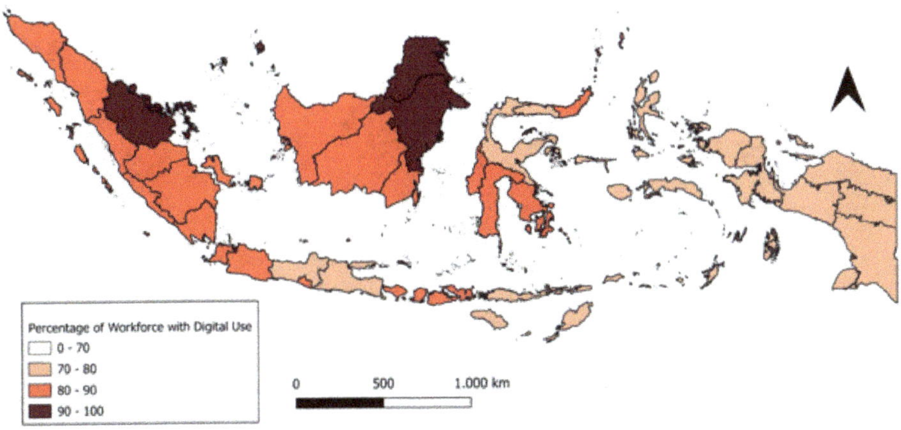

The age-group map of Indonesian provinces reveals clear demographic differences across the western, central, and eastern parts of the country. In North Sumatra, East Kalimantan, and most of Papua, most residents are under 30 years old. In contrast, Java, Bali, and South Sumatra are largely populated by people aged 30–39 years. Only a few provinces, such as small areas in Sulawesi and Nusa Tenggara, show a dominance of the 40-49 age group. The high concentration of people under 30 in Papua, East Kalimantan, and North Sumatra is due to relatively high birth rates and the attraction of cities that draw young migrants, particularly in sectors such as industry and natural resources, as seen in cities like Balikpapan, Samarinda, and Medan.

This situation indicates a potentially significant demographic dividend but also creates challenges in creating jobs and expanding higher-education opportunities. The predominance of the 30-39 age group in Java, Bali, and South Sumatra signals a demographic transition in which the population is at the peak of its productive age. This pattern is typical of regions with high urbanization, better access to health services, and more effective family-planning programs. The presence of most people aged 40-49 in some areas may reflect economic stagnation, out-migration of younger generations, and an aging population structure. The map suggests that Indonesia is experiencing an uneven demographic transition, requiring development policies that consider regional disparities.

Figure 10. Major age groups by province

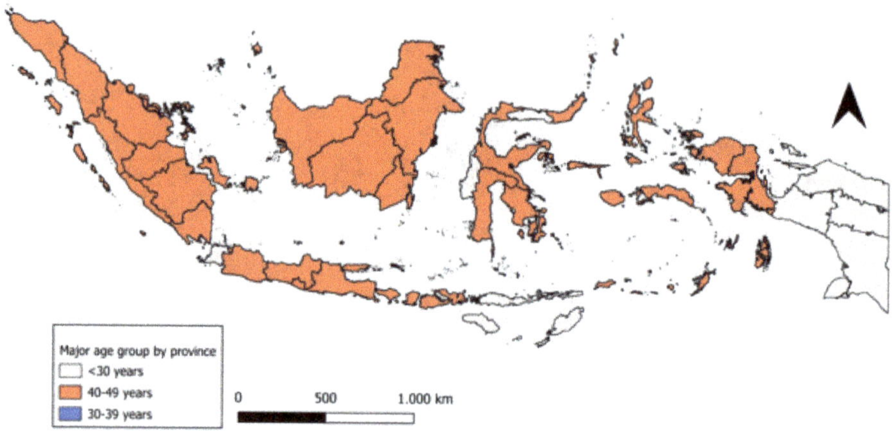

The percentage of workers using digital devices, whether computers, the internet, or mobile phones, reveal a pronounced digital divide across Indonesian provinces. Most provinces in Sumatra, Kalimantan, Sulawesi, and eastern Indonesia fall into the lowest category, with 0-70 percent of employees using digital tools. In contrast, the highest percentages, 90-100 percent, are concentrated in Java, particularly in the Special Capital Region of Jakarta, West Java, Banten, and the Special Region of Yogyakarta. Provinces such as Bali, Riau, and the Riau Islands occupy the middle range, 70-90 percent.

The concentration of digital usage in Java reflects disparities in digital infrastructure, internet access, and regional economic structures. Java hosts most offices, modern services, creative industries, and information technology firms, all of which demand digital tools for daily work. Outside Java, sectors dominated by agriculture, fishing, and mining generate lower demand for digital devices and consequently lower adoption rates. Overall, the map shows that digital adoption in the workplace remains highly uneven and is largely centered in western Indonesia, especially Java. This indicates a need for equitable development of digital infrastructure, sector-specific digital literacy training, and incentives for businesses outside Java to pursue digital transformation, so that productivity gaps between regions do not widen further.

Figure 11. Percentage of the working population with digital use

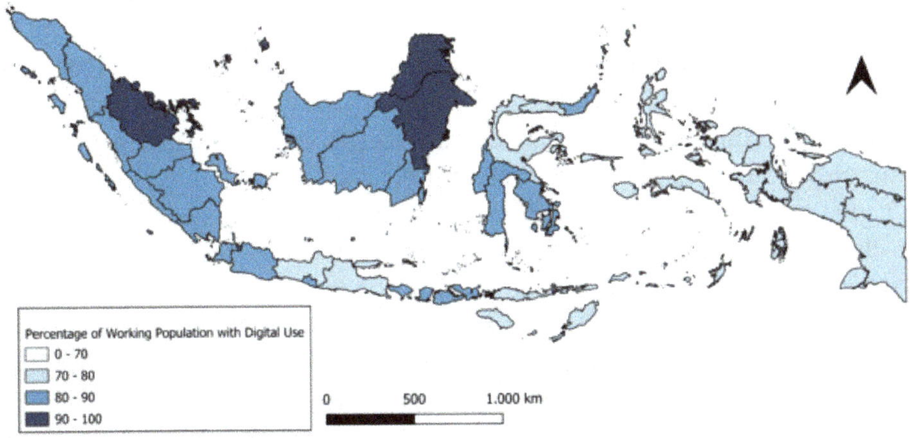

SOLUTIONS AND RECOMMENDATIONS

The increasing number of older workers in Indonesia, during the increasing use of digital technology in the industrial sector, poses challenges in improving workforce quality. Older workers have limited digital skills. The increasingly widespread use of digital technology demands that they master it. If they cannot keep pace with digital technology, older workers may be placed in positions that require limited digital use. Digital competency is increasingly vital across various sectors in Indonesia as the country navigates the complexities of the digital era. The public sector government must overcome significant hurdles to increase digital competence among civil servants, requiring upgrades to technology infrastructure, employee training, and a shift in workplace culture (Cahyarini & Ladiatno Samsara, 2021).

One sector that is lagging in using digital technology is the agricultural sector. As the sector with the lowest level of digital tool use, the agricultural sector needs to be prioritized in digital capability improvement programs. However, the digital transformation of agriculture in Indonesia faces several challenges that must be addressed to unlock its potential fully. Key obstacles include the need for enhanced digital infrastructure, improved digital literacy among farmers, and the establishment of supportive government policies (Beksultanova et al., 2023). The Indonesian government has taken steps to boost digital skills among agricultural producers, a vital factor in creating an environment that fosters digital innovation (Beksultanova et al., 2023; Rasyid & Kusumawaty, 2022). A major obstacle to smallholder farmers' access to information is the disparity in access to digital resources between urban and rural areas, where many still rely on basic technologies such as mobile phones and radios (Abdulai et al., 2023).

The telecommunications industry has also acknowledged the need for digital competencies, with companies identifying significant gaps in areas such as information management, communication, content creation, cybersecurity, and problem-solving (Aisyah & Susanty, 2017). For pre-service teachers, possessing digital competence is a vital requirement in the education sector, serving as a key indicator of literacy levels and having a profound impact on learning outcomes and teacher efficiency (Akbar et al., 2022). The digital transformation in the public sector has resulted in significant public service and policymaking process changes, and raises concerns over data protection and security (Hening & Ghozali Harda Kumara, 2019). These developments underscore the need for a comprehensive strategy to enhance digital competencies across sectors, ensuring that the workforce is well-equipped to meet the demands of an increasingly digital landscape.

This increase in competency capacity is balanced with equal digital access across regions. Furthermore, there must be a differentiated approach based on the age of the worker. Digital access capabilities for those under 40 are certainly different from those over 40. This is because the acceleration in competency development also differs with respect to digital. Furthermore, increasing digital access equitably across all regions will help workers and job seekers improve their competencies. On the other hand, companies must also be able to adapt to digital developments. Therefore, managers provide knowledge and technology transfer training to workers to improve their quality and contribute to the company (Bilanakos et al., 2018). If skills development does not align with the needs of the industrial world, workers will be marginalised by a capitalist system that demands productivity and adaptability to changing labour market conditions. Martin et al. (2016) propose that development encompasses both risks, including job losses, devaluation of skills, and enhanced employee monitoring, and opportunities, such as the increased significance of the human factor and improvements in manufacturing ergonomics. Therefore, adaptive digital technology skills capacity-building solutions are essential to address changes in the industrial ecosystem.

FUTURE RESEARCH DIRECTIONS

Based on the gaps and limitations identified in this manuscript, eight clusters of Future Research Directions can be developed as follows:

1. Longitudinal studies are the most methodologically urgent, as all findings in the manuscript represent a single-point-in-time snapshot. Without panel data, it is impossible to determine whether the digital competency gap among older workers is permanent or can be narrowed through targeted intervention.
2. The manuscript stops short of prescribing proven training approaches, instead only diagnosing the gap, with particular limitations in addressing the unique learning needs of older workers.
3. Gender Disparities in Digital Literacy Development warrant closer examination beyond the descriptive gap identified among older workers in this study: future research should investigate the mechanisms, such as differential access to training, intra-household time allocation, and occupational segregation that produce and sustain this disparity, and assess which interventions are effective in narrowing it.
4. Agriculture and the Informal Sector are highly relevant given that most of Indonesia's older workforce is concentrated precisely in these sectors, which simultaneously record the lowest levels of digital access nationwide.
5. Regional Anomalies is important for more nuanced policy understanding: why does East Java, despite its large economy, lag digitally? Why does South Sulawesi outperform other eastern provinces? These questions remain unanswered.
6. The study's methodology relies on established measurement principles, but the Susenas indicators used are severely limited, thereby restricting the analytical scope and preventing an accurate representation of the true digital competency landscape.
7. The manuscript identifies digitally competent individuals, but it does not yet examine the impact of this competence on wages, job opportunities, and overall well-being for older workers.
8. AI-Driven Workforce Transformation, Employer-Initiated Training, and Cross-Country Comparison represent a final cluster of open questions: how generative AI and automation will reshape the digital-skill demands facing older workers, whether employer-led training programs can close the gaps identified in this study more effectively than government-led initiatives, and how Indonesia's aging-workforce digital divide compares with patterns observed in other newly industrializing economies facing similar demographic transitions.

CONCLUSIONS

An aging workforce in the digital era of technology has implications for the world of work. Older generations tend to exhibit lower levels of digital competence, a phenomenon likely attributable to the rapid pace of technological advancements that challenge them to keep up. Additionally, the rural-urban divide intensifies these inequalities, as rural areas, often associated with underdevelopment, experience lower levels of digital device access and digital competencies. The trend is also apparent in disparities between employment sectors, with traditional sectors such as agriculture having less digital access than industrial sectors, government services, and those working in information and communication technology.

The study underscores that the quality of infrastructure, age, and employment sector influence digital competencies. For Indonesian policymakers, the priority should be to ensure equitable digital access for all segments of society, regardless of location, age, or educational level. Such access is a critical starting point for leveraging digital technologies to improve social and economic outcomes. Enhancing human capital through a multifaceted approach that integrates digital skills into education systems, provides targeted professional development for educators, and creates supportive institutional environments is essential for fostering widespread digital competence.

Institutional support plays a pivotal role in cultivating digital competence. Educational institutions must foster environments that build self-efficacy and promote positive attitudes toward digital tools. Strategic initiatives for developing digital competencies are equally crucial. Gulyak (2024) emphasizes the need for supplementary educational programs that focus on enhancing teachers' digital skills, which in turn lead to broader applications in teaching practices. Quttainah (2024) emphasizes that management education should incorporate digital competency-building strategies to improve employee performance and drive innovation. Similarly, Mihus (2023) advocates systematic evaluations of digital competencies within organizations to inform human resource strategies.

Increasing access to and knowledge of digital technology requires consideration of the population's age spectrum. The approaches used will certainly differ, as older adults, especially those from the baby boomer generation, tend to be less familiar with digital technology than younger age groups. In contrast, younger demographics, particularly Generation Z, were raised in environments where digital technology was prevalent. As a result, they generally demonstrate greater familiarity and adaptability to emerging technologies. However, some members of this younger generation also experience negative consequences from technology due to unwise use.

The younger generation, particularly those aged 15-29, exhibits a higher inclination to use digital technology, with 96.60 percent of users in this age group, in contrast to the lowest proportion of users found among older individuals at 43.23 percent. Therefore, in developing digital competency, age considerations are crucial. For older people, the approach must be tailored to their work needs. For older workers, the demands are at least less severe than for younger workers. This is because competition for young people in this productive age group presents greater challenges. Besides age, another factor to consider is the business sector.

Based on the primary sector, the service sector has the highest use of digital devices. Digital competence in Indonesia's service sector is increasingly viewed as a vital factor for enhancing productivity, sustainability, and resilience in the face of challenges such as market volatility and technological advancements. Digital technology is revolutionizing industrial practices by equipping workers with access to critical information and resources, thereby improving decision-making processes and operational efficiency. Improving the competence of workers, including older workers, poses several challenges. Indonesia is still undergoing an uneven demographic transition, necessitating adjustments to development policies to account for regional disparities. Second, the uneven distribution of digital infrastructure. To prevent the productivity gap between regions from growing, equitable digital infrastructure development, sector-specific digital literacy training, and incentives for businesses outside Java to undertake digital transformation are required.

REFERENCES

Abdulai, A., Quarshie, P., Duncan, E., & Fraser, E. (2023). Is agricultural digitization a reality among smallholder farmers in Africa? Unpacking farmers' lived realities of engagement with digital tools and services in rural northern Ghana. *Agriculture & Food Security, 12*(1), 11. Advance online publication. DOI: 10.1186/s40066-023-00416-6

Aisyah, S.N., A. Susanty. (2017). Measurement Gap of Competency in Preparing Employees for a Digital Company (A Case Study of a Telecommunication Company in Indonesia)

Akbar, Hengky M., Biyanto. (2022). Role of Digital Competence for Pre-Service Teachers in Higher Education in Indonesia. *AL-ISHLAH: Jurnal Pendidikan*

An, C., He, X., & Zhang, L. (2023). The coordinated impacts of agricultural insurance and digital financial inclusion on agricultural output: Evidence from China. *Heliyon, 9*(2), e13546. DOI: 10.1016/j.heliyon.2023.e13546 PMID: 36846666

Ariyanti, S. (2013). Study of digital divide measurement in Indonesia. Puslitbang Resources and Devices Post and Informatics, 281–292.

Audrin, B., Audrin, C., & Salamin, X. (2024). Digital skills at work - Conceptual development and empirical validation of a measurement scale. *Technological Forecasting and Social Change, 202*(February), 123279. DOI: 10.1016/j.techfore.2024.123279

Beksultanova, A., Dzhankhotova, P., & Shardan, S. (2023). Problems of digital transformation in agriculture and instruments of state support. *IOP Conference Series. Earth and Environmental Science, 1154*(1), 012061. DOI: 10.1088/1755-1315/1154/1/012061

Bilanakos, C., Heywood, J. S., Sessions, J., & Theodoropoulos, N. (2018). Does demand for product quality increase worker training? *Journal of Economic Behavior & Organization, 155*, 159–177. DOI: 10.1016/j.jebo.2018.08.018

Binus. (2022). https://onlinelearning.binus.ac.id/2021/12/06/begini-perbedaan-generasibaby-boomers-x-y-z-dan-alpha/ (accessed May 12, 2022)

BPS. (2020). Indonesia [Population Census Results, BPS Jakarta, Indonesia]. *Population Projections*, 2020–2050.

BPS. (2024). Average monthly per capita expenditure by commodity group and region of residence the (rupiah), 2023-Statistical Tables-Centraleau of Statistics of Indonesia (bps.go.id)

Cahyarini, B. R., Ladiatno Samsara. (2021). The Challenges of Digital Competency Implementation Towards World-Class Bureaucracy. *Jurnal Borneo Administrator*

Castillo de Mesa, J., Gómez-Jacinto, L., López Peláez, A., & Erro-Garcés, A. (2020). Social networking sites and youth transition: The use of Facebook and personal well-being of social work young graduates. *Frontiers in Psychology*, *11*, 230. DOI: 10.3389/fpsyg.2020.00230 PMID: 32132959

Conde-Jiménez, J. (2018). Digital competence as an indicator of the impact of ICT educational policies: Validation of a theoretical model using PLS. *Research on Education and Media*, *10*(2), 37–44. DOI: 10.1515/rem-2018-0013

Erumban, A. A. (2024). Informality and aggregate labor productivity growth: Does ICT Moderate the Relationship? *Telecommunications Policy*, *48*(1), 102681. DOI: 10.1016/j.telpol.2023.102681

Gulyak, I. (2024). Strategy of designing additional educational programs in the field of teachers' digital competencies of the higher agricultural education. Bio Web of Conferences, 84, 01009. DOI: 10.1051/bioconf/20248401009

Hening, P. & Ghozali Harda Kumara. (2019). Public Sector Transformation in the Digital Age: Obstacles and Challenges for Governance Indonesia. *IAPA Proceedings Conference*

Herdiansyah, H., Antriyandarti, E., Rosyada, A., Arista, N., Soesilo, T., & Ernawati, N. (2023). Evaluation of conventional and mechanization methods towards precision agriculture in Indonesia. *Sustainability (Basel)*, *15*(12), 9592. DOI: 10.3390/su15129592

Kaifi, B. A., Nafei, W. A., Khanfar, N., & Kaifi, M. M. (2012). A Multi-Generational Workforce: Managing and Understanding Millennials. *International Journal of Business and Management*, *7*(24), 2012. DOI: 10.5539/ijbm.v7n24p88

Krzywdzinski, Martin, Ulrich Jürgens, and Sabine Pfeiffer. 2016. The Fourth Revolution: The Transformation of Manufacturing Work in the Age of Digitalization. WZB Report 2016. Diunduh 10 Oktober 2018. file:///C:/Users/S/Downloads/2016industrie40.pdf

Mihus, I. (2023). Strategic management of human resources of enterprises based on digital competencies. *Scientific Notes of the University*, (2), 131–138. DOI: 10.31732/2663-2209-2022-70-131-138

Ngadi, N., Zaelany, A. A., Latifa, A., Harfina, D., Asiati, D., Setiawan, B., Ibnu, F., Triyono, T., & Rajagukguk, Z. (2023). Challenge of Agriculture Development in Indonesia: Rural Youth Mobility and Aging Workers in Agriculture Sector. *Sustainability (Basel), 15*(2), 922. DOI: 10.3390/su15020922

Oberländer, M., Beinicke, A., & Bipp, T. (2020). Digital competencies: A review of the literature and applications in the workplace. *Computers and Education, 146* (September 2019). https://doi.org/DOI: 10.1016/j.compedu.2019.103752

Rasyid, H., & Mumpuni Ningsih, G. (2024). The role of digital technology in the transformation of agriculture toward smart farming. *Journal of Wood Science, 3*(1), 1–7. DOI: 10.58344/jws.v3i1.523

Rasyid, T., & Kusumawaty, Y. (2022). Omnibus law and the challenges of the Indonesian agricultural sector: An Islamic perspective. *Jurnal Kajian Peradaban Islam, 5*(1), 49–61. DOI: 10.47076/jkpis.v5i1.119

Schroeder, T., Dodds, L., Georgiou, A., Gewald, H., & Siette, J. (2023). Older Adults and New Technology: Mapping Review of the Factors Associated With Older Adults'. *Intention to Adopt Digital Technologies JMIR Aging, 6*, e44564. PMID: 37191976

Singh, N., Sunitha, N. H., Tripathi, G., Saikanth, D. R. K., Sharma, A., Jose, A. E., & Mary, M. V. K. J. (2023). Impact of digital technologies in agricultural extension. *Asian Journal of Agricultural Extension Economics & Sociology, 41*(9), 963–970. DOI: 10.9734/ajaees/2023/v41i92127

Tayo, O., Thompson, R., & Thompson, E. (2016). Impact of the digital divide on computer use and internet access on the poor in Nigeria. *Journal of Education and Learning, 5*(1), 1–6. DOI: 10.5539/jel.v5n1p1

Tempo. (2023). From Boomers to Generation Z, How Long Have Indonesians Been on the Internet? - Techno Tempo. co

Tishman, F. M., Van Looy, S., & Bruyère, S. M. (2012). Employer Strategies for Responding to an Aging Workforce (pp. 1–39, Rep. New Brunswick, NJ: NTAR Leadership Center.

Van Laar, E., van Deursen, A. J. A. M., van Dijk, J. A. G. M., & de Haan, J. (2018). 21st-century digital skills instrument aimed at working professionals: Conceptual development and empirical validation. *Telematics and Informatics, 35*(8), 2184–2200. DOI: 10.1016/j.tele.2018.08.006

Vaportzis, E., Giatsi Clausen, M., & Gow, A. J. (2017). *Older Adults' Perceptions of Technology and Barriers to Interacting with Tablet Computers: A Focus Group Study. Qingchuan Li and Yan Luximon. (2016). Older Adults and Digital Technology: A study of user perception and usage behavior*. Springer International Publishing Switzerland.

Widiastuti, T., Sukmaningrum, P., Rani, L., Mustofa, M., & Ardiani, N. (2022). Economic empowerment of dhuafa families through digital business and financial management based on maqashid sharia in Tambakrigadung, Lamongan. *Jurnal Pengabdian Kepada Masyarakat*, *8*(3), 155. DOI: 10.22146/jpkm.67976

Yazdani-Darki, M., Rahemi, Z., Adib-Hajbaghery, M., & Izadi-Avanji, F. S. (2020). A qualitative study of older adults' barriers to using technology in daily life. *Nursing and Midwifery Studies*, *9*, 229–236.

Chapter 14

Adapting Cross-Training Programs to Changing Labor Market Conditions

Ashish Gupta
http://orcid.org/0009-0002-4460-6605
Institute of Technology and Management, Gwalior, India

Saidjon Islamov
Kimyo International University in Tashkent, Uzbekistan

Jumanov Azizbek
Tashkent State University of Economics, Uzbekistan

Buriboev Tolibjon
Alfraganus University, Tashkent, Uzbekistan

Ilyos Khursandov
Termez University of Economics and Service, Uzbekistan

Saidov Xayotjon
Denov Institute of Entrepreneurship and Pedagogy, Uzbekistan

Aripov Aziz
http://orcid.org/0009-0002-5153-534X
Kimyo International University in Tashkent, Uzbekistan

Phearak Pok
http://orcid.org/0009-0008-9159-521X
Royal University of Law and Economics (RULE), Cambodia

Sopheak Kong
Royal University of Law and Economics (RULE), Cambodia

Kimleng Hing
http://orcid.org/0009-0007-2697-3475
Royal University of Law and Economics (RULE), Cambodia

ABSTRACT

The volatility of contemporary labor markets—shaped by the Great Resignation, technological disruption, and persistent skill shortages—requires organizations to

DOI: 10.4018/979-8-3373-5327-2.ch014

ght © 2027, IGI Global Scientific Publishing. Copying or distributing in print or electronic forms without written permission of IGI Global Scientific Publishing is prohibited. Use of this chapter to n generative artificial intelligence (AI) technologies is expressly prohibited. The publisher reserves all rights to license its use for generative AI training and machine learning model development.

reconfigure how they develop and deploy human capital. Cross-training programs, historically used for operational continuity, must evolve into strategic instruments addressing workforce agility, knowledge retention, and career development. This chapter examines how effective cross-training adaptation requires integrating labor market diagnostics, evidence-based training transfer mechanisms, and manager-coaching infrastructure. Drawing on empirical research across petrochemical, automotive, retail, and public sectors, the chapter develops a framework for adaptive cross-training design and outlines implications for human resource practitioners. Organizations aligning cross-training with labor market signals are better positioned to sustain competitive advantage.

1. INTRODUCTION

The years following 2020 have fundamentally altered the landscape of workforce management. Organizations across industries have confronted labor shortages of historic proportions, characterized by what economists have termed the Great Resignation—a phenomenon denoting the mass voluntary departure of workers seeking improved conditions, compensation, and meaning in their professional lives (Amanor-Boadu, 2022; Gittleman, 2022). The consequences of this upheaval have been compounded by accelerating technological change, including the widespread integration of artificial intelligence, automation, and advanced manufacturing platforms that collectively redefine the skill profiles required for productive employment (Li, 2022; Morandini et al., 2023).

Within this turbulent context, cross-training programs—defined broadly as structured efforts to develop employee competencies across multiple roles, functions, or tasks—have attracted renewed attention as a potential strategic response. Traditionally positioned as operational tools for achieving flexibility and continuity coverage, cross-training initiatives are increasingly recognized as mechanisms through which organizations can simultaneously address workforce agility, knowledge transfer, and employee career development (Rizan et al., 2025; Hanu et al., 2023). However, the evidence base suggests that many cross-training programs remain anchored to designs that were conceived under more stable labor market conditions and have not been systematically adapted to contemporary realities (Alizadeh Majd et al., 2024).

This chapter addresses that gap. It argues that effective cross-training under current labor market conditions requires not merely program expansion but a fundamental reconceptualization of how training is designed, delivered, supported, and evaluated. Three interrelated arguments structure the analysis. First, labor market diagnostics must be integrated into the front-end design of cross-training programs rather than treated as contextual background. Second, the quality of training transfer—the degree to which learning from cross-training situations is applied in practice—is a critical and frequently underestimated mediating variable between program investment and organizational outcomes. Third, the role of managers as active architects of learning ecosystems rather than passive program administrators is decisive in determining whether cross-training investment yields sustainable returns.

The escalating cost and complexity of contemporary talent management further underscore the urgency of cross-training redesign. Ma et al. (2024) provide macroeconomic evidence that on-the-job training constitutes a significant and underappreciated component of human capital development in market economies, with returns distributed across both individual earnings trajectories and firm-level productivity. Their findings situate cross-training within a broader human capital investment framework, legitimizing the argument that organizations should apply rigorous investment logic—including attention to design quality, transfer conditions, and outcome measurement—to their cross-training portfolios rather than treating them as low-stakes operational programs.

The chapter proceeds as follows. Section 2 situates the discussion within the contemporary labor market context. Section 3 examines the theoretical foundations of cross-training and its mechanisms of effect. Section 4 presents an adaptive framework for cross-training design. Section 5 addresses training transfer and the social infrastructure that enables it. Section 6 considers measurement and evaluation imperatives. Section 7 offers practical implications for human resource professionals. Section 8 concludes with a reflection on future directions.

2. LABOR MARKET CONDITIONS AND THE IMPERATIVE FOR ADAPTIVE CROSS-TRAINING

2.1 The Great Resignation and Its Structural Implications

The Great Resignation, while often discussed in popular discourse as a transient behavioral phenomenon, reflects deeper structural shifts in the relationship between employees and organizations. Analyses published in the Monthly Labor Review establish that voluntary separation rates across the United States reached unprecedented levels between 2021 and 2023, with particularly severe impacts in healthcare, retail, hospitality, and manufacturing sectors (Amanor-Boadu, 2022; Gittleman, 2022). These departures have not simply created vacancies; they have generated knowledge gaps, disrupted institutional memory, and accelerated cycles of recruitment and replacement that impose significant direct and indirect costs.

From a workforce development perspective, the structural significance of these trends lies in the revelation that traditional approaches to talent retention—

compensation adjustments, benefit enhancements, and conventional career pathing—have demonstrated limited effectiveness in isolation. Employees departing in large numbers have frequently cited the absence of growth opportunities, lack of meaningful developmental experiences, and perceived career stagnation as primary motivators for exit (Wang & Hasan, 2024). This insight points directly toward cross-training programs as an underutilized lever: when designed with deliberate attention to employee career development and skill enrichment, cross-training initiatives may simultaneously address the supply-side problem of skill availability and the demand-side problem of employee disengagement.

Critically, the institutional knowledge lost through mass departures is not merely a quantitative reduction in staffing levels. The tacit knowledge embedded in experienced employees—operational heuristics, client relationship intelligence, process improvement insights—represents an accumulation of organizational learning that cannot be rapidly replicated through recruitment alone. Al-Zoubi et al. (2025) document the particular vulnerability of tacit knowledge to disruption during periods of high turnover, establishing that organizations without deliberate knowledge transfer mechanisms are disproportionately exposed to performance degradation when experienced employees depart. This vulnerability amplifies the strategic urgency of cross-training programs designed with explicit knowledge transfer objectives.

2.2 Technological Disruption and the Reskilling Mandate

Concurrent with demographic labor market disruptions, the accelerating integration of Industry 4.0 technologies has fundamentally redefined skill requirements across sectors. Li (2022) documents how automation, artificial intelligence, and digitization have created dual pressures: the obsolescence of existing technical competencies and the emergence of new skill demands that traditional recruitment pipelines struggle to fill. Morandini et al. (2023) extend this analysis to demonstrate that AI-driven work transformation is not confined to technical roles but permeates service, administrative, and management functions, broadening the scope of reskilling needs considerably.

The implications for cross-training design are significant. Programs historically designed around narrowly defined role competencies must now incorporate broader digital literacy components, adaptive problem-solving capacities, and cross-functional collaboration skills. Chong and Zainal (2024) provide empirical evidence that employee agility—encompassing the ability to rapidly acquire new competencies and apply them across shifting work contexts—mediates the relationship between individual capability development and job performance outcomes. This finding suggests that the strategic value of cross-training programs may extend beyond immediate skill acquisition to the cultivation of an underlying agility disposition that enhances long-term performance resilience.

Deming and Silliman (2024) further establish that human capital investment through structured on-the-job learning produces returns that are particularly pronounced in contexts of rapid technological change, precisely because such environments create continuous demand for competency adaptation. This economic evidence reinforces the strategic case for robust cross-training infrastructure as a form of organizational capability investment rather than merely a tactical operational response. The practical implication for program designers is that cross-training curricula must be treated as living documents subject to periodic revision rather than fixed templates insulated from market feedback.

2.3 Tight Labor Markets and the Retention Premium

The convergence of demographic shifts, technological disruption, and post-pandemic behavioral changes has produced labor markets characterized by persistent tightness across multiple sectors and geographies. In such environments, the cost of employee turnover escalates dramatically, both because replacement candidates are scarcer and because the knowledge embedded in departing employees is more difficult to reconstruct under compressed recruiting timelines (Letmathe & Schinner, 2022). Organizations that can retain existing talent while systematically expanding its capabilities gain a compounding advantage relative to competitors reliant on external recruitment cycles.

Cross-training programs contribute to this retention premium through multiple mechanisms. Zhu and Gao (2023) demonstrate that employees perceiving organizational career growth opportunities—of which cross-training participation is a primary indicator—exhibit stronger organizational commitment and lower voluntary separation intentions. Wang and Hasan (2024) extend this finding through a systematic literature review establishing that perceived career growth mediates the relationship between developmental practices and employee engagement. These findings establish an empirical basis for positioning cross-training not merely as an operational tool but as a strategic retention investment with measurable behavioral outcomes.

The protean career orientation of contemporary workers further amplifies the retention value of well-designed cross-training programs. Zhu and Gao (2023) document that employees with proactive, self-directed career orientations are particularly responsive to organizational cross-training opportunities, perceiving participation as evidence of organizational investment in their professional futures. This finding suggests that the communication and framing of cross-training programs—not only their substantive content—plays a decisive role in determining whether they generate retention benefits or are perceived as merely operational convenience measures.

2.4 Cross-Sector Evidence and Generalizability

While much of the foundational research on cross-training effects originates from manufacturing and industrial contexts, a growing body of evidence establishes the generalizability of adaptive cross-training principles across sectors. Ludviga and Kalvina (2023) demonstrate meaningful agility and engagement effects in public sector organizations. Hanu et al. (2023) document learning and agility outcomes in service industry contexts. Jackson et al. (2023) report health and productivity benefits in labor-intensive service settings. The cross-sector consistency of findings regarding the importance of mentoring, manager support, and structured reflection in cross-training programs provides confidence that the adaptive framework developed in this chapter has broad applicability, notwithstanding the need for context-sensitive program implementation.

3. THEORETICAL FOUNDATIONS OF CROSS-TRAINING IN DYNAMIC ENVIRONMENTS

3.1 Job Rotation as a Primary Cross-Training Mechanism

Job rotation constitutes one of the most extensively studied mechanisms of cross-training delivery. Alizadeh Majd et al. (2024) provide empirical evidence from the petrochemical industry demonstrating that job rotation programs improve employee performance when mediated through effective human resource strategy alignment and structured training support. Their finding that neither rotation nor training alone produces optimal outcomes—but that their interaction does—underscores the importance of treating cross-training as a systemic intervention rather than a standalone program.

Al-Zoubi et al. (2025) expand the conceptual scope of job rotation research by investigating its contribution to tacit knowledge transfer. Their findings indicate that job rotation, when combined with structured on-the-job training and mentoring relationships, creates conditions particularly favorable for the transmission of knowledge that resists formal codification—precisely the type of knowledge most at risk of organizational loss during periods of high turnover. This insight carries important practical implications: the design of job rotation sequences should be informed not only by skills mapping objectives but also by an explicit analysis of where critical tacit knowledge resides within the organization and which knowledge custodians are at highest flight risk.

Jackson et al. (2023) approach job rotation from an occupational health perspective, demonstrating that rotation programs designed with attention to physical and psychosocial work demands can yield improvements in employee well-being alongside productivity outcomes. This broadened conception of rotation benefits is particularly relevant in tight labor markets where employer branding and employee experience are competitive differentials in attraction and retention. The implication is that rotation scheduling and role sequencing decisions should incorporate ergonomic and psychosocial considerations alongside technical skill development objectives.

3.2 Kolb's Experiential Learning and Cross-Training Efficacy

Rizan et al. (2025) apply Kolb's experiential learning theory to the analysis of job rotation programs in organizational contexts, demonstrating that the concrete experience, reflective observation, abstract conceptualization, and active experimentation cycle provides a theoretically coherent explanation for why rotational cross-training yields learning outcomes that exceed those of more passive training modalities. The experiential framework suggests that cross-training programs must be designed to incorporate structured reflection opportunities—often absent in operationally driven rotation designs—if the full learning potential of role transitions is to be realized.

The experiential learning cycle has particular resonance in cross-training contexts because role transitions inherently generate dissonance between prior knowledge structures and the demands of new functional environments. This productive dissonance—when managed through adequate support structures—catalyzes the cognitive reorganization that produces transferable expertise rather than merely additive role-specific skill. Cross-training designers who attend to this dynamic will prioritize the quality and timeliness of reflection support as much as the technical content of rotation assignments (Rizan et al., 2025).

Decius et al. (2024) add an important dimension to this analysis by distinguishing between different forms of work-related learning and their differential effects on perceived employability. Their findings suggest that the reputational and career capital benefits of cross-training participation are strongest when the learning is perceived as intentional and developmental rather than merely operational, reinforcing the importance of framing and communication in cross-training program design. Organizations that position cross-training as a visible element of their employee value proposition—rather than an internal operational adjustment—are likely to realize stronger retention and engagement dividends from equivalent program investments.

3.3 Workforce Agility as a Strategic Cross-Training Outcome

The concept of workforce agility has emerged as a central organizing principle in contemporary talent management scholarship. Das et al. (2023) conceptualize workforce agility as comprising sensing, responding, and learning capabilities that enable organizations to reconfigure their human capital in response to environmental shifts. Gouda and Tiwari (2022, 2024) provide empirical evidence from the Indian automobile industry demonstrating that talent agility positively influences innovation adoption and sustainable business performance, while simultaneously identifying structural barriers—including inadequate cross-functional exposure and insufficient knowledge-sharing infrastructure—that impede agility development.

Hanu et al. (2023) specifically examine the relationship between work-based learning and employee agility, demonstrating that cross-functional learning experiences differentially affect agility, ambidexterity, and proactive goal generation. Their finding that not all forms of work-based learning yield equivalent agility outcomes suggests the need for careful design attention: cross-training programs must be structured to expose participants to genuine complexity, uncertainty, and problem-solving demands if agility cultivation is an intended outcome. Rotation designs that merely cycle employees through familiar tasks in unfamiliar settings will produce limited agility returns regardless of their duration or frequency.

Ludviga and Kalvina (2023) extend the organizational agility concept to the public sector, demonstrating that employee perceptions of strategic agility at the organizational level foster work engagement and well-being—outcomes that are themselves predictors of retention in tight labor markets. This cross-sector evidence reinforces the generalizability of agility-oriented cross-training logic beyond private sector manufacturing contexts. Reinhold (2024) further establishes that small and medium enterprises can systematically build agility through structured cross-training investments, providing an important corrective to assumptions that agility infrastructure is only viable at scale in large organizations.

3.4 Human Capital Theory and the Economics of Cross-Training Investment

Economic frameworks for understanding cross-training investments draw substantially on human capital theory, which distinguishes between general human capital (competencies valuable across multiple employers) and firm-specific human capital (competencies primarily valuable to the current employer). Ma et al. (2024) provide an integrative treatment of on-the-job training within macroeconomic models of labor market dynamics, demonstrating that firm-sponsored training generates returns for both the firm and the worker, with the distribution of returns depending on labor market competitiveness and the degree of skill portability. Their analysis suggests that in tight labor markets, firms face a fundamental tension between investing in training—which raises worker productivity and therefore retention—and creating general human capital that may enhance worker outside options and voluntary departure rates.

Deming and Silliman (2024) extend this analysis with labor market-level evidence demonstrating that skill investments calibrated to technological change trajectories yield the highest returns for both workers and employers. Their findings have direct implications for cross-training portfolio design: programs should deliberately balance general skill development (which enhances employee value in external labor markets and thus serves retention objectives) with firm-specific knowledge transfer (which creates mutual dependency that reduces attrition risk). The adaptive cross-training framework proposed in Section 4 attempts to operationalize this balance through a tripartite competency architecture.

4. AN ADAPTIVE FRAMEWORK FOR CROSS-TRAINING PROGRAM DESIGN

4.1 Environmental Scanning and Labor Market Intelligence

The first distinctive feature of adaptive cross-training design is its explicit integration of environmental scanning processes into the program development cycle. Traditional training needs assessments focus primarily on internal competency gaps derived from role analysis and performance data. Adaptive cross-training extends this diagnostic lens to encompass external labor market signals—including occupational demand forecasts, sector-specific skill shortages, wage trend data, and technological adoption trajectories—that inform both the content and sequencing of cross-training interventions.

This environmental intelligence function is particularly critical in tight labor markets because the opportunity cost of cross-training misalignment is magnified when replacement talent is scarce and expensive. An organization that invests in cross-training employees toward competency domains of declining labor market relevance compounds its human capital problem; conversely, organizations that align cross-training curricula with emerging skill demands position their employees as increasingly scarce assets whose retention becomes both more important and more achievable (Deming & Silliman, 2024; Li, 2022). Environmental scanning should therefore be institutionalized as a recurring input to program design review cycles rather than a one-time design-phase activity.

Figure 1. Cross-Training Program Adaptation Framework

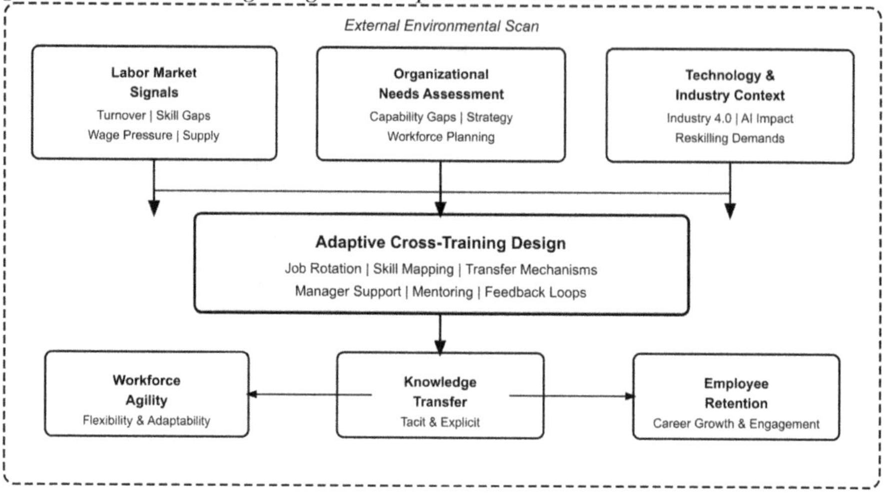

Figure 1 illustrate the depicts three environmental input streams — labor market signals (turnover rates, skill gaps, wage pressure), organizational needs assessment (capability gaps, workforce planning, strategic priorities), and technology and industry context (Industry 4.0 adoption, AI impact, reskilling demands) — that converge into an Adaptive Cross-Training Design layer encompassing job rotation, skill mapping, transfer mechanisms, manager support, mentoring, and feedback loops.

4.2 Skills Mapping and Competency Architecture

The second component of adaptive cross-training design involves the construction of dynamic competency architectures that specify not merely what skills employees need today but which skill clusters will generate the highest returns across a range of plausible future states. Letmathe and Schinner (2022) provide a formal model for workforce planning that integrates training investment decisions with demand volatility projections, demonstrating that flexible training designs—those capable of modulating intensity and focus in response to demand signals—outperform fixed curriculum designs across a wide range of market scenarios.

Skills mapping in adaptive cross-training contexts must distinguish between core competencies (foundational capabilities stable across role transitions), transferable competencies (skills that generate value across multiple functional contexts), and emerging competencies (capabilities relevant to anticipated technological or market developments). The architecture of a well-designed cross-training sequence should create deliberate exposure pathways across all three competency categories, with sequencing informed by both individual development trajectories and organizational capability gaps (Mababu Mukiur & Gomez Lega, 2025).

Mababu Mukiur and Gomez Lega (2025) offer particular theoretical guidance on this architecture by analyzing the mental processes through which technical and non-technical skills transfer across workplace contexts. Their framework identifies cognitive schemas, procedural knowledge structures, and metacognitive monitoring capacities as the primary mechanisms mediating skill transfer effectiveness, with important implications for how cross-training content should be organized to maximize schema activation and procedural generalization. Cross-training designers who apply this framework will sequence rotation assignments to build on existing cognitive structures rather than overwhelming participants with contextually alien competency demands.

4.3 Mentoring and Social Learning Infrastructure

The third structural component of adaptive cross-training design concerns the social learning infrastructure through which competency development is supported. Al-Zoubi et al. (2025) establish that mentoring relationships serve as critical conduits for tacit knowledge transfer in job rotation contexts, effectively converting individual cross-training experiences into organizational knowledge assets. The design of mentoring relationships within cross-training programs must therefore be treated as a core program element rather than an optional supplement.

Mehner et al. (2024) provide mixed-method evidence that social support—encompassing peer networks, supervisory coaching, and formal mentoring—constitutes the primary determinant of whether learning achieved during cross-training is transferred to practice. Their finding that knowledge sharing within social learning networks amplifies transfer effectiveness suggests that cross-training program designs should actively cultivate peer learning structures, including communities of practice, cross-functional project assignments, and structured after-action reflection forums. These structures do not arise organically from rotation program participation alone; they require deliberate architectural investment and managerial facilitation.

Kahl et al. (2023) contribute a complementary perspective by demonstrating that the degree of autonomy granted to organizational units mediates the relationship between learning investments and agility outcomes. Programs that combine cross-training exposure with meaningful empowerment to apply new skills in consequential contexts yield substantially stronger agility development than those that restrict transferred competencies to narrowly defined application windows. This finding has direct implications for the design of post-rotation job contexts as well as the rotation experience itself: the value of cross-training is contingently dependent on the degree to which organizational structures allow transferred competencies to be exercised with meaningful responsibility.

The infrastructure for social learning must extend beyond formal mentoring dyads to encompass broader knowledge-sharing ecosystems. Berg et al. (2023) provide a systemic framework for connecting personnel development activities with organizational development objectives through impact models that specify the causal pathways linking training investments to collective capability shifts. Applied to cross-training, this framework suggests that program designers should explicitly map the knowledge-sharing pathways through which individual rotation learning is expected to diffuse across the organization, and design program structures—including knowledge documentation practices, cross-functional communities, and mentoring networks—to facilitate that diffusion.

4.4 Program Sequencing and Rotation Design Principles

Effective adaptive cross-training programs require deliberate attention to the sequencing and duration of rotation assignments, which are among the most consequential and least theorized design variables in the cross-training literature. Al-Zoubi et al. (2025) find that the effectiveness of job rotation for tacit knowledge transfer is significantly conditioned by the duration of rotation assignments: rotations too brief to allow meaningful immersion in the target function generate surface-level exposure rather than substantive competency development, while rotations of excessive duration may reduce the breadth of cross-functional exposure that is the primary strategic rationale for rotation programs.

Alizadeh Majd et al. (2024) document that the sequencing of rotation assignments relative to formal training interventions is a critical determinant of outcome effectiveness. Rotation experiences that follow relevant formal training—allowing participants to apply newly acquired conceptual knowledge in contextually authentic settings—consistently outperform rotations conducted without prior grounding in the target competency domain. This finding suggests an optimal sequencing logic: formal knowledge acquisition, followed by supervised rotation with active mentoring, followed by autonomous application with structured reflection support. This three-phase sequencing operationalizes the Kolbian experiential learning cycle in practical rotation program architecture.

5. TRAINING TRANSFER: THE CRITICAL MEDIATING VARIABLE

5.1 The Transfer Problem in Cross-Training Contexts

Despite decades of research and organizational investment in training, the transfer of learning from structured training environments to actual work performance remains stubbornly incomplete. Meta-analytic evidence consistently suggests that a substantial proportion of training investment fails to translate into sustained behavioral change in work contexts (Blume et al., 2024). This transfer problem is particularly acute in cross-training programs because the knowledge and skills targeted are often complex, tacit, and context-sensitive—characteristics that resist straightforward encoding and retrieval.

Ardondi et al. (2025) conduct a systematic scoping review of evaluation tools for workplace training transfer in adult learning contexts, finding significant heterogeneity in how transfer is conceptualized and measured across organizational settings. Their synthesis highlights the need for multi-level evaluation frameworks that capture not only immediate behavioral indicators of transfer but also longer-term performance and organizational impact dimensions. The absence of robust transfer evaluation practices represents a significant blind spot in many cross-training programs: organizations cannot improve what they cannot reliably measure.

Shukla and Kumar (2024) extend the transfer analysis to online training formats, developing a taxonomic framework that identifies individual, program design, and organizational climate factors as the primary antecedents of transfer effectiveness. Their taxonomy has direct applicability to blended and digital cross-training modalities that have proliferated following the COVID-19 pandemic. The implication is that organizations designing hybrid cross-training programs must attend systematically to each factor category rather than assuming that content quality alone will drive transfer. Individual readiness for transfer—including motivation, self-efficacy, and cognitive load capacity—is as consequential as program design quality in determining transfer outcomes.

Figure 2. Training Transfer Ecosystem in Tight Labor Markets

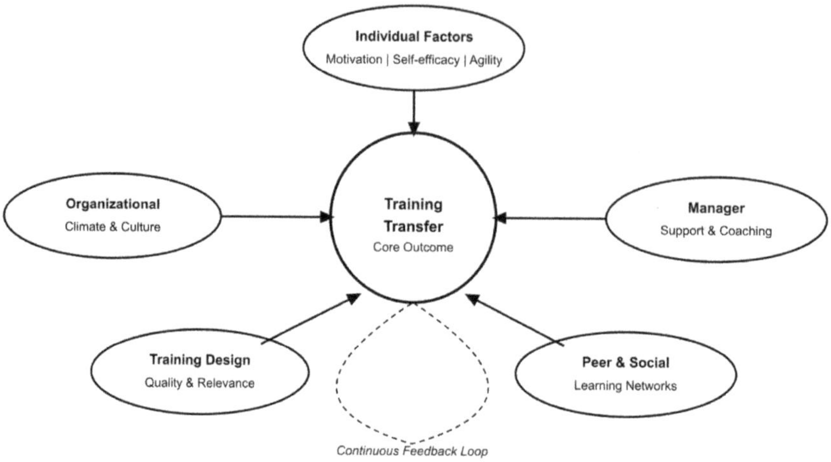

Figure 2 illustrate the ecosystem model depicts five convergent factor domains determining training transfer effectiveness: (1) Individual Factors (2) Organizational Climate and Culture (3) Manager Support and Coaching (4) Training Design Quality and Relevance (5) Peer and Social Learning Networks

5.2 Manager Support as the Critical Enabler

Across multiple empirical studies, manager support consistently emerges as the single most powerful organizational moderator of training transfer outcomes. Blume et al. (2024) demonstrate that manager support in informal learning contexts links learning activity to performance outcomes through reinforcement, opportunity provision, and accountability mechanisms. Their finding that manager behaviors in the post-training period are more predictive of transfer than training design characteristics challenges conventional wisdom that locates transfer primarily as a function of program quality.

Mehner et al. (2024) provide complementary evidence from a mixed-method study demonstrating that manager-facilitated knowledge sharing amplifies the transfer impact of formal training, creating a social multiplier effect whereby individual cross-training experiences generate collective competency gains. This finding suggests a reframing of the manager's role in cross-training programs: rather than functioning primarily as an approver of employee participation and an assessor of post-training performance, the manager must be actively engaged as an architect of the learning ecosystem that surrounds and extends the formal training experience.

Berg et al. (2023) provide a theoretical framework for integrating personnel development with organizational development through impact models that clarify the causal pathways through which training investments generate organizational outcomes. Their framework, applied to cross-training contexts, illuminates how manager behaviors function as critical linkage mechanisms between individual learning activities and collective organizational capability shifts. Managers who are themselves participants in cross-training design and evaluation processes—rather than passive recipients of HR-designed programs—demonstrate substantially stronger transfer facilitation behaviors than those positioned as external stakeholders.

5.3 Informal Learning and Transfer Complementarities

A growing body of evidence establishes that informal learning—unstructured, experience-driven learning that occurs in the flow of work—complements and amplifies the transfer of formal cross-training investments. Blume et al. (2024) demonstrate that informal learning activities and formal training programs function as substitutes in some contexts and complements in others, with the substitution or complementarity relationship determined primarily by the degree of manager support available. In high-support environments, informal and formal learning reinforce one another; in low-support environments, informal learning may partially compensate for transfer failures from formal programs.

Decius et al. (2024) extend this analysis by demonstrating that different types of work-related learning generate distinct employability perceptions, with formal cross-training producing stronger external employability signals and informal learning generating stronger internal employability benefits. This distinction is practically important because it suggests that adaptive cross-training programs should be designed to produce both formal certification of competency acquisition and informal learning opportunities that build contextually embedded expertise. A portfolio approach combining formal rotation assignments with structured informal learning activities—including job shadowing, cross-functional project participation, and peer knowledge-exchange sessions—is likely to maximize both transfer effectiveness and employee value perception.

The complementarity of informal and formal learning has particular relevance for small and medium enterprises operating with constrained training budgets. Reinhold (2024) establishes that SME workforce agility can be meaningfully developed through informal cross-training mechanisms even in the absence of elaborate formal rotation programs, provided that managerial support for informal skill application and knowledge sharing is deliberately cultivated. This finding democratizes the adaptive cross-training logic by demonstrating that its core principles can be operationalized with resource-proportionate investment across organizational sizes.

6. MEASUREMENT, EVALUATION, AND CONTINUOUS IMPROVEMENT

6.1 Multi-Level Evaluation Frameworks

The evaluation of cross-training programs in contemporary labor market contexts requires moving beyond the conventional Kirkpatrick four-level model toward frameworks capable of capturing the complex, time-distributed, and socially mediated nature of cross-training outcomes. Ardondi et al. (2025) identify a critical gap in the current evaluation toolkit: most instruments assess either immediate reaction and learning outcomes or long-term behavioral change, but few provide reliable measurement of the intermediate transfer mechanisms through which learning moves from training contexts to performance contexts.

An adaptive cross-training evaluation framework must therefore encompass at minimum four measurement dimensions: (1) learning fidelity, assessing the degree to which participants acquire targeted competencies during the cross-training experience; (2) transfer readiness, evaluating the organizational conditions—manager support, opportunity availability, social reinforcement—that either enable or constrain transfer; (3) application effectiveness, measuring the extent to which acquired competencies are demonstrably deployed in post-training work contexts; and (4) organizational impact, tracking the contribution of cross-training investments to organizational outcomes including productivity, agility indicators, retention metrics, and knowledge distribution.

The temporal dimension of evaluation deserves particular emphasis. Cross-training outcomes are characteristically time-distributed: some competency gains manifest immediately in post-rotation performance, while others—particularly those involving tacit knowledge integration and cross-functional perspective-taking—emerge gradually over months or years of application experience. Evaluation systems that rely exclusively on short-term post-rotation assessments will systematically underestimate the long-run value of well-designed cross-training programs, potentially leading to premature program termination or resource reallocation decisions based on incomplete evidence.

6.2 Agility and Resilience as Key Performance Indicators

The conventional performance indicators applied to cross-training evaluation—productivity metrics, error rates, training completion statistics—are inadequate for capturing the full value proposition of adaptive cross-training in tight labor market contexts. Das et al. (2023) propose a conceptualization of workforce agility that encompasses sensing, responding, and learning dimensions, each of which requires distinct measurement approaches. Gouda and Tiwari (2024) provide empirical modeling of talent agility barriers, identifying measurement infrastructure deficits as a significant impediment to agility-oriented talent development in practice.

Zhou et al. (2022) establish that high-performance work systems—of which robust cross-training programs are a central component—contribute to organizational resilience capability in SMEs through mechanisms including enhanced employee flexibility, strengthened knowledge redundancy, and improved adaptive capacity. Their finding that resilience outcomes are mediated by employee commitment suggests that cross-training evaluation frameworks should incorporate engagement and commitment indicators alongside traditional performance metrics. The connection between cross-training participation, perceived organizational support, and employee commitment creates a virtuous cycle that evaluation systems must be capable of detecting if the full strategic value of cross-training investment is to be recognized.

Reinhold (2024) further articulates the pillars of workforce agility at both organizational and individual levels in SME contexts, providing a framework for evaluation that distinguishes between structural agility enablers (training investments, work design flexibility, knowledge management systems) and behavioral agility outcomes (response speed, learning velocity, cross-functional collaboration effectiveness). This distinction is practically useful for cross-training program managers seeking to identify which program elements are generating agility returns and which require redesign. A balanced scorecard approach incorporating both structural enabler metrics and behavioral outcome metrics would provide a more complete picture of cross-training program effectiveness than single-dimension performance assessment.

6.3 Comparative Overview of Traditional and Adaptive Cross-Training

Table 1. Comparative Characteristics of Traditional and Adaptive Cross-Training Programs

Dimension	Traditional Cross-Training	Adaptive Cross-Training	Key References
Program Design	Fixed, curriculum-based rotations	Responsive, needs-driven and iterative rotations	Rizan et al. (2025); Alizadeh Majd et al. (2024)
Labor Market Alignment	Periodic and infrequent reviews	Real-time integration of market signals	Deming & Silliman (2024); Li (2022)
Knowledge Transfer Mechanism	Primarily explicit and codified	Tacit and explicit; mentoring-enriched	Al-Zoubi et al. (2025); Mababu Mukiur & Gomez Lega (2025)

continued on following page

Table 1. Continued

Dimension	Traditional Cross-Training	Adaptive Cross-Training	Key References
Manager Role	Administrative oversight	Active coaching and transfer support	Blume et al. (2024); Mehner et al. (2024)
Employee Agility	Incidental outcome	Deliberate and measured goal	Das et al. (2023); Hanu et al. (2023)
Evaluation	End-of-program assessment	Continuous, multi-level transfer evaluation	Ardondi et al. (2025); Shukla & Kumar (2024)
Technology Integration	Low; classroom-centric	High; digital and blended formats	Morandini et al. (2023); Chong & Zainal (2024)
Retention Impact	Indirect and long-term	Direct, measurable career growth linkage	Wang & Hasan (2024); Zhu & Gao (2023)

Figure 3. Comparative Outcome Performance: Traditional vs. Adaptive Cross-Training Programs

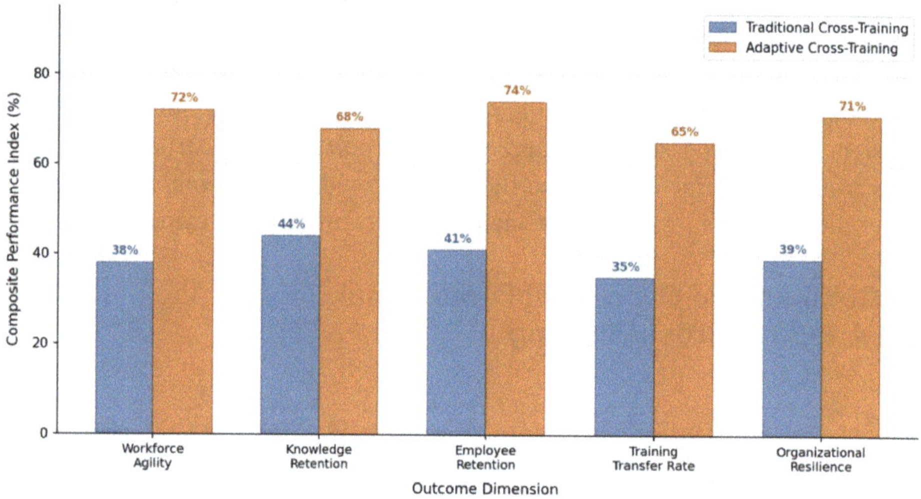

Note: Values represent illustrative composite indices synthesized from empirical findings in the literature reviewed in this chapter (e.g., Alizadeh Majd et al., 2024; Hanu et al., 2023; Mehner et al., 2024). Actual outcomes vary by organizational context, industry, and program design quality.

Figure 3 illustrate the grouped bar chart presents illustrative composite performance indices across five strategic outcome dimensions derived from the empirical literature reviewed in this chapter: Workforce Agility, Knowledge Retention, Employee Retention, Training Transfer Rate, and Organizational Resilience. Adaptive cross-training programs (orange bars) consistently outperform traditional cross-training designs (blue bars) across all five dimensions, with particularly pronounced differentials in Workforce Agility (+34 percentage points) and Employee Retention (+33 percentage points).

7. PRACTICAL IMPLICATIONS FOR HUMAN RESOURCE PROFESSIONALS

7.1 Designing Adaptive Cross-Training Programs

Human resource professionals seeking to implement adaptive cross-training programs in tight labor market contexts should begin by establishing a systematic environmental scanning function that translates external labor market data into actionable program design inputs. This function need not be elaborate; at a minimum, it involves quarterly reviews of sector-specific occupational demand data, internal turnover analytics segmented by function and level, and technology adoption roadmaps from business strategy documentation. The output of this scanning process should directly inform decisions about which role transitions to prioritize in cross-training sequences and which emerging competency domains to incorporate into rotation curricula.

Skills mapping processes should be reconceptualized from static competency inventories to dynamic architectures that explicitly distinguish between current, transferable, and future-oriented competencies. Mababu Mukiur and Gomez Lega (2025) provide a framework grounded in mental process analysis of skill transfer that is particularly useful for identifying which technical and non-technical skills are most amenable to cross-functional transfer and which require more intensive developmental investment. HR professionals should use this type of framework to design rotation sequences that create deliberate cross-pollination between competency domains rather than exposing employees to sequential role experiences without an underlying transfer logic.

Program structure should build in deliberate reflection intervals—scheduled opportunities for participants to make sense of their cross-training experiences with guidance from mentors or peer networks. Rizan et al. (2025) establish that the absence of structured reflection is among the primary reasons why job rotation programs fail to realize their full learning potential, as the experiential learning cycle is incomplete without the reflective observation and abstract conceptualization phases that transform experience into transferable knowledge. Practical reflection structures might include weekly learning journals reviewed with mentors, monthly cross-functional peer debrief sessions, and mid-rotation structured conversations between participants and host function managers.

The governance architecture surrounding cross-training programs deserves particular attention in tight labor market contexts. Programs that lack clear executive sponsorship, defined budget commitments, and explicit linkages to business strategy are vulnerable to resource reallocation during operational pressures—precisely the moments when cross-training investment is most strategically important. HR professionals should position adaptive cross-training programs within their organizations' formal strategic workforce planning processes, ensuring that program continuation is protected through the same governance mechanisms that protect other strategic capital investments (Letmathe & Schinner, 2022).

7.2 Building Manager Capability for Training Transfer Support

The evidence reviewed in this chapter converges on a consistent finding: the quality of manager support in the post-training period is among the most powerful determinants of cross-training return on investment. Yet most organizations continue to design cross-training programs as employee-facing interventions without corresponding investment in the manager capabilities required to support transfer. HR professionals should address this misalignment by developing manager-specific competency frameworks for learning support, incorporating transfer facilitation behaviors into manager performance evaluation criteria, and providing managers with practical tools for the coaching conversations that accelerate transfer (Blume et al., 2024; Mehner et al., 2024).

Specific manager behaviors that have demonstrated transfer support efficacy in the empirical literature include: proactively creating opportunities for transferred skills application within the first 30 days of rotation completion; providing specific performance feedback on transferred skill application rather than generic performance ratings; facilitating connections between cross-training participants and subject matter experts whose expertise can deepen application; and publicly recognizing instances of successful cross-functional competency deployment as signals to organizational peers of the program's value (Blume et al., 2024).

Manager capability development for cross-training support should itself be treated as a cross-training challenge. Managers who have personally experienced multi-functional rotation programs demonstrate substantially stronger empathy for the dissonance and learning demands experienced by cross-training participants, and consequently provide more effective post-rotation coaching support. Organizations can leverage this insight by deliberately designing manager development programs to include cross-functional exposure, creating a self-reinforcing culture of cross-functional curiosity that cascades from leadership through the organization. Berg et al. (2023) provide theoretical grounding for this logic through their treatment of leadership as a critical conduit between strategic learning ambitions and operational learning behaviors.

7.3 Managing Workforce Resilience Through Cross-Training Portfolio Design

In tight labor markets characterized by demand volatility, organizations face the challenge of cross-training investment allocation: which cross-training configurations maximize organizational resilience across a range of plausible demand scenarios? Letmathe and Schinner (2022) provide a formal model for this allocation problem, demonstrating that the optimal cross-training portfolio in volatile demand environments is characterized by breadth (ensuring multiple employees hold any critical competency), redundancy (ensuring no single rotation sequence leaves critical knowledge in the hands of only recently trained individuals), and scalability (designing rotation architectures that can be accelerated or decelerated as demand conditions shift).

Zhou et al. (2022) establish that high-performance work systems, including well-designed cross-training programs, generate organizational resilience through mechanisms that include both capability redundancy (multiple employees able to perform critical functions) and adaptive capacity (employees with cross-functional exposure better able to identify and implement innovative responses to novel challenges). HR professionals should treat cross-training portfolio design as a resilience engineering exercise, mapping coverage of critical organizational competencies against rotation participation to identify both over- and under-coverage risks.

Vapiwala and Pandita (2024) contribute an important cautionary note by demonstrating that defensive communication patterns among employees—including resistance to skill sharing born of job security concerns—can undermine cross-training program effectiveness. HR professionals implementing adaptive cross-training in tight labor market contexts should anticipate and proactively address these concerns through transparent communication about the career development rather than replacement logic of cross-training participation, structural protections against involuntary role displacement during training periods, and visible leadership endorsement of cross-training as a retention rather than a restructuring mechanism.

The portfolio design challenge has a temporal dimension that is frequently overlooked in cross-training program planning. Knowledge redundancy achieved through rotation programs degrades over time as trained employees forget unused competencies, change roles, or depart the organization. HR professionals should establish rotation refresh cycles that systematically renew the organization's cross-competency coverage, rather than treating initial rotation program completion as a permanent organizational capability enhancement. Gouda and Tiwari (2024) document that organizations failing to maintain ongoing cross-training investment—even after establishing initial agility capability—experience significant degradation in agility indicators over two-to-three-year horizons, suggesting that adaptive cross-training is best understood as a continuous organizational practice rather than a discrete program initiative.

7.4 Addressing Equity and Inclusion in Cross-Training Access

The strategic benefits of adaptive cross-training can only be fully realized if program access is equitably distributed across the workforce. Research on organizational career development consistently documents that cross-training and developmental rotation opportunities are more frequently extended to employees who are already perceived as high performers or high-potential candidates, creating Matthew effects in which advantaged employees accumulate further advantages through preferential developmental investment (Wang & Hasan, 2024). In tight labor markets, this inequity is not only ethically problematic but strategically counterproductive: organizations that restrict cross-training participation to existing high performers leave substantial untapped capability in their broader workforce.

Jackson et al. (2023) provide evidence from a longitudinal case study that job rotation programs designed with explicit attention to social equity considerations—including equitable assignment of physically demanding tasks, transparent rotation selection criteria, and proactive outreach to employees in roles with limited natural rotation pathways—generate broader organizational engagement benefits alongside their direct competency development outcomes. HR professionals should therefore design cross-training program access processes with deliberate attention to representation, ensuring that employees across functional levels, demographic groups, and performance categories have meaningful access to developmental rotation opportunities. The long-run return on this inclusive design will manifest in broader organizational capability distributions, reduced dependency on a small cadre of cross-trained individuals, and stronger organizational resilience across workforce transition events.

8. FUTURE RESEARCH DIRECTIONS AND CONCLUSION

8.1 Gaps in Current Knowledge

Despite significant recent progress in the empirical and conceptual foundations of cross-training research, several important knowledge gaps remain. First, the majority of empirical studies on job rotation and cross-training effects are conducted in single-industry or single-country contexts, limiting the generalizability of findings across labor market environments with different institutional configurations, skill ecosystem characteristics, and employment relation norms. Future research should pursue comparative designs that explicitly test whether adaptive cross-training frameworks developed in one context translate to materially different labor market environments, including high-regulation economies, emerging market contexts, and gig economy structures where employment relationships are less stable.

Second, the longitudinal dynamics of cross-training effects on workforce agility and organizational resilience remain understudied. Most available evidence captures outcomes at a single post-training measurement point, making it difficult to assess whether agility benefits from cross-training are sustained, amplified, or attenuated over time. Longitudinal research designs capable of tracking the careers of cross-training participants across multiple rotation cycles and role transitions would substantially advance practical understanding of how to sequence and sustain cross-training investments for maximum long-term return.

Third, the intersection of artificial intelligence tools and cross-training program design represents an emerging research frontier of considerable practical importance. As AI-enabled talent analytics, adaptive learning platforms, and intelligent mentoring systems become more widely available, the design possibilities for adaptive cross-training programs expand dramatically. Research investigating the conditions under which technology augmentation of cross-training programs enhances versus displaces the human social learning dynamics that appear most critical to transfer effectiveness would generate highly actionable insights for practitioners. The risk that algorithmic matching of employees to rotation assignments will underweight tacit knowledge transfer objectives in favor of operationally legible competency metrics is a specific concern meriting empirical attention.

Fourth, the equity dimensions of adaptive cross-training access represent an underdeveloped research area with substantial practical implications. Systematic investigation of the individual, organizational, and structural factors that determine which employees access developmental cross-training opportunities—and the long-run career and capability consequences of differential access—would provide the evidential foundation for more equitable cross-training program design. Research in this area should attend particularly to the intersection of cross-training access patterns with gender, ethnicity, educational background, and organizational level.

8.2 Conclusion

Contemporary labor market conditions have elevated workforce cross-training from an operational convenience to a strategic imperative. The convergence of the Great Resignation, accelerating technological disruption, and persistent skill shortages has created an environment in which organizations cannot afford cross-training programs that remain static in design, ambiguous in purpose, or disconnected from the external signals that should inform their content. The adaptive cross-training framework developed in this chapter provides a conceptual architecture for the redesign of cross-training programs as dynamic, environmentally responsive instruments of workforce capability development.

The key arguments advanced in this chapter can be summarized as follows. First, effective cross-training under current conditions requires systematic integration of labor market intelligence into program design processes, replacing the conventional assumption that competency requirements are stable with an explicit planning logic that anticipates and responds to skill demand evolution. Second, training transfer—the often-neglected bridge between learning acquisition and performance application—is the critical mediating variable determining whether cross-training investment generates organizational returns, and improving transfer effectiveness requires simultaneous attention to program design quality, organizational climate, peer learning networks, and manager support capability. Third, managers occupy a pivotal structural role in adaptive cross-training systems not as passive administrators but as active architects of learning ecosystems, and their capacity to fulfill this role requires deliberate organizational investment in coaching skill development and accountability structures.

A fourth integrating insight emerges from the cross-sector evidence reviewed in this chapter: the social infrastructure surrounding cross-training programs—mentoring relationships, peer learning networks, knowledge-sharing forums, and manager facilitation behaviors—is at least as consequential for program effectiveness as the technical content of rotation assignments. Organizations that invest heavily in curriculum design while underinvesting in the social architecture through which learning is shared, applied, and reinforced will consistently underperform relative to their cross-training investment potential. Adaptive cross-training design is fundamentally a social systems design challenge as much as a learning design challenge.

Organizations that succeed in building adaptive cross-training capabilities will gain compounding advantages in tight labor markets: a workforce whose breadth of competency enables operational resilience across demand fluctuations, whose development experiences generate the career satisfaction that drives retention, and whose knowledge distribution architecture reduces the organizational vulnerability associated with concentrated expertise. These advantages do not accrue automatically from program participation; they require the deliberate, evidence-informed, and continuously evaluated design architecture that this chapter has sought to articulate. In an era defined by labor market volatility and accelerating skill obsolescence, the investment in such architecture represents not merely a human resource management best practice but a foundational strategic capability on which sustainable organizational performance depends.

REFERENCES

Al-Zoubi, M. O., Masa'deh, R., & Twaissi, N. M. (2025). Exploring the relationship among structured on-the-job training, mentoring, job rotation, work environment factors and tacit knowledge transfer. *VINE Journal of Information and Knowledge Management Systems*, *55*(1), 240–267. DOI: 10.1108/VJIKMS-06-2022-0199

Alizadeh Majd, A., Bell, R., Ali, S., Davoodi, A., & Nasirifar, A. (2024). The effect of job rotation on employee performance: The mediating role of HR strategy and training in the petrochemical industry. *Industrial and Commercial Training*, *56*(2), 93–105. DOI: 10.1108/ICT-10-2023-0074

Amanor-Boadu, V. (2022). *Empirical evidence for the "Great Resignation." Monthly Labor Review*. U.S. Bureau of Labor Statistics., DOI: 10.21916/mlr.2022.29

Ardondi, M., Fortunato, E., Ruozi, C., Di Fronzo, P., Saffioti, A., Ferrari, I., Bassi, M. C., Ghirotto, L., & Pedroni, C. (2025). Workplace training transfer: A systematic scoping review of evaluation tools for adult learning. *Journal of Workplace Learning*. Advance online publication. DOI: 10.1108/JWL-03-2025-0068

Berg, A.-K., Schulte, E. M., Schultz, A., & Kauffeld, S. (2023). Transformationsprozesse gestalten und evaluieren: Wirkmodelle als Ansatz um strategische Personalentwicklung mit Organisationsentwicklung zu verbinden. Gruppe. Interaktion. Organisation. *Zeitschrift für Angewandte Organisationspsychologie*, *54*(3), 371–389. DOI: 10.1007/s11612-023-00695-4

Blume, B. D., Ford, J. K., & Huang, J. L. (2024). Transfer of informal learning: The role of manager support in linking learning to performance. *Business Horizons*, *67*(2), 125–136. DOI: 10.1016/j.bushor.2023.12.001

Chong, Y. K., & Zainal, S. R. M. (2024). Employee agility's mediating role on the link between employee vitality, digital literacy and transformational leadership with job performance: An empirical study. *Cogent Business & Management*, *11*(1), 2337447. Advance online publication. DOI: 10.1080/23311975.2024.2337447

Das, K. P., Mukhopadhyay, S., & Suar, D. (2023). Enablers of workforce agility, firm performance, and corporate reputation. *Asia Pacific Management Review*, *28*(1), 33–44. DOI: 10.1016/j.apmrv.2022.01.006

Decius, J., Knappstein, M., & Klug, K. (2024). Which way of learning benefits your career? The role of different forms of work-related learning for different types of perceived employability. *European Journal of Work and Organizational Psychology*, *33*(1), 24–39. DOI: 10.1080/1359432X.2023.2191846

Deming, D. J., & Silliman, M. I. (2024). Skills and human capital in the labor market (NBER Working Paper No. 32908). National Bureau of Economic Research. DOI: 10.3386/w32908

Gittleman, M. (2022). *The "Great Resignation" in perspective. Monthly Labor Review*. U.S. Bureau of Labor Statistics., DOI: 10.21916/mlr.2022.20

Gouda, G. K., & Tiwari, B. (2022). Talent agility, innovation adoption and sustainable business performance: Empirical evidences from Indian automobile industry. *International Journal of Productivity and Performance Management*, *71*(6), 2582–2604. DOI: 10.1108/IJPPM-02-2021-0071

Gouda, G. K., & Tiwari, B. (2024). Modelling the barriers of talent agility in Indian automobile industry in the era of industry 4.0. *Journal of Modelling in Management*, *19*(4), 1343–1368. DOI: 10.1108/JM2-06-2023-0124

Hanu, C., Amegbe, H., Yawson, M. D. T. A., & Mensah, P. (2023). Differential impact of work-based learning on employee agility, ambidexterity and proactive goal generation. *Journal of Workplace Learning*, *35*(1), 92–111. DOI: 10.1108/JWL-01-2022-0005

Jackson, J. A., Sund, M., Barlari Lobos, G., Melin, L., & Mathiassen, S. (2023). Assessing the efficacy of a job rotation for improving occupational physical and psychosocial work environment, musculoskeletal health, social equality, production quality, and resilience at a commercial laundromat: Protocol for a longitudinal case study. *BMJ Open*, *13*(5), e067633. DOI: 10.1136/bmjopen-2022-067633 PMID: 37173106

Kahl, J., de Klerk, S., & Whiteoak, J. (2023). Managing empowerment: Adjusting organisational units' autonomy to achieve corporate agility. Journal of Organizational Effectiveness: People and Performance. Advance online publication. DOI: 10.1108/JOEPP-05-2022-0126

Letmathe, P., & Schinner, M. (2022). Workforce planning in production with flexible or budgeted employee training and volatile demand. *Journal of Business Economics*, *92*(7), 1147–1183. DOI: 10.1007/s11573-022-01090-z

Li, L. (2022). Reskilling and upskilling the future-ready workforce for industry 4.0 and beyond. *Information Systems Frontiers*, *24*(6), 1697–1712. DOI: 10.1007/s10796-022-10308-y PMID: 35855776

Ludviga, I., & Kalvina, A. (2023). Organizational agility during crisis: Do employees' perceptions of public sector organizations' strategic agility foster employees' work engagement and well-being? *Employee Responsibilities and Rights Journal*, *35*(4), 295–316. DOI: 10.1007/s10672-023-09442-9 PMID: 40479364

Ma, X., Nakab, A., & Vidart, D. (2024). Human capital investment and development: The role of on-the-job training. *Journal of Political Economy Macroeconomics*, *2*(1), 107–148. DOI: 10.1086/728667

Mababu Mukiur, R., & Gómez Lega, J. L. (2025). Transfer of technical skills and non-technical skills in the workplace: An analysis from the perspective of mental processes of learning. *Human Resource Development Review*, 15344843251403110. Advance online publication. DOI: 10.1177/15344843251403110

Mehner, L., Rothenbusch, S., & Kauffeld, S. (2024). How to maximize the impact of workplace training: A mixed-method analysis of social support, training transfer and knowledge sharing. *European Journal of Work and Organizational Psychology*, *33*(2), 201–217. DOI: 10.1080/1359432X.2024.2319082

Morandini, S., Fraboni, F., De Angelis, M., Puzzo, G., Giusino, D., & Pietrantoni, L. (2023). The impact of artificial intelligence on workers' skills: Upskilling and reskilling in organisations. Informing Science. *Informing Science*, *26*, 39–68. DOI: 10.28945/5078

Reinhold, K. (2024). Building resilience: Pillars of workforce agility at organizational and individual levels in SMEs. In Durst, S., & Henschel, T. (Eds.), *Small and Medium-Sized Enterprise (SME) Resilience. Management for Professionals*. Springer., DOI: 10.1007/978-3-031-50836-3_11

Rizan, C., & Saikrishna, M. B. (2025). Leveraging job rotation programs for experiential learning in organizations through the lens of Kolb's experiential learning theory. *Development and Learning in Organizations*, *39*(6), 24–27. Advance online publication. DOI: 10.1108/DLO-09-2024-0272

Shukla, A., & Kumar, A. (2024). Factors affecting transfer of online training: A systematic literature review and proposed taxonomy. *Human Resource Development Quarterly*, *35*(2), 187–218. DOI: 10.1002/hrdq.21518

Vapiwala, F., & Pandita, D. (2024). Conflicts and defensive communication: Investigating the mature, neurotic and immature defences of service professionals. *International Journal of Conflict Management*, *35*(4), 633–657. DOI: 10.1108/IJCMA-12-2022-0211

Wang, L., & Hasan, N. A. (2024). Exploring organizational career growth: A systematic literature review and future research directions. *Cogent Business & Management*, *11*(1), 2398728. Advance online publication. DOI: 10.1080/23311975.2024.2398728

Zhou, Q., Edafioghor, T., Wu, C.-H., & Doherty, B. (2022). Building organizational resilience capability in small and medium-sized enterprises: The role of high-performance work systems. *Human Resource Management Journal*, *33*(2), 371–393. DOI: 10.1111/1748-8583.12479

Zhu, L. N., & Gao, Y. (2023). Protean career orientation, supervisor perceptions and organizational career growth: A moderated mediation model. *Current Psychology*, *43*(10), 8913–8930. DOI: 10.1007/s12144-023-05021-1

KEY TERMS AND DEFINITIONS

Cross-Training: The practice of training employees to perform multiple roles or tasks beyond their primary job responsibilities. It enhances flexibility, reduces dependency on specific individuals, and improves organizational efficiency by enabling workers to fill in during absences or shifting workload demands.

Job Rotation: A human resource strategy where employees are periodically moved between different roles or departments. It helps develop diverse skills, reduces monotony, increases job satisfaction, and prepares employees for broader responsibilities within the organization.

Labor Market Conditions: Refers to the overall state of supply and demand for labor in an economy, including employment rates, wage levels, job availability, and skill requirements. These conditions influence hiring practices, workforce planning, and opportunities available to job seekers.

Training Transfer: The extent to which skills, knowledge, and behaviors learned during training are effectively applied in the workplace. Successful transfer depends on factors like training design, workplace support, and employee motivation, ensuring that learning leads to improved job performance.

Workforce Agility: The ability of an organization's employees to quickly adapt to changing business needs, technologies, and environments. It involves flexibility, continuous learning, and responsiveness, allowing the workforce to handle new challenges, roles, or market conditions effectively and maintain productivity.

Chapter 15

Advanced Cross-Training Management and Cross-Border Talent Mobility in Severely Restricted Work Contexts

Jose De Jesus Reyes-Sánchez
http://orcid.org/0000-0002-3866-2363
TECNM Instituto Tecnologico Superior De Fresnillo, Mexico

Juan Antonio Gonzalez Saenz
http://orcid.org/0000-0003-2247-754X
TECNM Instituto Tecnologico Superior De Fresnillo, Mexico

Hugo Jimenez Alvarez
http://orcid.org/0009-0002-4497-0327
TECNM Instituto Tecnologico Superior De Fresnillo, Mexico

Jannet Maricela Barrientos Luján
http://orcid.org/0009-0009-3244-5016
TECNM Instituto Tecnologico Superior De Fresnillo, Mexico

Rosalinda Ramos Murillo
http://orcid.org/0009-0007-6572-9440
TECNM Instituto Tecnologico Superior De Fresnillo, Mexico

DOI: 10.4018/979-8-3373-5327-2.ch015

ght © 2027, IGI Global Scientific Publishing. Copying or distributing in print or electronic forms without written permission of IGI Global Scientific Publishing is prohibited. Use of this chapter to n generative artificial intelligence (AI) technologies is expressly prohibited. The publisher reserves all rights to license its use for generative AI training and machine learning model development.

ABSTRACT

The study examines how cross-training and cross-border talent mobility are integrated to sustain operations in severely restricted work contexts, demonstrating that the synergy between training flexibility and border permeability is a condition for maintaining innovation and operational continuity. It is argued that resilience arises when human capital is managed as a collective resource, supported by situated pedagogies, traceable digital platforms, flexible regulatory agreements, and transparent analytics that avoid bias and preserve psychosocial well-being. Gaps remain: regulatory fragmentation, difficulties in measuring the intangible value of learning, and ethical risks in decision automation.

INTRODUCTION

In the legal frontiers of the 21st century, the advanced management of cross-training and cross-border mobility of talent has become a strategic device to sustain the competitiveness of organizations operating under severe labor restrictions. Barriers to the movement of people have reconfigured the map of the supply and demand of skills, forcing employers to optimize the value of each training path and each professional itinerary. Companies that have thrived in this volatile environment share one trait: they have merged cross-training program design with talent architectures capable of navigating geopolitical, regulatory, and biosanitary constraints without sacrificing organizational agility. Such convergence has been evident both in the financial sector and in essential services, where pandemic peaks forced the entire workforce to be reconverted in a matter of days. The literature shows, for example, that sandbox frameworks, by enabling the validation of training practices in protected environments, reduce the risks of non-compliance and accelerate the absorption of critical skills (Zetzsche et al., 2020).

In turn, the cross-skilling programs implemented in British health systems during COVID-19 confirm that versatility can be developed with ultra-fast methodologies and without compromising clinical safety; by deploying reinduction modules in less than 72 hours, a referral hospital managed to mobilize hundreds of professionals to critical units without reducing mortality indicators or burnout metrics (Hettle, Sutherland, Miles, & Allanby, 2020). At the same time, bibliometric studies on scientific collaboration show that international co-production generates an impact dividend that grows when the flows of researchers overcome diplomatic barriers; analysis of 350,000 AI authors indicates that non-American teams produce articles with greater novelty and citation than domestic ones, even under trade tensions. This evidence suggests that the synergy between training flexibility and border permeability is not an academic luxury, but a prerequisite to sustain innovation in highly restrictive scenarios.

The convergence of these findings forces us to rethink the classic notion of talent mobility as a mere geographical transfer. Today it is a complex practice that articulates situated pedagogies, digital infrastructures and multilateral agreements capable of de-anchoring learning from the physical territory. Global companies that anticipated this trend have invested in competency analytics platforms to map skills gaps in real-time while simultaneously negotiating alternative migration routes that mitigate labor regulation bottlenecks. Empirical evidence suggests that this pair correlates with sustained productivity gains, as well as a reduction in the cost of vacancy in critical positions, even in jurisdictions subject to intermittent border controls (Lengnick-Hall, et al., 2011).

Against this backdrop, this research delves into the mechanisms by which cross-skilling and cross-border mobility can be managed in an integrated, ethical and resilient way. Based on the analysis of the original document and contemporary literature, vectors of action are outlined ranging from curricular engineering and algorithmic talent governance to the management of reputational risks associated with the relocation of personnel. An interdisciplinary perspective is adopted that combines principles of the political economy of migration, dynamic capabilities theory, and the psychology of organizational learning, with the ultimate goal of offering verifiable solutions to decision-makers facing severe regulatory constraints.

STATEMENT OF THE PROBLEM

Organizations that operate under severe labor restrictions face the paradox of needing extreme agility to sustain their processes and, at the same time, moving in a fragmented regulatory framework that limits the physical circulation of talent and conditions the validity of the training obtained in different territories. The apparent solution comes up against ethical, cognitive and political tensions that put at risk the internal and external legitimacy of decisions about who learns, who moves and under what conditions this learning is recognized. The literature reviewed shows that organizational resilience emerges when human capital is managed as a collective and dynamic resource, but also that such management requires transparency, social protection, and robust metrics capable of capturing intangible value without neglecting psychosocial well-being. (Lengnick-Hall, et al., 2011; Zetzsche et al., 2017).

The central problem deepens when observing that socio-technical devices designed to accelerate learning can become inflated catalogs or opaque algorithms that reproduce historical biases, while geographical dispersion erodes the informal channels of transmission of tacit knowledge. The pressure to retrain quickly raises cognitive load and fuels digital fatigue, generating an emotional toll that is rarely incorporated into return indicators. In the absence of rigorous pedagogical curation, clear rules of algorithmic governance, and deliberate spaces to preserve experiential knowledge, the promise of cross-training will degenerate into digital bureaucracy with no operational impact. (Barocas & Selbst, 2016; Argote & Ingram, 2000).

At the same time, the search for regulatory flexibility through sandboxes or bilateral agreements requires explicit social pacts: decent work standards, co-evaluation mechanisms with unions and communities of practice, and inclusive leadership that guarantees a voice to minorities usually excluded from mobility circuits. When inclusion is reduced to discourse, diversity does not produce innovation and mobility reproduces previous hierarchies; When psychological safety and transparency are institutionalized, regulation ceases to be an obstacle and becomes a device for collective learning. (Zetzsche et al., 2017; Nishii, 2013; Edmondson & Lei, 2014; Shore et al., 2011).

Rigorously measuring the impact of these strategies remains a critical knot. The benefits are expressed in operational resilience, density of collaboration networks and risk reduction, dimensions that do not fit into linear financial metrics. Hence the need for hybrid assessment models that combine network analysis, learning narratives and longitudinal traceability, avoiding confusing short-term results with sustainable dynamic capacities.

Based on this panorama, three guiding questions are formulated that seek to order the complexity described and offer a framework for strategic decision-making: How to coherently integrate cross-training and cross-border mobility to sustain the operation and, at the same time, guarantee equity and psychosocial protection in contexts of high restriction? What combinations of digital infrastructures, regulatory frameworks and algorithmic governance practices allow tacit knowledge to be transferred and bias to be avoided in the allocation of training and mobility opportunities, and finally, how can the real value of these strategies be assessed when the results are manifested in resilience, collaboration and cumulative learning rather than in immediate financial indicators?

Answering these questions implies recognizing that the effective integration between cross-training and mobility requires a pedagogical design anchored in real problems, accompanied by regulatory agreements that legitimize the circulation of talent and ensure basic rights, as well as transparent analytical systems that guide decisions without supplanting expert judgment or making vulnerable groups invisible; Only when these dimensions are taken care of simultaneously does the organization manage to recombine people and processes with agility, without sacrificing well-being or trust. (Edmondson & Lei, 2014).

BACKGROUND

Genealogy of Specialized Labor Migration

The relative freedom with which master craftsmen moved between European principalities during the transition from feudalism to incipient capitalism laid the foundations for a transnational labour market before the modern concept of frontier existed. Swiss watchmakers and Germanic blacksmiths, driven by the growing demand for precision in arms manufacturing, colonized trade corridors connecting the fairs of Lyon with the shipyards of Amsterdam. In this itinerant framework, a first notion of networks of practical knowledge germinated, since the guilds demanded the sharing of methods of tempering, alloys and machining in exchange for access to local clientele, a dynamic that heralded future industrial conglomerates based on the geographical specialization of know-how.

The consolidation of nation states and the emergence of the second industrial revolution caused this cognitive flow to be institutionalized through standardized skill tests by engineering academies and technical schools. Towards the end of the nineteenth century, these tests made it possible to obtain portable credentials valid at different customs, turning the skill into legal recognition and, by extension, an economic passport. At the same time, the World Exposes disseminated inventions and manufacturing processes that reinforced the idea that progress depended on the open circulation of experts (Kerr et al., 2016).

The Bracero program developed by the United States and the Labor Import Schemes designed by Canada reconfigured the labor geography of North America by absorbing contingents of Latin American farmers, welders and operators, while the European powers resorted to colonial recruitment to fill gaps in teaching, health and metallurgy. At the same time, the initiative known as Operation Paperclip corroborated that governments were willing to compete for rival scientists as a factor of technological supremacy.

With the digitalization of the end of the last century and the consequent expansion of transoceanic bandwidth, a phase emerged that some authors call cognitive telemigration. Collaborative platforms began to tender software, design or consulting projects without the provider leaving their country, inaugurating a form of mobility where what travels is not the body but the compiled algorithm. At the same time, the skilled diaspora began to serve as a bridge for soft knowledge transfer, articulating incubators, venture capital, and mentoring programs that fertilize innovation ecosystems at source.

Birth of Cross-Training in the Fordist Factory

The transformation of the assembly line in Highland Park introduced a rotation logic that allowed the operator to move from the riveter to the adjustment area and then to painting without interrupting the overall flow; That operational flexibility mitigated bottlenecks and led to a significant decrease in stoppages, while reinforcing the notion of uninterrupted flow that would later be associated with lean production. By shifting the focus from the fixed position to the circulation of tasks, manufacturing engineers laid the foundations for versatile work as a tool to sustain cadence and protect quality in the face of demand variability.

Industrial ergonomics soon endorsed this practice by verifying that the systematic alternation of movements distributes the musculoskeletal load among different anatomical groups, dilutes localized fatigue and delays the appearance of repetitive microtraumas. The most recent studies on biomechanical hazards corroborate that well-designed turnover reduces cumulative exposure to critical forces, increases job satisfaction, and consequently increases overall productivity by decreasing absenteeism from non-traumatic injuries (Padula et al., 2017).

When the lean production philosophy matured in post-war Japan, the multi-skill matrix became a mainstay of the just-in-time system. In practice, Toyota required each employee to master several processes and be able to assume them immediately in the event of model changes or alterations in the sequence of orders; This ensured continuity of flow and prevented bottlenecks without resorting to safety inventories.

As global corporations internalized those principles, training spaces of their own dedicated to certifying progressive levels of versatility emerged. These platforms evolved from face-to-face workshops to digital itineraries traced by microcredentials that record the possession of tactical, cognitive and relational skills with blockchain traceability.

Health and Geopolitical Crises as Catalysts for Mobile Talent

The influenza epidemic that swept the world in the year 1918 forced the owners of textile workshops and factories in Worcester and other industrial cities to redesign their shifts in strips that avoided the simultaneous congregation of large crews and, in parallel, to train seamstresses in steam cutting and ironing in an accelerated manner so that they could cover massive absences without stopping production. That preventive rotation strategy articulated the first formal catalogues of transferable skills on record and demonstrated that versatility not only preserves operational continuity but also reduces individual exposure to contagion by avoiding prolonged concentrations in the same position, a finding that would later be taken up by the International Labour Organization as an exemplary occupational safety practice.

The sudden rise in the price of crude oil during the oil crisis of 1973 caused engineering and refineries in North America and Europe to transfer experienced personnel to the emerging extraction hubs in the Persian Gulf, where the urgency to increase refining capacity required highly skilled labor in cryogenic pipe welding and control circuit design(Nykänen et al., 2020).

The emergence of the Severe Acute Respiratory Syndrome that broke out on the Asian continent during the year 2003 acted as a laboratory at scale for the early adoption of teleworking in port and insurance firms in Hong Kong and Singapore. Quarantines restricted physical transit, but logistical continuity was preserved thanks to the expeditious transfer of risk analysts and operations managers to virtual environments, demonstrating that digital connectivity could replace, at least partially, physical presence in sensitive supply chains.

The global impact of the disease caused by the new coronavirus in 2020 deepened this logic by forcing university hospitals to reconvert hotel managers into coordinators of the supply of protective equipment and to train aeronautical technicians as supervisors of mechanical ventilators in a matter of days. Experience has shown that express retraining is based on viable inventories of transitive skills and on upskilling platforms capable of combining augmented reality simulation with verifiable micro-credentials (Nykänen et al., 2020).

Digital Training Infrastructures and Their Global Expansion

The first computer-aided training solutions emerged at the dawn of the 1990s, when the floppy disk made it possible to bring multimedia lessons to the assembly line and substantially shorten the interval that separated the hiring of an operator from its full deployment in the plant. Automakers integrated these modules with enterprise resource planning systems, so that the learner's progress was reflected in real-time within the competency store and triggered automatic job reassignment (Adams et al., 2013).

As universities replicated this scheme, the delivery of content through virtual environments that linked asynchronous forums with automatic evaluation calendars became widespread. The turning point came during the second decade of the current century, when massive online courses multiplied the student population and fragmented programs into reusable units of competence that could be independently certified.

The standardization of metadata allowed microcredentials to become building blocks of personalized pathways, supported by blockchains that ensure the integrity of the training history from the origin to the final employer. This architecture promotes interoperability between educational platforms, as each badge encodes evidence of performance in virtual labs, collaborative projects, or situated simulations. The result is an ecosystem in which learning analytics diagnoses deficits based on the organization's strategic requirements and prescribes trajectories that are continuously updated as market needs shift toward new combinations of tacit and explicit knowledge (Nykänen et al., 2020).

The emergence of virtual reality and augmented reality extended these possibilities to the high-risk environment. Mining companies, for example, use digital twins that recreate underground galleries to test explosive charge maneuvers and evacuation protocols without exposing personnel or disrupting production. Motion sensors, haptics, and eye tracking feed algorithms that adjust the difficulty according to the expertise demonstrated, making the learning curve steep in minutes of immersive practice (Scorgie et al., 2024).

Internationalization of Migration Regulatory Frameworks

The opening negotiated within the World Trade Organization culminated in the Uruguay Round and, by incorporating the General Agreement on Trade in Services, inaugurated the so-called Mode Four, a figure that authorizes the temporary movement of natural persons to provide services without acquiring permanent residence. By recognizing this modality, states materialized for the first time the legal equivalence between a flow of human knowledge and a flow of trade, anticipating the logic of global value chains based on cognitive specialization (Winters et al., 2003).

The transition from theory to practice took place when the North American integration treaties introduced specific professional categories that allowed engineers, actuaries and designers to move quickly between manufacturing plants and research centers. The subsequent renewal of the agreement, renamed USMCA, strengthened the principle of document portability and linked eligibility to occupations linked to science, technology, engineering, and mathematics, reinforcing the synergy between skilled mobility and smart supply chains (Kerr et al., 2016).

In parallel, the consolidation of the Schengen area instituted free movement of labour within Europe and opened the door to a gradual harmonisation of admission criteria from third countries. The directive known as the Blue Card established uniform salary thresholds and minimum academic requirements, granting highly qualified personnel a plurinational residence permit that avoids duplicating procedures every time they change subsidiaries. In doing so, the European Union tested a supranational model of talent attraction that combines regulatory convergence with respect to national competences in terms of quotas and calibrated the governance of mobility at the level of economic citizenship (Shachar et al., 2017).

Beyond the West, several high-income economies experimented with experimental visas that mix scientific criteria with metrics of impact on innovation. Singapore launched the Tech Pass, a permit that requires having directed start-ups valued at more than one billion Singapore dollars or accrediting indexed publications with a high h-index, with which the document becomes an incentive for technology transfer and not just a migratory safe-conduct. Similarly, talent routes managed by state-owned points platforms in Australia, New Zealand, and Canada weigh patents granted, capital raised, and leadership in disruptive projects, demonstrating that selection with research and development indicators strengthens national applied science ecosystems (Mattoo et al., 2020).

The latest wave of regulations has incorporated the emergence of ubiquitous remote work and the so-called digital nomad visas, which authorise long-term stays for professionals capable of generating foreign currency without entering the domestic labour market. This shift blurs the line between economic migration and cross-border provision of services, as the contract can be executed entirely in the cloud and fiscal oversight shifts from the employer to payment platforms (Kerr et al., 2016; Winters et al., 2003; Testaverde et al., 2016).

Convergence Between Innovation Policies and Talent Attraction

Innovation policies in advanced and emerging economies have been incorporating migration instruments designed to capture critical knowledge and accelerate technology transfer. H1B visas in the United States consolidated ecosystems such as Silicon Valley by bringing together programmers, engineers, and data scientists around universities and companies with high investment in R+D; At the same time, the rigidity of their quotas pushed many firms and professionals to look for alternatives in neighboring poles, where the admission rules were more predictable and faster. The result has been a mobility architecture that combines formal qualification criteria with metrics of impact on innovation, so that the entry permit is no longer just a migratory procedure and becomes an instrument of scientific policy (Kerr et al., 2016; Winters et al., 2003; Testaverde et al., 2016).

Recent initiatives show a convergence between attraction instruments and retention mechanisms: accelerated processing schemes, partial exemptions from administrative requirements and clear routes to permanent residence are articulated with tax incentives for research and the creation of technology-based companies. In this framework, Canada positioned itself as a bridge for specialists trained or employed in the United States, while programs in Asia combine executive experience requirements in high-growth companies with academic trajectories quantified through the h-index and other bibliometric metrics (Winters et al., 2003; Kerr et al., 2016).

Emerging economies, on the other hand, have experimented with return policies that include tax deductions, preferential access to financing for technological ventures, and shareholding in public or mixed innovation companies. These instruments aim to transform the one-way outflow into a circular circuit where the diaspora acts as an investor, mentor, and strategic partner (Testaverde et al., 2016; Winters et al., 2003).

Evolution of Corporate Governance of Human Capital

The transition from the old personnel department to a strategic approach to human capital management meant recognizing the worker as the bearer of dynamic capabilities that can be reconfigured to sustain innovation. In this framework, the theory of dynamic capabilities emphasizes the need to detect opportunities, mobilize resources, and reconfigure competencies in the face of accelerated technological changes. Organizations that embody these principles integrate continuous learning practices with planned rotation mechanisms and competency maps that allow people to be moved quickly between critical projects without sacrificing occupational health or cultural cohesion. (Kerr et al., 2016; Winters et al., 2003; Testaverde et al., 2016).

The consolidation of people analytics expanded this strategic shift by incorporating machine learning algorithms on performance, collaboration, and well-being databases. Analysing productivity, turnover and engagement patterns in diverse workforces allows projects to be assigned according to technological affinity and digital maturity, but it also requires the development of ethical frameworks to avoid bias and ensure transparency. The intersection between advanced analytics and work ergonomics revalues the matrix of polyvalent skills: turnover is no longer only preventive against injuries, but also a mechanism for expanding the cognitive repertoire and relational capital.

At the same time, management models are oriented towards global pools of competencies that transcend organizational and geographical borders. The assignment of tasks is supported by collaborative platforms that integrate data on previous experience, languages, leadership styles and time availability; this requires governance frameworks capable of balancing flexibility with legal and psychological certainty (Mikalef et al., 2018;).

Transitioning From Face-to-Face Work to Remote Hybrid

The software industry tested distributed teams since the 1990s, but subsequent financial and health crises accelerated the adoption of remote work as an accepted norm. The COVID pandemic forced the reconfiguration of work processes, technologies, and cultures in a matter of weeks, validating asynchronous collaboration and deliverable management instead of face-to-face control.

The consolidation of hybrid schemes posed unprecedented regulatory challenges: bilateral agreements to avoid double taxation, coordination of social security systems, and clarification of the applicable jurisdiction in labor disputes. Discussions on Mode 4 of the GATS, originally designed for the temporary provision of services, provide a legal basis for understanding the mobility of professionals operating from countries other than their employer (Winters et al., 2003; Kerr et al., 2016).

The emergence of intermediaries acting as employers of record in multiple countries facilitates regulatory compliance and allows organizations to focus on coordinating the value created. These platforms, combined with advanced analytics, help map legal risks, tax burdens, and cultural compatibility, bridging the gap between corporate strategy and the day-to-day reality of distributed work (Mikalef et al., 2018).

THEORETICAL FRAMEWORK

Dynamic Capabilities Theory and Organizational Adaptation

The notion of dynamic capacities refers to the institutional competence to perceive discontinuities, interpret them with a strategic sense and reconfigure resources, structures and routines in order to sustain performance in changing environments, integrating processes of exploration, appropriation and transformation that act as a coherent system of collective learning and organizational renewal.

The sensing, seizing and transforming scheme is understood today as a continuous cycle rather than as sequential stages, since technological and market surveillance feeds investment and organizational design decisions, while the subsequent reconfiguration generates new information for the next cycle, so that strategic agility depends both on the quality of interpretation and on the speed to institutionalize changes without eroding cultural coherence.

Behavioral microfoundations incorporate managerial attention, the absorption of external knowledge, deliberate experimentation, and the coordination of dispersed competencies, so that dynamic capacity emerges from multiscale interactions between individuals, teams, and technological systems that configure flexible routines without falling into permanent improvisation.

Path dependence operates as a limit and simultaneous asset, since the paths traveled constrain the range of options but also provide organizational memory that can be creatively recombined if there are mechanisms of unlearning, internal variation, and critical reflection on the routines that are taken for granted.

The measurement of dynamic capabilities requires distinguishing them from operational capabilities, so configurational models that integrate structure, strategy and environment are used, and scales that capture processes such as resource orchestration, knowledge integration and business model renewal, avoiding confusing performance results with the underlying capacity that enables them.

The link between dynamic capacities and organizational resilience is expressed in the ability to absorb shocks, recompose supply chains, and redirect investments without losing purpose, which requires governance structures that legitimize quick decisions, digital platforms that accelerate the flow of information, and cultures that tolerate error as a learning input.

Human Capital and Intellectual Capital in Transnational Contexts

Human capital acquires the status of intellectual capital when it is integrated into networks that allow individual skills to be transformed into collective value, articulating tacit and explicit knowledge through shared practices, reciprocity norms and platforms that facilitate the codification and reuse of knowledge on a global scale.

The discussion between talent loss and global circulation shows that the departure of professionals can become a virtuous flow when institutional ties are established that facilitate mentoring, co-investment and temporary return, so that the knowledge accumulated in innovation poles is reinjected at the source through collaborative projects and networks of trust. (Meyer et al., 2001).

The conversion between tacit and explicit knowledge in distributed teams requires rich contexts of interaction, collaborative technologies, and leaderships capable of translating local practices into common languages, so organizations design cross-border communities of practice and psychological contracts that recognize expectations for development, mobility, and participation in results to maintain engagement at a distance.

Retention and repatriation strategies combine material incentives with symbolic recognition and clear professional trajectories, so that the decision to return or remain linked does not depend only on salary, but on the possibility of influencing research agendas, undertaking with institutional support and maintaining transnational professional identity. (Meyer et al., 2001).

The relational value of intellectual capital is enhanced when the organization acts as a node that connects dispersed experts, integrates performance and collaboration data, and adjusts its processes so that cultural diversity is a source of innovation and not conflict, which implies metrics that capture collective contributions and governance systems that balance flexibility with legal and psychological security.

Strategic Knowledge Management and Inter-Organizational Transfer

Strategic knowledge management is based on a scaffolding of social processes that translate individual experiences into collective assets through socialization, externalization, combination, and internalization, but its real effectiveness depends on extending the SECI model to multiple geographies where cooperation and competition coexist and where trust is built with governance mechanisms that reduce hostility to exchange and align incentives between partners Organizational; In this framework, the socio-technical architecture must enable cycles of observation, translation and continuous reconfiguration of knowledge so that routines are not fossilized and reciprocity can be sustained even when the actors belong to different corporate cultures (Faraj et al., 2016).

Virtual communities of practice and open innovation consortia act as privileged vehicles for sharing specialized knowledge as long as there is a balance between symbolic recognition, clear intellectual property rules, and digital platforms that reduce communicative friction; The creation of practice landscapes that connect diverse professional fields and the controlled opening of organizational boundaries allow the flow of knowledge to be oriented towards both exploration and exploitation, integrating collective contribution metrics and appropriation protocols that avoid the dilution of the value created. (Faraj et al., 2016).

Effective transfer between organizations requires absorption capacity, understood as the set of routines to recognize, assimilate and exploit external knowledge, which means investing in technological scanning instruments, appropriability metrics and relational structures that facilitate two-way flows without eroding competitive advantage; This capacity is operationalized through scales that distinguish potential and realized dimensions, and is reinforced when work design, motivation, and engagement mechanisms decrease hostility to exchange and promote the circulation of tacit and explicit knowledge. (Flatten et al., 2011).

When cooperation crosses institutional borders, knowledge governance requires combining formal and social instruments: contracts that clarify rights over results, networks of trust that legitimize the vulnerability necessary to share errors, and algorithmic mechanisms that recommend connections and content without reproducing biases; The result is an ecosystem where interorganizational transfer depends not only on initial agreements, but on the ability to adjust rules, roles, and technologies as new opportunities and tensions emerge. (Chesbrough et al., 2014).

International Human Resources Mobility

The mobility of qualified personnel can no longer be described only from the classic figure of the expatriate sent by the company for extended stays, because self-managed trajectories emerge that seek brief experiences, combine remote work with face-to-face periods and configure careers that cross multiple organizations and jurisdictions; This diversity includes professionals who negotiate their own packages, consultants who alternate global projects and employees who move virtually through digital platforms, which forces us to rethink the systems of selection, development and performance evaluation to capture value from non-linear trajectories and simultaneous belongings.

The transition to self-initiated modalities is sustained by a logic of individual agency where the professional assumes the costs and risks of mobility to obtain career capital, networks and international visibility, while the company benefits from already proven competencies without incurring the full expenses of a traditional assignment; At the same time, the models of short assignment, frequent travel and virtual work demand different support policies in mental health, family reconciliation and continuous learning, since spatial dispersion increases coordination complexity and reduces direct supervision, so that retention depends on the quality of the psychological bond rather than on physical permanence.

Circular migration is consolidated as a mechanism that allows the skills accumulated in high-tech destinations to periodically return to the organization or country of origin, creating a cumulative learning circuit where the individual acts as a cognitive and social bridge; This pattern is strengthened when there are institutional incentives for temporary return, credential recognition frameworks, and platforms that facilitate collaborative projects at a distance, so that the exit is no longer interpreted as a definitive loss and becomes a distributed investment in human capital (Padula et al., 2017; Adams et al., 2013; Nykänen et al., 2020).

The design of hybrid travel contracts and the adoption of center-type structures and spokes require legal clarity on the applicable law, coordinated social security agreements and metrics that allow value to be attributed when the professional reports to more than one site or delivers results from a third country; Hierarchical authority is blurred in the face of project networks, so management shifts towards the orchestration of resources and the construction of distributed trust, relying on monitoring tools that integrate productivity, collaboration and well-being without invading privacy (Padula et al., 2017).

The effectiveness of these configurations depends on contractual and technological devices that measure contributions in contexts where physical presence is no longer a sufficient criterion, so indicators of knowledge transfer, relational density and ability to solve problems in multicultural teams are required, in addition to legal and fiscal risk assessments that contemplate double taxation. immigration compliance and data protection; The result is a mobility architecture that integrates normative governance with organizational design and learning, aimed at preserving competitive advantage without sacrificing the integrity of people.

Accelerated Organizational Learning Paradigms

Accelerated learning relies on short units of content that are consumed in short intervals, anchored in real problems, and offer immediate feedback, so that retention and transfer are maximized when that micro-content is linked to strategic indicators and performance metrics that guide daily practice towards verifiable objectives; Instructional design must combine task analysis, semantic segmentation, and continuous formative assessment so that tacit knowledge emerges and is codified without saturating working memory or fragmenting the meaning of the educational process.

The use of simulations and digital twins in risk environments makes it possible to recreate critical situations with contextual fidelity, accelerate the acquisition of procedural skills and consolidate response habits through deliberate practice and situated repetition, while performance sensors feed algorithms that adjust the difficulty to the level of expertise demonstrated by the person; By transferring the experience to synthetic scenarios, exposure to incidents is reduced and transfer to the real terrain is increased thanks to controlled emotional activation and immediate reinforcement of correct behavior. (Scorgie et al., 2024).

The action-learning approach articulates teams that work on specific problems, alternate cycles of reflection and execution and document the findings so that they are transformed into institutional knowledge, stimulating metacognition, the construction of shared meaning and collective responsibility for results; In this way, the organization learns to learn in short periods of time because the process integrates critical analysis, controlled experimentation, and social feedback that strengthens organizational memory (Padula et al., 2017; Adams et al., 2013; Nykänen et al., 2020).

Algorithmic Talent Governance and Predictive Analytics

The exploitation of large volumes of data on performance, collaboration and learning makes it possible to anticipate skills gaps, prescribe personalised training itineraries and optimise the allocation of people to critical projects, but introduces ethical dilemmas related to transparency, informed consent, model explainability and statistical biases that can reproduce structural inequalities; Governance must incorporate principles of fairness, accountability and auditability so that analytics do not erode trust or make the worker an opaque object of automatic decisions. (Mittelstadt et al., 2016).

Career path recommendation systems can perpetuate gender, race, or national origin gaps when trained with biased histories or when they optimize narrow efficiency metrics, making it imperative to conduct equity audits, open decision logic to expert human review, and combine predictions with contextualized judgments that recognize the cultural and cognitive diversity of the workforce; Continuous impact evaluation and the participation of affected groups in the design of algorithms are minimum conditions to legitimize their use. (Veale, et al., 2018; Selbst et al., 2019; Greene et al., 2019).

Effective algorithmic governance requires regulatory frameworks that define responsibilities of developers and employers, interoperability standards between platforms and competency profile portability rights so that each person retains control over their learning evidence throughout their global journey; The formulation of ethical principles must be translated into operating procedures, auditable metrics and sanctioning mechanisms that make the protection of autonomy and dignity enforceable in contexts of digital talent management. (Floridi et al., 2018; Jobin et al., 2019).

Political Economy of Migration Regulation

Migration policies crystallize tensions between labor protectionism and productivity needs, expressed in visa quotas by sector, clauses for the mutual recognition of credentials, and diplomatic strategies aimed at attracting specialists in science and technology; Negotiation between state, business and trade union actors determines the degree of openness, while deep trade agreements incorporate chapters on temporary mobility that connect knowledge flows with global value chains. (Shachar et al., 2017; Winters et al., 2003; Mattoo et al., 2020).

Talent diplomacy arises when governments compete for researchers and entrepreneurs with comprehensive packages that combine immigration facilities, seed funding, access to laboratories, and collaboration networks, so that industrial and migration policy are intertwined to sustain national competitive advantages; selection becomes strategic by weighting patents, publications, and leadership in disruptive projects as admission criteria, and return programs transform the brain drain into virtuous circulation. (Kerr, et al., 2016).

Border controls generate transaction costs and potential losses of innovation by retaining human capital in contexts of low technological absorption or by making it difficult to efficiently match competencies and productive demands, so welfare analyses must incorporate indirect effects on productivity, entrepreneurship and dissemination of knowledge; Assessing these externalities requires models that integrate international economics, sociology of migration, and innovation studies. (Czaika & Parsons, 2017; Ortega & Peri, 2014).

Neuroscience and Cognitive Plasticity Applied to Multifunctional Work

Neuroplasticity describes the brain's ability to reorganize synaptic connections in response to new demands, which constitutes the biological basis of rapid learning and the reconversion of skills required by organizations in scenarios of continuous change; Neuroimaging studies show increases in gray matter and functional modifications after short periods of intensive practice, evidencing that the brain structure is sensitive to diversified work experience. (Draganski et al., 2004; Pascual-Leone et al., 2005).

The theory of cognitive load warns that learning in high-pressure environments must modulate the volume of new information and the level of complexity so as not to saturate working memory, so instructional designs adjust the difficulty to previous expertise through progressive scaffolding and spaced practice; Controlling the intrinsic and extrinsic load becomes key so that speed does not compromise the quality of learning or the mental health of the employee (Young, et al., 2014; Kirschner et al., 2006; Paas et al., 2004).

The construct learning agility refers to the willingness and ability to learn from experience and apply that learning in unprecedented situations, integrating psychological resilience, self-regulation and curiosity as components of future employability; Measuring and developing this agility requires validated psychometric instruments, reflective mentoring and environments that legitimize error as a resource for growth, thus reinforcing the sustainability of individual and collective dynamic capacities (Pulakos et al., 2000).

Theory of Networks and Ecosystems of Global Innovation

Competitive advantage based on networks emerges when mobile actors occupy intermediation positions that connect distant epistemic communities, allowing knowledge to be recombined and innovation cycles in distributed value chains to be shortened; Centrality, brokerage, and structural diversity become key attributes to explain the scientific and technological productivity of organizations and regions.

Open innovation extends this principle by integrating customers, suppliers, universities, and start-ups into collaborative processes where intellectual property is negotiated and trust is institutionalized through flexible contracts and digital platforms, configuring ecosystems that transcend the individual signature and require polycentric governance to balance openness and ownership. (Chesbrough et al., 2014).

The scientific diaspora acts as a technological bridge by transferring tacit knowledge, expanding collaboration networks and facilitating the circulation of projects between laboratories, so that the skilled migrant becomes an agent of systemic development beyond his or her individual productivity; Policies that recognize this function enhance the density and quality of linkages, producing multiplied returns for origin and destination (Meyer, et al., 2001).

Risk Management in the Relocation of Personnel

Relocation involves legal, health, and reputational risks that must be managed with multi-jurisdictional due diligence, health and safety protocols, and contingency plans that ensure the timely evacuation of talent in critical situations; The systematic identification and evaluation of legal, fiscal and social threats becomes essential when the company operates with distributed structures and personnel that alternate locations.

Transnational regulatory compliance requires mapping differences in labor legislation, taxation, and social protection, in addition to articulating agreements with local suppliers that guarantee ethical standards and avoid discriminatory or coercive practices in recruitment; Coordination between legal, human resources and corporate social responsibility departments makes it possible to prevent litigation and sanctions, as well as to protect institutional reputation. (Bader et al., 2015).

The reputational risk associated with failures in migration management can erode the employer brand and the trust of local communities, so transparency, two-way communication and accountability are integrated into crisis response frameworks; Organizational legitimacy depends on demonstrating coherence between discourse and practice, especially when displaced talent faces vulnerability. (Bundy et al., 2017).

Corporate Social Responsibility and Ethics of Labour Mobility

Social responsibility in mobility requires principles of fair recruitment, absence of coercion and respect for diversity, equity and inclusion, so that transfer and assignment decisions do not reproduce inequalities of gender, race or nationality; Integrating these principles into operational policies and procedures ensures that the human capital strategy is consistent with declared values and international standards.

The comprehensive well-being of mobile workers requires psychosocial support, access to health services, family accompaniment and mechanisms to maintain social networks of origin, avoiding the emotional isolation that usually accompanies geographical and cultural transitions; Investing in cultural adaptation programs and expat communities of practice increases retention and reduces psychological burnout (Caligiuri et al., 2020; Stahl et al., 2002; Lazarova et al., 2010).

Transparency in the talent supply chain involves reporting mobility practices in sustainability reports, including human development indicators, and subjecting international recruitment processes to independent audits that show the social impact of the human capital strategy; Integrated reporting frameworks link financial and social performance, strengthening legitimacy in the eyes of investors and communities (Eccles et al., 2014; Kölbel et al., 2020; Gond et al., 2012; Baumgartner & Ebner, 2010).

CHALLENGES FACED BY ORGANIZATIONS OR INSTITUTIONS

Organizations and institutions today operate on a global chessboard marked by labor, tax, and social security rules that change by border, while digitizing their talent management and safeguarding growing volumes of sensitive data. At the same time, they must retrain quickly without saturating the cognitive capacity of their teams and contain the digital fatigue that arises from permanent connectivity.

Regulatory Fragmentation and Multi-Jurisdictional Coordination

The expansion of cross-border remote work and hybrid assignments exposes organizations to a patchwork of labor, tax, and social security rules that rarely dialogue with each other; Coordinating what legislation applies, how contributions are calculated, and which authority can audit requires investing in specialized legal teams and monitoring tools that integrate regulatory changes in real time, because a minimal error can translate into penalties, double taxation, or loss of coverage for the employee, affecting reputation and operational continuity.

Data Protection and Cybersecurity in HR Tech Ecosystems

The digitalisation of talent management concentrates biometric, psychometric and performance data on platforms that operate across multiple countries, which makes it necessary to make frameworks such as the European GDPR compatible with heterogeneous sectoral and state regulations; In addition, the increase in ransomware attacks on human resources databases shows that privacy is not only legal compliance, but a strategic asset that demands advanced encryption, minimization principles and periodic audits of cloud providers (Martin et al., 2017).

Speed of Reskilling and Training Exhaustion

The pressure to retrain the workforce at the pace of automation and artificial intelligence generates accelerated resumes that often saturate the cognitive capacity of employees and dilute the effective transfer to the position; Sustaining reskilling programs requires diagnosing real gaps, dosing learning through significant microcycles and guaranteeing contextualized practice times to prevent training from becoming an additional burden that erodes commitment and mental health.

Digital Fatigue, Psychosocial Health and Limits of Connectivity

The hyperconnectivity of distributed work increases information overload, extends the working day to domestic spaces and leads to digital fatigue that is expressed in insomnia, irritability and decreased creative productivity; Organizations must design disconnection policies, redesign communication flows, and train leaders to recognize early signs of burnout, otherwise turnover and absenteeism increase while the climate of trust deteriorates.

Transfer of Tacit Knowledge in Dispersed Teams

When teams are distributed geographically, the tacit knowledge that previously circulated in face-to-face interaction loses natural channels of transmission; sustaining it requires deliberate digital rituals, time rotations, asynchronous mentoring, and devices that capture narratives of experience without reducing them to checklists, because competitive advantage lies in those nuances that manuals do not codify (Argote & Ingram, 2000; Leonardi, 2021).

Measuring the Value and Return of Cross-Training

Demonstrating the impact of multi-purpose training and internal mobilities continues to be a methodological challenge: the benefits are often intangible, expressed in operational resilience or in the reduction of downtime, and are not always captured in traditional financial indicators; therefore, mixed models that combine projective ROI, adoption metrics, quality of decision-making, and density of collaborative networks are recommended as complementary approaches (Salas et al., 2012).

Algorithmic Biases and the Legitimacy of Predictive Analytics

Trajectory recommendation systems and automated selection tools can amplify pre-existing inequalities if they are trained with biased historical data or if they optimize efficiency variables on principles of justice; Sustaining the social legitimacy of talent analytics requires independent audits, model explainability, and hybrid processes where informed human judgment corrects automated decisions.

Equity of Access and Cultural Cohesion in Mobility

Access to international mobility opportunities and cross-cutting training programs tends to favor already privileged profiles if clear criteria and inclusion metrics are not established; In addition, the cultural integration of hybrid teams depends on recognizing asymmetries of symbolic power and creating spaces for legitimate voice for minorities, preventing diversity from being treated as compliance and not as a source of innovation (Nishii, 2013; Ferdman & Deane, 2014).

EXAMPLES OF IMPLEMENTATION IN COMPANIES OR ORGANIZATIONS

Toyota Motor Manufacturing Kentucky, Airbus in Hamburg and Embraer in São José dos Campos integrated skill matrices to rotate technicians between welding, assembly and testing, relying on ergonomic redesign and digital boards that show coverage by process and activate immediate replacements; This practice stabilizes the flow, reduces unemployment and turns lateral mobility into a path of professional development validated by union agreements and operational quality metrics (Adler et al., 1999).

IBM promoted an ecosystem of digital microcredentials that certifies technical and leadership skills with open traceability, while AT&T financed a massive program of reconversion towards data and cybersecurity profiles and Banco Santander articulated its corporate university with external itineraries to accelerate upskilling in financial analytics and regulation; They all combine learning analytics with internal tutors to ensure transfer to the position (Noe et al., 2013; Gašević et al., 2015).

Rio Tinto and BHP adopted digital twins and virtual reality to train explosive charge maneuvers and underground evacuation, Shell simulated plant stoppages in immersive environments to reduce incidents, and Maersk replicated port operations in collaborative simulators that capture biomechanical metrics; Performance data fuels adaptive adjustments that accelerate the learning curve without putting teams at risk (Radianti et al., 2020; Makransky, Terkildsen, & Mayer, 2019; McGaghie et al., 2011; Moro et al., 2017).

GitLab and Automattic operate with total distributed work and open repositories that document decisions, Spotify combined remote squads with synchronous rituals to preserve team identity and Shopify migrated to a digital model by default redefining evaluation criteria by results; These experiences show that the success of remote learning requires redesigning coordination, disconnection rights, and spaces to socialize tacit knowledge (Choudhury et al., 2021; Mazmanian et al., 2013; Bloom et al., 2015).

Unilever integrated people analytics to align international mobility with diversity goals, Nestlé used predictive dashboards to plan global successions, Deloitte cross-referenced project data and skills to assign consultants to cross-border missions, and Microsoft audited its internal algorithms to reduce bias in promotions; All four companies show that the legitimacy of analytics depends on audits of fairness, explainability, and stakeholder engagement (Tambe et al., 2019; Boudreau & Cascio, 2017).

DHL Supply Chain designed multi-jurisdictional compliance programs for logistics mobility, Novartis harmonized benefits and social security in short assignments of researchers, Siemens created a global center of legal excellence for cross-border telework and Ericsson implemented framework agreements to avoid double taxation on short trips; These initiatives show that legal coordination is inseparable from the global talent strateg (Mayer et al., 2021).

RESULTS

The qualitative analysis reveals that organizations that linked cross-training with international mobility trajectories were able to sustain operations even under severe restrictions, because they did not limit themselves to moving personnel but activated repertoires of shared skills and networks of trust capable of redistributing critical tasks without degrading quality or safety standards. Resilience appeared as an emerging property of a human capital conceived as a collective resource, in constant recombination and learning, rather than as a set of isolated specialists in rigid functions (Lengnick-Hall et al., 2011; Ployhart & Moliterno, 2011).

The contrast between physical risk industries and knowledge-based sectors showed that micro-credential ecosystems, virtual reality and learning analytics accelerate contextual competence acquisition when modules are connected to concrete problems and are rigorously curated pedagogical; without this anchorage, catalogs proliferate that do not translate into observable performance or effective transfer. Immersive simulations and digital twins provided deliberate practice without exposing them to incidents, although their effectiveness depends on adaptive metrics that adjust the difficulty to the real level of expertise and on spaces for collective reflection that transform data into organizational learning.

Several companies negotiated with authorities and multilateral organizations experimental frameworks of flexible regulation that reduced validation and litigation times, but these benefits were conditional on explicit commitments to social protection and transparency. The comparison between finance and manufacturing suggests that regulatory sandboxes operate as institutional learning devices only when they include decent work standards and co-evaluation mechanisms with unions and communities of practice, transforming regulation into a strategic resource rather than an obstacle (Zetzsche et al., 2017).

The use of predictive models to assign projects, prioritize training, and anticipate skills gaps increased the speed of response, although it opened up an ethical dilemma: technical accuracy does not guarantee legitimacy if algorithms work as black boxes or replicate biases present in historical data. Organizations that incorporated independent audits, technical explainability, and opportunities to challenge recommendations strengthened internal trust, while those that delegated critical decisions to opaque systems generated new inequities in access to opportunities and internal mobility (Barocas & Selbst, 2016; Mittelstadt et al., 2019).

The accelerated pace of retraining and the dissolution of temporal boundaries in distributed work produced cognitive fatigue and emotional exhaustion that, if left unattended, erode the continuity of performance and retention. The cases with the best results combined effective disconnection policies, spaced microlearning, and spaces for conversation that legitimize error as an input for improvement; the affective dimension was shown to be a condition for training investment not to be diluted in turnover or apathy.

Measuring the value of multipurpose training was challenging, because the benefits manifest themselves as operational resilience, density of collaborative networks or risk reduction, dimensions difficult to capture with traditional financial indicators. Teams that incorporated network analysis, evaluative narratives, and longitudinal metrics complemented the classic ROI with cumulative learning evidence, offering a truer picture of the complexity of the phenomenon (Youndt et al., 2004).

The geographical dispersion of the teams hindered the circulation of tacit knowledge that was previously transmitted in everyday interaction. Sustaining this intangible required deliberate digital rituals, temporal rotations, asynchronous mentoring, and technologies capable of capturing stories of experience without reducing them to checklists; the competitive advantage rested on nuances that the manuals do not codify and that require spaces for storytelling, observation, and peer accompaniment to endure (Kellogg et al., 2020).

Access to international mobility and transversal training tended to concentrate on privileged profiles when transparent criteria and inclusion metrics were lacking; In addition, the cultural cohesion of hybrid teams depended on recognizing asymmetries of symbolic power and opening spaces of legitimate voice for minority groups, preventing diversity from being reduced to formal compliance. Innovation associated with diversity appeared when it was incorporated into routines, recognition systems, and strategic decisions, not when it was confined to declarative campaigns (Nishii, 2013; Shore et al., 2011).

The cross-sectional synthesis of the findings suggests that the most effective practices integrate four inseparable layers: pedagogical design linked to real problems, transparent and auditable technological architecture, normative governance built in dialogue with social actors, and sustained care for the psychosocial dimension.

The evidence analyzed shows that the conscious articulation between cross-training and cross-border mobility of talent allows operational continuity to be sustained in contexts of severe restriction because it activates collective repertoires of skills and networks of trust that redistribute critical tasks without sacrificing quality or safety standards, revealing that resilience is an emerging property of human capital managed as a dynamic resource and not as the sum of isolated specializations (Lengnick-Hall et al., 2011).

The effectiveness of digital training infrastructures depends less on technological novelty than on their alignment with specific problems and on pedagogical curation that avoids inflated catalogs without translation into performance; Microcredentials, immersive simulations, and learning analytics accelerate the contextual acquisition of competencies when integrated into reflective processes that convert data into organizational knowledge and preserve tacit knowledge that does not fit on checklists (Argote & Ingram, 2000).

The search for regulatory flexibility through sandboxes, bilateral agreements or figures such as Mode Four of trade in services only becomes a strategic lever when it is accompanied by explicit commitments to decent work, transparency and the participation of social actors; in this scenario, regulation ceases to operate as a brake and becomes an institutional learning device that reduces litigation and accelerates the validation of credentials without eroding rights.

The deployment of predictive analytics to assign projects and prioritize training increases the speed of response, but its legitimacy is sustained by the explainability of the models, independent audits and the possibility of challenging automated recommendations; without these counterweights, the biases embedded in historical data translate into new inequities and damage the internal trust that analytics itself seeks to strengthen (Barocas & Selbst, 2016; Mittelstadt et al., 2019).

The accelerated pace of reskilling and the dissolution of temporal boundaries in distributed work generate cognitive fatigue and emotional exhaustion that, if left unattended, dilute the benefits of training investment; the most solid cases combined real policies of disconnection, spaced microlearning, and collective spaces for reflection that legitimize error as input, demonstrating that the affective dimension is a condition of possibility for the sustainability of learning.

The circulation of tacit knowledge is complicated when teams are geographically dispersed; sustaining it requires deliberate digital rituals, asynchronous mentoring, and temporal rotations that keep alive the stories of experience and practical nuances that manuals do not capture, reaffirming that competitive advantage rests on the combination of collaborative technologies and meaningful human bonds (Leonardi, 2021; Kellogg et al., 2020; Argote & Ingram, 2000).

Measuring the real value of multipurpose training requires going beyond the immediate financial return and incorporating indicators of operational resilience, relational density and cumulative learning; approaches that integrate network analysis, evaluative narratives, and longitudinal traceability offer a more accurate representation of the ability to absorb shocks and reconfigure resources than linear models of return calculation.

Equity of access to mobility and transversal training continues to be a blind spot when selection criteria are not transparent and when diversity is managed as symbolic compliance; innovation associated with heterogeneous workforces appears when inclusion is institutionalized through legitimate voice, psychological safety, and recognition systems that value diverse contributions to everyday practice.

In summary, building organizational resilience in the face of severe constraints requires integrating four interdependent layers: pedagogical design anchored in real problems, transparent and auditable technological architecture, normative governance co-built with social actors, and sustained care for psychosocial well-being. Only when these dimensions are articulated do dynamic capacities emerge to perceive discontinuities, reconfigure resources, and sustain performance without losing legitimacy in the eyes of stakeholders.

Coherently integrating cross-training and cross-border mobility involves designing situated training itineraries that connect with specific operational needs, negotiating regulatory frameworks that legitimise the circulation of talent and guarantee social protection, and sustaining emotional support ecosystems that prevent fatigue derived from hyperconnectivity; in this way, the organization combines agility with equity and takes care of the human dimension of change.

The right mix of digital infrastructures, clear rules, and algorithmic governance is achieved when microcredential and analytics platforms undergo equity audits, when sandboxes incorporate decent work standards, and when communities of practice become bridges to tacit knowledge, avoiding biases and preserving the contextual richness of knowledge (Barocas & Selbst, 2016; Shachar et al., 2017; Kellogg et al., 2020).

The evaluation of the value generated demands hybrid metrics that capture resilience, collaboration, and cumulative institutional learning, integrating network analysis and longitudinal narratives to show that the return lies in the ability to recombine people and processes in the face of uncertainty, rather than in immediate increases in financial productivity (Youndt et al., 2004).

RECOMMENDATIONS FOR FUTURE RESEARCH

Future research should build longitudinal assessments that mix network analysis, digital ethnographic narratives, and resilience metrics to capture the intangible value of cross-learning and mobility, avoiding financial reductionisms that mask cumulative learning and collaboration. Comparing sectors and geographies will make it possible to identify patterns of emergence of dynamic capacities and translate them into useful tools for strategy (Youndt et al., 2004).

It is worth delving into experimental regulatory frameworks and bilateral agreements that enable the temporary movement of professionals, analysing how decent work standards, recognition of credentials and social protection, as well as risks of regulatory capture, are negotiated.

Algorithmic governance requires studies that combine fairness audits with legitimacy and trust analyses, comparing interpretable models with black boxes to set ethical and operational risk thresholds (Barocas & Selbst, 2016).

It is key to investigate the psychosocial dimension of accelerated reskilling and distributed work through mixed designs that include stress biomarkers and experience diaries, in order to propose pedagogical rhythms and evidence-based disconnection policies.

The transfer of tacit knowledge in dispersed teams requires virtual ethnography, digital traces, and rotation experiments to understand what rituals and artifacts sustain that know-how.

It is also necessary to examine the pedagogical architecture of microcredentials, virtual reality and learning analytics from their coherence with real problems and their curation, differentiating when they enhance performance and when they generate digital bureaucracy.

Equity in access to mobility and transversal training opens a field to study the relationship between selection criteria, inclusion climates and innovation results, showing how diversity produces advantage when it permeates routines and evaluation systems.

Coherently integrating cross-training and cross-border mobility requires situated itineraries, legitimized regulatory frameworks and psychosocial care so that agility does not become human exhaustion; thus, talent moves along with rights and support. The right mix of digital infrastructures, clear rules, and algorithmic governance appears when platforms are audited for fairness, their logic is explained, and communities of practice keep tacit knowledge alive. Assessing the real value of these strategies demands hybrid metrics that capture resilience, collaboration, and cumulative learning, showing that return is reflected in the ability to recombine people and processes in the face of uncertainty rather than in immediate financial gains.

REFERENCES

Adams, A. A., Liyanagunawardena, T. R., Rassool, N., & Williams, S. (2013). Use of open educational resources in higher education. *British Journal of Educational Technology*, *44*(5), E149–E150. DOI: 10.1111/bjet.12014

Adler, P. S., Goldoftas, B., & Levine, D. I. (1999). Flexibility versus efficiency? A case study of model changeovers in the Toyota production system. *Organization Science*, *10*(1), 43–68. DOI: 10.1287/orsc.10.1.43

Argote, L., & Ingram, P. (2000). Knowledge transfer: A basis for competitive advantage in firms. *Organizational Behavior and Human Decision Processes*, *82*(1), 150–169. DOI: 10.1006/obhd.2000.2893

Bader, B., Berg, N., & Holtbrügge, D. (2015). Expatriate performance in terrorism-endangered countries: The role of family and organizational support. *International Business Review*, *24*(5), 849–860. DOI: 10.1016/j.ibusrev.2015.03.005

Barocas, S., & Selbst, A. D. (2016). Big data's disparate impact. *SSRN*, *104*(3), 671–732. DOI: 10.2139/ssrn.2477899

Baumgartner, R. J., & Ebner, D. (2010). Corporate sustainability strategies: Sustainability profiles and maturity levels. *Sustainable Development (Bradford)*, *18*(2), 76–89. DOI: 10.1002/sd.447

Bloom, N., Liang, J., Roberts, J., & Ying, Z. J. (2015). Does working from home work? Evidence from a Chinese experiment. *The Quarterly Journal of Economics*, *130*(1), 165–218. DOI: 10.1093/qje/qju032

Boudreau, J. W., & Cascio, W. F. (2017). Human capital analytics: Why are we not there? *Journal of Organizational Effectiveness: People and Performance*, *4*(2), 119–126. DOI: 10.1108/JOEPP-03-2017-0021

Bundy, J., Pfarrer, M. D., Short, C. E., & Coombs, W. T. (2017). Crises and crisis management: Integration, interpretation, and research development. *Journal of Management*, *43*(6), 1661–1692. DOI: 10.1177/0149206316680030

Caligiuri, P., De Cieri, H., Minbaeva, D., Verbeke, A., & Zimmermann, A. (2020). International HRM insights for navigating the COVID-19 pandemic: Implications for future research and practice. *Journal of International Business Studies*, *51*(5), 697–713. DOI: 10.1057/s41267-020-00335-9 PMID: 32836500

Chesbrough, H., Vanhaverbeke, W., West, J., & Bogers, M. (Eds.). (2014). *New frontiers in open innovation*. Oxford University Press., DOI: 10.1093/acprof:oso/9780199682461.001.0001

Choudhury, P., Foroughi, C., & Larson, B. Z. (2021). Work from anywhere: The productivity effects of geographic flexibility. *Strategic Management Journal*, *42*(4), 655–683. DOI: 10.1002/smj.3251

Czaika, M., & Parsons, C. R. (2017). The gravity of high-skilled migration policies. *Demography*, *54*(2), 603–630. DOI: 10.1007/s13524-017-0559-1 PMID: 28290123

Draganski, B., Gaser, C., Busch, V., Schuierer, G., Bogdahn, U., & May, A. (2004). Neuroplasticity: Changes in grey matter induced by training. *Nature*, *427*(6972), 311–312. DOI: 10.1038/427311a PMID: 14737157

Eccles, R. G., Ioannou, I., Serafeim, G., & Chee, K. (2014). The impact of a corporate culture of sustainability on corporate behavior and performance. *Management Science*, *60*(11), 2835–2857. DOI: 10.1287/mnsc.2014.1984

Edmondson, A. C., & Lei, Z. (2014). Psychological safety: The history, renaissance, and future of an interpersonal construct. *Annual Review of Organizational Psychology and Organizational Behavior*, *1*(1), 23–43. DOI: 10.1146/annurev-orgpsych-031413-091305

Faraj, S., von Krogh, G., Monteiro, E., & Lakhani, K. R. (2016). Online community as space for knowledge flows. *Information Systems Research*, *27*(4), 668–684. DOI: 10.1287/isre.2016.0682

Ferdman, B. M., & Deane, B. R. (Eds.). (2014). *Diversity at work: The practice of inclusion*. Wiley., DOI: 10.1002/9781118764282

Flatten, T. C., Engelen, A., Zahra, S. A., & Brettel, M. (2011). A measure of absorptive capacity: Scale development and validation. *European Management Journal*, *29*(2), 98–116. DOI: 10.1016/j.emj.2010.11.002

Floridi, L., Cowls, J., Beltrametti, M., Chatila, R., & Chiaraviglio, L. (2018). AI4People—An ethical framework for a good AI society: Opportunities, risks, principles, and recommendations. *Minds and Machines*, *28*(4), 689–707. DOI: 10.1007/s11023-018-9482-5 PMID: 30930541

Gašević, D., Dawson, S., & Siemens, G. (2015). Let's not forget: Learning analytics are about learning. *TechTrends*, *59*(1), 64–71. DOI: 10.1007/s11528-014-0822-x

Gond, J. P., Grubnic, S., Herzig, C., & Moon, J. (2012). Configuring management control systems: Theorizing the integration of strategy and sustainability. *Management Accounting Research*, *23*(3), 205–223. DOI: 10.1016/j.mar.2012.06.003

Greene, D., Hoffmann, A. L., Stark, L., & Crawford, K. (2019). Better, nicer, clearer, fairer: A critical assessment of the movement for ethical AI and ML. *Proceedings of the 52nd Hawaii International Conference on System Sciences*, 2122–2131. https://doi.org/DOI: 10.24251/HICSS.2019.258

Jobin, A., Ienca, M., & Vayena, E. (2019). The global landscape of AI ethics guidelines. *Nature Machine Intelligence*, *1*(9), 389–399. DOI: 10.1038/s42256-019-0088-2

Kellogg, K. C., Valentine, M. A., & Christin, A. (2020). Algorithms at work: The new contested terrain of control. *The Academy of Management Annals*, *14*(1), 366–410. DOI: 10.5465/annals.2018.0174

Kerr, S. P., Kerr, W. R., Özden, Ç., & Parsons, C. (2016). Global talent flows. *The Journal of Economic Perspectives*, *30*(4), 83–106. DOI: 10.1257/jep.30.4.83

Kirschner, P. A., Sweller, J., Clark, R. E., & Ayres, P. (2006). Why minimal guidance during instruction does not work. *Educational Psychologist*, *41*(2), 75–86. DOI: 10.1207/s15326985ep4102_1

Kölbel, J. F., Heeb, F., Paetzold, F., & Busch, T. (2020). Can sustainable investing save the world? Reviewing the mechanisms of investor impact. *Organization & Environment*, *33*(4), 554–574. DOI: 10.1177/1086026620919202

Lazarova, M., Westman, M., & Shaffer, M. A. (2010). Elucidating the positive side of the work–family interface on international assignments: A model of expatriate work and family performance. *Academy of Management Review*, *35*(1), 93–117. DOI: 10.5465/amr.35.1.zok93

Lengnick-Hall, C. A., Beck, T. E., & Lengnick-Hall, M. L. (2011). Developing a capacity for organizational resilience through strategic human resource management. *Human Resource Management Review*, *21*(3), 243–255. DOI: 10.1016/j.hrmr.2010.07.001

Leonardi, P. M. (2021). COVID-19 and the new technologies of organizing: Digital exhaust, digital footprints, and artificial intelligence in the wake of remote work. *Journal of Management Studies*, *58*(1), 249–253. DOI: 10.1111/joms.12648

Makransky, G., Terkildsen, T. S., & Mayer, R. E. (2019). Adding immersive virtual reality to a science lab simulation causes more presence but less learning. *Learning and Instruction*, *60*, 225–236. DOI: 10.1016/j.learninstruc.2017.12.007

Martin, K. D., Borah, A., & Palmatier, R. W. (2017). Data privacy: Effects on customer and firm performance. *Journal of Marketing*, *81*(1), 36–58. DOI: 10.1509/jm.15.0497

Mattoo, A., Rocha, N., Ruta, M., & Kowalski, P. (2020). Movement of capital and people in deep trade agreements. In Mattoo, A. (Eds.), *Handbook of deep trade agreements* (pp. 177–223). World Bank., DOI: 10.1596/978-1-4648-1539-3

Mazmanian, M., Orlikowski, W. J., & Yates, J. (2013). The autonomy paradox: The implications of mobile email devices for knowledge professionals. *Organization Science*, *24*(5), 1337–1357. DOI: 10.1287/orsc.1120.0806

McGaghie, W. C., Issenberg, S. B., Cohen, E. R., Barsuk, J. H., & Wayne, D. B. (2011). Does simulation-based medical education with deliberate practice yield better results than traditional clinical education? A meta-analytic comparative review of the evidence. *Academic Medicine : Journal of the Association of American Medical Colleges*, *86*(6), 706–711. DOI: 10.1097/ACM.0b013e318217e119 PMID: 21512370

Meyer, J. B., Kaplan, D., & Charum, J. (2001). Scientific nomadism and the new geopolitics of knowledge. *International Social Science Journal*, *53*(168), 309–321. DOI: 10.1111/1468-2451.00317

Mikalef, P., Pappas, I. O., Krogstie, J., & Giannakos, M. (2018). Big data analytics capabilities: A systematic literature review and research agenda. *Information Systems and e-Business Management*, *16*(3), 547–578. DOI: 10.1007/s10257-017-0362-y

Mittelstadt, B. D., Allo, P., Taddeo, M., Wachter, S., & Floridi, L. (2016). The ethics of algorithms: Mapping the debate. *Big Data & Society*, *3*(2), 1–21. DOI: 10.1177/2053951716679679

Mittelstadt, B. D., Russell, C., & Wachter, S. (2019). Explaining explanations in AI. *Proceedings of the Conference on Fairness, Accountability, and Transparency*, 279–288. https://doi.org/DOI: 10.1145/3287560.3287574

Moro, C., Štromberga, Z., Raikos, A., & Stirling, A. (2017). The effectiveness of virtual and augmented reality in health sciences and medical anatomy. *Anatomical Sciences Education*, *10*(6), 549–559. DOI: 10.1002/ase.1696 PMID: 28419750

Nishii, L. H. (2013). The benefits of climate for inclusion for gender-diverse groups. *Academy of Management Journal*, *56*(6), 1754–1774. DOI: 10.5465/amj.2009.0823

Noe, R. A., Tews, M. J., & Marand, A. D. (2013). Individual differences and informal learning in the workplace. *Journal of Vocational Behavior*, *83*(3), 327–335. DOI: 10.1016/j.jvb.2013.06.009

Nykänen, M., Puro, V., Tiikkaja, M., & Kannisto, H. (2020). Implementing novel safety training: Benefits of virtual reality and 3D simulation in construction. *Journal of Safety Research, 75*, 205–221. DOI: 10.1016/j.jsr.2020.09.015 PMID: 33334479

Ortega, F., & Peri, G. (2014). Openness and income: The roles of trade and migration. *Journal of International Economics, 92*(2), 231–251. DOI: 10.1016/j.jinteco.2013.11.008

Paas, F., Renkl, A., & Sweller, J. (2004). Cognitive load theory: Instructional implications of the interaction between information structures and cognitive architecture. *Educational Psychologist, 38*(1), 1–4. DOI: 10.1207/S15326985EP3801_1

Padula, R. S., Comper, M. L. C., Sparer, E. H., & Dennerlein, J. T. (2017). Job rotation designed to prevent musculoskeletal disorders and control risk in manufacturing: A systematic review. *Applied Ergonomics, 58*, 386–397. DOI: 10.1016/j.apergo.2016.07.018 PMID: 27633235

Pascual-Leone, A., Amedi, A., Fregni, F., & Merabet, L. B. (2005). The plastic human brain cortex. *Annual Review of Neuroscience, 28*(1), 377–401. DOI: 10.1146/annurev.neuro.27.070203.144216 PMID: 16022601

Ployhart, R. E., & Moliterno, T. P. (2011). Emergence of the human capital resource: A multilevel model. *Academy of Management Review, 36*(1), 127–150. DOI: 10.5465/amr.2009.0318

Pulakos, E. D., Arad, S., Donovan, M. A., & Plamondon, K. E. (2000). Adaptability in the workplace: Development of a taxonomy of adaptive performance. *The Journal of Applied Psychology, 85*(4), 612–624. DOI: 10.1037/0021-9010.85.4.612 PMID: 10948805

Radianti, J., Majchrzak, T. A., Fromm, J., & Wohlgenannt, I. (2020). A systematic review of immersive virtual reality applications for higher education: Design elements, lessons learned, and research agenda. *Computers & Education, 147*, 103778. DOI: 10.1016/j.compedu.2019.103778

Salas, E., Tannenbaum, S. I., Kraiger, K., & Smith-Jentsch, K. A. (2012). The science of training and development in organizations: What matters in practice. *Psychological Science in the Public Interest : A Journal of the American Psychological Society, 13*(2), 74–101. DOI: 10.1177/1529100612436661 PMID: 26173283

Scorgie, D. G., Feng, Z., Paes, D., Parisi, F., Yiu, T. W., & Lovreglio, R. (2024). Virtual reality for safety training: A systematic review and meta-analysis. *Safety Science, 171*, 106372. DOI: 10.1016/j.ssci.2023.106372

Selbst, A. D., Boyd, D., Friedler, S. A., Venkatasubramanian, S., & Vertesi, J. (2019). Fairness and abstraction in sociotechnical systems. *Proceedings of the Conference on Fairness, Accountability, and Transparency*, 59–68. https://doi.org/DOI: 10.1145/3287560.3287598

Shachar, A., Bauböck, R., Bloemraad, I., & Vink, M. P. (Eds.). (2017). *The Oxford handbook of citizenship*. Oxford University Press., DOI: 10.1093/oxfordhb/9780198805854.001.0001

Shore, L. M., Randel, A. E., Chung, B. G., Dean, M. A., Ehrhart, K. H., & Singh, G. (2011). Inclusion and diversity in work groups: A review and model for future research. *Journal of Management*, *37*(4), 1262–1299. DOI: 10.1177/0149206310385943

Stahl, G. K., Miller, E. L., & Tung, R. L. (2002). Toward the boundaryless career: A closer look at the expatriate career concept and the perceived implications of an international assignment. *Journal of World Business*, *37*(3), 216–227. DOI: 10.1016/S1090-9516(02)00080-9

Tambe, P., Cappelli, P., & Yakubovich, V. (2019). Artificial intelligence in human resources management: Challenges and a path forward. *California Management Review*, *61*(4), 15–42. DOI: 10.1177/0008125619867910

Testaverde, M., Del Carpio, X. V., Wagner, M., & Özden, Ç. (2016). Global migration of talent and tax incentives: Evidence from Malaysia's returning expert program. *World Bank Policy Research Working Paper, 7875*. https://doi.org/DOI: 10.1596/1813-9450-7875

Veale, M., Van Kleek, M., & Binns, R. (2018). Fairness and accountability design needs for algorithmic support in high-stakes public sector decision-making. *Proceedings of the 2018 CHI Conference on Human Factors in Computing Systems*, Paper 88. https://doi.org/DOI: 10.1145/3173574.3174014

Winters, L. A., Walmsley, T. L., Wang, Z. K., & Grynberg, R. (2003). Liberalising temporary movement of natural persons: An agenda for the development round. *World Economy*, *26*(8), 1137–1161. DOI: 10.1111/1467-9701.00566

Youndt, M. A., Subramaniam, M., & Snell, S. A. (2004). Intellectual capital profiles: An examination of investments and returns. *Journal of Management Studies*, *41*(2), 335–361. DOI: 10.1111/j.1467-6486.2004.00435.x

Young, J. Q., Van Merriënboer, J., Durning, S., & Ten Cate, O. (2014). Cognitive load theory: Implications for medical education. *Medical Teacher*, *36*(5), 371–384. DOI: 10.3109/0142159X.2014.889290 PMID: 24593808

Zetzsche, D. A., Buckley, R. P., Arner, D. W., & Barberis, J. N. (2017). Regulating a revolution: From regulatory sandboxes to smart regulation. *SSRN*, *23*(1), 31–103. DOI: 10.2139/ssrn.3018534

Compilation of References

Abdou, A. H., Hassan, T. H., Salem, A. E., Albakhit, A. I., Almakhayitah, M. Y., & Salama, W. (2022). The nexus between environmentally sustainable practices, green satisfaction, and customer citizenship behavior in eco-friendly hotels: A social exchange theory approach. *Sustainability (Basel)*, *14*(19), 12791. DOI: 10.3390/su141912791

Abdulai, A., Quarshie, P., Duncan, E., & Fraser, E. (2023). Is agricultural digitization a reality among smallholder farmers in Africa? Unpacking farmers' lived realities of engagement with digital tools and services in rural northern Ghana. *Agriculture & Food Security*, *12*(1), 11. Advance online publication. DOI: 10.1186/s40066-023-00416-6

Abrams, C., & Berge, Z. (2010). Workforce cross training: A re-emerging trend in tough times. *Journal of Workplace Learning*, *22*(8), 522–529. DOI: 10.1108/13665621011082882

Absorb, L. M. S. (2026). The ultimate guide to hybrid learning vs. blended learning. https://www.absorblms.com/blog/what-is-the-difference-between-hybrid-and-blended-learning

Abubakar, A. M., Rezapouraghdam, H., Behravesh, E., & Megeirhi, H. A. (2022). Burnout or boreout: A meta-analytic review and synthesis of burnout and boreout literature in hospitality and tourism. *Journal of Hospitality Marketing & Management*, *31*(4), 458–503. DOI: 10.1080/19368623.2022.1996304

Abuhassna, H., Adnan, M. A. B. M., & Awae, F. (2024). Exploring the synergy between instructional design models and learning theories: A systematic literature review. *Contemporary Educational Technology*, *16*(2), ep499. DOI: 10.30935/cedtech/14289

Accenture. (2024). Resilience redefined: From readiness to reinvention. https://www.accenture.com/content/dam/accenture/final/accenture-com/document-3/Accenture-Resilience-Redefined-From-Readiness-to-Reinvention.pdf

Acemoglu, D., & Autor, D. (2011). Skills, tasks and technologies: Implications for employment and earnings. In Ashenfelter, O., & Card, D. (Eds.), *Handbook of labor economics* (Vol. 4, pp. 1043–1171). Elsevier., DOI: 10.1016/S0169-7218(11)02410-5

Acemoglu, D., & Pischke, J. S. (1999). The structure of wages and investment in general training. *Journal of Political Economy, 107*(3), 539–572. DOI: 10.1086/250071

Acemoglu, D., & Restrepo, P. (2018). The race between man and machine: Implications of technology for growth, factor shares, and employment. *The American Economic Review, 108*(6), 1488–1542. DOI: 10.1257/aer.20160696

Acemoglu, D., & Restrepo, P. (2019). Automation and new tasks: How technology displaces and reinstates labor. *The Journal of Economic Perspectives, 33*(2), 3–30. DOI: 10.1257/jep.33.2.3

Acemoglu, D., & Restrepo, P. (2020). Robots and jobs: Evidence from US labor markets. *Journal of Political Economy, 128*(6), 2188–2244. DOI: 10.1086/705716

Acemoglu, D., & Restrepo, P. (2022). Tasks, automation, and the rise in U.S. wage inequality. *Econometrica, 90*(5), 1973–2016. DOI: 10.3982/ECTA19815

Adams, A. A., Liyanagunawardena, T. R., Rassool, N., & Williams, S. (2013). Use of open educational resources in higher education. *British Journal of Educational Technology, 44*(5), E149–E150. DOI: 10.1111/bjet.12014

Adhika, I. N. R. (2024). Sustainable HR practices: Examining the connection between organisational resilience and green HRM in the hospitality sector. *Society, 12*(2), 1022–1034. DOI: 10.33019/society.v12i2.782

Adler, P. S., & Clark, K. B. (1991). Behind the learning curve: A sketch of the learning process. *Management Science, 37*(3), 267–281. DOI: 10.1287/mnsc.37.3.267

Adler, P. S., & Cole, R. E. (1993). Designed for learning: A tale of two auto plants. *Sloan Management Review, 34*(3), 85–94.

Adler, P. S., Goldoftas, B., & Levine, D. I. (1999). Flexibility versus efficiency? A case study of model changeovers in the Toyota production system. *Organization Science, 10*(1), 43–68. DOI: 10.1287/orsc.10.1.43

Adtani, R., Neelam, N., Raut, R., Deshpande, A., & Mittal, A. (2025). Embracing ICT in academia: Adopting and adapting to the new normal pedagogy. *Global Knowledge, Memory and Communication*, *74*(3-4), 806–823. DOI: 10.1108/GKMC-03-2023-0089

Adwan, S., Goncharenko, G., & Liu, S. (2024). The impact of employee satisfaction on company's labour investment efficiency. *International Review of Financial Analysis*, *96*, 103570. Advance online publication. DOI: 10.1016/j.irfa.2024.103570

Aggarwal, A., Mittal, A., Sharma, I., Chand, P. K., & Deshpande, A. (2025). Success doesn't come to you, you go to it: The role of self-perceived employability among engineering graduates. *Industrial and Commercial Training*, *57*(4), 361–387. DOI: 10.1108/ICT-07-2024-0073

Aghion, P., Antonin, C., & Bunel, S. (2024). Artificial intelligence, growth, and employment: The role of innovation. *The Journal of Economic Perspectives*, *38*(1), 3–30.

Aguilera, R. V., Correa, J. A. A., & Castillo, M. R. (2025). The influence of shareholder activism on global workforce practices. *Organizational Dynamics, 54*(3P1). DOI: 10.1016/j.orgdyn.2025.101141

Aguilera, R. V., Rupp, D. E., Williams, C. A., & Ganapathi, J. (2007). Putting the S back in corporate social responsibility: A multilevel theory of social change in organizations. *Academy of Management Review*, *32*(3), 836–863. DOI: 10.5465/amr.2007.25275678

Aguinis, H., & Glavas, A. (2012). What we know and don't know about corporate social responsibility: A review and research agenda. *Journal of Management*, *38*(4), 932–968. DOI: 10.1177/0149206311436079

Aguinis, H., & Kraiger, K. (2009). Benefits of training and development for individuals and teams, organizations, and society. *Annual Review of Psychology*, *60*(1), 451–474. DOI: 10.1146/annurev.psych.60.110707.163505 PMID: 18976113

Ahmadi, A., Cantini, A., Frías, V. G., & Staudacher, A. P. (2025). The impact of labor flexibility on operational efficiency in industry 5.0: A systematic literature review. *International Journal of Production Research*, •••, 1–26. DOI: 10.1080/00207543.2025.2516770

Aiken, L. H., Sermeus, W., Van den Heede, K., Sloane, D. M., Busse, R., McKee, M., Bruyneel, L., Rafferty, A. M., Griffiths, P., Moreno-Casbas, M. T., Tishelman, C., Scott, A., Brzostek, T., Kinnunen, J., Schwendimann, R., Heinen, M., Zikos, D., Sjetne, I. S., Smith, H. L., & Kutney-Lee, A. (2012). Patient safety, satisfaction, and quality of hospital care: Cross sectional surveys of nurses and patients in 12 countries in Europe and the United States. *BMJ (Clinical Research Ed.)*, *344*(mar20 2), e1717. Advance online publication. DOI: 10.1136/bmj.e1717 PMID: 22434089

Aisyah, S.N., A. Susanty. (2017). Measurement Gap of Competency in Preparing Employees for a Digital Company (A Case Study of a Telecommunication Company in Indonesia)

Ajgaonkar, S., Neelam, N. G., & Wiemann, J. (2021a). Drivers of workforce agility: A dynamic capability perspective. *The International Journal of Organizational Analysis*, *30*(4), 951–982. DOI: 10.1108/IJOA-11-2020-2507

Akbar, Hengky M., Biyanto. (2022). Role of Digital Competence for Pre-Service Teachers in Higher Education in Indonesia. *AL-ISHLAH: Jurnal Pendidikan*

Akhilesh, & Kumar, P. (2025). Impact of Artificial Intelligence on Employment and Skill Requirements in the Tourism Sector. In *Transforming the Service Sector With New Technology* (pp. 167–190). IGI Global Scientific Publishing. DOI: 10.4018/979-8-3693-7447-4.ch011

Alabi, O. A., Ajayi, F. A., Udeh, C. A., & Efunniyi, C. P. (2024). Predictive Analytics in Human Resources: Enhancing Workforce Planning and Customer Experience. *International Journal of Innovation and Scientific Research*, *XI*(IX), 149–158. DOI: 10.51244/IJRSI.2024.1109016

Alblihed, M., & Alzghaibi, H. A. (2022). The Impact of Job Stress, Role Ambiguity and Work-Life Imbalance on Turnover Intention during COVID-19: A Case Study of Frontline Health Workers in Saudi Arabia. *International Journal of Environmental Research and Public Health*, *19*(20), 13132. DOI: 10.3390/ijerph192013132 PMID: 36293713

Aldrich, H., & Herker, D. (1977). Boundary spanning roles and organization structure. *Academy of Management Review*, *2*(2), 217–230. DOI: 10.2307/257905

Alizadeh Majd, A., Bell, R., Ali, S., Davoodi, A., & Nasirifar, A. (2024). The effect of job rotation on employee performance: The mediating role of HR strategy and training in the petrochemical industry. *Industrial and Commercial Training*, *56*(2), 93–105. DOI: 10.1108/ICT-10-2023-0074

Aljohani, A. (2023). Predictive Analytics and Machine Learning for Real-Time Supply Chain Risk Mitigation and Agility. *Sustainability (Basel), 15*(20), 15088. DOI: 10.3390/su152015088

Allen, D. G., Bryant, P. C., & Vardaman, J. M. (2010). Retaining talent: Replacing misconceptions with evidence-based strategies. *The Academy of Management Perspectives, 24*(2), 48–64.

Allen, D. G., Peltokorpi, V., & Rubenstein, A. L. (2020). When "embedded" means "stuck": The dark side of job embeddedness. *The Academy of Management Annals, 14*(2), 143–168.

Al-Romeedy, B. S., & Alharethi, T. (2025). Leveraging green human resource management for sustainable tourism and hospitality: A mediation model for enhancing green reputation. *Discover Sustainability, 6*(1), 67. DOI: 10.1007/s43621-025-00829-2

Al-Twal, A., Alawamleh, M., & Jarrar, D. M. (2024). An investigation of the role of wasta social capital in enhancing employee loyalty and innovation in organisations. *Journal of Innovation and Entrepreneurship, 13*(1), 12. DOI: 10.1186/s13731-024-00372-w

Alviani, D., Hilmiana, , Widianto, S., & Muizu, W. O. Z. (2024). Workforce agility: A systematic literature review and research agenda. *Frontiers in Psychology, 15*, 1376399. DOI: 10.3389/fpsyg.2024.1376399 PMID: 39323587

Al-Zoubi, M. O., Masa'deh, R., & Twaissi, N. M. (2025). Exploring the relationship among structured on-the-job training, mentoring, job rotation, work environment factors and tacit knowledge transfer. *VINE Journal of Information and Knowledge Management Systems, 55*(1), 240–267. DOI: 10.1108/VJIKMS-06-2022-0199

Amanor-Boadu, V. (2022). *Empirical evidence for the "Great Resignation." Monthly Labor Review*. U.S. Bureau of Labor Statistics., DOI: 10.21916/mlr.2022.29

Anbalagan, B. (2023). Proactive Failover and Automation Frameworks for Mission-Critical Workloads: Lessons from Manufacturing Industry. *International Journal of Research and Applied Innovations, 6*(1), 8279–8296. DOI: 10.15662/IJRAI.2023.0601004

An, C., He, X., & Zhang, L. (2023). The coordinated impacts of agricultural insurance and digital financial inclusion on agricultural output: Evidence from China. *Heliyon, 9*(2), e13546. DOI: 10.1016/j.heliyon.2023.e13546 PMID: 36846666

Andrews, J., & Higson, H. (2008). Graduate employability, 'soft skills' versus 'hard' business knowledge: A European study. *European Business Review, 20*(4), 350–364. DOI: 10.1108/09555340810887579

Ap, J. (1992). Residents' perceptions on tourism impacts. *Annals of Tourism Research, 19*(4), 665–690. DOI: 10.1016/0160-7383(92)90060-3

Appelbaum, E., Bailey, T., Berg, P., & Kalleberg, A. L. (2000). *Manufacturing advantage: Why high-performance work systems pay off.* Cornell University Press.

Arasanmi, C. N., & Krishna, A. (2019). Linking the employee value proposition (EVP) to employee behavioural outcomes. *Industrial and Commercial Training, 51*(7-8), 387–395. DOI: 10.1108/ICT-05-2019-0043

Ardondi, M., Fortunato, E., Ruozi, C., Di Fronzo, P., Saffioti, A., Ferrari, I., Bassi, M. C., Ghirotto, L., & Pedroni, C. (2025). Workplace training transfer: A systematic scoping review of evaluation tools for adult learning. *Journal of Workplace Learning*. Advance online publication. DOI: 10.1108/JWL-03-2025-0068

Argote, L. (2024). Knowledge transfer within organizations: Mechanisms, motivation, and consideration. *Annual Review of Psychology, 75*(1), 405–431. DOI: 10.1146/annurev-psych-022123-105424 PMID: 37788572

Argote, L., & Ingram, P. (2000). Knowledge transfer: A basis for competitive advantage in firms. *Organizational Behavior and Human Decision Processes, 82*(1), 150–169. DOI: 10.1006/obhd.2000.2893

Argyris, C., & Schön, D. A. (1978). *Organizational learning: A theory of action perspective*. Addison-Wesley.

Aristotle. (350 BCE). *Nicomachean ethics*.

Ariyanti, S. (2013). Study of digital divide measurement in Indonesia. Puslitbang Resources and Devices Post and Informatics, 281–292.

Arntz, M., Gregory, T., & Zierahn, U. (2016). The risk of automation for jobs in OECD countries: A comparative analysis. *OECD Social, Employment and Migration Working Papers, No. 189*. OECD Publishing. DOI: 10.1787/1815199X

Assefa, Y., Mengistu, M., Moges, B. T., & Tilwani, S. A. (2023). The mediating role of lifelong learning in the structural relationship between workplace environment and staff engagement in higher education. *Cogent Social Sciences, 9*(2), 2272373. DOI: 10.1080/23311886.2023.2272373

Ast, J., & Nyhuis, P. (2022). Approach for determining functional flexibility of the workforce based on training losses and employee specific risks. *Procedia CIRP, 107*, 839–844. DOI: 10.1016/j.procir.2022.05.072

Ast, J., & Nyhuis, P. (2023). A Theoretical Approach for Considering Practice Effects when Determining Deployment Schedules. *Manufacturing Letters*, *36*, 26–29. DOI: 10.1016/j.mfglet.2022.12.005

Atkinson, J. (1984). Manpower strategies for flexible organisations. Personnel management, 16(8), 28-31. https://www.stonebridge.uk.com/uploads/courses/566.pdf

Atkinson, J. (1984). Manpower strategies for flexible organizations. *Personnel Management*, *16*(8), 28–31.

Atluri, A. (2024). The 2030 HR Landscape: Oracle HCM's Vision for Future-Ready Organizations. *International Journal of AI, BigData. Computational and Management Studies*, *5*(4), 31–40. DOI: 10.63282/3050-9416.IJAIBDCMS-V5I4P104

Audrin, B., Audrin, C., & Salamin, X. (2024). Digital skills at work - Conceptual development and empirical validation of a measurement scale. *Technological Forecasting and Social Change*, *202*(February), 123279. DOI: 10.1016/j.techfore.2024.123279

Auer, P., & Fortuny, M. (2000). *Ageing of the labour force in OECD countries: Economic and social consequences* (Employment Paper No. 2000/2). International Labour Office.

Autor, D. (2022). *Labor Market Impacts of Technological Change*. National Bureau of Economic Research.

Autor, D. H. (2015). Why are there still so many jobs? The history and future of workplace automation. *The Journal of Economic Perspectives*, *29*(3), 3–30. DOI: 10.1257/jep.29.3.3

Autor, D. H. (2022). The labor market impacts of technological change: From unbridled optimism to qualified optimism. *The Journal of Economic Perspectives*, *36*(1), 3–30.

Autor, D. H., & Dorn, D. (2013). The growth of low-skill service jobs and the polarization of the US labor market. *The American Economic Review*, *103*(5), 1553–1597. DOI: 10.1257/aer.103.5.1553

Autor, D. H., Dorn, D., & Hanson, G. (2016). The China shock: Learning from labor-market adjustment to large changes in trade. *Annual Review of Economics*, *8*(1), 205–240. DOI: 10.1146/annurev-economics-080315-015041

Autor, D. H., Levy, F., & Murnane, R. J. (2003). The skill content of recent technological change: An empirical exploration. *The Quarterly Journal of Economics*, *118*(4), 1279–1333. DOI: 10.1162/003355303322552801

Autor, D. H., Mindell, D. A., & Reynolds, E. B. (2023). *The work of the future: Building better jobs in an age of intelligent machines.* MIT Press.

Autor, D. H., & Salomons, A. (2018). Is automation labor-displacing? Productivity growth, employment, and the labor share. *Brookings Papers on Economic Activity, 2018*(1), 1–87. DOI: 10.1353/eca.2018.0000

Bader, B., Berg, N., & Holtbrügge, D. (2015). Expatriate performance in terrorism-endangered countries: The role of family and organizational support. *International Business Review, 24*(5), 849–860. DOI: 10.1016/j.ibusrev.2015.03.005

Baiocchetti, G., Scotti, F., & Iapadre, P. L. (2024). The impact of natural disasters: How the 2009 earthquake transformed the economy of L'Aquila's labour market area. *Papers in Regional Science, 103*(6), 100058. Advance online publication. DOI: 10.1016/j.pirs.2024.100058

Bakker, A. B., & Albrecht, S. (2018). Work engagement: Current trends. *Career Development International, 23*(1), 4–11. DOI: 10.1108/CDI-11-2017-0207

Bakker, A. B., & Demerouti, E. (2007). The job demands–resources model: State of the art. *Journal of Managerial Psychology, 22*(3), 309–328. DOI: 10.1108/02683940710733115

Bakker, A. B., & Demerouti, E. (2017). Job Demands–Resources theory: Taking stock and looking forward. *Journal of Occupational Health Psychology, 22*(3), 273–285. DOI: 10.1037/ocp0000056 PMID: 27732008

Bakker, A. B., Demerouti, E., & Sanz-Vergel, A. I. (2023). Burnout and work engagement: The JD-R approach. *Annual Review of Organizational Psychology, 10*, 35–60.

Bakker, A. B., Tims, M., & Derks, D. (2012). Proactive personality and job performance: The role of job crafting and work engagement. *Human Relations; Studies Towards the Integration of the Social Sciences, 65*(10), 1359–1378. DOI: 10.1177/0018726712453471

Balkin, D. B., & Werner, S. (2023). Theorizing the relationship between discretionary employee benefits and individual performance. *Human Resource Management Review, 33*(1), 100901. DOI: 10.1016/j.hrmr.2022.100901

Bandura, A. (1997). *Self-efficacy: The exercise of control* (Vol. 11). Freeman.

Bandura, A. (1997). Self-efficacy: The exercise of control. *The Freeman.*

Bangladesh Labour Foundation, BRAC University, & Solidaridad Network Asia. (2024). *Assessment of technological transition in the apparel sector of Bangladesh and its impact on the workers.* Bangladesh Labour Foundation.

Barney, J. B. (1991). Firm resources and sustained competitive advantage. https://doi.org/DOI: 10.1016/S0742-3322(00)17018-4

Barney, J. (1991). Firm resources and sustained competitive advantage. *Journal of Management, 17*(1), 99–120. DOI: 10.1177/014920639101700108

Barocas, S., & Selbst, A. D. (2016). Big data's disparate impact. *SSRN, 104*(3), 671–732. DOI: 10.2139/ssrn.2477899

Barrero, J. M., Bloom, N., & Davis, S. J. (2023). The evolution of work from home. *The Journal of Economic Perspectives, 37*(4), 23–49. DOI: 10.1257/jep.37.4.23

Bass, B. M., & Bass Bernard, M. (1985). *No. 3* (Vol. 25). Leadership and performance beyond expectations. Free press.

Batista-Toledo, S., & Gavilan, D. (2025). A blended learning future: COVID-19 lessons for "phygital" higher education. *International Review of Research in Open and Distance Learning, 26*(1), 45–62. DOI: 10.19173/irrodl.v26i2.8259

Battisti, M., Del Gatto, M., & Parmeter, C. F. (2022). Skill-biased technological change and productivity dynamics. *Journal of Economic Dynamics & Control, 139*, 104377.

Batt, R. (2002). Managing customer services: Human resource practices, quit rates, and sales growth. *Academy of Management Journal, 45*(3), 587–597. DOI: 10.2307/3069383

Baumgartner, R. J., & Ebner, D. (2010). Corporate sustainability strategies: Sustainability profiles and maturity levels. *Sustainable Development (Bradford), 18*(2), 76–89. DOI: 10.1002/sd.447

Baumol, W. J. (1967). Macroeconomics of unbalanced growth: The anatomy of urban crisis. *The American Economic Review, 57*(3), 415–426.

Baum, T. (1995). *Managing human resources in the European tourism and hospitality industry*. Chapman & Hall.

Baum, T. (2006). *Human resource management for tourism, hospitality and leisure: An international perspective*. Thomson.

Baum, T. (2018). Sustainable human resource management as a driver in tourism policy and planning: A serious sin of omission? *Journal of Sustainable Tourism, 26*(6), 873–889. DOI: 10.1080/09669582.2017.1423318

Baum, T., Mooney, S. K., Robinson, R. N., & Solnet, D. (2020). COVID-19's impact on the hospitality workforce: New crisis or amplification of the norm? *International Journal of Contemporary Hospitality Management*, *32*(9), 2813–2829. DOI: 10.1108/IJCHM-04-2020-0314

Baum, T., & Szivas, E. (2008). HRD in tourism: A role for government? *Tourism Management*, *29*(4), 783–794. DOI: 10.1016/j.tourman.2007.09.002

BCG. (2024, May 8). How governments can improve the Global Skills Market. How Governments Can Improve the Global Skills Market. https://www.bcg.com/publications/2024/how-governments-can-improve-global-skills-market

Becker, G. S. (1993). Human capital. The concise encyclopedia of economics, 2, 1-12.

Becker, B. E., & Huselid, M. A. (1998). High performance work systems and firm performance: A synthesis of research and managerial implications. *Research in Personnel and Human Resources Management*, *16*, 53–101.

Becker, G. S. (1964). *Human capital: A theoretical and empirical analysis, with special reference to education*. University of Chicago Press.

Begum, S., Ashfaq, M., Xia, E., & Awan, U. (2022). Does green transformational leadership lead to green innovation? The role of green thinking and creative process engagement. *Business Strategy and the Environment*, *31*(1), 580–597. DOI: 10.1002/bse.2911

Bejarano-Murillo, E. (2025). Digital Governance Across Continents: Cases From Diverse National Strategies. In *Data-Driven Governance Through AI, Digital Marketing, and the Privacy Interplay* (pp. 1–30). IGI Global Scientific Publishing. DOI: 10.4018/979-8-3693-6945-6.ch001

Beksultanova, A., Dzhankhotova, P., & Shardan, S. (2023). Problems of digital transformation in agriculture and instruments of state support. *IOP Conference Series. Earth and Environmental Science*, *1154*(1), 012061. DOI: 10.1088/1755-1315/1154/1/012061

Belias, D., & Trihas, N. (2023). The role of SHRM in navigating the hospitality sector during a crisis. In Masouras, A., Papademetriou, C., Belias, D., & Anastasiadou, S. (Eds.), *Sustainable growth strategies for entrepreneurial venture tourism and regional development* (pp. 60–76). IGI Global Scientific Publishing., DOI: 10.4018/978-1-6684-6055-9.ch004

Ben-Porath, Y. (1967). The production of human capital and the life cycle of earnings. *Journal of Political Economy*, *75*(4), 352–365. DOI: 10.1086/259291

Benson, G. S., & Dundis, S. P. (2003). Understanding and motivating health care employees: Integrating Maslow's hierarchy of needs, training and technology. *Journal of Nursing Management, 11*(5), 315–320. DOI: 10.1046/j.1365-2834.2003.00409.x PMID: 12930537

Berg, A.-K., Schulte, E. M., Schultz, A., & Kauffeld, S. (2023). Transformationsprozesse gestalten und evaluieren: Wirkmodelle als Ansatz um strategische Personalentwicklung mit Organisationsentwicklung zu verbinden. Gruppe. Interaktion. Organisation. *Zeitschrift für Angewandte Organisationspsychologie, 54*(3), 371–389. DOI: 10.1007/s11612-023-00695-4

Berge, Z. L. (2022). Designing workplace training for generational differences: Does it matter? *Merits, 2*(4), 400–407. DOI: 10.3390/merits2040028

Bergman, A., David, G., & Song, H. (2023). "I Quit": Schedule Volatility as a Driver of Voluntary Employee Turnover. *Manufacturing & Service Operations Management, 25*(4), 1416–1435. DOI: 10.1287/msom.2023.1205

Berkery, E., Peretz, H., Tiernan, S., & Morley, M. J. (2025). The impact of flexi-time uptake on organizational outcomes and the moderating role of formal and informal institutions across 22 countries. *European Management Journal, 43*(4), 640–649. DOI: 10.1016/j.emj.2024.05.007

Bessen, J. (2022). *AI and jobs: The role of demand* (NBER Working Paper No. 24235). National Bureau of Economic Research.

Bhamidipaty, V., Bhamidipaty, D. L., & Guntoory, I. Bhamidipaty, Kdp., Iyengar, K. P., Botchu, B., & Botchu, R. (2025). Revolutionizing Healthcare: The Impact of AI-Powered Sensors. In *Generative Artificial Intelligence for Biomedical and Smart Health Informatics* (pp. 355–373). John Wiley & Sons, Ltd. DOI: 10.1002/9781394280735.ch18

Bhatia, S., & Shrivastava, S. (2022). Cross Training and its Impact on Employees in Manufacturing Industry. *Academy of Marketing Studies Journal, 26*(5), 1–6.

Bhatt, P., & Muduli, A. (2022). Artificial intelligence in learning and development: A systematic literature review. *European Journal of Training and Development, 47*(7–8), 677–694. DOI: 10.1108/EJTD-09-2021-0143

Bidwell, M. (2011). Paying more to get less: The effects of external hiring versus internal mobility. *Administrative Science Quarterly, 56*(3), 369–407. DOI: 10.1177/0001839211433562

Bidwell, M., & Keller, J. R. (2014). Within or without? How firms combine internal and external labor markets to fill jobs. *Academy of Management Journal, 57*(4), 1035–1055. DOI: 10.5465/amj.2012.0119

Bijja Vishwanath, Surendar Vaddepalli. (2023). The Future of Work: Implications of Artificial Intelligence on Hr Practices. *Tuijin Jishu/Journal of Propulsion Technology, 44*(3), 1711–1724. DOI: 10.52783/tjjpt.v44.i3.562

Bilanakos, C., Heywood, J. S., Sessions, J., & Theodoropoulos, N. (2018). Does demand for product quality increase worker training? *Journal of Economic Behavior & Organization, 155*, 159–177. DOI: 10.1016/j.jebo.2018.08.018

Binns, R. (2018). Fairness in machine learning: Lessons from political philosophy. In *Proceedings of the Conference on Fairness, Accountability, and Transparency (FAT*)* (pp. 149–159).

Binus. (2022). https://onlinelearning.binus.ac.id/2021/12/06/begini-perbedaan-generasibaby-boomers-x-y-z-dan-alpha/ (accessed May 12, 2022)

Black, J. S., & Mendenhall, M. (1990). Cross-cultural training effectiveness: A review and a theoretical framework for future research. *Academy of Management Review, 15*(1), 113–136. DOI: 10.2307/258109

Blackman, T. (2025). Performing the future of work: Examining discourses of the future of work and the ideal worker through event ethnographies. *Geoforum, 167*, 104461. DOI: 10.1016/j.geoforum.2025.104461

Blanchard, O., Jaumotte, F., & Loungani, P. (2014). *Labor market policies and IMF advice in advanced economies during the Great Recession* (IMF Staff Discussion Note). International Monetary Fund.

Blau, P. (1964). *Exchange and power in social life*. Wiley.

Blau, P. M. (1964). *Exchange and Power in Social Life*. John Wiley.

Blickensderfer, E., Cannon-Bowers, J. A., & Salas, E. (1998). Cross-training and team performance. In Cannon-Bowers, J. A., & Salas, E. (Eds.), *Making decisions under stress: Implications for individual and team training* (pp. 299–311). American Psychological Association., DOI: 10.1037/10278-011

Bloom, B. S. (1956). *Taxonomy of educational objectives: The classification of educational goals. Handbook I: Cognitive domain*. Longmans Green.

Bloom, D. E., Kuhn, M., & Prettner, K. (2023). The macroeconomic effects of population aging and fertility decline. *Journal of Economic Literature, 61*(3), 1020–1063.

Bloom, N., Liang, J., Roberts, J., & Ying, Z. J. (2015). Does working from home work? Evidence from a Chinese experiment. *The Quarterly Journal of Economics*, *130*(1), 165–218. DOI: 10.1093/qje/qju032

Blume, B. D., Ford, J. K., & Huang, J. L. (2024). Transfer of informal learning: The role of manager support in linking learning to performance. *Business Horizons*, *67*(2), 125–136. DOI: 10.1016/j.bushor.2023.12.001

Bokhorst, J. A. C., & Slomp, J. (2007). Design and operation of a cross-trained workforce. In D. A. Nembhard (Ed.), *Workforce Cross-Training* (pp. 3–64). CRC Press, Taylor & Francis Group. DOI: 10.1201/9781420005349.ch1

Bone, J., Lambourne, A., & Codreanu, A. (2023). Skill-based hiring and labor market transformation. *Labour Economics*, *83*, 102345.

Boora, N., & Bishnoi, S. (2025). Skill-biased technological change and wage inequality in developing economies. *International Journal of Economics and Labour Studies*, *12*(1), 45–62.

Borghans, L., & ter Weel, B. (2007). The division of labour, worker organisation, and technological change. *Economic Journal (London)*, *117*(519), F45–F72. DOI: 10.1111/j.1468-0297.2007.02011.x

Boudreau, J. W., & Cascio, W. F. (2017). Human capital analytics: Why are we not there? *Journal of Organizational Effectiveness: People and Performance*, *4*(2), 119–126. DOI: 10.1108/JOEPP-03-2017-0021

Boudreau, J. W., & Cascio, W. F. (2021). *Investing in people: Financial impact of human resource initiatives* (3rd ed.). Pearson.

Boxall, P., & Macky, K. (2009). Research and theory on high-performance work systems: Progressing the high-involvement stream. *Human Resource Management Journal*, *19*(1), 3–23. DOI: 10.1111/j.1748-8583.2008.00082.x

Boxall, P., & Purcell, J. (2016). *Strategy and human resource management* (4th ed.). Palgrave Macmillan. DOI: 10.1007/978-1-137-40765-8

Boyatzis, R. E. (1982). *The competent manager: A model for effective performance*. John Wiley & Sons.

BPS. (2020). Indonesia [Population Census Results, BPS Jakarta, Indonesia]. *Population Projections*, 2020–2050.

BPS. (2024). Average monthly per capita expenditure by commodity group and region of residence the (rupiah), 2023-Statistical Tables-Centraleau of Statistics of Indonesia (bps.go.id)

Bramwell, B., & Lane, B. (2011). Critical research on tourism and governance. *Journal of Sustainable Tourism, 19*(4–5), 411–421. DOI: 10.1080/09669582.2011.580586

Brandl, J., & Neyer, A.-K. (2009). Applying cognitive adjustment theory to cross-cultural training for global virtual teams. *Human Resource Management, 48*(3), 341–353. DOI: 10.1002/hrm.20284

Brassey, J., De Smet, A., Maor, D., & Rabipour, S. (2024, December 6). *Developing a resilient, adaptable workforce for an uncertain future*. McKinsey & Company. https://www.mckinsey.com/capabilities/people-and-organizational-performance/our-insights/developing-a-resilient-adaptable-workforce-for-an-uncertain-future

Braun, V., & Clarke, V. (2022). Thematic analysis: A practical guide. *Sage (Atlanta, Ga.)*.

Bresnahan, T. F., Brynjolfsson, E., & Hitt, L. M. (2002). Information technology, workplace organization, and the demand for skilled labor: Firm-level evidence. *The Quarterly Journal of Economics, 117*(1), 339–376. DOI: 10.1162/003355302753399526

Brewster, C., Mayrhofer, W., & Farndale, E. (2018). *Handbook of research on comparative human resource management* (2nd ed.). Edward Elgar Publishing., DOI: 10.4337/9781784711139

Bridgstock, R. (2009). The graduate attributes we've overlooked: Enhancing graduate employability through career management skills. *Higher Education Research & Development, 28*(1), 31–41. DOI: 10.1080/07294360802444347

Brossoit, R. M., Hammer, L. B., Bodner, T. E., Mohr, C. D., Allen, S. J., Crain, T. L., Brockwood, K. J., & Adler, A. B. (2024). Transfer of a leadership training intervention prior to COVID-19 on leadership support during the pandemic. *Journal of Managerial Psychology, 39*(7), 930–946. DOI: 10.1108/JMP-10-2023-0582 PMID: 41737586

Brunow, S., Fuchs, M., & Weyh, A. (2022). Wage growth in tight labor markets: Evidence from Germany. *Empirical Economics, 63*(2), 873–902.

Brusco, M. J., Johns, T. R., & Reed, J. H. (1998). Cross-Utilization of a Two-Skilled Workforce. *International Journal of Operations & Production Management, 18*(6), 555–564. DOI: 10.1108/01443579810370116

Brynjolfsson, E., & McAfee, A. (2014). *The second machine age: Work, progress, and prosperity in a time of brilliant technologies*. W. W. Norton & Company.

Brynjolfsson, E., Mitchell, T., & Rock, D. (2018). What can machines learn, and what does it mean for occupations and the economy? *AEA Papers and Proceedings. American Economic Association, 108*, 43–47. DOI: 10.1257/pandp.20181019

Brynjolfsson, E., Rock, D., & Syverson, C. (2019). Artificial intelligence and the modern productivity paradox: A clash of expectations and statistics. In Agrawal, A., Gans, J., & Goldfarb, A. (Eds.), *The economics of artificial intelligence: An agenda* (pp. 23–57). University of Chicago Press., DOI: 10.7208/chicago/9780226613475.003.0001

Bundy, J., Pfarrer, M. D., Short, C. E., & Coombs, W. T. (2017). Crises and crisis management: Integration, interpretation, and research development. *Journal of Management, 43*(6), 1661–1692. DOI: 10.1177/0149206316680030

Burnett, J. R., & Lisk, T. C. (2021). The Future of Employee Engagement: Real-Time Monitoring and Digital Tools for Engaging a Workforce. In *International Perspectives on Employee Engagement*. Routledge. DOI: 10.4324/9781003142492-9

Caballero, C. L., & Walker, A. (2010). Work readiness in graduate recruitment and selection: A review of current assessment methods. *Journal of Teaching and Learning for Graduate Employability, 1*(1), 13–25. DOI: 10.21153/jtlge2010vol1no1art546

Cabrera Noriega, L. E. (2014). Síndrome de Boreout: Diseño, confabilidad y validación preliminar de un instrumento para su medición. *Revista de la Universidad Industrial de Santander. Salud (Barranquilla), 46*(3), 259–265.

Cahyarini, B. R., Ladiatno Samsara. (2021). The Challenges of Digital Competency Implementation Towards World-Class Bureaucracy. *Jurnal Borneo Administrator*

Caligiuri, P., De Cieri, H., Minbaeva, D., Verbeke, A., & Zimmermann, A. (2020). International HRM insights for navigating the COVID-19 pandemic: Implications for future research and practice. *Journal of International Business Studies, 51*(5), 697–713. DOI: 10.1057/s41267-020-00335-9 PMID: 32836500

Campion, M. A., Cheraskin, L., & Stevens, M. J. (1994). Career-related antecedents and outcomes of job rotation. *Academy of Management Journal, 37*(6), 1518–1542. DOI: 10.2307/256797

Campion, M. A., Fink, A. A., Ruggeberg, B. J., Carr, L., Phillips, G. M., & Odman, R. B. (2011). Doing competencies well: Best practices in competency modeling. *Personnel Psychology, 64*(1), 225–262. DOI: 10.1111/j.1744-6570.2010.01207.x

Cannon-Bowers, J. A., Salas, E., Blickensderfer, E., & Bowers, C. A. (1998). The impact of cross-training and workload on team functioning: A replication and extension of initial findings. *Human Factors, 40*(1), 92–101. DOI: 10.1518/001872098779480550

Cannon-Bowers, J. A., Tannenbaum, S. I., Salas, E., & Volpe, C. E. (1995). Defining competencies and establishing team training requirements. In Guzzo, R. A., & Salas, E. (Eds.), *Team effectiveness and decision making in organizations* (pp. 333–380). Jossey-Bass.

Cappelli, P. (2015). Skill gaps, skill shortages, and skill mismatches: Evidence and arguments for the United States. *Industrial & Labor Relations Review, 68*(2), 251–290. DOI: 10.1177/0019793914564961

Cappelli, P. (2022). *The future of the office: Work from home, remote work, and the hard choices we all face.* Oxford University Press.

Cappelli, P. (2023). Talent management: Conceptual approaches and practical challenges. *Human Resource Management Journal, 33*(2), 203–219.

Cappelli, P., & Keller, J. R. (2013). Classifying work in the new economy. *Academy of Management Review, 38*(4), 575–596. DOI: 10.5465/amr.2011.0302

Cappelli, P., & Neumark, D. (2001). Do "high-performance" work practices improve establishment-level outcomes? *Industrial & Labor Relations Review, 54*(4), 737–775. DOI: 10.1177/001979390105400402

Caribou, & Genesis Analytics. (2024). *AI's potential impact on Africa's tech-outsourcing sector.* Report prepared in partnership with the Mastercard Foundation.

Carnevale, J. B., & Hatak, I. (2020). Employee adjustment and well-being in the era of COVID-19: Implications for human resource management. *Journal of Business Research, 116*, 183–187. DOI: 10.1016/j.jbusres.2020.05.037 PMID: 32501303

Carroll, A. B., & Shabana, K. M. (2010). The business case for corporate social responsibility: A review of concepts, research and practice. *International Journal of Management Reviews, 12*(1), 85–105. DOI: 10.1111/j.1468-2370.2009.00275.x

Cascio, W. F., & Aguinis, H. (2023). *Applied psychology in talent management* (9th ed.). SAGE Publications.

Castillo de Mesa, J., Gómez-Jacinto, L., López Peláez, A., & Erro-Garcés, A. (2020). Social networking sites and youth transition: The use of Facebook and personal well-being of social work young graduates. *Frontiers in Psychology, 11*, 230. DOI: 10.3389/fpsyg.2020.00230 PMID: 32132959

Cath, C., Wachter, S., Mittelstadt, B., Taddeo, M., & Floridi, L. (2018). Artificial intelligence and the "good society": The US, EU, and UK approach. *Science and Engineering Ethics, 24*(2), 505–528. DOI: 10.1007/s11948-017-9901-7 PMID: 28353045

Causa, O., Cavalleri, M. C., Luu, N., & Toth, A. (2025). *Labour and skills shortages in OECD countries* (OECD Economics Department Working Papers). OECD Publishing.

Cazes, S., Verick, S., & Hussami, F. (2011). Diverging trends in unemployment in the United States and Europe: Evidence from Okun's law and the global financial crisis. *Employment Working Paper*. International Labour Office.

Chan, E. S. W., & Hsu, C. H. C. (2016). Environmental management research in hospitality. *International Journal of Contemporary Hospitality Management, 28*(5), 886–923. DOI: 10.1108/IJCHM-02-2015-0076

Cheng, H., Guo, H., & Shi, Y. (2024). Multifactor conditional equity premium model: Evidence from China's stock market. *Journal of Banking & Finance, 161*, 107117. Advance online publication. DOI: 10.1016/j.jbankfin.2024.107117

Chen, H., Fang, T., Liu, F., Pang, L., Wen, Y., Chen, S., & Gu, X. (2020). Career Adaptability Research: A Literature Review with Scientific Knowledge Mapping in Web of Science. *International Journal of Environmental Research and Public Health, 17*(16), 5986. DOI: 10.3390/ijerph17165986 PMID: 32824717

Chen, L., & Tseng, C. (2012). Benefits of cross-functional training: Three departments of hotel line supervisors in Taiwan. *Journal of Hospitality and Tourism Management, 19*(1), 115–122. DOI: 10.1017/jht.2012.13

Chen, Z. (2024). Responsible AI in Organizational Training: Applications, Implications, and Recommendations for Future Development. *Human Resource Development Review, 23*(4), 498–521. DOI: 10.1177/15344843241273316

Chesbrough, H., Vanhaverbeke, W., West, J., & Bogers, M. (Eds.). (2014). *New frontiers in open innovation*. Oxford University Press., DOI: 10.1093/acprof:oso/9780199682461.001.0001

Chiaburu, D. S., & Harrison, D. A. (2008). Do peers make the place? Conceptual synthesis and meta-analysis of coworker effects on perceptions, attitudes, OCBs, and performance. *The Journal of Applied Psychology, 93*(5), 1082–1103. DOI: 10.1037/0021-9010.93.5.1082 PMID: 18808227

Chong, Y. K., & Zainal, S. R. M. (2024). Employee agility's mediating role on the link between employee vitality, digital literacy and transformational leadership with job performance: An empirical study. *Cogent Business & Management, 11*(1), 2337447. Advance online publication. DOI: 10.1080/23311975.2024.2337447

Choudhury, P., Foroughi, C., & Larson, B. Z. (2021). Work from anywhere: The productivity effects of geographic flexibility. *Strategic Management Journal, 42*(4), 655–683. DOI: 10.1002/smj.3251

Clarke, M. (2018). Rethinking graduate employability: The role of capital, individual attributes and context. *Studies in Higher Education, 43*(11), 1923–1937. DOI: 10.1080/03075079.2017.1294152

Cohen, W. M., & Levinthal, D. A. (1990). Absorptive capacity: A new perspective on learning and innovation. *Administrative Science Quarterly, 35*(1), 128–152. DOI: 10.2307/2393553

Collings, D. G., McMackin, J., Nyberg, A. J., & Wright, P. M. (2022). Strategic human resource management and performance: A review and research agenda. *Human Resource Management Journal, 32*(1), 1–20. DOI: 10.1111/j.1748-8583.2011.00189.x

Collings, D. G., & Mellahi, K. (2009). Strategic talent management: A review and research agenda. *Human Resource Management Review, 19*(4), 304–313. DOI: 10.1016/j.hrmr.2009.04.001

Collings, D. G., Mellahi, K., & Cascio, W. F. (2018). Global talent management and performance in multinational enterprises: A multilevel perspective. *Journal of Management, 45*(2), 540–566. DOI: 10.1177/0149206318757018

Collings, D. G., Nyberg, A. J., Wright, P. M., & McMackin, J. (2021). Leading through paradox in a COVID-19 world: Human resources comes of age. *Human Resource Management Journal, 31*(4), 819–833. DOI: 10.1111/1748-8583.12343

Collins, J. (2012). *Good to great: Why some companies make the leap and others don't.* HarperBusiness.

Colman, H. (2026, March 18). *Cross-Training Employees: Key Benefits and Strategies.* Ispring. https://www.ispring.com/knowledge-hub/cross-training-employees?

Colquitt, J. A., LePine, J. A., & Noe, R. A. (2000). Toward an integrative theory of training motivation: A meta-analytic path analysis of 20 years of research. *The Journal of Applied Psychology, 85*(5), 678–707. https://psycnet.apa.org/doi/10.1037/0021-9010.85.5.678. DOI: 10.1037/0021-9010.85.5.678 PMID: 11055143

Colquitt, J. A., LePine, J. A., & Wesson, M. J. (2021). *Organizational behavior: Improving performance and commitment in the workplace* (7th ed.). McGraw-Hill Education.

Conde-Jiménez, J. (2018). Digital competence as an indicator of the impact of ICT educational policies: Validation of a theoretical model using PLS. *Research on Education and Media, 10*(2), 37–44. DOI: 10.1515/rem-2018-0013

Connelly, C. E., Zweig, D., Webster, J., & Trougakos, J. P. (2012). Knowledge hiding in organizations. *Journal of Organizational Behavior, 33*(1), 64–88. DOI: 10.1002/job.737

Cordery, J., Soo, C., Kirkman, B., Rosen, B., & Mathieu, J. (2010). Leading parallel global virtual teams: Lessons from Alcoa. *Organizational Dynamics, 39*(3), 204–216. DOI: 10.1016/j.orgdyn.2009.04.002

Costa, F., Thürer, M., & Portioli-Staudacher, A. (2023). Heterogeneous worker multi-functionality and efficiency in dual resource constrained manufacturing lines: An assessment by simulation. *Operations Management Research : Advancing Practice Through Research, 16*(3), 1476–1489. DOI: 10.1007/s12063-023-00371-2

Cotton, J. L., Vollrath, D. A., Froggatt, K. L., Lengnick-Hall, M. L., & Jennings, K. R. (1988). Employee participation: Diverse forms and different outcomes. *Academy of Management Review, 13*(1), 8–22. DOI: 10.2307/258351

Creswell, J. W., & Creswell, J. D. (2024). *Research design: Qualitative, quantitative, and mixed methods approaches* (6th ed.). SAGE Publications.

Creswell, J. W., & Poth, C. N. (2025). *Qualitative inquiry and research design: Choosing among five approaches* (6th ed.). SAGE Publications.

Cropanzano, R., & Mitchell, M. S. (2005). Social exchange theory: An interdisciplinary review. *Journal of Management, 31*(6), 874–900. DOI: 10.1177/0149206305279602

Cross, R., & Parker, A. (2004). *The hidden power of social networks: Understanding how work really gets done in organizations*. Harvard Business School Press.

Czaika, M., & Parsons, C. R. (2017). The gravity of high-skilled migration policies. *Demography, 54*(2), 603–630. DOI: 10.1007/s13524-017-0559-1 PMID: 28290123

D, D., & M, J. P. P. (2023). *A Brief Study of Privacy-Preserving Practices (PPP) in Data Mining* (No. arXiv:2304.14607). arXiv. https://doi.org//arXiv.2304.14607DOI: 10.48550

Dafoe, A. (2018). *AI governance: A research agenda*. Future of Humanity Institute, University of Oxford. https://www.fhi.ox.ac.uk/wp-content/uploads/AI-Governance-Research-Agenda.pdf

Das, M., & Hilgenstock, B. (2022). *Labour markets and inequality in developing economies* (World Bank Policy Research Working Paper No. 10045). World Bank.

Das, K. P., Mukhopadhyay, S., & Suar, D. (2023). Enablers of workforce agility, firm performance, and corporate reputation. *Asia Pacific Management Review, 28*(1), 33–44. DOI: 10.1016/j.apmrv.2022.01.006

Daugherty, P. R., & Wilson, H. J. (2018). *Human + machine: Reimagining work in the age of AI.* Harvard Business Review Press.

Dauth, W., Findeisen, S., Südekum, J., & Woessner, N. (2021). The adjustment of labor markets to robots. *Journal of the European Economic Association, 19*(6), 3104–3153. DOI: 10.1093/jeea/jvab012

Davenport, T. H., & Prusak, L. (1998). *Working knowledge: Managing what your organization knows.* Harvard Business School Press.

Day, D. V. (2001). Leadership development: A review in context. *The Leadership Quarterly, 11*(4), 581–613. DOI: 10.1016/S1048-9843(00)00061-8

De Vos, A., & Cambré, B. (2017). Career management in high-performing organizations: A set-theoretic approach. *Human Resource Management, 56*(3), 501–518. DOI: 10.1002/hrm.21786

Deci, E. L., & Ryan, R. M. (1985). *Intrinsic motivation and self-determination in human behavior.* Springer. DOI: 10.1007/978-1-4899-2271-7

Deci, E. L., & Ryan, R. M. (2000). Self-determination theory and the facilitation of intrinsic motivation, social development, and well-being. *The American Psychologist, 55*(1), 68–78. DOI: 10.1037/0003-066X.55.1.68 PMID: 11392867

Deci, E. L., & Ryan, R. M. (2000). The "what" and "why" of goal pursuits: Human needs and the self-determination of behavior. *Psychological Inquiry, 11*(4), 227–268. DOI: 10.1207/S15327965PLI1104_01

Decius, J., Knappstein, M., & Klug, K. (2024). Which way of learning benefits your career? The role of different forms of work-related learning for different types of perceived employability. *European Journal of Work and Organizational Psychology, 33*(1), 24–39. DOI: 10.1080/1359432X.2023.2191846

Deloitte. (2025). 2025 Global Human Capital Trends: "Turning tensions into triumphs": Deloitte Southeast Asia. 2025 Global Human Capital Trends. https://www.deloitte.com/southeast-asia/en/services/consulting/perspectives/2025-human-capital-trends.html

Demanuele, L. M. (2025). (2025). *Recruitment and selection: An evidence based approach.* https://www.um.edu.mt/library/oar/handle/123456789/132894

Deming, D. J., & Silliman, M. I. (2024). Skills and human capital in the labor market (NBER Working Paper No. 32908). National Bureau of Economic Research. DOI: 10.3386/w32908

Deming, D. J. (2017). The growing importance of social skills in the labor market. *The Quarterly Journal of Economics*, *132*(4), 1593–1640. DOI: 10.1093/qje/qjx022

Deming, D. J. (2023). Four facts about human capital. *The Journal of Economic Perspectives*, *37*(2), 75–102.

De, S., Mukherjee, D., & Ray, J. (2025). Skill in Indian Labour Market: Current Trends and Estimating Future Gaps. *Arthaniti: Journal of Economic Theory and Practice*, *24*(1), 103–129. DOI: 10.1177/09767479221138961

Desalegn, E. G., Guedes, M. J. C., Gomes, J. F. D. S., & Tebeka, S. M. (2024).

Deshpande, A., Raut, R., Gupta, K., Mittal, A., Raheja, D., Ekbote, N., & Kaul, N. (2024). Predictors of continued intention of working professionals for pursuing e-learning courses for career advancement. *Information Discovery and Delivery*, *52*(2), 175–184. DOI: 10.1108/IDD-11-2022-0120

Dessein, W., & Santos, T. (2006). Adaptive organizations. *Journal of Political Economy*, *114*(5), 956–995. DOI: 10.1086/508031

Di Stefano, G., Peteraf, M., & Verona, G. (2014). The organizational drivetrain: A road to integration of dynamic capabilities research. *The Academy of Management Perspectives*, *28*(4), 307–327. DOI: 10.5465/amp.2013.0100

Dirks, J. L., Lough, M. E., & Moungey, S. J. (1995). Cross-training across acuity levels. *Critical Care Nurse*, *15*(1), 68–74. DOI: 10.4037/ccn1995.15.1.68 PMID: 7712821

Doeringer, P. B., & Piore, M. J. (1971). *Internal labor markets and manpower analysis*. D.C. Heath.

Doz, Y. L., & Kosonen, M. (2010). Embedding strategic agility: A leadership agenda for accelerating business model renewal. *Long Range Planning*, *43*(2-3), 370–382. DOI: 10.1016/j.lrp.2009.07.006

Draganski, B., Gaser, C., Busch, V., Schuierer, G., Bogdahn, U., & May, A. (2004). Neuroplasticity: Changes in grey matter induced by training. *Nature*, *427*(6972), 311–312. DOI: 10.1038/427311a PMID: 14737157

Duchek, S. (2020). Organizational resilience: A capability-based conceptualization. *Business Research*, *13*(1), 215–246. DOI: 10.1007/s40685-019-0085-7

Dunphy, D., & Bryant, B. (1996). Teams: Panaceas or prescriptions for improved performance? *Human Relations; Studies Towards the Integration of the Social Sciences*, *49*(5), 677–699. DOI: 10.1177/001872679604900507

Dustmann, C., Schönberg, U., & Stuhler, J. (2023). The impact of immigration: Why do studies reach such different results? *The Journal of Economic Perspectives*, *37*(1), 31–56.

Duval, R., & Loungani, P. (2021). *Designing labor market institutions in emerging and developing economies: Evidence and policy options* (IMF Working Paper). International Monetary Fund.

Dweck, C. S. (2006). *Mindset: The new psychology of success*. Random House.

Easygenerator. (2025). Cross-training employees: 5 benefits you can't ignore. https://www.easygenerator.com/en/blog/employee-generated-learning/cross-training-employees/

Eccles, R. G., Ioannou, I., Serafeim, G., & Chee, K. (2014). The impact of a corporate culture of sustainability on corporate behavior and performance. *Management Science*, *60*(11), 2835–2857. DOI: 10.1287/mnsc.2014.1984

Edinger-Schöns, L. M., Lengler-Graiff, L., Scheidler, S., & Wieseke, J. (2019). Frontline employees as corporate social responsibility (CSR) ambassadors: A quasi-field experiment. *Journal of Business Ethics*, *157*(2), 359–373. DOI: 10.1007/s10551-018-3790-9

Edmondson, A. (1999). Psychological safety and learning behavior in work teams. *Administrative Science Quarterly*, *44*(2), 350–383. DOI: 10.2307/2666999

Edmondson, A. C., & Lei, Z. (2014). Psychological safety: The history, renaissance, and future of an interpersonal construct. *Annual Review of Organizational Psychology and Organizational Behavior*, *1*(1), 23–43. DOI: 10.1146/annurev-orgpsych-031413-091305

Egana-delSol, P., Bustelo, M., Ripani, L., Soler, N., & Viollaz, M. (2022). Automation in Latin America: Are Women at Higher Risk of Losing Their Jobs? *Technological Forecasting and Social Change*, *175*, 121333. DOI: 10.1016/j.techfore.2021.121333

Ehnert, I., Parsa, S., Roper, I., Wagner, M., & Müller-Camen, M. (2016). Reporting on sustainability and HRM: A comparative study of sustainability reporting practices by the world's largest companies. *International Journal of Human Resource Management*, *27*(1), 88–108. DOI: 10.1080/09585192.2015.1024157

Ehnes, D., Schweizer, L., & Storz, C. (2025a). Labour-cost retrenchment strategies in times of crisis: Comparing market reactions to flexible and rigid strategies. *Long Range Planning*, *58*(3), 102509. Advance online publication. DOI: 10.1016/j.lrp.2025.102509

Eichenseer, P., Hans, L., & Winkler, H. (2025). A data-driven machine learning model for forecasting delivery positions in logistics for workforce planning. *Supply Chain Analytics*, *9*, 100099. DOI: 10.1016/j.sca.2024.100099

Eisenberger, R., Huntington, R., Hutchison, S., & Sowa, D. (1986). Perceived organizational support. *The Journal of Applied Psychology*, *71*(3), 500–507. DOI: 10.1037/0021-9010.71.3.500

Eisenberger, R., Malone, G. P., & Presson, W. D. (2020). Optimizing perceived organizational support to enhance employee engagement. *Society for Human Resource Management*, *73*(2), 1–25.

Eisenberger, R., & Stinglhamber, F. (2011). *Perceived organizational support: Fostering enthusiastic and productive employees*. American Psychological Association. DOI: 10.1037/12318-000

Eisenhardt, K. M., & Martin, J. A. (2000). Dynamic capabilities. *Strategic Management Journal*, *21*(10–11), 1105–1121. DOI: 10.1002/1097-0266(200010/11)21:10/11<1105::AID-SMJ133>3.0.CO;2-E

Eldor, L., & Harpaz, I. (2016). A process model of employee engagement: The learning climate and its relationship with extra-role performance behaviors. *Journal of Organizational Behavior*, *37*(2), 213–235. DOI: 10.1002/job.2037

Elgeddawy, M., & Abouraia, M. (2024). Pragmatism as a research paradigm. *In Proceedings of the European Conference on Research Methodology for Business and Management Studies* (Vol. 23, No. 1). https://doi.org/DOI: 10.34190/ecrm.23.1.2444

Ellström, P. E. (2001). Integrating learning and work: Problems and prospects. *Human Resource Development Quarterly*, *12*(4), 421–435. DOI: 10.1002/hrdq.1006

Elm Learning. (2023). The hybrid learning framework: Adopt it for corporate training? https://elmlearning.com/blog/hybrid-learning-framework-for-corporate-training/

Epstein, M. J., & Buhovac, A. R. (2014). *Making sustainability work: Best practices in managing and measuring corporate social, environmental and economic impacts* (2nd ed.). Berrett-Koehler.

Ernst, E., & Feist, M. (2024). *Labour shortages and the future of work*. International Labour Organization.

Erumban, A. A. (2024). Informality and aggregate labor productivity growth: Does ICT Moderate the Relationship? *Telecommunications Policy*, *48*(1), 102681. DOI: 10.1016/j.telpol.2023.102681

Fan, M., Soomro, S., Soomro, S., Sohu, J. M., Shah, S. B., & Shaikh, S. N. (2025). The human side of AI adoption: Exploring technostress, training and employee well-being in manufacturing SMEs. *Journal of Manufacturing Technology Management*, •••, 1–22. DOI: 10.1108/JMTM-02-2025-0120

Faraj, S., von Krogh, G., Monteiro, E., & Lakhani, K. R. (2016). Online community as space for knowledge flows. *Information Systems Research*, *27*(4), 668–684. DOI: 10.1287/isre.2016.0682

Farr, J. L., & Tesluk, P. E. (1997). Process and outcome feedback as learning mechanisms during technical skill acquisition. In Quinones, M. A., & Ehrenstein, A. (Eds.), *Training for a rapidly changing workplace.* American Psychological Association.

Feist, M. (2024). *Structural labour shortages: Challenges and policy responses.* ILO Policy Brief.

Fenwick, T. (2010). (Re)thinking the 'learning organization': A proleptic glimpse at the emergent field. *Journal of European Industrial Training*, *26*(2), 70–82. DOI: 10.1108/03090590210421009

Ferdman, B. M., & Deane, B. R. (Eds.). (2014). *Diversity at work: The practice of inclusion.* Wiley., DOI: 10.1002/9781118764282

Ferrer-Serrano, M., Fuentelsaz, L., & Latorre-Martinez, M. P. (2022). Examining knowledge transfer and networks: An overview of the last twenty years. *Journal of Knowledge Management*, *26*(8), 2007–2037. DOI: 10.1108/JKM-04-2021-0265

Filippucci, F., Gal, P., Jona Lasinio, C. S., & Alvaro Leandro And Giuseppe Nicoletti. (2024). *The impact of Artificial Intelligence on productivity, distribution and growth.* DOI: 10.1787/dee339a8-en

Fındık, L. Y. (2025). Adult Learning Theories. In *Exploring Adult Education Through Learning Theory* (pp. 29–54). IGI Global Scientific Publishing., DOI: 10.4018/979-8-3693-5812-2.ch002

Flatten, T. C., Engelen, A., Zahra, S. A., & Brettel, M. (2011). A measure of absorptive capacity: Scale development and validation. *European Management Journal*, *29*(2), 98–116. DOI: 10.1016/j.emj.2010.11.002

Floridi, L., Cowls, J., Beltrametti, M., Chatila, R., & Chiaraviglio, L. (2018). AI4People—An ethical framework for a good AI society: Opportunities, risks, principles, and recommendations. *Minds and Machines*, *28*(4), 689–707. DOI: 10.1007/s11023-018-9482-5 PMID: 30930541

Fomude, A. H., Yang, C., Agordzo, G. K., Serwah, A. V., & Abangbila, L. (2023). AI Model to Improve HR Decision-Making with Machine Learning Predictions Algorithm. *2023 25th International Conference on Advanced Communication Technology (ICACT)*, 206–212. DOI: 10.23919/ICACT56868.2023.10079282

Fotiadis, I., Salepaki, A., Angelou, I., & Kourkouridis, D. (2025). Human resource strategies in Greek tourism businesses: Perspectives and challenges. *SA Journal of Human Resource Management*, *23*(0), a2911. DOI: 10.4102/sajhrm.v23i0.2911

Freeman, J. M., & Ellis, J. (2025). The Expert Behind the Desk: Collaborative Cross-Training in Unlocking Potential in Frontline Academic Library Staff. *Journal of Library Administration*, *65*(6-7), 1–21. DOI: 10.1080/01930826.2025.2518007

Frey, C. B., & Osborne, M. A. (2017). The future of employment: How susceptible are jobs to computerisation? *Technological Forecasting and Social Change*, *114*, 254–280. DOI: 10.1016/j.techfore.2016.08.019

Fukuda, K. (2019). Science, technology and innovation ecosystem transformation toward society 5.0. *International Journal of Production Economics*, *220*, 107460. DOI: 10.1016/j.ijpe.2019.07.033

Fuller, J. B., Raman, M., Sage-Gavin, E., & Hines, K. (2022). *The emerging degree reset: How the shift to skills-based hiring holds the keys to growing the U.S. workforce*. Harvard Business School Project on Managing the Future of Work.

Fung, H. G., Li, T., Lu, C., & Wen, M. M. (2025a). The inevitable disclosure doctrine: A facade or a curse in the CEO labor market. *Journal of Banking & Finance*, *179*, 107540. Advance online publication. DOI: 10.1016/j.jbankfin.2025.107540

Gagné, M.. (2015). The multidimensional work motivation scale: Validation and evidence across countries. *European Journal of Work and Organizational Psychology*, *24*(2), 178–196. DOI: 10.1080/1359432X.2013.877892

Gagné, M.. (2022). The motivation at work scale–revised. *Motivation and Emotion*, *46*(2), 180–203.

Gagné, M., & Deci, E. L. (2005). Self-determination theory and work motivation. *Journal of Organizational Behavior*, *26*(4), 331–362. DOI: 10.1002/job.322

Gallup. (2023). *State of the global workplace report*. Gallup.

Gallup. (2024). State of the global workplace: 2024 report. https://www.gallup.com/workplace/349484/state-of-the-global-workplace.aspx

Garavan, T. N., Carbery, R., & Rock, A. (2012). Mapping talent development: Definition, scope and architecture. *European Journal of Training and Development, 36*(1), 5–24. DOI: 10.1108/03090591211192601

Garavan, T. N., & McGuire, D. (2001). Competencies and workplace learning: Some reflections on the rhetoric and the reality. *Journal of Workplace Learning, 13*(4), 144–163. DOI: 10.1108/13665620110391097

Gašević, D., Dawson, S., & Siemens, G. (2015). Let's not forget: Learning analytics are about learning. *TechTrends, 59*(1), 64–71. DOI: 10.1007/s11528-014-0822-x

George, D. A. S., & George, A. S. H. (2024). Towards a Super Smart Society 5.0: Opportunities and Challenges of Integrating Emerging Technologies for Social Innovation. *Partners Universal International Research Journal, 3*(2), 01–29. DOI: 10.5281/zenodo.11522048

George, D. A. S. (2024a). AI-Enabled Intelligent Manufacturing: A Path to Increased Productivity, Quality, and Insights. *Partners Universal Innovative Research Publication, 2*(4), 50–63. DOI: 10.5281/zenodo.13338085

George, D. A. S. (2024b). Artificial Intelligence and the Future of Work: Job Shifting Not Job Loss. *Partners Universal Innovative Research Publication, 2*(2), 17–37. DOI: 10.5281/zenodo.10936490

Ghosh, P., Rai, A., & Sinha, A. (2013). Organizational justice and employee engagement: Exploring the linkage in public sector banks in India. *Personnel Review, 43*(4), 628–652. DOI: 10.1108/PR-08-2013-0148

Gibb, S. (2014). Soft skills assessment: Theory development and the research agenda. *International Journal of Lifelong Education, 33*(4), 455–471. DOI: 10.1080/02601370.2013.867546

Gilligan, C. (1982). *In a different voice: Psychological theory and women's development.* Harvard University Press.

Gittleman, M. (2022). *The "Great Resignation" in perspective. Monthly Labor Review.* U.S. Bureau of Labor Statistics., DOI: 10.21916/mlr.2022.20

Global Sustainable Tourism Council. (2022). GSTC criteria for destinations (version 2.0). https://www.gstcouncil.org/gstc-criteria/

Goldman Sachs. (2023). *The potentially large effects of artificial intelligence on economic growth.* Goldman Sachs Economic Research.

Goldstein, I. L., & Ford, J. K. (2002). *Training in organizations: Needs assessment, development, and evaluation* (4th ed.). Wadsworth.

Goleman, D. (1995). *Emotional intelligence: Why it can matter more than IQ*. Bantam Books.

Gond, J. P., Grubnic, S., Herzig, C., & Moon, J. (2012). Configuring management control systems: Theorizing the integration of strategy and sustainability. *Management Accounting Research, 23*(3), 205–223. DOI: 10.1016/j.mar.2012.06.003

Goos, M., Manning, A., & Salomons, A. (2014). Explaining job polarization: Routine-biased technological change and offshoring. *The American Economic Review, 104*(8), 2509–2526. DOI: 10.1257/aer.104.8.2509

Göranzon, B., & Josefson, I. (2012). *Knowledge, Skill and Artificial Intelligence*. Springer Science & Business Media.

Gouda, G. K., & Tiwari, B. (2022). Talent agility, innovation adoption and sustainable business performance: Empirical evidences from Indian automobile industry. *International Journal of Productivity and Performance Management, 71*(6), 2582–2604. DOI: 10.1108/IJPPM-02-2021-0071

Gouda, G. K., & Tiwari, B. (2024). Modelling the barriers of talent agility in Indian automobile industry in the era of industry 4.0. *Journal of Modelling in Management, 19*(4), 1343–1368. DOI: 10.1108/JM2-06-2023-0124

Govaerts, N., Kyndt, E., Dochy, F., & Baert, H. (2011). Influence of learning and working climate on the retention of talented employees. Journal of workplace learning, 23(1), 35-55https://DOI: 10.1108/13665621111097245

Grant, A. M. (2008). The significance of task significance: Job performance effects, relational mechanisms, and boundary conditions. *The Journal of Applied Psychology, 93*(1), 108–124. DOI: 10.1037/0021-9010.93.1.108 PMID: 18211139

Grant, A. M. (2012). Leading with meaning: Beneficiary contact, prosocial impact, and the performance effects of transformational leadership. *Academy of Management Journal, 55*(2), 458–476. DOI: 10.5465/amj.2010.0588

Grant, A. M., & Parker, S. K. (2009). Redesigning work design theories: The rise of relational and proactive perspectives. *The Academy of Management Annals, 3*(1), 317–375. DOI: 10.5465/19416520903047327

Grant, R. M. (1996). Toward a knowledge-based theory of the firm. *Strategic Management Journal, 17*(52), 109–122. DOI: 10.1002/smj.4250171110

Greasidou, M., & Valachis, I. (2022). The role of human resource management in service quality improvement of hotel businesses. *Enlightening Tourism: A Pathmaking Journal, 12*(3), 105–135. https://doi.org/DOI: 10.33776/et.v12i3.7277

Greene, D., Hoffmann, A. L., Stark, L., & Crawford, K. (2019). Better, nicer, clearer, fairer: A critical assessment of the movement for ethical AI and ML. *Proceedings of the 52nd Hawaii International Conference on System Sciences*, 2122–2131. https://doi.org/DOI: 10.24251/HICSS.2019.258

Greenhaus, J. H., & Callanan, G. A. (2006). Cross-training. In *Encyclopedia of career development* (pp. 208–208). SAGE Publications, Inc., DOI: 10.4135/9781412952675.n76

Greenwood, M. (2013). Ethical analysis of HRM: A review and research agenda. *Journal of Business Ethics, 114*(2), 355–366. DOI: 10.1007/s10551-012-1354-y

Groh, K. (2026, February 5). *Cross-training employees: A smarter way to build agility and engagement*. Valamis. https://www.valamis.com/blog/cross-training-employees

Gruenewald, H., & Mueller, M. (2025). *Reskilling and Upskilling in a Globalized Economy: Essential Strategies for Workforce Transformation*. Springer Nature. DOI: 10.1007/978-3-658-48384-5

Gudykunst, W. B. (1998). Applying anxiety/uncertainty management (AUM) theory to intercultural adjustment training. *International Journal of Intercultural Relations, 22*(2), 227–250. DOI: 10.1016/S0147-1767(98)00005-4

Guest, D. (1991). The Hunt is on for the Renaissance Man of Computing. *The Independent (London)*, 17 September.

Guest, D. E. (2017). Human resource management and employee well-being: Towards a new analytic framework. *Human Resource Management Journal, 27*(1), 22–38. DOI: 10.1111/1748-8583.12139

Gulyak, I. (2024). Strategy of designing additional educational programs in the field of teachers' digital competencies of the higher agricultural education. Bio Web of Conferences, 84, 01009. DOI: 10.1051/bioconf/20248401009

Gupta, P., Gupta, D., & Gupta, M. (2025). Unleashing human capital analytics for data-driven workforce management. In *Human Capital Analytics: Exploring the HR Spectrum in Industry 5.0* (pp. 143–163). https://doi.org/DOI: 10.1002/9781394238354.ch7

Hackman, J. R., & Oldham, G. R. (1976). Motivation through the design of work: Test of a theory. *Organizational Behavior and Human Performance, 16*(2), 250–279. DOI: 10.1016/0030-5073(76)90016-7

Hager, P., & Holland, S. (Eds.). (2006). *Graduate attributes, learning and employability*. Springer.

Hald, A. N., Enemark, U., Mwale, M. L., & Burau, V. (2025). Conceptualising the Primary Health Care Workforce: A Meta-Narrative-Inspired Review of Stakeholder Perspectives in Denmark. *Health Policy (Amsterdam)*, *105474*, 105474. Advance online publication. DOI: 10.1016/j.healthpol.2025.105474

Hall, C. M. (2011). A typology of governance and its implications for tourism policy analysis. *Journal of Sustainable Tourism*, *19*(4–5), 437–457. DOI: 10.1080/09669582.2011.570346

Hall, J. A. (2022). A Problem-Centered Approach to Designing Blended Courses: Unifying Online and Face-to-Face Modalities. *Education Sciences*, *12*(10), 689. DOI: 10.3390/educsci12100689

Hamdi, S., Silong, A. D., Omar, Z. B., & Mohd Rasdi, R. (Nisar, T. Reviewing Editor) (2016). Impact of T-shaped skill and top management support on innovation speed; The moderating role of technology uncertainty. *Cogent Business & Management*, *3*(1), 1153768. https://doi.org/DOI: 10.1080/23311975.2016.1153768

Hamza, K. (2025). *Emerging Markets and the Digital Economy: A Framework for Enhancing Global Competitiveness*. Taylor & Francis. DOI: 10.4324/9781003596868

Hanna, M. G., Pantanowitz, L., Jackson, B., Palmer, O., Visweswaran, S., Pantanowitz, J., Deebajah, M., & Rashidi, H. H. (2025). Ethical and Bias Considerations in Artificial Intelligence/Machine Learning. *Modern Pathology*, *38*(3), 100686. DOI: 10.1016/j.modpat.2024.100686 PMID: 39694331

Hanu, C., Amegbe, H., Yawson, M. D. T. A., & Mensah, P. (2023). Differential impact of work-based learning on employee agility, ambidexterity and proactive goal generation. *Journal of Workplace Learning*, *35*(1), 92–111. DOI: 10.1108/JWL-01-2022-0005

Harvey, L. (2001). Defining and measuring employability. *Quality in Higher Education*, *7*(2), 97–109. DOI: 10.1080/13538320120059990

Hasan, M. (2024). Upskilling and reskilling in a rapidly changing job market. European Journal of Business and Management Research. https://eu-opensci.org/index.php/ejbmr/article/view/52502

Hass, C., Rodriguez, A. M., Glover, R., & Goodrum, P. (2001). Implementing a multiskilled workforce. *Construction Management and Economics*, *19*(6), 633–641. DOI: 10.1080/01446190110050936

Heckman, J. J., & Kautz, T. (2012). Hard evidence on soft skills. *Labour Economics, 19*(4), 451–464. DOI: 10.1016/j.labeco.2012.05.014 PMID: 23559694

Henao, C. A., Mercado, Y. A., Gonzales, V. I., & Luer-Villagra, A. (2023). Multiskilled personnel assignment with k-chaining considering the learning-forgetting phenomena. *International Journal of Production Economics, 265*, 109018. DOI: 10.1016/j.ijpe.2023.109018

Hening, P. & Ghozali Harda Kumara. (2019). Public Sector Transformation in the Digital Age: Obstacles and Challenges for Governance Indonesia. *IAPA Proceedings Conference*

Henke, J. B., ... (2022). Skills and abilities to thrive in remote work: What have we learned? PMC. https://pmc.ncbi.nlm.nih.gov/articles/PMC9807077/

Henseler, J., Ringle, C. M., & Sarstedt, M. (2015). A new criterion for assessing discriminant validity in variance-based structural equation modeling. *Journal of the Academy of Marketing Science, 43*(1), 115–135. DOI: 10.1007/s11747-014-0403-8

Herdiansyah, H., Antriyandarti, E., Rosyada, A., Arista, N., Soesilo, T., & Ernawati, N. (2023). Evaluation of conventional and mechanization methods towards precision agriculture in Indonesia. *Sustainability (Basel), 15*(12), 9592. DOI: 10.3390/su15129592

Hernaus, T., Černe, M., & Škerlavaj, M. (2021). The interplay between relational job design and cross-training in predicting employee job/task citizenship performance. *Human Resource Development Quarterly, 32*(4), 625–646. DOI: 10.1002/hrdq.21427

Hershbein, B., & Kahn, L. B. (2023). Do recessions accelerate routine-biased technological change? Evidence from vacancy postings. *The American Economic Review, 113*(2), 400–435.

Heskett, J. L., Jones, T. O., Loveman, G. W., Sasser, W. E., & Schlesinger, L. A. (1994). Putting the service-profit chain to work. *Harvard Business Review, 72*(2), 164–174.

Heslin, P. A. (2005). Conceptualizing and evaluating career success. *Journal of Organizational Behavior, 26*(2), 113–136. DOI: 10.1002/job.270

Heuser, P., Letmathe, P., & Schinner, M. (2022). Workforce planning in production with flexible or budgeted employee training and volatile demand. *Journal of Business Economics, 92*(7), 1093–1124. https://doi.org/. DOI: 10.1007/s11573-022-01090-z

Hite, L. M., & McDonald, K. S. (2008). A New Era for Career Development and HRD. *Advances in Developing Human Resources, 10*(1), 3–7. DOI: 10.1177/1523422307310103

Hofer, A. (2026). Beyond Job Insecurity: The Role of Global Occupation Insecurity in Shaping Happiness, Health, and Performance. *Journal of Business and Psychology*. Advance online publication. DOI: 10.1007/s10869-026-10113-3

Holbeche, L. (2023). *The Agile Organization: How to Build an Engaged, Innovative and Resilient Business*. Kogan Page Publishers.

Holzinger, A., Zatloukal, K., & Müller, H. (2025). Is human oversight to AI systems still possible? *New Biotechnology, 85*, 59–62. DOI: 10.1016/j.nbt.2024.12.003 PMID: 39675423

Hom, P. W., Lee, T. W., Shaw, J. D., & Hausknecht, J. P. (2017). One hundred years of employee turnover theory and research. *The Journal of Applied Psychology, 102*(3), 530–545. https://psycnet.apa.org/doi/10.1037/apl0000103. DOI: 10.1037/apl0000103 PMID: 28125259

Honey, P., & Mumford, A. (1986). *The manual of learning styles*. Peter Honey.

Hopp, W. J., & Spearman, M. L. (2008). *Basic factory dynamics. Factory Physics* (3rd ed.). McGraw-Hill.

Houseman, S. N. (2001). Why employers use flexible staffing arrangements: Evidence from an establishment survey. *Industrial & Labor Relations Review, 55*(1), 149–170. DOI: 10.1177/001979390105500109

HUANG, Q., & HANAOKA, S. (. (2025). Dynamic Workforce Allocation for Train-Based Crowd-Shipping: Multi-Period Optimization Incorporating Transit Discomfort Costs. *Multimodal Transportation, 100269*. Advance online publication. DOI: 10.1016/j.multra.2025.100269

Humphrey, S. E., Nahrgang, J. D., & Morgeson, F. P. (2007). Integrating motivational, social, and contextual work design features: A meta-analytic summary and theoretical extension of the work design literature. *The Journal of Applied Psychology, 92*(5), 1332–1356. https://psycnet.apa.org/buy/2007-12832-011. DOI: 10.1037/0021-9010.92.5.1332 PMID: 17845089

Huselid, M. A. (2018). The science and practice of workforce analytics: Introduction to the HRM special issue. *Human Resource Management, 57*(3), 679–684. DOI: 10.1002/hrm.21916

Hutson, J., & Ceballos, J. (2023). Rethinking Education in the Age of AI: The Importance of Developing Durable Skills in the Industry 4.0. *Journal of Information Economics*, *1*(2), 26–35. Advance online publication. DOI: 10.58567/jie01020002

Ichniowski, C., Shaw, K., & Prennushi, G. (1997). The effects of human resource management practices on productivity: A study of steel finishing lines. *The American Economic Review*, *87*(3), 291–313.

Illeris, K. (2011). *The fundamentals of workplace learning: Understanding how people learn in working life*. Routledge.

ILO. (2023)... *World Employment and Social Outlook*. Advance online publication. DOI: 10.54394/SNCP1637

International Labour Organization (ILO). (2023). *Global employment trends 2023*. ILO.

International Labour Organization. (2018). *World employment and social outlook: Trends 2018*. ILO.

International Labour Organization. (2020). *World employment and social outlook: Trends 2020*. ILO.

International Labour Organization. (2021). *World employment and social outlook: The role of digital labour platforms in transforming the world of work*. ILO.

International Labour Organization. (2023). *Global employment trends and the future of work*. ILO.

International Labour Organization. (2023). *World employment and social outlook: Trends 2023*. International Labour Office. https://www.ilo.org/global/research/global-reports/weso/WCMS_865332/lang--en/index.htm

International Monetary Fund (IMF). (2023). *World economic outlook: Navigating global divergences*. IMF.

Ishaq, M. I., Sarwar, H., Franzoni, S., & Palermo, O. (2025). The nexus of human resource management, corporate social responsibility, and sustainable performance in upscale hotels: A mixed-method study. *International Journal of Emerging Markets*, *20*(13), 1–29. DOI: 10.1108/IJOEM-04-2022-0714

Islam, E., Loriot, B., & Rahman, L. (2025). The impact of product market competition on workplace safety. *Journal of Corporate Finance*, *93*, 102778. Advance online publication. DOI: 10.1016/j.jcorpfin.2025.102778

Jaakkola, E. (2020). Designing conceptual articles: Four approaches. *AMS Review*, *10*(1–2), 18–26. DOI: 10.1007/s13162-020-00161-0

Jackson, J. A., Sund, M., Barlari Lobos, G., Melin, L., & Mathiassen, S. (2023). Assessing the efficacy of a job rotation for improving occupational physical and psychosocial work environment, musculoskeletal health, social equality, production quality, and resilience at a commercial laundromat: Protocol for a longitudinal case study. *BMJ Open*, *13*(5), e067633. DOI: 10.1136/bmjopen-2022-067633 PMID: 37173106

Jain, P., Tripathi, V., Malladi, R., & Khang, A. (2023). Data-Driven Artificial Intelligence (AI) Models in the Workforce Development Planning. In *Designing Workforce Management Systems for Industry 4.0*. CRC Press. DOI: 10.1201/9781003357070-10

Jay, S. (n.d.). *Cross-Training Employees: 9 Practical Tips for Your Organization*. Academy to Innovate HR. https://www.aihr.com/blog/cross-training-employees/

Jehanzeb, K., & Bashir, N. A. (2017). Training and development programs and employee job satisfaction and retention: Evidence from the banking sector. *Frontiers in Psychology*, *8*, 939.

Jiang, K., Lepak, D. P., Hu, J., & Baer, J. C. (2012). How does human resource management influence organizational outcomes? A meta-analytic investigation of mediating mechanisms. *Academy of Management Journal*, *55*(6), 1264–1294. DOI: 10.5465/amj.2011.0088

Jingsheng, W. (2024). Cross-Training. In *The ECPH Encyclopedia of Psychology* (pp. 358–358). Springer., DOI: 10.1007/978-981-97-7874-4_1294

Jobin, A., Ienca, M., & Vayena, E. (2019). The global landscape of AI ethics guidelines. *Nature Machine Intelligence*, *1*(9), 389–399. DOI: 10.1038/s42256-019-0088-2

Johnston, S. (2004). Teaching Any Time, Any Place, Any Pace. In *Development and Management of Virtual Schools: Issues and Trends* (pp. 116–134). IGI Global Scientific Publishing. DOI: 10.4018/978-1-59140-154-4.ch006

Joo, B. K. (2010). Executive coaching: A conceptual framework from an integrative review of practice and research. *Human Resource Development Review*, *4*(4), 462–488. DOI: 10.1177/1534484305280866

Jordan, W. C., & Graves, S. C. (1995). Principles on the benefits of manufacturing process flexibility. *Management Science*, *41*(4), 577–594. DOI: 10.1287/mnsc.41.4.577

Jordan, W., Inman, R., & Blumenfeld, D. (2004). Chained cross-training of workers for robust performance. *IIE Transactions, 36*(10), 953–967. DOI: 10.1080/07408170490487713

Kagermann, H., Wahlster, W., & Helbig, J. (2013). *Recommendations for implementing the strategic initiative Industrie 4.0*. National Academy of Science and Engineering (Acatech).

Kahkesh, V. (2024, November 14). *Cross-training employees: what it is, tips, and benefits*. https://www.rippling.com/blog/cross-training-employees

Kahl, J., de Klerk, S., & Whiteoak, J. (2023). Managing empowerment: Adjusting organisational units' autonomy to achieve corporate agility. Journal of Organizational Effectiveness: People and Performance. Advance online publication. DOI: 10.1108/JOEPP-05-2022-0126

Kahn, W. A. (1990). Psychological conditions of personal engagement and disengagement. *Academy of Management Journal, 33*(4), 692–724. DOI: 10.2307/256287

Kaifi, B. A., Nafei, W. A., Khanfar, N., & Kaifi, M. M. (2012). A Multi-Generational Workforce: Managing and Understanding Millennials. *International Journal of Business and Management, 7*(24), 2012. DOI: 10.5539/ijbm.v7n24p88

Kaine, S., & Josserand, E. (2019). The organisation and experience of work in the gig economy. *The Journal of Industrial Relations, 61*(4), 479–501. DOI: 10.1177/0022185619865480

Kant, I. (1785). *Groundwork of the metaphysics of morals*.

Kantabutra, S., & Ketprapakorn, N. (2021). Toward an Organizational Theory of Resilience: An Interim Struggle. *Sustainability (Basel), 13*(23), 13137. DOI: 10.3390/su132313137

Karatepe, O. M., & Olugbade, O. A. (2016). The mediating role of work engagement in the relationship between high-performance work practices and job outcomes of employees in Nigeria. *International Journal of Contemporary Hospitality Management, 28*(10), 2350–2371. DOI: 10.1108/IJCHM-03-2015-0145

Karhapää, M. (2024). Hybrid work and workforce adaptability: Developing competencies for cross-functional collaboration in digital environments. *Journal of Organizational Learning and Development, 18*(2), 145–162. DOI: 10.1080/jorld.2024.01824

Karuppiah, S. P., & Kumaran, S. (2025, July). AI-powered talent acquisition: Enhancing recruitment and workforce analytics using machine learning. In *2025 IEEE 4th World Conference on Applied Intelligence and Computing (AIC)* (pp. 179–184). IEEE. https://doi.org/DOI: 10.1109/AIC66080.2025.11212065

Karuppiah, S. P., & Sriramakrishnan, R. RJ, E. B., & Kumaran, S. (2025, July). Employee retention analytics: Predictive modeling for workforce stability and talent management. In *2025 IEEE 4th World Conference on Applied Intelligence and Computing (AIC)* (pp. 420–425). IEEE. https://doi.org/DOI: 10.1109/AIC66080.2025.11212141

Katz, R., & Allen, T. J. (1985). Project performance and the locus of influence in the R&D matrix. *Academy of Management Journal*, *28*(1), 67–87. DOI: 10.2307/256062

Kaufman, B. E. (2015). *Theoretical perspectives on work and the employment relationship*. Industrial Relations Research Association.

Kegan, R. (1994). *In over our heads: The mental demands of modern life*. Harvard University Press.

Kehoe, R. R., & Wright, P. M. (2013). The impact of high-performance human resource practices on employees' attitudes and behaviors. *Journal of Management*, *39*(2), 366–391. DOI: 10.1177/0149206310365901

Kellogg, K. C., Valentine, M. A., & Christin, A. (2020). Algorithms at work: The new contested terrain of control. *The Academy of Management Annals*, *14*(1), 366–410. DOI: 10.5465/annals.2018.0174

Kerr, S. P., Kerr, W. R., Özden, Ç., & Parsons, C. (2016). Global talent flows. *The Journal of Economic Perspectives*, *30*(4), 83–106. DOI: 10.1257/jep.30.4.83

Khalil, O. E., & Seleim, A. (2010). Culture and knowledge transfer capacity: A cross-national study. [IJKM]. *International Journal of Knowledge Management*, *6*(4), 60–86. DOI: 10.4018/jkm.2010100104

Khamis, R. (2024). *AI-Powered Learning Experience Platforms: Investigating Personalized Learning in the Workplace*. https://gupea.ub.gu.se/handle/2077/83632

Khatib, M. E., Almarzooqi, S., Almarzooqi, E., & Alzaidan, S. (2024). Strategic Collaborations and Ecosystem Integration-DT Insights from Deloitte Case Studies. [IJTOP]. *International Journal of Theory of Organization and Practice*, *4*(2), 109–121. DOI: 10.54489/c9ef8m28

Kher, H. V. (2000). Examination of flexibility acquisition policies in dual resource constrained job shops with simultaneous worker learning and forgetting effect. *The Journal of the Operational Research Society*, *51*(5), 592–601. DOI: 10.1057/palgrave.jors.2600935

Kim, M., & Beehr, T. A. (2018). Challenge and hindrance demands lead to employees' health and behaviors through intrinsic motivation. *Motivation and Emotion*, *42*(4), 465–481.

Kinicki, A., & Fugate, M. (2018). *Organizational Behavior. A Practical, Problem-Solving Approach*. McGraw-Hill Education.

Kirkman, B. L., Rosen, B., Tesluk, P. E., & Gibson, C. B. (2019). Enhancing the transfer of learning through cross-training: A resource-based view of team development. *Academy of Management Review*, *44*(3), 583–606.

Kirkpatrick, D. L. (1994). *Evaluating training programs: The four levels*. Berrett-Koehler.

Kirkpatrick, D. L. (1998). The Four Levels of Evaluation. In Brown, S. M., & Seidner, C. J. (Eds.), *Evaluating Corporate Training: Models and Issues. Evaluation in Education and Human Services* (Vol. 46). Springer., DOI: 10.1007/978-94-011-4850-4_5

Kirkpatrick, J. D., & Kirkpatrick, W. K. (2016). *Kirkpatrick's four levels of training evaluation*. ATD Press.

Kirschner, P. A., Sweller, J., Clark, R. E., & Ayres, P. (2006). Why minimal guidance during instruction does not work. *Educational Psychologist*, *41*(2), 75–86. DOI: 10.1207/s15326985ep4102_1

Klein, M., & Smith, J. (2024). Matching workers to jobs: Recruitment, selection and labour market efficiency. *Journal of Labor Economics*.

Kline, R. B. (2023). *Principles and practice of structural equation modeling* (5th ed.). Guilford Press.

Kniffin, K. M., Narayanan, J., Anseel, F., Antonakis, J., Ashford, S. P., Bakker, A. B., Bamberger, P., Bapuji, H., Bhave, D. P., Choi, V. K., Creary, S. J., Demerouti, E., Flynn, F. J., Gelfand, M. J., Greer, L. L., Johns, G., Kesebir, S., Klein, P. G., Lee, S. Y., & van Vugt, M. (2021). COVID-19 and the workplace: Implications, issues, and insights for future research and action. *The American Psychologist*, *76*(1), 63–77. DOI: 10.1037/amp0000716 PMID: 32772537

Koçak, Ö., Levinthal, D. A., & Puranam, P. (2023). The dual challenge of search and coordination for organizational adaptation. *Organization Science*, *34*(2), 851–869. DOI: 10.1287/orsc.2022.1601

Kolb, A. Y., & Kolb, D. A. (2005). Learning styles and learning spaces: Enhancing experiential learning in higher education. *Academy of Management Learning & Education*, *4*(2), 193–212. DOI: 10.5465/amle.2005.17268566

Kolb, D. A. (1984). *Experiential learning: Experience as the source of learning and development*. Prentice-Hall.

Kölbel, J. F., Heeb, F., Paetzold, F., & Busch, T. (2020). Can sustainable investing save the world? Reviewing the mechanisms of investor impact. *Organization & Environment*, *33*(4), 554–574. DOI: 10.1177/1086026620919202

Kölling, A. (2022). Labor shortages and wage responses: Evidence from German establishments. *Journal for Labour Market Research*, *56*(1), 1–18.

Koopmans, L., van den Tooren, M., & Preenen, P. (2025). Long-term effects of on-the-job skills (mis)match on employee wellbeing and employability: A 7-wave longitudinal study. *Frontiers in Psychology*, *16*, 1591769. DOI: 10.3389/fpsyg.2025.1591769 PMID: 41479979

Koren, M., & Pető, R. (2023). Business disruptions from social distancing. *Journal of Economic Dynamics & Control*, *138*, 104320.

Kotter, J. P. (1996). Leading change. Harvard business press.

Kraimer, M. L., Seibert, S. E., Wayne, S. J., Liden, R. C., & Bravo, J. (2011). Antecedents and outcomes of organizational support for development: The critical role of career opportunities. *The Journal of Applied Psychology*, *96*(3), 485–500. DOI: 10.1037/a0021452 PMID: 21114356

Kramar, R. (2014). Beyond strategic human resource management: Is sustainable human resource management the next approach? *International Journal of Human Resource Management*, *25*(8), 1069–1089. DOI: 10.1080/09585192.2013.816863

Kryscynski, D., & Coff, R. (2024). Empirical opportunities for advancing theory and research on strategic human capital. *Journal of Management Scientific Reports*, *2*(2), 168–178. DOI: 10.1177/27550311241249947

Krzywdzinski, Martin, Ulrich Jürgens, and Sabine Pfeiffer. 2016. The Fourth Revolution: The Transformation of Manufacturing Work in the Age of Digitalization. WZB Report 2016. Diunduh 10 Oktober 2018. file:///C:/Users/S/Downloads/2016industrie40.pdf

Kulkarni, P. M., Appasaba, L. V., Gokhale, P., & Tigadi, B. (2022). Role of digital simulation in employee training. *Global Transitions Proceedings*, *3*(1), 149–156. DOI: 10.1016/j.gltp.2022.04.014

Kunze, F., Boehm, S., & Bruch, H. (2013). Age, resistance to change, and job performance. *Journal of Managerial Psychology*, *28*(7/8), 741–760. DOI: 10.1108/JMP-06-2013-0194

Kurki, A.-L., Koskela, I., & Yli-Kaitala, K. (2024). Collaborative development on a digital learning platform: The potential of AI tools for facilitation. *Human Technology*, *20*(3), 3. Advance online publication. DOI: 10.14254/1795-6889.2024.20-3.5

Kwok, L. (2022). Labor shortage: A critical reflection and a call for industry-academia collaboration. *International Journal of Contemporary Hospitality Management*, *34*(11), 3929–3943. DOI: 10.1108/IJCHM-01-2022-0103

Labus, P., & Lukić Nikolić, J. (2025). The Mediating Role of Employee Engagement in the Relationship Between Organisational Climate and Turnover Intentions: A Study among Hospitality Employees. *Journal for East European Management Studies*, *30*(4), 49104. DOI: 10.31083/JEEMS49104

Labus, P., Ostojić, B., & Lukić Nikolić, J. (2026). The impact of marital and parental status on burnout and wellbeing among hospitality employees. *The European Journal of Applied Economics*, *23*(1), 113–125. DOI: 10.5937/EJAE23-62934

Lado, A. A., & Wilson, M. C. (1994). Human resource systems and sustained competitive advantage: A competency-based perspective. *Academy of Management Review*, *19*(4), 699–727. DOI: 10.2307/258742

Laker, D. R., & Powell, J. L. (2011). The differences between hard and soft skills and their relative impact on training transfer. *Human Resource Development Quarterly*, *22*(1), 111–122. DOI: 10.1002/hrdq.20063

Lancaster, C., Gilreath, H., Mallick, R., & McNeese, N. J. (2024). Evaluating cross-training's impact on perceived teaming outcomes for human–AI teams. *Proceedings of the Human Factors and Ergonomics Society Annual Meeting*, *68*(1), 1469–1472. Advance online publication. DOI: 10.1177/10711813241262033

Lasi, H., Fettke, P., Kemper, H. G., Feld, T., & Hoffmann, M. (2014). Industry 4.0. *Business & Information Systems Engineering*, *6*(4), 239–242. DOI: 10.1007/s12599-014-0334-4

Lau, C. M., & Ngo, H. Y. (2004). The HR system, organizational culture, and product innovation. *International Business Review*, *13*(6), 685–703. DOI: 10.1016/j.ibusrev.2004.08.001

Lazarova, M., Westman, M., & Shaffer, M. A. (2010). Elucidating the positive side of the work–family interface on international assignments: A model of expatriate work and family performance. *Academy of Management Review, 35*(1), 93–117. DOI: 10.5465/amr.35.1.zok93

Lazear, E. P. (2009). Firm-specific human capital: A skill-weights approach. *Journal of Political Economy, 117*(5), 914–940. DOI: 10.1086/648671

Lee, A. N., & Nie, Y. (2024). Future-Oriented Learning and Continuous Skills Development: Developing a Resilient Workforce in Changing Times. In Lee, A. N., & Nie, Y. (Eds.), *Future-oriented Learning and Skills Development for Employability: Insights from Singapore and Some Asia-Pacific Contexts* (pp. 3–15). Springer Nature., DOI: 10.1007/978-981-97-8584-1_1

Lee, T. W., & Bruvold, N. T. (2003). Creating value for employees: Investment in employee development. *International Journal of Human Resource Management, 14*(6), 981–1000. DOI: 10.1080/0958519032000106173

Leger, M. (2023). *Building High-Trust Workplaces: The Role of Employee Resource Groups in Fostering Stronger Employee-Employer Relationships*. American Enterprise Institute. https://www.jstor.org/stable/resrep55292

Lehmann, R., & Vogt, B. (2024). Improving Likert scale big data analysis in psychometric health economics: Reliability of the new compositional data approach. *Brain Informatics, 11*(1), 19. DOI: 10.1186/s40708-024-00232-z PMID: 38987395

Lengnick-Hall, C. A., & Beck, T. E. (2005). Adaptive fit versus robust transformation: How organizations respond to environmental change. *Journal of Management, 31*(5), 738–757. DOI: 10.1177/0149206305279367

Lengnick-Hall, C. A., Beck, T. E., & Lengnick-Hall, M. L. (2011). Developing a capacity for organizational resilience through strategic human resource management. *Human Resource Management Review, 21*(3), 243–255. DOI: 10.1016/j.hrmr.2010.07.001

Leonardi, P. M. (2021). COVID-19 and the new technologies of organizing: Digital exhaust, digital footprints, and artificial intelligence in the wake of remote work. *Journal of Management Studies, 58*(1), 249–253. DOI: 10.1111/joms.12648

Levandowski, S. (2025). Adult Learning Theory. In *Routledge Companion to Occupational Therapy*. Routledge. DOI: 10.4324/9781003526766-54

Levy, F., & Murnane, R. J. (2004). *The new division of labor: How computers are creating the next job market*. Princeton University Press. DOI: 10.1515/9781400845927

Lewicki, R. J., Saunders, D. M., & Barry, B. (2003). *Negotiation* (4th ed.). McGraw-Hill.

Li, L. (2022). Reskilling and upskilling the future-ready workforce. Frontiers in Psychology. https://pmc.ncbi.nlm.nih.gov/articles/PMC9278314/

Liang, G. (2024). Skill Shifts and Retraining Initiatives: Adapting to Post-Pandemic Labor Market Dynamics. *Law and Economy*, *3*(1), 58–61. DOI: 10.56397/LE.2024.01.06

Li, H., Ma, S., & Pan, X. (2025a). The influence of stock market liberalization on labor investment decisions: Evidence from China. *Pacific-Basin Finance Journal*, *93*, 102859. Advance online publication. DOI: 10.1016/j.pacfin.2025.102859

Li, J., Bonn, M. A., & Ye, B. H. (2019). Hotel employees' artificial intelligence and robotics awareness and its impact on turnover intention. *Tourism Management*, *73*, 172–181. DOI: 10.1016/j.tourman.2019.02.006

Li, L. (2024). Reskilling and upskilling the future-ready workforce for Industry 4.0 and beyond. *Information Systems Frontiers*, *26*(5), 1697–1712. DOI: 10.1007/s10796-022-10308-y PMID: 35855776

Lima, S. A., & Rahman, M. M. (2025). Generational diversity and inclusion: HRM challenges and opportunities in multigenerational workforces. [IJHSSM]. *SSRN*, *5*(3), 704–710. DOI: 10.2139/ssrn.5330092

Littrell, L. N., Salas, E., Hess, K. P., Paley, M., & Riedel, S. (2006). Expatriate preparation: A critical analysis of 25 years of cross-cultural training research. *Human Resource Development Review*, *5*(3), 355–388. DOI: 10.1177/1534484306290106

Liu, R., & Yin, H. (2024). How algorithmic management influences gig workers' job crafting. *Behavioral Sciences (Basel, Switzerland)*, *14*(10), 952. DOI: 10.3390/bs14100952 PMID: 39457824

Lokesha, M. U., & Siddegowda, Y. S. (2009). Training and development practices: A comparative study of public and private sector industries. *Prabandhan: Indian Journal of Management*, *2*(6), 17–26. DOI: 10.17010/pijom/2009/v2i6/61033

London, M., & Smither, J. W. (1995). Can multi-source feedback change perceptions of goal accomplishment, self-evaluations, and performance-related outcomes? Theory-based applications and directions for research. *Personnel Psychology*, *48*(4), 803–839. DOI: 10.1111/j.1744-6570.1995.tb01782.x

López, S. P., Peón, J. M. M., & Ordás, C. J. V. (2005). Managing knowledge: The link between culture and organizational learning. *Journal of Knowledge Management, 8*(6), 93–104. DOI: 10.1108/13673270410567657

Lo, T. T. S., Chen, Y., Lai, T. Y., & Goodman, A. (2024). Phygital workspace: A systematic review in developing a new typological work environment using XR technology to reduce the carbon footprint. *Frontiers in Built Environment, 10*, 1370423. DOI: 10.3389/fbuil.2024.1370423

Ludviga, I., & Kalvina, A. (2023). Organizational agility during crisis: Do employees' perceptions of public sector organizations' strategic agility foster employees' work engagement and well-being? *Employee Responsibilities and Rights Journal, 35*(4), 295–316. DOI: 10.1007/s10672-023-09442-9 PMID: 40479364

Lukić Nikolić, J., & Labus, P. (2024). The mediating role of the glass-ceiling phenomenon in the relationship between career opportunities and employee engagement within the hospitality. *Hotel and Tourism Management, 12*(2), 25–39. https://doo.org/10.5937/menhottur2400011L

Lukić Nikolić, J. (2024). Perceived Effects of Robotic Process Automation on Work Tasks and Processes: A Study of an IT Company in the Republic of Serbia. [JSIR]. *Journal of Scientific and Industrial Research, 83*(11), 1236–1245. DOI: 10.56042/jsir.v83i11.5466

Lukić Nikolić, J., & Andrian Sredojević, S. (2025). The future of work in Banking 5.0: Examining the impact of automation and artificial intelligence on employees in Serbian banks. *EMC Review, 29*(1), 127–143. DOI: 10.7251/EMC2501127N

Lukić Nikolić, J., Dudić, B., & Mirković, V. (2024). The impact of employee engagement on organizational agility in the digital age: A case study of the software development company. *International Review (Steubenville, Ohio), 1–2*(1-2), 15–25. DOI: 10.5937/intrev2401015N

Lukić Nikolić, J., & Mirković, V. (2023). Occupational burnout among employees in Serbian banking sector: Evidence during Covid-19 pandemic. *Inzinerine Ekonomika –. The Engineering Economist, 34*(5), 500–513. DOI: 10.5755/j01.ee.34.5.31558

Luthans, F. (2002). The need for and meaning of positive organizational behavior. *Journal of Organizational Behavior, 23*(6), 695–706. DOI: 10.1002/job.165

Luthans, F., Youssef, C. M., & Avolio, B. J. (2006). *Psychological capital: Developing the human competitive edge*. Oxford university press. DOI: 10.1093/acprof:oso/9780195187526.001.0001

Mababu Mukiur, R., & Gómez Lega, J. L. (2025). Transfer of technical skills and non-technical skills in the workplace: An analysis from the perspective of mental processes of learning. *Human Resource Development Review*, 15344843251403110. Advance online publication. DOI: 10.1177/15344843251403110

MacDuffie, J. P. (1995). Human resource bundles and manufacturing performance: Organizational logic and flexible production systems in the world auto industry. ilr. *Industrial & Labor Relations Review*, *48*(2), 197–221. DOI: 10.1177/001979399504800201

Maclaren, S. (2016, May 16). *How Investing in Employee Training Benefits Your Business*. https://mena.entrepreneur.com/growth-strategies/how-investing-in-employee-training-benefits-your-business/275842

Madhumita, G., & Dolly Diana, P. PC, N., Narendra Kiran, P. B., Aggarwal, S., & Satish Nargunde, A. (2024). AI-powered Performance Management: Driving Employee Success and Organizational Growth. *2024 5th International Conference on Recent Trends in Computer Science and Technology (ICRTCST)*, 204–209. DOI: 10.1109/ICRTCST61793.2024.10578371

Maestas, N., Mullen, K. J., & Powell, D. (2023). The effect of population aging on economic growth, the labor force, and productivity. *American Economic Journal. Macroeconomics*, *15*(2), 306–332. DOI: 10.1257/mac.20190196

Makransky, G., Terkildsen, T. S., & Mayer, R. E. (2019). Adding immersive virtual reality to a science lab simulation causes more presence but less learning. *Learning and Instruction*, *60*, 225–236. DOI: 10.1016/j.learninstruc.2017.12.007

Malhotra, M. K., Fry, T. D., Kher, H. V., & Donohue, J. M. (1993). The impact of learning and labor attrition on worker flexibility in dual constrained job shops. *Decision Sciences*, *24*(3), 641–663. DOI: 10.1111/j.1540-5915.1993.tb01296.x

Malhotra, M. K., & Ritzman, L. P. (1990). Resource flexibility issues in multistage manufacturing. *Decision Sciences*, *21*(4), 673–690. DOI: 10.1111/j.1540-5915.1990.tb01243.x

Manyika, J., Chui, M., Miremadi, M., Bughin, J., George, K., Willmott, P., & Dewhurst, M. (2017). *A future that works: Automation, employment, and productivity*. McKinsey Global Institute.

Marinakou, E., & Giousmpasoglou, C. (2019). Talent management and retention strategies in luxury hotels: Evidence from four countries. *International Journal of Contemporary Hospitality Management*, *31*(10), 3855–3878. DOI: 10.1108/IJCHM-10-2018-0862

Márquez Stone, V., & Sandoval Cabrera, S. V. (2024). Effects of automation on Mexican automotive employment: 2013–2022. *The Indian Journal of Labour Economics : The Quarterly Journal of the Indian Society of Labour Economics, 67*(3), 661–680. DOI: 10.1007/s41027-024-00505-5

Marsick, V. J., & Watkins, K. E. (2003). Demonstrating value of learning culture. *Advances in Developing Human Resources, 5*(2), 132–151. DOI: 10.1177/1523422303005002002

Martin, K. D., Borah, A., & Palmatier, R. W. (2017). Data privacy: Effects on customer and firm performance. *Journal of Marketing, 81*(1), 36–58. DOI: 10.1509/jm.15.0497

Maslach, C., & Leiter, M. P. (2016). Understanding the burnout experience: Recent research and its implications for psychiatry. *World Psychiatry; Official Journal of the World Psychiatric Association (WPA), 15*(2), 103–111. DOI: 10.1002/wps.20311 PMID: 27265691

Mathrani, S., & Edwards, B. (2020). Knowledge-Sharing Strategies in Distributed Collaborative Product Development. *Journal of Open Innovation, 6*(4), 194. DOI: 10.3390/joitmc6040194

Mattoo, A., Rocha, N., Ruta, M., & Kowalski, P. (2020). Movement of capital and people in deep trade agreements. In Mattoo, A. (Eds.), *Handbook of deep trade agreements* (pp. 177–223). World Bank., DOI: 10.1596/978-1-4648-1539-3

Ma, X., Nakab, A., & Vidart, D. (2024). Human capital investment and development: The role of on-the-job training. *Journal of Political Economy Macroeconomics, 2*(1), 107–148. DOI: 10.1086/728667

Mayer, J. D., & Salovey, P. (1997). What is emotional intelligence? In Salovey, P., & Sluyter, D. J. (Eds.), *Emotional development and emotional intelligence*. Basic Books.

Mayer, K. U., Ritschard, G., & Oris, M. (2010). *Longitudinal analysis and life course research*. Springer.

Maynard, M. T., Luciano, M. M., D'Innocenzo, L., Mathieu, J. E., & Dean, M. D. (2012). Modeling team empowerment: An integrative multilevel model. *Human Resource Management Review, 22*(2), 127–139.

Mazmanian, M., Orlikowski, W. J., & Yates, J. (2013). The autonomy paradox: The implications of mobile email devices for knowledge professionals. *Organization Science, 24*(5), 1337–1357. DOI: 10.1287/orsc.1120.0806

McGaghie, W. C., Issenberg, S. B., Cohen, E. R., Barsuk, J. H., & Wayne, D. B. (2011). Does simulation-based medical education with deliberate practice yield better results than traditional clinical education? A meta-analytic comparative review of the evidence. *Academic Medicine : Journal of the Association of American Medical Colleges, 86*(6), 706–711. DOI: 10.1097/ACM.0b013e318217e119 PMID: 21512370

McKee, M. C., & Froelich, K. A. (2016). Does cross-training improve retention? The role of workload and perceived fairness. *Human Resource Development Quarterly, 27*(3), 345–364.

McKinsey & Company. (2023). *Future of work report.* https://www.mckinsey.com/featured-insights/future-of-work

McKinsey Global Institute. (2017). *Jobs lost, jobs gained: Workforce transitions in a time of automation.* McKinsey & Company.

McKinsey Global Institute. (2023). *The future of work in a post-pandemic economy.* McKinsey & Company.

McLagan, P. A. (1997). Competencies: The next generation. *Training & Development, 51*(5), 40–47.

Meerman, J., van Casteren, P. A. J., Brouwers, E. P. M., van Dam, A., & van der Klink, J. J. L. (2022). A capability perspective on sustainable employability: A Dutch focus group study on organizational, work and personal conversion factors. *PLoS One, 17*(10), e0274000. DOI: 10.1371/journal.pone.0274000 PMID: 36269699

Mehler, M., Balint, E., Gralla, M., Nater, U. M., & Claudia, M. (2024). Training emotional competencies at the workplace: A systematic review and meta-analysis. *BMC Psychology, 12*(1), 718. DOI: 10.1186/s40359-024-02198-3 PMID: 39627880

Mehner, L., Rothenbusch, S., & Kauffeld, S. (2025). How to maximize the impact of workplace training: A mixed-method analysis of social support, training transfer and knowledge sharing. *European Journal of Work and Organizational Psychology, 34*(2), 201–217. DOI: 10.1080/1359432X.2024.2319082

Meyer, B. H., Prescott, B., & Sheng, X. S. (2022). The impact of the COVID-19 pandemic on business expectations. *International Journal of Forecasting, 38*(2), 529–544. DOI: 10.1016/j.ijforecast.2021.02.009 PMID: 35185229

Meyer, J. B., Kaplan, D., & Charum, J. (2001). Scientific nomadism and the new geopolitics of knowledge. *International Social Science Journal, 53*(168), 309–321. DOI: 10.1111/1468-2451.00317

Meyer, J. P., & Allen, N. J. (1997). Commitment in the workplace: Theory, research, and application. *Sage (Atlanta, Ga.)*. Advance online publication. DOI: 10.4135/9781452231556

Mezirow, J. (1991). *Transformative dimensions of adult learning*. Jossey-Bass.

Miah, M. T., Erdei-Gally, S., Dancs, A., & Fekete-Farkas, M. (2024). A systematic review of Industry 4.0 technology on workforce employability and skills: Driving success factors and challenges in South Asia. *Economies (Basel)*, *12*(2), 35. DOI: 10.3390/economies12020035

Microsoft. (2024). Working in a phygital world: Why businesses need to rethink their workspace experiences now. Microsoft Inside Track. https://www.microsoft.com/insidetrack/blog/working-in-a-phygital-world-why-businesses-need-to-rethink-their-workspace-experiences-now/

Mihus, I. (2023). Strategic management of human resources of enterprises based on digital competencies. *Scientific Notes of the University*, (2), 131–138. DOI: 10.31732/2663-2209-2022-70-131-138

Mikalef, P., Pappas, I. O., Krogstie, J., & Giannakos, M. (2018). Big data analytics capabilities: A systematic literature review and research agenda. *Information Systems and e-Business Management*, *16*(3), 547–578. DOI: 10.1007/s10257-017-0362-y

Milkovich, G. T., Newman, J. M., & Gerhart, B. (2014). *Compensation* (11th ed.). McGraw-Hill.

Mill, J. S. (1863). *Utilitarianism*.

Mittelstadt, B. D., Allo, P., Taddeo, M., Wachter, S., & Floridi, L. (2016). The ethics of algorithms: Mapping the debate. *Big Data & Society*, *3*(2), 1–21. DOI: 10.1177/2053951716679679

Mittelstadt, B. D., Russell, C., & Wachter, S. (2019). Explaining explanations in AI. *Proceedings of the Conference on Fairness, Accountability, and Transparency*, 279–288. https://doi.org/DOI: 10.1145/3287560.3287574

Mitterbacher, K., Fleiß, J., & Palan, S. (2024). Reciprocity in migration policy and labor market integration: A lab experiment. *Economic Analysis and Policy*, *81*, 1–16. DOI: 10.1016/j.eap.2023.11.008

Moedt, K., Lechner, C., & Khapova, S. (2024). Growing pains during scale-up hypergrowth: Integration and future research agenda. *Technological Forecasting and Social Change*, *209*, 123779. DOI: 10.1016/j.techfore.2024.123779

Mohammadi, N., & Mohammadian, B. (2025). Employee value proposition mining: A novel approach to employer brand development based on social media data using aspect-based sentiment analysis. *Results in Engineering*, *28*, 107973. DOI: 10.1016/j.rineng.2025.107973

Mohammed, N. A., Mohammed, D., & Gana, J. (2022). THE IMPACT OF TRAINING AND DEVELOPMENT ON EMPLOYEE PRODUCTIVITY IN THE 21ST CENTURY. *African Journal of Management and Business Research*, *3*(1), 41–58.

Mohebianfar, E. (2025). *An AI-driven approach to improve talent retention and mobility* [fi=Ylempi AMK-opinnäytetyö|sv=Högre YH-examensarbete|en=Master's thesis|]. https://www.theseus.fi/handle/10024/883116

Moi, L. (2026). Phygital dynamic capabilities: Microfoundations and their implications for organizations. *Technological Forecasting and Social Change*. Advance online publication. DOI: 10.1016/j.techfore.2025.124423

Montgomery, R. M. (2024). *The Rise of Inequality and Artificial Intelligence: Impacts, Challenges, and Opportunities in a Globalized Economy* (SSRN Scholarly Paper No. 4964094). Social Science Research Network. DOI: 10.2139/ssrn.4964094

Morandini, S., Fraboni, F., De Angelis, M., Puzzo, G., Giusino, D., & Pietrantoni, L. (2023). *The Impact of Artificial Intelligence on Workers' Skills: Upskilling and Reskilling in Organisations*. DOI: 10.28945/5078

Moro, C., Štromberga, Z., Raikos, A., & Stirling, A. (2017). The effectiveness of virtual and augmented reality in health sciences and medical anatomy. *Anatomical Sciences Education*, *10*(6), 549–559. DOI: 10.1002/ase.1696 PMID: 28419750

Mouw, T., Kalleberg, A. L., & Schultz, M. A. (2024). "Stepping-Stone" versus "Dead-End" jobs: Occupational structure, work experience, and mobility out of low-wage jobs. *American Sociological Review*, *89*(2), 298–345. DOI: 10.1177/00031224241232957

Mutawa, A. M., & Sruthi, S. (2025). UNESCO's AI Competency Framework: Challenges and Opportunities in Educational Settings. In *Impacts of Generative AI on the Future of Research and Education* (pp. 75–96). IGI Global Scientific Publishing. DOI: 10.4018/979-8-3693-0884-4.ch004

Mwakyusa, J. R. P., & Mcharo, E. W. (2024). Role ambiguity and role conflict effects on employees' emotional exhaustion in healthcare services in Tanzania. *Cogent Business & Management*, *11*(1), 2326237. DOI: 10.1080/23311975.2024.2326237

Naguib, A., & Fouad, K. M. (2024). Database Security: Current Challenges and Effective Protection Strategies. *2024 6th International Conference on Computing and Informatics (ICCI)*, 120–130. DOI: 10.1109/ICCI61671.2024.10485182

Nahapiet, J., & Ghoshal, S. (1998). Social capital, intellectual capital, and the organizational advantage. *Academy of Management Review, 23*(2), 242–266. DOI: 10.2307/259373

Near, J. P., & Miceli, M. P. (1995). Effective whistle-blowing. *Academy of Management Review, 20*(3), 679–708. DOI: 10.2307/258791

Nelson, R. T. (1967). Labor and Machine Limited Production Systems. *Management Science, 13*(9), 648–671. DOI: 10.1287/mnsc.13.9.648

Nembhard, D. A., & Prichanont, K. (2007). Factors affecting cross-training performance in serial production systems. In D. A. Nembhard (Ed.), *Workforce cross training* (pp. 87–109). CRS Press, Taylor & Francis Group.

Nembhard, D. A., Black Nembhard, H., & Qin, R. (2005). A real options model for workforce cross-training. *The Engineering Economist, 50*(2), 95–116. DOI: 10.1080/00137910590949850

Nettle, R., Vikas, A., Lin, P., & Santhanam-Martin, M. (2025). Review: Attracting and retaining a farm workforce for the pork industry. *Animal, 101670*, 101670. Advance online publication. DOI: 10.1016/j.animal.2025.101670 PMID: 41176510

Ngadi, N., Zaelany, A. A., Latifa, A., Harfina, D., Asiati, D., Setiawan, B., Ibnu, F., Triyono, T., & Rajagukguk, Z. (2023). Challenge of Agriculture Development in Indonesia: Rural Youth Mobility and Aging Workers in Agriculture Sector. *Sustainability (Basel), 15*(2), 922. DOI: 10.3390/su15020922

Ng, T. W., Eby, L. T., Sorensen, K. L., & Feldman, D. C. (2005). Predictors of objective and subjective career success: A meta-analysis. *Personnel Psychology, 58*(2), 367–408. DOI: 10.1111/j.1744-6570.2005.00515.x

Nguyen, T., Le, C. V., Nguyen, M., Nguyen, G., Lien, T. T. H., & Nguyen, O. (2025). The organisational impact of agility: A systematic literature review. *Management Review Quarterly, 75*(3), 2709–2757. DOI: 10.1007/s11301-024-00446-9

Ninan, N., Roy, J. C., & Thomas, M. R. (2019). Benefits of Cross-Training: Scale Development and Validity. *Prabandhan: Indian Journal of Management, 12*(6), 41–56. https://doi.org/DOI: 10.17010/pijom/2019/v12i6/144935

Nishii, L. H. (2013). The benefits of climate for inclusion for gender-diverse groups. *Academy of Management Journal, 56*(6), 1754–1774. DOI: 10.5465/amj.2009.0823

Niyaz, M. T., Qorri, D., Kovács, K., & Juhasz, C. (2025). Research trends in workforce planning in the automotive sector: A comprehensive review. *Administrative Sciences*, *15*(4), 140. DOI: 10.3390/admsci15040140

Noe, R. A. (2017). *Employee training and development* (7th ed.). McGraw-Hill Education.

Noe, R. A., Clarke, A. D., & Klein, H. J. (2014). Learning in the twenty-first-century workplace. *Annual Review of Organizational Psychology and Organizational Behavior*, *1*(1), 245–275. DOI: 10.1146/annurev-orgpsych-031413-091321

Noe, R. A., Hollenbeck, J. R., Gerhart, B., & Wright, P. M. (2023). *Fundamentals of human resource management* (10th ed.). McGraw-Hill.

Noe, R. A., Hollenbeck, J. R., Gerhart, B., & Wright, P. M. (2023). *Human resource management: Gaining a competitive advantage* (13th ed.). McGraw Hill.

Noe, R. A., Tews, M. J., & Marand, A. D. (2013). Individual differences and informal learning in the workplace. *Journal of Vocational Behavior*, *83*(3), 327–335. DOI: 10.1016/j.jvb.2013.06.009

Nonaka, I., & Takeuchi, H. (1995). *The knowledge-creating company: How Japanese companies create the dynamics of innovation*. Oxford University Press. DOI: 10.1093/oso/9780195092691.001.0001

North, D. C. (1990). *Institutions, institutional change and economic performance*. Cambridge University Press. DOI: 10.1017/CBO9780511808678

Notestein, F. W. (1945). Population—the long view. In Schultz, T. W. (Ed.), *Food for the world* (pp. 36–57). University of Chicago Press.

Nunkoo, R. (2017). Governance and sustainable tourism: What is the role of trust, power, and social capital? *Journal of Destination Marketing & Management*, *6*(4), 277–285. DOI: 10.1016/j.jdmm.2017.10.003

Nunkoo, R., & Ramkissoon, H. (2012). Power, trust, social exchange and community support. *Annals of Tourism Research*, *39*(2), 997–1023. DOI: 10.1016/j.annals.2011.11.017

Nykänen, M., Puro, V., Tiikkaja, M., & Kannisto, H. (2020). Implementing novel safety training: Benefits of virtual reality and 3D simulation in construction. *Journal of Safety Research*, *75*, 205–221. DOI: 10.1016/j.jsr.2020.09.015 PMID: 33334479

O'Reilly, C. A.III, & Tushman, M. L. (2013). Organizational ambidexterity: Past, present, and future. *The Academy of Management Perspectives*, *27*(4), 324–338. DOI: 10.5465/amp.2013.0025

Oberländer, M., Beinicke, A., & Bipp, T. (2020). Digital competencies: A review of the literature and applications in the workplace. *Computers and Education, 146* (September 2019). https://doi.org/DOI: 10.1016/j.compedu.2019.103752

ODI. (2025). *The AI time bomb: 2.5 million jobs at risk, is Kenya ready?* ODI: Think Change.

OECD AI Outlook. (2024, May 14). *OECD Digital Economy Outlook 2024 (Volume 1).* OECD. https://www.oecd.org/en/publications/oecd-digital-economy-outlook-2024-volume-1_a1689dc5-en.html

OECD. (2019). *OECD skills outlook 2019: Thriving in a digital world.* OECD Publishing., DOI: 10.1787/df80bc12-

OECD. (2024). *OECD Employment Outlook 2024: The Net-Zero Transition and the Labour Market.* OECD Publishing., DOI: 10.1787/ac8b3538-

OECD. (2024a). *Artificial intelligence and education and skills.* OECD. https://www.oecd.org/en/topics/artificial-intelligence-and-education-and-skills.html

OECD. (2024b, December 4). *OECD Economic Outlook, Volume 2024 Issue 2.* OECD. https://www.oecd.org/en/publications/oecd-economic-outlook-volume-2024-issue-2_d8814e8b-en.html

Ojambati, T. S., Akinbile, B. F., & Abiola-Falemu, J. O. (2012). Personnel training and development: A vital tool for construction worker's performance. *Journal of Emerging Trends in Engineering and Applied Sciences, 3*(6), 996–1004.

Olivella, J., & Nembhard, D. (2016). Calibrating cross-training to meet demand mix variation and employee absence. *European Journal of Operational Research, 248*(2), 462–472. DOI: 10.1016/j.ejor.2015.07.036

Oreg, S. (2006). Personality, context, and resistance to organizational change. *European Journal of Work and Organizational Psychology, 15*(1), 73–101. DOI: 10.1080/13594320500451247

Organisation for Economic Co-operation and Development (OECD). (2019). *OECD employment outlook 2019: The future of work.* OECD Publishing.

Organisation for Economic Co-operation and Development (OECD). (2020). *OECD employment outlook 2020: Worker security and the COVID-19 crisis.* OECD Publishing.

Organisation for Economic Co-operation and Development (OECD). (2021). [*OECD indicators.* OECD Publishing.]. *Health at a Glance*, •••, 2021.

Organisation for Economic Co-operation and Development (OECD). (2022). *Labour market and skills shortages in the OECD*. OECD Publishing.

Organisation for Economic Co-operation and Development (OECD). (2024). *Adapting labour market institutions for an ageing workforce*. OECD Publishing.

Organisation for Economic Co-operation and Development (OECD). (2024). *OECD employment outlook 2024*. OECD Publishing.

Organisation for Economic Co-operation and Development. (OECD). (2021). OECD skills outlook 2021: Learning for life. OECD Publishing. DOI: 10.1787/0ae365b4-en

Ortega, F., & Peri, G. (2014). Openness and income: The roles of trade and migration. *Journal of International Economics*, *92*(2), 231–251. DOI: 10.1016/j.jinteco.2013.11.008

Orth, C. D., Wilkinson, H. E., & Benfari, R. C. (1987). The manager's role as coach and mentor. *Organizational Dynamics*, *15*(4), 66–74. DOI: 10.1016/0090-2616(87)90045-3

Osterman, P. (1994). How common is workplace transformation and who adopts it? *Industrial & Labor Relations Review*, *47*(2), 173–188. DOI: 10.1177/001979399404700202

Ostovari, A., Benyoucef, L., & Haddou-Benderbal, H. (2025). Multi-objective production scheduling and workforce planning in sustainable reconfigurable manufacturing system. [IJIDeM]. *International Journal on Interactive Design and Manufacturing*, *19*(5), 3803–3823. DOI: 10.1007/s12008-024-02010-x

Owino, D. (2023). *Employee cross-training as a tool for addressing employee loyalty and business environment uncertainties* [fi=Ylempi AMK-opinnäytetyö|sv=Högre YH-examensarbete|en=Master's thesis|]. https://www.theseus.fi/handle/10024/814262

Paas, F., Renkl, A., & Sweller, J. (2004). Cognitive load theory: Instructional implications of the interaction between information structures and cognitive architecture. *Educational Psychologist*, *38*(1), 1–4. DOI: 10.1207/S15326985EP3801_1

Padula, R. S., Comper, M. L. C., Sparer, E. H., & Dennerlein, J. T. (2017). Job rotation designed to prevent musculoskeletal disorders and control risk in manufacturing: A systematic review. *Applied Ergonomics*, *58*, 386–397. DOI: 10.1016/j.apergo.2016.07.018 PMID: 27633235

Pajares, F. (1997). Current directions in self-efficacy research. In Maehr, M., & Pintrich, P. R. (Eds.), Advances in motivation and achievement: Vol. 10. *JAI Press*.

Pan, D., Zhao, D., Pu, Y., Wang, L., & Zhang, Y. (2024). Use of cross-training in human–robot collaborative rescue. *Human Factors and Ergonomics in Manufacturing, 34*(3), 261–276. DOI: 10.1002/hfm.21025

Pandya, B., & Boukareva, B. (2025). Empowerment of digital start ups in the gig economy through digital employees: A systematic review. *International Journal of Entrepreneurship and Innovation*, 14657503251400965. Advance online publication. DOI: 10.1177/14657503251400965

Panopto. (2021). Upskilling and reskilling your hybrid workforce. https://www.panopto.com/blog/learning-and-development-reskilling-upskilling-cross-skilling-hybrid-workforce/

Parasuraman, A., Zeithaml, V. A., & Berry, L. L. (1988). SERVQUAL: A multiple-item scale for measuring consumer perceptions of service quality. *Journal of Retailing, 64*(1), 12–40.

Parker, S. K., Bindl, U. K., & Strauss, K. (2010). Making things happen: A model of proactive motivation. *Journal of Management, 36*(4), 827–856. DOI: 10.1177/0149206310363732

Park, P. S., & Bobrowski, P. M. (1989). Job Release and Labor Flexibility in a Dual Resource Constrained Job Shop. *Journal of Operations Management, 8*(3), 230–249. DOI: 10.1016/0272-6963(89)90026-0

Park, S. P. (1991). The Examination of Worker Cross-Training in a Dual Resource Constrained Job Shop. *European Journal of Operational Research, 52*(3), 291–299. DOI: 10.1016/0377-2217(91)90164-Q

Park, T. Y., & Shaw, J. D. (2013). Turnover rates and organizational performance: A meta-analysis. *The Journal of Applied Psychology, 98*(2), 268–309. DOI: 10.1037/a0030723 PMID: 23244224

Pascual-Leone, A., Amedi, A., Fregni, F., & Merabet, L. B. (2005). The plastic human brain cortex. *Annual Review of Neuroscience, 28*(1), 377–401. DOI: 10.1146/annurev.neuro.27.070203.144216 PMID: 16022601

Peck, W. J. (2025). Workforce planning: A review of methodologies. *Annals of Operations Research, 352*(1), 251–294. DOI: 10.1007/s10479-025-06734-1

Peri, G. (2022). Immigration and labor markets. *Annual Review of Economics, 14*, 607–635.

Perone, G. (2024). The relationship between labor market institutions and innovation in 177 European regions over the period 2000–2015. *Structural Change and Economic Dynamics, 70*, 128–149. DOI: 10.1016/j.strueco.2023.12.016

Pfeffer, J. (1998). *The human equation: Building profits by putting people first.* Harvard Business School Press.

Pink, D. H. (2009). *Drive: The surprising truth about what motivates us*. Riverhead Books.

Pinker, E., & Shumsky, R. (2000). The efficiency-quality trade-off of cross- trained workers. *Manufacturing & Service Operations Management, 2*(1), 32–48. DOI: 10.1287/msom.2.1.32.23268

Ployhart, R. E. (2021). Resources for what? Understanding performance in the resource-based view and strategic human capital resource literatures. *Journal of Management, 47*(7), 1771–1786. DOI: 10.1177/01492063211003137

Ployhart, R. E., & Hale, D. (2014). The fascinating psychological microfoundations of human capital resources. *Annual Review of Organizational Psychology and Organizational Behavior, 1*, 145–172. DOI: 10.1146/annurev-orgpsych-031413-091312

Ployhart, R. E., & Moliterno, T. P. (2011). Emergence of the human capital resource: A multilevel model. *Academy of Management Review, 36*(1), 127–150. DOI: 10.5465/amr.2009.0318

Poell, R. F. (2017). Time to 'flip' the training transfer tradition: Employees create learning paths strategically. *Human Resource Development Quarterly, 28*(1), 9–15. DOI: 10.1002/hrdq.21279

Porter, M. E., & Kramer, M. R. (2006). Strategy and society: The link between competitive advantage and corporate social responsibility. *Harvard Business Review, 84*(12), 78–92. PMID: 17183795

Poudel, S., Basyal, D. K., Devkota, N., Paudel, U. R., Lawaju, P., & Danuwar, R. K. (2024). Using social exchange theory to predict residents' perspective on factors influencing tourism development in Pokhara. *Smart Tourism, 5*(1), 2561. DOI: 10.54517/st.v5i1.2561

Prahalad, C. K., & Hamel, G. (1990). The core competence of the corporation. *Harvard Business Review, 68*(3), 79–91.

Pulakos, E. D., Arad, S., Donovan, M. A., & Plamondon, K. E. (2000). Adaptability in the workplace: Development of a taxonomy of adaptive performance. *The Journal of Applied Psychology*, *85*(4), 612–624. DOI: 10.1037/0021-9010.85.4.612 PMID: 10948805

Putnam, R. D. (2000). *Bowling alone: The collapse and revival of American community*. Simon & Schuster.

Qin, R., Nembhard, D. A., & Barnes, W. L.II. (2015). Workforce flexibility in operations management. *Surveys in Operations Research and Management Science*, *20*(1), 19–33. DOI: 10.1016/j.sorms.2015.04.001

Radianti, J., Majchrzak, T. A., Fromm, J., & Wohlgenannt, I. (2020). A systematic review of immersive virtual reality applications for higher education: Design elements, lessons learned, and research agenda. *Computers & Education*, *147*, 103778. DOI: 10.1016/j.compedu.2019.103778

Rainbird, H., Fuller, A., & Munro, A. (Eds.). (2004). *Workplace learning in context*. Routledge.

Rajoli, S. B., & Manoharan, G. (2023). Artificial Intelligence in Recruitment–The Future of Talent Acquisition. In AI and Innovation in HRM (pp. 276-293). Routledge.

Ramachandran, K. K., Apsara Saleth Mary, A., Hawladar, S., Asokk, D., Bhaskar, B., & Pitroda, J. R. (2022). Machine learning and role of artificial intelligence in optimizing work performance and employee behavior. *Materials Today: Proceedings*, *51*, 2327–2331. DOI: 10.1016/j.matpr.2021.11.544

Ranasinghe, T., Grosse, E. H., Glock, C. H., & Jaber, M. Y. (2024). Never too late to learn: Unlocking the potential of aging workforce in manufacturing and service industries. *International Journal of Production Economics*, *270*, 109193. DOI: 10.1016/j.ijpe.2024.109193

Rao, S., Gupta, U., Ramanujam, A., Knoble, A., Gondi, I., Gowda, P., Reddy, C., Shah, K., Amatya, A., Kalaunee, A., Rajbhandari, R., Henkar, R., Shah, M., Khan, S., Jesudian, G., Vora, K., Jindal, R. M., Suroy, A., Ghosh, D., & Zadey, S. (2026). Capacity building through workforce training and community engagement for surgical, obstetric, trauma, and anaesthesia (SOTA) care: Case studies from South Asia. *Dialogues in Health*, *100295*, 100295. Advance online publication. DOI: 10.1016/j.dialog.2026.100295 PMID: 41908516

Rasyid, H., & Mumpuni Ningsih, G. (2024). The role of digital technology in the transformation of agriculture toward smart farming. *Journal of Wood Science*, *3*(1), 1–7. DOI: 10.58344/jws.v3i1.523

Rasyid, T., & Kusumawaty, Y. (2022). Omnibus law and the challenges of the Indonesian agricultural sector: An Islamic perspective. *Jurnal Kajian Peradaban Islam*, *5*(1), 49–61. DOI: 10.47076/jkpis.v5i1.119

Reinhold, K. (2024). Building resilience: Pillars of workforce agility at organizational and individual levels in SMEs. In Durst, S., & Henschel, T. (Eds.), *Small and Medium-Sized Enterprise (SME) Resilience. Management for Professionals*. Springer., DOI: 10.1007/978-3-031-50836-3_11

Reinsberg, B., Kentikelenis, A., Stubbs, T., & King, L. (2019). The political economy of IMF conditionality. *The Journal of Development Studies*, *55*(6), 1–18.

Rest, J. (1986). *Moral development: Advances in research and theory*. Praeger.

Rhoades, L., & Eisenberger, R. (2002). Perceived organizational support: A review of the literature. *The Journal of Applied Psychology*, *87*(4), 698–714. DOI: 10.1037/0021-9010.87.4.698 PMID: 12184574

Riley, M., Ladkin, A., & Szivas, E. (2002). *Tourism employment: Analysis and planning*. Channel View Publications. DOI: 10.21832/9781873150382

Rizan, C., & Saikrishna, M. B. (2025). Leveraging job rotation programs for experiential learning in organizations through the lens of Kolb's experiential learning theory. *Development and Learning in Organizations*, *39*(6), 24–27. Advance online publication. DOI: 10.1108/DLO-09-2024-0272

Robles, M. M. (2012). Executive perceptions of the top 10 soft skills needed in today's workplace. *Business Communication Quarterly*, *75*(4), 453–465. DOI: 10.1177/1080569912460400

Roth, P. L., Purvis, K. L., & Bobko, P. (2012). A Meta-Analysis of Gender Group Differences for Measures of Job Performance in Field Studies. *Journal of Management*, *38*(2), 719–739. DOI: 10.1177/0149206310374774

Rousseau, D. M. (1995). Psychological contracts in organizations: Understanding written and unwritten agreements. *Sage (Atlanta, Ga.)*. Advance online publication. DOI: 10.4135/9781452231594

Rousseau, D. M. (2000). *Psychological Contract Inventory Technical Report*. Carnegie Mellon University.

Rowe, A. K., Rowe, S. Y., Peters, D. H., Holloway, K. A., & Ross-Degnan, D. (2021). The effectiveness of training strategies to improve healthcare provider practices in low- and middle-income countries. *BMJ Global Health*, *6*(1), e003229. DOI: 10.1136/bmjgh-2020-003229 PMID: 33452138

Ruhs, M. (2013). *The price of rights: Regulating international labor migration*. Princeton University Press.

Rupcic, N. (2024). Working and learning in a hybrid workplace: Challenges and opportunities. *The Learning Organization*, *31*(2), 276–283. DOI: 10.1108/TLO-02-2024-303

Rutovitz, J., Langdon, R., Lara, H. B., Briggs, C., Singha, D., Davies, E., & Whelan, J. (2025). Predicting workforce requirements for energy efficiency and electrification from energy scenarios. *Energy Reports*, *14*, 1548–1561. DOI: 10.1016/j.egyr.2025.07.040

Ryan, R. M., & Deci, E. L. (2017). *Self-determination theory: Basic psychological needs in motivation, development, and wellness*. Guilford Press. DOI: 10.1521/978.14625/28806

Ryan, R. M., & Deci, E. L. (2019). Brick by brick: The origins, development, and future of self-determination theory. *Advances in Motivation Science*, *6*, 111–156. DOI: 10.1016/bs.adms.2019.01.001

Rychen, D. S., & Salganik, L. H. (Eds.). (2003). *Key competencies for a successful life and a well-functioning society*. Hogrefe & Huber.

Sabharwal, M. (2014). Is diversity management sufficient? Organizational inclusion to further performance. *Public Personnel Management*, *43*(2), 197–217. DOI: 10.1177/0091026014522202

Saini, G., & Baba, M. M. (2024). Psychological expedient of multimedia in blended learning and metamemory satisfaction. *The Learning Organization*, *31*(1), 68–87. DOI: 10.1108/TLO-11-2022-0130

Saks, A. M. (2019). Antecedents and consequences of employee engagement revisited. *Journal of Organizational Effectiveness*, *6*(1), 19–38. DOI: 10.1108/JOEPP-06-2018-0034

Salanova, M., Schaufeli, W. B., Xanthopoulou, D., & Bakker, A. B. (2010). The gain spiral of resources and work engagement. *Journal of Vocational Behavior*, *77*(2), 225–236.

Salari, N., Beiromvand, M., Hosseinian-Far, A., Habibi, J., Babajani, F., & Mohammadi, M. (2025a). Impacts of generative artificial intelligence on the future of labor market: A systematic review. In *Computers in Human Behavior Reports* (Vol. 18). Elsevier B.V., DOI: 10.1016/j.chbr.2025.100652

Salas, E., Nichols, D. R., & Driskell, J. E. (2007). Testing three team training strategies in intact teams: A meta-analysis. *Small Group Research, 38*(4), 471–488. DOI: 10.1177/1046496407304332

Salas, E., Tannenbaum, S. I., Kraiger, K., & Smith-Jentsch, K. A. (2012). The science of training and development in organizations: What matters in practice. *Psychological Science in the Public Interest : A Journal of the American Psychological Society, 13*(2), 74–101. DOI: 10.1177/1529100612436661 PMID: 26173283

Salem, I. E.-B., & Abdien, M. K. (2017). Implementation of employee cross-training during perilous conditions in hotels. *Tourism Management Perspectives, 23*, 68–74. DOI: 10.1016/j.tmp.2017.05.005

Sarmiento Falla, J. F., Karwowski, W., Jahani, S., Rabelo, L., & Hancock, P. A. (2025). Agile healthcare: The role of information technology ambidexterity and human resource practices fostering workforce agility and job performance. *International Journal of Industrial Ergonomics, 110*, 103818. Advance online publication. DOI: 10.1016/j.ergon.2025.103818

Sarstedt, M., Ringle, C. M., & Hair, J. F. (2022). Partial least squares structural equation modeling. In C. Homburg, M. Klarmann, & A. Vomberg (Eds.), *Handbook of market research* (pp. 587–632). Springer. https://doi.org/DOI: 10.1007/978-3-319-57413-4_15

Sarstedt, M., Hair, J. F.Jr, & Ringle, C. M. (2023). "PLS-SEM: Indeed a silver bullet" – Retrospective observations and recent advances. *Journal of Marketing Theory and Practice, 31*(3), 261–275. DOI: 10.1080/10696679.2022.2056488

Scharron, C. (2025). *Examining Adoption Factors of AI-Enabled Workplace Training Through the Lens of the UTAUT2 and Extended Factors*. https://hdl.handle.net/20.500.12264/714

Schaufeli, W. B. (2013). What is engagement? In Truss, C., Alfes, K., Delbridge, R., Shantz, A., & Soane, E. (Eds.), *Employee Engagement in Theory and Practice* (pp. 15–35). Routledge.

Schilke, O., Hu, S., & Helfat, C. E. (2018). Quo vadis, dynamic capabilities? A content-analytic review of the current state of knowledge and recommendations for future research. *The Academy of Management Annals, 12*(1), 390–439. DOI: 10.5465/annals.2016.0014

Schmidt, F. L., & Hunter, J. E. (1998). The validity and utility of selection methods in personnel psychology: Practical and theoretical implications of 85 years of research findings. *Psychological Bulletin, 124*(2), 262–274. DOI: 10.1037/0033-2909.124.2.262

Schon, D. A. (1983). *The reflective practitioner: How professionals think in action.* Basic Books.

Schroeder, T., Dodds, L., Georgiou, A., Gewald, H., & Siette, J. (2023). Older Adults and New Technology: Mapping Review of the Factors Associated With Older Adults'. *Intention to Adopt Digital Technologies JMIR Aging, 6*, e44564. PMID: 37191976

Schuler, M. S., Coffman, D. L., Stuart, E. A., Nguyen, T. Q., Vegetabile, B. G., & McCaffrey, D. F. (2025). Practical challenges in mediation analysis: A guide for applied researchers. *Health Services and Outcomes Research Methodology, 25*(1), 57–84. DOI: 10.1007/s10742-024-00327-4 PMID: 39958808

Schultz, T. W. (1961). Investment in human capital. *The American Economic Review, 51*(1), 1–17.

Schultz, T. W. (1961). Investment in human capital. *The Economic Review, 51*(1), 1–17.

Schulz, B. (2008). The importance of soft skills: Education beyond academic knowledge. *NAWA Journal of Language and Communication, 2*(1), 146–154.

Schwab, K. (2016). *The fourth industrial revolution*. World Economic Forum.

Schwartz, B. (2013). *Practical wisdom: The right way to do the right thing*. Bloomsbury.

Scorgie, D. G., Feng, Z., Paes, D., Parisi, F., Yiu, T. W., & Lovreglio, R. (2024). Virtual reality for safety training: A systematic review and meta-analysis. *Safety Science, 171*, 106372. DOI: 10.1016/j.ssci.2023.106372

Scott, S. G., & Bruce, R. A. (1994). Determinants of innovative behavior: A path model of individual innovation in the workplace. *Academy of Management Journal, 37*(3), 580–607. DOI: 10.2307/256701

Selbst, A. D., Boyd, D., Friedler, S. A., Venkatasubramanian, S., & Vertesi, J. (2019). Fairness and abstraction in sociotechnical systems. *Proceedings of the Conference on Fairness, Accountability, and Transparency*, 59–68. https://doi.org/ DOI: 10.1145/3287560.3287598

Senge, P. (1990). *The fifth discipline Doubleday.*

Senge, P. M. (1990). *The fifth discipline: The art and practice of the learning organization*. Doubleday.

Serenko, A. (2019). Knowledge sabotage as an extreme form of counterproductive knowledge behavior: Conceptualization, typology, and empirical demonstration. *Journal of Knowledge Management, 23*(7), 1260–1288. DOI: 10.1108/JKM-01-2018-0007

Shachar, A., Bauböck, R., Bloemraad, I., & Vink, M. P. (Eds.). (2017). *The Oxford handbook of citizenship*. Oxford University Press., DOI: 10.1093/oxfordhb/9780198805854.001.0001

Shao, Y., Fang, Y., & Wang, M. (2022). Reskilling and upskilling for the digital era: A cross-country study. *Human Resource Development International, 25*(2), 158–180.

Shdema, I., Mor, Y., & Abu-Rayya, H. M. (2025). Conflicting identities and labour market outcomes of minorities: Evidence from Arabs in Israel. *International Journal of Intercultural Relations, 109*, 102309. DOI: 10.1016/j.ijintrel.2025.102309

Shen, Y., Lythreatis, S., Singh, S. K., & Cooke, F. L. (2025). A meta-analysis of knowledge hiding behavior in organizations: Antecedents, consequences, and boundary conditions. *Journal of Business Research, 186*, 114963. DOI: 10.1016/j.jbusres.2024.114963

Sherehiy, B., & Karwowski, W. (2014). The relationship between work organization and workforce agility in small manufacturing enterprises. *International Journal of Industrial Ergonomics, 44*(3), 466–473. DOI: 10.1016/j.ergon.2014.01.002

Shiferaw, R. M., & Kero, C. A. (2024). Dynamic capabilities view practices of business firms: A systematic literature review. *Cogent Business & Management, 11*(1), 2336309. Advance online publication. DOI: 10.1080/23311975.2024.2336309

Shore, L. M., Randel, A. E., Chung, B. G., Dean, M. A., Ehrhart, K. H., & Singh, G. (2011). Inclusion and diversity in work groups: A review and model for future research. *Journal of Management, 37*(4), 1262–1299. DOI: 10.1177/0149206310385943

SHRM. (2023). Workforce report. https://www.shrm.org/content/dam/en/shrm/executive-network/SOTW-23-24Enterprise-Solutions.pdf

Shukla, A., & Kumar, A. (2024). Factors affecting transfer of online training: A systematic literature review and proposed taxonomy. *Human Resource Development Quarterly, 35*(2), 187–218. DOI: 10.1002/hrdq.21518

Shukla, P., & Garg, A. (2022). Sentiment Analysis of Online Learners in Higher Education: A Learning Perspective through Unstructured Data. In *Intelligent System Algorithms and Applications in Science and Technology*. Apple Academic Press.

Sila, A. (2014). Relationship between training and performance: A case study of Kenya women finance trust eastern Nyanza region, Kenya. *European Journal of Business and Social Sciences*, *3*(1), 95–117.

Sims, D. E., Salas, E., & Burke, C. S. (2005). Promoting effective team performance through training. In Wheelan, S. A. (Ed.), *The handbook of group research and practice* (pp. 407–426). Sage.

Singh, A., & Ehlers, T. (2020). Human capital development and economic growth in emerging markets. *Journal of Human Capital Development*.

Singh, A., Wu, P., Komaraju, B., Okwudire, C. E., & Banu, M. (2025). Hybrid education and training approaches enabling workforce development in additive manufacturing. *Manufacturing Letters*, *46*, 65–71. Advance online publication. DOI: 10.1016/j.mfglet.2025.10.007

Singh, N., Sunitha, N. H., Tripathi, G., Saikanth, D. R. K., Sharma, A., Jose, A. E., & Mary, M. V. K. J. (2023). Impact of digital technologies in agricultural extension. *Asian Journal of Agricultural Extension Economics & Sociology*, *41*(9), 963–970. DOI: 10.9734/ajaees/2023/v41i92127

Singh, V., Singh, G., & Sharma, G. (2025). The Future of the Healthcare Workforce in the Age of Automation. In *Driving Global Health and Sustainable Development Goals With Smart Technology* (pp. 453–472). IGI Global Scientific Publishing., DOI: 10.4018/979-8-3373-0240-9.ch019

Slomp, J., & Molleman, E. (2002). Cross-training policies and team performance. *International Journal of Production Research*, *40*(5), 1193–1219. DOI: 10.1080/00207540110098823

Soomro, S., Fan, M., Sohu, J. M., Soomro, S., & Shaikh, S. N. (2024). AI adoption: A bridge or a barrier? The moderating role of organizational support in the path toward employee well-being. *Kybernetes, ahead-of-print*(ahead-of-print). DOI: 10.1108/K-07-2024-1889

Spencer, L. M., & Spencer, S. M. (1993). *Competence at work: Models for superior performance*. John Wiley & Sons.

Spender, J. C. (1996). Making knowledge the basis of a dynamic theory of the firm. *Strategic Management Journal*, *17*(52), 45–62. DOI: 10.1002/smj.4250171106

Spreitzer, G. M. (1995). Psychological empowerment in the workplace: Dimensions, measurement, and validation. *Academy of Management Journal*, *38*(5), 1442–1465. DOI: 10.2307/256865

Spurk, D., Hofer, A., Hirschi, A., De Cuyper, N., & De Witte, H. (2022). Conceptualizing career insecurity: Towards a better understanding and measurement of a multidimensional construct. *Personnel Psychology*, *75*(2), 253–294. DOI: 10.1111/peps.12493

Stahl, G. K., Miller, E. L., & Tung, R. L. (2002). Toward the boundaryless career: A closer look at the expatriate career concept and the perceived implications of an international assignment. *Journal of World Business*, *37*(3), 216–227. DOI: 10.1016/S1090-9516(02)00080-9

Stek, K., Lefers, L., & Belotti Pedroso, C. (2025). Strengthening innovation capacity in health and care workforce: A role-based framework for the procurement professionals. *Health Policy (Amsterdam)*, *161*, 105423. Advance online publication. DOI: 10.1016/j.healthpol.2025.105423 PMID: 40912179

Stock, R. M. (2015). Is boreout a threat to frontline employees' innovative work behavior? *Journal of Product Innovation Management*, *32*(4), 574–592. DOI: 10.1111/jpim.12239

Subrahmanyam, S., & Hamadamin, Z. F. (2019). The Role of Supportive Organisational Culture in Strategic Success: A Research in Private Hospitals in Erbil City. *Pacific Business Review International*, Volume-11 | Issue-11, 50-60. https://www.pbr.co.in/2019/May.aspx

Subrahmanyam, S. (2025). Human Factors and Workforce Adaptation in Digital Transition. In Martínez-Falcó, J., Sánchez-García, E., & Marco-Lajara, B. (Eds.), *Navigating Digital Transformation Through Business Process Management* (pp. 95–126). IGI Global Scientific Publishing., DOI: 10.4018/979-8-3373-3336-6.ch005

Subrahmanyam, S. (2025). Shaping Tomorrow's Talent Strategies with Predictive Workforce Intelligence. In Badouch, M., & Boutaounte, M. (Eds.), *Emerging Technologies for Recruitment Strategy and Practice* (pp. 211–236). IGI Global Scientific Publishing., DOI: 10.4018/979-8-3373-6516-9.ch008

Subrahmanyam, S. (2025). Using AI-Driven Analysis for Training and Leadership Growth. In Mrabet, J., Boudagga, S., Sharma, R., & Bansal, R. (Eds.), *Harnessing Emotion AI for Customer Support and Employee Wellbeing* (pp. 321–352). IGI Global Scientific Publishing., DOI: 10.4018/979-8-3373-3658-9.ch013

Su, G., Zhong, H., & Zhang, J. (2025). Integrated training course planning and hierarchical multi-skilled employee scheduling in the workforce skill transformation context. *International Journal of Production Economics, 286*, 109642. DOI: 10.1016/j.ijpe.2025.109642

Suleman, F. (2018). The employability skills of higher education graduates: Insights into conceptual frameworks and methodological options. *Higher Education, 76*(2), 263–278. DOI: 10.1007/s10734-017-0207-0

Tafese, T., Lay, J., & Tran, V. (2025a). From fields to factories: Special economic zones, foreign direct investment, and labour markets in Vietnam. *Journal of Development Economics, 174*, 103467. Advance online publication. DOI: 10.1016/j.jdeveco.2025.103467

Taheri Hosseinkhani, N. (2025). *Economic and Social Implications of AI-Driven Automation and Workforce Transformation.* https://aurora.auburn.edu/handle/11200/50713

Talent, L. M. S. (2024). The state of upskilling & reskilling: 2024 research. https://www.talentlms.com/research/employee-upskilling-and-reskilling-report

Tambe, P., Cappelli, P., & Yakubovich, V. (2019). Artificial intelligence in human resources management: Challenges and a path forward. *California Management Review, 61*(4), 15–42. DOI: 10.1177/0008125619867910

Tarí, J. J., Pertusa-Ortega, E. M., López-Gamero, M. D., & Pereira-Moliner, J. (2025). Drivers of social sustainability practices: Quality management, human capital, and innovation. *International Journal of Contemporary Hospitality Management, 37*(2), 462–481. DOI: 10.1108/IJCHM-12-2023-1866

Tariq, M. U., Babar, M., Poulin, M., Khattak, A. S., Alshehri, M. D., & Kaleem, S. (2021). Human Behavior Analysis Using Intelligent Big Data Analytics. *Frontiers in Psychology, 12*, 686610. Advance online publication. DOI: 10.3389/fpsyg.2021.686610 PMID: 34295289

Taylor, R., Fakhimi, M., Ioannou, A., & Spanaki, K. (2024). Personalized learning in education: A machine learning and simulation approach. *Benchmarking*. Advance online publication. DOI: 10.1108/BIJ-06-2023-0380

Tayo, O., Thompson, R., & Thompson, E. (2016). Impact of the digital divide on computer use and internet access on the poor in Nigeria. *Journal of Education and Learning, 5*(1), 1–6. DOI: 10.5539/jel.v5n1p1

Teece, D. J. (2016). Dynamic capabilities and entrepreneurial management in large organizations: Toward a theory of the (entrepreneurial) firm. *European Economic Review*, *86*, 202–216. DOI: 10.1016/j.euroecorev.2015.11.006

Teece, D. J. (2018). Business models and dynamic capabilities. *Long Range Planning*, *51*(1), 40–49. DOI: 10.1016/j.lrp.2017.06.007

Teece, D. J. (2025). *Dynamic capabilities*. Cambridge University Press., DOI: 10.1017/9781009562713

Teece, D. J., Peteraf, M., & Leih, S. (2016). Dynamic capabilities and organizational agility: Risk, uncertainty, and strategy in the innovation economy. *California Management Review*, *58*(4), 13–35. DOI: 10.1525/cmr.2016.58.4.13

Teece, D. J., Pisano, G., & Shuen, A. (1997). Dynamic capabilities and strategic management. *Strategic Management Journal*, *18*(7), 509–533. https://sms.onlinelibrary.wiley.com/doi/10.1002/(SICI)1097-0266(199708)18:7%3C509:AID-SMJ882%3E3.0.CO;2-Z. DOI: 10.1002/(SICI)1097-0266(199708)18:7<509::AID-SMJ882>3.0.CO;2-Z

Tempo. (2023). From Boomers to Generation Z, How Long Have Indonesians Been on the Internet? - Techno Tempo. co

Terrazas, A. (2022, November 17). Workplace trends 2023. Workplace Trends 2023. https://www.glassdoor.com/blog/workplace-trends-2023/

Testaverde, M., Del Carpio, X. V., Wagner, M., & Özden, Ç. (2016). Global migration of talent and tax incentives: Evidence from Malaysia's returning expert program. *World Bank Policy Research Working Paper, 7875*. https://doi.org/DOI: 10.1596/1813-9450-7875

Tharenou, P., Saks, A. M., & Moore, C. (2007). A review and critique of research on training and organizational-level outcomes. *Human Resource Management Review*, *17*(3), 251–273. DOI: 10.1016/j.hrmr.2007.07.004

Thomas, A. (2025). The dynamics of knowledge behaviors: Exploring drivers, triggers and paradoxes in knowledge sharing, hiding, hoarding and sabotage. *Journal of Knowledge Management*, *29*(11), 117–144. DOI: 10.1108/JKM-03-2025-0399

Thomas, D. A. (1990). The impact of race on managers' experiences of developmental relationships (mentoring and sponsorship): An intraorganizational study. *Journal of Organizational Behavior*, *11*(6), 479–492. DOI: 10.1002/job.4030110608

Tishman, F. M., Van Looy, S., & Bruyère, S. M. (2012). Employer Strategies for Responding to an Aging Workforce (pp. 1–39, Rep. New Brunswick, NJ: NTAR Leadership Center.

Tomlinson, M. (2012). Graduate employability: A review of conceptual and empirical themes. *Education + Training*, *54*(4), 280–290. DOI: 10.1108/00400911211236621

Torrington, L. H. (2008). *Human resource management*. Pearson Education Limited.

Tosun, C. (2000). Limits to community participation in the tourism development process in developing countries. *Tourism Management*, *21*(6), 613–633. DOI: 10.1016/S0261-5177(00)00009-1

Tracey, J. B., Tannenbaum, S. I., & Kavanagh, M. J. (1995). Applying trained skills on the job: The importance of the work environment. *The Journal of Applied Psychology*, *80*(2), 239–252. DOI: 10.1037/0021-9010.80.2.239

Tracey, J. B., Way, S. A., & Tews, M. (2008). HR in the hospitality industry: Strategic frameworks and priorities. In Tesone, D. V. (Ed.), *Handbook of hospitality human resources management* (pp. 3–22). Butterworth-Heinemann. DOI: 10.1016/B978-0-08-045081-0.50004-5

Training Industry. (2022). Training a hybrid workforce? Consider these 3 best practices. https://trainingindustry.com/articles/workforce-development/training-a-hybrid-workforce-consider-these-3-best-practices/

Trépanier, S. G., Fernet, C., & Austin, S. (2019). A longitudinal investigation of workplace bullying, basic need satisfaction, and employee functioning. *Journal of Occupational Health Psychology*, *24*(1), 30–47. PMID: 25151460

Tseng, Y. J., Wu, M., Feng, Z. Y., & Tan, S. Y. (2025a). The effect of labor unions on capital markets: Evidence from seasoned equity offerings. *International Review of Economics & Finance*, *101*, 104190. Advance online publication. DOI: 10.1016/j.iref.2025.104190

Turker, D. (2009). How corporate social responsibility influences organizational commitment. *Journal of Business Ethics*, *89*(2), 189–204. DOI: 10.1007/s10551-008-9993-8

UNDP (United Nations Development Programme). 2024. Human Development Report 2023-24: Breaking the gridlock: Reimagining cooperation in a polarized world. New York. https://hdr.undp.org/content/human-development-report-2023-24

UNESCO. (2023a). *Global education monitoring report, 2023: Technology in education: A tool on whose terms? - UNESCO Digital Library*. https://unesdoc.unesco.org/ark:/48223/pf0000385723

UNESCO. (2023b). *Technology in education: GEM Report 2023 | Global Education Monitoring Report*. https://www.unesco.org/gem-report/en/publication/technology

United Nations. (2019). *World population prospects 2019: Highlights*. United Nations.

Urban, A. (2024). Clinical Trial Research Nurse New Employee Onboarding 30-60 -90 Day Checklist. *Master's Projects and Capstones*. https://repository.usfca.edu/capstone/1761

Valachis, I., & Skoultsos, S. (2026). Reframing sustainable human resource management in tourism: Education, social exchange, and destination governance. *Tourism and Hospitality*, *7*(5), 118. DOI: 10.3390/tourhosp7050118

Valachis, I., & Tachmatzidis, D. (2023). Employees' metacognitive knowledge and skills assessment in tourism and hospitality. *Journal of Tourism Management Research*, *10*(2), 123–139. DOI: 10.18488/31.v10i2.3418

Valachis, I., & Trihas, N. (2025). Tourist awareness in tourism development: Case study of the city of Veria, Greece. In Alkier, R., Catenazzo, G., Milojica, V., & Zając, A. (Eds.), *Cases on effective destination management* (pp. 57–81). IGI Global Scientific Publishing., DOI: 10.4018/979-8-3693-1548-4.ch003

Valentine, S., Godkin, L., Fleischman, G., & Kidwell, R. (2011). Corporate ethical values, group creativity, job satisfaction and turnover intention: The impact of work context on work response. *Journal of Business Ethics*, *98*(3), 353–372. DOI: 10.1007/s10551-010-0554-6

Van den Broeck, A., Ferris, D. L., Chang, C. H., & Rosen, C. C. (2016). A review of self-determination theory's basic psychological needs at work. *Journal of Management*, *42*(5), 1195–1229. DOI: 10.1177/0149206316632058

Van Laar, E., van Deursen, A. J. A. M., van Dijk, J. A. G. M., & de Haan, J. (2018). 21st-century digital skills instrument aimed at working professionals: Conceptual development and empirical validation. *Telematics and Informatics*, *35*(8), 2184–2200. DOI: 10.1016/j.tele.2018.08.006

Vapiwala, F., & Pandita, D. (2024). Conflicts and defensive communication: Investigating the mature, neurotic and immature defences of service professionals. *International Journal of Conflict Management*, *35*(4), 633–657. DOI: 10.1108/IJCMA-12-2022-0211

Vapiwala, F., Rastogi, S., & Pandita, D. (2025). Is workforce agility the new agenda? Perspectives on the role of constructive task conflicts. *Employee Responsibilities and Rights Journal*, •••, 1–20. DOI: 10.1007/s10672-025-09528-6

Vaportzis, E., Giatsi Clausen, M., & Gow, A. J. (2017). *Older Adults' Perceptions of Technology and Barriers to Interacting with Tablet Computers: A Focus Group Study. Qingchuan Li and Yan Luximon. (2016). Older Adults and Digital Technology: A study of user perception and usage behavior*. Springer International Publishing Switzerland.

Veale, M., Van Kleek, M., & Binns, R. (2018). Fairness and accountability design needs for algorithmic support in high-stakes public sector decision-making. *Proceedings of the 2018 CHI Conference on Human Factors in Computing Systems*, Paper 88. https://doi.org/DOI: 10.1145/3173574.3174014

Vial, G. (2019). Understanding digital transformation: A review and a research agenda. *The Journal of Strategic Information Systems*, *28*(2), 118–144. DOI: 10.1016/j.jsis.2019.01.003

Vihari, N. S., Yadav, M., Shah, S., Balodi, A., Tolani, M., & Mittal, S. (2024). Impact of sustainable human resource management on employee work wellbeing: Examining the mediating role of employee empowerment and moderating influence of organizational identification. *Employee Responsibilities and Rights Journal*. Advance online publication. DOI: 10.1007/s10672-024-09514-4

Volpe, C. E., Cannon-Bowers, J. A., Salas, E., & Spector, P. E. (1996). The Impact of Cross-Training on Team Functioning: An Empirical Investigation. *Human Factors*, *38*(1), 87–100. DOI: 10.1518/001872096778940741 PMID: 8682521

Vygotsky, L. S. (1978). *Mind in society: The development of higher psychological processes*. Harvard University Press.

Waizenegger, L., McKenna, B., Cai, W., & Bendz, T. (2020). An affordance perspective of team collaboration and enforced working from home during COVID-19. *European Journal of Information Systems*, *29*(4), 429–442. DOI: 10.1080/0960085X.2020.1800417

Wamba-Taguimdje, S.-L., Fosso Wamba, S., Kala Kamdjoug, J. R., & Tchatchouang Wanko, C.-E. (2020). Influence of artificial intelligence (AI) on firm performance: The business value of AI-based transformation projects. *Business Process Management Journal*, *26*(7), 1893–1924. DOI: 10.1108/BPMJ-10-2019-0411

Wang, J., & Solís, P. (2025). Identifying latent workforce capacities for extreme heat resilience: An artificial intelligence assisted approach. *Energy and AI*, *21*, 100580. Advance online publication. DOI: 10.1016/j.egyai.2025.100580

Wang, L., & Hasan, N. A. (2024). Exploring organizational career growth: A systematic literature review and future research directions. *Cogent Business & Management*, *11*(1), 2398728. Advance online publication. DOI: 10.1080/23311975.2024.2398728

Wang, S., & Noe, R. A. (2010). Knowledge sharing: A review and directions for future research. *Human Resource Management Review*, *20*(2), 115–131. DOI: 10.1016/j.hrmr.2009.10.001

Wani, N. U. H., Deshpande, A., Sidana, N., & Rasa, M. M. (2025). Determinants of higher education quality in Afghanistan's higher education sector: Insights from students' perceptions. *Journal of Applied Research in Higher Education*, *17*(1), 123–138. DOI: 10.1108/JARHE-06-2023-0231

Wenger, E. (1998). *Communities of practice: Learning, meaning, and identity*. Cambridge University Press. DOI: 10.1017/CBO9780511803932

Wesner, B. S. (2014). Managing cross-understanding: An extension of cross training. *Journal of Marketing and Management Research*, *16*(3), 1–16.

Wheelahan, L., & Moodie, G. (2021). Gig qualifications for the gig economy: Micro-credentials and the "hungry mile". *Higher Education*, *83*(6), 1279–1295. DOI: 10.1007/s10734-021-00742-3 PMID: 34366441

Widiastuti, T., Sukmaningrum, P., Rani, L., Mustofa, M., & Ardiani, N. (2022). Economic empowerment of dhuafa families through digital business and financial management based on maqashid sharia in Tambakrigadung, Lamongan. *Jurnal Pengabdian Kepada Masyarakat*, *8*(3), 155. DOI: 10.22146/jpkm.67976

Winters, L. A., Walmsley, T. L., Wang, Z. K., & Grynberg, R. (2003). Liberalising temporary movement of natural persons: An agenda for the development round. *World Economy*, *26*(8), 1137–1161. DOI: 10.1111/1467-9701.00566

Wood, A. J., Graham, M., Lehdonvirta, V., & Hjorth, I. (2019). Good gig, bad gig: Autonomy and algorithmic control in the global gig economy. *Work, Employment and Society*, *33*(1), 56–75. DOI: 10.1177/0950017018785616 PMID: 30886460

World Bank. (2023). *World development report 2023: Migrants, refugees, and societies*. World Bank.

World Economic Forum. (2020). *The future of jobs report 2020*. World Economic Forum

World Economic Forum. (2020). The future of jobs report 2020. World Economic Forum. https://www.weforum.org/reports/the-future-of-jobs-report-2020

World Economic Forum. (2023). *The Future of Jobs Report 2023*. World Economic Forum. https://www.weforum.org/publications/the-future-of-jobs-report-2023/

World Economic Forum. (2023). *The future of jobs report 2023*. World Economic Forum. https://www.weforum.org/reports/the-future-of-jobs-report-2023

World Economic Forum. (2025). *Future of jobs report*. https://www.weforum.org/publications/the-future-of-jobs-report-2025/

World Economic Forum. (2025). The future of jobs report 2025. https://www.weforum.org/publications/the-future-of-jobs-report-2025/

Wright, P. M., & McMahan, G. C. (2011). Exploring human capital: Putting 'human'back into strategic human resource management. *Human Resource Management Journal*, *21*(2), 93–104. DOI: 10.1111/j.1748-8583.2010.00165.x

Xanthopoulou, D., Bakker, A. B., Demerouti, E., & Schaufeli, W. B. (2009). Reciprocal relationships between job resources, personal resources, and work engagement. *Journal of Vocational Behavior*, *74*(3), 235–244. DOI: 10.1016/j.jvb.2008.11.003

Xu, Z. (2024). AI in education: Enhancing learning experiences and student outcomes. *Applied and Computational Engineering*, *51*(1), 104–111. DOI: 10.54254/2755-2721/51/20241187

Yang, Y., Li, X., Pan, G., Cai, Y., & Shi, W. (2024). The relationship between Machiavellianism and knowledge hoarding: A moderated mediation model. *Knowledge Management Research and Practice*, *22*(2), 148–161. DOI: 10.1080/14778238.2022.2155594

Yao, W., Arshad, M. A., Yang, Q., & Tan, J. (2025). Can employee training stabilise the workforce of frontline workers in construction firms? An empirical analysis of turnover intentions. *Buildings (Basel, Switzerland)*, *15*(2), 183. DOI: 10.3390/buildings15020183

Yazdani-Darki, M., Rahemi, Z., Adib-Hajbaghery, M., & Izadi-Avanji, F. S. (2020). A qualitative study of older adults' barriers to using technology in daily life. *Nursing and Midwifery Studies*, *9*, 229–236.

Yoo, D. Y. (2024). Eco-leadership in action: Integrating green HRM and ecological paradigms. *Sustainability*, *16*(20), 9044. DOI: 10.3390/su16209044

Youndt, M. A., Subramaniam, M., & Snell, S. A. (2004). Intellectual capital profiles: An examination of investments and returns. *Journal of Management Studies*, *41*(2), 335–361. DOI: 10.1111/j.1467-6486.2004.00435.x

Young, J. Q., Van Merriënboer, J., Durning, S., & Ten Cate, O. (2014). Cognitive load theory: Implications for medical education. *Medical Teacher*, *36*(5), 371–384. DOI: 10.3109/0142159X.2014.889290 PMID: 24593808

Yu, D. (2023). AI-Empowered Metaverse Learning Simulation Technology Application. *2023 International Conference on Intelligent Metaverse Technologies & Applications (iMETA)*, 1–6. DOI: 10.1109/iMETA59369.2023.10294830

Yue, H., Slomp, J., Molleman, E., & Van Der Zee, D. J. (2008). Worker flexibility in a parallel dual resource constrained job shop. *International Journal of Production Research*, *46*(2), 451–467. DOI: 10.1080/00207540601138510

Yukl, G. (2013). *Leadership in organizations* (8th ed.). Pearson.

Zahra, S. A., & George, G. (2002). Absorptive capacity: A review, reconceptualization, and extension. *Academy of Management Review*, *27*(2), 185–203. DOI: 10.2307/4134351

Zarb, F., & McNulty, J. P. (2025). Assessment of workforce availability, staffing, and education, and training requirements for radiographers across Europe as part of EU-REST project. *Radiography*, *31*(5), 103101. Advance online publication. DOI: 10.1016/j.radi.2025.103101 PMID: 40763392

Zenger, J., & Folkman, J. (2009). *The extraordinary leader: Turning good managers into great leaders*. McGraw-Hill.

Zerilli, J., Bhatt, U., & Weller, A. (2022). How transparency modulates trust in artificial intelligence. *Patterns (New York, N.Y.)*, *3*(4), 100455. Advance online publication. DOI: 10.1016/j.patter.2022.100455 PMID: 35465233

Zetzsche, D. A., Buckley, R. P., Arner, D. W., & Barberis, J. N. (2017). Regulating a revolution: From regulatory sandboxes to smart regulation. *SSRN*, *23*(1), 31–103. DOI: 10.2139/ssrn.3018534

Zhou, Q., Edafioghor, T., Wu, C.-H., & Doherty, B. (2022). Building organizational resilience capability in small and medium-sized enterprises: The role of high-performance work systems. *Human Resource Management Journal*, *33*(2), 371–393. DOI: 10.1111/1748-8583.12479

Zhu, L. N., & Gao, Y. (2023). Protean career orientation, supervisor perceptions and organizational career growth: A moderated mediation model. *Current Psychology, 43*(10), 8913–8930. DOI: 10.1007/s12144-023-05021-1

Zhu, T. (2025). Latent factor model in asset pricing: A deep learning approach in the Chinese stock market. *Finance Research Letters, 86*, 108519. Advance online publication. DOI: 10.1016/j.frl.2025.108519

Zirar, A., Ali, S. I., & Islam, N. (2023). Worker and workplace artificial intelligence (AI) coexistence: Emerging themes and research agenda. *Technovation, 124*, 102747. DOI: 10.1016/j.technovation.2023.102747

About the Contributors

Bryan Christiansen is a highly indexed author of 50 Reference books on topics ranging from cultural studies to organizational sociology. He is currently an Adjunct Professor of business at Southern New Hampshire University and the Chief Executive Officer of the management consultancy, Soluvex, LLC in New Mexico, USA. Professor Christiansen is fluent in Chinese, Japanese, and Spanish, and is currently learning Russian. He has presented his work at several universities in numerous countries including Oxford University in the United Kingdom in 2016. He earned an MBA from Capella University in 2003 and a BS in Marketing from the University of the State of New York in 1996.

Mehmet Ozbek has been working at the Narendra Paul Loomba Department of Management at the Zicklin School of Business, Baruch College, City University of New York since 2023, and the Department of Human Resource Management, Gumushane University, Turkey since 2009. Previously, I worked as a lecturer at the Department of Business Management, University of Economy and Enterprise, Kyrgyzstan a former Soviet Country from 2003 to 2009. I also worked as a research scholar at Eberly College of Business, IUP, at the Indiana University of Pennsylvania. USA in 2012- 2013. I have publications in the Journal of Business Ethics, Creativity and Innovation Management, Business Ethics, the Environment and Responsibility, and Journal of Business Research.

***

Anjali is an Assistant Professor in the Department of Management at Seth Jai Prakash Mukand Lal Institute of Engineering and Technology, India. She earned her Master of Business Administration as a gold medalist from Deenbandhu Chhotu Ram University of Science and Technology, Murthal, Over the past two years, she has taught undergraduate and postgraduate courses in Human Resource Management and Marketing Management, consistently earning top student evaluations for her engaging pedagogy. She has contributed to a Scopus-indexed publication and presented at national conference. Her research interests include talent management, employee engagement, and digital marketing strategies. Ms. Anjali is committed to advancing management education by integrating innovation, ethics, and emerging technologies into her teaching and scholarly work.

Viral S Ahire is a committed Research Scholar and Assistant Professor in Management, bringing over a decade of rich academic experience to her field. She is currently pursuing her Ph.D. in Human Resource Management at Bharati Vidyapeeth University, Pune. Her areas of specialization encompass Human Resource Management, Organizational Behavior, and Soft Skills, reflecting her strong foundation in both theoretical and practical dimensions of management education. A prolific academic contributor, Mrs. Ahire has published research articles in reputed national and international journals, including Scopus and IEEE-listed publications. She has also authored textbooks for Savitribai Phule Pune University (SPPU), further enriching the learning resources for students and scholars. In addition, she has served as a chapter editor for academic volumes and holds patents, highlighting her innovative mindset and research driven approach. Her academic philosophy is rooted in continuous learning, interdisciplinary growth, and fostering impactful knowledge dissemination.

Duggirala Aravind is currently associated with the Department of Aviation, ASET Institute of Science and Technology, Chennai, India. He previously completed his Bachelor's degree in Electrical and Electronics Engineering at MITS University. His research interests include aviation operations, renewable energy technologies in air transport, Artificial Intelligence, Computer Science, Logistics and Business management. (aravindaset.edu@gmail.com).

Sadhna Chauhan is the Head of the Department of Management at CT Group of Institutions, Jalandhar, India. She holds a Ph.D. in Management from Guru Jambheshwar University of Science and Technology, Hisar, and is a UGC-NET and JRF qualified scholar. With over nine years of academic and research experience, her expertise spans Human Resource Management, Organizational Behavior, and Marketing Management. Her research focuses on artificial intelligence applications in HR, knowledge management, and sustainable organizational practices. She has published and presented extensively in national and international conferences and journals, and contributed book chapters with Taylor & Francis, IGI Global, Emerald Publishing, and NOVA Science Publishers. Dr. Sadhna has received several distinctions, including the Best Paper Award (Kurukshetra University, 2023). Her current academic pursuits emphasize integrating ethics, innovation, and technology into contemporary management education and research.

Amruta Deshpande is a Professor at the School of Business, Indira University, and currently serves as the Associate Dean – Research and Development. With over 17 years of rich academic and research experience, Dr. Deshpande has made significant contributions to management education. Her teaching and research interests primarily span Organizational Behavior, Human Resource Management, Theory of Management, and Management Fundamentals, with a focus on mentoring postgraduate and master's students toward professional excellence. She is a Certified Emotional Intelligence Specialist, Executive Life Coach, and Psychometric Test Professional, and holds global credentials as a Master Trainer, Facilitator, and Performance & Competence Developer. She is also a Certified Microsoft Innovative Educator and has participated in the X-Culture Global Research Collaboration Project. To further strengthen her academic expertise, she has attended several Management Development Programmes (MDPs) at leading IIMs. Dr. Deshpande has published nearly 65+ research papers in reputable national and international journals indexed in Scopus, ABDC, and Web of Science (WoS) referred Journals, covering areas such as career management, contemporary HR practices, and emerging HR trends. She is also the author and co-author of multiple books and edited volumes. Recognized for her expertise, she serves on the editorial and review boards of over 25+ high-quality journals indexed in Scopus, ABDC, and WoS. Her ongoing contributions aim to bridge the gap between academic research and industry practices and to foster a research-driven culture in management education.

Silambarasan G possesses a comprehensive academic foundation, holding a Bachelor of Computer Applications (BCA) and a Master of Computer Applications (MCA), and Holds a Ph.D. in the Department of Computer Science from Periyar University, Salem, Tamil Nadu, India. With over 08 years of teaching experience and 02 years of industry exposure, he has consistently demonstrated excellence in both academic and technical domains. His professional journey reflects a strong commitment to research, innovation, and pedagogical advancement in the rapidly evolving field of computer science. Renowned for his expertise in network administration, system architecture, virtualization, and emerging computing technologies, Dr.Silambarasan G continues to contribute significantly to the integration of theory and practical application. His academic and research pursuits exemplify a passion for technological innovation and a steadfast dedication to advancing the frontiers of computer science education.

Beni Gunawan is a junior researcher at Research Centre for Population, BRIN, based in Jakarta, Indonesia. His research interests focus on labour and employment issues, particularly labour economics and the application of econometric methods in labour market analysis

M. Gurusamy, with a comprehensive academic background that includes an MBA, M.Phil, Ph.D., and a D.Litt. in Marketing, brings an impressive 21 years of teaching experience, alongside a brief stint in the industry of 9 months. Currently serving as Professor and Chairperson of Marketing and Entrepreneurship at the Adarsh Institute of Management and Information Technology in Bangalore, Karnataka, India, he has distinguished himself in both academic and research fields. Dr. Gurusamy has made significant contributions to the intellectual property domain, holding nine patents in India and five in Australia, which underscores his innovative approach to research and development. His scholarly output is remarkable, with 12 articles published in Web of Science journals, 40 in Scopus-indexed journals, and numerous articles in other national and international journals, as well as 40 books published. As an academic leader, he has evaluated Ph.D. theses and served as an external examiner, highlighting his expertise in guiding research scholars. Dr. Gurusamy's role as a resource person and chairperson in 90 instances, along with his editorial and reviewer memberships in 14 and 16 journals, respectively, reflects his esteemed position in the academic community. Additionally, his contributions extend to academic advisory boards and visiting professorships, demonstrating a commitment to enhancing educational standards. His achievements have been recognized with 30 awards, affirming his influence and excellence in marketing and research. Dr. Gurusamy's professional journey is a testament to his dedication to academia, research, and the practical applications of marketing principles in the evolving business landscape.

Sidharth Halder is an Assistant Professor in Amity School of Management & Commerce at Amity University Jharkhand, Ranchi. He brings over 26 years of academic and professional experience, having two master's degrees: one in Personnel Management and Industrial Relations and another in Computer Application with a Gold Medal from XISS, a Chemistry Hons graduate, and the University Topper. His decade-plus corporate experience spins into Training, Sales, and Marketing with MNCs and Fortune 500 companies. He has contributed to the academic fraternity by publishing 6 copyrights, 1 patent, 2 books as a testimony of his academic rigour. He has continuously upgraded his skills through a variety of professional certification like- HR Analytics, Compliance Risk Management & Financial Economic Crimes, Operational Risk Management, Basics of Investments, Anti-Fraud Awareness, SEO and Digital Marketing, Entrepreneurship etc. He recently completed the Leadership Programs from IIM Ranchi. His research focuses on AI augmented HR decision making, evidenced by his recent article "Investigating the Role of Artificial Intelligence in HR Decision Making Processes," published in Library Progress International (Vol. 44 No. 3, Jul–Dec 2024), BPAS Journals. He has also co-authored "Exploring the Effectiveness of Remote Work Arrangements on Productivity and Work Life Balance" in EEL (2024, 14, 1545–1553), demonstrating his interest in sustainable and flexible workplace models. Prof. Halder's work in Green HRM and sustainability includes developing AI-driven tools to monitor office energy usage and promote eco-friendly employee behaviours. He has presented these findings at national and international conferences, collaborating with industry partners to pilot AI-based HR solutions that enhance both operational efficiency and environmental stewardship. As a mentor, he supervises postgraduate research in digital transformation of HR and sustainable organizational practices, and teaches courses such as Organizational Behaviour, Training & Development, and Compensation Management. His interdisciplinary approach bridges HRM, AI, and sustainability, fostering ethical, inclusive, and future-ready workplace environments. As a Professor of HR and Research Scholar, you're not just teaching students; you're mentoring minds across organizational behaviour, management theory, training & development, and even life insurance. He has also mentored 4 startups in university. He is also Head of Placements in Management and Humanities and Head of Discipline. And he loves helping students in realizing their fullest potential and exploring beyond their beliefs.

Kimleng Hing is a dedicated public administration professional and scholar whose career reflects a strong commitment to effective governance, administrative excellence, and public sector development. With extensive experience serving in various administrative capacities, he has developed a comprehensive understanding of organizational management, policy implementation, institutional development, and public service delivery. Throughout his professional career, Dr. Hing has demonstrated exceptional leadership and administrative expertise, contributing to the improvement of public sector operations and governance practices. His practical experience has provided him with valuable insights into the challenges and opportunities facing modern public administration, enabling him to bridge the gap between theory and practice effectively. Complementing his professional achievements, Dr. Hing has pursued advanced academic studies in the field of public administration. He is currently undertaking a Doctor of Philosophy (Ph.D.) in Public Administration at the Faculty of Law and Economics, Khemarak University in Phnom Penh, Cambodia. His doctoral research reflects his dedication to advancing knowledge and promoting innovative approaches to governance, public policy, and administrative reform. Dr. Hing's academic interests encompass public governance, organizational leadership, public policy analysis, administrative reform, institutional effectiveness, and sustainable public sector development. Through rigorous research and scholarly engagement, he seeks to contribute to the enhancement of administrative systems and the promotion of good governance practices at local, national, and international levels. As both a practitioner and researcher, Dr. Hing is committed to fostering evidence-based decision-making and strengthening the capacity of public institutions. His unique combination of practical administrative experience and academic scholarship positions him as a valuable contributor to discussions on public administration and governance reform. Driven by a vision of efficient, transparent, and accountable public service, Dr. Hing continues to pursue excellence in both his professional and academic endeavors. Through his work, research, and leadership, he aims to make meaningful contributions to the advancement of public administration, supporting sustainable development and improved governance outcomes in Cambodia and beyond.

Khairul Ismed is a researcher at the Research Centre for Population, BRIN. He earned his doctorate in management science from Jakarta State University, and his research focuses on human resource economics, labour issues, labour protection and supervision. Prior to BRIN, he worked at the Ministry of Manpower of the Republic of Indonesia.

Jomon Jose M. is an Associate Professor and Research Supervisor at Sahrdaya Institute of Management Studies. He holds a Post-Doctoral qualification and specializes in marketing, consumer behavior, HRM, digital transformation, and sustainable business practices. His research contributions include Scopus-indexed publications, book chapters, and interdisciplinary studies focusing on AI, finance, branding, and strategic management.

Evangelina Joseph is a research scholar specializing in Human Resource Management (HRM) at CHRIST (Deemed to be University), Bengaluru. Holding an MBA in Human Resource Management, her academic foundation is complemented by a deep and current engagement with the field. Her primary research interests focus on the interdisciplinary aspects of Human Resource Development (HRD), Organizational Behaviour (OB), and Organizational Psychology. Her work aims to explore the empirical links between these areas to develop actionable strategies for enhancing workforce performance and organizational effectiveness. Furthermore, she actively contributes to academic discourse as a reviewer for peer-reviewed journals and book chapters, demonstrating a commitment to scholarly rigor and the advancement of knowledge within the domains of management and applied psychology.

Sopheak Kong is a law lecturer at the Royal University of Law and Economics (RULE) and a practicing lawyer registered with the Bar Association of the Kingdom of Cambodia since 2007. He holds a PhD in Law and combines academic expertise with practical legal experience. His research and professional interests include civil law, contract law, family law, and inheritance law. Dr. KONG is dedicated to advancing legal education and practice in Cambodia.

Jelena Lukić Nikolić began her academic journey in 2007, enrolling at the University of Belgrade, Republic of Serbia, Faculty of Economics. She earned her bachelor's degree in 2011 in International Economics and Foreign Trade, followed by a master's degree in 2012 in Business Administration, specializing in Organization and Human Resource Management. In 2017, she completed her PhD in Business Management at the same faculty, with a dissertation on the impact of Big Data technologies on organizational design. Her academic career started in 2014 at the College of Sports and Health in Belgrade, Republic of Serbia, where she worked until 2017 as an Assistant in the field of Sports Management. That same year, after completing her doctorate, she joined Modern Business School in Belgrade, Republic of Serbia, as an Assistant Professor (2017–2022), later serving as Assistant Director for International Cooperation (2018–2023). In 2022, she was promoted to Associate Professor, and in 2023 she became Head of the Department for Management and Marketing.

Avirup Mukherjee is presently serving as an Assistant Professor in the Department of Economics at Amity University, Jharkhand, where he is engaged in teaching, mentoring, and research activities that span across diverse domains of economics, Labour Market and finance. Over the years, he has been a consistent participant in debates, seminars, and research forums that address the complexities of financial systems, socio-economic policy, and inclusive growth. His professional experience is marked by a robust engagement with nationally and internationally recognized organizations. He has had the privilege of working on several prestigious projects commissioned by the Planning Commission of India, the Reserve Bank of India, Navajbai Ratan Tata Trust, Indian Council of Social Science Research (ICSSR), and UNICEF, New Delhi. Furthermore, he plays an instrumental role in the preparation of the Economic Survey and the State Budget for the Government of Jharkhand, where his expertise contributes to framing evidence-based policies aimed at promoting sustainable growth and welfare at the state level. In addition to his policy-oriented contributions, Prof. Avirup Mukherjee has established himself as an active scholar with a strong research record. He has authored numerous research articles, case studies, and review papers that have been published in reputed international journals, reflecting his commitment to advancing knowledge and engaging with contemporary debates in Labour economics and finance. His scholarly work is recognized for its blend of rigorous analysis, policy relevance, and practical applicability. By combining his academic pursuits with professional practice and policy involvement, he continues to play a significant role in shaping discourses on financial inclusion, market efficiency, and economic resilience.

Ngadi Ngadi is a senior researcher at the Research Centre for Population, BRIN since 2005. He is a Ph.D. candidate in Human Geography, at the University of Tokyo, Japan. He obtained a master's degree from Population and Employment Studies at the University of Indonesia (2005). His research interests relate to population and labour mobility, employment and human resources, demographic change and rural development. He has published more than 30 articles both as books and journals in national and international publisher. Scopus ID: 57682503500; 0000-0002-5249-0860

Phearak Pok is Deputy Head of the Department of International Relations at the Royal University of Law and Economics (RULE). He holds a PhD in Economics and a Master's in Business Administration. Since 2010, he has specialized in the interdisciplinary fields of economics, business, and politics, with teaching and research focused on integrating theory and practice. Dr. POK is committed to advancing knowledge and fostering critical dialogue in Cambodian academia.

Ramakrishnan Ramachandran, PhD in Stakeholder Management is a diplomat turned passionate research-oriented teacher with wide & varied experience in Indian Government /Private Enterprise. He has been associated with founding four B schools and is currently Chief Consultant, Vivin Consultants, Chennai. Author of six books ranging from TQM to Environmental Science to Ethics, he has written close to 100 papers.

Rosalinda Ramos Murillo is an Industrial Engineer with a Master's in Business Administration, bringing extensive experience in the private sector, specifically in manufacturing, quality assurance, planning, and logistics for multinational companies. A dedicated professor with over 20 years of experience in academia and leadership roles, I have successfully developed projects focused on updating curriculum plans and programs, optimizing production processes, enhancing quality and productivity, and managing quality systems in compliance with international standards such as ISO 9001:2015 and ISO 14001:2015.

Ali Raza is an Assistant Professor of Human Resource Management at Sukkur IBA University, specializing in HRM practices and organizational development. He holds a Ph.D. in Human Resource Management from Universiti Sains Malaysia, an

MSc in HRM from Glasgow Caledonian University, Scotland, and a BBA in HRM from Sukkur IBA. Dr. Raza has contributed to academic research with publications like New Wella Salon: Exploring Growth Opportunities and has been recognized with awards such as the QEC Appreciation by Sukkur IBA in 2015. As an associate member since 2010, he continues to excel in teaching, research, and mentoring in HRM.

José De Jesús Reyes-Sánchez, Ph.D. in senior management, has six master's degrees, in education, in management, professional soccer technique, in physical preparation, in professional soccer, in physical rehabilitation sciences, in sports sciences, as well as in coaching and integral well-being, who is a research professor at the TECNM Instituto Tecnológico Superior De Fresnillo, with more than 20 years of teaching experience, PRODEP profile and coordinator of the academic body with vast experience in conferences and workshops, currently novelist and writer.

Gautam Shivaraj, with a comprehensive academic background including a Bachelor's in Mechanical Engineering, Master of Engineering Management (Australia), MBA and also pursuing Ph.D, brings an impressive 07 years of teaching experience alongside a brief stint in the industry of 5 years. Currently serving as an Assistant Professor at the Adarsh Institute of Management and Information Technology in Bangalore, Karnataka, India, he has distinguished himself in the academic and research fields. Prof.Gautam Shivaraj professional journey is a testament to his dedication to academia, research, in the evolving world.

Safia Soomro holds an MPhil in Education from Sukkur IBA University and currently serves as a Lecturer at Begum Nusrat Bhutto Women University, Sukkur. Her research interests encompass educational leadership, educational psychology, and the integration of technology in teaching. With a specialization in assessment, she focuses on how emerging technologies particularly Artificial Intelligence can enhance assessment practices and promote effective learning outcomes. Through her academic work, she is committed to advancing innovative, evidence-based approaches in education, with the goal of shaping tech-enhanced learning environments and fostering progressive leadership in the educational sector.

Sanam Soomro holds an MS degree in Human Resource Management from Sukkur IBA University. Currently, she is pursuing a PhD at the School of Management, Jiangsu University, Zhenjiang, China. Her research interests include Artificial Intelligence, Human Resource Management, Work-Life Balance, Employee Well-being and Employee Performance. She is actively engaged in interdisciplinary research aimed at enhancing organizational effectiveness through innovative HR practices and technological integration. With a forward-thinking approach, she is committed to contributing to the future of work through innovative, data-driven insights that support both organizational growth and human flourishing.

Satya Subrahmanyam is a distinguished academic leader, researcher, and institutional strategist with over 28 years of experience in higher education, business research, leadership and management. He holds two PhDs and a Postdoctoral qualification from the Polytechnic Institute of Leiria, Portugal. Currently serving as Professor and Dean (Research) at Holy Spirit University of Kaslik (USEK), Lebanon, he spearheads research initiatives that enhance academic excellence and institutional reputation. He played a pivotal role in the development of the Catholic University in Erbil, Kurdistan, where he established new departments, led research programs, and collaborated on international educational projects. As a founding member and Managing Partner of Vignan Institute of Technology and Management, India, he contributed to its transformation into a premier institution. With expertise in AI-driven business strategies, HR analytics, and leadership in technology adoption, he has published extensively, guided PhD research, and led training programs in corporate and academic settings.

Triyono Triyono is a researcher at the Research Centre for Population, BRIN. His research interests include labour politics, wage policy and social security. He examines industrial relations and employment protection in Indonesia.

Index

A

C

D

S

T

W